French Novelists of Today

French Novelists of Today

HENRI PEYRE
Sterling Professor of French
Yale University

OXFORD UNIVERSITY PRESS
LONDON   OXFORD   NEW YORK

Preface

In 1955, an earlier version of this volume on the French novel of today was published by the Oxford University Press. The substance of the book consisted of the Mary Flexner lectures delivered some years earlier at Bryn Mawr College. The author is grateful to Bryn Mawr College for having permitted the reprinting of several chapters from the original volume, then entitled *The Contemporary French Novel,* in the present work.

Much has happened in French fiction between 1950 and 1967. Our perspective on the great figures of the twentieth century has been altered; Proust, Malraux, Green, Bernanos have grown in stature; others, even Gide and Camus, are now viewed more critically; the existentialist novel is no longer in the forefront; and the 'new novelists' launched in the late nineteen-fifties are challenged by even newer ones while the French public becomes increasingly cool to their over-publicized innovations. The temper of the nation which is mirrored, or distorted, in its fiction is strikingly different from what it was in the post-World War II era, when the French looked up to American fiction and felt deeply disturbed by their efforts to catch up with more stable and more prosperous nations.

Such changes, and many others, are reflected in this work, in which new chapters have been added on Camus, Simone de Beauvoir, and the 'new novelists.' Bibliographies have been brought up to date. A list of over one hundred novelists, with brief critical appraisals of their achievement, has been appended to the book and should prove useful to readers interested in gaining information and in seeing the author's evaluation of a number of living writers not discussed fully in the body of the text. The stress throughout is not on the technique of the novel as a *genre*, a province of criticism which the author believes to have been overworked by academic writers; but is rather on the individual novelists and on their works as they are related to life and as they afford a broadening of our culture, a liveliness of interest, an insight into the French mind and sensibility, and, hopefully, some pleasure.

Hamden, Conn.   H. P.
September 1966

Contents

Influence of Simone Weil. Outburst of feminist thought in France and growing rivalry between the sexes. Minor but representative women novelists of today. Simone de Beauvoir, her writings on 'the second sex' and her novels. Originality of two of them at least, in spite of excessive didactic preoccupations and of a fundamental lack of emotional and sensual warmth. Bibliographical Notes.

Acknowledgments

Acknowledgment is hereby made for permission to quote from the following:

The Atlantic Monthly and Jean-Paul Sartre, for a quotation from the article 'American Novelists in French Eyes,' in the issue of August 1946.

Commentary and Albert Camus, for a quotation from Camus's article 'The Artist as Witness of Freedom,' in the issue of December 1949.

Gallimard, Paris, and the authors, for quotations from Simone de Beauvoir, Albert Camus, André Gide, Jean Giono, André Malraux, Marcel Proust, Antoine de Saint-Exupéry, Jean-Paul Sartre, and Paul Valéry.

Bernard Grasset, Paris, and François Mauriac, for a quotation from Mauriac's works.

Harcourt, Brace and Company, for quotations from the novels of Saint-Exupéry, and Mr. Lewis Galantière for quotations fom his translations of Saint-Exupéry.

Harper & Brothers, and Aldous Huxley, for a quotation from Huxley's *Eyeless in Gaza*.

The Hogarth Press, London, and Raymond Mortimer, for a quotation fom Mortimer's *Channel Packet*.

Horizon and Cyril Connolly, for a quotation from an interview with André Malraux, in 1945.

Alfred A. Knopf, for quotations made from Simone de Beauvoir, André Gide, Roger Martin du Gard, and Jean-Paul Sartre.

The New York Times for quotations from Simone de Beauvoir's article 'An Existentialist Looks at America,' *The New York Times Magazine*, May 25, 1947.

The Philosophical Library, for quotations from Jean Cocteau's *Letter to Jacques Maritain.*

Random House and Robinson Jeffers, for a quotation from Jeffers's poem 'Joy.'

Theatre Arts, for a quotation from J.-P. Sartre's article of June 1946, 'Forgers of Myths.'

The Viking Press, for a quotation from D. H. Lawrence's *Phoenix.*

The Virginia Quarterly Review, for permission to reprint part of an article on 'American Literature through French Eyes,' published there by the author in the summer of 1947.

French Novelists of Today

I

The Crisis in French Fiction

It has long been a platitude to assert that the nineteenth century was
the golden age of fiction, supposedly because fiction portrayed the middle class (though seldom flatteringly) and because its audience was
chiefly recruited from that same middle class: so was naturally the audience for the drama, for musical symphonies, art exhibits, for the essay,
criticism, and even for poetry. Ever since the disappearance from the
European literary stage of Tolstoi, Zola, Henry James, Conrad, Hardy,
book reviewers and sociologists have monotonously proclaimed the death
of the novel and have duly accounted for it with cogent reasons, among
others the alleged disappearance of the bourgeoisie and the spread of
insecurity in modern man. But the bourgeoisie has seldom been stronger
than in the prosperous era which began with the second half of the
twentieth century in most of Europe and America; it openly boasts of
its technocratic supremacy and it clamors for political and administrative
regimes which would reflect its predominance. The old aristocracy and
the proletariat of the last century are fast becoming 'embourgeoisés,'
swelling the ranks of the expanding middle class. As to security, 'mortal's
chiefest enemy,' as Hecate calls it in *Macbeth*, we may yearn for more
of it today and dramatically allude to the nuclear Twilight of all the
Gods at every convention of writers and academics, but in truth never
has mankind enjoyed such personal, financial, economic, social, or political security as it does in the nineteen-sixties. Those who argue that
the novel could only prosper in a stable and harmonious society forget
the substance and the tone of fiction written by Stendhal, Balzac, Dos-

3

toevski, Melville, Zola, and Hardy: tragic insecurity indeed prevailed then. It is moreover more than doubtful whether people who feel insecure and anguished inevitably want to see their anxieties mirrored and dramatized in the literature which they read—occasionally for entertainment and for escape. 'He that drives fat oxen must himself be fat,' mocked Dr. Johnson two hundred years ago.

It may be natural for every innovator in every art, including such an impure and loose art as fiction, to imagine that he has composed the final masterpiece which will put an end to fiction forever. Proust, Joyce, Thomas Mann, Musil, Broch may have thought so; American giants have been diffident and modest in comparison. The novel nevertheless continues and is periodically reborn. It has even survived the direst of all perils: the avalanche of criticism of fiction as form, structure, technique, and of speculations on the great tradition and on the 'new' novel, on time, on symbolic secrets and on storytelling as a handmaid to metaphysics. Up to 1930 or so, the French could boast of next to nothing (besides Flaubert's *Correspondence*) on the craft of fiction to be even remotely compared to Henry James's Prefaces, to Percy Lubbock's *The Craft of Fiction*, to E. M. Forster's 1922 lectures *Aspects of the Novel* and to Virginia Woolf's ironical, lucid, and admirably suggestive essays in *The Common Reader* and her articles 'Phases of Fiction.' Proust and Gide had incorporated the best of their reflections on the subject in their long novels. Thibaudet, probably the most assiduous French critic of fiction before 1930, was too desultory as a critic and more addicted to entertaining classifications and rapprochements than to probing the arcana of the novelist's mind and art in depth.

Suddenly the gap was filled by a new generation of critics (several of them, such as Mauriac, Romains, Sartre, Blanchot, and Butor, being also practitioners of the craft of fiction). Every other critic of the novel, and every third novelist, since 1940, appears to have been trained in philosophy. Not a few of them have pondered phenomenology—Heidegger, Bachelard, and Sartre. The earnestness, the depth, and the arrogant vitality of that recent criticism of fiction in France and in Switzerland is in itself remarkable. American professors, if not the uncommon American common reader, have, since 1950, expressed their esteem for so much subtle disquisition, only voicing their timid fear that such relentless delving into metaphysical and technical depths might end in drying up creativeness altogether. A similar, even more abstract and ferociously analytical movement of critical dissection of the art of the novel had taken place earlier in the United States. But the peril to creative imagination was less serious on this side of the Atlantic, since few novelists here are in the habit of paying much attention to academic critics. French poets and novelists, like French painters, enjoy the dubious advantage of having a host of decipherers working their half-unconscious intentions and intuitions into an aesthetic body of thought. Those commentators are wont to weave veils, or thick blankets, of subtleties over the work which they ponder with high seriousness. They would deem themselves unequal to their self-assigned task if they did not discover philosophical and moral profundities in tales and stories which otherwise would not be worth their real attention. The novelists in their turn are impressed by their exegetes. Giono, a rustic Provençal, Bernanos, an insurance salesman, Claude Simon, a wine grower, Robbe-Grillet, an agronomist, confide to interviewers, draw up manifestoes, brief their disciples, and end up by writing elucidations of the mysteries which others have uncovered in them. 'Since those mysteries are beyond me, let us pretend to be the organizer of them,' says a shrewd character in Cocteau's *Les Mariés de la Tour Eiffel.*

The doubt which will often underlie the following chapters is whether the laborious, at times ponderous, critical work accumulated in the last thirty years about the novel of the past and of the present has truly served to understand it more or enhance the enjoyment of it. One of the trends has led toward structural analysis: it rather naïvely takes it for granted that the unfolding of a skillfully contrived structure, perceptible to none but the trained scholar who has patiently learned how to interpret signs and to translate symbols, is the highest aesthetic joy to be afforded by the reading of a novel. Another method, less intent on embracing the whole of a work of fiction but more searching in its concentration on a microcosm taken to be representative of the whole, has preferred the very close reading of a carefully selected passage. When practiced by a man of vast erudition and of discriminating taste, accustomed to analyzing style, like Leo Spitzer or Erich Auerbach, such an approach can be illuminating. Naturally, the passages thus ransacked for fruitful and far-reaching conclusions are selected with sedulous care, as were the experiments to which the tutor, in Rousseau's *Emile*, subjected his naïve disciple. Wielded by less learned and less ingenious tyros, or by dry students of language and mechanical accountants of key words and of recurring metaphors, that method of style analysis can remain exterior to the essence of the novel. Style, which is seldom all-important in fiction, tends to be overstressed; the novel is not espoused in its dynamic fluidity but carved into separate prose-passages to be scanned.

In truth, if the criticism of fiction was so superficial, and now has become so pedantic and full of jargon, lagging behind the criticism of tragedy and of poetry, it has many an excuse. As the keenest analyst of the craft of fiction, Percy Lubbock, pointed out, no other literary genre offers the same dilemmas to the reader. Any discussion of a long novel demands that we keep in the focus of our attention the whole of its complexity of plot and incidents, its digressions, its gradual unfolding of characters, and its latent philosophy. Individual episodes and snatches of lyricism cannot be isolated as they may be in the enjoyment of the epic. The most sophisticated reader should share the eager excitement of the plain reader who is tempted to rush to the dénouement breathlessly. Yet in comprehensive and continuous reading one must remain alert for revealing details, attentive to key passages: the reader must be seized by the witchcraft of Scheherazade without abdicating critical lucidity. There is a limit to the length and complexities allowed to a drama; there are none to a *roman-fleuve*, except that 'the weariest river winds somewhere safe to sea.'

The present writer's conviction is that there is no single approach that is infallible or systematically to be preferred when dealing with literature. Pluralism seems to me to be a far more fruitful attitude; the prejudice that brands eclecticism as insipid and a mere cloak for a lack of personal opinion has too long gone unchallenged. Any dogmatism, while it may provide the lover of systems with a cheaply acquired consistency and unity of point of view, soon proves detrimental to the most varied of human pursuits—the pursuit of beauty, truth, and 'greatness' in works of art. Fiction, even more than poetry, music, or painting, sets everything in motion in us: our senses (it would be hypocrisy to ignore the sensuous and erotic motivation of readers of fiction or lovers of pictures), our sensibility, our intellect, our religious, philosophical, and social views, our esthetic joys, our desire to know ourselves better and to penetrate into other lives. Any approach to the novel, therefore, that is honest and intelligently sustained is valid if it draws us nearer to the work of art or to its creator. Lawrence Durrell raised an outcry and was hooted by some of his sophisticated confrères as a Philistine when, at the International Writers' Conference of the Edinburgh Festival in 1962, he suggested that three plain questions be asked of a novel: 'Has it made me care? Has it brought me joy? Has it changed me at all?' Yet those questions are indeed the ones which will occur to any reader of fiction, whether he be an old fashioned Victorian or a post-Jamesian esthete. Was it not Henry James himself who, in an 1884 essay on 'The Art of Fiction' published in 1888 in *Partial Portraits,* proclaimed: 'The only reason for the existence of a novel is that it does attempt to represent life.'

The aesthetic approach, which pays due heed to the novelist's technique, should reasonably come first; it is the most detached and the most mature. But the biographical one, which traces the link—often an elusive one—between the man and his writings, his borrowings from life and from his life and the metamorphosis worked by his imagination, is not to be excluded: Stendhal, Balzac, Dostoevski, Proust fascinate us as much as their fictional characters. The exclusion of biography, on the pretext that it can at times be superficially anecdotal, has lately dehumanized literature in several lands and averted potential readers from books, which have been coldly dissected like marvels of pure engineering. A critic's task, or one of his tasks, is after all to stir up discussion around a work of art. Thomas Wolfe expressed more than the pathetic inflation of his ego when he remarked, in his preface to *Look Homeward, Angel,* that 'all serious work in fiction is autobiographical. . . . A more autobiographical work than *Gulliver's Travels* cannot easily be imagined.'

Equally valid is the philosophical study of fiction, or the consideration of the novelist as thinker. Maupassant, one of the least philosophical among the novelists of France, warned, in his famous preface to *Pierre et Jean,* that 'philosophy should be hidden in a book as it is hidden in reality under the facts of life.' Some readers may choose to leave it hidden and unexplored. Others feel compelled to interpret a story or a play as a philosophy expressed in a code; they will not stop until they have formulated and even systematized that philosophy: 'a novelistic technique,' according to Sartre, 'always leads us back to the metaphysics of the novelist. The critic's task is to elicit the latter before appraising the former.' It is not certain that existentialism has given France a great work of philosophical fiction, but it has encouraged philosophical criticism, which Sartre himself has practiced with brilliance. It has also given an impetus to psychological criticism and popularized the labels of phenomenological criticism and of existential psychoanalysis. Psychology has long constituted in France the warp and woof of many a fictional loom. It was one of the merits of the novel from Mme de La Fayette through Marivaux and Laclos to Stendhal when, in an age of ideas which

called into question the social order, the political organization, the
validity of ethics and of traditional religion, eighteenth-century fiction
shied away from those momentous issues and concentrated on the dissection of individuals.

One of the claims to greatness of the nineteenth-century French and
English novel is, on the contrary, to have dared be influential political
and social criticism. The 'pure novel' of which Gide dreamed around
1920, the novel of Hamlet-like adolescents which followed World War I,
the novel of 1950–65 in France which has proudly accepted the title of
'new' have all conspicuously eschewed political and social problems. They
have thereby severed many of the links which might have bound them
to the masses and made them less esoteric and rarefied. The 'social condition' is an almost unheard-of phrase while the 'human condition' has
invaded every sophomore's essay on literature. Nevertheless, and in
spite of much mishandling of literature envisaged solely as document in clumsy sociological theses, we believe that the social approach
to fiction is legitimate and needed. Readers from another country will
inevitably seek insight into Russian or French life, into the moods of
the Germans since World War II or of Americans during the Depression
years when approaching the novels of those countries. Malraux, Romains,
Aragon, Céline, Druon, Troyat will be valuable, in different degrees, for
the insight which they afford into French life. Modern historians proclaim today that the most faithful picture of the problems of the misery
of the working classes at the beginning of the industrial revolution in
France is offered, not by historians or social reformers, but by Balzac and
Victor Hugo. By surrendering all portrayal of manners to sociology, the
modern novel has deprived itself of powerful sources of inspiration and
of interest and has alienated thousands of readers, who flock to sociological studies instead of to fiction. A concern with man's fate and with
the tragic duel of our modern heroes with destiny should not blind us
altogether to the truth that we understand men better if we watch them
at work in collective undertakings. By dwelling on the universal absurdity
and our baffled anguish in an irrational world, fiction may have thought
it was growing more philosophical. But it abdicated in favor of science
which persists in eliciting some significance from a bewildering universe.

Any work of criticism, like any philosophical treatise, rests upon some
assumptions, which are in part arbitrary. The author should, in all fairness, state them briefly, at the risk of seeming to extend his prolegomena
with some complacence. Definitions are one half of criticism, and often
its better half.

Our first one is a platitude but, like all obvious statements, often disregarded. The modern novel, and specifically the modern French novel, as an entity, hardly exists. There are only contemporary novelists, some of whom are modern. There exist far wider gaps between two novels written in our age than there ever existed between two plays, two poems, even two essays, two symphonies, two churches.

Once this has been said, we shall not, however, shyly refrain from all generalizations about the novel in France. The process of abstracting and of generalizing is inseparable from that of thinking. A suggestive synthesis is more useful to scholarship than one more of those thorough, myopic, and infinitesimal analyses of an ever-diminishing topic. But we prefer concentrating our remarks around individuals who proposed and solved problems *in vivo* to breaking up the art of fiction into components such as narrative, description, dialogue, plot, conflict of characters, and so forth. E. M. Forster has ridiculed some of the textbooks on materials of fiction. He has opened the way to better ones. But the craft of fiction, or the understanding of fiction, or its enjoyment cannot be reduced to recipes.

Fiction, in any movement, trend, or period, is made by individuals. Thus a second pitfall lies before the critics. How will he make a choice among the recent and living authors who seem to have a claim upon his attention? The critic may wish to be polite to novelists who, of course, are also critics themselves and whom he will have to meet next month at some literary dinner party. Moreover, he is not absolutely sure of his own taste and will provide a guarantee against the gibes of posterity if he lists all those who may survive. Many works on contemporary literature, therefore, afraid of appearing schoolmasterish in ranking writers, take refuge in tedious enumerations, granting an honorable mention to every respectable talent. This may save embarrassment, but the criticism will read like a dictionary of names and titles.

Anyone who ventures to treat living literature must be ready to take risks and must abide by his own taste, while broadening it as best he can. Courage is as indispensable as intelligence in such matters. In the realm of fiction, more than in any other, a critic must be selective, for many more novels than any other kind of literature are included in monthly publishers' lists. Out of the fictional avalanche on a reviewer's desk, four or five novels in every decade, that is to say, one per cent or so, may some day emerge. The others are not all mediocre, and we owe to them a few hours of entertainment as well as some understanding of our age and of public taste. The chances are that the best-seller will be among these pleasing, soon-to-be-forgotten books. However, these books do not belong to the restricted and magical circle of 'works of literature.'

It is the critic's and often the professor's privilege to decide what literature is and what it is not. But the power of the professor is not arbitrary. He follows not his whim but a test, the most scrutinizing to which a contemporary novel or play can be subjected: Does the new writer stand up under the slow reading, the elaborate dissecting of three or four hours of lecture and of discussion of his work? The teacher and the students who struggle with his volume just off the press are also reading Sophocles, Racine, Tolstoi, Ibsen. To them they will compare Mr. Tennessee Williams, Mr. Christopher Fry, M. Jean-Paul Sartre, or M. Butor. Sad to confess, the rewarding writer who remains on the syllabus is the writer about whom the lecturer does not run dry after fifty minutes and whose solidity resists the irony and the severity of young apprentices.

But the professor is overwhelmed by his responsibility. He is prone to excessive prudence and often seeks refuge in well-established values in order to avoid the brutality of the present. He favors novels which are 'arty,' probably pretentious, and overwritten by an author too conscious of his calculated effects. A clique of an unhappy few may thus cry up Djuna Barnes's *Nightwood*, or Charles Morgan's novels of labored mysticism and impure chastity, or even Graham Greene's weird atmosphere, or, in France, Marcel Jouhandeau, Julien Gracq, and even Jean Giraudoux. They will not succeed in imposing their taste. For, less than any other means of literary expression, can the novel be severed from life for very long. Stylization may rule supreme in some other arts; it does not in fiction. The peril of excluding too much of life, as Henry James did, is greater than that of accepting it too liberally and of running the risk of presenting violence, vulgarity, and sadism as the whole of life.

The very general characteristics by which a novel may be broadly classified may take the place of a definition—necessarily a very loose one. The novel is a story, perhaps borrowed from reality, but reality transposed and reimagined, endowed with form, made fictitious. It is in prose, or it has been since the end of the Middle Ages. It has a certain length; there is no upper limit, apparently, to the number of pages or volumes that a novel may reach, but it should not be so short that it becomes a long short story. All other requirements that have been put forward by critics, those unacknowledged legislators, may be discarded, for they raise too many difficulties to win general approval. A narrative element used to be required in a novel, but it is no longer generally considered necessary. Many moderns are Platonists, who will not allow appearances to count for much, unless they suggest or reveal some deeper significance. Our age yearns for a world of essences transcending our phenomenal and temporal prison. Smooth, vivid, and entrancing storytelling, such as the Italians and Russians once practiced with special mastery, has lost vogue with us. Creation of character is also less essential than it was in the days of Fielding, Dickens, and Balzac. Around 1860–70, literature and art were rocked to their foundations by the writers' and artists' determination to change the world or to re-create a new universe with words, colors, and sounds, instead of placidly depicting reality or letting their picaresque heroes make the best of it and acquire experience, wisdom, and a few good memories thereby. Ever since, the novel has been seized by social and metaphysical ambitions. Some say that its great age then passed away.

Let us not be nostalgic. The greatness of literature, in countries like France, lies in its claim, often made good, of taking the place once filled by religion and dogmatic ethics. Matthew Arnold, in his essay on 'The Study of Poetry' had prophesied that 'most of what passed . . . for religion and philosophy will be replaced by poetry.' Charles Baudelaire, Arthur Rimbaud, and their successors among poets; stark and occasionally cruel novelists, from Flaubert to Sartre; historical writers, from Taine to modern historians, freed from consoling delusions, have poured the virile draught on which the youth of the country has been intoxicated. They did not respect traditions, and they did not encourage man to hope for another world or even for much improvement in this one. But they have steeled many a soul to bear evils with fortitude and, in a world where absurdities and iniquities are triumphant, to take arms against a sea of troubles and to endow a frail life with significance.

The French novel is thus, more than ever before, a novel of moralists more than of storytellers, of seekers of wisdom more than of creators of characters. It aims at increasing the reader's understanding of life, at sharpening his lucidity and his sincerity; indeed, with all its pessimism, it has enhanced the Frenchman's zest for living a life which authors have depicted as sombre, bristling with hostile temptations, unprotected by any providence, but the more exhilarating for all that.

The present volume deals with the French novelists who appear to be the most significant in the literature of the years 1920–65. In this sense they are modern, though not particularly modernistic—for, except in poetry and perhaps in music, the years 1925–50 were marked in France by much technical experimentation. With the second half of the century, innovating attempts have again flourished. New abysses of eroticism, abnormality, and cruelty have been explored but their apparent depth soon vanished. Lesbianism and pederasty have afforded some psychological enrichment, by now treasured, or squandered. The most original movement at present is the revolt against language. 'On a touché au vers,' declared Stéphane Mallarmé in 1895 before Oxford and Cambridge audiences awaiting the latest news from Paris. Fifty years later, prose, in its turn, was attacked in its very essence: communication and suggestion.

But experiment is not necessarily the road to the future. It often leads away from the real trend of literary evolution into paths that perhaps have been tried earlier and have proved to be blind alleys. It is possible that one of these paths, diverging from the main road, may one day become a spacious avenue, if a genius forces it wide open. Meanwhile, many experimenters are the martyrs of a lost cause, or of a cause that has not yet found itself. On the other hand, the forces of the past may only temporarily seem to have spent themselves; some genius may instill revolutionary dynamism into them tomorrow. This has often been the case in France.

The French are keenly conscious of their traditions, and no French writer, however iconoclastic he may be, has ever wholly neglected some reading of Racine, Pascal, Balzac, and Hugo. Happily for the French, they have not one but several traditions, which more often than not conflict with one another. Periodically, they sort out their legacy of a complex past and advocate a single current as beneficent; the rest become the object of eloquent vituperation.

The position adopted by a literary generation in respect to its past is therefore revealing. No writer worthy of the name and deserving a niche in the temple (or in the stables) of posterity is merely an imitator. Borrowings that may at one time have been permissible in other literary genres would not be tolerated in the art of fiction: the creative imitation of Theocritus by Virgil, of certain Spaniards by Corneille, of Plautus by Molière, of Bion and Moschus by Shelley. Even the patent adoption and utilization of foreign models, such as Lesage practiced with the Spanish picaresque tradition, and many Frenchmen with Samuel Richardson and Walter Scott, would today offend our literary conventions. The American novel has been caricatured in the last decades, somewhat unconsciously, by the Frenchmen who plundered it. But the number of fictional situations, even if a little larger than the restricted number of dramatic situations, is, after all, limited. It is not easy to create a miser or an old man devoured by his fatherly love for his daughters without having Balzac thrown at one's face; a sentimental, cynical young upstart without inviting comparison with Stendhal; a middle-aged, dissatisfied, and tempted lady without conjuring up Emma Bovary. More than in subject matter, the influence of certain past novelists looked upon as masters appears in the tone assumed by some of the moderns. An original history of literature could be written by classifying families of minds in separate chapels, with the name of some patron saint of earlier eras inscribed on the pediment.

The novelists of the past whose prestige and influence in France (and not necessarily elsewhere) have sunk lowest are Anatole France and Guy de Maupassant. The naturalists have not yet regained favor, and many of them hardly deserve it. Joris-Karl Huysmans, who is too often grouped with them, deserves to return to popularity, more so, in our eyes, than do Léon Bloy or Barbey d'Aurevilly, two Catholic but uncharitable souls and novelists of some power. Zola suffered, at least among the self-styled elite, from the trend away from naturalism. He remains, however, with Victor Hugo, the only French novelist of the nineteenth century to have reached the masses and to be actually bought and read widely by the 'common reader.' [1]

Zola is now also winning the admiration of scholars, and one may safely predict a wave of dissertations (*tout finit en Sorbonne,* as a Frenchman remarked) on the structure of *Germinal* or of *La Débâcle* and on the stylistic effects of *La Faute de l'Abbé Mouret.* Few subjects would be richer. It is revealing that one of the warmest admirers of Zola was Mallarmé, the purest and least realistic of poets. Henry James could not help envying Zola's power of dealing with crowds, numbers, confused gregarious movements. In *Notes on Novelists,* he compared him, with more sympathy than irony, to 'some mighty animal, a beast of a corrugated hide and a portentous snout, soaking with joy in the warm ooze of an

---

1. We are, of course, omitting novelists whom we, and others, do not consider to have a rank in literature: Eugène Sue, Emile Gaboriau, Alexandre Dumas, Georges Ohnet. They once delighted the middle-class reading public; they are still read and published serially in newspapers, and preferably in Communist ones. *Habent sua fata libelli.*

African riverside.' Arthur Symons, the priest of the symbolist movement, was also partial to Zola; Edmund Gosse, the respectable critic par excellence, who was severe on Charles Dickens's vulgarity and ironical about George Eliot, proclaimed Zola in 1893, in *Questions at Issue*, 'one of the leading men of genius in the second half of the nineteenth century, one of the strongest novelists of the world.'

Flaubert has had to withstand attacks on several scores. His style, on which he had expended much labor and on which he had pinned all his faith, convinced that all else was vanity in a loveless and godless world, meets with few champions among us. Marcel Proust was one of the first to deride its painstaking failure. Paul Valéry mocked Flaubert's ponderousness and his rather weak intellectual grasp (so rules the creator of M. Teste, self-defined by his motto 'stupidity is not my strong point'), which made him an easy prey to the snares of erudition and to the naïve claims of realism. His characters, especially those whom he tried to resuscitate from an archaeological past, are passive and papery. André Gide would not rank Flaubert's novels among the few he would select to bear yearly rereading on the imaginary desert island. André Malraux, in his preface to *Le Temps du mépris* (*Days of Wrath*), and Jean-Paul Sartre, in his manifesto for the opening of *Les Temps modernes,* have been even more blatantly unjust to Flaubert. Some greater measure of justice is now being meted out to him, as it has always been among the English and American novelists, whose allegiance he has not lost. But it is doubtful whether he will ever be restored to a supreme place.

Balzac's greatness is overpowering. The number and the quality of the books written about him between 1935 and 1960 exceed any other body of admirative criticism about any French writer. He has traversed most of the avenues which may tempt the modern novelist. Visionary novelists hail Balzac as their ancestor and master; so do several illuminists, occultists, and fervents of mystical correspondences. But Balzac is also the master of those who undertake to embrace in several volumes the social, economic, and sentimental life of a whole generation. Authors who attempt to create monstrous monomaniacs, or to explore the world of financiers, inventors, and even of homosexuals are easily called Balzacian. François Mauriac has confessed his admiration for Balzac; Proust was fascinated by him, and probably reoriented the course of his fictional epic out of admiration for the *Comédie humaine.* Butor writes on him as the supreme master. Still, because he is too enormous, baffling, and exasperating, and also because his technique, which is subtle despite appearances to the contrary, is closely linked to an imagination that few can emulate, Balzac has not found many imitators in the modern novel. His secrets cannot be appropriated from the outside; and his unsure taste, his liberal digressions, his omniscient generalizations, and his violent or angelic women would impede any disciple.

Stendhal clearly is today, and has been ever since 1920 or so, the novelist of the past who is most, and perhaps too much, with us. Outside France, especially in English-speaking countries, the very small band of the devotees of Stendhal has at last succeeded in making converts among the youth. But French cultists of Stendhal, like the worshippers of Racine, love their hero all the more devotedly as their passion is shared by few foreign initiates. The psychology of love embodied in Stendhal's novels (which is often remote from the theory of love and its crystallization proposed in the same author's treatise on the subject) together with Proust's portrayal of love obsess younger novelists.

Stendhal's attitude toward his heroes, his nonchalantly adroit manner of intervening in his narrative and of taking us into his confidence as accomplices, his hardly concealed romanticism reveling in passion, violence, and generosity, have left their imprint upon French fiction since Gide. The analytical restraint of his style, classical in appearance but vibrating with tingling emotion, has seduced many moderns to revolt against the barrier of words and especially the lush and vague adjectives that, in the more eloquent writers, interpose a screen between the reader and the object presented to him by the author.

Yet Stendhal can be a perilous master. His models of analytical lucidity and of stylistic sobriety may have proved beneficial to a few authors like Albert Camus who, born to the passionate enjoyment of shapes and colors, needed the lesson of restraint and bareness that Stendhal can teach. 'If I am not clear, my whole universe crumbles into nothingness,' declared Stendhal in one of those lapidary sentences admired by Gide and Camus. However, Stendhal fortunately did not banish shade, mystery, and the whisperings of the subconscious from his novels. His most unforgettable scenes in *Lucien Leuwen*, those showing Fabrice in his prison tower, or Julien and Mathilde fighting with each other's pride in the library of the *Hôtel de la Môle*, are instinct with passion all the more fervid for being analyzed. Stendhal's imitators have seldom pierced through to the romantic ebullience in him, which had to be tamed. They have copied the exterior features of his novels and even some of his mannerisms. However, there is, in most recent novels inspired by Stendhal, a dryness and an excessive fear of being the dupe of feelings and of senses, which betray the secret flaw of many a French novelist: lack of faith in his creation and lack of a true novelist's vocation. As Somerset Maugham once remarked, literature, and especially fiction, is in France a *moyen de parvenir,* quicker than politics, surer than business. Hence there is a proliferation of writers who, in other lands, would be hunting foxes, playing cricket, or selling bonds and television sets. Like all Frenchmen, they are adroit and adept at self-analysis.

Stendhal's influence has been paralleled by the acclaim granted to three earlier novelists, who have lately ceased to be labeled as minor. Indeed, they have displaced many of the once famous classics of fiction in our admiration of mid-century: Mme de La Fayette, Choderlos de Laclos, and the Marquis de Sade. Sade seems to be grossly overrated as a novelist. Yet an absurd prejudice terrifies many who, for good aesthetic reasons as well as on grounds of common sense and—why not?—taste, see little in Sade, in Henry Miller, in Raymond Guérin, or even in Jean Genet. They are, however, so afraid of appearing to be old-fashioned that they will pay insincere lip service to the cult of these nether-world deities. Laclos is a much greater artist and a keener psychologist than Sade. André Suarés, André Malraux, Jean Giraudoux, and Albert Camus have paid him glowing tribute. His limitations are serious, since they range from some sterility of imagination and lack of narrative skill to a certain poverty of expression and a total lack of that poetical conception of characters in which Stendhal is triumphant. Within these limits, the *Liaisons dangereuses* is a minor masterpiece and perhaps the best novel of the eighteenth century in France.

As to the *Princesse de Clèves,* it deserves unstinted historical admiration as the first good European novel written after *Don Quixote.* It is the pioneer of a long line of French psychological novels treating of the fear of love in a feminine heart and of a Cornelian struggle within a character who is close to some of Racine's heroines. It is a novel by a woman selecting as her heroine an intelligent woman who ironically and vainly seeks moral guidance in her husband, in a lukewarm or nonexistent religious faith, and in a lover who does little to conquer and therefore to silence her scruples, a lover whom she cannot love truly because she does not esteem him fully. Written in 1678, this novel remains the best written in French by a woman. Its imitators, however, have been exclusively men, from Sendhal's *Armance* to Raymond Radiguet's second novel. Stories of love and self-respect at odds with each other, or tales of fear of love cramping the desire for it are favorite subjects with French dramatists and novelists. After Mme de La Fayette, French women writers, beginning with Mme de Lespinasse, from George Sand to Mme de Noailles, Rachilde, Colette, and Violette Leduc, have seldom balked at impudicity, and men, who prefer to retain the monopoly of sensuality in literature or prefer sobbing feminine ones to feminine hearts laid bare, have not easily forgiven women novelists for their boldness.

Are there a few features of the French novel that have persisted to our day and that may help us evaluate it in its recent metamorphoses? The senseless but convenient saying that exceptions are always to be found to confirm a rule may embolden one to venture a few generalizations.

First, there is order, structure, or, as we prefer to call it, an architectural sense, equally present in French music, painting, drama, landscape gardening, poetry and, naturally, in the foremost French art, that of cooking and of relishing well-composed meals and sipping the attending wines according to a rigid and yet ever-surprising pattern. 'Order the beauty even of beauty is,' said, not a Frenchman, but a Welsh clergyman and rather formless poet, Thomas Traherne, whom Mrs. Wharton liked to quote. John Galsworthy remarked in a vivacious little volume, *Castles in Spain and Other Scripts* (1927), that 'the English novel, though on the whole perhaps more varied and rich than that of any other country, has—from *Clarissa Harlowe* to *Ulysses*—been inclined to self-indulgence: it often goes to bed drunk.' As an antidote, the feeling of enclosure, of planned and self-conscious limitation, which is experienced in Flaubert, has afforded many British novelists a rare and subtle pleasure. 'Never, perhaps, can we hope to bring forth a novelist of such imaginative perfection, so polished, and at the same time so full of fire, as Flaubert,' confessed Osbert Sitwell in *Trio* in 1938—a confession which can but remain unconvincing to a modern Frenchman. The French, who are taught rhetorical composition and analytical clarity from their infancy on, are apt to have less admiration for a fairly common virtue that is easily turned into a fault.

The French have rebelled in our time against the worship of composition, which may lead to a dead order and block the irruption of life, which frightens overcareful planners. Paul Bourget's novels were, in a sense, most elaborately composed but also lifeless, for they failed to rest the synthetic organization of the characters upon a previous intuition of those characters. They banish chance, mystery, irrationality, and life itself. Jules Romains is guilty of the same delusion that a character can be welded together out of several fragments elaborately pieced together. Mauriac himself, hard as he tried to avoid becoming another Bourget and to stress poetry in his fiction, constructed some of his bad novels (he wrote a few bad ones) according to a pattern which left nothing to surprise, not even the unfathomable ways of God converting a sinner.

It is easy to assail the teaching of Flaubert, Bourget, and their successors and to point to the greatest novels, *Le Rouge et le noir, War and Peace,* and *The Brothers Karamazov* as being, almost purposely, ill-composed. Genius has always defeated all generalizations. Many French novelists annoy us with their emphasis on too obvious structural effects and with their economy which borders on poverty. But there remain many others (Louis-Ferdinand Céline, Jean Giono, Georges Bernanos, Robert Pinget in *L'Inquisitoire,* Michel Butor in *Degrés,* are among the most gifted of the moderns) who have spoiled a powerful talent and a significant theme for lack of attention to elimination, selection, and grouping. The structure of any work of art must be its own and must be in harmony with the content of subject matter or temperament expressed in that work. It must not be amenable to set rules. The only truth about the French novel as distinct from some others is that it is more sensitive than the American, the Russian, or the German novel to what Walter Pater called 'the necessity of mind in style.' [2]

This may well be, as has often been contended, the legacy of French classical tragedy to the French novel. For the novel appeared as an autonomous and full-fledged art form at the very time when the last great French classical tragedy, *Phèdre,* had been produced on the Parisian stage (1677). To tragedy, it owed its favorite theme: the analysis of couples, with the help of one or more adjuncts, torn by their loves and hatreds, their jealousies, their ambition to possess, be possessed, or elude possession, achieved through a peculiar intensity of self-exploration. To tragedy it owed also the primacy given to women characters in the earliest masterpieces of French fiction; *La Princesse de Clèves* (1678), *Manon Lescaut* (1735), *Vie de Marianne* (1741), *La Religieuse,* and *La Nouvelle Héloïse* (in the early 1760's) all have one heroine. (In the

2. Pater defined it as 'structure . . . that architectural conception of work which foresees the end in the beginning and never loses sight of it, and in every part is conscious of all the rest, till the last sentence does but, with undiminished vigor, unfold and justify the first.' ('Style,' in *Appreciations.*) Such an ideal does not seem desirable in a novel and has not saved Pater's own novel or tales from the threat of oblivion. Even in a poem it might seem too rigid and too naïve.

following century only, with René, Adolphe and Julien Sorel in *Le Rouge et le noir*, will young men displace women as protagonists.) To the tragedy of Corneille and Racine the French novel also owed its relative artistic purity, its avoidance of humorous or comic episodes, multiplied in the works of Fielding, Smollett, and Dickens, and its linear development.

Giraudoux once sketched an entertaining parallel between the French novel, *une nouvelle manquée*, a short story which, getting out of hand, became a novel, and the English novel, an abortive epic, multiplying digressions and episodes and rambling leisurely along. He called the effect of the French novel that of a shower, while he compared the English to a bath in which one steeps oneself to one's heart's content and slowly absorbs the benign effects of the tepid water. From Rousseau, a Swiss, to Proust, a Parisian, and Romains, a son of Auvergne, there have appeared many French novelists undaunted by length. Patience seems to have grown in the reading public since Romain Rolland, beating Balzac and Zola at their own game, let his Jean-Christophe wander for ten volumes in search of himself and his loves.

But these long sagas also are often made up of separate volumes that retain unity and some autonomy. It probably remains true that, even when they disregard it, French novelists feel behind and around them the presence of a tradition of brevity, tenseness, and linear development with one plot and a few characters. Periodically, they return to it, as Mauriac, Green, and Camus did. Among those born after 1910, the one who has stated the case for classical virtues in the novel most forcibly, Camus, takes as symbolic of that tradition the answer of a guard to Louis XVI when the King, being led to the guillotine, begged the man to accept a message for the Queen: 'I am not here to do your errands, but to take you straight to the scaffold.'[3] The essential classical virtue is aptly called by him a passionate monotony. Novelists, like dramatists, treat the same subject over and over again.

Next to the need for a framework in which to insert and set off the variegated unruliness of life, and to the passion for brevity and stylization meant to make art more intense than actual life, the stress on analysis is doubtless the third chief characteristic of French fiction. Existentialist

3. The essay by Camus is to be found in an important volume of essays on the novel, prepared during World War II and published in 1943, *Problèmes du roman* (Confluences, Lyon et Paris). Jean Prévost, killed in the *maquis* a year later, supervised and edited it.

writers have lately taken the French novel to task for its probing into motives and past regrets; they have seen in it an impediment to projection into the future, which alone can form the nucleus of a free personality. They have set up the American novel as a model for a more virile type of fiction. Their reaction was a healthy one. It surprised not a few Americans, who felt that their native fiction, from Ernest Hemingway to John O'Hara and John Steinbeck, could well do with a little more mature analysis of life and a few more nuances in laying bare the secret springs of behavior.

But the best French writers have seldom been able to follow their American models closely. They have already reverted to a compromise between American imports and their own tradition: the exploration of inner life, the weaving of absurd events into an almost orderly pattern, the intellectual dissociation of ideas, feelings, and subconscious promptings of men and women.

The point needs no laboring. The emphasis on man and, within man, on his ability to see through himself, to yield to desire, greed, crime, charity, or heroism only after clearly realizing why and how he does so has always been the central force in French literature and art, from Chrétien de Troyes, the Proust of the twelfth century as his ardent admirers call him, and from the painter Jean Fouquet in the fourteenth. *Voir clair dans son cœur,* to read clearly in one's heart, is the constant preoccupation of heroines in French comedy, from Marivaux to Anouilh, in Corneille's Pauline and in Racine's Andromaque, as it is that of Adolphe and of the innumerable progeny of that sterile character in modern French fiction. Emphasis on introspection has been fostered by the Catholic confessional, by the reading of ancient authors at school, by the arts of conversation and letter writing (both so often and so delightfully egocentric) and by the quest for multiple affairs of the heart, which however deceptive or painful, are at least taken to further one profitable end—the lover's progress in his own self-exploration.

Its drawbacks are obvious: one of them is that the story is too often made subservient to the complacent self-analysis of the author; the second, the author's diffidence of unreality, of fantastic or imaginary stories, of epic tales, of mystical novels, in which character portrayal tends to disappear and the links with real life and all-too-human men and women are severed. But the positive contribution of the French analytical novel has amply compensated for any deficiencies. The tradition of the French in fiction, and to some extent also that of the Russians and

the Germans, has led them to the perilous, yet valid, temptation of composing novels of ideas. The history of that genre is strewn with misfits.
It may degenerate into an over-conscious allegory or favor characters
who are mere puppets pulled to and fro by the author's tyranny over his
creations; it is thus drawn to the Voltairian philosophical tale, to the
pleasant but shallow dissertations of Anatole France, and the excessive
self-awareness of Aldous Huxley.

It is dangerous indeed to portray a character bulging with ideas, because the ideas will probably be identified as the author's own and will
intrude into the narrative. While brilliant paradoxes are bandied back
and forth, life may remain in the background. But the distrust of the
intellect in the art of fiction has proved a worse peril still, one which has
seduced too easily many half-cultured storytellers. After all, the great
conflicts of our age are conflicts of ideas, or of myths, that is, of ideas
made vital and impelling men to action. The novel has become willy-
nilly the most powerful vehicle for the expression of ideas or for their
popularization. Even more than history, it has been for fifty years intellectual dynamite. Behind much fiction by Gide, Mann, Malraux, and
Camus, there echoes the voice of Nietzsche and that peculiar tragic emotion of our age that the French term *le tragique de l'intellect*. These
novelists, with Proust, Joyce, Hermann Broch, Hermann Hesse, and
Sartre of course, are men of unusual intelligence, teeming with ideas, and
their fiction gains by this fact even if it loses in naïveté. Ideas are lived
by them, 'felt in the blood, and felt along the heart,' and are not translated into terms of fiction but conceived in those very terms and imper-
sonated before they appear consciously to the author.

Indeed, the difference between Thomas Hardy, Theodore Dreiser, and
Sinclair Lewis and the giants of the novel, between Francis Carco,
Georges Simenon, and Jean Giraudoux and their greater French contemporaries is a difference of intellectual as well as of imaginative power.
Herman Melville and Henry James appear to us today (since James's
death in 1916 and Melville's centenary in 1919, which ended his prolonged stay in Purgatory) as towering above other novelists of the
American nineteenth century for the same reason. Melville's intellectual
energy, while primarily that of a storyteller and a maker of myths, was
also expressed in pregnant reflections on his art, such as are casually
scattered in *The Confidence Man*. James's prefaces and letters are famous. Well could he declare with some pride: 'No good novel ever proceeded from a superficial mind.'

Absorption in ideas or in intellectual reactions and in their elucidation by a searching mind has harmed many a French novelist and led him to distrust imagination overmuch. Gide's youthful confession, in his diary of 1893, points to the weakness inherent in an excessive clear-sightedness. 'With me, imagination rarely precedes the idea . . . I have the idea of a work several years before I then imagine it.' Stendhal, in a famous confession, had perceived the foible of that national turn of mind that, with all his worship of energy and passion, was his too. 'I always lay my nets too high; nothing low is ever caught in them.'

Such a charge proffered against the French novel may appear as a paradox to those who remember how often it has been accused of immorality. Traditionally, since George Sand and Balzac, French novelists have been feared by the British as corrupters. A certain sanity and mature courage in refusing to eschew love scenes or to throw a veil over some climaxes which can be the object of serious and even poetical delineation characterize French novels. Sex is treated frankly by the French, and such frankness perhaps indicates more respect than does some of the ponderous sentimentalization frequent in German fiction or the timidity of very brutal American novelists of recent years. In fact, no other nation has probably treated the subject of love with such gravity as do the French. It is usually accompanied by tenderness, that delightful 'rest from passion,' by mutual esteem, and comradeship; and the physical communion is seldom unaccompanied by the play of the intellect, which watches, understands, analyzes, and occasionally ennobles.

The word by which Frenchmen like to characterize their novelists is hardly translatable; its English counterpart, 'moralists,' fails to convey all that it connotes in French. The ultimate justification of literature for most French people is moral, in the sense that it must push ever further man's knowledge of man, and be easily condensed into precepts that may enable readers to act 'morally,' that is to say, more lucidly and more sincerely. Jean Cocteau, André Breton, Mauriac, and Camus have all proclaimed their concern with *la morale,* which, in the feminine gender, becomes for them a muse, a mistress, the one idol that withstands all assaults. No Frenchman can resist scattering in his larger works a few epigrammatic thoughts summing up his experience of life and his vision of human affairs, with cynicism occasionally but more often than not with earnestness. Through these tablets of compressed wisdom, he naïvely expects to cure some of the illusions, if not some of the diseases, of mankind.

A breviary of higher wisdom can thus be extracted, not only from professional moralists like Montaigne and Pascal, but from Balzac, Proust, Malraux, and Cocteau. These maxims are incisive, polished, pared down to a few explosive words. Like La Fontaine's fables, they denounce vanity, insecurity, fickleness, and imprudence in the civilized garden of life, from which the Frenchman fondly hopes to expel hazards, blind passions, wild beasts, and obtrusive neighbors. Behind his veneer of irony, which is a mild revenge on life from him who preaches and perhaps practices virtue, the optimistic Frenchman expects that his wisdom, gained through hardships, may keep his readers and their children from venturing into paths of danger. His instinct for economy makes him believe that the experience of one generation can be handed down intact to another in a few neat formulas and save the new generation trial and error. The Anglo-Saxon is a truer cynic. Neither Ernest Hemingway nor Norman Mailer, neither James Joyce nor Virginia Woolf foolishly hoped that, by inserting some such condensed reflections into their tales of war, love, and spiritual adventure, they would ever deter their readers and their readers' sons from stumbling into folly and despair.

Modern philosophers are fond of disserting on values. It is hardly in the novelist's role to propose general reflections on the subject. Yet his art, while primarily concerned with storytelling and giving life to characters, is also a creation of values. He weaves a pattern out of the baffling contradictions of reality; he endows with some consistency those strange creatures who surround him in life and seem now empty, now bewilderingly erratic, now steeped in the full logic of unpoetical lives. He singles out a few significant events from the disconcerting disorder of chance happenings, establishes some relation of cause and effect where Fate, with its ironical irrelevancies, appeared to intervene arbitrarily. In so doing, he lays bare the true man in us—a truer man than is heard declaiming on the radio, seen moving jitteringly about on a screen, and myopically observed or belittled by journalists, travelers, and letter writers. And because such a man is a knot of relations, an individual linked by subtle ties to his physical and social environment, willingly held in check by shifting but impressive ethical codes to which he bows even when he disobeys them, the novelist is in our age a worthy successor to the priest and to the moralist. D. H. Lawrence, as good a storyteller as appeared in our century in England, often proved a turgid and apocalyptic reasoner; but he was clear-sighted when, like Proust, Mauriac, Giono, Saint-Exupéry, Malraux, Montherlant, Camus, and Sartre, he perceived the advantages that a novelist who remains an imaginative artist can derive from posing moral problems. He wrote, in a fragment collected in *Phœnix:*

> Morality is that delicate, forever trembling and changing balance between me and my circumambient universe, which precedes and accompanies a true relatedness . . . The novel is the highest example of subtle inter-relatedness that man has discovered. Everything is true in its own time, place, circumstance, and untrue outside of its own place, time, circumstance. If you try to nail anything down in the novel, either it kills the novel or the novel gets up and walks away with the tale.

The last decade of the nineteenth century and the first decade of the twentieth appear to us today as a low point in the history of French fiction. Books published in Paris continued indeed to be sold by the thousands all over the world; Anatole France was for many years identified with all that was subtle and mildly perverse in Gallic letters; Romain Rolland seemed to denationalize and deprovincialize French fiction, and his *Jean-Christophe* drew tears from many eyes. Paul Bourget was proposing first moral problems, then social ones, with convincing dialectic and a few scientific terms attuned to the pre-Freudian era. Henry Bordeaux, René Bazin, and a few other pillars of traditionalism perceived the possibilities of the novel for maintaining scions of noble families, future parish priests, and convent-educated, genteel young ladies on the path to virtue and resignation. Pierre Loti, plaintively tossing his disenchanted soul on strange seas and searching for picturesque feminine puppets and passionate sailors amid exotic climes, carried on the genre of romantic fiction. Maurice Barrès, the least popular abroad of these five masters of French romance, probably the best stylist of them all, and today the least antiquated, attempted a curious experiment in collective fiction with *Les Déracinés* (1897), and, in *La Colline inspirée* (1913), offered the original achievement of a Catholic and mystical novel written by an unbeliever. But ideas that are not transmuted into emotions by the alchemy of imagination soon make a novel monotonous and lifeless. The generation that had been powerfully moved by the Dreyfus trial did not succeed in achieving the significant novel on politics that France awaited. A true novelist needs more faith and less irony, perhaps even a little more vulgarity and occasional stupidity, than these refined and fashionable observers of human folly possessed.

Parallel with this emphasis on the mind and on the psychological novel as opposed to the realistic and naturalistic one, the symbolist trend, in the years 1890–1910, set other pitfalls for fiction. It perceived ethereal and profound symbols behind most appearances. It took flight from earth, its mud, its real men and women, toward blessed damozels, sexless angelic creatures, imaginary polar settings, and perpetual yearning for the Idea underlying all faint representations that reached our prisoners' cave. 'No! bodies are not indispensable interpreters!' exclaims a young character in Gide's earliest volume of prose. And Gide delighted in describing the allegorical *Voyage d'Urien* in which, as the pun in the title suggests, neither scenery nor character has any reality. Symbolist fiction may be credited with a few curious attempts at personal analysis of a young man's soul (in *Valbert,* by T. de Wyzewa, in Edouard Dujardin's *Les Lauriers sont coupés,* which since has won fame as the systematic interior monologue that may have helped James Joyce's *Ulysses*) and with some original, but overwritten and overeloquent, novels, by Joris-Karl Huysmans and Elémir Bourges. But an excessive and 'arty' self-consciousness, a prophetic and declamatory tone, and a uniform haze, muffling all the characters and perfidiously dulling the reader's attention, seem to afflict most of the symbolist novels attempted in any language (and America is not immune from the peril, as readers who have remained allergic to Djuna Barnes's *Nightwood* or to William Goyen's *The House of Breath* will recall). In a splendid series of articles published in 1913 in the *Nouvelle Revue Française,* later collected in the posthumous *Nouvelles Etudes,* Jacques Rivière, then a young critic of twenty-eight, denounced the pernicious influence of symbolism upon fiction. Soon after, when Proust's first volume appeared, it was imbued with symbolist influences, but the author had assimilated and outgrown them and had made them subservient to his purpose as a novelist.

The French novel in particular stood in need of new blood in the years preceding World War I. It was then wading through one of the low-water tides of its history and ran the serious danger of perishing from drought. Naturalism, whatever we may think of it in retrospect (and returns to it are staged periodically), had brought about a triumph for French fiction. But the new vogue for the Russian novel was already, in France at least, undermining the success of Zola and his disciples. Eugène Melchior de Vogüé's book *Le Roman russe* (1882) had made a deep impression; no less a personage than Taine declared soon after to Vogüé that 'Zola, Daudet, Goncourt and others are not worthy to untie the shoelaces of that man [Dostoevski].'

In France, the years 1910–30 have as much unity as any literary period can assume. Elsewhere [4] we proposed the view, which has since won fairly general acceptance, that the new physics (Max Planck and Albert Einstein), the new psychology (Sigmund Freud and his followers), the reactions against Henri Bergson in philosophy and the advocacy of neo-Thomism, the scientific study of literary history and of history (Gustave Lanson, Victor Langlois, and Charles Seignobos), the renewal of socio-logical, anthropological, religious, and ethical studies (by Emile Durk-heim's disciples: Lévy-Bruhl, Rauh, and others) were accompanied around 1910, indeed preceded, by a revolution in literature and the arts. Guillaume Apollinaire sensed the significance of that revolution and was instrumental in effecting it in painting and poetry. Arthur Rimbaud and Stéphane Mallarmé suddenly came into their own, and from their exam-ple the surrealists and Paul Valéry were to derive theoretical conse-quences and felicitous inspiration. Paul Cézanne's lesson at last was proving fruitful, and the post-impressionists were recognized and praised. The superficial drama of the boulevards was battered. New periodicals appeared, new critics took stock of the legacy of symbolism (Albert Thi-baudet, André Suarès, Jacques Rivière) and encouraged bolder steps forward. Men who had long waited for an audience (André Gide, Paul Claudel, Charles Péguy, Marcel Proust) suddenly sprang to the fore between 1910 and the outbreak of World War I. Almost all of those who were to be acclaimed in the postwar years began to give substantial proof of their talent around 1910–11. Their names are: Bernanos, Char-donne, Cocteau, Duhamel, Alain-Fournier, Giraudoux, Jouhandeau, Jouve, Larbaud, Martin du Gard, Mauriac, Maurois, Morand, Paulhan, Reverdy, Rivière, Romains, St.-John Perse, Vildrac. Fiction, too, in France in the years 1910–30, is marked by a few features that will naturally leave their imprint upon the subsequent span of forty years that it is our purpose to discuss.

But first, a brief epitaph on a few graves. The historical novel seems to be dead and gone—deader in France than in English-speaking coun-tries, where Margaret Mitchell and, after a fashion, Robert Penn Warren or Robert Graves have revived the genre with a measure of success. A case could be made for historical fiction, at a time when history proper has often hedged itself around with footnotes and documents and has ceased to be a part of the reading of cultured men and women.

4. In a volume, now out of print, entitled *Hommes et œuvres du XXe siècle* (Corrêa, 1939) and in an essay on '1914: annus mirabilis,' *The Baltimore Museum of Art*, October–November 1964.

Romanticized biography has stepped in where historical novels used to reign supreme a century and a quarter ago, when Walter Scott provided Balzac with his impetus and launched Leopold von Ranke on the path to accurate history. Not even nostalgic regret for a glorious past, during the tragic ordeal of the two world wars and of a decline in French power, has succeeded in luring French novelists to their Revolution, their Age of Louis XIV, or the romantic Middle Ages, staged by Gore Vidal in this country as a symbolic setting for his *Search for the King*. The only exception is a Russian-born French novelist, Zoë Oldenbourg, whose novels in a medieval setting, *Argile et Cendres* (1947), *La Pierre angulaire* (1953), *Catherine the Great* showed skill and narrative talent.

The poetical novel, also dear to the romantics, has likewise disappeared. What in Shakespeare and in Racine is taken to be an effective aesthetic device becomes intolerable in a novel and in prose. Proust, Giraudoux, and Giono have at times ventured dangerously close to the poetical novel; they have been saved, the first by the originality of his psychology, the second by his irony, the third by his robustness as a *surmâle*, as the French word puts it. Description has become a lost art. The influence of painting, then of the cinema has been immense, if seldom recognized, on the reading public far more than on the novelists. Landscape in literature has been divested of its estate.

Finally, the plot as such counts far less than it used to. There again, the movies and the detective story have lightened the weight that used to be borne by the novels of Balzac, Dickens, and Dostoevski. Breathless surprises, thrills of suspense before and after a murder, and patient questioning about when and how the chaste heroine would let her virtue be defeated, appear unsophisticated to many a novel reader today. He enjoys these devices in detective stories read as relaxation, and as a geometrical combination to satisfy his logical brain, seeking a cause for every effect and trying to identify murderers of victims who were never very much alive in any case, at least psychologically. But intricacies of plot, subtle progression toward a climax, and unraveling of the knotted threads in the conclusion seem naïve to most modern novelists. What happens is secondary to the question: How are the characters changing under the impact of incidents? In Mauriac, Camus, Sartre, and, to a lesser degree, in André Malraux and Julien Green, the unfolding of events can be guessed from the start or is revealed from the start if the author works back from the present to a reminiscence of the events and motives that resulted in a crime, a trial, a great passion, or a great remorse.

More recent novelists, such as Philippe Sollers, Jean-Pierre Faye, even

Michel Simon, have been even less concerned in focusing the interest
of their condescending novels on plot or the conflict of characters, or
on anything recalling an imitation of reality. They have been in love
with language and introduced a Racinian stylization into fiction, in a
manner which might have fulfilled Leonardo's dictum that the most
difficult of all arts is that which best transposes the real into speech.

Several times since 1910, or perhaps since Rivière's articles in 1913,
critics have called for a renaissance of the novel of adventure. They
hoped that Pierre MacOrlan or Francis Carco might provide it, after the
works of Claude Farrère and Pierre Benoît had ceased to be regarded as
literature. Their hopes have hardly been fulfilled. The only adventure
that has inspired good novels, from Alain-Fournier's *Le Grand Meaulnes*
to Saint-Exupéry, has been psychological. Men's lives have not been
devoid of hazards and contingency in our age, and neither historical
determinism nor the revelation of blind impulses from our libido and
from primeval forces lingering in us has banished the mystery of *res
adventura*, of what is yet to come and surprise us. But the novelist's
purpose is to endow the contingent with a certain necessity, to integrate
chance accidents into the total and fairly consistent pattern of a man's
life, as accepted and even as wanted by him. Adventures in *La Chartreuse de Parme*, in which the structure of the plot counts for little compared with the invention lavished by the author on individual scenes,
have delighted many a modern reader whom Balzac's laborious schemes
left unimpressed. Many good modern novels are Stendhalian in the sense
that they neglect the central plot and the structure and scaffoldings that
should support them, but lavish their art on individual scenes that alone
will remain engraved in the reader's memory.

On the positive side, the revolution that began in French fiction
around 1910 (and that is closely paralleled by a renewal in English
fiction about the same time) may be summed up in the word 'disintegration,' stripped of all disparaging connotations. It was, first of all, a disintegration of our idea of reality. Science was then effecting a similar
disintegration, which was to usher in the atomic age. But literature owed
nothing to science; if anything, the literary revolution preceded the
change in scientific thought. Poets and novelists like to be called prophetic, and indeed they have been. French fiction had climbed on the
band wagon of science in 1860–90, only to discover that scientific truth
is the most ephemeral of all truths. As a German, J. von Uexhüll, declared in 1909: 'A scientific truth is but the error of tomorrow.' Proust,
Giraudoux, Virginia Woolf, and Kafka remained unaware of the new

physics, probably to their dying day. But they brought about the definitive break with realism in the novel that liberated modern fiction.

Proust attacked realism scathingly in the last volume of *Le Temps retrouvé:* 'The kind of literature which is content with describing things, while it calls itself realistic, is the furthest removed from reality.' Giraudoux and Cocteau depicted life as a pointillist and delightfully confusing welter of impressions. Virginia Woolf, in her entertaining essay railing at Arnold Bennett and his contemporaries H. G. Wells and John Galsworthy, all painstakingly bent upon rendering houses, furniture, silverware, and upholstery of London men of property, inhabitants of the five towns, or of the world of William Clissold, asserted: 'On or about December, 1910, human character changed.' [5] The liberation from too coarse a conception of reality was badly needed at the beginning of the twentieth century. It was effected, thanks to the generation of novelists reaching their manhood or womanhood around 1910. They opened up richer possibilities to fiction as an art.

The second disintegration, now linked with the great name of Freud, was that of our classical idea of man. The notions of libido, the id, the ego, and the superego have not, however, become integrated into the culture of the French common reader as they have in America. Many writers remained unaware of Freud's discoveries or impervious to them as late as 1925 and even 1935. Proust probably never knew anything precise about psychoanalysis. But there again novelists have been ahead of science. They broke up the classical concept of the unity of man, which Stendhal and then Dostoevski had already severely damaged. They freely juxtaposed insoluble contradictions in their characters and sought what Baudelaire had already called antithetic, yet simultaneous, directions toward God and toward Satan. They delved into the subconscious and became fascinated by eroticism. They became especially conscious of the sadistic-masochistic impulses dormant in most normal people and often co-existing with moral principles and saintly behavior. To be sure, there was much sadism already, not only in Sade, who was read by only a few until the last decades, but in Balzac, and Emily Brontë, and especially in Charles Dickens (*Nicholas Nickleby, Barnaby Rudge, Dombey and Son*), who was fascinated by it while condemning it. But our vision of man has been immensely enriched by the novelists of our century, who have torn many of the soothing illusions that used to veil our lower selves from our vision.

5. *Mr. Bennett and Mrs. Brown* (Hogarth Press, London, 1928).

This disintegration of our classical notion of personality was helped by World War I, in which many novelists participated (Giraudoux, Mauriac, Duhamel, Drieu La Rochelle, Aragon), while others watched it eagerly, repelled and fascinated (Romains, Colette, Cocteau, young Radiguet). The war itself is treated in far fewer French than American novels. It seems to have inspired many Americans to write, especially ambulance drivers. Nor did it evoke among French writers the same horrified disgust of civilized and sportive gentlemen as it did in English literature (Ralph Mottram, Robert Graves, Richard Aldington, and D. H. Lawrence; and Siegfried Sassoon, Wilfred Owen, and Edward Thomas among the poets). André Gide, François Mauriac, Jean Cocteau, Paul Morand, and Valéry Larbaud preferred to ignore the subject. But the wound was deeper in France than elsewhere, too deep for literary expression, and much of the cruelty and the cynicism depicted in fiction since 1920 originated in the display of man's inhumanity to man that haunted the survivors of Verdun and the Somme.

Linked with the atomization of man's personality, which characterized fiction between 1910 and 1930, is the predominance of two themes or types of characters that gives many of the novels of that age their main tonality. Most of the heroes are devoid of will power and delight in the resulting lack of any axis in their personality, and the majority of them are adolescents, usually of the male sex, if not of an ambiguous or ambidextrous one.

Hamlet has been hailed as the inspirer or the model of many French writers until 1930 or so, and their disease is currently called in France 'hamletism.' Ever since the romantics, the French had been obsessed by the Shakespearean hero. But what had been a literary vogue spread to a larger number of Frenchmen when, after 1918, they were confronted by the need to act and live up to their Pyrrhic victory and also by the unpredictable consequences of their action. The world overestimated French power and even spoke of French hegemony in Europe; diplomats concluded a net-work of treaties to make themselves believe that time could be stopped and life crystallized by legalistic agreements. But the men of letters, as usual, were more clear-sighted and fifteen years ahead of other observers. They realized that their victory was only luring them into postponing reforms or the needed revolution, that their country was weaker than it appeared to the world, and that the slaughter of a million and a half young men had left their comrades frightened in the presence of the gigantic task expected of them.

Hence the invasion of the novel by young men, devoid of will, weighing on a vast Elsinore platform the skulls of their friends fallen in battle, as Valéry was to say in a famous article. They distrusted propaganda, because war had fed them with official lies; they distrusted politics, since politicians had not averted the war; they distrusted women, because they had helped the patriotic propaganda and admired heroes in uniform and been the mainstay of the pressure of public opinion to encourage men to fight; they distrusted themselves most of all, and the generous but ill-starred *élan* of the youth of 1914. They set about rebuilding the ruins; they rushed to dancing halls, musical *cafés,* jazz orchestras, and cosmopolitan and Bohemian sets populated Montparnasse, and paraded a *joie de vivre* that half concealed their surprise at finding themselves alive after the long ordeal. Like their predecessors, the Julien Sorels and the Rastignacs who grew to manhood after the Napoleonic wars, they rushed insolently to the means of power left after the years of battle: money-making and unscrupulous *arrivisme.* But they lacked the vigor of their romantic ancestors, who, while reading Alphonse de Lamartine and George Sand and carrying their hearts in a sling, had achieved the first French industrial revolution. They took greater delight in pitiless self-analysis than in action. They were sought after by the postwar women in the bustle of the marriage mart, where men were outnumbered and could select, and change their minds or their partners. They disarticulated themselves, and in their novels they complacently analyzed their self-pity, their hesitations, and the finer nuances of their ego.[6]

The primacy of the adolescent in French fiction from Proust's *Du côté de chez Swann,* Alain-Fournier's *Grand Meaulnes,* Giraudoux's *Simon le pathétique,* and Radiguet's and Cocteau's teenagers to Mauriac and Martin du Gard's young heroes is a strange phenomenon, which has been studied in an excellent monograph by Justin O'Brien and, from another angle, by Mauriac in a revealing little book, *Le Jeune Homme* (1926). Adolescents were not scarce in ancient literature. They had haunted the imagination of many a painter, such as Leonardo and Bronzino. But they had hardly ever been analyzed in their contradictions and in their violent impulses to despair, to revolt, and to idealism as they

6. Typical illustrations are many understudies of Gide's Lafcadio in the novel of those years; also, the characters in Edouard Estaunié, Jacques Rivière's two analytical novels, in Jacques de Lacretelle; Phillippe Soupault, Marcel Arland, the early Henri de Montherlant, Paul Morand, Betz's *L'Incertain,* Robert de Traz's *L'Ecorché,* Pierre Drieu la Rochelle's *L'Homme couvert de femmes.* Joseph Kessel's *Le Tour du malheur* belatedly (in 1949) depicts the same era and its moods.

have been in recent French fiction. They have displaced not only the *jeune fille*, who never held a great fascination for French novelists, but their former favorite characters, the mature woman troubled by her 'noonday demon,' and the middle-aged Don Juan unweariedly playing his part of Bel-Ami.

Goethe's Wilhelm Meister, Balzac's Rubempré, and Stendhal's heroes in his three main novels were somewhat different from the adolescents of sixteen to nineteen who have invaded modern fiction. Novelists then preferred to start with the early years of manhood, when the young man, having put on his *toga praetexta*, was completing his education through war, politics, and the affairs of the stage, of literature, or of the heart. George Sand, whose story of her life reveals a much keener psychologist than many of her romantic novels, was the first to remark, in the early chapters of her autobiography, that poets and novelists had unduly neglected the rich subject of the adolescent, worshipping his mother and not yet severed from her spiritually, but ready to transfer to another woman and to another plane some of his feelings, often ugly, rebellious, spiteful, but nevertheless shy and athirst for poetry. Dostoevski's novel *The Adolescent* influenced the modern French more than George Sand's prophetic passage, which Justin O'Brien rediscovered. But the French, however hard they try, seldom can unreservedly subscribe to the hysterical behavior and to the antics, apparently sincere, that Dostoevski's heroes, and still more his heroines, can stage with much ease. Gide was a more direct inspirer of the French portrayers of adolescence who had been struck by his Nathanael, his prodigal son, and his Lafcadio.

Twentieth-century fiction in France, soon imitated by fiction in other countries, thought it had charted one of those unknown and metaphorically fertile fields in the theme of homosexuality. The theme had been central, twenty centuries or more before, in the literature of antiquity. But it had not assumed the tragic character it received when religion, society, and our prevailing mores, outlawing homosexuality, made it a glamorous forbidden fruit for some, the mark of an ineluctable pursuit by fate for others. If one judges it purely on the literary plane, the theme of homosexual love offers undoubted advantages to the novelist. It lends itself to an atmosphere of secrecy, dear to many readers of detective stories. It affords the thrill of breaking social codes, at a time when adultery and so-called illicit sex relations seem to have lost much of the glamor that surrounded them when *Madame Bovary* revolted French taste in 1857. It cuts across ordinary social strata, and, when men on the wrong side of forty, no longer able to rely upon their charm alone, have to seek their victims or their partners among servants, sailors, and young men whom they bribe, it takes on the pitiful form of social *déclassement*, of venality, and of cruel disparity of ages, well known to readers of Proust and Gide. It has, more, perhaps, than any other single factor, contributed to the predominance of a new type in modern French fiction: *l'homme traqué*, the man hunted by fate, by his passions, by his vice, by his tragic solitude, and yearning for the beauty and formal serenity of a work of art to escape from the night in which he is doomed to grope his guilty way.

Sociologists, who are slow at learning from the insight of fictional works, in which a keener and unhappier sensibility than theirs often senses the most acute problem of the age, may some day look for social, perhaps even economic, causes to explain the vogue of pederasty as a literary subject and the apparently larger proportion of homosexuals to be found among creative writers than among other men, and especially among creative writers since the era of Walter Pater, Oscar Wilde, Paul Verlaine, Pierre Loti, and Marcel Proust. Has the custom of early marriage (often in the early twenties) among students and young men of letters and the consequent financial pressure on them driven the gifted heterosexual writers to pursuits other than literature, leaving the field to those who did not seek the responsibilities of a wife and children? Has the growing comradeship between the sexes and often the effort on the part of the young woman to behave, talk, think like a man divested the woman of some of her traditional charm and convinced some disciples of Plato that intellectual beauty, if it must be sought behind the deceptive appearance of the bodily envelope, can be found more abundantly in young males? Such explorations obviously do not go deep enough. The secret is psychological and individual in the first place. But the increase of self-confessed homosexuals among the gifted men of letters is also in part a social phenomenon, in which imitation and closely knit *confréries* of persons so inclined praising and pushing each other's works may well have a share. The subject cannot be ignored, since it has contributed to the tragic loneliness of many modern heroes and to the now common picture of the family as a prison from which one escapes and no longer as a nucleus around which everything converges.[7]

7. John Aldridge, in *After the Lost Generation* (McGraw-Hill Book Company, 1951), notes (p. 100) the intrusion of the same theme of homosexuality in several contem-

Paradoxically, at the very time when the novel was taking as its assumptions the disintegration of reality as formerly conceived, the disintegration of personality, and the disintegration of the ultimate social cell, the family, it was also returning to a long, devious, meandering type of epic fiction in several volumes, often grouped around one or several families, the *roman-fleuve*. The reasons for such a vogue are complex. Critics often make the mistake of ignoring the fact that literature is, if not conditioned by, at least produced for a public and for specific publishers aware of the public's buying habits, by authors who have to make a living. A French book will be published, and apparently will be bought, more readily if it falls under a series; fanciful titles for these 'collections' enliven the catalogues of French publishers. Similarly, it was thought, and apparently with good reason, since Romain Rolland's and Marcel Proust's fictional avalanches, that the collector or the thrifty bourgeois who has ventured to purchase the first four or five volumes of a saga-novel would not wish to see his investment interrupted. He might even—who knows?—be so thrilled after volume eight or fourteen that the good will of his purse would continue to respond *in saecula saeculorum*.

But literary motives may also be adduced to account for the extraordinary vogue of the *roman-fleuve*. First, especially after 1920 or thereabouts, the French novelists desired to compete on equal terms with their Russian and English confreres. Parisian publishers had long worked on the assumption that the French, being a light, fickle, and impatient race, should have their novels brief, compressed, and selective; or that, being self-proclaimed masters in the knowledge of the human, and particularly of the feminine heart, they insisted on their fiction being stripped of all that was not 'psychology.' Then they discovered that the public was ready to welcome *War and Peace, The Brothers Karamazov*, and almost any long novel translated from the English, and, later on, from the German and American. They blamed the decadence of taste and the decline of culture, which were discarding the great classical lesson, the art of omission, and destroying the intelligent group of

porary American novels by Frederick Buechner, Vance Bourjaily, Truman Capote, J. H. Burns, Gore Vidal, and others. British fiction is now coming to the same subject with *Hemlock and After* by Angus Wilson (Viking Press, 1952) and the extraordinary story of a British officer in Burma by Walter Baxter, *Look Down in Mercy* (G. P. Putnam's Sons, 1951). The most superb example of a novel about a man haunted not by homosexuality but by alcoholism is *Under the Volcano* (Reynal and Hitchcock, 1947), by Malcolm Lowry.

readers who scorned violent effects and superabundance of details. Incidentally, they forgot all about Balzac and Hugo and a number of Frenchmen whose long serial novels and lavishness of words and over-stressed effects had not repelled an earlier public.

Many Frenchmen thus became convinced that a true novel must be long and that their traditional fiction was much too stripped of essential nonessentials, too linear in its hasty ascent to a climax and subsequent descent, too dramatic in its elimination of all that, in the characters, did not bear directly on the central crisis in which they would be the fever-ish actors.

While the French *roman-fleuve* was often eager to rival Dostoevski in its profusion of seemingly irrelevant details and in its juxtaposition of unreconciled contradictions in men's motives and actions, it also pursued another end; it attempted, in the years that followed the Dreyfus case and seemed to herald the triumph of both sociology and of socialism, to abandon the narrow analysis of one individual, usually telling the story of some episode in his life in the first person singular. The more thoughtful among the French novelists have reflected much, at the time of Proust and since, on the perils of the so-called autobiographical novel, in truth a contradiction in terms. The advantages in credibility and consistency to be gained by memoirs are obvious; the unity of the point of view is easily achieved; the author may yield to poetical evocations, to self-pity, and even more to self-vindication; he leads events and characters safely to a preordained conclusion, which is his present mood of serenity and complacency. But the loss is immense; the multiplicity of possibilities and the thrilling sense for the reader that the novelist is unsure of the future and of the forthcoming development of his characters disappear. Events are relived by memory, but they are not re-created into an animated whole. And the sincerity of the storyteller can be much greater than that of the reminiscing autobiographical author, hemmed in on all sides by factual truth and unable to reach toward the deeper, symbolic truth that fictional creatures of Stendhal or Proust achieve.[8] Hence the ambition to flee from the self-analytical ego and from the intimate diary, the perpetual pitfall for French fiction, and to

8. See especially Duhamel, *Remarques sur les mémoires imaginaires* (Mercure de France, 1934); Gide's obsession with the problem in his *Journal*, in *Si le grain ne meurt* (If It Die), and elsewhere; Martin-Chauffier's acute essay on 'Proust and the Double I,' *Partisan Review*, October 1949. I have written at greater length on the subject in *Literature and Sincerity* (Yale University Press, 1963).

embrace the vast picture of changing scene through a score of years.

The best known of the *romans-fleuves,* reminiscent of Zola's Rougon-Macquart series more than of Balzac's recurring characters in his portrayal of the whole of France, are Romains's *Les Hommes de bonne volonté* (*Men of Good Will*), Martin du, Gard's *Les Thibault* (*The World of the Thibaults*), Duhamel's *Chronique des Pasquiers.* René Béhaine has his admirers, but he has failed to win an audience, outside of a very small French circle, for his *Histoire d'une société.* Lacretelle embarked on a *roman-fleuve* with his *Hauts-Ponts* (1932–33) and stopped after the fourth volume, out of breath and deserted by most of his readers. The French Academy, however, soon rewarded him for his portrayal of a woman's obstinate attachment to her family estate. Later still, a lingering desire to depict French society between the two wars inspired Joseph Kessel in *Le Tour du malheur,* Maurice Druon in *Les Grandes Familles,* Paul Vialar in *La Mort est un commencement,* two series of saga novels set in Russia and in France by Henri Troyat, and even J.-P. Sartre. It may be confessed, however, that the sociological ambitions of the French novel have been frustrated, and that its portrayal of French society holds hardly more interest for younger readers today than do *The Forsyte Saga* and its sequels or H. G. Wells's novels for the new generations of the English. The novel is probably a better document when it is one without the author's being aware of the fact or when, like Balzac's *Comédie humaine,* it distorts what it renders so powerfully that it becomes the truth of tomorrow.

After 1930, the social ambition of the novel gave way, in France and soon in other countries, to its metaphysical ambition. Joyce confessed that he wished to free himself from the nightmare of history; ironically, our successors may someday admire him primarily as the portrayer of Dublin. Kafka became the model most oppressive for younger novelists; Mann of *Buddenbrooks,* probably his best artistic achievement and his most durable one, was almost forgotten for the philosophical speculations of *The Magic Mountain* and of *Doctor Faustus.* In France, from Malraux to Sartre and from Cocteau to Genet, no self-respecting writer would sketch a novel without scaling the heights of the difficulty of being, of assuming freedom and responsibility, and of organizing a frail existence constantly threatened by disintegration and nothingness.

II

Martin du Gard, Duhamel,
Romains, and Radiguet

The most embarrassing predicament that a critic of recent literature finds
himself in is having to take a stand and to select, with not a little arbi-
trariness, the authors whom he deems worthy of being read, reread, and
therefore characteristic, important, great perhaps, and likely to survive.
To balk before such a task and instead to enumerate a confusingly vast
list of names is cowardly and turns a volume of critical information into
a dictionary. To retain solely the novelists whom the critic or historian
considers as falling within the exclusive perspective that a dogmatic view
of literature forces upon him would be a mark of arrogance, and unfair
to the dissenting reader. A list of the French novelists of some significance,
with a brief characterization of their talent, is appended to this book and
should prove useful. In these chapters, a choice had to be made which
reflects the author's judgment and his temperamental preferences. Labels
and categories such as 'the Catholic novel,' 'the psychological novel,'
'the social or collective fiction' have been avoided. This book deals with
novelists and not with the art of the novel in general. Any division into
schools or into periods would be artificial. The critical dates around
which a new trend appears to have asserted itself in the literary evolution of France fall, as it happens, at intervals of roughly twenty years.
The year 1910, when the new century truly found its originality, is our
starting point. The artistic, musical, literary movements then initiated
by the experimenters in those arts were not stopped, nor were they drastically renovated, by World War I: but they had expended themselves

37

by 1930 or so, when new influences were brought to bear upon French intellectual life. Again, World War II matured the general reader for the ideas and art forms which had made their way in 1930 or thereabout; but it did not create anything drastically new. Sartre, Camus, Anouilh had already been writing in the late 'thirties. A broad unity may be seen to encompass the score of years which covered, from 1930 to 1950, the Depression, the Spanish Civil War, World War II, and its aftermath of hopes and disappointments. After 1950, new moods as well as new talents appeared; the patriarchs of literature of the previous two generations were dying (in 1944-45, Saint-Exupéry, Giraudoux, Valéry, Romain Rolland; in 1948, Bernanos; in 1951, Gide; Eluard, the following year; Colette in 1954, Claudel in 1955, Martin du Gard in 1958, and Céline in 1961). Existentialism had ceased to be in the ascendant and its leaders were indulging in wistful reminiscences of their youth. By 1970, the majority of French people will have but a faint actual memory, if any, of World War II and will grow accustomed to the much advertised, but in truth comfortable anguish of the atomic age. Being comfortable, it is likely to clamor for a literary and artistic, as well as political, renovation or revolution.

The novelists of the very early years of the twentieth century, whose star began to wane with the advent of a bold and vocal avant-garde around 1910, were Pierre Loti, Anatole France, Paul Bourget, Maurice Barrès, and Romain Rolland. (A sixth one, never widely read abroad, but emotionally deeper and technically more of an innovator than any of these, Edouard Estaunié, deserves to be reappraised.) These big five have lain long enough in limbo, and scholars will probably soon try to direct our interest to them again. Bourget's early novels throw a curious light on the atmosphere which Proust breathed when he searched for his vocation as a man of letters; they are seldom read now for their own sake. Anatole France lacked imagination and passionate involvement in his characters to a degree seldom forgiven by posterity. The man in Romain Rolland, as revealed in several posthumous volumes of letters, was more engrossing than the novelist of the contrived and thin adventures of Jean-Christophe that moved our forefathers to tears or to anger. While none of his novels can be ranked among the powerfully imaginative works which live with us after we have closed them, Barrès survives best of this group as an artist and as the exemplar of an ardent sensibility, which lives again in De Gaulle and Montherlant, Mauriac, Malraux, and

Camus. Colette's world of boudoirs and of bedrooms of feline women and of brainless gigolos seems antediluvian today; her artistry was impressive but is wearing in its strained monotony. Her niche is probably assured in anthologies of French prose, but her place as a French novelist is not secure. Alain-Fournier's *Le Grand Meaulnes*, with its quest for the lost paradise of childhood dreams and loves, and its aura of rustic charm, proves to have been the most lastingly influential of the novels published before World War I, next to those of Gide and Proust. It is however hardly more than a period piece, somewhat effete in its grace, unconvincing in its characterization.[1]

Others among the French writers who sprang to fame on the eve of World War I and enjoyed long years of eminence after 1920 have to be left out of this book: Giraudoux because he is much more successful as a dramatist, Cocteau whose best medium was poetry, Larbaud, Maurois, Morand, Chardonne, Schlumberger because they have not left a single novel of genuine power and were at their best in some other medium: the essay, the short story, the biography, the thin sentimental or analytical tale. The careers of three authors of long saga-novels, Martin du Gard, Duhamel, Romains, and, briefly, the very youthful portrayer of an adolescent, Radiguet—all of the immediate postwar period—will be sketched in this chapter.

Roger Martin du Gard was ten and twelve years younger than Proust and Gide respectively. He was born near Paris in 1881 and lived much of his life in isolation in central France. Neither his technique, nor his preoccupations and implicit philosophy, rank him as a contemporary of the existentialists or of other newcomers in the field of the novel, whose vision of man is more tragic and whose tone is that of bitter individual revolt. But for anyone who disregards the flux of fashions, the author of *Les Thibault* stands as the most faithful imaginative portrayer of the conflicts that tore the French conscience between 1880 and 1930. 'The sick conscience is the theatre of modern fatality' is the epigraph from the essayist André Suarès which Martin du Gard selected for *Jean Barois*. No history of the Third Republic has yet succeeded in bringing to life the significance of those French crises, which also became crises

1. We have treated less succinctly of Colette in an article on 'Contemporary Feminine Literature in France,' *Yale French Studies*, no. 27, Spring 1961, 47–65, and of *Le Grand Meaulnes* in an introduction to an illustrated translation of that volume (Heritage Press, New York, 1958), pp. xi–xxx.

for the rest of the Western world, as have the novels of this man trained in history, but who contended in a letter to Claude Roy that 'the novelist does nothing good with reality . . . only good reporting.'

Martin du Gard has consistently been the most discreet of all French men of letters in his age. Very few private letters by him have been published. He is almost alone among the moderns in never having written or revealed a private diary or memoirs. He has kept to himself whatever opinions he may have entertained on the present and the future of the novel, on his fellow novelists (we do know that Gide heeded his advice), and on his own aims and technique. His acceptance speech of the Nobel Prize was conspicuously reserved on these subjects. Critics who often balk at dissecting a work of fiction and prefer to branch off on the writer's opinions and avowals have been baffled by his exemplary discretion. Very few have written on him. Vercors, Prévost, Ikor, and Camus (in his fine introduction to the Pléiade edition of Martin du Gard's fictional saga) have paid him a moving tribute. Young men have relived the sorrows and yearnings of the teenage hero of *Les Thibault*. Literary craftsmen have respected him. His work has worn less thin than that of Duhamel and Romains, and will probably outlive Gide's *Counterfeiters*.

His early training, like that of Mauriac and Malraux, was in history and in archaeology. He wrote a thesis for the *Ecole des Chartes* on the Norman abbey of Jumièges. He had thus learned how to consult and interpret documents; his subsequent reconstruction of the Dreyfus debate and of the impact of the war in 1914 was supported by an impeccable, almost obtrusive utilization of the most faithful contemporary accounts. He also mastered the more valuable art of submitting to his characters as he had created them and to his narrative as it logically and smoothly unfolded. Hence his equanimity appears almost inhuman to some readers who today prefer the vituperations of Georges Bernanos or Louis-Ferdinand Céline and wax impatient at the serene impartiality of a novelist who refuses to intervene and tell us what he thinks of his heroes. The style itself has a uniform transparency, which reveals events and moods without any willful distortion on the author's part.

Some of the volumes in *Les Thibault* have been linked with the French naturalists, especially when Martin du Gard depicts, with clinical precision, a doctor's workday or the onslaught of disease and death upon old Oscar Thibault, then upon Antoine, the war-wounded doctor. The author's latent view of man cherishing the pursuit of truth, spurning many of the solaces of traditional religion, and stressing clear-headedness and the senseless inhumanity of war and of fanaticism has reminded some of the positivism of the earlier French naturalists. The analogy is superficial. Unlike the naturalists, Martin du Gard derives no joy from exploring the lower side of man or from exposing the selfish meanness of the bourgeois class. His novel or volume of sketches on peasant life, *La Vieille France,* is doubtless somewhat reminiscent of Zola in its satirical onslaught on the agrarian myth. Sentimental idyls are not to the taste of that clear-sighted observer. But if such a great name is not too over-powering, Tolstoi is the writer with whom Martin du Gard has most in common—except for Tolstoi's faith and crusade. *The Death of Ivan Ilyich,* that extraordinary record of a man feeling himself dying of cancer, is the model, unconsciously perhaps, for the death scenes in *Les Thibault* and in many subsequent French novels. A tone of pity and of generosity, only half audible but excluding cynical contempt for man, a creature more stupid than criminal, and sinned against by fate more than sin-ning, is the tone of Martin du Gard. Camus, in the following generation more fond of displaying its philosophical reading and more vocal in its revolt, will not be remote from the author of *Les Thibault.*

Lucidity, humanity, and sorrowful, but perforce resigned, evocation of the agony of all his men characters and of prewar Europe are the chief virtues of the fine saga-novel, which it is not our purpose here to analyze or to discuss at length. In spite of some overstressed symmetry, especially in the earlier volumes, between the two families delineated, the novel eschews the characterization of social classes as such. It scathes the tyrannical family pride and hypocrisy of the bourgeoisie, but even the self-righteous old Thibault is treated with sympathy.. (Indeed, what services the much-maligned bourgeois have rendered modern fiction, not only by purchasing it but by providing it with three-fourths of its best characters and unweariedly absorbing its fiercest blows!) It moves according to a plan that the author nowhere has made too obvious or too rigid, and the reader remains in suspense and shares in the spon-taneity the novelist has maintained in his characters. Though less am-bitiously comprehensive than his successor Jules Romains, Martin du Gard has avoided the peril of venturing to describe environments and scenes that he did not know through imagination and feeling. He realized how inadequate is knowledge of the intellect alone, even supported by documents. The limitations of the author are real: he is not enough of a poet in the deeper sense of the word, and his most effective scenes lack the visionary *élan,* the mysterious thrill that alone could engrave them unforgettably upon our memories; and his lighting is probably too uniform, his effects of chiaroscuro or of lurid abysses of night illuminated by sparse rays from the author's projector are too few or too weak. The series of volumes is thus prevented, in spite of the not undeserved Nobel Prize, from ranking among the great masterpieces of fiction. His own discretion and overready submission to a traditional form of narrative may well have been a disservice to the author.

These limitations, which will be even more conspicuous in other *romans-fleuves*, are perhaps inseparable from the genre itself. No one, except a feverishly inspired genius like Balzac, can turn out one or two novels a year steadily. The author of a long saga-novel inevitably suffers from lapses of inspiration and phases of sterility. He then lets a few years go by without resuming his convict's forced labor, and the sweep of the work, the inspired unity, are compromised. This was true of the earlier volumes of *Les Thibault,* begun 1922, interrupted after 1928, and resumed only in 1936 with the series about the summer of 1914. The tone then was altered; the gloom weighing over a universe in which little hope was left for man crushed by physical forces had become all-pervading; the freshness of the scenes of adolescence and love had wilted. In spite of the deep pity of the author for his characters, who are all brooding victims of a monstrous game in which the dice are loaded against man's kindness and courage, we fret at his impassive portrayal of their defeats. Other novelists have proved far less intellectually honest in their description of modern man, less coolly objective; but we find them less disconsolate, for they at least imply that sin exists and therefore perhaps redemption also, that some grace may call their characters from the most horrible abysses of vice. Evil to them, even to Mauriac and Genet, Céline and Gide, assumes the appearance of a positive, diabolical force, and it is depicted with such truculence that we may, upon closing the book, imagine that *we* are immune from such a violent condemnation. The author of *Les Thibault* leaves us with no such illusion. Science, progress, knowledge, and good will alone could have turned this into a better world; and man has misused them irretrievably. There is no hell; but we are all sick, and no faith illuminates our dismal hospital abode.

Some critics have consequently dismissed Martin du Gard as a man of the nineteenth century who had accepted the benefit neither of neo-Thomism nor of existentialism. Such labels are absurd, for the faith in the possibilities once offered by science was no less valid than the assertion that man's freedom is all-powerful; the disappointment of those who were forced to disbelieve in progress and in ethical behavior severed from religion is no more old-fashioned than the trust of a later generation in a religious, Freudian, or Marxist *mystique*. Physical suffering, stressed by Martin du Gard, is just as revolting and humiliating (perhaps more tragic even if monotonously ancient) as the philosophical anguish of more recent fictional heroes in pondering over the problems of language or of total sincerity. The comparison between our war-ridden twentieth century, with its fanatical clashes of ideas (as we pompously call our propagandized assumptions and our complacently lauded ways of life), and the one that preceded it may well put ours to shame.

Artistically, Martin du Gard had doubtless achieved a greater success with his less ambitious *Jean Barois* (1913). Through its rich content and its symbolical significance, the book may well be one of the most important novels of the years 1900–1918, along with Gide's *La Porte étroite* and Proust's *Swann*. The author experimented with the form of a novel transposed into a dramatic dialogue, which enabled him to avoid some of the smoothness of his later narratives as an omniscient novelist. The conversations between the characters faithfully express the style, the emotions, and the behavior of the interlocutors, without the novelist's having to intrude with comments of his own. High lights can thus be focused sharply, while didactic parts (on the background and details of the Dreyfus case) and especially descriptions, the dead weight in so many novels of Balzac and Dostoevski, are cut short. A few stage directions conjure up the setting of the main scenes.

Such a technique, however, cannot avoid some artificial devices or some monotony. Martin du Gard, who has written farces for the stage with marked dramatic flair and is not without a bitter comic sense, does not succeed in animating some of his crucial scenes. His women characters in particular are too reserved, closer, even in their scenes of anger and protest, to women as men want them to be in life—composed, outwardly resigned, inwardly sure of their own ultimate victory—than to woman as men like to find her depicted in novels of other nations—hysterical, as in Dostoevski, shrieking with orgiastic laughter, clinging to the man who has scorned her most and following him to Siberia after his inevitable crime. The passions that impel Jean Barois, Luce, and the other characters are mainly intellectual. The love element is restricted. The noble impartiality of the novelist disconcerts readers who like to have the author's position stated unambiguously.

This dramatized novel is likely to remain as the most vivid portrayal of the two crises lived by the author and by France between 1880 and 1910: the struggle waged between Catholicism and science, and the loss of the traditional faith in many minds that had received a historical and exegetic training; and the Dreyfus case, which drove some of the same minds to anticlericalism. These crises go a long way toward elucidating the attitude of France even in 1965 and help explain how, to this day, Frenchmen may, in the face of grave exterior perils, refuse to compromise on such questions as the state support of clerical schools.

The drama of Jean Barois lies in his anxiety to fill the gap left by the breakdown of the Catholic faith of his youth, shattered by the study of natural history and exegesis. The rigidity of Church dogmas and his own uncompromising temperament drive him to an active crusade for new values, which he cherishes and which he opposes to traditional Christianity. He soon clashes with his pious wife, Cécile, whose religion has become narrow and superstitious. They separate. The Dreyfus affair breaks out. Jean Barois plunges into it on the side of the defenders of Dreyfus and, even more, on the side of liberalism and abstract justice. After seven years of trial and retrial, of organized lying by the anti-Semites and by the defenders of the army, prone, as Goethe once confessed he was, to prefer an injustice to disorder, Dreyfus is vindicated. Socialism, tinged with anticlericalism and antimilitarism, triumphs. The noble *mystique* of liberal champions of justice and truth has to give way to a spoils system in which the army is weakened, the Church is persecuted, and the mediocrity of profiteers of politics replaces the lofty dream of elevating the people and of teaching them socialism as an untarnished Messianic faith.

Jean Barois does not moralize on the event. The novel gives us insight into the minds of some of the fighters in that great duel of consciences. Jean himself has had his nerves shattered by the long fight. He sees death close to him in a carriage accident, and his lips voluntarily whisper a prayer memorized in his pious childhood. He admits that he fears death. His own daughter, whom his wife alone has brought up, chooses to be a nun. Her father realizes that any onslaught on dogmas and rites, any historical and philosophical refutation leave the will to believe, the hope of triumphing over death, and the solitude of human beings yearning for charity and love untouched in many a heart. On his death bed he prays and is comforted. Roger Martin du Gard, who had the 'irony' of an artist and has never forsaken his intellectual honesty, avoided the naïveté of letting his own unbelief win in the denouement. The overtones of sadness in the final pages, however, half reveal his own sorrow at man's inability to act rationally.

To people who have read about the Dreyfus case only in history books, *Jean Barois,* better than any other novel written on that civil war, offers an accurate and vividly dramatized account of the problems of ethics and of conscience then posed to many Frenchmen. The last sections of *Les Thibault,* which deal with the summer of 1914 when all idealistic pacifist dreams were destroyed, and then with Antoine, the doctor, slowly dying from the gas which had corroded his lungs when he was at the front, are pregnant with restrained emotion and with melancholy anger at men's incurable folly. One thought inevitably recurs when those volumes are reread: the probity of the author is admirable. Nothing is unduly magnified. The novelist's objectivity is never forsaken. He effaces himself and conceals his passion and his pessimistic fear of death and of the future under a clarity lent equally to all scenes. The characters are presented in their relations with other men, horizontally as it were, but seldom vertically in relation to a presence above or in the act of delving into their own deeper and turbid darkness, for to convey an unforgettable impression of the chaos, of the absurdity, and of the greatness of war would have required more familiarity with mystery, perhaps more partiality, and even charlatanry, than Martin du Gard could have stooped to.

The influence of wars on literature has never been adequately studied; nor has the equally powerful impact of literature upon war, either to ridicule it and advocate pacifism (as have satirists ever since Aristophanes) or to glorify battle, as Tyrteus, Horace, and others whose bravery was in no way exemplary have enjoyed doing. Polemology should offer a challenge to the collaboration of strategists, scientists, psychologists, sociologists and, certainly, humanists. World War I was far more ghastly than the humiliating Second World War for the French nation; though the collapse was less total, the shame and the sense of guilt less widely spread, the disillusionment and the prolonged aftereffects went far deeper. For a number of French writers, imbued with a mystique of adventure (which their British counterparts hardly seem to have shared), the excitement of the immense struggle appeared like the prelude to a reconstruction of the souls and the fulfillment of a Nietzschean prophecy of perilous life. Apollinaire, Elie Faure, Teilhard de Chardin, Drieu La Rochelle, Montherlant, Giraudoux saw beauty and a mystical promise of regeneration in the squalor and the slaughter of the trenches. Others imparted to readers their horror at such futile absurdity: Barbusse, Dorgelès, Céline, Giono, the last two with Goyaesque visionary power. Radiguet and his mentor Cocteau (in *Thomas l'Imposteur*) treated the war with irony and as hardly capable of soiling the innocence of very young men just emerging from an awkward age; to them, it was not a tragedy, but 'long holidays' pleasantly delaying their assumption of the responsibilities of manhood. No masterpiece, worthy of Balzac or of Tolstoi, has yet been written on World War I and Dos Passos or Hemingway have perhaps come closer to writing such a striking book than any writer from England or France. But few have written on the war so movingly as Duhamel and none with such intellectual sharpness and clarity as Romains. Both had grown to manhood in the years which followed the vindication of Dreyfus and had witnessed both the soul-searching and the hopes of their countrymen then. To both, the shattering of many illusions followed fast upon the German invasion of Belgium and the rallying of the German social-democrats to the 'fresh and joyous war' in August 1914.

Georges Duhamel enjoyed the advantage of clear prose and an apparently effortless and smooth narrative, which designated him as the successor to Anatole France. His work, however, wore thin after he had drawn on his war experience and on his postwar vision of men bound by friendship and a kindly desire to rebuild a better world. His long and facile saga-novel, *Chronique des Pasquier,* in spite of occasional charm and freshness, fails to hold the attention of readers; Duhamel's one determined attempt to renovate his inspiration, after World War II, with *Le Voyage de Patrice Périot* (1951) resulted in an unconvincing picture of a doctor's family torn by ideological feuds and of naïve scientists becoming the playthings of political exploiters. These novels start auspiciously and are delineated in pleasing and precise outlines, displaying a gift for draftsmanship, which has become a rarity nowadays. They breathe a human warmth that is also rare in the pessimistic literature of our age. But they fail to expand and to be sustained to the end by sufficient creative fire. It is sad to have to confess once again that anger and hatred seem to nourish an author's energy more persistently than pity and love.

Duhamel's father was a doctor who started practicing medicine late, never became very successful for lack of order and efficiency in his life, and bequeathed little else to his family but the memory of an entertaining visionary buffeted by life but always obstinately smiling. He appears several times in the novels of his son. Duhamel was also a doctor, one of many in Europe who turned to literature; Céline and Luc Durtain were also medical men who won fame as novelists, as other doctors—Elie Faure, Henri Mondor, even Alexis Carrel—became outstanding essayists. 'Anatomists, physiologists, I find you everywhere!' exclaimed Sainte-Beuve, himself a former medical student, when reviewing Madame Bovary. It has been contended that doctors' sons (Flaubert, Proust, Mauriac) lean heavily to intense analytical study of life and to melancholy brooding over man's inability to escape from his physical and physiological limitations. If this is so, Duhamel is an exception among doctors and doctors' sons. But he owed much to the practice of medicine, the most fertile training ground for one who would be a novelist. He probed the secrets of men and women and diagnosed the psychological causes of some of their diseases. He observed the concrete instead of theorizing from books and systems. He visited people when they were off their guard, in a disorderly bedroom, with their hair, faces, and clothes unprepared for the social comedy that one plays in healthy life. He heard confessions from wives hating their husbands, from heartless husbands, and from human beings suddenly become abject in their fear of disease and of death. But that experience did not make Duhamel bitter or cynical. It did not even make him gruff and imperious, like many doctors who think they will be obeyed and respected more by their patients if they utter laconic oracles and scold with sharp finality. Pity is the controlling sentiment that Duhamel tried to reintroduce into literature, after the naturalists and certain intellectual cynics had disaccustomed readers to such an outmoded feeling.

Duhamel as a child had been poor, a not uncommon feature among men of letters, who are mostly drawn from the lower middle class. He neither resented his poverty nor revolted against it. Even less did he affect the worldly manners of young men who want to forget their origins and the sacrifices made by their families so that they may tempt fortune in Paris. Duhamel never made a specialty of the study of misery, as did the proletarian novelists and later a short-lived group of 'populist' novelists (Henri Poulaille, André Thérive, Eugène Dabit). He liked to choose his characters from among shabby office clerks and petty government employees, and he tried to steer halfway between the sentimental idealization of their mediocre lives and the propagandist tone of Upton Sinclair or of John Steinbeck that weaves misery and injustice into much too colorful an epic.

Duhamel succeeded where others failed, without having the inverted pride in his social origins that drove D. H. Lawrence, for example, to grant the monopoly of sexual attraction and potency to miners, soldiers, gamekeepers, and American Indians. The stumbling block of such a literature is sentimentality, and sentimentality, which occupies a large place in life, is granted only a small place in literature. Duhamel tempers his picture of man with humor. His sentimentality is closer to the tragic kind that is found in Russian fiction. His characters lay their hearts bare with humility and a passion for abject confession of their weaknesses and sins; but they do not revel in it with the pride of sinners who wish to unbosom their secrets so as to make room for more sins in their unburdened souls.

The lifelong concern of Duhamel, apparent in all his essays, reminiscences, and novels, is one that he shared with Charles Péguy, Romain Rolland, Jules Romains, and other writers of his period: an idealistic impulse to save men. Duhamel, like young Péguy, then an unbeliever, turned all his meditations around the categorical imperative inspired by Joan of Arc: 'One must save.' But save whom? For men are stubbornly reluctant to be saved. As the Utopian socialists had done, as Péguy did, Duhamel and some of his friends dreamed of harmonious life; in their youthful fervor they attempted life in common in the phalanstery of an old abbey. But the French, who are likely to cherish mankind in the abstract and to undertake distant crusades in the interest of humanity, are notoriously bad neighbors when it comes to silencing their individualism, their envy, and their irony. Duhamel smiles at the men and women whom he wants to continue loving in spite of themselves. He is not blind to the disappointments that an optimist must endure, and all his novels display the gradual collapse of a rosy dream. He will not seek a solution in an easy catchword, tendered by Christianity, which he respected but never professed, or in science, which he always admired, though he was aware of its limitations. Friendship is the feeling of which he spoke most nobly (in *Deux Hommes* especially); like Romains, Vildrac, and later Malraux and Saint-Exupéry, he would have liked to build a virile and warm regeneration of mankind upon friendship, that is, upon the most beautiful of all words and ideals proposed by humanism and by Christianity—fraternity.

After completing his medical studies, Duhamel had written plays, of

slight dramatic value, and critical essays, when World War I revealed
to him a new and richer vein of his own talent. In 1917, he brought out,
under a pseudonym then required by his position in the army, *La Vie
des martyrs;* he followed it up with a sequel, *Civilisation,* in 1918; and,
thirty years later, he returned to the same subject in one of the best
volumes of his old age, *Récits des temps d'affliction.*

Duhamel's point of view toward the gigantic catastrophe into which
Europe was plunged in 1914 is original. Others, most numerous, chose
to depict war as monstrous and ghastly, caused by the greed of states-
men and of industrialists. A few, found among the fighters as well as
among the profiteers and those who love to command from a safe desk
job, actually enjoyed the war and explained why in memorable books:
Ernst Jünger in Germany, Montherlant (*Le Songe*), Drieu la Rochelle
(*La Comédie de Charleroi*), Vercel (*Le Capitaine Conan*). Some, to
avoid being crushed by the inexorable and devouring machine, undertook to laugh the strain off by stressing the humorous or entertaining
moments in the soldiers' lives; thus did André Maurois who, like Duhamel, hit upon his best vein in his two war books of conversations with
Colonel Bramble and Dr. O'Grady. Giraudoux pretended that he enjoyed
the war because it was a liberation from prosaic life, an opportunity to
dream freely about women, transfigured by the soldiers' love-starved
imagination, an ordeal pleasantly interrupted by furloughs and hospitals.
The poet Apollinaire, before he died from his wounds, likewise sang the
romance of modern war, of galloping artillery horses and 'phallic' antiaircraft guns pointing to the sky.

Duhamel was a doctor in the front lines. He had no ax to grind, having
no political cause to uphold. He was not naïve enough to believe wars
to be the contrivance of munitions makers. He did not attempt a panoramic picture of the war, with the strategic plans of generals and the
intricate transmission of orders and an elaborate analysis of the emotions
of men before and after an attack. Like Stendhal in his famous account
of Waterloo, he was determined to describe only what he saw. As a
doctor, operating in an ambulance close to the line of battle, in a war
in which the medical corps was conspicuous for its poor organization,
he saw wounded and dying men. To weld those fragments of experience
into a continuous novel would have been untrue to the author's purpose.
He did not compose a novel, which would have been more vivid perhaps
than reality but which would have betrayed the bare testimony of a
witness and destroyed the gloomy unity of the author's experience, ob-

sessed by so much suffering. The war books of Duhamel are composed of vignettes and short stories, with a minimum of touching up. They are told dramatically, because Duhamel's artistic sense prompted him to restore to reality, through literary skill, some of the tragedy it contains. But the author expressed himself in the first person, an eyewitness who, as an army doctor, participated in the scenes enacted and endured.

Those war books are an impassioned, though restrained, indictment of war. They use satire effectively to scathe the ridiculousness of hierarchy and discipline and the vanity of otherwise intelligent men, who fondly believe that they belonged to 'the most intelligent people' on earth and suddenly, having donned a uniform, abdicate all critical spirit. Doctors, who were accustomed to following exacting professional standards, become fascinated by gold braid on a cap and the voice of a higher officer who may hold their promotion in the palm of his hand. Men whose survival cannot be reasonably hoped for deceive themselves stubbornly unto the last and expect a miracle. Gravely disabled soldiers, for whom life can be only a slow death, cling to the hideous wreck that is their maimed body. They even laugh at their own martyrdom and joke about their misery. The resilience of men is the most eloquent challenge to pessimism about the human race.

While sparing no realistic details, Duhamel is moved by devotion and sympathy for the new martyrs whose flesh was tortured in the bloodiest war in history. Moralists and preachers have given physical suffering too much credit for its reforming effects. It can sober up and mature a few sufferers who might otherwise remain plain hedonists (a beautiful word, which we have allowed to degenerate into one of opprobrium), unconcerned with an afterlife. But how degrading sickness and pain are to our bodies and to our minds! These ills are unjust, stupid, humiliating, and, especially if inflicted through war, a mockery of all the hopes and aspirations of mankind. Duhamel's first war book was merely descriptive. The second becomes more bitter as it develops and, discreetly, suggests the author's message. In an operating room, the most handsome men of France, cavalry soldiers transferred to the infantry, have been pouring in since morning, wounded in the lungs, in the stomach, in the head; the surgical tools shine resplendent on all sides, devised by the ingenious techniques of modern 'civilization.' Negro stretcher-bearers from those black regiments that France had recruited all over Africa to come and take part in the slaughter of 'civilized' whites by other whites come and go, silently and gently carrying the groaning men. The author looks at that nightmarish scene, ashamed of what may be going through the dim consciousness of those African soldiers, ashamed of his own race. The lofty words of our religion, to which we have been paying lip service for almost two thousand years, sound ironically in his ears: 'Love ye one another'; 'Thou shalt not kill.' His whole being shudders in protest. Civilization does not lie in the tools of the surgeon or in the perfected anesthetics of the operating room. 'If it lie not in the heart of man, it is nowhere.'

Duhamel's qualities appear most conspicuously in the best novel (in our opinion), which he wrote after his war books: the central book in the Salavin series entitled *Journal de Salavin.* The subject is one of the most commonly treated in fiction: the failure of an ideal and eventually of a life. Duhamel handles it deftly, with kindly, though frank, humor and without the obstinate insistence on crushing men's aspirations that marked the French naturalists, American pessimists like John Dos Passos, and even the author of *Of Human Bondage.*

Salavin is a well-meaning, honest, thoughtful man of about forty, essentially undistinguished but determined to rise above his own mediocrity. He decides to keep a diary and realizes in so doing that his life thus far has been empty and useless. He will rise, not through money, for which he cares little; not through action, for he is not ambitious and is hardly the stuff of which heroes are made; not through art, for he is not gifted. Failing those, he will try to become a saint. His inability to have any religious faith fails to deter him. Saints, the dictionary informs him, have done good and lived in humility and devoted themselves to others. He will do as they do and record his saint's progress in his diary. He promises to himself the utmost sincerity.

His mother is puzzled when he declares to her that he wants to be good. His wife, noticing that he no longer protests at the dishes he used to dislike and that he rises earlier in the morning, thinks he is sick or queer. He is forced to lie to the two good ladies. Saints have borne suffering; he inures himself to pain by inserting his finger between the door and the doorframe every morning and closing the door on it a little more each day until it hurts. But his wife, unsuspecting, one day slams the door and his finger is crushed. He goes about the streets of Paris looking for old ladies carrying parcels whom he may assist, since helping young ones might be misinterpreted, and lepers whom one may kiss in brotherhood have become rare in our cities. He goes into movie houses, hoping for the day when a fire may break out and he will extinguish it, help the audience to escape, and save them from the stampede. When a fire once actually occurs, he must confess in his diary that his reactions were not those he had rehearsed; he had scurried toward the door, forgetting about women and children to be rescued. A fellow employee at his company had been stealing for some time. Salavin deprives himself and his wife to give him money, so that he may restore what he had subtracted from the cashier's desk. He thus becomes party to an offense, and the culprit never reforms. Telling the truth to others, he soon discovers, brings only embarrassment and ill will to them and to him.

Salavin must confess that he is a failure. It is hard to be a lay saint. Religious faith would help him if only he could acquire it. He visits a Protestant pastor famous for his influence, who hurriedly psychoanalyzes him and sees a crank in him. He goes from the Protestant pastor to a Catholic priest, expecting much from the atmosphere of the Church and from the confession. The priest pities him, offers to take upon himself the burden of Salavin's mistakes, and suggests prayer as a cure. The solution is too easy for the unquiet soul of the would-be saint. Will not God bestow a sign upon him and help him in his spiritual ascent? More confused than ever, he wanders in the snow, distraught, and awakes in a hospital bed, feverish, disillusioned, and ready for further crises of remorse and aspirations, which will fill the last volumes of the Salavin series. The very abnegation of that pathetic character was tainted with pride. His sincerity only wrought havoc around him and failed to satisfy him. He acted upon a system instead of truly loving with a spontaneous overflow of his heart. He wanted to be humble, but humility also can be false and affected or exaggerated. In that entertaining and skillfully drawn portrait Duhamel has delineated one of the typical characters of the postwar era, eager to reform a world bent upon its own perdition, pitifully incapable of achieving too overwhelming a task and admitting his failure.

Jules Romains appeared for some time likely to rank as the most important French novelist of his age group. He possessed the breadth of culture and knowledge, having early mastered philosophy, literature, and even natural history, traveled in several lands, observed varied environments, and even evolved a philosophical system of his own, which attracted and deserved notice. He had attempted poetry with determination, if not with an inspired gift, and seemed capable of putting poetry in a broad sense into the novel. Several of his plays had met with success;

they held the promise of a novelist who would perceive the comic potentialities of situations and was endowed with one of the primary gifts of a creator of fiction, the gift of mimicry. Lastly, Romains (whose real name was Louis Farigoule and who, some scoffers have hinted, had chosen the first name of Julius Caesar and an impressive pseudonym suggestive of Roman grandeur) met at least one of the requisites of genius, an infinite capacity for taking pains. His *Les Hommes de bonne volonté* (*Men of Good Will*) sprawled over twenty-seven volumes in the French original and might well have been extended still further if the good will of the readers had responded to the dauntless obstinacy of the author.

Novels hailed as timeless masterpieces age quickly in our century. Many flaws have appeared in the ambitious fabric of that long saga. The author has provided his readers with weapons against himself in the artificiality of his composition and the papery thinness of many of his hundreds of characters stretched across seven thousand five hundred pages. Such an immense undertaking required far more imaginative sweep than Jules Romains possessed; its ups and downs are too painfully obvious, and he ups do not carry one along loftily enough to help one forget all the swampy stretches that must be waded through. But some ultimate failures are not only more courageous but also more informative than successes easily achieved through fear of risks. Romains has fulfilled at least one of the ambitions of many *romans-fleuves*—he is to be reckoned with, through sheer weight and comprehensiveness. And his very shortcomings have taught his successors some lessons.

The son of a schoolteacher from the center of France, on the border of the Auvergne, Romains spent his childhood and adolescence in the busiest and most populous districts of Paris, on the right bank near Montmartre. He showed great promise as a schoolboy and student, being equally proficient in the humanities, in philosophy, and in science. He entered the celebrated École Normale Supérieure, took his advanced degree in philosophy, did experiments in biology and experimental psychology, and wrote a scientific treatise on the paroptic, or extraretinal, vision, which failed to convince many biologists but attracted a few among them. He had also, although he has been reluctant to acknowledge it and was perhaps unaware of it, been influenced by the startling development in sociology associated with Gabriel Tarde, who saw in imitation the most powerful factor explaining the behavior of human beings (a doctrine that denied sociology properly speaking, since it started from individual phenomena, which spread through contagion), and with Emile Durkheim, who tried to give the new science its laws and its rules. When Romains was studying in Paris (he was twenty in 1905), sociology was renovating the study of history, anthropology, and several branches of law. It was natural for literature to react against the cult of the individual and to analyze groups and the forces that endow groups with a semi-mystical power incommensurate with that of the individuals whose gathering around some creeds constitutes a group.

Romains always maintained, and there is no reason to doubt his word, that his literary work had not originated in any preconceived theory or been subjected to philosophical influences, but that it had stemmed from observation of the concrete and from an almost mystical intuition. Like many moderns who do not subscribe to Christian faith but try to find substitutes for religious experience in poetical experience, like Rimbaud and Proust, among others, Romains has secularized mysticism. Repeatedly, in his early works, even in some of his farces, then in several volumes of *Les Hommes de bonne volonté*, he has depicted the action of a few individuals giving a soul to a group or controlling their own bodies, even the mechanism of their breathing or the beating of their hearts. And he has described their hallucinations. He is a mystic, not only without God (not an uncommon occurrence after all) but with more rationality than sensibility and with an unflagging practical sense. He has related how, at the age of eighteen, walking along the rue d'Amsterdam, near the Saint-Lazare station, at the end of the afternoon, while *midinettes* rushed to their buses or to their rendezvous, commuters to their trains, loafers to their favorite *cafés*, he had experienced a trance. Suddenly, he had become conscious of the crowd in its bustle and confused unity; he had merged his own identity into that of the group. His calling was then decided; he would become the literary interpreter of the group and unleash the explosive forces latent in gatherings of men.

He had the good fortune to coin a word for his intuition, which soon became a reasoned and consistent view of men—'unanimism.' The original significance of the Latin words enclosed in that '-ism' must not be lost sight of: single-minded, or one-souled. Social environments and huge collective events are not, for the founder of unanimism, a mere series of diverse settings in which his stories may be laid. He also discards the invention of character and incident conceived as an illustration of the play of those social forces, for, thus conceived, individuals dwindle and tend to become types. Romains aimed at being the magician unleashing and controlling spiritual forces latent in groups. He always contended that he was not an analyst of social phenomena but a captor of magnetic currents passing through and electrifying crowds and transfiguring them into conscious, dynamic organisms with a collective soul.

His most conspicuous success was in rendering the life of a street or of a quarter of Paris. There his greatness is assured. He blended knowledge of all the haunts of the big city with tender sympathy for its little people and an intense perception of the erotic thrill of men and women seeking each other in desire and passion, as Lucretius evoked them in the woods under the sway of Aphrodite. The fourth volume of *Les Hommes de bonne volonté*, entitled *Eros de Paris*, is in that respect among the freshest and most tender in the whole work. But in all his writings, plays, short stories, poems (if Romains's prosaic and desperately wingless verse can thus be called), the founder of unanimism has pursued the implications of the truth that had been revealed to him one afternoon in a Paris street. If he is, as he likes to be considered, an inspired mystic first, Jules Romains is also an adept at dissociating ideas and at reasoning. He has repeatedly and very deftly laid bare the mechanism through which a random gathering of persons in a school, in the army, in an audience, in a bus, or in a railway carriage is suddenly transformed, turned into a unanimist group, with a soul, or a 'divine' presence, different in nature from each of the individuals merged into the group, yet present in each member of the group and endowing him with a new personality. The two persons who make up a couple are three and not two, for a third living being, the couple, hovers between them and molds them. The five members of a family are all permeated by the spirit of the family, a sixth being more potent than each of them separately. A new and higher symbolic, yet living, presence pervades the mediocre, isolated, soulless human beings who were gathered in a bus or in a street (as in John Steinbeck's *The Wayward Bus* and in Waldo Frank's *City Block*, which indirectly owe much to unanimism). They become endowed with a collective soul, enhancing their individual personalities.

Romains gave the most successful illustrations of his unanimist view of man in his early and brief stories, like *Le Bourg régénéré* (1906), *L'Armée dans la ville* (1911), and *Sur les quais de la Villette* (1914). He never recaptured their contagious humor and their robust concreteness. As is to be expected, unanimism was more effective in rendering humor than sorrow, and the process of giving a soul to a group is more easily practiced in a comic spirit than in the lyrical or tragic mood; *Les Copains* is one of the very few excellent works of comedy of an age that has not displayed much mastery in rivaling Molière. *Mort de quelqu'un*, which was translated into English by Desmond MacCarthy as *The Death of a Nobody*, was more ambitious. It delineated the concentric zones of spiritual influence, forging unanimist groups around a banal incident: the solitary death, in Paris, of a retired employee, who had remained without friends and without any unanimist radiation while he was alive. His old father in his native village takes a train to Paris; he is afflicted by the death of his son, yet proud of the important news, which he must share with his fellow travelers in the railway carriage. Gradually, until the burial takes place with mourners, neighbors, and sympathetic onlookers, a new group consciousness is momentarily aroused around a man who had been a mere somebody or nobody when he lived alone and left everyone unconcerned.

Later on, especially in his trilogy, *Psyché*, Romains tried to raise unanimism to the plane of mysticism. After a first volume, which was modest and rich in restrained poetry, *Lucienne*, the author attempted, with *Le Dieu des corps*, a description of the physical mutual adoration of a man and his wife, which is as infelicitous as all the erotic scenes in *Les Hommes de bonne volonté*. (There are many, regularly scattered here and there, as if to help the sales of each volume.) The third volume, *Quand le navire*, is a totally unconvincing, though painstaking, description of a hallucination, by which the husband, traveling on the seas, conjures up his absent and ardently loved wife. Repeatedly, Romains ventures into the zones that lie beyond consciousness and rationality, and into the realms of communication with the unknown. It is difficult, however, to be a mystic without faith and without some naïveté. Those excursions into the mysteries of the beyond, into which the prophet of the unanimist religion was lured repeatedly, have been ill-starred. A later work along those lines, which takes place in New York, *Violation de frontières*, is among his poorest pieces of writing (1950). It is a melancholy sight to observe almost every writer bent upon verifying at his own expense the saying of Ruskin that 'no great man ever stops working till he has reached his point of failure.'

Romains's wish was to stand or fall, as a writer, by his huge cyclic novel, *Les Hommes de bonne volonté*, one of the most determined and intellectually powerful fictional attempts of the century in France. In it, Romains undertook to be the Balzac or the Zola of his age. The similarity between his ambitions and theirs led many a critic to compare him, much too hastily, to those giants of the last century and probably induced Romains to take the comparison too seriously. Unlike Balzac, however, Romains wished to write a collective novel that would not be just a collection of separate parts on the army, the church, provincial life, the peasantry, and so forth. It would have a unity of its own, at the risk (which it ran, alas, too liberally and hardly victoriously) of depriving itself of the fresh *élan* of a new work, loosely, if at all, tied to its predecessors. Unlike Zola, he wanted to avoid the easy trick of a family, with its several members serving as pretexts for exploring a different segment of life in the country at a certain time.

Romains has boldly attempted to avoid the single hero going through an incredible variety of experiences and environments, and the family or the selected group of friends to which earlier novelists limited their field of vision. He chose to create an extremely large number of characters, with no one of them being for long 'above the rest proudly eminent.' He took them from a purposely bewildering variety of social environments: students, scientists, writers, actresses, aristocrats, journalists, murderers, workmen, priests, politicians. An index appended to every other volume enabled the reader to thread his way among the successive plots and the thousand small and big characters. The action would vary, at times resembling or aping a detective story, at times disappearing altogether to make room for the Battle of Verdun or the idyllic life of the survivors of the war rediscovering the *'douceur de la vie.'* Romains tried to steer midway between purely objective recording of the behavior of the characters and supposedly deep probing into their inner secrets, which several contemporaries have sought through the interior monologue. The first method could hardly satisfy a writer who insists upon understanding mysteries and upon reconciling some of the contradictory manners in which men behave with some concealed or semiconscious unity. Romains found it easy and a little cheap to multiply strange actions and unpredictable behavior in his characters, as some Russians, many Americans, and even Joseph Conrad do in their fiction, and then to gape at the profundity of their contradictory, hence unfathomable, creations. On the other hand, he found fault with the systematic use of the interior monologue made by Valéry Larbaud in France, by James Joyce in Ireland, and by their followers. For that monologue seizes only what flits through the consciousness as words, but hardly or not at all what cannot be formulated in words and often lies much deeper. What is worse, it puts everything indiscriminately on the same plane, the silly unuttered jabbering with ourselves in which we indulge when walking on a street and monologuing about a dog, a fly, a speck of dust, a letter we have forgotten to write, the shape of a body we may desire, as well as the deeper emotions, the original thoughts in us, which may also be part of our stream of consciousness.[2] The possibilities offered by the interior monologue, which seemed revolutionary when Joyce first came into fashion, have indeed narrowed down to an occasional and often artificial device to which a novelist may resort. It cannot, any more than the novel written as an intimate journal (also the object of Romains's sarcasm), replace the narrative of events and the analysis of character by the novelist himself.

It would be idle and carping criticism that would find fault with Romains's saga-novel because the novelist's method is not revolutionary, certainly much less revolutionary than he himself assumed. The results have to be assessed independently from the method and from the doctrine of unanimism, which may for all practical purposes be ignored by the reader of those novels. In the best volumes, like *Verdun,* neither theories nor technique are primary. We have an acute and extremely intelligent study, in imaginative form, of the reasons why men fight and continue to fight in a war, of the impact of war upon soldiers and generals, upon civilians, including profiteers, upon women, and upon the forces (gigantic even more than collective, tragic, and baneful, and no longer comic and partly or pseudo divine) that buffet human creatures at odds with hostile fate. The book came out at an opportune moment: in France just at the time of Munich (in the fall of 1938), in America in the fall of 1939 when the reality of another war faced the West. The praise lavished on the book was almost boundless. In December 1939 *The New Yorker* critic, typical of many others, called it 'the most adult' of books written about World War I, 'a war novel in the grand style,' able to 'see war steadily and see it whole.'

Much of the praise still seems deserved, after the lapse of another 25 years and the completion of another world war. The behavior of the traders supplying the army, of the workmen turned into fattened bourgeois by their war profits, of the ladies selling patriotism in the salons, of the generals, some cowardly and grotesque, some well meaning but

2. Romains slipped many of his views on the novel into his *Les Hommes de bonne volonté* sometimes under the guise of satire of his fellow writers. He has expressed himself in lectures on his own work, not yet collected into a volume, notably, as concerns the interior monologue, in *Les Annales-Conferencia* (November 1950).

crushed by the enormous task to be accomplished, has been observed by a sarcastic and lucid eye. The discussions on strategy are said to have satisfied many a staff officer; the precise details of the French units fighting at Verdun, on the geography of the battlefield, on the thousand local fights that went into the bloodiest battle of the bloodiest of wars; the letters and conversations of the two intellectuals discussing the wherefore and the how of war—all have met with the approval of those who actually fought at Verdun. Romains himself was not there and does not speak as an eyewitness, though he nowhere mentions straightforwardly the fact that he depicts war at second hand.

The undoubted merits of the author are his intellectual equipment and his broad sympathy, as well as his gift for lucid narrative. The book is impeccably documented. He studied newspapers of the time, memoirs of soldiers, diaries of officers, logbooks and histories of regiments and divisions. He reconstitutes events logically and integrates them into a pattern, distributing light evenly, shifting impartially from the French front of battle to the German lines, from Verdun to the rear, from officers to privates. He explains, with commendable didactic talent, the motives for the actions of some individuals and, with even greater skill, the motives that cause soldiers to fight: patriotism, to be sure, and an ideological attachment to a way of life, to a cultural past, to the soil and the landscape and the eating habits of their country; a sense for risk, which cannot be underrated and to which many conquerors and dictators have appealed; and an exaltation toward greatness to which even cynics occasionally respond. But Romains does not overlook the liberation that army life brings to young men; they are suddenly uprooted from their families, from their wives and home life, from their small towns and the conventional watch of society, of women, of group meetings, of professional behavior. Wars are caused by far different forces, but they compensate the pitifully inadequate appeal that modern life makes to imagination. All the boyish instincts for destruction, the adolescent instincts for male comradeship, coarseness of language, violent sport, and the male instinct for polygamy seem to be unleashed by war.

Verdun is a valuable historical document. It is remarkably lucid, exact, and exhaustive as psychological analysis. It is impartial even when it is ironical, and it leaves the reader with respect for the author's intellect and for the range of his knowledge and the acuteness of his dialectic. But is it a very great book? Our own answer must be negative, and that is not disparaging a fine work, for very great books are scarce. It is exact as history, painstakingly documented, but it lacks the kind of poetry that would be truer than history, the lie inherent in all art that makes art not just a copy but a new truth parallel to reality and more meaningful. The profound truth of the Verdun battle, which even the humblest participants in that fight experienced, was one that eludes Romains through his patient explanations: soldiers and civilians alike felt then that the decisive moment of the war had come, that they had to resist at all costs, with a unanimist and grim determination that made their silent heroism worthy of an epic. That epic, that concentration of energies around a *mystique*, called for an imaginative rendering, enhancing reality in order to express its latent *élan*. The founder of unanimism, when weighed against the immense subject he had assigned himself, is found wanting.

His very gifts of a clear intellect and the detachment of a cool professor expounding his view of history in an orderly fashion fail to serve the novelist in him. He knows too much about his characters, about the whys and the hows of war, and the fundamental irrationality of history and of men is consequently left out. If Romains's fiction aged fast in ten years, it is because he will not accept or depict the absurdity of man, which has become very dear to another generation. Even mystery is absent from his picture, as is shade. Everything receives an equal lighting and is pitilessly analyzed, as if by a professional psychologist. But less intellectual novelists have managed to reveal far deeper secrets with fewer words and less dissection; the secrets of human beings flash to us through a smile, a gesture, the way a person walks or sits down, his drawn features, a gleam in his eye. Romains fails to render the physical or spiritual presence of his characters. His women in particular are all pitifully unconvincing. His art, in a word, is one of combination. He resembles a pharmacist or a grocer, taking a few ingredients from a shelf or from one glass jar, then another, and eventually concocting his panacea. A more cruel reviewer (a woman) has even compared him to a manufacturer of synthetic rubber, drawing his elongated or overextended plastic material through volume after volume. But the intuition of life, the sudden creation that does not juxtapose fragments of observation but makes them spring alive, the global synthesis that is not made up of a conglomeration of neatly cleaned and sized-up particles—those gifts are not primarily those of the author of *Les Hommes de bonne volonté*.

Even if it has not yet created masterpieces of fictional literature, unanimism has been a significant force in the first half of the twentieth century and one of the most determined attempts to broaden a limited field, which writer after writer has been content with tilling. The nineteenth century had not ignored the play of great social forces: Zola had animated crowds, in *La Débâcle* and in *Lourdes,* as few novelists have been able to do; Balzac deserved the praise of Karl Marx, who saw a revolutionary delineation of the corruption of the bourgeoisie in the novels of that monarchist and conservative. But it remains true that the collective factors were hardly sought by most authors and by most heroes in the literature that extends from Chateaubriand and Byron to Ibsen and the symbolists. The favorite characters, from Byron's Childe Harold, Vigny's Moses, Stendhal's and Balzac's young men rushing to the conquest of Paris, to Baudelaire's cursed poet and Ibsen's enemy of the people, were those who branded the masses and almost any group as contemptible and deified the man who chose solitude. The hero was 'immovably centered,' as Baudelaire defined him after Emerson, reluctant or unable to establish communication with others even in love. When a reaction against the romantics set in, men began feeling nostalgic for earlier ages, which, as they fondly imagined, had witnessed a closer communion between the creative individual and the group inspiring him, supporting him, interpreted by him: ancient Greece and the age of the cathedrals. Their social conscience, after the Dreyfus case and the 'democratic' wars of the new century, tormented them. Was it right, and was it beneficial to literature, to continue enjoying the advantages of a culture and of a civilization without contributing anything to its spiritual enrichment? Were not the essential forces, which are collective in our gregarious age, to be captured by writers powerful enough to renounce the easy self-analysis of a lonely individual, to attempt the tragic subject of what has been called 'a lonely crowd'? The fear of solitude and the fear of insecurity have become such anguishing motives in the lives of moderns in the second half of our century that hymns to solitude and odes to the spirit of adventure have become as unthinkable in modern poetry as odes to enthusiasm and vituperations against an unfaithful mistress. Poems in praise of wine have likewise regrettably disappeared, while drinking has become general but unpoetical. Novels are boldly attempting to depict men, in search of fraternity, huddled together in labor unions, army squadrons, suburban communities—and hating each other more bitterly than ever before. Never was hatred of man for man— ideological, political, sexual, racial—so bitter as it has become in our era, which preaches the virtues of getting along with people and of mutual assistance and international understanding.

If Martin du Gard, Duhamel, and Romains counted, perhaps mistakenly, on the massive impact of their sagas upon posterity, Raymond Radiguet owes his survival to two slim, youthful, yet extraordinarily precocious, novels. Death carried him off at the age of twenty. Whether he would have matured into a full-blown novelist, creating a world of his own and perhaps rivaling Stendhal, or would have lapsed into overconscious analysis and the tricks of a moralist writing novels in the classical tradition must remain matter for speculation. It is dangerous for a gifted writer not to have passed through a romantic phase, with some unsure or bad taste, an unpruned growth of sentiments and unruly emotions, and an undisciplined abundance. But it would be ungracious to be squeamish about the achievement of Radiguet. Many Frenchmen consider his *Bal du Comte d'Orgel* a masterpiece to be ranked with *La Princesse de Clèves*, which was obviously Radiguet's model. I do not, and I confess that disbelief when reading that novel is constantly aroused by the author's intrusions into his narrative and by the sententious tone of these reflections of a very young man who thinks he has nothing more to learn about life and love. The tradition of the psychological novel, which French schoolboys are taught to admire from their lycée classes on, is responsible for some linear dryness and thinness in stories, too expert too soon and too sedulously eschewing disorder and chaos, that they write when out of college. Françoise Sagan, Françoise Mallet-Joris, and other girl-prodigies have thus composed frighteningly sophisticated precocious novels, after which they have incurred the danger either of decline before reaching maturity or of repetitiousness. Mauriac, who praised that 'psychological game of chess' (the phrase was coined by Thibaudet) of Radiguet's second and last novel, was right to add that its slight dryness is that of a young author who is as yet only 'a splendidly gifted brain, but whose heart has not yet been enriched and mellowed by life.' The mechanism, learned in *La Princesse de Clèves*, *Adolphe*, and *Le Rouge et le noir*, is made to function too perfectly, when some awkwardness and intrusions from rebellious life would be more natural.

On the other hand, the earlier novel, *Le Diable au corps* (1922), which was transposed to the screen in 1947 with Gerard Philipe and Micheline Presle, remains a masterpiece of adolescent fiction. Max Jacob wrote privately to the author: 'It is a wonder that at your age you should have redone Laclos without even suspecting it.' The author, born in 1903 in the suburbs of Paris, along the river Marne, in the very setting of his novel, had, at fifteen, composed some delicate poems, collected in 1920 in *Les Joues en feu.* Jean Cocteau admired them profusely and compared the youthful prodigy to Rimbaud. But Radiguet was impatient with his youth and resented it: growing old quickly was his most fervent ambition. *Le Diable au corps,* whose title suggests not *Devil in the Flesh,* as it was rendered in 1932, but the feverish impatience of a boy eager to sow his wild oats and to become a man through a convulsive love affair, appeared in 1922. A year later, on December 12, 1923, Raymond Radiguet died of typhoid fever. Three days earlier he had whispered to his friend Jean Cocteau: 'Listen to something dreadful. In three days, I shall be shot by the soldiers of God.' Cocteau, Lacretelle, and Mauriac mourned him as one of the 'inheritors of unfulfilled renown.' Aldous Huxley, prefacing Kay Boyle's translation of *Le Diable au corps,* recalled young Mozart and remarked that the author 'set out in possession of those literary virtues with which most writers end.'

Precocious as he was, Radiguet could not but write an autobiographical novel under a disguise. But most of the usual faults of adolescent writing have been avoided by the youthful author, except a tendency to summarize the lessons of his experience in those neat, imperious maxims of which French novelists have always been fond. The book has been called a '*Daphnis and Chloé* in modern dress,' and the author himself mentions the falsely naïve Greek pastoral that his mistress and he are living over again. But the idyl becomes a tragic one, and the adolescent blends cynicism and cruelty with tenderness. It assumes universal value by the remarkable talent for selection of significant details displayed by an author in his teens who had read Mme de La Fayette, Stendhal, and perhaps Mérimée. It is the definitive portrayal of the adolescent in wartime, rushed into manhood and unequal to the emotional demands and responsibilities thrust upon him.

War is mentioned in the opening sentence of the book; to the boys then entering their teens, it was a four-year holiday, with freedom prematurely won from their parents, who spoiled their sons, threatened by the draft; the young women, temporarily deprived of their husbands, were prompt to initiate these youngsters to love.

The narrator is still a child who has to creep out of his home stealthily at night for his first rendezvous and to forge lies to conceal that he has missed school. He tries hard to appear cynical, but he faints when he watches, with the crowd of his little town, a mad woman leap from the roof of a house. He meets Marthe, who is a few years older, engaged to an officer, and very much of a 'petite bourgeoise.' A common interest in literature arouses their curiosity about each other. He skips school to accompany her when she buys furniture for her future home. He imposes his own taste upon her, and he naïvely wonders at her feminine pleasure in yielding to his self-assured male reasoning. He meets her again after she has married, having been invited to look at the bedroom decoration he selected for her. He has now lost his pose and his cynicism in playing at inspiring love. He is the shy and clumsy adolescent, fearful of the mystery in the woman, intimidated by his own body and the gestures of profanation that love seems to require. She leads him tenderly to physical union, after the subtle gradation from 'vous' to 'tu,' from respect to carnal union, and from passion to the tenderness that outlives and justifies the physical passion. Some details of the idyl, such as the basket filled with eatables that the boy had to accept from his mother; his fear of ridicule; his arrival, soaked from the rain, when Marthe has to make him undress and don her husband's dressing gown; the fire of olivewood beside which they lie down in silence—all are exquisitely selected and treated with skill.

But the adolescent is still a child intent upon breaking up his toy and killing his happiness. There is no sense of sin or remorse in him, but an unexplained cruelty, as of a boy bent on hurting his devoted mother and jealously picking quarrels on the flimsiest pretexts. A demon of analysis, instilled by literature, makes him question whether he really loves her. He becomes impatient over her angelic look when she wakes up beside him or after she has become pregnant. Their love, meanwhile, has become a scandal in the little suburban town. She must go and stay with her family. Once Marthe and he attempt a trip to Paris for a night; in an unforgettable scene of boyish cruelty, he makes her walk for hours (she is then pregnant) in search of a hotel, while he is too shy to ask for a double room. She catches a lung affliction and dies soon after. Her young lover faints when his younger brothers break the news to him. 'My jealousy,' he confesses when tragedy has at last overwhelmed him, 'pursued her even in the grave, and I hoped that there would be nothing after death.' He understands that he was probably never really happy but that he loved Marthe profoundly, even if their love was doomed in advance by all the conventions of their class and the ineluctable necessities of life.

This study of analysis of love and of a self-tormenting adolescent hurting the woman who has unreservedly given herself to him shows flashes of deep insight, but it is not woven into a finished artistic whole, as are Gide's shorter novels or Proust's poetical developments. It is remarkable for its restraint and its structural organization, with episodes, concrete details, and symbolic incidents marking the phases of an implacable tragedy of love and death. Except for the few unpleasant didactic remarks strewn here and there, the novel stands out for its perfect naturalness; the adolescent and the woman accept themselves as they are, submit to their love and its consequences, quietly ignore and challenge society, and reach a bareness in stating their feelings, as they discover them, which was to remain unequaled in the novels of the decade 1920–30.

There is more tenderness and more sincerity, more art, in its naïve excess of sophistication, and more mystery in this little book than in most of the more ambitious volumes of Romains, Duhamel, and even Martin du Gard. Once again, a novel may survive owing to the restrained poetry that breaks through in patches in spite of the author's endeavor to be a detached and lucid moralist. Radiguet's promises were great indeed. Like Rimbaud, to whom he is often and unfairly compared, like Cocteau himself, who became, for a brief while, a convert following Radiguet's death, the author of *Le Diable au corps* was athirst for purity when he analyzed himself and others most mercilessly, a fallen angel or, as Cocteau put it, a glove of heaven:

> You know what I call 'gloves of heaven': To touch us without soiling itself heaven sometimes puts on gloves. Radiguet was a glove of heaven. His form fitted heaven like a glove. When heaven takes out its hand, it is death.

Bibliographical Notes

General works on the fiction of the years 1910–30 are listed in the General Bibliography.

Both *Jean Barois* and *Les Thibault* are published in English translation by The Viking Press, New York. One or two able reviews of *Les Thibault* were written by Jean Prévost and Benjamin Crémieux, both victims of World War II. The essay by André Rousseaux in *Littérature du vingtième siècle* (Albin Michel, 1938–53, 5 vols.) is neither distinguished nor very informative. René Lalou has a slim pamphlet on Martin du Gard (Gallimard, 1938), Howard C. Rice wrote one in English (The Viking Press, 1941), R. Gibson a third one published by Hillary House, New York, in 1961 and Bower, London. The only illuminating discussions of Martin du Gard are those by Claude-Edmonde Magny in her *Histoire du roman français* (Editions du Seuil, 1950), by Jean Prévost in *Problèmes du roman* (Lyon et Paris: Confluences, 1943, pp. 95–100), by Roger Ikor, 'Humanité des Thibault,' *Europe*, June 1946, 28–47, and Léon Roudiez, 'Situation de Martin du Gard,' *The French Review*, XXXIV, 1, October 1960, 13–25. After his death, Martin du

Gard was treated at greater length in a special number of *La Nouvelle Revue Française* (September 1957) and by Denis Boak, in English, *Roger Martin du Gard*, The Clarendon Press, Oxford, 1963.

Marcel Saurin published, in 1951, at the Mercure de France, a very useful bibliography of Duhamel's writings, interestingly prefaced by Duhamel himself. Articles on Duhamel are very numerous; a special number of *Le Capitole* was devoted to him in 1927. Little books on Duhamel have been written by Luc Durtain in 1920, André Thérive in 1925, and Achille Ouy in 1927. A collective work on *Duhamel et nous* (by Claudel, Madaule, Archambault, and others) constituted one of the 'Cahiers de la Nouvelle Journée' (Bloud et Gay, 1938). Other essays useful to consult are by Henri Massis (*Revue Universelle*, March 15, 1922, 738–61), Christian Sénéchal (*La Vie des peuples*, July and August 1924, 456–83 and 681–716), by André Rousseau (in *Ames et visages du vingtième siècle*, Grasset, 1932), and by Louis Chaigne (*Etudes*, December 20, 1935, 721–35). The most recent books in French are *Georges Duhamel ou le bourgeois sauvé* by Pierre Henri Simon (Le Temps présent, 1947) and, by William Falls, *Le Message humain de Duhamel* (Boivin, 1948). Other admirers and interpreters of Duhamel in America have been Hélène Harvitt and Clark Keating. Duhamel himself wrote a suggestive, though slight, essay on the novel, *Essai sur le roman* (Marcelle Lesage, 1925), and some interesting considerations on the 'I' in fiction and memoirs in *Remarques sur les mémoires imaginaires* (Mercure de France, 1934).

Jules Romains has not lacked enthusiastic critics. The first volumes of *Les Hommes de bonne volonté* were warmly and intelligently appraised by Benjamin Crémieux, Jean Prévost, and Marcel Thiébaut. Reference is made in the text to the remarks of the woman critic Claude-Edmonde Magny (*Esprit*, February 1941) and to a review of *Verdun* by Clifton Fadiman (*The New Yorker*, December 30, 1939, pp. 53–5).

André Cuisenier has two solid books on Romains: *Jules Romains et l'unanisme* (Flammarion, 1935) and *L'Art de Jules Romains* (Flammarion, 1952). Other monographs are by Marie-Louise Richli-Bidal, *Après le symbolisme: retour à l'humain* (Presses modernes, 1938), W. Ehrenfels, *Das unanimistische Bewusstsein im Werke J. Romains* (Greifswald, 1940), Henri Blaser, *De l'influence alternée et simultanée des éléments sensible et intellectuel dans les oeuvres de Jules Romains* (Zurich 1941), Madeleine Berry, *Jules Romains, sa vie, son oeuvre* (Le Conquistador, 1953), and Madeleine Israel, *Jules Romains* (Kra, 1931). André Figueras presented a selection of Romains's poetry, published by Seghers in 1953; Peter Norrish published a volume on his unanimist plays at the Cambridge University Press in 1958; André Bourin wrote a volume, approved by Romains, which was published by Flammarion in 1961.

Radiguet's two novels have been translated: *Devil in the Flesh* appeared as a Signet Book (New York); *The Count's Ball* has been published by New Directions (Norfolk, Connecticut). An Australian, Keith Goesch, presented a Sorbonne thesis on Radiguet in 1952 containing many curious texts and documents, but little critical appraisal. It was published in 1955 by La Palatine, Paris.

III

The Legacy of Proust and Gide

Marcel Proust died in November 1922. There can be little question, fifty years or more after his death, that his place is secure among the French novelists, indeed, that he must rank with the four or five greatest among them. Gide, born two years before Proust, survived him by almost twenty-nine years. Gide's influence on French novelists and probably on French life was wider. His literary activity was diverse, and his polymorphous personality stood at many a crossroad of religion, psychology, politics, aesthetics, and ethics. He was a great prose writer and a *touche-à-tout* of genius, such as Voltaire had been and such as Sartre is today. But Gide's ultimate position as a novelist and as a writer is likely to be a far more modest one than Proust's. He appears more remote from us today. No novelist in the present century, not even Thomas Mann, James Joyce, Joseph Conrad, or William Faulkner, has left a gallery of characters— tragic and ludicrous, vain or pitiful, profoundly analyzed or fleetingly episodic—as rich and as teeming with life as the hundred or so characters of *A la Recherche du temps perdu* (*Remembrance of Things Past*). Balzac, Dostoevski, and perhaps, though it is doubtful, Tolstoi and Dickens alone tower above Proust in that respect.

Proust's untimely death in his fiftieth year, only fifteen years or so after he had decisively embarked upon his career as a novelist, left the second half of his monumental work imperfect; but there is perhaps greater originality in those last volumes, as there is in the last six books of the *Aeneid*, than in the better known early part. His early death proved a boon for Proust's ultimate reputation. He was not afforded the

time to attempt paler copies of his own great work or to caricature its
subtlety, occasional morbidity, or its stylistic mannerisms, as has been the
sad lot of aging writers. After his death, his novel was submitted to many
attacks. Since adversaries are proverbially more clear-sighted than admirers, they helped rid the Proustian monument of much superfluous
accretion and shift the emphasis away from secondary features to the
more vital ones, where Proust victoriously resisted both criticism and the
corroding of time. Several alternate, if not necessarily conflicting, interpretations of the greatness of Proust have been proposed since 1922. The
first test of literary immortality has been met: the ability of a work to
assume different faces for succeeding generations and to lend itself, with
the sovereign indifference of beauty, to a variety of transfigurations.

English critics and admirers were, characteristically, the first to pay
Proust discerning and enthusiastic homage; a volume entitled *An English
Tribute*, published as early as 1923, contains valuable contributions by
Clive Bell, Joseph Conrad, Compton Mackenzie, Middleton Murry, Lo-
gan Pearsall Smith, Arthur Symons, Alec Waugh, and others. Several of
the best recent appraisals of Proust have come from Great Britain and
America (in one single year, 1964–65, those of Wallace Fowlie, George
Painter, Philip Kolb, and Leo Bersani). Between 1930 and the year 1941,
when war-ridden England welcomed the two-volume new edition of *Remembrance of Things Past* (Random House, 1941), ironical or severe
attacks against the adulation of Proust poured in from English pens.
A certain moral revulsion from the Proustian obsession with abnormal
love was to be expected, even from post-Puritan England, and the lack
in Proust of a social conscience or of any political enthusiasm for a better
world was to be resented by the young Englishmen who 'thought continually of those who were truly great' and were inflamed by the Russian
five-year plans and the Spanish republican cause. W. H. Auden and
Louis MacNeice, venturing to appraise the literary stock market in their
Letters from Iceland, prophesied—wrongly—'some further weakening in
Proust.' Philip Guedalla had, much earlier, coined one of his bons mots
in announcing that the vogue for Proust would hardly outlast a 'Marcel
wave.' 'Water jelly,' exclaimed D. H. Lawrence to characterize that
strange coldblooded animal who scientifically and patiently dissociated
ideas, emotions, and sensations. 'Ploughing a field with knitting needles'
was George Moore's description of Proust. Aldous Huxley, one of the
very few living writers who had the honor of a flattering mention in
Proust's novel, placed some ungrateful lines in the mouth of one of his
characters in *Eyeless in Gaza*.

> How I hate old Proust! . . . that asthmatic seeker of lost time
> squatting, horribly white and flabby, with breasts almost female but
> fledged with long black hairs, for ever squatting in the tepid bath
> of his remembered past . . . There he sat, a pale repellent invalid,
> taking up spongefuls of his own thick soup and squeezing it over
> his face . . .

The disappointment and the impatience that many expressed between 1930 and 1940, when the newness of Proust's psychology and poetry had worn off, can easily be explained by several converging causes. First came the mechanical working of one of the few effective laws of literature: the law of reaction of one generation against the previous one. Proust had appeared impossibly difficult in 1913—to the point where Gide himself had refused the manuscript for the Gallimard firm and where critic after critic confessed he could make neither head nor tail of *Du côté de chez Swann* (*Swann's Way*). But obscurity is short-lived in modern letters and was in this case. Ten years after Proust's death, most young readers declared Proust's writing occasionally involved and needlessly exacting, but hardly obscure—in fact, not enough so. Too many passages are too well written to suit the present fashion for bare simplicity, and for some the author falls too readily in line with the French tradition, which stems from Chateaubriand or even from Montaigne. Kafka and Joyce seem to many young readers to retain their 'virtue' of obscurity longer than Proust, now read as a classic the world over and revered as a model prose writer in many anthologies.

The personality of Proust as it came to be half revealed after his death (many letters probably still remain to be unearthed and many ugly secrets still to be brought to light) was a second source of disappointment for the early admirers of the novelist. It dawned on many that the author had lent much of himself not only to the narrator as a child crying for his mother's kiss and spoiled by his grandmother while vacationing in Balbec, but perhaps also to Mme Vinteuil indulging in sadistic profanation of her father's image, to the morbid inquisitor into Albertine's past debauchery after the girl's death, and even to Morel, Jupien, and some of the most dubious or frankly discreditable characters in fiction. There were glaring contrasts in Proust's personality, polite to a fault and treating his friends to sumptuous aristocratic dinners, then repairing to some shady establishment where he would evince more concrete admiration for the handsome or vicious servants of the dukes and barons with whom he had associated. That ambivalence of the man in Proust obviously served the artist in him. He had good reason for forcing his own fictional characters into sudden contradictions or abrupt changes of personality that no gradual evolution could account for. Staid critics have been repelled or unconvinced by those dramatic metamorphoses that plunged Saint Loup or Gilberte into vice and exalted a former prostitute like Rachel to the pedestal of an actress loved and idealized by one of the most intelligent members of the aristocracy. In *La Prisonnière* (*The Captive*) Proust expressed his admiration for the buffoons and the women in Dostoevski, similar to people painted by Rembrandt, alternately exuberant in their humility and haughtily insolent, charitable to a point that hurts our Western idea of self-respect, then suddenly lecherous or drunken.[1] He compared Dostoevski's fantastic creatures to Rembrandt's 'Night Watch,' and implied, with his own characters in mind, that only the lighting and the costumes exalted to the status of visionary phantoms people who were perhaps average men and women.

Revelations, at first half-whispered and lately more frank, from friends and acquaintances of Proust threw some light on facets of Proust's personality that could not but disappoint the least squeamish among his readers. His high-flown compliments to women concealed a profound lack of interest in all but the superficial aspects of their nature. His interest in servants, chauffeurs, butlers, and elevator boys hardly sprang from social charity. Even his proverbially lavish tips were an unpleasant manifestation of his desire to be liked and to pay for his loves or for friendship. The publication of Proust's letters proved especially harmful to the cult that might have developed for the author of the most intimate novel of the century. He reserved his genius for his book, fearful as he was of dying before he would complete it, and veiled his life under a screen of flattering politeness that was little more than a defense reaction. There was a rare gift for mimicry in Proust's ability to observe and reproduce other people's idiosyncrasies, and not a little hypocrisy in the adolescent who had cultivated his disease in order to retain his mother's lenient love and who had to conceal from his beloved mother and from all those who were dear to him the less orthodox sides of his nature.

Other grievances harbored by many readers of Proust concerned his excessive preoccupation with sexual abnormality and his snobbery. Our moral notions are, it is well known, elastic, and the literature of the last

1. Claudel likewise acknowledged Dostoevski's enormous influence over him; he admired in him the rapid and sudden changes in the characters, through which they discover elements in themselves that simply were not there before—the way stressed by the biologist De Vries in which nature proceeds in its sudden mutations.

two decades has accustomed many of us to a more than frank treatment of sodomy and Lesbianism. Jean Genet makes Marcel Proust appear rather tame. But even the broadest-minded among Proust's readers may protest, on aesthetic grounds, against a vision of the world that sets up abnormality as the norm. When practically every character in Proust turns homosexual in the latter part of the novel, we remain unconvinced and wonder how 'universal' such a vision can be. Proust, perhaps fascinated by Balzac, and in terms Flaubert or Zola might have used, defined himself in his last volume as an 'anatomist' and quietly wrote to one of his friends: 'I obey a general truth which prevents me from being concerned with friend and foe alike. The praise of sadists will distress the man in me when my book comes out. It cannot alter the conditions under which I experiment with truth and which I do not choose arbitrarily.'

Only naïve sociologists will demand from an artist that he depict the world as it is and be true to statistical proportions established by scientists. Obviously, the world of Balzac, that of Dostoevski, or that of Faulkner are no more normal, in other respects, than that of Proust. Even the France of Louis Philippe was less preoccupied with money than the characters in the *Comédie humaine* appear to be; and Temple Drake must have few prototypes among Southern American college girls. But Proust's saga-novel rests upon the assumption, occasionally made explicit by the author, that sexual anomaly and sadism are linked with moral goodness and superior intelligence. M. de Guermantes, unhappy enough to be afflicted with normal love habits, is a fool when compared with his extraordinary brother, M. de Charlus. Jupien, Proust assures us, was in truth highly gifted, whatever the average reader may think of the use to which he put his talents. The scene in *Swann* that shocked Edith Wharton and many French friends of Proust, where Mlle Vinteuil lets her friend spit upon her dead father's picture when indulging in Lesbian caresses, is strangely followed by an apology for sadism, in which Proust betrayed his hidden purpose. A sadist like her, he explains to his reader, is an artist in evil. She is a purely sentimental creature, naturally inclined to virtue, and, when yielding to evil momentarily, she merely 'escapes from her scrupulous and tender soul into the inhuman world of pleasure.' Elsewhere, in *A l'ombre des jeunes filles en fleurs* (*Within a Budding Grove*), he asserts that 'only in truly vicious lives can the moral problem be posed with its full anxious force.' There is much didacticism in Proust, and too much of it, less blatantly but more perfidiously than in Gide's *Corydon*, is devoted to proposing a justification

of unorthodox sexual behavior and of effeminacy in some men, which some
of us still refuse to acclaim as a sign of especial grace and as the privilege of genius.

It seems hardly to be denied that Proust, in his youth at least, was a
snob. He strove hard and long, he, a half-Jew, to be received into the
most aristocratic Parisian circles. To this end he spared no effort of his
naturally kind personality. He was almost obsequiously anxious to please;
he was generous, yet convinced that any affection is venal and could be
purchased with enough presents and favors. But hundreds of writers in
the past have been snobs and many are today, or inverted snobs in their
brutality toward wealthy and well-mannered people and in their courting the popularity of the uncultured. Proust denied, in letters to Paul
Souday and to his English friend Sidney Schiff (alias Stephen Hudson),
that he was a snob. And he certainly outgrew most of his early admiration
for the fashions, etiquette, and conventionality of the Faubourg Saint-
Germain. He became ruthless in displaying their selfishness and their
vanity. But he lost also 'whatever poetry there may be in snobbery,' as
he had called it in writing to Lucien Daudet. In any case, snobbery
exists; it is a powerful social force, occasionally a force for good. Proust
deserves no blame for having turned his telescope, as he liked to call
it, on that phenomenon.

He has, however, been severely taken to task for concentrating almost
exclusively on the feudal nobility, the bourgeoisie, and the servant class.
The charge is naïve and rests upon a misunderstanding. Neither Racine
nor Kafka has depicted workmen on strike or humble housewives struggling with the Monday-morning laundry, and the depth and the truth
of their work have not suffered thereby. Kitchenmaids and milliners
have been known to admire such 'class products' as the Duchess of
Guermantes and Gilberte; a New York commissioner of police, in 1950,
was depicted by a weekly magazine as reading Proust at night in his
kitchen while drinking (was it an antidote?) a glass of milk before re-
tiring to bed. British prisoners of war, in 1940–44, displayed a passion
for reading Proust, and it is reported that Proust had to be branded
officially as dangerous to communism and as too subtly corrupt, even
as an example of the decadent bourgeoisie, when his success in Russian
translation frightened Moscow's cultural masters; proletarians had to be
protected against his insidious poison.

Several brave critics, however, between 1930 and 1940, announced
that Proust's fame was on the wane because he had sadly lacked a social

conscience. Others ventured the thesis, in 1940, that he would remain
as an illustration of French decadence and provide the key to France's
failure of nerves and to Vichy. Sociological maniacs, who flourish in some
academic circles, maintained that Proust's survival would be attributable
to his description of the ascending bourgeoisie absorbing the descending
aristocracy. They overlooked similar assertions, which had characterized
in closely parallel terms the memoirs of Saint-Simon, the satirical portraits of La Bruyère, Balzac's fiction, and many other famous works. In
truth, the vision of the narrator, and of the author, having become gradually blurred by pessimism and by the stress on abnormality, is responsible for the changes in the characters and groups delineated by Proust.
The fusion of the middle and upper classes had occurred a long time
before Proust and would not have been a very original subject for a
novelist. Just as convincing a case could be made for Proust as the champion of the servant class! He is tender to Jupien and Morel, lyrical in his
irony over Françoise's culinary talents, and when a certain young man
who had served him as a chauffeur died in 1914 in a seaplane accident,
Proust praised him in a letter to Gide as a 'young man with a delightful
intelligence' who, with no culture and of a lowly estate, had written him
'letters which are those of a great writer.'

Proust's fame has survived these charges and others; it has emerged
unscathed from World War II, from the new stress on *littérature engagée*
and on man's freedom in his denial of a God on whom to lean, and
finally from the admiration for unanalytical American novels. If the con-
vergent attention granted to a writer by scholars of all ages and by
critics is a sign of his continued reputation, Proust has certainly received
that tribute. At least twenty full books on him have been published in
French and English since 1940. Proust's niece, by distilling very spar-
ingly the notebooks left by Proust and hinting at further revelations,[2]

2. Other letters of moderate interest came out in 1952–53. The most important
posthumous work is *Jean Santeuil*, published in 1952, a long manuscript apparently
composed between 1892 and 1903 or perhaps 1908 (and not just 1896–9 as
claimed by the publisher). It was unfortunately badly edited, put together very
arbitrarily and preceded, thus far, by a very inadequate introduction. It can be
called a novel only in parts, for many of its chapters rather resemble portraits,
sketches, comments on literature and politics. But several parts already give evidence
of Proust's stylistic gifts and of his early awareness of some of the essential themes
of his future work: the mother's kiss, the conventionality of the father, the son's
revolt against his parents, the ambivalence between sadism and kindness in the
imaginary novelist portrayed, the children's loves in the Champs Elysées, the death
of love, jealousy. But neither Saint Loup, Charlus, Swann, nor Vinteuil is yet

has increased the curiosity of many for the details of Proust's life and the mysterious and critical years between twenty-five and forty when he elaborated his future work through fruitful waste of time. But the emphasis is no longer on the man, obsequious, tormented, hypocritical, self-centered, nasty as he may have been, and equally kindhearted, sensitive, secretly courageous, and extraordinarily intelligent. It stresses the long novel created by Proust, which proved to be greater than its creator.

An interesting French novel, in 1949, *Une Lecture* by Roland Cailleux, turned the Proustian novel itself into a fictional character. The protagonist of that book actually had his whole life changed by reading Proust. The author, Cailleux, and many who agreed with him, confessed that their own and many other lives had been determined at some critical moment by the intrusion of Proust's characters into their own careers. Only Balzacian creatures seem ever to have fascinated French readers to such a perilous extent. Contrary to what suspicious critics might expect, it is not the homosexual obsession suddenly irrupting into 'normal' lives that acted most potently upon devotees of Proust. For it soon dawns on the reader that, while Proust derives much that is universally valid and profound from his delineation of abnormal love, he has established those truths upon a fundamental lie; his most impressive scenes, such as those in which Albertine is kept prisoner, are too obviously incredible in their data. The hero of Cailleux's novel and many readers of Proust in actual life are much more struck by the critical about-face of the narrator in *A la Recherche du temps perdu*. After many years seemingly wasted in social vanities and the melancholy conviction that he was unfit to devote himself to any serious achievement, the Proustian narrator suddenly shifted from the past to the future. He vanquished death, perceived the serpentine but sure direction of all his past life, and embarked upon artistic creation. Future Ph.D.'s will most certainly write theses on the beneficent moral influence of Proust's stubborn pursuit of a vocation. It is regrettable that the poetical English title, drawn from

present. And Proust has not yet developed the type of fictional technique that felicitously blends the directness and intimacy of memoirs in the first person singular and the novelist's art through which he assigns full significance to the remembered past and recreates it imaginatively. *Jean Santeuil,* valuable as some of its chapters are, fails to come to life as a whole and to be lightened of the weight afflicting memoirs that adhere to reality too closely. Philip Kolb has studied Proust's early novel most accurately and ingeniously in *Saggi e Ricerche di letteratura francese* (Turin, vol. IV, 1963).

the thirtieth of Shakespeare's *Sonnets*, should fail to convey the notion of a search for a vocation through time apparently lost.

The admirer of Proust need have little worry about the survival of Proust among the most eminent novelists. The difficulty lies rather in determining the most lasting reasons for that survival. We have enumerated the main grounds on which Proust could well antagonize or disgust the generations that followed him. Other flimsy assertions have been neglected, such as the prophecy, advanced by Léon Pierre-Quint in a disappointed or defeatist article in *Europe*, in 1935, that new generations being brought up in sports would find Proust distasteful. By the same reasoning, Joyce, Kafka, Eliot, and Sartre would hardly appeal to those who have practiced boxing, football, golf, and cricket! Proust has enjoyed an advantage that has not often been granted to great works and that the four authors just mentioned have been denied: he has had practically no imitators. Jean Stafford's *Boston Adventure* in America and Stephen Hudson's *A True Story* in England have been described as Proustian novels. In French, it would be hard to quote one book written unambiguously under Proust's influence. Proust has thus been spared the harmful tribute of disciples who caricature a great work and popularize it, a tribute from which Debussy, Cézanne, Matisse, and Gide have not been saved.

The legacy that Proust bequeathed French literature is as rich and diverse as the whole of his extant work and as the series of conflicting interpretations and misconstructions of which that work is susceptible. Among the manifold aspects from which one may look admiringly and with renewed wonder at Proust, a few, however, seem to us to deserve being singled out, thirty years after Proust's death. Others, which immediate successors of Proust had stressed, were soon dwindling into relative insignificance; or rather, they may well be the 'wrong reasons' that have always at first attracted the earliest admirers of great innovators to their least significant merits, as was the case, for instance, with Diderot, Baudelaire, Mallarmé, Henry James, and Yeats. Thus the so-called philosophy of Proust, which has been repeatedly referred to Plato, Schopenhauer, Schelling, and Bergson, seems to us today a secondary factor in Proust's originality. Hailing Proust as a 'forerunner' of Freud, whom chronologically he followed, or as a rediscoverer of Freudianism, of which he had probably never heard, is similarly irrelevant and injurious to Proust since Freudian psychoanalysis, epoch-making as it is likely to remain, is being superseded by other doctrines and newer forms of soul therapeutics. It was equally naïve to multiply articles on the impeccable composition of Proust's novel, variously termed 'Wagnerian,' 'en rosace,' 'circular,' even a model of 'a perfect circle,' and 'Gothic,' like a cathedral of Ile de France. It is true that Proust stressed the ingeniousness of some of the props on which he was raising his structure, rich in gargoyles and buttresses and dark, suspicious aisles, and built many of his volumes with a view to the final aesthetic revelation of *Le Temps retrouvé*. But it is none the less true that few great novels, even Russian and American ones, are so liberally encumbered with digressions and extraneous accretions. We may be grateful that they are not impeccable pieces of structural engineering at which some professors naïvely marvel, but as unpredictable and irrational and 'unstructural' as life at its liveliest.

Organic structure, for those of us who do not approach literature with the mind, or the ax, of an engineer, is a dubious virtue in the art of fiction. The far too famous 'petite madeleine' dipped into the cup of tea is responsible for much indigestion in squeamish stomachs which relish other Proustian nourishment with intense delight. Proust's games of *petites phrases* and leitmotivs and foreshadowings of the future evolution of his characters are tricks and clumsy devices used by a writer who was far too mindful of the traditional French stress on composition and who could not help respecting Flaubert, Anatole France, and even Bourget (Bergotte has all the letters of Bourget's name but one) far too much. Lastly, to define Proust's position in literature as the crowning achievement of symbolism, as Edmund Wilson did, is to over-emphasize one of the aspects of the early Proust and his theoretical aesthetics. Only rarely was Proustian symbolism artificial and intellectual, as the search for subtlety in correspondences had often proved to be with the minor symbolist poets. Proust himself liked to stress the naturalness and inevitability of metaphors not only in style but in our very perception and sensibility. 'Is it not logical,' he asks somewhere in his novel, 'through no device of symbolism but through a sincere return to the very root of the impression, to represent an object by another which, in the flash of an original illusion, we had mistaken for it?' But Proust, whatever he may have said in praise of dreams, of the imagination, of the magic lantern of his childhood reminiscences, of ethereal women's dresses, and of languid flowers, also stands the furthest removed from Henri de Régnier, Albert Samain, Maurice Maeterlinck, and other symbolists. A virile intellect, a relentless mental courage, comic realism, a grasp upon prosaic life, and the awareness that women are not blessed damozels nor marmoreal Herodiades, that men and even children are not angels of purity and innocent Pelleases—these were Proust's gifts also.

Proust possessed the primary privilege of the great novelist: he could, and did, create a variegated and haunting gallery of characters, the richest in French literature next to Balzac's. In spite of the philosophy that is generously lent to him, in spite of the psychological and moral didacticism, of which he was often guilty, and of the aesthetic theorizing in his last volume, Proust never created his characters in order to illustrate pre-existing views or as mouthpieces of his own ideas. Even Bergotte and Elstir are primarily real people. Elstir is the most complex and profound painter ever portrayed in fiction. Proustian characters are not all as convincing. The women who are loved (in what strange ways!) seem to have been endowed with the most elusive characterization. Odette and Albertine are almost negative in this respect. But Andrée, Oriane de Guermantes, Françoise (in spite of Proust's wearisome obsession with the language of his characters), the old aunts at Combray, Mme de Villeparisis, the narrator's grandmother—all are splendidly alive.

So are the 'flat' characters, as E. M. Forster calls them, of which any novel must count a good many, because they are actually flat in real life and are likely to become easily adopted as types. We dare laugh at them as we cannot do when we have discovered the true complexity of M. de Charlus or the tragedy of Swann frittering his life away not only, as he confesses somewhere, on a woman who was not worth it, but on empty social values from which he could not free himself. Proust is probably the greatest master of comedy since Dickens. M. de Norpois will for many decades remain the fatuous diplomat, Cottard the pompous doctor. Legrandin's nose, M. and Mme Verdurin's gestures, cruelty, and silliness are unforgettable. Proustian readers have actually been known to shed tears at St. Loup's disappointing evolution and death, and others to choke with sobs when reading the brave pages in *La Prisonnière* on Vinteuil's greatness or the Dantesque passage where Swann recognizes his own tearful eyes in a mirror while listening to the *petite phrase* and living over again his disappointed love for Odette in his torturing memory.

While Charlus is the incomparable hero of Proustian fiction, perhaps of twentieth-century fiction altogether, Swann, though less dominant in the saga, lays bare more clearly Proust's process of character presentation and delineation. Like all the others, he is a blend of several persons observed by the author in reality. He first appears to the narrator when the latter, a sensitive child, surrounds him with mystery and accumulates baffling contradictions on the wealthy neighbor of Combray. Proust depicts his physique in rapid touches, renders his language, gradually suggests him among his family, his sets of friends. Like most Proustian characters, Swann leads a double life and is himself ambivalent. He is one of the very few exceptions who, perhaps because he dies before the middle of the work, is never carried away in the infernal homosexual round. But he cherishes dolorous and languid women, Botticelli-like, in art, yet, in real life, concretely embraces Rubens-like cooks, servants, and unrefined country girls. He is addicted to dreaming and sharpens his acute nervous sensitiveness to the point of welcoming pain, but he is not capable of the efforts needed to mature in solitude and to create a work of art. He thus fills an essential function in the novel. He opens up the world of art to Marcel but fails to show him how to penetrate deeply into it, as Elstir will teach him. He points to the peril of living a purely mundane life and of being engulfed by it to the point of losing the ability to concentrate and to create. And he prefigures for Marcel all the tortures of sickly love, anguish, lack of will, and jealousy that will punctuate with their monotonous burden every subsequent passionate pilgrimage within the long novel. In the revelation of his characters, which is never continuously dramatic, Proust is gradual, second to no novelist, except perhaps Dostoevski. The character is imagined and magnified by the narrator long before he appears; then he reveals his several facets, always keeping some mysteries in reserve, and to the last he retains his capacity to astonish us and baffle us. Well may a discerning English critic, Raymond Mortimer, have declared:

> No novelist has made his characters more real to us than Proust, and we know much more about them than about any other figure in fiction. For this reason alone, I believe him to be incomparably the greatest writer who has flourished in my lifetime.

Much will doubtless continue to be written on Proust's psychological revelation and on his aesthetics, the two aspects of his work best calculated to tempt commentators. Both the psychology and the aesthetics of Proust contain much that is already being assimilated by other novelists and by a large portion of the public, even if that public has not actually read Proust. Our way of looking at nature and our manner of falling in and out of love and complacently undergoing the tortures of jealousy have today become definitely Proustian, so much so that the originality of the finest Proustian analyses are already blurred for the generations that have grown up in a Proustian climate. The secrets Marcel read in the sudden thrusts of involuntary memory have likewise lost some of their magic for us. Too many of us have thought ourselves favored with a Proustian revelation because dipping our cake into a cup of tea, smelling a woman's perfume, hearing the distant hum of a train in the night, or stumbling on a flagstone have, thanks to Proust, become meaningful events laden with what we seriously take to be half-mystical ecstasies. In truth, these multiplied episodes in which an involuntary reminiscence releases the Proustian narrator from his anguish and interrupts the otherwise inexorable flow of time do not constitute the most lasting part of Proust's revelation. They may indeed appear to some as a very frail and artificial foundation for the immense cathedral they have to support. Only the unusual depth of Proust's analysis and his poetical gift of transfiguration have saved such episodes, in the last volume, from appearing somewhat childish and arousing our disbelief.

Placed, however, in the course of the novel in general, these flashes of involuntary memory take on a different significance. The Dantesque voyage of the narrator through his childhood and his loves, through the turmoil and vanity of social life, even through the revelations of the spires of Martinville, of the hawthorn and of the medieval stones will end in futility. Society people are empty and cruel; the bevy of girls cycling about the beach is just as heartless; loved ones are mere pegs on which our illusions are hung for a brief respite; death is preying on us from all sides. But one involuntary memory suddenly reveals to the narrator the pattern for which his life had in vain striven. The past is recaptured, the essences shine from behind the painted veil of appearances, the hero's vocation is at last discovered. He composes his work and triumphs over death.

We have also disfigured Proust by our unjustified harping on the theme of his unconscious or latent Bergsonism. Since the task of men teaching young men is apparently to explain more than can be explained and to present annoyingly unpredictable masterpieces as linked to a society or to a philosophy, scholars and critics like to stress the unity of a culture or of an age. Their keenest joy is to discover a philosopher (Descartes, Hegel, Comte, Freud, or Dewey) who will be considered, preferably once he has been safely tucked in his grave, as having formulated the creed from which artistic creations of that age radiated. Bergson has been that scapegoat for the symbolist movement and for the aftermath of symbolism, with Claudel and Proust, even Valéry, presented as his astonished disciples. Proust's repeated denials availed but little, for a touchy author is always suspected of denying most vehemently what secretly pinches him most. The question of Proust's Bergsonism is highly complex and concerns us little here. Clearly, however, Proust does not stem from Bergson and cannot be explained by him. He differs from the philosopher of *Matière et mémoire* (*Matter and Memory*) radically in his conception of memory, in his neglect of the Bergsonian theses on freedom and on the heterogeneousness of cerebral and psychical elements in us, in his stress upon the past, and in his total disinterest in will power, in contrast with Bergson's orientation toward the future and toward action. Proustian aesthetics may remind us of the all-too-scarce passages in which Bergson (notably in *Le Rire* and in *La Pensée et le mouvant*, translated as *The Creative Mind*) had some lineaments of a Bergsonian aesthetics. But there again the parallel should not be strained.

Proust may more convincingly be presented as the Christ heralded by Bergson the Baptist. He was the novelist whom Bergson might have wished to appear and might have announced, even if the prophet did not hail the Messiah with enthusiasm when he finally arrived. For, however perfidiously Bergson may have been lauded by other philosophers for his literary style—a double or multi-edged compliment on their lips—he himself never confused the two separate provinces of philosophy and literature. In a passage of *La Pensée et le mouvant,* he declared: 'It is the province of literature to undertake . . . the study of the soul in the concrete, upon individual examples; the duty of philosophy, it seemed to me, was to lay down the general conditions of the direct, immediate observation of oneself by oneself.' In the same volume, in an essay on 'La Perception du changement,' Bergson had granted the artist a privileged function and added: 'What is the object of art if not to make us discover . . . outside and within ourselves, a vast number of things which did not clearly strike our senses?' And in his first work, *Les Données immédiates,* translated as *Time and Free Will,* he had praised the anonymous, bold novelist who might tear the deftly woven cloth of our conventional self and put us back in the presence of ourselves.

Proust's original vision may well remain priceless where it indeed rent the delusive veil that conceals true life from us. He escaped from the dull narcotic of habit, removed the superficial layers we have allowed to accumulate over our perception, espoused essences, and arrested time. He belonged, through some features of his genius, to the same family of minds that included Bergson, Rousseau, and Montaigne. He uttered diffident warnings against intelligence, also ingloriously treated by Bergson in *L'Evolution créatrice*. It is a saving grace for France, as Etienne Gilson has remarked, to count periodically some prophets who bid their countrymen to distrust the intellect and flout reason. But for them, it would be harder for Frenchmen to remain intelligent with the due corrective of humanity.

More aptly than the much-abused adjective 'Bergsonian,' the broader word 'romantic' would designate the best in the Proustian vision. The romantics restored 'the pleasures of imagination' to the forefront. Romantic heroes, and, even more, romantic heroines, enjoyed the expectation of all joys, and particularly the sinful ones, far more than the fullfillment of such expectations; for reality regularly disappointed them. Like Emma Bovary after she had decided to seek the realization of her bookish dreams with pitifully selfish lovers, they confessed to 'experiencing nothing extraordinary' even in forbidden pleasures. But, and on another plane, imagination was the goddess worshipped by Coleridge, Poe, Baudelaire, and Proust. It alone constituted the whole of love according to Proust; it lay at its source in any case, and it provoked all other pleasures, transfiguring to secondary characters fleetingly colored by the narrator's magic lantern persons from M. de Charlus, Mme de Guermantes, la Berma, and Bergotte to Mlle de Stermaria or the dairy girl of whom he caught a glimpse from the train taking him to Balbec. Proust's claim to greatness lies in part in that irradiation of imagination, enriched by a retentive and transfiguring memory, which turns a weight of matter into gold, and transmutes vices, jealousies, and suspicions into beauty. The lyrical novel, in every language, has usually ended in failure. The Germans, the French (from Chateaubriand to Barrès), the English, including Walter Pater, George Moore, perhaps James Joyce himself, have usually failed in their attempt to incorporate lyricism and a highly wrought prose into fiction. In his poetization of objects, persons, the cries of street vendors in Paris, and the butlers and lackeys standing in the antechamber of Mme de Saint-Euverte, Proust has succeeded in remaining a convincing and fascinating novelist and in filling the novel with all the poetry it can hold.

But Proust, like all writers who tower above mere talents and who retain their freshness through and despite generations of commentators, cannot be reduced to one formula. He unites in himself contradictory qualities. He 'pushed analysis to the point where it becomes creative,' said one of his earliest English admirers. On the one hand, he belongs with the romantics and the symbolists and goes beyond all of them in centering the whole of life and the whole of his long novel on art. The world, his own remorseful loss of past time, and his plunging into disease and vice receive their only possible justification in being suddenly raised, by the artist's magic wand, to the plane of an aesthetic phenomenon. On the other hand, Proust is a pitiless analyst of all that he uncovers in man, and of himself. He had been compared by the man who understood him most deeply among his contemporaries, Jacques Rivière, with Kepler, Galileo, or Newton. His sharp and cruel vision pierces through all our illusions. He dissociates, even more lucidly and relentlessly than the founders of psychoanalysis, the emotions of love, before which most philosophers, except perhaps Plato and Schopenhauer, had recoiled.

The miracle is that such analytical dissociation is not affected by separating the object from the subject but by a more intimate penetration into the object itself and a spiritualization of matter, which breaks up its material substance into atomic particles and infuses new life into them. The greatest virtue that Proust possesses can probably be best represented by one word—depth. Where others would have passed by, content with rendering the world of appearances, Proust dislocates, assimilates the shattered fragments, and reconstructs them. Like his hero Elstir, he spares no effort to 'dissolve that aggregate of reasonings that we call vision.' His own vision has the newness and the same quality of wonder as that of a child. But it is supplemented by memory, by knowledge of other artists who have already penetrated into the secrets of reality, by an intense concentration of the attention, and by knowledge. Proust probably appreciated the impressionists most among the painters of his age, but Cézanne, and before him Chardin, are those to whom he stands closest. His treatment of concrete objects (the brioches eaten at Combray after the Sunday Mass, the asparagus on Françoise's table, the telephone set at Doncières when he hears his grandmother's voice transfigured by the instrument) has all the solidity and the multidimensional quality of a post-impressionist painting. And it retains motion or the potentiality of motion, grace, and elusiveness as well.

In a curious preface to *Tendres Stocks,* by Paul Morand, Proust wrote lines that may well apply to his own unique gift.

> In all the arts, it seems as if talent consisted in a greater closeness between the artist and the object to be expressed. As long as the closeness of the one to the other is not complete, the task is unfinished . . . In other centuries, we feel that there always had re-

mained a certain remoteness dividing the object from the highest
minds which hold discourse about it.

These words may well be the most fitting to designate the unique
features of Proust's eminence as a novelist. He has most of the other
qualities for which we praise the greatest of novelists. In range, he cannot
rank with Dickens, Balzac, and Dostoevski. In naturalness, Tolstoi out-
shines him. But his deep penetration both into reality and into man's
emotions and thoughts is hardly equaled anywhere. As a foreign commentator, and one who is not partial to fiction or to French literature, the
Spaniard José Ortega y Gasset declared:

> He [Proust] stands as the inventor of a new distance between
> things and ourselves . . . The whole of the novel that preceded him
> suddenly appears like a bird's eye literature, crudely panoramic,
> when compared to that delightfully near-sighted genius.

'My function is to disturb,' Gide was fond of saying. His influence has
been profound and always a seminal one, partly because Gide's own
achievement seldom reached such greatness as would discourage emula-
tion in others but also because he willingly sacrificed some of his potentialities to teaching others how to become more truly themselves.
His own artistic failures or his limitations have in that sense
proved more valuable than several of his better-known volumes.
Indeed, the triumphant Gide, the one whose *La Symphonie pastorale* was
adapted to the screen with great skill and whose *Caves du Vatican*,
staged at the *Comédie Française*, reached new and wider layers of the
public, struck his truest admirers as a dissonance. There were not a few
lapses of taste in the elder Gide. The most glaring one was *Robert ou
l'intérêt général*, a ludicrously mediocre and uninspired play, which his
critical self should have strangled before it reached the printer. His compilation of a banal and conventional *Anthology of French Verse* was
another mistake, which revealed how one of the acutest of critics could
err in dealing with his own literature, as he had erred repeatedly when
carried away with enthusiasm for Rabindranath Tagore and the lesser
poems of Robert Browning, for Arnold Bennett or Dashiell Hammett.
His flippant *Thésée* was hardly better inspired; and even the claim to
sincerity failed to excuse the publication of long, dull stretches of Gide's
later diaries. Early in his career Gide sensed that the peril for him would
lie in replacing the vibrating fervor of desire, transfiguring the whole of
life, with the didactic utterances of a moralist. He has not always kept

clear of it. But Gide seems to have been bent, through some Protestant passion for self-mortification, upon providing his critics or his enemies with a plentiful arsenal of weapons against himself. Some even suspect him of coquettishness (he was occasionally guilty of that charming minor vice) in disarming eventual critics by handing over to them the weapons with which to assail him. His future biographers may look back nostalgically upon the earlier part of Gide's career, when he struggled in vain for public recognition and veiled his avowals and his conflicts under artistic restraint. He might well have heeded Proust's advice to him that a writer may say anything provided he takes care not to use the first person singular. Our own conviction is that Gide's *Journals,* which have been hailed in Europe, then in America in Justin O'Brien's excellent translation, as his main achievement, have been dangerously overrated. Only a slim anthology containing the most significant excerpts from that collection of notes, maxims, and confessions jotted down over sixty years of an overlong career and, added to them, the dozen or so critical and aesthetic articles in which Gide has proved a singularly perspicacious critic might be likely to reach posterity. Not a few chapters of Gide's autobiography, *Si le grain ne meurt,* already rank as classics of French prose. *Gidisme* like *Beylisme* or *Renanisme,* is likely to remain as a typically French illustration of the influence of literature upon life. Like Voltaire, or rather like Goethe, to whom he prefers to be compared, Gide never summed up his very diverse gifts into one or several masterpieces that might survive independently of the author and of his life. The potentialities that one detects in him remain superior to his actual achievement. Perhaps his preoccupation with his own problems and with the ethical and aesthetic solution he pursued for them, while it communicated a peculiar *Schaudern* to Gide's writings, prevented him from cutting the navel cord, as the French like to put it, and hampered the expansion of his inventive gifts.

The case of Gide is by no means an isolated one in French literature, although an infrequent one in other literary traditions in which fewer writers attempt to compose novels while not especially endowed with the conventional gifts of the novelist. The gradual loss of the essay— literary, fanciful, whimsical, polished, even political and philosophical— for which our periodicals apparently no longer find the space or the patience, is responsible for many twentieth-century men of letters embodying their abortive or repressed essays into a work of fiction. The parallel disrepute into which the short story has fallen forces these writers to compose novels when they should have been content with a more constricting and deepening framework. *Philoctète* and *Le Retour de l'enfant prodigue,* perhaps also *Saul,* may remain as the finest works of Gide to reach posterity. *Les Nourritures terrestres (The Fruits of the Earth)* would have gained by being cut to half its length.

But it would be a senseless mutilation to insist that a literature be reduced to the very few great works of fiction for which their authors seemed to be predestined. 'What is great in a great book?' is a question no theorist of literature has ever yet answered adequately. Many of us, mildly impressed by the ballyhoo surrounding the hundred best books in the world, would gladly remain blissfully ignorant of two-thirds of those recognized or loudly publicized 'classics' and grant our partiality to works just below the greatest. Gide's novels have moved generations of readers to their depths, in part because they were not the easy outpouring of a born novelist but a painful conquest over obstacles and over himself. Their author endeavored to load what he reluctantly called fiction with dialogues and digressions on religious, ethical, and technical questions, all of them leading to the search for greater authenticity. Saint-Exupéry, Malraux, even ungrateful successors such as Sartre and Camus, will in that respect be Gide's heirs. Like him, they also forsook the novel for the essay or for memoirs. Can the French novel bear that burden of moral scruples, metaphysical and political discussion, and anguished pursuit of total sincerity with which Russian or Germanic fiction likes to afflict itself? The answer to the question is as yet unclear.

Gide *had* to compose novels in order to escape from the pitfall of solipsism, to which not only his own physical temperament and his education but the example of many self-centered symbolists in Paris *cénacles* exposed him. Only through half-imaginary creatures could he, at first, prolong and liberate some of the obsessions that tormented him. Only thus could he solve in some measure the dilemma posed by his search for sincerity. But Gide's sincerity never went quite so far as to condemn him or caricature him remorselessly. His novels remain, under several insidious disguises and in spite of some prefaces (not too genuine, like that of *L'Immoraliste*) and of Gide's insistence on the critical or ironical character of his books, self-defenses. That rebel against Protestantism could never rid himself, any more than could Rousseau, of the lurking conviction that he was right and that his most abject avowals ultimately would vindicate him.

If that elusive 'synthetic and magical power,' imagination, is the primary gift of the born novelist, Gide was not one of its recipients; neither were many of the most respected novelists of several Western literatures. But few acknowledged it as nakedly as did Gide, for imagination, even more than taste, is the last quality of which a writer or an artist may confess to being deprived. As early as 1893, Gide jotted down in his *Journals* that imagination, with him, rarely preceded the idea. He would conceive the idea of a work and even its organization before his imagination took fire. He paid himself elsewhere the dubious compliment: 'And then, I do not know how to invent anything,' and, at the very end of that strained and stilted satirical tale. *Paludes,* for which the author has expressed such surprising tenderness, he half-ironically noted: 'My aesthetic principles are opposed to conceiving a novel.'

Not a few important works of fiction, to begin with *Don Quixote* and *Joseph Andrews,* were born from a satirical intent. Their very irony became creative. After he outpoured the fervor of his *Les Nourritures terrestres,* Gide wrote nothing, as he himself confessed, but 'critical' and ironical works. But the irony in *L'Immoraliste* and in *La Porte étroite* (*Strait Is the Gate*) is not of the Voltairian kind. It is so artfully conveyed that many a reader has shed tears at reading these strangely ironical works, in which the half-stifled sobs of the author's ardent sympathy break through his suggested criticism of his characters. Gide's chief virtue as a novelist is probably his ever-renewed capacity for sympathy. His friends have often portrayed him in society or at gatherings of intellectuals, listening intently to all that others glibly uttered, sharing their eagerness, lending himself generously to them, hardly able to resist the first impulse of admiration and even of self-humiliation. He would soon after, when alone with his thoughts or with his diary, withdraw with equal eagerness—like a kiss, said Rivière of his ability to give himself and take himself back again—and revenge himself for having rushed to admiration too soon. In his diary, he has recorded more than once how he would open a volume with raptures of joy or even of tears, then would lay it down and take it up again with disenchanted boredom. Indeed, his gift of sympathy, which enabled him to become all his characters as he wrote his novels instead of modeling his characters after their creator, was matched only by what Cocteau has pointed out as his gravest flaw as a novelist, his ability patiently to bear boredom.

A writer of fiction probably should possess a more plentiful supply of patient tolerance toward his characters than Gide displays toward his imaginary counterfeiters or even toward the parson in the *Symphonie*

pastorale. But many other novelists have knelt down ecstatically before
the children of their brain and marveled at their own inexhaustible fertility. It is refreshing to come across a novelist who, at the risk of being
less authentic, also remains humorous and intelligent and stubbornly
rejects paludal stagnation. Gide is not a powerful thinker, and his fiction
may suffer thereby. But one of his most precious messages has been that
of continuous development, through contradictions, sharp about-faces,
and impious denials. He adopted as one of his mottoes the beautiful
sentence of John Keats: 'Better be imprudent moveables than prudent
fixtures!' He spurned all systems as prisons for willing captives. He
ridiculed the pompous attitudes in which literary potentates often consent
to posture. He stood on the lookout for new small facts, historical, biolo-
gical, psychological, through which the pretentious edifice of a system
collapses. Passionately, he hoped to lead into uncharted lands. His early
Les Nourritures terrestres was a canticle to joy; but he soon repudiated
any joy, any happiness that would fail to be progressive. And he soon
discovered that through restraint and voluntary impoverishment alone
can our joys take on an ever-new intensity.

Gide the novelist should be judged by three volumes: *L'Immoraliste*
(*The Immoralist*) (1902), *La Porte étroite* (*Strait Is the Gate*) (1909),
and *Les Faux-Monnayeurs* (*The Counterfeiters*) (1925). *La Symphonie
pastorale* (*The Pastoral Symphony*) (1919), while exemplary within its
limits, suffers from an excessive haste in the development of the plot and
from some improbability in the denouement. The lyrical vein has been
silenced by the author; sobriety and simplicity are carried almost to the
point of asceticism. The symmetry between the spiritual blindness of the
pastor and the gradual discovery of light, of love, of evil by the blind
girl is too deftly contrived. The irony toward the ecclesiastical unctu-
ousness of the clergyman undergoing a second youth and rationalizing his
impulses is a trifle facile; the controversy against the alleged distortion
of Christ's message by St. Paul is too obstrusive. Yet, once again, Gide only
half-disguised the deep personal tragedy of his own life from which he
was trying to find deliverance in a work of art: his own passionate affection for a young person, called Michel (in truth, Marc) in Gide's diary,
with whom he traveled in 1917–18, and whom he attempted to mold
amorously, and the consequent sorrow of his wife to whom the pastor's
wife, Amélie, is not unrelated.[3] *Thésée* may be dismissed as a skillful

3. It is not indiscreet to hint at the living sources of *La Symphonie pastorale* after
Gide's death and *Et nunc manet in te.* A very acute literary historian, A. Adam, has

neoclassical pastiche, lacking in force and naturalness. *L'Ecole des femmes* (*The School for Women*) and its two brief sequels are, in our eyes, an uninspired attempt to write within the tradition of the analytical novel, of which Constant's *Adolphe* is the model but also the *ne plus ultra* beyond which lies the peril of dryness, a tradition that has misled more than one French novelist. *Les Caves du Vatican* is entertaining buffoonery.

L'Immoraliste was slowly and probably too laboriously composed by Gide. Several incidents, easily identifiable, are borrowed directly from life, obviously a legitimate procedure; but the author may have respected their literal data overmuch, instead of transfiguring them through some impetuous rush of an imaginary re-creation. Gide repeatedly reported that he discovered the work of Nietzsche while he was writing that novel and rejoiced that Nietzsche had said before him much of what he, Gide, was thinking; the novel could thus be lightened of an unwelcome burden of didacticism. Indeed, the weight is not all gone, and the preaching by Ménalque to his friend in search of his own liberation constitutes a super-fluous and unconvincing hors-d'oeuvre. The preface, written in a some-what stilted manner, offers the author's plea that he be dissociated from his hero and that his book be judged as an objective work of art, in which, as Flaubert had taught the young admirer of his correspondence, the artistry alone matters and no conclusion need be sought. The conclusion of the novel also betrays traces of imperfection. But Gide is fond of intriguing denouements that, untying little (the plot was frail in any case), seem to prolong the story into the reader's perturbed mind. But elsewhere, in the descriptions of Normandy, in the slow recovery of the hero in North Africa, and in his naïve egotism asserting itself at the expense of his wife's very existence, the book reaches one of the few summits of Gide's career. It is indeed, as Charles du Bos aptly called it, 'the masterpiece of luminous cruelty.'

The themes woven into the novel are complex, although they hardly enter into struggle with one another. Gide keeps sedulously shy of con-flicts in his strangely anti-novelistic novels. On the surface, *L'Immoraliste* is the portrayal of the individualist who breaks free from his past, from his education, and from his environment and asserts his determination to live authentically. Such a subject was hardly original and has today

analyzed the critical years of Gide's life (1915–23) in an excellent article in *Revue des Sciences Humaines* (Lille) (No. 67, July–September 1952, pp. 247–72). See also Léon Pierre-Quint's excellent volume on Gide (1951) and its valuable appendix.

become a current one in international fiction, from Franz Kafka to Georges Simenon. The liberated individualist in this case is a scholar who, like Gide in his earlier crisis, rapturously celebrated in *Les Nourritures terrestres*, bidding farewell to his youth, realizes that true life has passed him by. Michel decides to scratch beneath the varnish of culture and to embrace a more primitive mode of life, to flee both the aridity of scholarship and the effete existence of the salons. His journeys to more sunny climates are flights away from his earlier and tamed self, responses of a Faust hardly of epic stature to some Mephistophelic calls, and yearnings for some Walpurgis night.

Gide, not unmindful of his own private life, smoothed the path of his hero's liberation beyond the bounds of psychological verisimilitude. Michel has married, impelled by no particular passion or affection. He has loved no other women and thought it natural not to experience any particular warmth toward his fiancée. He then gradually discovers, with some astonishment, that his bride has a personality of her own. He falls gravely sick while traveling in North Africa. She nurses him with admirable devotion and restores him to health. Meanwhile, he has belatedly become conscious of his own body. He absorbs with voracious joy the sunlight, the gentle African winter air, and the fragrance of the night. And he becomes aware of the special charm that young adolescents and especially 'the sunlight that lingers on tawny skins' hold for him. An Arab boy whom he had seen stealing his wife's scissors especially fascinates him. (Michel knew that the boy knew he had been seen stealing.)

The second part of the novel, too symmetrically contrived in relation to the first, relates Michel's new passion for all that is primitive, robust, spontaneous vice, including wrestling with handsome young farmers and poaching on his own estate. Ménalque, a predicating and not too witty Oscar Wilde, teaches Michel in ponderous formulas to believe in his own pleasure and to cultivate his own uniqueness. He incites the former archaeologist to forget all yesterdays and to welcome every hour that strikes as virginally novel. Meanwhile his wife falls gravely ill. He takes her to Switzerland; but, impatient with the dull honesty and the unimaginativeness of the Swiss, he sets off with her southward. While she pines alone on her sick bed, distressed by the doctrine now preached by her husband, which advocates the suppression of the weak, he worships 'an unknown god.' He gives free rein to his homosexual bent and rises at last beyond conventional good and evil. 'In every being, the worst instinct appeared to me as the most sincere.' His wife dies in desperate solitude. Thus each man kills the thing he loves. Gide's message had not essentially varied since *Les Nourritures terrestres* and would vary but little in years to come: liberation is arduous and perhaps genuine only if it is bought with the suffering of others. One must not indulge possession after possession has ceased being an enrichment and has become a stale prison; for then one is in truth possessed by what one loved. Gide was ready for the message that he was, some ten years later, to hail in Blake: "Sooner murder an infant in its cradle than nurse unacted desires.'

To a correspondent who praised *L'Immoraliste* with exaggeration, at the expense of his next novel, Gide replied, as he reports in 1909 in his *Journals:* 'If I were but the author of *L'Immoraliste* which you admire so much, then truly would I feel myself shrinking.' Although Gide, in his Goethean ambition, always refused to let himself be summed up by one single work and coyly dissented from admirers who singled out one of his volumes for their eulogy, he may well remain for future ages the novelist of *La Porte étroite*. Once again, the book may be biblically said to be 'a bone of his bones and flesh of his own flesh.' There is little invention in it, as there was little in many eclogues and epics and tales of the classical ages; but the incidents and the dreams of his own youth are harmoniously fused by the author into one of the most restrainedly tragic novels of the century.

The elements Gide borrowed from his own peculiar inclinations are here transmuted into universal motives. The fear of love is also the fear of all the accumulation of mediocre habits, banal gestures, half-sincere formulas, and legalized boredom that bourgeois married life may bring. The dream of the two young people is that of many couples in the present age, obsessed by Rimbaud's disturbing cry: Love is to be reinvented. Too often love is a comedy in which the pursuer attempts to conceal the bestial avidity of his face and of his desire under soothing romantic assurances, and the pursued one practices elegant feints and coquettish wiles, combining what Laclos has called 'the glory of defense and the pleasure of defeat, woman's two favorite passions.' Yet some women insist upon being esteemed in their own uniqueness and respected as minds and souls, while sought for their physical charm; they include not only the *précieuses* of all ages but many of the noblest idealists of their sex. But an ominous severance of pleasure from sentiment, of the senses from the respectful and spiritual love may take place in the pursuer. It did in Gide. And, rather than become exposed to such a dereliction and to the wreckage of their youthful dreams, some young women, like the heroine of this novel, may prefer to enter the narrow gates of saintliness and of spiritual widowhood.

Gide's limitations as a writer of fiction are here turned to actual advantages. The type of novel attempted in *La Porte étroite* required a minimum of incidents, few or no exterior intrusions, an extreme purity of structure, and the effective use of silent pauses. The souls of the protagonists had to be engaged in an inward exploration of their own depths in order to offer to each other the noblest of tributes: a clearer insight into themselves and a fervent striving after perfection; laid at each other's feet. It was thus natural for Alissa, Jérome, and Juliette to avoid the brutal explanation or configuration of scenes, to shun the harsh words, the swoonings, or the hysterical flow of tears dear to earlier fictional heroines or to Dostoevskian ones. Gide's rather easy device, the laying bare of the private diary invariably kept by the leading character, thus becomes fully natural here, as does the exchange of letters indulged in by the idealistic lovers. 'More than kisses, letters mingle souls,' said Donne. The Jamesian question of the point of view is happily solved by the device of the narrative in the first person singular, which appears fully natural and even inevitable in *La Porte étroite*. Jérome, the witness and recorder of the tragic story of failure, had to have, as seemed natural in his case, a discreet, modest, even a weak, personality. He had to be intelligent and analytical, but neither avidly possessive nor scathingly ironical. He only half understood the drama in which he was a semi-passive actor, and Gide was thus able to launch his reader on several divergent tracks without ever imposing one set of symbols or of explanations upon him. The extreme brevity of the volume enhanced its beauty further; for, unlike Balzac and the novelists who insist upon leaving nothing unsaid, Gide wants to remain as far as possible from the perilous effect of saturation produced by Richardson, Zola, or Dostoevski. The past is subtly guessed. A few sentences suffice to conjure up Lucile Bucolin, the only sinner in the family, to whom perversely curious readers would have liked a whole chapter devoted. Juliette's life of resigned domestic bliss is left for us to imagine. The natural scenery and the passing of the seasons are conjured up in a few haunting poetical touches.

La Porte étroite stands in some respects closer to some of the late nineteenth-century novels than to more recent ones, in which obstacles laid before the fulfillment of passion spring from physiological or psychoanalytical motives, seldom from spiritual aspirations. In very few of the great French novels (neither in *La Princesse de Cléves,* in *Manon Lescaut,* nor in Rousseau, neither in Stendhal, in Balzac, nor even Mauriac) did love enter into conflict with religion. It wrestled with honor, ambition, pride (Mlle de la Môle), maternal affection, social conventions, the fear of hell occasionally, or even the sense of duty to one's spouse, but seldom with the aspiration toward saintliness. Alissa spurns, like her creator, any happiness that would be easy to reach. 'What one undertakes above one's strength is what goes by the name of virtue' was the Protestant saying uttered by a Greek character in Gide's *Philoctète.* She will not marry and then play to herself the comedy of conjugal happiness, even less carry over a complacent self-satisfaction to her children and forsake her earnest, girlish ideals. Her idea of happiness is a steep and perilous one. It must, like true love, feed on the sacrifices that it entails. She cherishes difficulty, wants a human happiness that leads not away from Christ but closer to mystical love. The dream proves an impossible one, and she mutilates herself in pursuit of inhuman purity.

But Alissa is more complex than that. The fire that burns within her soul stirs also within her body. Her father, early in the novel, remarked how closely she resembled her sinful mother, who eloped long before, but is not wholly forgotten by those who now keep their lips sealed about her. Alissa is ashamed and afraid of her heredity. She had, very early, to substitute for her absent mother and to assume the responsibility of the household. Her acquired seriousness has not, however, killed her zest for life. There are dormant possibilities in her that love might awaken.

She has not yielded to them up to the present. Her implacable Protestant habit of soul-searching has taught her to be lucid and has given her the pride of dignified self-sacrifice in favor of her more earthly and less exacting sister Juliette. She tries to persuade Jérome to marry Juliette and be content with banal domestic happiness. But Jérome loves Alissa, and Juliette marries a worthy, uninspiring man of affairs. She fears she may be too old for Jérome, for she is indeed not only a few years older but wiser, more cerebral, more clear-sighted. Does he love her with the whole of his nature or only with a noble chivalrous exaltation mixed with some pity, for he was aware of the grief caused in her by her mother's irregularities? Will he not someday dissociate desire from respect, physical passion from tender affection, and cruelly wreck her ideals? Will he not turn—like Michel—and, belatedly, discover that another kind of love is more meaningful to him? Nothing in the novel entitles one to surmise, as critics have done, that Jérome may be afflicted with impotence, like the hero of Stendhal's *Armance,* or with latent homosexuality. But nothing precludes such a conjecture, however crude it may seem where such a masterpiece of delicate understatement is concerned.

Jérome is an essential agent in the development of the volume, even if a passive one. It would have taken the tricks of a coquette or the harmless poutings and whims of an average girl to stimulate him into less cerebral a passion and to hasten the marriage he steadfastly but shyly contemplated. He quotes reams of poetry to Alissa, dreams of kisses of the soul and spiritual bonds. He studies ancient poets at the university, and perhaps Virgil's third *Eclogue,* in which Galatea throws an apple at the young shepherd and flees toward the willows, wishing first to be seen. But he will not read between the lines of Alissa's letters. She bids him not to come, and he naïvely refrains from coming. 'Suddenly,' she writes him, 'I wished you right here, I felt you here, close to me, with such violence that you will perhaps have shared it.' Later, she distressedly remarks to him that each of them in his letters writes to himself alone and seeks a mirror, and she expresses her diagnosis that his love 'was mostly in his brain, a fine intellectual obstinacy in tenderness and fidelity.' He does not reply, does not even rush to the train to come and deny the indictment. Only later will he read in dead Alissa's diary 'Poor Jérome! And yet if he knew that at times he would have only a gesture to make, and a gesture which at times I pray for . . .' Gide has never written more heart-rending pages than those that follow the tragic mis-understanding between two exalted natures, perhaps not born for happi-ness, and too averse to anything low or vulgar ever to reach it at the expense of their spiritual or religious ideal. Alissa's slow death was a prefiguration of the premature aging and forlornness of Gide's own wife, as his posthumous revelation of Mme Gide has showed. Never did Gide explore the abysses of sorrow more tragically than when he turned her irretrievably away from him. But he knew the Goethean art of converting sorrow into art. 'We make out of the quarrel with others, rhetoric, but of the quarrel with ourselves, poetry.' [4]

During the fifteen years that elasped between *La Porte étroitè* and *Les Faux-Monnayeurs,* Gide went through several crises. The first was intellectual, the impact of Dostoevski, which revolutionized many of his views on the novel and drove him to seek for more complexity in the multiplicity of plots, to prefer surprise to continuity of effect, and to

4. W. B. Yeats in *Per Amica Silentia Lunae* (Macmillan, 1918).

forsake the Western dogma of the essential unity of man. 'Oh do not
believe in the unity of man!' is among the Russian master's pronouncements. The years of World War I also coincided with a profound sensual
and religious as well as sentimental upheaval in Gide, from which he
emerged, after a bitter struggle, more self-assured, determined to reject
religious conversion and to flout the conventional censorship of pederasty
through the publication of *Corydon* and of his memoirs. The youthful
uncertainty and the frailty of the young novelist, as yet unsure of himself,
communicating his own vibration to his tales and instilling poetry into
them gave way, in *Les Faux-Monnayeurs,* to a prolonged intellectual
attempt and to a work that springs from will power as much as from
inspiration. The mastery of the craftsman is evident. The elaborate organization and the utmost care spent over details concealed under an
apparent nonchalance have caused the novel to be compared with the
three greatest works of the years 1920–26; *Ulysses, A la Recherche du
temps perdu,* and *The Magic Mountain.* The comparison, however, can
only bring out Gide's lesser power. The value of *Les Faux-Monnayeurs,*
more than forty years after its appearance, probably lies in the ingeniousness of its psychology and its technical lessons for novelists and
students of the novel.

The unity of a single plot and the intimacy of a narrative in the first
person, which marked Gide's earlier novels—or *récits* as he was to call
them according to a *distinguo* that we need not adopt—are gone. There
are as many as five or six separate stories in *Les Faux-Monnayeurs,* and
the links established among them remain tenuous. Gide sought new starts
with every chapter and attempted very hard not to take advantage of
any earlier and cumulative *élan.* The tone itself is no longer as clear and
bright as that which irradiated Gide's early prose. There is something
abrupt and disconcerting in the succession of the chapters and in the
very last sentence, which does not close the book but with which Gide
delights in appearing as the demoralizer. The structure of *Les Faux-
Monnayeurs,* also, even judged by its own laws, is not above reproach.
Far too much has to be presented through Edouard's diary and is colored
through his tinted glasses. But there is much also that could not be thus
encompassed, and the fusion of heterogeneous data is not felicitous. The
omniscient author himself asserts his presence and pulls the strings of
his puppets with some irony. One is too deeply conscious that he had
earlier selected the material his characters have observed. The characters
are very artificially linked to one another by the busybody Edouard, who

reads Vincent's last book and Laura's letter, and receives Bernard's and Olivier's secrets. Old La Pérouse, borrowed from life, is movingly true but hardly essential to the plot. Passavant, perhaps a caricature of Cocteau, and Lady Griffith are hardly convincing. Gide's purpose, however, was not so much to create characters able to compete with the *Etat civil*, like those of Balzac, but to depict the characters' own progressive self-discovery. The author purposely wanted them to remain unfinished, endowed with diverse and unexhausted possibilities and, if not like those of Pirandello in search of their author, at least in search of the reader of good will who would prolong their frail existence.

The chief interest of the novel, next to its delineation of the complex psychology of adolescents, has been found to lie in its being a novelists' novel; its theme is 'the rivalry between the real world and the representation we make of it,' as Gide formulated it. A sophisticated modern novel must comprehend within itself the critique of the novel and its own genesis: how reality can become stylized into art. Such is the contention of self-conscious or technique-intoxicated readers, who rejoice in a novel about a novelist writing a novel about a novelist trying to write a novel. We confess to a mild interest in such disquisitions when carried outside the critical seminar where they rightly belong.

Stronger features of *Les Faux-Monnayeurs* are the central symbol of counterfeit coin and the dramatized position of the question that permeated all the meditations of Gide in his last thirty years and that will probably remain the most valued part of his legacy to the world, the question of sincerity. Most of the characters in the book are themselves counterfeit: Robert de Passavant and Lady Griffith most of all, for they do not even know what it is to be sincere; but so are Vincent, who lacks the strength to become himself, Olivier who, after brushing past suicide, is driven back to Edouard, La Pérouse, whose married life has been futile and who was a dupe always, and others, such as the Pastor and Azaïs, whose professions should have implied the practice of truth and virtue. Bernard himself rebelled vigorously against hypocrisy but exhausted his vigor in the process and failed to live his love for Laura. However, many people go through life without having ever been sincere in the sense of being authentically themselves. The true hypocrite, as Gide remarked in one of his many reflections on the subject, 'is he who is no longer even aware of a lie, who lies with sincerity.' His name in our midst is legion. All our moralists, Berdiaev, Pirandello, Aldous Huxley, Kafka, but none more consistently than Gide, have denounced the prevalence of insincerity toward oneself as the gravest of all our intellectual and moral lapses.

Gide is the novelist of sincerity. Therein lies his chief claim to the gratitude of moderns who are determined not to live forged lives and who wish to throw away the forged coins of social conventionality, of religious conformity, of sexual Pharisaism, of literary and rhetorical embellishment. Montaigne, La Rochefoucauld, and Rousseau had paved the way for him. For, in spite of the Socratic message and of the Roman elegiacs, even of St. Augustine and of the Christian analysts of the tormented human conscience, it was hardly before Montaigne that the ideal of sincerity became the *unum necessarium* of modern letters, as it is today in France. Most of Gide's novels and all his intimate journals and confessional writings have revolved around that question, which colored all others. Among these other questions was, first, style. Can style cease being an adornment, a sumptuous drapery folded over the object, become bare and apparently artless, and yet not betray thereby the intensity of the feeling to be expressed, the force of the idea? And is spontaneous, speedy, almost automatic writing the more faithful, or writing that, through art, succeeds in curbing and concealing art? Gide oscillated between the two poles.

He also pondered the next obvious question. Does sincerity demand that we reject all that was acquired through education, reading, social adaptation, moral censorship, and that we restore in ourselves the primitive, presumably the violent and the irrational? Is there more truth in the heart than in the brain, or in the solar plexus as D. H. Lawrence contended, or in what in ourselves used to be considered base? The Olympian Goethe confessed, in a remark that was to haunt Gide, that there was 'no crime, however monstrous, of which he did not feel himself to be capable.' Gide attempted to find the core of one's sincerity in gratuitous acts, unexplained crimes, waves of folly surging beyond the dull routine of habit, beyond repression and logic.

'Who will deliver my spirit from the heavy chains of logic?' Gide cried, in a Rimbaldian *élan*, in his sequel to *Les Nourritures terrestres* in 1935. To him, as to most of his logic-conditioned compatriots, sincerity lay beyond clarity, beyond consistency and neatly aligned ideas. He chided Corneille, Descartes, Balzac, and the influence of society life, which tends to laugh our naturalness away, and the traditional teaching, which assigns to us a model personality according to which we try to build ourselves. Gide cherished contradictions, sudden upheavals originating in

our senses or in imperious desires, disintegrations of our personality pre-
luding a rebirth and going away with what he called 'clear-cut ideas, the
most perilous of all, for they are in ourselves a premature death.'

The search for sincerity is perilous, for the Devil may lurk behind it,
as he does in *Les Faux-Monnayeurs*. He may suggest to us that indulging
our vices, gratifying our desires, and rebelling against laws observed by
more conventional members of our society are forms of sincerity. He
may lead us to mistake 'sincerity' in crude avowals and shameless confessions for a moral virtue and hold that all that is boastfully confessed
is thereby purified. Sincerity may also lead us to mistake a momentary
exaltation for our truest mood, as Gide did when he thought he was
undergoing religious ardor (in *Numquid et Tu*), or Communist fervor, or
some short-lived literary admiration. It tends (this is even more dangerous for our art) to reduce literature to the direct expression of the
ego; but memoirs, confessions, and private diaries are often the most
mendacious of writings. They boast or they disparage, they reinterpret
the past in the light of the present, they stress the silliest deeds or gestures
of Pepys, Boswell, Rousseau, or Gide. But they leave out the dreams
that reality may have aroused, the imaginary lives that have often meant
more than our mediocre existences, the imaginative liberation that the
writing of a novel or a poem will afford us. Writing inevitably implies a
public, hence a pose, and Claudel, whose theological virtues have been
other than charity, may not have been far wrong when he stigmatized
his great contemporary and rival as a man fascinated by mirrors and
trying out attitudes before others and himself. Narcissus is one of the
undying myths of literature.

Bibliographical Notes

Essential titles on Marcel Proust as a novelist are listed below. None prior to
1939 is included. Consult A. L. Bisson's excellent review of recent Proust
criticism in *French Studies* (Oxford), I, 3, July 1947, 191–217.

Barker, Richard H., *Proust: A Biography*. Criterion Books, 1958.
Bell, William S., *Proust's Nocturnal Muse*. Columbia University Press, 1962.
Bersani, Leo, *M. Proust. The Fictions of Life and of Art*. New York: Oxford
    University Press, 1965.
Brée, Germaine, *Du temps perdu au temps retrouvé*. Belles-Lettres, 1951.
———, *Marcel Proust and the Deliverance from Time*. New Brunswick: Rut-
    gers University Press, 1956.

Bret, Jacques, *Marcel Proust, étude critique*. Geneva: Editions du Mont Blanc, 1946.

Chernowitz, Maurice, *Proust and Painting*. Columbia University Press, 1944.

Cohn, Robert G., *The Winter's Way in France*. Philadelphia: University of Pennsylvania Press, 1960.

Coleman, Elliott, *The Golden Angel*. Coley Taylor, 1954.

Deleuze, Gilles, *Proust et les Signes*. Presses Universitaires Françaises, 1963.

Etiemble, René, *Proust et la crise de l'intelligence*. Alexandria: Editions du Scarabée, 1945.

Fardwell, Frances V., *Landscape in the Works of Proust*. Washington, D.C.: Catholic University of America Press, 1948.

Fernandez, Ramon, *Proust*. Nouvelle Revue Critique, 1943.

Fowlie, Wallace, *A Reading of Proust*. Doubleday & Co., 1964.

Girard, René, *Marcel Proust: A Collection of Critical Essays*. Englewood Cliffs: Prentice Hall, 1962.

Golstine, Enid, 'La Renommée et l'influence de Proust en Angleterre,' Paris, 1949. (Unpublished Thesis.)

Green, F. C., *The Mind of Proust*. Cambridge, England: Cambridge University Press, 1949.

Haldane, Charlotte, *Marcel Proust*. London: Arthur Barker, 1951.

Hindus, Milton, *The Proustian Vision*. Columbia University Press, 1954.

Kolb, Philip, *La Correspondance de Proust*. Urbana: Illinois University Press, 1949.

Leon, Derrick, *Introduction to Proust: His Life, His Circle and His Work*. London: Kegan Paul, 1940.

Levin, Harry, *The Gates of Horn*. New York: Oxford University Press, 1963.

March, Harold, *The Two Worlds of Marcel Proust*. Philadelphia: University of Pennsylvania Press, 1948.

Maurois, André, *Marcel Proust: Portrait of a Genius*. Harper and Brothers, 1950. (In French: *A la recherche de Marcel Proust*. Hachette, 1949. English translation: *The Quest for Proust*. London: Jonathan Cape, 1950.)

Mouton, Jean, *Le Style de Proust*. Corrêa, 1948.

O'Brien, Justin, 'La Mémoire involontaire avant Proust,' *Revue de Littérature Comparée*, XIX, 1, January 1939, 19–36.

————, *The Maxims of Marcel Proust*. Columbia University Press, 1948.

Painter, George D., *Proust: The Early Years; The Later Years*. Boston: Little, Brown & Co. Two volumes: 1959 and 1965.

Pícon, Gaëtan, *L'Usage de la lecture*. Mercure de France, 1963.

Piroué, Georges, *Proust et la musique du devenir*. Denoël, 1960.

Revel, Jean F., *Sur Proust*, Julliard, 1960.

Rivane, Georges, *Influence de l'asthme sur l'oeuvre de Marcel Proust*. La Nouvelle Edition, 1945.

Rivière, Jacques, *The Ideal Reader*. Meridian Books, 1961.

Shattuck, Roger, *Proust's Binoculars*. Random House, 1963.

Spitzer, Leo, *Marcel Proust e altri saggi di letteratura francese*. Einaudi, 1959.

Strauss, Walter, *Proust and Literature*. Cambridge, Mass.: Harvard University Press, 1957.

Taumann, Léon, *Marcel Proust: une vie et une synthèse*. A. Colin, 1949.

Vigneron, Robert, several important articles, not yet collected into a volume, in *Revue d'Histoire de la Philosophie* (Lille), 1937; *Modern Philology*, May 1945, November 1946, February 1948; *The French Review*, May 1946.

Allusion is made in our text to Léon Pierre-Quint's articles, 'Une Nouvelle Lecture: Marcel Proust et la jeunesse d'aujourd'hui,' *Europe*, XXXIX, 1935, 185–98 and 382–99; to Roland Cailleux's *Une Lecture* (Gallimard, 1949); to Raymond Mortimer's *Channel Packet* (London: Hogarth Press, 1943); and to a superficial article by Edwin B. Burgum, 'Into the Night: Proust's Account of the Collapse of French Civilization,' *Accent*, Summer 1941, 202–12.

The important works by Gide (except for the beautiful *Le Retour de l'enfant prodigue*) are all available in translation. A very abundant biographical and critical literature has accumulated in the last few years on a writer who concealed little about his own life and earnestly wished to interest and to disturb after his death. Much of it is ephemeral: the books by Pierre Herbart, Maurice Lime, Maurice Sachs, for example, and even the imposing but disappointing special number of the *Nouvelle Revue Française* devoted to Gide in 1951. The *Conversations* with Gide by Claude Mauriac (Albin Michel, 1952) and especially the brief *Notes sur André Gide* (Gallimard, 1951) by Roger Martin du Gard are the most valuable posthumous testimonials.

Among the special numbers of periodicals in which a varied crop of articles on Gide may be found, two deserve to be set apart: *Le Capitole, Hommage à Gide* (1928) and *Yale French Studies* (No. 7, 1951).

The most useful bibliographical items will be found to be the following, Hytier's and Pierre-Quint's being the most valuable of all:

Adam, A., 'Quelques années de la vie de Gide,' *Revue des Sciences Humaines*, No. 67, July–September 1952, 247–72.

Alibert, François-Paul, *En Marge d'André Gide*. Oeuvres Représentatives, 1930.

Arland, Marcel, *Essais critiques*. Gallimard, 1931.

Bendz, Ernst, *Gide et l'art d'écrire*. Goteborg: Elanders, 1939.

Brée, Germaine, *Gide, l'insaisissable Protée*. Les Belles-Lettres, 1953. Translated as *Gide*, New Brunswick: Rutgers University Press, 1963.

Davet, Yvonne, *Histoire des nourritures terrestres*. Gallimard, 1948.

Delay, Jean, *La Jeunesse de Gide*. Gallimard, 1956, 2 vols. Translated as *The Youth of Gide*. Chicago: Chicago University Press, 1963.

Du Bos, Charles, *Dialogue avec André Gide*. Au Sans Pareil, 1929.

Estève, Claude, *Etudes philosophiques sur l'expression littéraire*. Vrin, 1938.

Fayer, Mischa H., *Gide, Freedom, and Dostoevski*. Middlebury, Vermont: Lane Press, 1946.

Fowlie, Wallace, *Gide. His Life and Art*. New York: Macmillan; London, Collier-Macmillan, 1965.

Gandon, Yves, *Le Démon du Style*. Plon, 1938.

Guérard, Albert J., *André Gide*. Cambridge, Mass.: Harvard University Press, 1951.

Hytier, Jean, *André Gide*, rev. ed., Alger Charlot, 1945.

Lafille, Pierre, *André Gide romancier*. Hachette, 1954.

Lalou, René, *André Gide*. Strasbourg: Heissler, 1928.

Lang, Renée, *André Gide et la pensée allemande*. Egloff, 1949.

Lièvre, Pierre, *Esquisses critiques*. Le Divan, 1929.

Mann, Klaus, *André Gide and the Crisis of Modern Thought*. Creative Age Press, 1943.

March, Harold, *André Gide and the Hound of Heaven*. Philadelphia: University of Pennsylvania Press, 1952.

Michaud, Guy, 'Genèse des Faux-Monnayeurs. L'Art de la fugue. Morphologie-Syntaxe,' *Dialogues*, II, 2, January 1951, 37–86.

O'Brien, Justin, *A Portrait of André Gide*. Alfred A. Knopf, 1953.

Peyre, Henri, *Hommes et oeuvres du vingtième siècle*. Corrêa, 1938.

Peyre, Henri, *Literature and Sincerity*. New Haven: Yale University Press, 1963.

Pierre-Quint, Léon, *André Gide*. Stock, 1951.

Rivière, Jacques, *Etudes*, Nouvelle Revue Française, 1911, and articles in *Chronique des Lettres Françaises*, January–June 1926.

Schwob, René, *Le Vrai Drame d'André Gide*. Grasset, 1932.

Scott, J. D., 'André Gide,' *Horizon*, No. 64, April 1945, 267–79.

Thomas, D. L., *André Gide*. London: Secker and Warburg, 1951.

Wilson, Edmund, *The Wound and the Bow: Seven Studies in Literature*. Boston: Houghton Mifflin, 1941; new printing with corrections, New York: Oxford University Press, 1947.

IV

François Mauriac

If the French critics of 1930–45 had been asked which novelist, in their estimation, was the most likely to outlive the wreckage of time and to rank next to Proust in greatness, more votes would probably have been cast for Mauriac than for any other living French writer, his rivals being Malraux, Giono, and Bernanos, probably in that order. Mauriac's eminence remained comparatively unrecognized in English-speaking countries, long after his election to the French Academy in 1933 and even after the Nobel Prize had been bestowed upon him. Translations of his works have been coming out timidly. The utmost tribute, that of a Pocket Books edition with a seductive or a sickening cover (as tastes may go), came to the *Desert of Love* only in 1953. The brevity of Mauriac's *récits* may have appeared unorthodox to publishers who like a novel to conform to the supposed demands of solid readers who insist that they get their money's worth in weight. The poetic finish of his style may have frightened off translators. But the pessimism of Mauriac's novels and their Roman Catholic view of sin and of love must have proved the chief deterrent to Anglo-Saxon readers. Pessimism, to be sure, abounds in their own fiction, but it dons youthful violence, and evil is somehow depicted in glaring and alluring colors.

There were signs of a change in the tastes of many educated readers, at the very time (since 1945 or thereabout) when the compatriots of Mauriac tended to dimiss him as a classical writer who, afraid of spoiling his earlier successes through imitating himself, was driven to dramas and to journalism. Many students in American colleges were fascinated by Mauriac as a craftsman and also by the use he has made of the religious theme. Religion once again has become fashionable in fiction. It has been found by reassured critics to permeate James Joyce's work, to explain William Faulkner's portrayal of an evil that was original and hence ennobling, and to give a Catholic hue to Eugene O'Neill's plays and James T. Farrell's saga. The adjective 'Catholic' paired with the word 'novelist,' has, in the eyes of some readers, enhanced the stature of Graham Greene and Evelyn Waugh. Somerset Maugham made skillful use of the theme in *The Razor's Edge,* and Aldous Huxley wrote fondly of Machiavellian mystics like Father Joseph. But Mauriac's place in contemporary letters owes little to sectarianism or to tides of changing taste. Out of the score of novels he has published, four or five seem clearly destined for survival. Few are the novelists in any language of whom such a prophecy could be ventured.

If the factors at work at any time in life and in art may be grouped into the conflicting forces of tradition and of experiment, Mauriac seems to rank with those novelists who have shunned the loudly advertised paths of experimentation. At a time when the *roman-fleuve* appeared as the order of the day and when juggling with the old-fashioned structural unity and with the continuous flow of time had become the first gesture of a writer asserting his modernity, Mauriac chose to compose isolated novels, strictly organized, with few of those contradictions and violent plunges into the unconscious that other Frenchmen took as evidence that they lived in a post-Dostoevskian era. Once or twice, the same characters recur in two different books. But their creator had enough humility not to presume that his readers might, after several years, remember the earlier doings of certain women of ill repute or of angelic adolescents. He rightly feared the lack of freshness and the artificiality of novelists who have chained themselves, volume after volume, to the drawn-out career of a Forsyte or of a Jean-Christophe. Every one of Mauriac's novels is a fresh attempt and an adventure into the unknown, though every one of them ends monotonously with the gift of grace that the novelist insists upon imparting to his sinners.

Mauriac's fiction has been charged with monotony. It moves in a world that indeed is, geographically and socially, narrowly limited. It revolves around the same perennial obsessions with money, property, the enticements of the flesh, and the wages of sin. Within these confines, however, it explores in depth. What is more, it conjures up that diseased and haunted world, and gains in vivid intensity what is sacrificed in diversity. In contrast with several experimenters among contemporary novelists, Mauriac stands as the upholder of the traditional virtues of the French novel. He is fully aware of the new complexity that Stendhal, Dostoevski, and Proust have led us to expect from fiction. But his purpose is not to experiment with new fictional forms or to explore recesses of the unconscious with awe, or with the naïveté of one who has lately discovered the jargon of clinical psychology. He writes because he must rid himself of the obsession of his characters and endow with shapes and sounds the desolate world that he carries within his imagination. The traditional form of the French novel, condensed, linear in its development, and strongly tempted to return to the unities of the classical tragedy, suited his talent as it did the themes he treated. Like Racine's plays, his novels are dramatic presentations of a psychological crisis. The plot permits very few incidents, and only those that help bring out new aspects of the characters. His novels move swiftly to a relentless denouement. Indeed, their tension is so feverish that they could hardly last longer without becoming painful to the reader. They are no more relieved by humor, by the restful oasis of pure description or of lyrical escape than is Racinian tragedy. Within the traditional mold of the French novel, classical in its economy, swift in its pace, written with elaborate care for stylistic values, Mauriac subtly casts the molten lead of dark motives and destructive passions, such as we have come to expect from modern fiction since Balzac, Melville, and the great Russians.

Mauriac's date of birth, 1885, makes him one of the group of gifted French novelists who were to reach full manhood on the eve of World War I and to stage, in the years 1910–13, a literary renaissance in Paris. Martin du Gard, Giraudoux, Duhamel, Romains, Maurois, Alain-Fournier, Jouhandeau, and Bernanos belong to the same age group. Their ascendancy over French letters reached its height in 1925–35, when, with the exception of Alain-Fournier, who was killed in the war, they were to meet with an audience attuned to their music, and to produce their most accomplished work. Most of them belonged to the middle or lower strata of the bourgeoisie, whose creative vitality has remained astounding in France, despite savage attacks repeatedly launched against it by its own scions, from Flaubert to Mauriac himself. Most of them were provincials; and Mauriac's fiction, even after he had taken up residence in Paris, fed on the observations and memories accumulated in his provincial childhood.

The area of France to which he belongs with all his being had already given birth to many men of letters, most of them of a cheerful and humorous disposition, inclined to skeptical enjoyment of the varieties and inconsistencies of mankind. But Mauriac has little in common with Montaigne or Montesquieu, even with elusive Fénelon or with Rivière, also born in Bordeaux, in 1886, who searched for faith with the secret fear of being imprisoned in it if he once found it. The power of literature is such that the Bordeaux region and its inhabitants will henceforth appear to many in the gloomy hues lent to them by Mauriac's fiction, as Georgia and Mississippi have been stamped as lands of oppressive tragedy by contemporary American novelists. The traditional Gascon, with his bravado or with the playful irony that Renan thought he owed to his Gascon mother, the smiling beauty of his vineyards, and his Epicurean delight in choice food, never appear in Mauriac's stories of frustration and of remorse.

Yet Mauriac loves his native city of Bordeaux, its wine merchants and its lawyers, its *cafés* and its public gardens, where his characters repair, pleasure bound, when they leave their country estates to celebrate a rich crop or an advantageous sale of timber. Rather, he hates Bordeaux because he loves it too much, as he confessed at the conclusion of his unfinished autobiography, *Commencements d'une vie*. 'We hate our city as we do the being whom we love, for all that is usurped by that being, for the limits which it imposes upon us; it sets irreparable bounds upon our existence, and defrauds us of a higher fate.' His debt to his provincial childhood has been loudly and repeatedly proclaimed.

In fact, he confessed his inability to place any of his novels in a setting other than the one in which he grew; he compared the fascination thus wrought over him by his province to the blinding of a mule doomed to grind corn in its circular prison. When his characters rush to Paris, eager to escape for a brief respite from the passions that hold them captive in their drab familiar surroundings, they appear suddenly less real. The dance halls or the *cafés*, where they attempt to drown their regret for their childhood and for their native village, are depicted as some devil's den in a modern Babylon. The characters who had hoped to escape from themselves remain provincials in exile. 'The provinces are Pharisaic,' said Mauriac in a small book of notes and maxims on that subject, *La Province*. 'Only in the provinces do people know to hate well . . . The provinces condemn most women to chastity.[1] How many of them lacked

1. The French word is nobler or more pretentious—*la vertu*. Nietzsche scathingly remarked somewhere how the term that used to denote the virile courage of man had been degraded to signify a 'merely negative' attribute of some women.

the vocation for it . . . Every writer leaving his province for Paris is a fugitive Emma Bovary.' But life is more intense because it is less subject to idle diversion than in Paris. The human heart can be more easily laid bare to one who, in his teens, had silently observed his elders, dreamed about women whom he would never approach, tamed his wild desires, and stifled his rebellious sobs.

The child, in Mauriac, is father of the man. He was molded by his early memories. Malagar, the country house in which he takes refuge every summer, has been repeatedly transfigured by him into a setting for his stories. Langon, which has become a gloomy abode of the dying wife and of the domineering mother-in-law in *Genitrix*, situated near the railway line between Bordeaux and Sète, was his grandfather's property. That grandfather, stubborn and anticlerical, who was converted on his dying day, has provided his grandson with a few features of the pathetic old man in *Le Nœud de vipères* (*Viper's Tangle*). Thérèse's house, named Argelouse in the novel, was that of Mauriac's maternal grandmother. The rumbling, packed streetcar in which, every evening, young Courrèges first met Maria Cross, was familiar to Mauriac when he was completing his secondary school in Bordeaux. Mauriac's own father died when he was but eighteen months old. The child, along with three brothers and one sister, was brought up entirely by the young widow. The father had been an unbeliever, the mother was sternly religious, with a deep tinge of Jansenism to her Roman Catholic faith. The evening prayer, uttered by the mother with her five children gathered around her under the crucifix, was a solemn rite. Then the children would go to sleep, their arms crossed on their breasts, as demanded by God. They scrupulously observed the strictest rules, to the point of not eating the crust of their bread on Friday if it appeared slightly yellow, hence tainted with the yolk of eggs, thus infringing upon the observance of fasting. The fear of sin, first conceived as disobedience, haunted them; God was the formidable chastiser of the Old Testament rather than the merciful forgiver of the Gospels. Death was often present to them, as the dire event that might at any moment force them to appear before their Creator in a state of unreadiness.

Yet Mauriac's childhood was a happy one. He liked solitude and found it, even at school, where he seldom took part in games and sports. His faith was a source of deep inner joy to him. His meditative habits developed in him a precocious sensitiveness to nature. He feared the beauty of the fields and the hills, yet drank it avidly. Unlike the psalmist, he could not read the glory of God's bounty in the starry nights and the fragrant orchards in springtime. 'Cybele has more worshippers in France than has Christ,' he wrote, denouncing the religion of the earth as the most potent religion among French peasants. He, too, was swayed by that pagan cult; the struggle between earthly and earthy attachments and a thirst for divine grace is an ever-recurring one in his characters. His early studies in a religious school near home developed religious sensibility in him and the other schoolboys but did little toward fostering religious intelligence, as he later remarked. Pascal was the favorite writer of the youth; although he later took him to task for his Jansenism, Mauriac remained his spiritual descendant. His fiction has aptly and skillfully been defined, by those who defended its orthodoxy against timid souls who smelled heresy in it, as the concrete expansion of a title suggested by Pascal for a whole section of his *Pensées*: 'Misery of the world without God.'

Mauriac completed his secondary studies at the *lycée* of Bordeaux. He passed his baccalaureate and went to Paris to pursue his scholarly education. Paleography and medieval archaeology then attracted him, and, after passing the required tests, he entered the *Ecole des Chartes,* where curators of French archives and medievalists are trained. However, he soon resigned from the *Ecole des Chartes*. His was not the scholar's patient and modest gift. He carried an ardent world within him, made up of memories of his province, of human desires and temptations, and, even more, of an impossible conflict between human and divine love. His ambition was to translate that inner universe into words.

Along with Pascal and Racine, who were, among the French classics, the chief builders of his soul, the writers he admired were the more sincere and the more tormented of the romantics. He admired Alfred de Vigny, whose thoughtful poetry attracted him in spite of, or perhaps because of, its passionate revolt against God, which Mauriac tended to prefer to conservative religious complacency. He felt close to Mauriac de Guérin (1810–39), who worshipped nature with a burning fervor that set him apart from other French romantics. Guérin was a pagan and a pantheist tempted by Christ, struggling to be a true Christian but engulfed by the worship of the elements celebrated in his famous prose poem, *Le Centaure*. A centaur himself, he aspired toward the serenity of the heavens but was held back by animal life and earthly beauty. Jean Lacordaire and Félicité de Lamennais were also spiritual and literary intercessors, the first for his eloquent charity and because 'he dares call human love by its name; the flesh and the blood are not silenced by him,' the second because he rejected the placid comfort of orthodoxy and a religion unmoved by the sufferings of the poor. Baudelaire's fame was spreading among the French youth in 1905–10, when Mauriac was himself courting the muse. One of his early essays vindicated *Les Fleurs du mal* against the Catholic critics who tried to reject such poetry on account of the poet's life or his occasional blasphemies. Mauriac, already, advanced the assertion that a sinner who half repenteth or who, like Baudelaire, with remorse and anguish damns himself is more truly Christian than many a virtuous man who has, like the philosopher Taine, led an impeccable life.

Among the writers then living, Mauriac, on the threshold of his literary career, was attracted by Barrès. At the age of sixteen, he drew comfort from a formula in *Un Homme libre,* one of Barrès's early novels, which described what the provincial adolescent was then practicing: 'to feel as much as possible while analyzing oneself as much as possible.' Mauriac rejoiced in his youthful sorrows, which made him a younger brother of those men of letters whose biographies he was devouring at that time. During his solitary years in Bordeaux and later among the temptations of the metropolis, the young Mauriac was followed by his familiar daemon, the daemon of self-knowledge (the title of his most searching short story was 'Le Démon de la connaissance'). Soon, however, he discovered, like all born novelists, that it is easier to know oneself by lending one's own feelings to imaginary creatures and developing them to the full than by remaining confined to complacent introspection. He cultivated in himself 'the fondness for taking a voluptuous interest in souls' that he attributed to one of the characters in his earliest novel.

Mauriac's literary debut, with two volumes of verse, was hailed by Barrès in 1909 and 1911. Soon after, the young poet, having married, gave up formal poetry, in which he felt his style was always cramped, and adopted the form of the novel. He returned to poetry only after his fiftieth year, in *Atys*. His early attempts at fiction, *L'Enfant chargé de chaines* (1913) and *La Robe prétexte* (1914), are immature and over-inclined to lyrical exuberance, which detracts from the convincingness that the plot and characters might have had. The author, already the father of a child, served in the army during World War I. The war, as a theme, left little trace in his work; but, in its gloomiest year, while a member of the expeditionary force on the Macedonian front in 1917, he meditated on the French moralists of whom he knew himself to be the heir. He strengthened his resolve to follow in their footsteps. But his ambition was to be a Christian moralist because he considered the Christian as the truest of all humanists since, 'to reach God, he must cross the whole of himself, and see the light dawn only through and beyond his own heart.' [2]

On his return to civilian life, Mauriac brought out two brief, ardent, but still unconvincing and youthful novels: *La Chair et le sang* (1920) and *Préséances* (1921). They, as well as a stronger work, *Le Fleuve de feu* (1923), are permeated with the obsession of the flesh. The delight of the senses is depicted as mysteriously entrancing, driving the characters to wild forsaking of all self-control and even to suicide. Yet those carnal pleasures are not merely the snares of the Devil. The power of love is great because we are aware of its frailty, we desperately try to embrace a beautiful body and to discover a soul behind it because we dread soon to be deprived of such ephemeral loveliness. Fear of the passing of time and of our own hasty march toward old age and death, search for self-oblivion in the abysses of passion, dim realization that the sufferings of love and the disgust of our sins draw us nearer to religion—such are the feelings lurking in the frantic adolescents depicted in Mauriac's early novels.

With *Le Baiser au lépreux* (1922), Mauriac composed his first masterpiece. Weaker novels were still to alternate with others of rare finish and power. *Destins* (1928), *Ce qui était perdu* (1930), *Le Mystère Frontenac* (1933), *Le Mal* (1935), *Les Anges noirs* (1936), *Les Chemins de la mer* (1939) are considered definitely feeble products of the novelist's pen. Even *La Fin de la nuit* (1935), 'Insomnie,' and 'Thérèse chez le docteur,' two striking, long short stories included in *Plongées* (1938), and *La Pharisienne* (1941), while far from negligible, suffer from blemishes that impair their effectiveness as a whole. The best of Mauriac lies, for us, in the five works to which closer attention will be given in these pages.

Jean Péloueyre, the lamentable hero of *Le Baiser au lépreux*, is depicted with relentless lucidity by Mauriac. He is hideously ugly, tortured by shyness and the consciousness of his ridiculousness, afraid of girls; he resorts to religion and especially to confession as a refuge from his inferiority. He discovers one day a page of Nietzsche branding the inferior breed of 'slaves' as ready prey for Christian ethics and exalting the will

2. Preface to *Petits Essais de psychologie religieuse* (Société littéraire de France, 1920), written during Mauriac's service on the Eastern front.

to power in man.[3] He resolves to shake his gnawing timidity and to ask a young woman, from a poorer peasant family, to marry him. She cannot say no, for the Péloueyres are a well-to-do family, envied and respected in the district, and as the priest explains to her, 'one does not refuse a Péloueyre.' Noémi, the husky peasant girl, like most of Mauriac's hero-ines, hardly looks for any physical pleasure in marriage; she will obey the law of religion and of her husband, and retain, through several pregnancies, a candid and almost virginal innocence. But the ugliness of Noémi's husband, the leper, whose soul, haunted by desire, becomes even more repulsive than his face, is too much even for her naïve good will. She embraces him, solely out of pity, and he, aware of the horror that he inspires, convinced that he never will be loved, flees to Paris for an impossible respite. He languishes away from her and from his familiar country surroundings, returns thin and pale, while she has involuntarily thrived in his absence. He dies, mourned by his wife, to whom he has bequeathed his fortune on the condition that she shall not marry again. Repressing her buried youth and silencing the call of her flesh, she re-signs herself to the eternal mourning clothes of the provincial widows and enters the only path open to her, that of self-denial.

In that brief, inhumanly hard novel, all the greatness of Mauriac's art is already fully developed. The vision of nature is vividly suggested, con-trasting in its magnificence with the cringing and self-ashamed hideous-ness of the hero. The characters are powerfully sketched in their physical personality with a few harsh touches. The stifling rites of bourgeois existence imprison in a strait jacket the latent paganism of those who dare not rebel against them. The tone of the novelist is one of satire blended with pity and enhanced by poetry.

Genitrix (1923) is laid in the same setting of a gloomy country house near Bordeaux. Fernand Cazenave is the son of a domineering mother, who eyed his marriage with suspicion and treated his bride with hostility. Her animosity grew when the young woman became pregnant; she feared that her son would then escape her for good. The baby, fortunately, was stillborn, and Cazenave's wife is now dying in a solitary room in the bleak, cold house. Her whole past appears in the mind's eye of the

3. Mauriac, broad-minded and often unorthodox Catholic that he is, has confessed to a curious fondness for Nietzsche. He wrote in *Le Bâillon dénoué* (Grasset, 1946) that 'no philosopher had remained dearer to him than Nietzsche, the poor antichrist' and that, although Voltaire always repelled him, he counted more than one friend in the posterity of Voltaire: Stendhal, for example, and Giraudoux on whom the Voltairian smile, no longer 'hideous,' sat like a radiant light.

abandoned woman: her melancholy childhood spent in poverty, her marriage to a man older by a good many years who trembles like a little child before his authoritarian mother. He had consented to be lured into wedlock through a futile effort to free himself from the maternal tyranny. But he had never given his wife the slightest joy. 'This body of hers was soon to be consumed by death, and it had not known love. No annihilation in the ecstasy of caresses had prepared her for the eternal dissolution.' She dies. Her memory will henceforth live with her weakling husband; it is so much easier to love the dead, as Mauriac says somewhere, for they do not annoy us any more. Remorse, bitterness against the engrossing love of his mother who can think only of watching his appetite, his sleep, his clothes, his comfort, and of coddling him as if he were still a little child, and contempt for his own selfishness and avarice now turn him against the triumphant Genitrix. She, who thought she had recaptured her son with the death of her daughter-in-law, now finds herself rejected. She dies in her turn and leaves her son to his solitude. He, like many a man, should have gone through life without even trying to know what love is.

Genitrix is, in its condensed beauty, almost unbearably harsh; the theme of maternal love driven to tyrannical excesses, worthy of Greek tragedy, has seldom been approached by a novelist with such stark courage. The three characters are depicted with cruel truth, unrelieved by any touch of irony or tenderness. The beauty of the flesh and the fond transfiguration of the loved one by the lover have little place in such a novel. Children and domestic animals hardly ever seem to inhabit Mauriac's world. Only the changing seasons or the tragic grandeur of the night, with the whistle of express trains in the distance and the sounds of the owls or the nightingales in the garden, bring a momentary vision of external beauty, contrasting with the feverish emotions of the characters, bent on mutual torture.

Le Désert de l'amour has more ample scope. Not only is the novel longer, with changes in place and time, but it offers a subtle orchestration of diverse themes and varies the novelist's focus by presenting three protagonists of almost equal importance. Dr. Courrèges has led a life of incessant labor; his wife, absorbed by the material worries of daily living, has gradually lost all spiritual companionship with her husband. Professional success has come to him, but he is profoundly lonely. He, who has pierced through the secrets of many patients and listened to their confessions, cannot break through the wall of shyness and misunderstanding that separates him from his own son. The latter, an un-couth and gawky adolescent, frets in the atmosphere of cold suspicion that prevails in the home; he neglects his studies, affects a brutal cynicism, and awaits the experience of love, which might transform him.

When the novel opens, fourteen years after the events, Raymond Courrèges is sitting in a bar in Paris. A woman enters with an older man. He recognizes her as an old acquaintance from Bordeaux, Maria Cross. The train of memories takes him back to his life as a schoolboy of eight-een, when he used to take the evening streetcar back to the suburbs of Bordeaux. On it he met Maria Cross, a woman of doubtful reputation, kept by some rich merchant. Maria Cross was no lady of vice, not even a coquettish or sensuous woman. She had fallen into her existence out of weariness; she harbored sentimental yearnings and became fondly and maternally attached to the clumsy lad who, every evening, sat op-posite her in the dingy streetcar. At the same time, his father, the doctor, was falling in love with her, respectfully and naïvely, like a man of science having suddenly, in middle age, discovered romantic tenderness. The woman worshipped the doctor as a saint and fondly accepted the affection of the adolescent until, one afternoon, he brutally tried to rape her. He was repulsed and mocked. Vexed in his male pride and hurt in having been judged both silly and repellent, he left her, eager to take revenge upon other women for the wound inflicted upon his vanity. He embarked on a dissolute life but never would forget or forgive the woman who had treated him like the clumsy child that he was.

The last pages of the volume take us back to the bar in Paris. Maria Cross, after years of a semi-respectable liaison, is now married. She has recognized Raymond, vaguely recalled the ridiculous adventure that, for her, never counted. Her husband is suddenly seized by a stroke. And it is the old Dr. Courrèges, who had telegraphed his son that same morning to announce his visit to Paris, who is called by him to attend to the sick man. Father and son briefly meet near the woman whom they both had fondly dreamed of, still vainly trying to understand each other, solitary pilgrims in the desert of love.

A similar technique of relating the events in retrospect, as they flash upon the memory of the chief actor reliving every gesture, every sensa-tion or thought that once was his, is used to superb advantage in *Thérèse Desqueyroux*. The point of view of the protagonist is thus adopted with-out any artificiality, and the reader shares the sense of solitude that afflicted the heroine, to the point of excusing her criminal attempt. Of all his women characters, Mauriac has drawn Thérèse with the deepest sympathy and with the finest nuances of convincing verisimilitude. Twice he felt impelled to return to the same heroine and perhaps to bring her to God. He shrank, however, before the conversion that might have saved Thérèse in the religious sense but would have imperiled her complex humanity.

Thérèse was a provincial *jeune fille*, the daughter of wealthy proprietors of acres of pines and vineyards, who accepted marriage, with no more love than is customary in such unions, to Bernard Desqueyroux, a landowner who seemed cultured and handsome. But Thérèse finds no happiness in married life, not even in maternity. She reads, thinks, smokes cigarettes, and judges her mediocre husband with lucidity, soon with severity and hostility. He is brutal and animal in his physical seizure of his bride; her senses are repelled by his complacent male coarseness. Every one of his thoughts revolves around the land and the family. Thérèse feels forever imprisoned in a dreary cage. Hatred for her husband creeps into her heart, and fear that her own daughter may have inherited too much of the paternal coarseness and conventionality haunts her. One day, while a fire was raging outside, in the pine forests, Bernard unwittingly pours himself a double dose of the arsenic that had been prescribed for him. She fails to warn him. She then is tempted to pour poison herself for her husband, and she falsifies the doctor's prescription to obtain it. Her husband survives, and her crime is discovered. She is saved from a prison sentence by Bernard's wish that the family be spared such a scandal. She is taken back to her husband's house and sequestered there until, one day, stifling in her prison, she decides to break away and live by herself in Paris. Appearances have been preserved. The family can exult, and Bernard can go back to his truest concerns, those of a landowner, sportsman, and voracious eater.

Thérèse, the sinner, the unbeliever, is the heroine of Mauriac. For she has suffered and revolted; and she is lamentably misunderstood by her middle-class family, who are aghast that one of them should insist upon thinking and acting in her own way. Mauriac delineated her with tender care, while apologizing for not creating characters 'streaming with virtue and pure in heart.' He presented her with the most precious gift a novelist can make to his heroes: he endowed her with mystery. She herself never knew what had impelled her to poison her husband. Shade plays with light, and half-shades with more glaring color in Thérèse, the most subtle and the most pitiful of Mauriac's oppressed women.

Mauriac's most successful novels eschew the confusing turbulence of the fiction in which life seems constantly to erupt with fresh incident and new characters. The novelist's most powerful stories are also the barest. Artistic unity is achieved through our perceiving every detail through the lens of one central character. But our vision remains impartial, for the protagonist who tells the tale is pitiless to his own failings. The form of reminiscences or of a diary occasionally interposes remoteness between the events remembered and the reader, keeping the reader at a distance and in a state of tranquility. In Mauriac's use of the form, on the contrary, the reader is carried away by the torrent overflowing from the tormented heart of the protagonist. The feverish, broken-up style of the interior monologue wins the reader's participation in sordid calculations and venomous hatreds.

Le Nœud de vipères is an artistic masterpiece, somber as a Shakespearean tragedy without comic relief and momentary escape into the ecstasy of the lyric. The hero is a King Lear with no Cordelia at his side, a Balzacian miser without the fierce passion for gold that transfigures Père Grandet. Everything in the middle-class family described by Mauriac is sordid. Jealousy, hatred, spying on one another, lying, and the sadistic infliction of wounds through words poison the family circle, which Mauriac, himself the happiest of family heads, refuses to see in rosy hues. But the true viper's tangle is the heart of the old man, Louis, who has kept a diary for years so that his wife might one day peruse it and marvel at how much he scorned and distrusted her.

Her 'crime' was that she had married him for money, after having broken an earlier engagement into which, presumably, she had poured more sincere feeling than she was ever to experience for her husband Louis. She belonged to an old family, which had lost its fortune, and she thought she honored Louis by accepting his hand, for he was but a son of peasants who had risen through their stubborn thrift. He had received a good education, had worked with zeal to be able to eclipse in intellectual achievement the young men whose greater social ease and worldly success he envied. Succeeded he had, and when he discovered that his bride had married him solely for his position and his money, while scorning his humbler origin and clumsy manners, he was wounded for life. Money-making became for him the only joy; or rather, a wild drive for possession of material good replaced in him the affections of the heart. His wife raised their children against him, as her potential allies; she nurtured them in a conformist and Pharisaic religious attitude, which professed horror at the father's unbelief. He lived on in his alienated home, surrounded by children and grandchildren who feared him and who speculated avidly on the amount that the old man was likely to leave them on the day of his death. He, in the bitterness of his heart, fed on revenge and plotted to hand most of his securities to an illegitimate child he had once had and thus deprive his family of the coveted legacy. The scheme is foiled through the cowardice of the bastard son.

His wife, for whom the venomous diary was intended, died before him. To the old man, long starved for affection, who had been waylaid by possessiveness and retaliation for the blows he had suffered early in life, another path now opened. Like most people, he had deceived himself only to be able to live. Hatred and vengeance had been vain pursuits for him. 'I have always been mistaken as to the object of my desires. We do not know what we desire, we do not love what we think we love.' Beneath the vipers entangled in his hardened heart was a nugget of charity. He inscribed in his mournful diary the name of the one true Love; he was drawn to Christ by his sufferings and sins, before he died.

But for its final pages, where the move toward divine charity appears too sudden and unexplained—a common feature of literary works in which supernatural grace invades a soul through an illumination, which can neither be prepared nor accounted for rationally—*Le Nœud de vipères* ranks among the most masterly novels of the century. Within a brief compass and through a voluntarily restricted technical medium, Mauriac has explored depths of evil and potentialities for good in a human creature. He has given concrete form to a vision of life and of man that is dark but is lighted up by charity. Without any elaborate description or ideological digression, he has afforded his reader an insight into social problems proposed by a middle class gnawed by avarice, Pharisaism, conventionality, and relentless selfishness.

Only one other of Mauriac's novels, in our opinion, ranks among his best, and even in that one the flaws are more conspicuous than in the earlier masterpieces, and the emphasis on the Catholic psychology of the characters is overstressed for the non-Catholic reader. The novel is *La Pharisienne* (*A Woman of the Pharisees*). The leading character, Brigitte Pian, is a deeply religious woman who might be called an unconscious or a sincere hypocrite. She forces others to practice virtue and thus drives them to revolt or hatred. She ruins a priest whose faith she finds too weak, dooms a frail young woman who insists upon knowing love of the flesh,[4] and turns her own religion into a caricature of Christian mercy. With his usual subtlety, Mauriac allows us to infer only that impure elements may enter into the making of such an imperious propagandist of enforced virtue, who may combine greed for power over souls, sexual unbalance perhaps, and sincere striving after saintliness. But he refrains from intrusive analysis and from the comments of a moralist. Several paths are opened before the reader down which he may venture to seek an interpretation of the novel. The technique differs from the retrospection or from the diary device of most earlier stories. A narrator is introduced, who participates in the action yet abstracts herself from it at times to interpret it to the readers. Some of the stark unity of Mauriac's more vivid masterpieces is thus lost.

Much in Mauriac must be explained by his determination not to become another Bourget, who preached the validity of Christianity for political and social reasons and praised Catholicism as an adjunct of order and an instrument for discipline. The author of *The Pharisienne* is Catholic but not clerical. Faith is, to him, not a haven of security and serene joy. Good does not reign on earth, and the hearts of the faithful are far remote from the purity of little children. Indeed, St. Francis celebrating the naïve beauty of birds and flowers, and Christ pointing to the lilies of the field are infrequent visitations in modern Catholic literature. Evil lurks behind every shape and perfume that is beautiful; the ultimate descent of grace into disturbed hearts takes place most surely once sin has paved the way to regeneration. Mauriac's Catholic novel insists upon remaining bold and powerful; it is Catholic and Christian because it respects the ugly truth of life and conforms to reality. Its characters are not docile believers bent at will by their creator; they resist him, rebel against being led to Paradise. In a little book written in memory of a friend of his youth who died during World War I, Mauriac clearly defined his purpose: 'A certain literature of edification falsifies life. The transcendence of Christianity appears most manifest in its conformity with reality. Do not then fake reality. To depict man in all his

4. Mauriac lends to the narrator of the story in *La Pharisienne* the following words, which reveals one of his obsessions and explains the ardent and constant attraction and repulsion that the theme of love holds for him: 'I believe that all the miseries of our human conditions spring from our inability to remain chaste and that human beings vowed to chastity would not be afflicted with most of the evils that oppress them.'

misery is to unmask the abyss opened, in the modern world, by God's absence.' [5]

It is strange that it should be in our time, when faith is less widespread than in the past centuries, that Catholic literature, long relegated to an unenviable place, has regained ascendancy with Péguy, Claudel, Bernanos, Mauriac, and certain Catholic writers of note in England and America. Catholicism, by once more placing disquietude at the core of religious literature, has tapped the sources for a new tragic feeling for life.

The advantages derived by Mauriac from his Catholic conception of the world are to perceive life as unceasingly torn between contrary forces and to picture man as restlessly preyed upon by the powers of Evil. Christianity, says Mauriac, enters into souls in order to divide them. The world is an arena for the struggle in which the Devil fights against God, vice against virtue, the animal part of ourselves against the call of the spirit. To the honest observer, virtue is not triumphant, as it may be in edifying novels; nor can vice win in the end, for that would be a denial of Providence. Thus a conflict is perpetually being waged. Man finds in his own ability to doom himself the very proof of his freedom. He revolts against God; but the life he makes for himself is, but for a few unreal moments of bodily and sensuous exultation, afflicted with an oppressive sense of dereliction.

Life assumes a significance to the Catholic novelist, in contrast with the naturalist author in whose fiction one felt only the slow, meaningless gnawing of an average existence, abandoned to forces of heredity, environment, and instinct. The Catholic novel portrays a struggle, with an end at least dimly perceived, sometimes attained with the help of divine grace. Sin also takes on a significance.

The Catholic novel rests on a sharp distinction between Good and Evil. Man surrenders to the call of his desires or to the violence of his passions voluntarily and, what is more, fully conscious that he is breaking a moral law. 'La conscience dans le mal' [6] gives added zest to his pleasures, but works for his remorse, and in some cases for his salvation. Mauriac goes much further. Sinning appears in his fiction as the prereq-

---

5. *La Vie et la mort d'un poète* (André Lafont), Bloud et Gay, Paris, 1924, p. 32.
6. The line concludes one of the darkest poems in *Les Fleurs du mal*, 'L'Irrémédiable.' Mauriac's affinities with Baudelaire can hardly be exaggerated. See his youthful essay on that French poet, translated in *Baudelaire* (Twentieth Century Views), Prentice-Hall, 1962.

uisite for entering through the strait gate and winning 'more room in Heaven' after the sinner will have atoned for the sin by repentance. This concept reassures his disturbed characters that they were not born to the conventional existence of a timid Pharisee; they are not, therefore, incapable of the élan that plunges them into hell only to raise them all the more securely into the abode of the elect.

> Those who seem vowed to evil were perhaps elect before all others, and the depths of their fall measure the extent to which they have betrayed the task to which they were destined. There would be no blessed in Heaven if they had not received the power to damn themselves; it may be that they alone rush into perdition who might have become saints.[7]

The doctrine is not without its dangers, which moralists could denounce.[8] But it offers unambiguous advantages to the Catholic novelist, who uncovers snares laid by demons in the beauty of an April morning, in the loveliness of a youthful face, in the encounter of a young man and a young woman in a restaurant or on a bathing beach. While Anatole France and many another novelist traditionally called Gallic accepted the pleasures of the flesh as the most valuable adornment of our brief life, Mauriac pictures them as unreal and followed by unspeakable misery, 'Christianity makes no allowance for the flesh; it suppresses it,' asserts the theologian-novelist. And, as he elsewhere adds, we cannot love both Cybele and Christ. Conflict waged against one half of ourselves and vigilance against all in outward nature that could seduce us into paganism give Mauriac's novels a tragic meaningfulness that Epicureans and skeptics seldom achieve in fiction.

Not all Catholic readers feel secure in the presence of such stories of temptation and subsequent remorse. Some openly regret that this Frenchman from the south should be relentlessly oppressed by the vision of sin. They would prefer the harmonious balance between the flesh and the spirit achieved by Hellenic culture and attempted by humanism after its discovery of antiquity They contrast the hideousness of caresses exchanged between lepers in Mauriac's world with the splendor of the kiss bestowed by Cleopatra on Antony in Shakespeare's play, when the Queen

---

7. Mauriac, *The Mask of Innocence* (Farrar, Straus and Young, 1953, p. 138).

8. Indeed, a moralist had denounced the doctrine in the second century A.D., for the view that sin gives the sinner a moral superiority and a prior claim to the Kingdom of Heaven is as ancient as Christianity—the pagan apologist Celsus, as reported by Origen in *Contra Celsum*.

of Egypt, who had mastered the art of sinning with grace, proclaimed herself and her lover peerless before the world.[9] Others, less nonchalant in their tolerance of the charming evils that flesh is heir to, have wondered which of the two phases often described alternately in Mauriac's novels was the more powerfully delineated and the more likely to remain engraved in the memory of young readers: the descent into the abysses of vice, or the ultimate dipping into holy water and the vistation of faith when sinners were no longer able to bear their strenuous life of sin?

Mauriac, in the sincerity of his faith, has pondered over some of these criticisms, of which his coreligionists have not been sparing. But he has remained convinced that his duty is to depict man as he sees him and to describe the world with the truth from which great Christian artists have seldom flinched. 'To dare say everything, but to dare say everything chastely. Not to divorce ardor from purity.' The most unchristian view of life would conceal the power of temptation to carry away the frail and even the most resolute of creatures. Like many Catholics and like many Frenchmen, Mauriac is primarily anti-Rousseau; man, to him, was not born good and can only with much effort become so, seldom through his own light. Not desire and lechery alone, but pride, avarice, bourgeois complacence, hatred of one's neighbors and family, the vanity of petty pleasures, and, most of all, the incurable stupidity of many human beings testify to the pervading influence of original sin. 'Men are all fools,' said another Catholic, an Englishman, G. K. Chesterton. 'This doctrine is sometimes called the doctrine of original sin. It may also be described as the natural equality of man.'

Mauriac's originality as a novelist lies in his Catholic vision of the world, in his analysis of love and especially of middle-aged women and adolescents led by a love affair to explore the bitter depths of love. It lies, too, in his craftsmanship, which, conscious and subtle as it is, contrives to leave in the novel the element by which it is most likely to challenge time—poetry.

Love hallowed by the sacrament of marriage and embellished by the devotion of the Christian couple to the service of God is hardly a theme for Catholic novelists. Happiness does not interest a creator. The radiating joy of lovers who might find an absolute in physical love is the foe Mauriac pursues relentlessly, either in the second act of *Tristan und*

9. The criticism was offered with others, in an ironic, yet sympathetic, speech delivered by André Chaumeix when he received Mauriac into the French Academy (November 17, 1933).

Isolde, where, to Mauriac's relief, the lovers' raptures can end only in death, or in *Lady Chatterley's Lover,* against which he has shot the arrows of his bitterest irony, in 'Eros,' *Journal* I and 'Une Gorgée de poison,' *Journal* II. To him, desire is always hideous. 'It transforms the person who draws near us into a monster that is no longer like him. Nothing then stands any longer between us and our accomplice.' His married women have, of course, ceased to expect any pleasure or joy. No mutual esteem, no admiration ever precedes or prolongs physical love. Love is nothing but a delusion that makes us feel our loneliness more acutely, or a fleeting sadistic impulse to humiliate our partner. More often still, with Mauriac, love is the inordinate power to torment us with which we have suddenly invested another creature. 'There's beggary in the love that can be reckoned,' whispered Shakespeare's Antony. The French novelist, listening to Wagner's opera, mourns: 'How can love ever be reckoned, except by the tears that we draw from our partner?'

Mauriac indicts the flesh because he fears its power. Like the ascetics, he brands its pleasures as lamentably brief and preposterously vain, since they rest on illusions about our partner and delusions about ourselves. Love cannot live on if the lovers renounce the martyrdom of separation. Let lovers understand their true role, which is that of being the executioner of one another, he exclaims in a very pregnant preface to *Trois Récits* (1929). Human love will fill its only true purpose if it serves as a tool to inflict suffering upon us, a hook to catch us unawares and lift us to the only love that disappoints not—divine love.

His partial view of passion, his denial of the mere possibility of happiness illustrates the limitations of Mauriac. He never aimed at universality and he did not claim objectivity. 'The novel does not reproduce reality; it transposes it' is one of the many lucid remarks made by the novelist on his art. The novel falsifies life for many a technical reason: for example, it cannot render silences, and must resort to dialogues far more than we do in life; and no fictional device is perhaps more artificial than the much-vaunted interior monologue, in which the novelist conceals his intervention and blends confusedly the perception of a series of events and the consciousness of such a perception. Mauriac cannot hold the mirror up to nature because he starts from an a priori vision of the world. The word metaphysician recurs in critical essays devoted to Mauriac, who is nevertheless hardly a philosophical mind, and he has used it himself in the most fitting characterization that he has made of himself in *Journal* II: 'I am a metaphysician working on the concrete.

Owing to a certain gift of atmosphere, I try to make the Catholic universe of evil perceptible, tangible, odorous. The theologians give us an abstract idea of the sinner; I give him flesh and blood.'

Not only must he resort to exaggeration and distortion but he must (or so Mauriac thinks) focus his lens on the inner man and on the isolated individual. Even the portrayal of a family is, with Mauriac, the portrayal of divergent members of one group, impatiently fretting at the prison where they must gather for meals or for the evening rest. They hardly ever communicate. Mauriac repeatedly contended that factory workers do not differ from duchesses in the quality or the manner of their feeling and that love and hatred are fundamentally the same in a farmer's daughter and in Racine's Hermione. He does not attempt to delineate groups or a whole society. He says of himself and of novelists in general, we 'can only depict with some adequacy beings oppressed by a law . . . The art of the novelist is a bankruptcy.'

Brevity is another self-imposed limitation with him. It keeps him from gaining for his stories the slow collaboration of time. The effect of the corrosion of the years on his characters does not interest Mauriac any more than it did the French tragic writers of the classical age. His manner, to use the Jamesian terminology, is not panoramic (except when characters survey their remembered past) and it is seldom dramatic in the literal sense, for there is very little drama enacted in the presence of the reader. Several of the best novels begin after the climax of the action has been reached, after Raymond Courrèges has lived his life of futility, after Thérèse has been judged for her attempt at poisoning, and after Louis has undone some of the viper's coils oppressing his heart. The passing of time matters less for Mauriac than the exploration in depth of the inner man. Variety in his gallery of characters matters less for him than grappling repeatedly with a few stubborn souls and unearthing more of their secrets.

Sartre, in a scathing article,[10] has pitilessly pointed out the truest weakness of Mauriac: the absence of freedom in his characters. Everything in them is predetermined by heredity, by the curse of original sin, and by their creator or by God. Mauriac once defined the novelist as 'the ape of God.' Sartre concludes his article with the oft-quoted words: 'God is no artist. Neither is Mauriac.' He charges Mauriac with first identifying

10. The article is listed in the bibliographical notes. Mauriac has never forgiven it and has seized every opportunity to attack Sartre in Le Figaro. Sartre, however, took issue with one of the less good, and less representative, novels by Mauriac.

himself with his characters, then suddenly forsaking them in order to act as a stern judge. Like God, he decrees that his wretched creatures be such and such, but he does not show them in the process of becoming what they are to be. The reader is not uncertain enough about the fate that will ultimately be meted out to them. The element of indetermination, which Sartre, the philosopher and the novelist of freedom, boasts of having restored to fictional characters, is indeed woefully lacking in Mauriac.

But he has other gifts, which compensate those he may lack: that of the tragic writer, hasty, feverish, eager to integrate the discoveries made by Dostoevski and Freud into the French mold of strict construction and swift, unrelenting ardor; that of the moralist, whose concern is to bring to light the still-unexplored or dark recesses of the human heart and to explore the perilous force of passions; above all others, that of the poet. In an interview with Frédéric Lefèvre, Mauriac indirectly hinted at his finest achievement when he declared:

> There is little danger in the novel's invading the rest of literature. I believe that only poetry counts, and that only through the poetical elements enclosed in a work of art of any genre whatever does that work deserve to last. A great novelist is first of all a great poet. Both Proust and Tolstoi were great, because their power of suggestion was boundless.

Bibliographical Notes

The most valuable material on Mauriac is that which he has untiringly provided himself, in many biographical essays: *Commencements d'une vie* (1932); 'Cinquante Ans,' *Nouvelle Revue Française*, No. 313, October 1939, 535–51; in the four volumes of his *Journal;* in his wartime essays *Le Bâillon dénoué* (1945); in excellent analytical essays on *Le Jeune Homme* (1926) and *La Province* (1926). Mauriac has published three important little books on the art of the novel as he envisages it: *Le Roman* (1928), *Dieu et Mammon* (1929, reprinted in 1935), and *Le Romancier et ses personnages* (1933).

No volume on him is thus far wholly satisfactory, not even Nelly Cormeau's, which Mauriac praised as the best on him. Useful information may be found in the following titles:

Bendz, Ernst, *François Mauriac, ébauche d'une figure*. Göteborg: Elanders, 1945.
Boerebach, 'La Place de la métaphysique dans le roman de Mauriac,' *Neophilologus*, October 1946, 151–64.

Catalogne, Gérard de, 'Mauriac ou le sens du péché,' in his book *Une Génération*. Le Rouge et le Noir, 1930.

Cormeau, Nelly, *L'Art de François Mauriac*. Grasset, 1951.

Fernandez, Ramon, introductory essay to the second edition of Mauriac's *Dieu et Mammon*. Catalogne, 1935.

Fillon, Amélie, *Mauriac*. Malfère, 1936.

Greene, Graham, 'Mauriac vu par un Anglais,' *La France libre*, April 16, 1945.

Hopkins, Gerard, 'Mauriac et les Anglais,' *Mercure de France*, April 1, 1948, 590–95.

Hourdin, Georges, *Mauriac romancier chrétien*. Le Temps présent, 1945.

Jaloux, Edmond, introductory essays to Mauriac's *Le Romancier et ses personnages*. Corrêa, 1933.

Magny, Claude-Edmonde, 'Un Romancier de la passivité, Mauriac,' *Esprit*, September 1949, 444–54.

Majault, Joseph, *Mauriac et l'art du roman*. Laffont, 1946.

O'Donnell, Donat, *Maria Cross: Imaginative Patterns in a Group of Modern Catholic Writers*. London: Chatto and Windus, 1954.

Palante, Alain, *Mauriac, le roman et la vie*. Le Portulan, 1946.

Prévost, Jean, 'De Mauriac à son œuvre,' *Nouvelle Revue Française*, I, 1930, 349–66.

Sartre, Jean-Paul, 'Mauriac et la liberté,' *Nouvelle Revue Française*, I, 1939, 212–32, reprinted in *Situations*, Gallimard, 1947, I, pp. 36–57.

Hommage à François Mauriac, La Revue du Siècle, July–August 1933.

In 1959, Mauriac published one of his most revealing and best written volumes on his own life, *Mémoires intérieurs*, Flammarion, translated under the same title by Gerard Hopkins (Farrar, Straus and Cudahy, 1960). A second volume followed in 1965.

V

Jean Giono

Historians and philosophers, with their faculty for proposing impressive generalizations, will some day speculate on the 'necessary' correlation between society and literature in France during the period between the two world wars. In the view of these thinkers, artists and writers stand in close dependence upon the environment in which they have grown up and reflect the prevailing mood of their age. Those who have remained aloof are ruled out as solitary exceptions confirming the common rule, as the absurd saying puts it; or they are branded as dwellers in an ivory tower, who refused their duty to society.

The truth is that the spirit of an age as it is reflected in history is often contradicted by the image of the same era mirrored in its art and letters. In western Europe the period from 1919 to 1930 was a time of economic reconstruction, of relative political stability, of social optimism, and of the pursuit of prosperity. Yet the literature of the period was characterized by an all-pervading sadness, even when it advocated hedonism. This generation cared little about stability and unambiguously dismissed any concern with eternal values. While official prophets celebrated the creed of social service and the steady improvement of man and his world, the rebels of letters bewailed the solitude of the modern civilized individual, and his failure to reach harmony with others and find peace within himself. The writers stressed introspective self-analysis as never before. When many declared that woman had at last come of age and would henceforth share man's role in the world, heroines practically disappeared from literature or were depicted with ferocious severity.

While the world, one was told, was entering upon a century of indefinite progress, literature expressed discouragement, describing the disintegration of man and his world and the disintegration of the novel and other art forms.

France was struck last by the economic crisis of 1929–33, and for a time she seemed only mildly affected. Yet a worm undermining her political structure was gnawing more and more deeply. A cleavage was widening daily between antagonistic social elements. The country, with her nostalgic attachment to the past and her innate turbulence, avid for innovations, seemed reluctant to accept the modern world, with its methods of mass production, its faith in machines, and its worship of efficiency. While other nations were artificially fostering their much-advertised 'dynamism,' they revived the old accusation that France was backward and 'decadent.' Yet intelligence, subtlety, humor, and originality were as abundant as ever in Paris. Unfortunately, action seemed to be divorced from intelligence, and subtle minds seemed unable to envision the forces of the future and to harness them in the interest of their country and of mankind.

At the very moment when her political and economic leaders seemed powerless to avert an impending catastrophe, France produced a number of writers whose robust audacity and faith were scarcely equaled elsewhere in Europe. Jean Giono is probably the most original among these men; his appearance in the French literary firmament was truly meteoric. At the very time when Marcel Proust seemed to have established his supremacy in French fiction and to have oriented it toward the minute analysis of man's remembrance of things past, when Jules Romains, Jacques de Lacretelle, and André Maurois were delighting in the delineation of hypercerebral and sensual characters, when François Mauriac was populating his fervid *récits* with miserly bourgeois men and love-starved wives frantically seeking God to put an end to their isolation, a new voice rang from the remote Alpine countryside. It sang of nature, of the starry skies, of the wind, of ardent and simple creatures, and of intoxicating sensations, with the accents of a primitive bard. The novels of that newcomer to literature were not skillfully built; they ignored academic subtleties and the fashions of the day. Their heroes were not poisoned by complexes, nor did they blend desire and hatred in 'that mutual torture,' which was, for Proust, synonymous with love. In them the tone of a psychological dissector had given way to that of a poetical master of suggestive language and an epic storyteller.

Giono was also a prophet, and his message was soon acclaimed by eager disciples. He rejected much of our urban and analytical civilization; but he held out hope for despairing moderns. He aimed at rebuilding a new unity in man and endeavored to instil in him the sweet, or bitter, 'lore that nature brings.' The shades of other prophets of revolt were recalled by critics: Rabelais, Rousseau, Rimbaud. Once again, indeed, from the land most famous for analytical introspection and destructive irony, there sounded an appeal to listen to nature alone and to delve into the mysteries of precivilized life. This new hymn to nature and to joy at once found echoes in other lands. Giono's prose, unusually difficult because of its wealth of vigorous words, was enthusiastically deciphered by students in foreign universities. The screen consecrated first *Harvest* (*Regain*), then the *Baker's Wife* (inspired by an episode in *Jean le bleu*), a typically Gallic picture, which caused American journalists and commentators to throw moderation to the winds in their praise.

Giono is a Frenchman of the south, but there are many varied domains within the vast and vague realm called 'southern France.' His *petite patrie* is not the playful Southwest of Montaigne, Montesquieu, and Gobineau, nor the mysterious land of the Basques. It is not the Provence of the cavalcades and of the *Félibres*, of colorful costumes and a sonorous language revived, not without some artifice, by Mistral and his circle. Alphonse Daudet's graceful tales, fragrant with rosemary and thyme, are pale sketches when placed beside Giono's flamboyant description of mountains and storms and floods. The ferocious logic of Charles Maurras and of other southern Royalists clinging to a bygone order, or the subtle Greek intellectuality of Paul Valéry, are no less alien to this new romantic. Although Giono's native city is not many miles distant from the Mont Sainte-Victoire, now familiar to museum-goers of two continents, his luxuriousness seems to set his landscape in a different world from that of Cézanne's essential sobriety. With Zola, Cézanne's compatriot, Giono seems at first to have more in common. But he embellishes reality and exalts man, while Zola, a romantic at heart, found bitter rejoicing in the somber poetry of vice and too often cultivated ugliness.

Giono is not merely a provincial novelist or what the French call *un écrivain du terroir*. His appeal is to all modern men, as is Thomas Hardy's or William Faulkner's, even though the setting and the characters of their books are narrowly localized. But Giono's reader cannot divorce the message implicit in his books or in the beings to whom he gives life from the landscape, which is always part and parcel of the story. His Provence is not the conventional Riviera with its cosmopolitan tourists, its equable climate gentle to invalids, retired officials, and undersexed esthetes. It is not the Provence of imposing Roman ruins or of pine-clad promontories still haunted by Greek memories. It stretches between the Durance Valley and the Italian frontier, north of Aix and Draguignan. Its soil is poor; indeed the Basses-Alpes, being one of the least favored of all the French departments, has remained unspoiled by industry and by the tourist trade.

Manosque, Giono's birthplace, is a town of some five thousand inhabitants, whose history, as a few picturesque relics still testify, goes back to the Middle Ages. Its narrow lands, contained within the perimeter of old fortified walls, afford vistas of the countryside studded with dark tapering cypresses, long rows of century-old ashen-gray olive trees, and, in the early spring, the delicate beauty of almond trees in bloom. Beyond stands the mountain of Lure, a familiar presence in Giono's novels. On its slopes there are scattered farmhouses with their ancient wells shaded by a broad fig tree, and a threshing ground for the wheat that grows sturdily in the dry, red earth. Farther up, there stretch green pasture lands to which shepherds repair in the summer with their flocks, after driving their sheep and a few male goats along the dusty roads of the plain all the way from Camargue. Stags and birds, depicted with an uncanny insight into their physical being and their wild, delicate nature in some of Giono's books, haunt the many glades, which resound at night with their calls. The fauna of Giono's landscapes is bewilderingly rich: swarms of insects buzzing in the trembling noonday heat, partridges and larks and nightingales, rabbits, martins, and weasels appear in his stories, not as a pretext for elaborate descriptions, but briefly characterized in the felicitous images of a sensuous pantheist. Snakes are especially dear to him, as they were to Shelley, for their strange gracefulness and peaceful communion with the earth in which they wind and burrow. The river Durance is ever present; now almost dried up by the summer drought, with innumerable islets overgrown with osier and tall, marshy grasses in which the baker's wife and her lover take refuge; now impetuously overflowing the plains, swollen with the thaw of Alpine snows and swinging against its banks in wrath.

The chief actors in Giono's stories are the great elemental forces: the wind, the torrents of spring unleashed over field and marsh, the parched earth in summer, the Dionysian dance of reeling odors, which intoxicate his men and his women, and above all, the stars that guide their works and their humble meditations. The novelist's purpose is to create living beings not unworthy of such a simple and yet grandiose setting, and the best of Giono's books are those in which he has conjured up the people who enchanted his childhood and taught him the meaning of life and the acceptance of fate. They are his father, a few women with their wise intuition and their revelations of the mysteries of physical delight and of spiritual otherness, an occasional artisan or peasant, now and then a village healer or an itinerant acrobat who attempted to cure the evil in souls. These characters are robust children of nature, hardly literate, little addicted to pondering mental problems or to repressing their healthy enjoyment of all senses by inhibitions of religion or culture. Yet they are never coarse, like the degraded peasants of Zola or of Erskine Caldwell. Their passions are ardent when aroused, but they never become abnormal nor indelicate. Clumsily but with earnest good will, they grope toward an end; and that end is almost always charity, the gift of themselves to others, the fraternal desire to help their fellow creatures reach joy. Idealized though they may be, and sweet-tongued or figurative in their language, they seldom appear false to those who are familiar with their native province. The humble shoemaker in *Jean le bleu*, the simple and devoted journeyman from Baumugnes, the farm laborers in *Que ma joie demeure*, even the more primitive men and women struggling against fate and against each other in *Le Chant du monde* are as true to life as any other peasants in French literature.

Giono was born at Manosque on March 30, 1895, the first of a brilliant group of writers who came into the world before the dawn of the new century. His father, who died in 1920, was a shoemaker in his small town. Giono learned much from watching his father at work with his leather, awl, and cobbler's wax, and from listening to his slow, thoughtful conversation with friends and customers. Unlike other writers born in humble condition, who hasten to become members of the middle class or to knock at the doors of salons and academies, Giono always took pride in his humble origins. His semifictional autobiography, *Jean le bleu*, movingly portrays his father guiding his son through the awakening of adolescence to the shrewd wisdom of inner contentment and fraternity. He has often alluded to three other French writers of some repute (Jean Guéhenno, Louis Guilloux, and Lucien Jacques), also sons of shoemakers, as constituting with him the brotherhood of cobblers in present-day literature.

Giono's father, like Zola's father and Valéry's mother, was of Italian descent. His grandfather, who had conspired with other Italian *carbonari*, had fled from Italy across the French Alps, then served with the French in Algeria in 1835. Giono's father, born near Marseille, had eventually settled at Manosque; there he married, in 1892, Pauline Pourcin, whose father came from Provence and whose mother came from Picardy. She was a laundress by trade, and *Jean le bleu* as a child roamed from the tools of the shoemaker's workshop to the lower floor of the laundry where the smell of clean linen, of hot irons, and, as he proclaims, of perspiring women delighted his precocious adolescence.

His father was his most influential teacher. To him Giono owes a spirit of indomitable independence in his political and social views, a seriousness of purpose, which may have been strengthened by certain leanings in his father toward Protestantism, and a durable attachment to the concrete and the palpable in life, which recalls a craftsman plying his wood, leather, and thread. Giono's sense of touch is second only to his extraordinary sense of smell. The boy went to school in Manosque from the age of six to that of sixteen, then entered a local bank as a petty clerk and remained there until the war broke out. His amazing mastery over one of the richest stores of words ever handled by any French writer was apparently acquired not in lecture rooms and university libraries but at the truest fountains of language: a few great books, read and reread, and the talk of peasants, shepherds, and artisans.

Little is known about Giono's sources, and even the most inquisitive scholar need not know much more; except for a few reminiscences of Gide's *Nourritures terrestres,* Giono owes little to the works of his contemporaries. The two great events in his youth were his discovery of the classics and his initiation into music, related with emotion and humor in the early chapters of *Jean le bleu.* To his love of music, especially that of Bach and Mozart, different as Giono is from them, some of his ideological essays will later bear witness. His novels, with their alternating phrases of sonorous exuberance and of slender flutelike melody, occasionally recall musical symphonies. They certainly aim at seizing the whole of the reader's sensibility and they unleash the same elemental forms that Beethoven and Wagner translated into sounds. They hardly reflect the preference for design, often accompanied by too sharp a relief given to lines and too conscious a control of one's material, that has marked the French novel since Stendhal.

The reading of ancient poets in translation was for the young Jean the supreme revelation. Others, born comfortably into the middle class with the advantages of a liberal education, have derived nothing but boredom from their enforced construing of the lines of Homer and Sophocles. Giono had not learned Greek, but he grew up in a land where peasants to this day winnow their grain, pluck their olives, and milk their goats much as their Mediterranean forefathers did in the time of Ulysses or Theocritus. He felt the classics spontaneously and lived them in his body. They gave him, according to his favorite phrase, 'a kick in the stomach.' They aroused in him at fifteen an impulse to write, which he was to obey only many years later. In one of the few passages in which he has enlightened us on his training and technique, Giono declared:

> Born in a poor family, the son of a shoemaker, then a small clerk in a bank, I bought one day the ancient classics in the cheap Garnier collection. The Greeks were revealed to my dazzled mind . . . I have revived, or rather I have made actual, the heroes of Homer and of Sophocles whom I found unchanged in my native province . . . From that day on, I had found my path: to renew the great Greek tragedies.[1]

In his autobiographical novel, *Jean le bleu* (blue because he loves to close his eyes and to feel his dizzy head all filled with blue), he recalls the intoxication of his fourteenth year. Once, at harvest time, a mysterious farm laborer lent him a copy of the *Iliad* in translation. He read it among the yellow ears of wheat, while scythes were creaking and long forks were pitching the sheaves. The text penetrated into his very senses and marrow. 'Into me was Antilochus throwing the spear. Into me was Achilles ramming the soil of his tent, trampling in the wrath of his heavy feet. In me was Patroclus shedding his blood.'

Homer, Aeschylus, Sophocles, and Aristophanes are still the authors most often taken from their shelves; then Shakespeare and Spinoza. Hardly any of the French classics and only, among the moderns, Melville (for whom he wrote an eloquent preface, *Pour saluer Melville*, in 1940), and Walt Whitman, whom he has frequently read aloud to the peasants of Provence. With the Old Testament he is obviously familiar, and some

1. The passage is from an interview given to *Les Nouvelles Littéraires* on March 13, 1937. Most of the other details about Giono's family, his manner of living, his reading, and about the successive drafts of his novels, as well as several very valuable quotations from unpublished manuscripts, are to be found in the earliest good book on Giono, *Jean Giono et les religions de la terre*, by Christian Michelfelder (Gallimard, 1938). For subsequent volumes of biography and criticism see the bibliographical notes at the end of this chapter.

of its myths have lately haunted his imagination. Unlike many of his contemporaries, he refrains from belittling Hellenic themes with irony and facile anachronism when he goes to them for his inspiration; he also refrains from technical tricks and from such manipulations with time, syntax, and words as have tempted many moderns, naïve in their sophisticated desire to disconcert their readers. His only principle is to grasp the subject fully, squarely, banishing all subterfuge; the rest follows slowly but surely.

When the war suddenly broke out in 1914, the bank clerk, then nineteen, was soon called to the colors. For almost four years he served as a private in an infantry regiment, exposed to the sordidness of mud and carrion, watching men intoxicate themselves with the smell of blood or resort to the lowest pleasures in order to forget. Miraculously, he escaped wounds and death. But he saw his dearest comrades fall in combat by his side; he returned home on brief furloughs, to watch desolate parents and widows pining in grief and to count the friends of his youth whom war was ravishing one after the other. Giono hated war. His anger against Christianity springs in part from the lamentable record of modern history, with war condoned or incited by religion. Leaving Nietzschean hymns to the virtues of the dangerous life and the heroism of hard-hearted warriors to the lucky or timid ones who had stayed behind at their desks, he spoke as a plain soldier who had seen too much actual shedding of blood ever to celebrate the mystical value of that rite. 'I have stayed at Fort de Vaux [near Verdun] for forty-two days, and it is difficult for me to get excited over a corpse . . . The stupidity of war is what disgusts me most in it. I love life.' Indeed, his war stories, ferocious in their bitter emphasis on the grim aspects of the fighting, contain some of the most haunting evocations of the butchery of Verdun and Kemmel. But the bruised flesh and the eyes of dead soldiers eaten up by rats and vultures revolted Giono less than the immense waste that characterizes war. Peasant that he is, he cannot be reconciled to the senseless mowing down of young bodies and ripe crops and cattle, and the laying waste of old trees and carefully tended meadows.

In 1919, Giono finally came back to Manosque, sad in mind although unharmed in body. Other young men who had shared the same experience were driven by the lust of escape to exotic lands; or they were eager to make up for their lost years and rushed to Paris, the eternal goal of all provincial Frenchman with literary, political, or financial ambitions. Giono did not share in the postwar race for pleasure, speed, and 'intense living.' He quietly took up his former position at the local bank, worked underground in the vaults at the *Service des Coupons,* endlessly clipping off bits of strangely colored and engraved paper and crediting them in big ledgers. But a banker he was never meant to be. He resigned from the bank when, in 1929, his company offered to send him to Antibes to direct a new branch there. Money inspired him with neither respect nor greed. He will later contrast 'the true riches' with those squares of green-backed or yellowish thin paper that most men worship. In 1920, he had married and soon had had two daughters.

After he had resigned from the bank, he devoted most of his day to writing. He began by composing poetical tales of nature and delicate eclogues set in the Manosque region, then a more ambitious volume inspired by the *Odyssey,* or rather reinterpreting the old epic imaginatively, *La Naissance de l'Odyssée* (1930). His friend Lucien Jacques took one of his manuscripts to Marseille and had it published there. He was thus encouraged and in 1929, *Colline,* printed in a Parisian review, revealed him as a writer of original talent. The doors of the literary world suddenly swung wide open.

Giono did not rush to conquer the salons and the *cénacles* of the French capital. He chose to remain a provincial. The streets of the busy metropolis appeared inhuman to him, for they were filled only with vacant eyes and the hurried steps of people who had lost contact with trees and rocks, horses and foxes, even with the sun and the sky. He traveled there seldom, to visit his publisher or to watch the performance of his plays, two of which were given on the Parisian stage with scant success, for Giono's talent is not truly dramatic. He avoided literary circles, but fame came to him as it had come to few modern French writers since Proust and Valéry. Still Giono lived on in his old house in Manosque, writing in his 'lighthouse' as he calls his clear sunny room overlooking the valley. His friends remained the humble folk of the country: the postman, the grocer, the shepherd, and their wives, whom he persuaded for a while to bake their own bread, as the first step to the recovery of pristine wisdom.

Giono, however, is no modest hermit singing in unadorned language of simple life and the joys of the earth. He soon became conscious of his rare power over words; at times he became intoxicated with it. He was not content with portraying what he saw or writing of the feelings and the sensations that he imagined. His later tales had a message, and the message was in danger of devouring the tale. In the years immediately preceding World War II, Giono turned into a Tolstoyan prophet. Many men and women of France, and still larger numbers from central Europe, flocked to Manosque to seek the counsel of the sage. Tourists on their way to the Riviera included Manosque in their journey and came in the luxurious comfort of their automobiles to revere the advocate of simple living. Enthusiasts, reported Ernst E. Noth, a German friend of Giono who became a French writer of no mean talent, even claimed that pilgrims to the Giono abode should not walk or ride but crawl on their knees from the railway station to his house!

Giono's career was, from 1929 to 1937, an uninterrupted flowering, which brought forth over a dozen volumes and probably another dozen that have remained in manuscript to this day. These works can, without too much artifice, be divided into several groups.

In his first attempts, the sage from Manosque was trying his hand at stories of limited length, sketching only a few characters but already investing his tales with symbolic significance and discovering his gift for the earthy, striking metaphor. Along with *Naissance de l'Odyssée*, a fanciful tale of Ulysses' home coming (written five years before its publication in 1930), Giono first revealed himself with a collection of short stories, *Solitude de la pitié*. Several of them are intensely moving because of the simplicity of the theme and the directness of the style. The two words linked in the title point toward the leitmotivs of the book. Giono has none of the impassive objectivity of Guy de Maupassant. He is less intent on building his stories up to a dramatic climax; he seems to whisper his tale into the reader's ear with a heart-rending, though unsentimental, force of emotion, rare in the short-story writers of our century. Giono already draws upon some of the mainsprings of his inspiration: his hatred of urban civilization and of Paris, against which he launches a burning anathema (in 'Destruction de Paris'); the visitation of Pan, herald of rapturous joy, to a village ('Prélude de Pan'); and his ambition to write a book in which man will be merged into the surrounding world, attuned to its supreme harmony ('Le Chant du monde'), a brief tale with the same title as the novel.

Soon after, three short novels appeared, which Giono grouped as the *Trilogie de Pan: Colline* (1929), *Un de Baumugnes* (1929), and *Regain* (1930). The second of these volumes was translated into English as *Lovers Are Never Losers,* and the third is known as *Harvest;* both were made famous by screen adaptations. This trilogy revealed Giono to be a master of adroit stylistic effects; his sentences are short and concise and seem to grasp the object in its very shape and mass and odor. They render, more faithfully than Giono's later exuberance succeeded in doing, the dry heat of upper Provence and the parched earth strewn with pine needles. Great God Pan, reborn after centuries of Christianity, or, rather, never dead in spite of Plutarch's sailor hearing the voice announcing his end, reigns supreme in that pagan land. *Colline* is a tale of peasant witchcraft as well as a hymn to the true life that flows in communion with nature. *Regain* is the new grass growing on reclaimed meadows and again mown, and the new crop of wheat in fields that had long remained untilled: a victory of man over the earth he had misunderstood and over his own selfish and bitter solitude. The story ends in fairy-tale fashion, with too obvious a moral lesson, which detracts from the artistic quality but was made more palatable in the moving picture.

The middle book of the trilogy, *Un de Baumugnes,* on the contrary, is a masterpiece of its kind. The novel has a moral purpose, but it is not obtrusive, and the tale in itself is breath-taking. The scenery is suggested with subtle restraint, so that the description remains secondary to the plot and creation of character. The story is told in the first person by a farm laborer who, at harvest time, met in the village *café* a tall young man with a heavy weight on his heart. He is Albin, from the village of Baumugnes (Vaugnières is the real name of the village on the map, but it has also been identified as St. Julien en Beauchêne, where Giono occasionally spent the summer months), a silent, clumsy, kindhearted giant, who inherited from his Huguenot ancestors an uncanny gift for playing the harmonica. Persecuted by the people of the plain because they clung to their different religion, these Huguenots had had the tip of their tongues cut off by their Catholic enemies during the religious wars, so that they would no longer be able to sing their hymns. They fled to the mountains, and, unable to speak, they called each other through the music of their harmonicas.

Albin was strolling in the village one evening after work when he was struck by the apparition of a tall, slim girl from one of the farms. But another lad had seen her too, a rascal from Marseilles, who was eager to earn his living more speedily, if less honestly, than by threshing corn. More wily and eloquent than Albin, he lost no time in arranging a meeting with the girl, Angèle, lured her with mendacious promises away from her home, and, after a child was born to her and she was ashamed to go back to her parents, forced her to sell herself to other men. When she broke away and returned with her fatherless baby to the farm where she was born, her parents, nearly crazy with shame, imprisoned her in a silo so that she would never again be seen. But Albin could not forget the vision of Angèle. His friend, the narrator of the story, undertook to discover her; he had himself hired at the desolate farm and, risking the wrath and the gun of the old father, discovered at last the subterranean prison and called for Albin. Albin's harmonica, played at night with skill and with feeling, revealed to Angèle the faithful young man who had once gazed at her. The novel ends when, after eluding the attacks of the old maniac, Angèle eloped with Albin, taking her baby, which became his. They went to the mountain village to live happily ever after. The story is simple but told with consummate art, with none of the complex layers of motives and desires dear to the novels of the nineteen-thirties. It is credible throughout, flowing with life. Unashamedly, it portrayed in postwar literature a man who was sincerely and naïvely in love and a woman worthy of being loved.

These early novels of Giono reflected the radiant search for joy of a young man exulting in his rediscovered bonds with the mythical forces of nature and eager to rebuild a new communion through love. Soon, however, the author became obsessed with the memories of war. Giono is the author of two war books, *Le Grand Troupeau* (1931) and *Refus d'obéissance* (1937). A third one, *Jean le bleu* (1933), receives its full significance from the last chapters on the tragic massacre that buried the rosy dreams of his adolescence. 'Beyond this book, there is the huge gaping wound by which all men of my age are gangrened,' he writes as a mournful conclusion to that enchanted autobiography.

Refus d'obéissance is vitiated by too crude an emphasis on the blood-curdling aspects of the carnage in the trenches; its propagandist intention almost defeats its own purpose. It recalls the era when well-meaning pacifists thought they would undermine fascist appeals to the heroism of battle by dwelling on the horrors of gore and blown-out brains. The war scenes in *Le Grand Troupeau* are horrifying too, but so was the reality they describe; they do not try to provoke or convert the reader, and they strike one as graphically true to life. But the splendid part of this book is the delineation of civilians; for example, the opening scene with its epic descent of the flock of sheep through the dusty Alpine villages, the solitude of women dreaming of their absent husbands after the day of hard physical labor on the farm, haunted, in Giono's usual manner, by odors: 'When he was undressing, it would swell your nose; an odor of leather and of perspiring hair on his body. It smelt as when one prepares the dressing for the big Summer salads and crushes vinegar and garlic and powdered mustard in the salad bowl.' The volume, which is less a novel than a series of disconnected vignettes of the front and the villages in the remote rear, with the omnipresence of death contrasted with the resilience of life, ends when an old shepherd visits a newborn baby on the farm and wishes for him the true blessings of life.

> If God may listen to me, it will be thy lot to love slowly, slowly in all thy loves, like one who holds the arms of the plow and digs a little more deeply every day.
> Thou wilt never weep the watery tear through thy eyes, but, like the vine, through the cleft opened at random.
> Thou wilt often carry the burden of others, and be by the roadside like a fountain.
> And thou wilt love the stars!

The last word of the grim war book is an appeal to lead the great flock of men, not let oneself be led, a message of hope, which Giono will henceforth regularly propose to his contemporaries.

Jean le bleu similarly lacks the well-balanced unity of a carefully composed novel. It meanders among the profuse reminiscences of the author's childhood and adolescence, treasures the sounds and the smells through which young Jean awoke to the exterior world, and conjures up, in an order as capriciously alien to time sequence as that of Proust's saga, visions of nature, farmers, animals, all reeling in a dizzy feast of the senses, amid the pagan setting of upper Provence. The book overflows with vitality; its very images are heavy, like pendant clusters of grapes. Yet there is wisdom in that debauchery of sensations, and purity in the pagan naturalness with which these peasants face the basic realities of life. The personality of Giono's father, the reflective shoemaker, dominates the book. Toward the end, the old man, his heart weakened, feels death approaching. In magnificent language, he explains to his son the meaning of the words 'God,' 'Death,' 'Life,' and tells him how much more difficult it is to suffer all alone than to live all alone, and how soothing it would be to invent God to console one's suffering if one has failed actually to find Him.

The news had just reached the quiet Southern village of the American who had succeeded in keeping in the air for one hundred and fifty feet. Some day it would be one hundred and fifty miles and many more, but the village sages nod their heads dubiously.

> All that will not change anything, for the happiness of man is enclosed in small valleys.

Close to us, against the wall, there were swallows' nests, and
mother-birds came to feed the little ones . . .

The tragic thing about our lives is that we are nothing but halves.
As long as inventions are made in mechanics and not in love, men
will not reach happiness. We are still only halves. The curse of
heaven on us had been to make our hearts single. One for each.
Once halved in two, you must find your exact counterpart, or else
you will remain alone all your life . . . You are not any the happier
for these magical inventions, for you have invented nothing new in
the call you send around you for the other half of your heart.

And while the milk of the earth streams through all the blades of
grass, while tree and beast are in all their glory of early summer, the
young men leave for war, singing. Half of them will never again gaze
at the beauty of this world.

Giono had proved himself a master of the robust idyl in *Un de
Baumugnes* and had given in *Jean le bleu* a happy blending of fancy and
of warm and senuous realism. His next masterpieces, *Le Chant du monde*
(*The Song of the World*) and *Que ma joie demeure* (*Joy of Man's
Desiring*), can best be defined as epic novels. Giono was predestined
among the French novelists of the century to attempt an epic novel. His
humble origins and his obstinate determination to remain a provincial
and a man of the people preserved him from the cleverness that gives a
veneer of charm, but nothing more, to many brief French novels. He did
not aim at speed and did not shrink from the plodding gait of the farmer
pacing his furrow. His gift was one of the imagination rather than of
analysis, and his instinct kept shy of the studies of desire, passion, and
jealousy in which his compatriots think they excel. He had no cynicism
and hardly any irony, not even much of a sense of humor, which is a
saving grace in some writers but which occasionally paralyzes creation.

Le Serpent d'étoiles, published in 1933, is a strange tale of Provençal
and Piedmontese shepherds gathering their flocks on the high pastures
of the Alps during the summer. At the end of their long trip across the
parched plains, they improvise a splendid epic drama in which the
dialogues and the choruses leap with the untrammeled freedom of primitive inspiration. If, as he avers, Giono has preserved the original integrity
of these folk songs and folk dramas, the book contains some of the most
unique documents ever recorded in popular and spontaneous literature.
The setting is described with a splendor of imagery that recalls the
greatest of primitive epics, the *Vedas* and *The Iliad*. The reader feels
the wind graze the palm of his hand, drinks the sky in long gulps, sniffs

the smell of the hay in rapture, marvels at the multitudinous stars 'sown into the night as from a sack of rice' and as brightly pure as if they had never before twinkled in the luminous darkness. In this book, Giono first decided to apply to his writings the Whitmanian question: 'Can your work face the open countryside and the ocean shores?'

Le Chant du monde (1934) takes us back to the world of man with its passions and hatreds. It is, of all Giono's works, the one nearest to our idea of a novel, with characters presented in motion, struggling against each other, and integrated into a closely woven plot. Antonio, a fisherman, starts on a expedition along the river banks to a high mountain, with an older man, Matelot. The latter, having lost one of his twin sons in some wild fray, has resolved to explore the country for the other twin, a red-haired young man who has lately mysteriously disappeared. The pasture lands above the valley and the fantastic city halfway up the mountain are ruled over by a much-feared tyrant by the name of Maudru. Cowherds for leagues around obey Maudru's bidding. Antonio and Matelot reach the town and repair to the house of a hunchback, who is versed in old books, herbs, and plasters. The hunchback, who has been frustrated in some early love, had retired into that spacious house, the old palace of the bishops, and had devoted his life to healing the sick and the lunatics, who flock to him in long caravans from the countryside. There he had given refuge to the red-haired twin, who had dared fall in love with Gina, a girl of the Maudru family, and had eloped with her, after killing her fiancé, Maudru's own nephew, in a fight. He had promised her escape into the plains far away, freedom, and joy. But freedom is slow in coming; and the girl's hot blood boils while she is kept in concealment by her husband. But the couple cannot face the wrath of Maudru and his vassals in midwinter. They must wait until the snow melts and uncovers a raft, which the husband has built and concealed in a lonely creek.

Meanwhile, Matelot is killed in an ambush by Maudru's men, who have sniffed an enemy in him. His son, outraged and furious, with Antonio's help, sets fire to Maudru's stables and frees the bulls, which maddened by the smell of fire, race wildly across the fields and overpower the cowherds. Then, while the great disorder of spring sends off steaming clouds from the forests of firs, quickens their trunks with sparkling sap, and thaws the face of the earth into rivulets and swamps, the two men launch their raft and float down the swollen river. Gina at last sees her dream of freedom fulfilled and admires in her husband the

fearless killer, as tender in his love as he was furious in battle. With
Antonio is a blind woman, Clara, whom he had met one day in the woods,
while she was giving birth to a baby. He had tended her clumsily but
devotedly and had accepted her insight and her faithful gratitude, while
she worshipped his smell of a robust male. The two young couples sail
down the river on their Noah's ark, as if determined to remold their
own lives and the world. Slowly the blind woman deciphers the names
of the trees, of the mud, of the stars, through the eyes of her lover; and
he listens to her strange metaphors, which translate nature through other
senses than sight; through her, he learns that seeing is deceptive. The
secrets of life have to be questioned patiently, in humble submission.

Throughout the novel, the forces of nature—mountain and river and
snow and the tender spring buds—are united with the wild passions of
men, clan hatreds, vengeance, and desire. The story takes on a frantic
violence at times, then subsides in the end, where the dominant feelings
are those of protective love bestowed on the frail by the strong and of
tender pity for the meek. The actors, except Toussaint, the healer, the
meditative character who always appears among Giono's primitive souls,
are above the common stature of men. They are epic heroes not because
they accumulate feats in violent battle but because they are the very
forces of nature embodied in simple, strong creatures; they echo the
song of the world.

Each pair of lovers, at the end of *Le Chant du monde*, reaches happiness in mutual love and in bowing humbly to nature in her moods of
fury or of gentleness. But man cannot long ignore other men; even the
senses and the passionate desire that fully rewarded love had momentarily appeased will soon aspire beyond the walls of their selfish retreat.

Que ma joie demeure, published one year later, in 1935, is a more ambitious attempt. It portrays a group of diversified human beings who
want to reach happiness and to preserve it when once won. The title is
taken from the opening of Bach's chorale, from which the first word,
Jesus, considered by Giono as a limitation, has been erased. The volume,
an ample and at times meandering novel of five hundred pages, is one
long, surging aspiration toward joy. The plot is too loose to be sum-
marized. A peasant has risen in the middle of the night to plough his
field, vaguely disturbed by a brooding sense of the incompleteness of
his own life and of that of the farmers around him. Suddenly a stranger
appears on the ploughed furrow, under the dance of the stars, asks him to
look up at Orion so like a carrot flower, questions him on his secret

sorrow, and promises joy to him: let him leave some strips of land unsown, and grow lavish daffodils, and daisies, and merry hawthorn. The thrifty farmer listens, and obeys. And his neighbors, amused at first, also fall under the sway of Bobi the stranger, a mountebank and a prophet. They understand that to live is not to economize and to hoard in selfish possession. To live is to seek joy and to find it in what is useless. 'Youth is a passion for what is useless.'

The new faith spreads. The farmers banish the mutual diffidence that had caused them to live like lepers. They learn to cooperate and to trust each other and to listen to nature. Their consecration of a new community bond is sealed at an epic dinner, in which meat and game and fragrant herbs and wines pour out with Rabelaisian lavishness. Their senses and their hearts vibrate with the new fraternity. They let their colts and mares roam free about the pastures; they uproot the fences that jealously enclosed their fields; they harvest their wheat and mow their hay in communal glee. Bobi had brought with him a stag. The men start on an expedition to a nearby forest, described by Giono with exuberance and splendor; they surround and catch hinds as companions for the stag. It is like the dawn of a new world.

Tragedy soon breaks the idyllic dream. Aurore, a girl in her teens, an Ophelia-like creature, who has secretly fallen in love with Bobi, the wise man working his natural magic, commits suicide in her grief at seeing her love unrequited. Hearts are stung with jealousy. Greed proves hard to eradicate. Joy, easily attained in an *élan* of youthful faith, is hard to retain. Bobi knows that he has gone too fast and aimed too high. The world cannot be transformed overnight. His message must, once sown, slowly germinate. He decides to go away. He is ascending a mountain path, alone, when a storm gathers around him. Rain streams on his body, gusts of wind buffet his back; he walks on; and a lightning stroke, like a dagger, pierces him between the shoulders.

Although the meaning of the novel is cloudy at times and contradictory, the book is made alive through Giono's splendid art. The ardent love of nature, the insight into the life of animals obeying sovereign forces, mating in the woods with a grave delight worthy of Lucretius' evocations, the portraying of the changing seasons and of the works and days of peasant life reminiscent of Hesiod—these are the finest merits of the book. Its magic descriptions unite the splendor of the epic with a familiar simplicity of dialogue that few realistic novels have struck so felicitously. The volume is probably too long and its plot too thin or too

unconventional, the behavior of the characters too insufficiently motivated and their pronouncements on life, joy, and fraternal love too
cryptic to rank *Que ma joie demeure* among the most satisfying novels
of this century. But nowhere has Giono risen higher than in certain
chapters of this book.

Batailles dans la montagne, which followed in 1937, is an even
more ambitious attempt at the epic and is even more disconcerting to the common reader of fiction, who expects the smooth
flow of narrative and true-to-life characters. The story leaps almost beyond human bounds; the actors are hardly made real. Saint-Jean, the chief
character, a carpenter who saves the village from a threatening flood, is
more a symbol than a living man: Jacob wrestling with the angel or
Prometheus defying the gods to serve men. After his superhuman feat,
he aspires only to the calm serenity of death. His epic stature alone fills
the novel; but the dramatic and even the plain human quality of Giono's
earlier works seems gone. Words are rich in sap and juicy as sunny
grapes, but their impetuous torrent appears no longer controlled by the
author. Giono's epic qualities have swollen dangerously.

The novelist then appeared to be attracted by another medium. The
next phase of his career was similar to that which came at the end of
Tolstoi's and D. H. Lawrence's literary careers. (In all likelihood, Giono's
evolution was accompanied by a loss of artistic creation similar to that
of Tolstoi and Lawrence.) More and more, as he became sensitive to
the evils of the world, the prophet in him triumphed over the teller of
tales.

His gift of style has not left him. His message, earnestly felt, is often
expressed with great force. An anthology of Giono's thoughts, detached
from a certain verbose repetitiousness, which weakens them in their
context, would include some of the most convincing denunciations of the
social and moral wrongs of modern life, couched in sumptuous language.
But Giono's books have become loose in structure, occasionally declamatory, and wearying in their revolt against the inevitable. The distinction
the Stoics make between evils that we may hope to cure and evils that
are not under our control is not observed by this old pagan wisdom.
Les Vraies Richesses (1936) recalls Gide's paean to the sensuous joy of
living in *Les Nourritures terrestres* and, even more, the Nietzschean
assertions of Zarathustra. It is an impassioned protest against the dehumanization of men in our industrial age and the ensuing reign of
greed and fear. *Le Poids du ciel*, published in 1938 with sumptuous

photographs of stars and interplanetary spaces, also contains pages of beautiful prose. Giono, Antaeus-like, seems to draw unto him the strength of the earth and, Atlas-like, carries with ease the weight of the skies on his shoulders. He interprets the lessons of nature with convincing eloquence. His reasoning is less cogent when he attacks our civilization indiscriminately, and it is difficult to think that he could have seriously believed that his message of nonresistance to war was timely preaching in 1938, before the Munich capitulation and when one half of Europe was bent upon annihilating the other half. 'All conquered people have become the masters of their conquerors. Violence and force may satisfy those who think only of what is temporary; it might be time to think of what is eternal.' These words of Giono were to bring little solace to Frenchmen in their years of oppression. His message was one of resignation to the inevitable enjoyment of the simple pleasures of life, of poetical familiarity with the great forces of nature; it was also one of peace at any price. At a time when tanks and airplanes were rumbling out of German factories, Giono became an ardent pacifist. When Austria and Czechoslovakia were suffering their supreme national humiliation, he was preaching passive resistance against the call to arms.

Only the greatest, that is, the humblest of masters can resist the wine of flattery, which worshipful disciples dispense to them. A group of rebels against modern civilization gathered around the sage of Manosque. With his friend Lucien Jacques, Giono founded *Les Cahiers du Contadour*, from the name of the plateau on which the new gospel was preached; communal living in harmony with nature was practiced there by these pagan cenobites. Much vain declamation was poured forth. Giono issued two small pamphlets to his friends the peasants: *Lettre aux paysans sur la pauvreté et la paix* and *Précisions* (1938 and 1939). These advocated resistance to war through nonobedience, resistance to the state, which serves nothing but its own tyranny, contempt for money and machines. 'No political regime ever gave men in a thousand years the thousandth part of the happiness which they find in one night's sleep.' In 1942, in a volume of long and rather diffuse reflections on the same themes, Giono, apparently unperturbed by the plight of his compariots who had lacked machines and had been crushed, continued his preaching. The logic of his position led him to espouse some of the doctrines of collaboration with the Nazis, for instance, to contribute to an abject periodical, *La Gerbe*, inspired by a traditionalist Breton nobleman who was also a gifted novelist and a blinded admirer of the 'New Order,' Alphonse de Chateaubriant. He was imprisoned for a little while after the liberation of France, but apparently left unharmed or ignored by the reprisals that ensued. His part as a leader of French youth or even as an inspired writer of epic fiction seems to have been brought to a close when World War II broke out. In 1947, he emerged from the war years a completely different writer, content once more to be a storyteller. Could he, at fifty, find himself attuned to a changed world?

Opinions vary greatly as to the merits of this pure storytelling by which Giono replaced his earlier search for a faith, in those postwar years when philosophy had become for some an escape, for others a quest for a possible course of action in an absurd universe. Some who had been overwhelmed by the verbal sumptuosity and the sentimental simplicity of the earlier novels welcomed the more nervous prose and the Stendhalian irony of the volumes which poured out from Giono's pen during the nineteen-fifties. Such was the opinion of several English critics, whose literature has never favored the lyrical novel (Henry Miller's fulsome praise of Giono as the mouthpiece of what was most alive in France, in 1944, had found few echoes in Britain). The warmth which had glowed in Giono's pantheistic and mythopœic pictures of nature gave way to a systematic desire to ignore the present, the moral and political problems which tortured Camus and the existentialists. The storyteller took refuge in the past and gave the subtitle of *Chroniques* to those evocations of Provence a century ago. The truculence of this kind of chronicle, in which picaresque adventures and colorful incidents are more prominent than the study of characters, had been presented in the tradition of Froissart. The naïveté of the fourteenth-century chronicler is however not easily recaptured by a modern. One is rather reminded of Alexandre Dumas (with more restraint and more style) and of Stendhal's joy in imagining the passionate reveries and the superb insolence of Fabrice. In the five volumes of *Chroniques*, the break with the prewar Giono is complete. The style is concise, bare, familiar; the exuberance of metaphors and of comparisons is gone. Gone also are the elaborate descriptions of nature. A few vignettes suffice to picture the colors of the dawn, the marvel of the stars, the smell of hay in the fields, the winter roads slippery with snow and ice. The trees and the rivers, whose impetuous life Giono used to recapture in torrents of imagery, are still the kings of his landscape, but sketchily evoked. The scene of the novels themselves is not specifically laid in the upper Provence dear to the earlier Giono. *Un Roi sans divertissement*, the first of the *Chroniques*, is a 'regionalist' story, supposed to have occurred in 1843, somewhere in Dauphiné. The fifth, *Les Grands Chemins,* shifts from some Alpine region to the Rhone valley and a landscape of dry bushes beaten by the wind. Nature has ceased to be the protagonist in Giono's novels. His manner, humorous and familiar, now cuts short all the poetical *élans* of the cosmic pagan. Eloquence is pursued and banished. The stories are usually told in the first person by some observer and narrator who has been an actor in the events related. His own language is rendered with some realistic accuracy; it is never coarse, as in many recent writers, but earthy, picturesque, close to the 'green' language of slang, and it moves in a swift tempo.

The volumes themselves are brief. They leave much unsaid, so much indeed that the inquisitive reader may think himself inadequately repaid. The novelist makes little effort to enter the minds of his most important characters (such as the dying old lady in *Mort d'un personnage,* the domineering peasant woman in *Les Ames fortes,* or the card player and thief who inspires the storyteller in *Les Grands Chemins* with a strange fraternal and maternal devotion until he is shot by him, almost tenderly). He alludes to some events, briefly sketches a scene, describes bewildering behavior, sometimes bordering on the fantastic (as in the short story, 'Faust au village'), then passes on. It would take extraordinary power in the novelist to win the credibility of his readers, and Giono does not always win it. The novels strike one as a little thin, their psychological depths insufficiently explored, told with ease and verve but not truly compelling belief.

The admirer of Giono is ready to concede that the author had to renovate his earlier manner, which had been in danger of stifling plot and characters with an overgrowth of poetry, allegory, and imagery, and that the cosmic or epic novel should not be attempted too often. He may also, however, resist the latest 'chronicles' of peasant life delineated by Giono and his attempt at sketching real characters. The most successful are those of *Mort d'un personnage,* with the skillful picture of a home for the blind in the late nineteenth century and of a strong and spiritually blind woman withdrawing from the visible world. Giono's mastery is that of a superb craftsman. His sensitiveness is more human, more attuned to our average statures, than it was in his former volumes. But none of the *Chroniques* thus far published would be enough to grant Giono an exalted place in French letters today. His portrayal seems strangely detached and cool. His narrative technique is too smooth.

Le Moulin de Pologne, published in 1953, is in our opinion equally remote from Giono's earlier achievement. Some scenes, that of the ball especially, are related with a rare skill for creating suspense, and the character of Monsieur Joseph, who baffles all the inhabitants of the slumbering provincial town, is delineated with much verve. The tragic story of an implacable series of misfortunes striking three or four genera-tions of the Coste family, owners of the 'Moulin de Pologne,' appears gratuitous. Too little is explained, and the pace is too swift for the reader to become absorbed in the tragicomic tale of Atrides or Amalecites trans-planted into Provence.

Le Hussard sur le toit (1952), which, unfortunately, Giono has followed up with a lengthy sequel, *Angelo,* is on the contrary one of the most youthful and freshest novels of the last fifteen years. The hero is a young Piedmontese and a colonel of hussars, a very close relative of Stendhal's Fabrice. He had to flee his country for political reasons in 1838 and, on returning home, he encounters a terrifying epidemic of cholera in upper Provence. He escapes from the hostile inhabitants over the roofs of the city, falls into the room of an aristocratic young lady, and meets her again on the road while escaping both the plague and the fury of the populace dreading contagion. They flee together, respect each other to the end, and their comradeship, their virile restraint and their chivalrous sense of humor prove stronger not only than love but than the plague and the wickedness of men. This long adventure novel does not win the reader's credence throughout; the contrast between the lurid scenes of drought and cholera and the fantastic heroism of the Italian colonel appear lacking in nuances; the Stendhalian tone is too conspicuous, and one wonders whether the author intended a historical novel or a pastiche of *The Charterhouse of Parma.* But alone among the seven or eight volumes published by Giono since 1946, *Le Hussard sur le toit* gives evidence of true original power and promise of a renewal in a novelist who was to become a sexagenarian in 1955. *Le Bonheur fou* in 1957, fulfilled those promises, with the pacifist author's revelling in tales of epic fights, and of chaste pursuit of heroic women, and in a very un-fashionable quest for what the moralist Joubert once called 'the finest of all courages, that of being happy.' The significant, and perhaps the great, Giono remains in our opinion that of the seven or eight books which preceded the murky and too lavish *Batailles dans la montagne* and the author's ill-starred 'engagement' of the war years.

Giono is significant in French letters because he is, primarily, a great artist. This son of a Provençal shoemaker enriched the French novel of his age with an infusion of virility and of poetry. He broke with the tradition of the psychological novel of Stendhal, Proust, and Gide, as well as with the tradition of huge realistic sagas that Roger Martin du Gard and Jules Romains had tried after Zola.

His first astonishing gift is sensation. Giono plunges into the world with a freshness of perception denied to most adults. But that freshness is not the delicate sensitiveness of children, which blends the concrete and the magical. His sensations are as robust and earthy as they are intense. They do not diffuse objects in a halo of evanescent glimmering light; they accept them whole and capture their essence, concrete and spiritual. The novelist's world is a world of smells, tastes, palpable masses and shapes, caressed by the body; visual sensations account for little, and the intellectual content of perceptions is sacrificed to their sensuous revelation.

What he has perceived is almost instantaneously rendered through images. Giono is one of the most prolific creators of images in modern literature. He has occasionally abused his gift, but he has seldom indulged in the tricky metaphorical phrases for which Jules Renard, then Paul Morand and Jean Giraudoux became famous. Giono's images do not aim at surprising the reader, even less at debasing the person or the object, as was the fashion when a 'gentleman' would compare his lady's pale complexion to 'that yellow paper in which butchers wrap up meat.' Giono's rarest gift is his inexhaustibility to create precise, yet expanding and soaring, images. He fixes the essence of reality through them and ennobles it at the same time; he simplifies, and yet transfigures.[2] Later, when he became conscious of his gift of coining metaphors and became more ambitiously epic, Giono developed his metaphors into ample comparisons. 'Intelligence is a miserable and stately Antigone: it appears, leading man by the hand . . .' And, in a passage of *Que ma joie demeure* not unworthy of Homer, the simple farmer gazing at the distant village at night, perceives fiery signs flickering; they are, of course, the rays of light filtered irregularly through the shutters. But before he realizes their origin, the old man slowly spells them like letters of the alphabet: '*L*',

2. Here are a few examples: 'Through the slit of the vale, one sees a country russet-red like a fox.' 'The air, full of flies, creaks like a greenfruit that is being sliced.' 'Aubignane clings to the edge of the plateau like a small nest of wasps.' 'That beautiful round breast is a hill.' 'The lizards sleep in the sun; then they jump, snap up and slowly chew bees which taste of honey. And they shed golden tears which sizzle on the burning-hot stone.' 'The transparent shade of the olive-trees holds in its spider's web the siesta of a little girl.'

f, o, m, l', f, o, m, . . . like one of those great shapeless words which must have designated the sun, the moon and the stars in the mouths of early men.'

Giono is no master of the art of fiction in the traditional sense of the word; and his wealth of digression and lavish use of description deprive his books of the purity of outline associated with many French novels. The structure and the pattern of his volumes (with two or three exceptions, such as *Un de Baumugnes* and *Le Chant du monde*) would not stand the strict critical scanning of a disciple of Henry James or Gustave Flaubert. They are often loosely built. Even in character creation, where Giono is far stronger, he can lay no claim to having molded individuals overflowing with life, as are the heroes of Balzac or Proust. His women in particular remain indistinct. We know much of what takes place in their sensations and, as it were, along and under their skin, but much less about their feelings and less still about the intellectual side of their nature, their moral or social reactions.

They are nevertheless real human beings and as true peasants as exist in fiction. It is not easy to give life to simple, robust, uncouth people, naïvely groping for joy, clumsy in the expression of their emotions, but unafflicted with the contagious disease of Gide's, Huxley's, and Mann's heroes, who discourse endlessly on their view of the world or conveniently reveal in a diary all the reader should know about them, and more. Giono's characters are not made of elaborate synthetical combinations of disconnected elements patiently pasted together; they surge into life at one stroke, as if impelled by a powerful creator to appear and haunt us. We may know little about them and their reflections and their inhabitions; but, as might be said of D. H. Lawrence's heroes, we become aware of their mysteriousness and live with them through three hundred pages.

Giono is also an artist with words. His vocabulary is extraordinarily varied—one of the richest in French since Balzac and Hugo. He seems to have the right word always ready at his disposal to express any part of a flower, of a tree, of an animal, or of a house, for the precise sensation received from the wind or the rain. His language is as robust as it is rich. The reader actually smells Giono's verbs, breathes the fragrance of his adjectives, feels the caress of his adverbs on his skin. A voluptuous artist was born in the son of the Manosque cobbler. 'Before I write a word,' he confessed to his biographer, 'I taste it as a cook tastes the ingredient that he is going to add to his sauce; I examine it against the light as a decorator gazes at the Chinese bowl that he will place in its proper setting.' Elsewhere one of his characters speaks of the magic of images that transfigure reality, of the legerdemain practiced, as by a dyer, by the artist in words, who changes the colors of objects. 'Poetry is the dynamite that blows up and tears away the rock.'

Where he has avoided the traditional pitfall of southerners, verbosity and lavish eloquence, Giono has indeed proved one of the finest masters of contemporary French prose. One is at times uncertain whether this primitive artist is not a false primitive, pretending to write clumsy dialogue or endeavoring not to compose his descriptions with the obvious artistry of a more conventional writer. But in his best moments, when rendering the cataclysms of nature or the sensations of men, Giono has succeeded in creating a style that appears devoid of artifice, more naïvely natural than the poetic prose of Chateaubriand or Barrès, more animated than Flaubert's dead cadences, less 'clever' and self-conscious than that of most moderns.

If art is the chief quality to be demanded from an artist, the artistic gift of creation and of expression that distinguishes a novelist like Giono is nevertheless nourished by a personality that feels and thinks. Giono's 'thought,' when reconstructed with some consistency by the critic, is neither profound nor original. Tolstoi's was no more so when he undertook to elucidate art or to comment on Shakespeare, nor Lawrence's when he pontificated on the fantasia of the unconscious and the 'dark mysteries' of sex. Even Shakespeare's pronouncements on life's brief candle and dusty death and self-slaughter, if translated into dull prose, would appear shallow or commonplace. The value of an artist's 'ideas' lies in the intensity with which they have been felt and clothed, and in the dramatic fitness with which they are expressed by the imaginary characters of the drama or the novel at a chosen moment. Giono feels his ideas with a burning ardor and makes his creatures live them.

But the critic's task is to restate in his own colorless language, and probably with clearer logic than his subject would like, a 'philosophy' that was merely implicit in the novelist or the poet. He cannot shirk this task if he studies writers like D. H. Lawrence and Giono, Claudel and Dostoevski; for their ideas, profound or shallow, trite or original, counted vitally for these men, and for their followers. Giono's message shook many a European in the early 'thirties; and its influence, assimilated and transformed, has probably not yet ceased acting as a ferment in the emotional aspiration of our age.

Giono, like Lawrence whom he often recalls (although the southern Frenchman, accepting sex with the sanity and restraint of the peasants of his country, is remote indeed from the mysticism of the flesh preached by the inverted Puritan of the Midlands), rejects the civilization that surrounds him. The modern world is utterly bad if it dooms man to be a cog in a crushing wheel. Greed, gregarious pleasures, meaningless ambitions, and aimless and soulless efficiency for efficiency's sake drive most modern men to a death-in-life worse than death. 'You must have been told,' Giono declares to his imaginary disciple in *Les Vraies Richesses*, 'that you should succeed in life; and I tell you that you should live: that is the one true success in the world.' And again: 'We have forgotten that our only purpose is to *live*, and this is a thing we must do every day, and at each hour of the day we fulfill our true Destiny if we live.' Let us therefore go back, and abandon the path of death and war which has misled us so lamentably. We can and we must recover deeper sources of life today, and thus make it possible for our sons to become harmonious beings once more.

Not only have we forgotten how to live, but we foolishly revel in our inner emptiness. We even lack the courage to look for the remedy, which lies within our reach. 'Modern times have not merely solved the problem of the disintegration of the atom; they have accomplished the disintegration of our beings, needlessly freeing and wasting spiritual forces that were necessary to us if we were to lead a human life.' We build and drive machines, we go to the bank and sign checks and clip off coupons, we read books and dissect them, we dictate from an office chair to a meek and neatly manicured secretary who obeys us punctually, and we give the name of life to that routine activity. But no true contact with the realities of life enters into that stultified existence. We devise mechanical contraptions that we force our customers to buy from us, through wars if need be; but we do not know how to make our own bread any more. We talk of mastering economic forces, but we have allowed the wind and the rain and the snow and the forests to be taken from us.

The secret of happiness is to recover our lost unity; the road lies through the restoration of a threefold communion. First, with nature. Such a communion, more necessary today than in Rousseau's times, as our urban lives have become more mechanized, is not to be effected through spending a few weeks at a seashore resort, not even through diligently mowing our lawns on weekends or sawing trees in a summer camp. Only through humility can we penetrate into the secrets of nature. 'Now

I understand why we are the salt of the earth,' exclaims the prophet of
Les Vraies Richesses. 'The wide still fields cannot of themselves express
their deep intentions; silently, they blow a foam of vegetals. The extraordinary thing about our human destiny is not the intelligence that we
have carefully molded for ourselves and that we direct at will like a
revolving beam . . . it is our power to fuse ourselves with things; it is
that divine part of ourselves, always in rebellion, which makes us the
mouthpiece of the world.' Earlier, in a preface to a deluxe edition of
Colline, Giono had already proclaimed in striking language: 'All the
errors of man spring from his imagining that he is treading a dead
earth, while his footsteps are imprinted in a flesh full of good will.'

The lessons of nature must bring us back to a sense of unity with the
world around us. But the storms that tear our own world are no less
tumultuous than the fierce rending in the clouds and the salubrious
gusts of mountain wind that sweep across Giono's novels. It is easier
to find contentment in submission to nature than to reconcile our own
inner conflicts. Ignoring the call of our senses or repressing it is a false
way of reaching an illusory peace with ourselves. Giono, to be sure,
never advocates gratification of the senses; his novels do not contain
precise love scenes, and bodily embrace and sexual indulgence are
remarkably absent from his stories. But he knows that true wisdom is
not of the intellect alone. Asceticism is to him a criminal mutilation. The
obsession of the senses is never worse than when the unhealthy lover has
to gird himself daily for the fight against his desires and his poisoned
thoughts. Full acceptance of one's body is more chaste and wiser, Giono
declares, echoing perhaps unconsciously Zarathustra's aphorism: [3] 'To
satisfy our intelligence is not difficult; to satisfy our mind is not difficult
either. But to satisfy our body seems to humiliate us. Yet the body alone
partakes of a dazzling knowledge.'

Thus the novelist who has rendered sensations with unrivaled vividness and reveled in their richness happens to be one of the least morbid
and least libertine in contemporary French literature. Giono does not
leave women out of his stories, as Malraux does, except for Malraux's
few scenes of eroticism. He is completely alien to the subtle perverseness
that fills many French stories of amorous friendships of adolescents.
Proust's sadism is equally remote from him, as well as the recent fashion
that, under the guise of friendship and equality of the sexes, reduced
many heroines to the role of willing partners to man's drinking bouts

3. 'There is more reason in thy body than in the best of all wisdoms.'

and amorous games. Giono's women do not resort to the hysterical screams dear to movie actresses, nor to the hardhearted calculations of would-be and accomplished spouses destined to arouse and maintain man's desire before and after marriage. His peasant women always win the esteem and affection of men, as well as their love. Seldom do their senses overpower their will; or rather the two hardly ever enter into conflict. There is little brutality and much mutual respect in the free giving and receiving of their love.

Yet it may be relatively easy to reach communion with another being in the passionate ecstasy of love or through the painted veil woven between lovers by the magic of desire. The truly rare communion is that which may spring from love between a man and a woman and outlive it, or link several men and women together in unreserved trust and the common pursuit of a higher goal. Giono, like Duhamel, Malraux, and Saint-Exupéry, is obsessed by the necessity of nurturing among us the plant of true friendship, rarer, as La Rochefoucauld once said, than true love. For friendship is more than comradeship of youth, of students or soldiers who have not yet been thrown into divergent paths by ambitions, selfish pursuits, or routine habits. It requires an unstinted sacrifice of our selfcenteredness, a victory over secret jealousy and spite, a determination to spread joy around us and to accept it from others. It is perhaps the highest fulfillment that men can accomplish, for it demands the greatest immolation of our pride. It should combine the spontaneous gift of oneself that youth is prone to offer with the patient tolerance and the wise humility that mature years alone can bring.

It is such a purification of the soul that Giono advocates in his disciples. This prophet of a new paganism [4] here concurs with the sages of Christianity and of oriental religions. He spurns the denial of the body, which is a mutilation of our being, but he decries no less vehemently the lavish attention paid by many to their feminine or effeminate bodies. Modern times provide us with luxurious pink, pistachio, and sky-blue bathtubs, with a whole pharmacopoeia of almond creams and odorous and deodorant perfumes and nail polishes. But who attends to the pustulant rash of our souls? Where are the hygienic experts to wash away their crust of filth?

4. Giono professes paganism, not atheism. 'The atheist says no; he is content with refusing. But the pagan wishes, wants, hence destroys and rebuilds . . . atheism retains something of the sour atmosphere of spiritualistic religions; paganism truly liberates.' Thus spoke Giono in a conversation reported by Christian Michelfelder.

This is the function of the artist. He creates beauty; but he must also extend his prophetic gaze beyond the narrow horizon of other men, discover and radiate joy, teach hope. 'The true artist always stands at the vanguard,' says Giono. 'He leans over from the top mast; he is the discoverer of new lands, of all the joys, the delights, and nourishment which await men—not for men to capture such riches greedily and shut them up in a safe, but for him to live with this treasure in a harmonious integration.' And again: 'The poet is a professor of hope . . . the horizon of men having fallen lower, his gaze flies far beyond, and the fragrance of stars is wafted to him.' Joy is the keynote of Giono's pagan message as it is of Claudel's Catholic teaching.

But can joy be long possessed? In the resplendence of his early creative years, Giono had seemed content with the delineation of humble characters reaching joy and living content in its fulfillment. That, however, gave an appearance of unreal idyls, almost of moral Sunday-school teaching, to his novels. For joy is not all.

> If joy is better than sorrow joy is not great;
> Peace is great, strength is great.
> Not for joy the stars burn, not for joy the vulture
> Spreads her gray sails on the air
> Over the mountain; not for joy the worn mountain
> Stands, while years like water
> Trench his long sides . . .

Thus, at the remotest end of the world from Giono's Provence, wrote Robinson Jeffers, the tragic pessimist of California in one of his finest short lyrics. In his more mature works. Giono became aware of suffering and of the inevitable brevity of joy. 'I believe that one cannot make joy last, and even that one should not desire it . . . Suffering is an inventor of remedies; an inventor of hope. When man suffers the most hopelessly, then also has he the most hope. Suffering is then an immense apple-orchard in Autumn, under the rain, with beautiful washed apples at the end of the branches.'

It is on that word 'hope' that Giono's message concludes. He realizes that no regression is possible for men; machines will not be scrapped and probably should not be; but 'the true riches' should be shared by many of those who are at present absorbed in machines. If we cannot deny or undo mechanical civilization, we can go beyond it. To the suffering man of today, oppressed by a load of monstrous drudgery and living in terror of fierce cataclysms, Giono extends words of solace and hope. 'I can no longer accept the works of art unless they serve man, and the sign of the highest is that they express at the same time the strange misfortune of man's fate and man's reasons for hope.'

A passionate protest against man's fate—this is the significance of Giono's work. Some will smile at these outbursts against modern civilization and affix the familiar labels: romanticism, primitivism, antiintellectualism. There will doubtless be a measure of truth in their scoffing. But Giono's art laughs in turn at such philosophers who treat man as a purely logical and reasoning animal, or rather as hardly an animal or plant at all, while he differs only in degree from trees and horses. His creed is not likely to be long discussed by professional thinkers or to be weighed carefully by experts on economic science. But it is the living faith of a poet, the passionate and anguished cry of a sensitive man protesting against 'what man has made of man.'

Giono, like Rousseau, Tolstoi, Thoreau, Rimbaud, and Gauguin,[5] has written about one of the most significant moods in the psychological history of mankind in the last two centuries: dissatisfaction with modern civilization. We have changed the face of the earth, filled the air with our engines and our sound waves, mastered explosive energy, but we have hardly scratched the surface of man's spirit. Can we not change man also and bridge the chasm that has too often separated our hearts and our heads, our religion and our philosophy? A Chinese sage of our time, Kou Houng Ming, has aptly expressed our tragic dilemma: 'Europe has a religion which satisfies its heart but does not satisfy its head, and a philosophy which satisfies its head but fails to satisfy its heart.'

Bibliographical Notes

The translations of Giono's earlier novels have been out of print since 1950 or so. *Regain* (*Harvest*) and *Un de Baumugnes* (*Lovers Are Never Losers*. London: Jarrold, 1932) had appeared in 1939. *Jean le bleu* was translated by Katherine Allen Clarke (*Blue Boy*, Viking Press, 1946), who had written a thesis in French on *Le Lyrisme dans l'œuvre de Giono* for the University of Grenoble in 1938. *Joy of Man's Desiring* was published by the Viking Press in 1946, where *The Song of the World* had also appeared in 1937. Alfred A.

5. As a prophet, Giono belongs with these men; as an artist, however, and as a powerful delineator of peasant life and of men living in harmony with nature, his spiritual family counts more central Europeans and Scandinavians than Frenchmen or even than English writers who, like Mary Webb, lack a certain robustness and elemental vigor. The Pole Ladislas Reymont, the Scandinavians, and the Swiss Charles Ramuz are perhaps nearest to Giono in modern literature.

Knopf brought out *Horseman on the Roof* in 1954 and *Angelo as The Straw Man* in 1959. Criterion Books published *The Malediction* (*Le Moulin de Pologne*) in 1953.

The books on Giono are those of Pierre de Boisdeffre (Gallimard, 1965), with a selection of texts and an excellent bibliography compiled by Jean Bottin; Claudine Chonez, *Giono par lui-même*. Seuil, 1956; a German thesis by Heinz Crossik, *Giono, Ein Dichter der Provence*. Posen, 1934; Bernard Marion, *A la rencontre de Giono*. Ghent: La Sixaine, 1947; Christian Michelfelder, *Jean Giono et les religions de la terre*. Gallimard, 1938; Jacques Pugnet, *Jean Giono*. Editions Universitaires, 1955; Romée de Villeneuve, *Giono ce solitaire*. Avignon: Presses Universelles, 1955. The most substantial articles are those of Marcel Arland, 'Le Chant du Monde,' *Nouvelle Revue Française*, I, 9, September 1953, 495–505; Henri Fluchère, in *Les Cahiers du Sud*, March 1932, 144–149 and July 1935, 588–591; Henri Pourrat, 'La pensée magique de Giono,' *Nouvelle Revue Française*, 51, No. 301, October 1938, 646–658; Jacques Robichon, 'Dialogue avec Giono à Manosque,' *La Table ronde*, No. 86, February 1955, 50–61; Pierre Robert, 'Giono et les Techniques du Roman,' *University of California Publications in Modern Philology*, Berkeley, vol. 56, 1961; Alphonse Roche, 'Les provençalismes et la question du régionalisme dans l'œuvre de Giono,' *P.M.L.A.*, LXIII, 4, December 1948, 1332–1342; Maxwell A. Smith, 'Giono's Trilogy of Pan,' *Tennessee Studies in Literature*, 2, 1957, 73–80; 'Giono's Use of the Ulysses Concept,' *The French Review*, XXXI, No. 1, October 1957, 41–46; Pierre Varillon, *Etudes*, vol. 230, 5 et 20, February 1937, 337–351 and 469–483; Hadlam Walker, 'Myth in *Chant du Monde*,' *Symposium*, XV, 2, Summer 1961, 139–146.

VI

Antoine de Saint-Exupery

Of all the French writers who sprang to fame around 1930 (Giono, Bernanos, Céline, Malraux), Antoine de Saint-Exupéry is the one whose popularity, not only in France but in other countries too, grew most suddenly. There was nothing spurious about the enthusiasm that acclaimed the author of *Terre des hommes* (*Wind, Sand and Stars*), no undue publicity encouraged it. Neither the stories that his books told nor the manner of telling tried to lure the reader with superficial charm. Their author shunned the publicity of newspapers and lecture rooms. It was clear that the chief concern of this aviator with a legendary past was that of a seeker after wisdom and of a classical craftsman.

Popular acclaim is no conclusive proof of greatness, nor in spite of some cynical scoffers, of mediocrity. We do not believe that Saint-Exupéry will go down as one of the truly great names of modern French letters. But piety and admiration surround his memory, some twenty years after the author disappeared, a new Icarus, flying over the Alps and German antiaircraft artillery. Saint-Exupéry's influence on the youth of France is deep. He is one of the very few of his immediate predecessors of whom Sartre, the philosopher of *What Is Literature?*, wrote with respect. The new province of literature that he opened, the literature of aviation, is proving to be an important one; but none of the French successors of Saint-Exupéry (Jules Roy and Pierre Clostermann are the most gifted), or Anne Morrow Lindbergh, or heroic Richard Hillary have eclipsed the pioneer. The significance of Saint-Exupéry transcends literature. He was the mouthpiece of some of the deepest aspirations of the French people, perhaps even of Western man, between 1930 and 1944. He sensed and concretely expressed some of the most harrowing problems of his age. He was less—and far more—than a novelist. Steeped as he was in Gide and Giraudoux, who had been among the purest men of letters of the decade 1920–30, prone to *préciosité* himself and to the cult of imagery, Saint-Exupéry nevertheless charged his writings with a new density. He eschewed politics, felt more at home in the sands of Africa than in Parisian *cafés,* and died before the phrase *littérature engagée* became the order of the day. But he had been among the first to realize that the era that saw Hitler crushing democracy at home and that saw Abyssinia, Spain, Austria, and Czechoslovakia falling prostrate and betrayed was entitled to more than the introspective complacency of the writer of 1920–30. The gravity of the moralist and the wrath of the prophet could hardly be out of place in the novel, even if it ceased to be the traditional fiction bent upon telling a story and upon creating characters similar to living men.

Saint-Exupéry's fiction is concerned with the anguish of man facing himself, war, and death rather than with the verisimilitude of a few puppets or the adroit contriving of a coherent plot. He is a moralist and a poet even more than a novelist. Three characteristics may be said to mark his anxious quest and that of many of his French contemporaries: intellectual lucidity, a profound sense of the tragedy of life, and unconquerable hope. Most of the writers of today are agnostics nostalgic for religious faith, or more curiously still, believers nostalgic for the inquietude and the torment of negators. They are also contemptuous of the easy delusions with which a previous century had imagined it had put an end to bloody wars and revolutions. Saint-Exupéry, Malraux, Sartre, and Montherlant never forsake intellectual lucidity, even when they desert clarity in their sentences and scorn the pedestrian linking of ideas.

Such a lucid gaze at the stark truths of life brings to modern writers a sense of tragedy. The word 'tragedy' is at present being discredited by being dragged into every book of criticism, every sermon, every philosophical article. But Saint-Exupéry, always modest and touchingly *pudique,* shied at such easy words. He lived tragedies and did not discourse about them. Death was close to him many times; he had grappled with its most excruciating forms, perishing from thirst and hunger, in the solitude of mountains. He returned from his overtures to death all the more eager to live and to endow life with a meaning. His hope for man and for his country never faltered. Not a professional thinker himself, although he toyed with the ambition of being one in his unwieldy posthumous volume, he meditated incessantly on some of the dilemmas that confront modern man. Dilemmas they are, rather than problems. For they can never be solved once and for all but only perceived intensely and, at best, embraced in a higher dialectical synthesis. Four such dilemmas seem to haunt the French writers of the years 1930–50, and most of all the moralist Saint-Exupéry.

The first is the necessity of conciliating the legacy of the past and the forces of the present. Western man today, and the Frenchman most of all, is obsessed by history; he is prone to lament all that has happened to his country after a certain date—1914, or 1870, or 1789. His nostalgic and reactionary attitude provokes other Frenchmen to assert that the true tradition of France is revolutionary. Hence the conflict that incessantly opposes those who are unable to prepare for the future or accept it imaginatively and those who scorn all earlier achievements, the paralytics and the epileptics fighting for the control of history, as Ortega y Gasset has called them.

The second dilemma is to reconcile thought and action, ideal and reality. A woeful divorce of the modern age is the growing rift between intelligence and politics, abstract thinking and the techniques of practical life. Idealists who expect to change man in the near future are often naïvely chimerical; pseudo-realists who accept him at his lowest and flatter Caliban in order to leave him to his low estate are cynics. Too much action, in politics and diplomacy, is futile because it has not been preceded by careful meditation.

Third is the antinomy between concern for the individual, respected as a human being, and subordination to a group, which should enrich him spiritually without forcing him into gregariousness. Historical evolution has, in the last hundred years, tended to enhance the power of the centralized state, and impressive results have been achieved. But the habit of herdlike thinking and of passive conformity has also poisoned many a soul. The Frenchman distrusts intellectual monotony, quantitative accumulation, and even the modern techniques of mass production and of efficient government. But he wonders today how long his individualism can survive. Saint-Exupéry, Malraux, and their contemporaries foresaw that the task of the second half of their century would be to evolve a synthesis between the individual, with his creative gifts and his dignity as a person, and the collectivity, claiming more and more sacrifices from its participants.

A fourth dilemma haunts these writers: the machine versus the soul. Men like Saint-Exupéry, Malraux, Kessel, and Chamson, who have flown thousands of miles in modern airplanes and witnessed the power, first of German, then of American, machines to enslave or to liberate men, do not scoff at the machine as Duhamel and an earlier generation did with some complacency. It is futile and probably foolish to declaim against modern mass media, as it once was to indict the cinema or photography or modern newspapers, which once drove Baudelaire to an abortive or a simulated suicide attempt. The task confronting us, however, is to utilize mechanical help to the full while remaining aware of its limits. Beauty, mystery, and sentiment have not been expelled from our world by the machine. The thinking man need not be awed into silence and submission by mechanical civilization. 'The airplane is a machine, but what a tool for analysis!' wrote Saint-Exupéry.

Around 1930, Antoine de Saint-Exupéry, whom no early essays had yet revealed to critics, was suddenly hailed as a writer marked for glory. Success came to him overnight; literary prizes crowned a man of action, who had remained innocent of all literary strategy. Then, with a grave volume that had none of the features of the usual best-seller, Saint-Exupéry conquered the North American public. Soon, the readers of ten countries praised in that Frenchman a writer with a sumptuous gift of style, who lavished images as in a shower of stars and renovated the traditional novel; a man of action, who had lived his stories and, describing his adventures without bravado or egotism, had annexed to literature the virgin domain of men conquering aerial space; psychologist and a moralist eager to probe into the secret springs of action; a poet in prose whose restrained fervor sang a hymn to friendship, to the earth, to men.

He was born with the century, on June 29, 1900, in Lyons, the fourth of a family of five children. His name suggests the nobility of his family. It is said that one of the ancestors of the twentieth-century flier had fought in the American War of Independence and had been present at the siege of Yorktown and the surrender of Cornwallis.

Little is known about the private life of 'Saint-Ex,' as he was usually called by his friends, and the discreet reserve of this spiritual son of the French classicists must be respected. His books, however, are all colored by what Baudelaire has called 'the green paradise of childhood loves.' The life of the man was irradiated, at times saddened, by the nostalgic memory of too happy a childhood. Repeatedly, when stranded in the desert or surrounded by the fire of enemy bullets, the airman was to remember the wide park in which he used to play with his sisters, the wild games they would invent, and the Tyrolean governess Paula, who took such good care to protect them against 'adventure.' From that sheltered world, he emerged to enter the most audacious career open to modern man and to face the most extreme hazards of a deadly war.

But the child in him never died, with its tenacious loyalty to comrades in peril and its silent wonder at the big words and vain discussions in which grown-ups feel they must periodically indulge. Saint-Exupéry always preserved jealously the integrity of his dreams against the intrusion of bleak reality. During the darkest days of his vigil of arms in New York in 1941–42, the famous writer would spend hours toying with complicated mechanical gadgets or flying small paper airplanes of his own making over the strollers in Central Park. Of many a poet and artist of our times, the saying of William Wordsworth seems truer than ever: 'The child is father of the man.' The first novel of Saint-Exupéry, *Courrier-Sud (Southern Mail)*, announced already his nostalgic concern with childhood, which his last published work will triumphantly proclaim. 'You have integrated the course of the star, O generation of laboratories, and you no longer know it . . . Your knowledge does not measure up to that of a small child.'

Two main influences molded Saint-Exupéry's formative years: Catholicism and humanism, the two, of course, meeting at many points. After his very early years at St. Maurice de Remens, near Ambérieu, he was educated at the Jesuit College of Notre Dame de Sainte Croix, at Le Mans, then at Fribourg in Switzerland. The dogmas and the ritual of the Catholic Church were not to play an important part in his later life; while his sisters remained deeply pious, their brother seemed detached from all strict orthodoxy. In the most critical moments of his career as recorded in his books, his preoccupations were not with a future life but with man and his world. But the lasting effect of his Roman Catholic upbringing is felt in more elusive ways; he never sloughed off the habit of moral stocktaking and of searching confession acquired in childhood. The letters which have been published since his death, *Lettres de jeunesse, 1923–1931*, addressed to Renée de Saussine (1953) and *Lettres à sa mère* (1955) reveal a perennial adolescent, in need of friendship, of adventure, easily discouraged, prone to transfiguring all his experiences into poetry. What was left of religion in him was similar to the Renanian shrine of lovely and vague synonyms replacing a personal God. 'What matters it to me that God does not exist! God endows man with divinity,' he wrote in his *Notebooks*. And again: 'If I have lost the benefit of the religious explanation, I must at any rate transpose the values which it held, for they are necessary and fruitful.'

The study of the classics strengthened his concern with the analysis of inner life and his emphasis on man as the measure of all things. These classics were, in the French use of the term, both the ancients (a pregnant density, reminiscent of Latin, marks his sentences) and the French writers of the age of Louis XIV. To Montaigne, Pascal, La Rochefoucauld, and others 'moralists,' Saint-Exupéry owed in part his refusal to allow the lucidity of his vision to be blurred by the rationalization of perfidious wishes of the heart.

Saint-Exupéry's school years came to an end while World War I was raging. His vocation for literature apparently dawned early and he had, while still a child, dreamed of writing poetry. The first book that he loved passionately was Andersen's *Tales*, then, a little later, *Les Indes noires* by Jules Verne, whose subterranean wanderings may have lingered in his memory when he wrote *Vol de nuit* (*Night Flight*).[1] Balzac's *Père Goriot* then fascinated him. In 1915 he discovered Dostoevski; it was a revelation. 'I felt at once that I had entered into communication with something vast, and I proceeded to read everything he had written, one book after the other, as I had done with Balzac.' This in no way implies that Saint-Exupéry's gifts lay in the direction of the imaginative giants; to admire is not to imitate. More than a creator of plot and characters, the author of *Wind, Sand and Stars* was a sensitive prose poet. He related himself how he was seized in his teens by the adolescent's passion for poetry and learned by heart many lines from Baudelaire, Leconte de Lisle, Heredia, and Mallarmé. Among his immediate contemporaries, Rilke charmed him by his feminine delicacy and plasticity and by the intensity of his inner life. He also cherished Giraudoux, especially in his early works such as *Simon le pathétique*, steeped in gentle and humorous emotion.

The desire of the future flier was to enter the French Naval Academy.

1. Saint-Exupéry confessed it himself in an article he wrote for *Harper's Bazaar* in April 1941. He has generally been very discreet on the subject of his reading or of influences by other writers. Quotations are conspicuously absent from his works. Yet one influence at least, that of Gide, is clearly felt in his early writings. Reminiscences published by Saint-Exupéry's friends since his death have added little to our knowledge of the man of letters in him.

Pierre Loti, Claude Farrère, and Alain-Fournier had similarly been attracted by the sea and the long meditative leisure of ocean voyages, conducive to literary labor. But the irony of fate (or the legend) would have it that young Saint-Exupéry, who excelled in mathematics, failed the entrance examination to the Naval Academy because of incompetence in French composition! He then turned to architecture for a brief time, served his term of military service in Strasbourg after the peace of Versailles, and contemplated vaguely and unenthusiastically a business career.

But aviation was his true mistress. He had already taken a few flying lessons; he received his pilot's license in 1921; in 1926, he was accepted as a regular air-mail pilot on the Toulouse-Casablanca line. Those years were the heroic era of French aviation: the planes were often antiquated; machinery was scarce; radio communication was lacking or in its incipient stage; but flying attracted daring young men all the more.

Saint-Exupéry was no rebel against society, no voluntary exile contemptuously shaking the dust of Europe off his feet. He went back to Paris on his furloughs and enjoyed the delicacies of life, especially the choice meals in which the gastronomes of his native city proverbially indulged. He was fond of the company and the conversation of women and was said to display his charm most when engaged in the playful sport of flirting. But the most refined human comedy soon appears ludicrous to a man whose profession it is to risk death. For a year, Saint-Exupéry was placed in charge of the airport at Cape Juby, where airplanes made brief stops in their flight from Casablanca to Dakar. The country around, poetically called the Rio de Oro, was far from safe. Many of the natives took their theoretical allegiance to Spain more than nonchalantly; to them, a stranded airman was a valuable captive to be held for ransom. Saint-Exupéry learned how to deal with the natives, and undertook many missions, as diplomatic as they were bold, to rescue pilots grounded among dissident tribes. He loved the chivalrous code of those natives, their virile pride, their loyalty to their friends, and their capacity for solitude.

While on that assignment, Saint-Exupéry made the acquaintance of the already legendary figure of Mermoz. The men who worked with Mermoz all revered him as a real hero of our time; they admired his daring and his skill, his unfailing devotion to his team, his unselfish pursuit of tasks for higher than individual reward. His little book, *Mes Vols*, reads at times like a fragmentary epic. Another French writer and airman,

Joseph Kessel, wrote the story of his life. For ten years, Mermoz, who served in the same air line as Saint-Exupéry, the Latecoère company, stood at the vanguard of all aeronautic progress. He opened the air-mail service to Dakar, then across the South Atlantic, then from Brazil to Argentina and, most perilous of all, across the Andes. Paris and Buenos Aires had thus been linked by five-day airplane communication. Then, on December 7, 1936, Mermoz, who had defied death repeatedly, disappeared with his crew while on his twenty-fourth flight across the South Atlantic. Saint-Exupéry was to succeed him in the admiration of French youth until he, too, mysteriously disappeared on another flight of Icarus.

During his years at Cape Juby, Saint-Exupéry enjoyed for the first time the leisure necessary to literary creation. His first book, published in 1929, was entitled *Courrier-Sud*. It met with moderate success. *Vol de Nuit*, two years later, brought him wide fame. Many another flier might then have exchanged his life of hazards for the comfort of a promising literary career. But Saint-Exupéry chose to remain silent for eight long years, thus setting an example rarely followed by modern novelists. That silence enabled him to enrich his experience of life and to mature his talent. The famous writer retained his modest simplicity and his freshness. He flew planes across the Atlantic Ocean and the South American continent, and became a pioneer of mail flights south of Buenos Aires through the dreary solitude of Patagonia. He gained administrative experience as director of the station of Commodoro-Rivadavia, in southern Argentina. A reorganization of the French air lines, which reduced the number of pilots, occurred in 1933. Saint-Exupéry made way for younger men, took to journalism, and visited Russia and most of Europe and the Near East. Late in 1935, he started on a record nonstop flight from Paris to Indo-China, against adverse meteorological conditions. He had to make a forced landing in the Libyan desert, was stranded without food or water, and for several days was given up as dead. Bedouins dramatically rescued him and his mechanic when thirst had conquered their resistance. Once more the flier-writer took up his itinerant career. He was sent to Spain as a correspondent from the daily *Paris-Soir* when Madrid was heroically holding against the troops of Franco.

In 1938, for the second time, Saint-Exupéry had a narrow escape from death. He had reached New York in a monoplane, which he planned to fly all the way down the American continent to Patagonia. But when taking off from Guatemala, his plane crashed to the ground and he suffered serious injury to his shoulder. He was then warned that he should never again attempt parachuting, for the shock might prove too much for his bruised shoulder. He did not, however, give up his passion for flying, and he had a third accident that nearly cost him his life: he was almost drowned in the bay of Saint-Raphael, in southern France, when trying a new hydroplane. Meanwhile, *Terre des hommes* had made him the literary hero of the year 1939, crowned by the French Academy, adopted by all the book clubs. He again courted danger, first in piloting a heavy flying boat from France to New York, then in insisting, in spite of his forty years, upon taking part as an active flier in World War II. Once again, during the disastrous days of June 1940, he miraculously escaped death. He survived to write a grave tribute to his torn country and to his friends of the French air force who had fallen in the fight.

While a semblance of order was succeeding the disorderly turmoil in France of the summer of 1940, Saint-Exupéry, spurning the advances of the Vichy regime, decided to settle in New York until events took a turn for the better. He spent two tormented years there. It was clear that, while impatient to re-enter the fight against the Germans, Saint-Exupéry was not altogether in sympathy with some supporters of the Free French cause in America and retained a prejudice against General de Gaulle. Only much later, when he heard the leader of Fighting France deliver an impassioned speech to the Provisional Assembly in Algiers, in that terse and lofty language that has won for him a place among the soldier-writers of his country, did Saint-Exupéry acknowledge that his prejudice had been unfounded.[2]

In America, Saint-Exupéry worked silently, avoiding many of his countrymen, whose idle talk angered him. He had seen with his own eyes the tragic inequality of forces, which had doomed the French to German bondage in 1940; he resented the *émigrés* who argued that the defeat might have been averted by some last-minute palliative. He knew that America's entry into the war could ultimately liberate France from the German yoke. But the reluctance of many Americans to admit that the cause of oppressed Europe was also their cause, that freedom and democracy were everywhere endangered, caused him, until Pearl Harbor, to be grieved by the attitude of a country he deeply admired and loved.

Saint-Exupéry traveled little about the United States. He refused most invitations to lecture. But he was working hard with his pen all the while. He labored patiently, as he always did on his manuscripts, over *Pilote*

2. See the article by André Gide, who then saw much of Saint-Exupéry in Algiers, as reported in *France-Amérique* (New York), March 25, 1945.

de guerre (*Flight to Arras*); he was also keeping the record of his thoughts in a thick notebook, which has become *Citadelle* (*The Wisdom of the Sands*). He had other books in mind, concerning spiritual and moral problems. He avoided the polemics then rife among Frenchmen in foreign countries; his own record in the battle of 1940 had spoken eloquently for him. In November 1942, when the Americans landed in North Africa, he published an open letter to Frenchmen abroad, in *The New York Times*. 'Let us be infinitely modest,' he told them. 'We do not represent France; all we can do is to serve her . . . Men of France, let us be reconciled in order to serve.' Some saw in these words an excessive leniency to the Vichy regime and a preference for General Giraud against General de Gaulle. The philosopher Jacques Maritain took the philosophically minded aviator to task with some bitterness. But such divisions, however important at the time, have already been blurred by events. Saint-Exupéry was to serve his country in one supreme task. He asked to leave for North Africa; he took up active service in the reconstituted French Air Force and insisted upon flying in spite of his forty-three years, although he was implored to stay with the ground forces. The integrity of his intentions was soon proved by his actions and ennobled by his death.

Saint-Exupéry literary output is comparatively scant: four volumes, which one may call novels by stretching the word a little; a fairy tale, *Le Petit Prince* (1942), more revealing of its author than many a page written in the first person singular; a slim collection of reflective essays, *Lettre à un otage* (1943), and posthumous reflections. This restraint is only another mark of Saint-Exupéry's stark sincerity. He never indulged in writing merely to retain the attention of the public or because of tempting contacts offered by publishers. He patiently waited until he had matured inwardly what he had to say and had mastered the form that would say it most adequately. Saint-Exupéry's books are usually brief, almost to a fault; there is no redundance in them, few irrelevant digressions, no trace of superfluous fat, as it were. In his rare moments of confiding in his readers, he would compare himself to a diamond cutter or to a sculptor, chiseling away from the first drafts of his writings all extraneous substance; or, better still, to a baker kneading his dough over and over again until it developed enough resistance for him to fight successfully against its plastic matter. Indeed, his manuscripts showed whole pages crossed out after successive and pitiless revisions.

Southern Mail (translated under this title by Stuart Gilbert in 1933) was composed while the author was stationed at Cape Juby. He read it, seated on his camp bed in the sun-baked tent, to the man whose approval he most earnestly desired, Mermoz. The book enjoyed moderate success, and so did the film based on it. It is faulty in many respects and immature in technique. Saint-Exupéry is not skilled in inventing incident interwoven with character or in handling the traditional form of the novel. But the gifts of the author as a stylist, and his concern with discovering a deeper purpose to human life are already discernible. The hero, Bernis, an air-mail pilot stationed in the West African desert, is obviously a projection of the writer. His story is told in part through laconic radiograms of weather reports and of the progress of his flight, in part through his own confession woven into a novel. The interest of this early work is twofold. It sheds light on the life and moods of a pilot, away from civilization, alone with his machine and with the clouds, restraining his regrets and his dreams to bow to a self-imposed discipline and to the biddings of fate. But Bernis is also the one character in Saint-Exupéry's works for whom love might almost challenge 'military servitude.' During a leave spent in France, he has met a former childhood friend, Geneviève. The only woman who plays any part in Saint-Exupéry's books, she is delineated with delicacy and tenderness. To the flier, she embodies the golden years of his boyhood. But she is not happy. Her husband is ambitious, selfish, and without understanding. When their son dies, his brutal behavior drives her to leave him in a rage; she seeks refuge with Bernis. For a brief while they try to recapture the beauty of their adolescent dreams. They leave Paris together and drive to a provincial city. But, realizing the sordidness of a conventional liaison, they decide to master the force that had drawn them together. Their love, perhaps, is too weak; all love, perhaps, is weakness; childhood visions, embellished by rosy memories, cannot be relived. Bernis also understands the meaning of his vocation. A flier is no longer a man like other men. Geneviève belongs to another world in which comfort, security, and serenity are real things. How could he ever draw her into his world? In spite of the sentimental link between them, they are separated 'by a gulf of a thousand years.' Bernis returns to his flying in Africa. A few days later, his plane is lost and his body is found in the desert.

The originality of this early volume lies in its sketchy but subtle portrait of Geneviève, frail, illogical, unhappy, yet tied down to her worldly life. In Bernis's career of aviation and exploration, love sinks into relative insignificance. After his first two books, woman disappears from Saint-Exupéry's work. She remains in the background, as the precious symbol of that other world to which the flier returns after his inhuman challenge of the hurricanes. He will concentrate on what he knows best. The meaning of life as perceived by men of action thrown together on some common adventure will be to him a more fitting subject than any interpretation of feminine psychology.

Vol de nuit is artistically far superior to *Courrier-Sud,* more strongly welded, with a skillful fusion of moral reflections and of dramatic action that the author was never again to accomplish as felicitously. The slim volume, a *récit* more than a novel, enjoyed a surprising success on its appearance, in 1931. It was soon translated into ten languages. Strangely enough, the author who had, through his introspective stories, his very frank confessions of the least orthodox aspects of his life, and his prestige with youth, symbolized the literature of the postwar years, André Gide, was the first to point out the significance of Saint-Exupéry's book. He seemed ready to burn what he had once adored when he declared in his preface to *Vol de nuit:*

> Too well we know man's weaknesses, his inner surrender and his shames, and recent literature has been only too skillful in exposing them: our need is for authors to show us how the force of will can lift man above his own self . . . I am grateful to Saint-Exupéry for having illustrated this paradoxical truth, that man's happiness lies not in freedom, but in his acceptance of a duty.

There are only three characters in the short novel: two men and a woman. The pilot, Fabien, is engaged on night flights between Buenos Aires and Patagonia or the Andes. These flights are perilous but indispensable if the air lines are to compete with ships and trains. In these pioneer days of aviation, many of the pilots flying at night will never return, but, because of the risks they have taken, others may one day safely carry business letters and lovers' messages with greater speed. The pilot has been married only a few weeks. One morning, before dawn, a telephone message orders him on a flying mission. His young bride watches him sleep a few more minutes, answer the call to duty, which rings for him alone in the silent city, glance at the moonlit darkness, and don his helmet and his leather breastplates. Like a medieval knight leaving on a single fight, he then goes. Fabien, carrying the mail from Patagonia, is surrounded by a hurricane. He loses his way in the clouds. The fuel tank shows that his respite is decreasing from one hour to half an hour, to a supreme quarter of an hour. The radio stations on the ground hear him no longer. Soon he has disappeared, forever.

Fabien's wife appears only fleetingly in the drama. She has counted the hours since her husband took off, felt reassured when the moon shone in a clear sky, disturbed whenever the overcast sky brought an omen of storm. He should by now have safely arrived. She calls up the air line, receives elliptic answers mentioning unforeseen delay. She understands and utters only an 'Ah!' from her wounded flesh. Revolt is vain. She represents the absolute of love and individual happiness, opposed to that of duty and action. She bows to the mysterious law that bids men play havoc with humble affections, gentle memories, the soft light of a lamp on a table, and the comfort of family life.

But the chief character in the book is not the flier or his wife, and the true conflict is not that of love and duty. Saint-Exupéry has avoided such conventionality. Rivière is the hero. He is the director of the office of the air lines. His task is to impose discipline, to defend the regulations as if they were sacrosanct, to order pilots on the night flights. He appears harsh, but it is only in order to extract from men their latent energy and to raise them above self-pity. He kneads them as virgin wax and instills a will into them. His curt language superficially recalls that of a Nietzschean superman, ordering an inferior race ruthlessly and singing the paean of Zarathustra—'Let us be hard.' In truth, he is deeply human. He will not display his sympathy for others in order to win their love. Events have to be controlled by men, and men must be emboldened so that they will conquer events. Repeatedly, Rivière, meditating upon the loss of human lives, ponders: 'Is this worth the life of one man? Is anything worth the life of a young man, carefully nurtured, patiently educated, tenderly loved?' And he replies: 'Human life may be priceless, but we always behave as if there were something higher in value than human life . . . But what is it?' When Fabien's plane is overdue, a pin is removed from the map in the office; a card is withdrawn from a drawer. Death is a victory. Through the unending task accomplished by successive men, aviation will conquer the night. As Renan used to say, man is like the worker at the Gobelins tapestry, weaving from the reverse a design that he does not perceive.

Vol de nuit is, in its condensed form, worthy of a classical tragedy. The theme itself recalls the torch race of the Greeks, in which relay runners pass the torch to each other with the spirit in which men and women devote themselves to a higher purpose dimly understood. The tone is that of a tragic dialogue, chary of words, devoid of declamation. There are three characters, as in the early Aeschylean plays, and they meditate while they act. Their struggle is not against each other; it is rather a threefold combat. Men challenge the elements, while the radio stations on land, sending messages across the air, seem to play the part of the chorus witnessing the doomed human challenge to fate. Man has to face woman and the values that she opposes to duty, profession, and risk. Man fights chiefly against himself, for it is in Fabien's and Rivière's very hearts that tenderness, pity, and love have to be ultimately mastered.

After eight years spent in accumulating varied experience and meditating on it, Saint-Exupéry published *Terre des hommes*. The new volume was acclaimed instantaneously. It brought its author the coveted reward of the Grand Prix du Roman, bestowed yearly by the French Academy. In it, however, Saint-Exupéry made no pretense of retaining the form of the novel. Man in general concerns him more than individuals; and his creative gift is more suitable to the presentation of suggestive details chiseled into striking images than to the invention of an arbitrary plot.

Terre des hommes is indeed primarily the work of an expert in the artistry of style, but is is not overwritten, as elaborate French prose is apt to be. Saint-Exupéry occasionally indulges in a perilous fondness for rhetorical questions and invocations to departed friends, but he soon restrains these expansive emotional outbursts. He is usually remote from the joyful exuberance of Gide's early prose and from the excessive dryness that marks imitators of Stendhal, from the unnerved and pale style of Maurois, and from the rigid prolonged tension of Malraux. His sentences are brief; the words are the simplest possible, with hardly any technical expressions. The cadences of poetic prose are sedulously avoided. The flavor of the style comes from the splendor of its imagery contrasting with the sobriety of the general tone. Whirlwinds tearing across the Atlantic skies are transfigured into pillars of an awesome temple or grotto inhabited by giants. The moon often pours its lurid light over the stormy scenes described by the author, now dying in the sky like pallid embers, now playing with the fog and the clouds. The earth and the sky are often merged into one vast indistinct substance hostile to the rash flier. At times also, he rejoices among the stars, shimmering as in green water, glittering like hard diamonds, or shooting across the blue darkness in a mad gambol.

For the volume, composed of separate vignettes linked by a profound unity of meaning, is that of a cosmic poet. The adjective has been abused, but to few men does it belong by birthright as to Saint-Exupéry. Shelley, Hugo, and Rimbaud had dreamed of wild rounds of planets in fantastic skies or had lent a voice to the clouds and the moon. Saint-Exupéry has actually conversed with these divinities, has received from them now guidance, now treacherous delusion, and he humanizes them in the simplicity of his prose. But his true theme is not the firmament; it is the earth. And the first essential word in the title of his book, unfortunately omitted in the English version, is *Terre*.[3] The lakes of twinkling diamonds and the wild tornadoes rending the sky are but a setting for the only abode that really counts, the earth. The originality of this poet-airman is that he has, through his adventures in the air, rediscovered the earth.

The earth seen from above is not the familiar and orderly landscape to which we are accustomed. It is only a small archipelago, hemmed in by oceans; and on that narrow stretch of land, spanned in a few hours of flight, how many expanses of hostile sand, of uninhabitable mountains and glaciers! The airplane alone could reveal to us our globe as it is, by lifting us out of our well-tilled plains, fertile valleys, and winding highways. To the flier swooping down in search of his landing field, the thatched roof of a farmhouse, a shepherd girl grazing her lambs near some Andalusian village, or a little fort guarded by a sergeant and four soldiers in the African wild appear suddenly invested with a frail and moving beauty. If the earth appears frail seen from the skies, men should revere it all the more tenderly; and tenderness is indeed the note that best describes many of Saint-Exupéry's evocations. Among his perilous cosmic wanderings, the warm security of a soft bed and, in the morning, hot *croissants* and *café au lait* appears as goods of unattainable, haunting value, which will again link the knight of the air to plain but dear realities: the flour and the wheat field recalled by the *croissants*, the cows that produced the milk and the butter, the poetry of the earth that is never dead.

Such was Saint-Exupéry's discovery, which renovated the literature of aviation. The miracle of the airplane, he writes, is that 'it plunges man straight into the heart of the mystery.' It even reveals mystery where man

3. Lewis Galantière has revealed, in a very interesting article in *The Atlantic Monthly* (April 1947), that Saint-Exupéry himself had chosen *Du vent, du sable, des étoiles* as the title of his manuscript, then changed his mind in the French edition so as to avoid appearing romantic or too literary.

had heretofore failed to perceive it. For years, loud innovators had proclaimed the advent of the machine age in literature; they had baptised 'futurism' a childish rendering of mechanical objects through broken-up phrases and juggled alliterations. They had encumbered their writings with blast furnaces and electric wires, worshipped dynamos and airplanes. Or else they had been intoxicated with the power that men draw from their illusory mastery over machines and, like an Italian flier bearing a famous name, they sang the rapturous joy of bombing defenseless Ethiopian villages. Saint-Exupéry is true to the traditions of his people in considering the machine as a tool, beautiful because of the materials of which it is built and because it attains the purity of a stripped body and a perfect simplicity of outline, as well as an exquisite fitness to its purpose. But, as he declares at the conclusion of his book:

> The airplane is a means, not an end. One does not risk one's life for an airplane any more than the peasant plows for the sake of his plow. But, through the airplane, one leaves cities and their accountants and recovers a peasant reality. One accomplishes a man's work and knows man's cares. One enters into contact with the wind, the stars, the night, the sand, the sea . . . one envisions the airport as a land of promise and questions the stars for one's truth.

Terre was the first essential word in the title of the book; *Hommes,* also omitted from the traitorous English title, is the second. And the true leitmotiv of the book is indeed men, in the plural. Through flying, charting new lands on his frail globe, and spanning boundless oceans, man makes one gain only: he is given the means of knowing himself more deeply. The ghost of Pascal haunts the reflections of the twentieth-century aviator. For man is weaker than a reed when tossed about by the winds, lost in the fog, stranded on a peak in the Andes, reduced to licking a few drops of dew on the wing of an airplane in the parched Libyan desert. His courage then rises to radiant summits.

Saint-Exupéry does not prize physical courage very highly; most men will develop it under the stress of circumstances and will endure what had seemed insufferable. The trite motto 'live dangerously' has more appeal to sickly philosophers muffled in their dressing gowns amid books than to true men of action. Saint-Exupéry despises the risk that gamblers with their lives incur for the mere thrill of it. Intense living is to him only a means of penetrating more deeply into the secrets of the universe and of developing a keener consciousness of our duties and potentialities as men. And, in man, reasoning counts little and seldom grasps the essentials. Logic too often remains a shell of ponderous words with which we disguise the real truth about ourselves and our living contradictions. Our truth is what fosters in us a grave sense of inward fulfillment, liberates us from the trivialities of life, and endows our smallest acts with a meaningful virtue. 'Spirit alone, blowing over the loam, creates man.'

Action enables man to know himself better and to define his conscious purpose in this life. It also brings men together. *Terre des hommes* and, indeed, every work of Saint-Exupéry, is in its essence a hymn to friendship. Flying over oceans, imprisoned in a solitary airport in Africa, sharing thirst, hunger, and extreme fatigue when thrown by a forced landing into a ravine that may be their grave, two or three men, stripped of every earthly good and almost of every hope, relish the treasure of true comradeship. Then they know and understand each other without effort. There is dignity and loyalty in their relation, unreserved mutual devotion, tolerance and even admiration for their differences, and an exaltation that comes from pursuing a common purpose together. The machine has helped create such friendship, as have sports and wars. Love dwindles to a selfish and anarchic or disturbing force when compared with the cool, restrained friendship enjoyed in the midst of ordeals; men will often yearn for friendship when rivalries, ambitions, the selfish exigencies of family life again draw them apart. The concluding pages of *Terres des hommes* sing the unique and well-nigh mystical joy of men who, freed in their perilous career from all the false values of life, suddenly become alien to hatreds, jealousies, and desires, and reach the true fraternity of co-operating, with body and soul, in a disinterested effort. 'When joined to our brothers by a common purpose which is placed outside ourselves, then only do we breathe and understand that to love is not to gaze into each other's eyes, but to look together in the same direction.' National rivalries and wars appear senseless at such moments. For if war does provide these grave and loyal comradeships, other experiences can create them at lesser cost.

'War deceives us. Hatred adds nothing to the exaltation of the race that we run. Why hate each other? We are all in the same solidarity, carried away by the same planet, as crew of the same ship. It is good indeed for civilization to compete in order to bring about new syntheses, but it is monstrous for them to devour each other.' Thus, a few months before World War II unleashed its orgy of destruction from the air, ran the message of one of the noblest fliers France had yet produced,[4] and the most thoughtful of them all, in a book hailed by a critic in *La Revue Hebdomadaire* as 'The Song of Roland' of our modern age.

Saint-Exupéry, who happened to be in New York in the spring of 1939, sensed that a war was inevitable and hurried back to France in time. He was soon attached to a reconnaissance squadron, one of the few in the French army. To his experiences in the fateful days when the whole of his country seemed to be disintegrating under the impact of the German Panzer divisions, we owe the finest prose work that World War II seems as yet to have produced. It appeared in French in New York in 1942 as *Pilote de guerre*[5] and in English as *Flight to Arras*.

It is not a conventional war book. The circumstances in which Saint-Exupéry wrote it were the most tragic in which his country, and perhaps mankind, had ever lived: in 1940–41, Russia and the United States had not yet been thrown into the conflict and a German victory seemed a dreaded possibility to all but a few dauntless optimists. The author, miraculously safe after a fierce though unequal fight, resented the lack of understanding with which many then spoke of the collapse of France and of her too-easy acceptance of her humiliation; a note of bitter impatience before much idle talk creeps at times into the volume.

But *Pilote de guerre* is primarily the objective record of a mission and the exposition of the author's philosophy. Few books are more stripped of all superfluous details. The classical principles of economy of means and of understatement have seldom been more strictly observed: no

4. There is only one other book that we would rank high among the works inspired by aviation: the moving autobiography of a British flier who met death in World War II, after having endured ghastly ordeals, *Falling through Space* (Reynal and Hitchcock, 1942), by Richard Hillary. (*The Last Enemy*, Macmillan & Co., London, 1943, was the title in the English edition.) Its artless charm and winning humor stand in contrast to Saint-Exupéry's gravity and studied artistry. In French, Jules Roy wrote a fine volume, *La Vallée heureuse* (Charlot, 1945), on the bombing of the Ruhr in which he took part; another pilot of the R.A.F., Pierre Clostermann, like Jules Roy an ardent admirer of Saint-Exupéry, has written *Le Grand Cirque* (Gallimard, 1948; *The Big Show*, Random House, New York, 1951), a fresh and unpretentious account of his airman's experiences, and *Feux du ciel* (1951), a more technical volume.

5. It was reprinted in French in Paris after the liberation. The Germans, having allowed it to circulate freely in France, banished it on the denunciation of a French collaborationist writing in *Je suis partout*, who pointed out to the master race that the book praised a Jewish aviator, Israel. Captain Israel was in fact one of the members of Saint-Exupéry's outfit in 1940; his name was not invented.

grandiloquence, no stylized imagery, not the faintest trace of pose. On one of the last days of May 1940, six reconnaissance groups out of twenty-three are left in the unit to which Captain de Saint-Exupéry belongs. The first phase of the war is already hopelessly lost for the French. German fighter planes outnumber them ten to one; and any information that French reconnaissance could bring back is clearly of no avail. The enemy himself does not conceal his position, while the French staff is disorganized, its telephone transmission cut off, and its orders delayed and inapplicable. But the cruel game of war has to be acted to the last: as glassfuls of water are poured over a huge forest fire, French crews are being ordered out one by one and, stoically, they fulfill their mission.

Saint-Exupéry's turn has come. He and his friends are stationed in a schoolhouse, among desks, maps and blackboards. A door is flung open now and then; an order is shouted, which calls for a crew to take to flight. The chances are exactly two to one against their returning alive. At night, at the officer's mess a laconic remark will be uttered: 'Tiens! so and so is not back at the base'; an oppressive silence will follow for a minute, and that will be all. The reconnaissance plane of Saint-Exupéry is given the mission to observe the enemy deployments over Arras; to do it, he must fly over the German lines, over roads clogged with refugees fleeing from the dive bombers, and face several barrages from German fighter planes enjoying unchallenged mastery of the air. Repeatedly, the fliers' lives seem to hang by a thread. The pilot's controls freeze when he has to climb to thirty-three thousand feet to escape enemy fighters; he drops to twenty thousand feet to watch Arras in flames. Bullets pierce his fuel tank, hit his wings; he runs the gauntlet of intense flak, goes up again, baffles his pursuers by losing himself in the setting sun, and miraculously returns to his base, where he has already been given up as lost. Within a few hours, packed with intense living and ardent thought, he has gone through the acts of a fierce tragedy, challenged fate and death, and accumulated enough reflections for him to ponder over for years.

The tragedy is not a merely personal one, however. The action of the book (a meditative action, for the author is all along a Hamlet, who welcomes action as a road to clearer self-knowledge) takes place on several levels. He returns alive, but with no exhilaration. For he has witnessed the defeat and misery of his country. From the air, he has seen the roads of France clogged with refugees fleeing toward an unknown fate, blindly obeying orders that bid them evacuate their villages, starve by the roadside, be shelled by German planes. The picture of that population fleeing in panic, mixing with the remnants of a broken army, driving in pitiful old cars, which soon will run short of gasoline and will be abandoned along the road as scrap iron, is sketched in lamentable and vivid colors. Babies are born in ditches, others vainly cry for milk, grandmothers perished exhausted. The whole of France is like a huge anthill kicked open, the ants swarming aimlessly. Yet no complaint is heard; it is war, and although the sacrifice is apparently useless and illogical, it has to be.

It would have been out of place for Saint-Exupéry to weave artistry out of such human misery. Once or twice he catches himself coining a precious image while pursued by the enemy fighters, imagining the wake of gossamers left behind his machine, and eluding his pursuers by skillful turnings, like a pretty lady proudly holding the train of her dress, spotted with stars of ice, and suddenly eluding her suitors. But he is the first to smile at his own far-fetched fancy. The poetry of *Pilote de guerre* is never super-added; it is harmoniously integrated with the book. It calls up idyllic memories of childhood, which contrast with the terrifying present, the joy of hearing a fire crackling in the hearth before jumping out of bed on an icy morning, the fighter planes around him like 'a people of jugglers throwing their missiles,' and the trajectory of the bullets is like a slender needle or a stalk of wheat.

> The German on the ground knows us by the pearly white scarf which every plane, flying at high altitude, trails behind like a bridal veil. The disturbance created by our meteoric flight crystallizes the watery vapor in the atmosphere. We unwind behind us a cirrus of icicles . . . our wake will thicken bit by bit and become an evening cloud over the countryside. The fighters are guided towards us by the ostentatious luxury of our white scarf. Nevertheless, we swim in an almost interplanetary emptiness.

Such is, in Lewis Galantière's very sensitive translation, a sample of the poetry woven by the flier out of peril and death, a moment's relief amid terror and pity. But *Flight to Arras* taken as a whole is not a serene work of art on the misfortunes of war. It is a book written in the throes of defeat by a Frenchman who fully accepted responsibility for his country's mistakes took pride in her moral greatness asserted in the midst of chaos, and tried to rise above national considerations to the formulation of a faith valid for all men. There is not one word of hatred in these

pages, composed while the Germans were plundering the land of France
and killing innocent hostages; not one boastful sentence, such as a soldier
who had risked his life might utter against those who stayed at home or
emigrated abroad and wrote books and articles on what should have
been done. Defeated army generals were then in Vichy bestowing
medals upon each other and laying the blame for the defeat on politicians; politicians were throwing the burden on their predecessors or on
the institutions of the Third Republic. Foreign observers, disappointed
by the debacle of the French army, which should have served as their
shield against the German menace, coldly sat back to remark that sacrifices had been too scant, that not enough bridges had been blown up,
not enough cities offered to destruction.

Saint-Exupéry's answers unite humility with nobleness. While flying
to and from Arras amid the tracer bullets, watching villages burn and
civilians shelled, he meditates on his country's right and wrong. Much,
to be sure, was wrong with France. But she had played her part and was
then helpless. She could not possibly have won in 1940 and she knew it;
she went to war against logic, and lost. In so doing, she was a victim,
and it was hardly fair of the outside world to look upon her as sinning
rather than sinned against. By her readiness for sacrifice she should be
judged. Because she plunged headlong into disaster, she did not betray
the conscience or the confidence of the world. For the final assault to be
successful, many a victim must first fall in the vanguard. The defeat of
France, fatal as it was, was made worse by incompetence and laxity.
But no Frenchman can disown responsibility for it; to his country and to
the whole world, he is bound by solidarity. 'Each is responsible for all.
Now for the first time I understand one of the mysteries of religion, from
which originated the civilization which I claim as mine. "Bear ye one
another's burdens." Each of us bears the burden of all men.'

But in that very defeat lie the seeds of rebirth and of spiritual victory.
Frenchmen, suffering together, discovered a new meaning to brotherly
communion, to charity, to love. When the evil consequences of starvation
and humiliation have been obliterated, Europe may well discover that
the lessons of the war have not been learned in vain. There was little
good to hope for in the world of 1933–38, and stagnation and fear
might still be ruling if, by some series of 'Munichs,' the war had been
averted. Russia in 1917 and Germany in 1918 had seemed even more
prostrate than France in 1940. They rose again. A defeat, or a victory, is
what we make it. 'One victory exalts, another corrupts. One defeat kills,

another brings life. Tell me what seed is lodged in your victory or your defeat, and I will tell you its future.'

Through this message of indomitable hope in his country's future, Saint-Exupéry rises to a broader lesson, addressed to all men. He is no professional philosopher, and he is no virtuoso player with abstractions. But his manifesto, diffuse and wordy at times, groping toward an approximation of his own truth, is a generous statement of faith; it rises to a strange greatness without being novel or profound, for it is the creed of a man of action who, while ready to give his life for a higher cause, discovers the meaning of the great struggle. Logic and intelligence are by themselves of little avail. Our key words—democracy, culture, religion—have gradually become emptied of their substance. We must imbue them again with fervor; each must strike new roots in a soil of reality. And the chief reality is that we are all bound together; we participate and commune, and, in Coleridge's words, 'we receive but what we give.'

But, 'in my civilization, he who differs from me, far from impoverishing me, enriches me.' The uniformity of spirits and their consequent leveling down are to be sedulously avoided. Differences bring us a truer gain; minorities, instead of being suppressed or even artificially assimilated, must be harmoniously fused so that they will retain some of their original essence while contributing to a larger whole. Men are equal in the dignity due to all of them, and political and social organization should help correct the natural inequalities that separate them. But equality in not identity. And equality, like liberty, should be conscious of a higher purpose, and enable men to reach, all together, new heights. The goal is not a collective deity that crushes men; it is rather the cult of Man, superior to isolated individuals. Charity and humility, generosity and self-devotion are revered virtues in the humanism propounded by Saint-Exupéry, which unites the best of the Christian teaching, transposed into lay formulas, with the best of ancient pagan wisdom, and endows with renovated meanings the most beautiful word ever coined by man—'fraternity.'

Such is the conclusion of this war volume in which a pilot in a defeated army, obsessed at first by the magnitude of his defeat, gradually vanquishes it in his soul, draws upon his deepest spiritual sources, and recovers his own center by redefining his reasons for living. He does not offer a doctrine, but forges new links between himself and other men. He has demonstrated nothing. His teaching retains no trace of sophistry; it eschews the much-vaunted French clarity; it proceeds slowly, at times confusedly. But it is worthy of the man who has lived it, fought for it; it fulfills the saying of the Spanish thinker of our day who defined true culture as lying not in the accumulation of knowledge or in the weaving of consistent reasonings, but in 'feeling more and more intensely a small number of mysteries.'

Le Petit Prince, published simultaneously in French and English in 1943, is a fairy tale of infinite charm, in which gentle satire of the dullness of grown-ups, of the pomposity of scientists, and of the aimless feverishness of businessmen is delicately blended with poetical evocations of the African desert and of cosmic wanderings among planets and stars. It illustrates the truth of Baudelaire's celebrated definition of genius as 'childhood recovered at will.' The Little Prince, whose fancy roams in interstellar spaces, also asks a few questions, intensely grave as children's questions can be. It incarnates Saint-Exupéry's passionate regret for the fervent faith of a child and his imaginative freedom, unspoiled by the hypocritical calculations of adults. The tale is written with a purity of outline and a terse simplicity of dialogue that recall the exquisite blending of reasonableness and supernaturalism that marks the seventeenth-century French fairy tales of Perrault. It makes no concessions to absurdity or cheapness of effect, as too many of our writings and films for children, unsuccessful imitations of *Alice in Wonderland* or of Walt Disney, are inclined to do. Its simple dialogue between a flier impatient with the evils of the world and a terse unsmiling child clinging to his dreams receives a tragic significance when read as the author's farewell to this gross earth over which millions of young men were then shedding their blood, their sweat, and their tears.

Saint-Exupéry published another little book in the year 1943: a slender collection of personal reminiscences and reflections, dedicated to a friend who had remained in France, one of the millions of 'hostages' before whom the flier, safe in America, bowed in humility; for they could only suffer in silence and wait for the long-wished-for dawn of their liberation. In his *Lettre à un otage,* Saint-Exupéry reiterated his philosophical message; its key words were 'weight' and 'substance,' designating the chief virtues that any man's thought must possess if it is not to lose itself in airy nothings; then 'friendship' and 'joy,' the latter to be experienced not in the conventional pleasures of social intercourse, not even in the ecstasies of mutual love, but in the rare moments of life when a man feels, through a smile or a radiant look, that he has forged bonds with another man.

Saint-Exupéry had had little opportunity to meditate on social and political problems. The discipline of the life of airmen waives many issues with which the civilian and the politician have to cope. But gradually his thought faced the complexities created by free men colliding against each other with their ambitions and their jealousies. He denounced the source of all that was most nefarious in fascism as contempt for man. Conversely, he reasserted that the prerequisite for democracy is respect for man.

Modern man must borrow from religions their keystone, sacrifice, and, endowing the word with a lay and humanized significance, recover respect for that free gift that, demanding nothing in return, kneads and molds the giver and makes him a man among men. A shortsighted psychology may lead many of our contemporaries to believe that the world, in its revolutions and its wars, is led by interest in the guise of 'economic causes.' A man who had, with few scruples, led many men through many wars, Napoleon himself, knew better when he admitted: 'Interest is the key to vulgar actions alone.' Saint-Exupéry, in his turn, in the very last message he sent to his American friends, formulated his creed as follows:

> Whatever I was paid for my work at the rate of a pilot's pay was never important . . . My work, even while it furnished me food and shelter, would have been of no value whatever if it had not made me one *of* something—pilot *of* the line, gardener *of* the garden, builder *of* the cathedral, soldier *of* France. The airline laid out by us, who were its first pilots, enriched us by virtue of the gifts it forced us to make—the line was born of our gifts. Once it was born, it bore us, made us men. Two weeks ago one of my fellow pilots of that line turned up in New York. 'Do you remember . . .' we said to each other. And we discovered that those had been marvelous years; for, having been woven together out of the common strands of our gifts, we were fellows, and we loved one another.

On July 31, 1944, Saint-Exupéry left Bastia, in Corsica, for a flight over Savoy. His plane mysteriously disappeared. His wife [6] and his friends hoped against hope that a miracle would once again save him. They waited. The war ended some months later. The flier was not among those who returned from prison camps. He had clearly met with the kind of death he had courted so often and would have chosen for himself if, as

6. Consuela de Saint-Exupéry, who is of Central-American origin, published a light and pleasant volume relating her life in France during the early months of German occupation, *Oppède* (Brentano's, New York, 1945), for which her husband was to have written a preface.

was Rilke's constant dream, men could elect the mode of dying most fitting to what their life had been. But his name lives on. He will not rank among the giants of the French novel; he has not made any new discoveries in man's psychological secrets or created a new style of writing. But he ranks high among those moralists who are to this day one of the most valuable contributions of France to world literature. Not only as a pioneer who has annexed the virgin domain of aviation to letters, but as a thoughtful writer who formulated anew, with force and beauty, some of the baffling problems facing man, he has won an enduring place among the champions of the true civilization, that of the soul.[7]

Bibliographical Notes

Much has been written on Saint-Exupéry, both in his lifetime (laudatory prefaces or articles by Benjamin Crémieux, André Gide, Jean Prévost) and since his death. *Citadelle* alone brought forth reservations on the part of critics and, except for a virulent attack, in poor taste, by Jean Cau, when a text of Saint-Exupéry was proposed for comment to the French baccalaureate candidates in July 1962, almost all the critical literature on him has been favorable. In August 1965, it was decided that an inscription would be engraved in the Pantheon in his memory. All he wrote has been published in English translation, and in a number of other languages.

Among the useful articles and volumes are: Daniel Anet, *Saint-Exupéry*. Corrêa, 1947; R. M. Albérès, *Saint-Exupéry*. La Nouvelle Edition, 1947; Louis Barjon, 'L'homme qui conquiert sa vérite,' *Etudes*, No. 244, February 1945, 145–166; Roger Caillois, introduction to the Pléiade volume, 1954; Pierre Chevrier, *Saint-Exupéry*. Gallimard, 1950; Maria de Crisenoy, *Saint-Exupéry, poète et aviateur*. Spes, 1948; André Devaux, 'Les grandes leçons du *Petit Prince*,' *Synthèses*, IX, July–August 1954, 83–93; Luc Estang, *Saint-Exupéry par lui-même*. Seuil, 1956; Antoine Fongaro, 'Saint-Exupéry, poète fourvoyé,' *Cahiers du Sud*, No. 336, August 1956, 270–288; Carlo François, *L'Esthétique de Saint-Exupéry*. Neuchatel: Delachaux, 1957; Jean Hugnet, *Saint-Exupéry ou l'enseignement du désert*. La Colombe, 1956; Jean-Claude Ibert, *Saint-Exupéry*. Editions universitaires, 1953; Marcel Migeo, *Saint-Exupéry*. London: Macdonald, 1961; Jules Roy, *Passion et Mort de Saint-Exupéry*. Julliard, 1951; Richard Rumbold and Lady Margaret Stewart,

---

7. *Citadelle* (Gallimard, 1948, *The Wisdom of the Sands*), a bulky collection of oracular utterances, grave maxims, mystical aphorisms, and meditations on man, is much admired by some followers of Saint-Exupéry; to others, with whom we align ourselves, it was a disappointing publication of a sadly unfinished work. In any case, it is a long series of allegories and parables, which occasionally elucidates Saint-Exupéry's thought but is of little concern to our point of view here, that of an interpreter of Saint-Exupéry's novels.

The Winged Life. London: Weidenfeld and Nicolson, 1954, and New York: David McKay, 1955; Maxwell A. Smith, *Knight of the Air*. London: Cassells, 1959, and New York: Pageant Press, 1956, and his article on *Citadelle*, *The French Review*, XXV, 1, October 1951, 16–22; Philip A. Wadsworth, 'Saint-Exupéry, Artist and Humanist,' *Modern Language Quarterly*, XII, No. 1, March 1951, 96–1–7; Léon Wencélius, on *Citadelle*, *Modern Language Notes*, LXVI, No. 5, May 1951, 289–295.

VII

Three Controversial Novelists: Bernanos, Céline, and Green

'One must hate,' was one of the battle cries oft repeated by that strange socialist and Catholic Charles Péguy, killed at the battle of the Marne in 1914 and revered as a saint by many Frenchmen during the Second World War and since. Throughout his pamphlets and his disorganized and repetitious philosophical essays, Péguy never wearied of asserting that he who allows an injustice or a crime to be committed is more contemptible than the one who has the courage to commit it, for he is an accomplice, and a coward to boot. 'A great philosophy,' he added at the end of his life (when he did not separate Bergson from Descartes in his enthusiasm), 'is not that which is never beaten. But a little philosophy is that which does not fight.' There have been among the Catholics of France some Franciscans, or spiritual brothers of St. François de Sales, meek and patiently ready to offer the other cheek. But the majority of the Catholics who were writers, or who set out to Christianize other lands and, today, the working classes, have been hardy and militant believers. Their sorrow was relieved by anger. Invectives and vituperations have been their daily fare. Léon Bloy is their patron saint. Bernanos is the novelist of this century whom they revere. To a number of Frenchmen, he appears as the French Dostoevski, tense, chaotic, prophetic, crudely injust, but a powerful visionary. Others are more impressed by all that in him is excessive, false, rhetorical, and inconsistent. Our conviction is that not more than one or two of his novels will be assured of survival. But, if he may ultimately fail to be among the great, no volume on the novelists of contemporary France could be deemed adequate that altogether ignores him.

He was born in Paris on February 20, 1888, but no Frenchman was ever less Parisian, if being Parisian implies refinement of manners, cynical irony, wit and humor, and the refusal to be taken in by any enthusiasm. His spiritual home and the setting of his best stories were in the lugubrious plains of northern France, amid a few arrogant rich isolated in their chateaux and by their greed, together with cattle-dealers, miners, and farmers. He was educated in the Jesuit college of the Rue de Vaugirard, but he absorbed little of their much vaunted, sometimes much indicted, sense for casuistry and compromise. It is said that there were Spaniards among his ancestors and even Lorraine relatives of Joan of Arc, as well as corsairs who had settled for a time in San Domingo and returned to France in 1787. Like Dreiser and George Moore before him, he was entranced and hallucinated in his youth by the reading of Balzac. He took degrees in letters and in law, was plunged into the adventure of the 1914 war first as a dragoon, then as one of Duhamel's and Giono's anonymous martyrs who dwelt in heroism, squalor, and fear in the trenches. He sold insurance after his return, in eastern France, sided with the Monarchist party whose paper, L'Action française, reveled in vituperation and invective. Disgust with the bourgeoisie and with the war-weary veterans' desire for return to normalcy incited him to write. In 1926 his strange novel in which the supernatural and Satan made a boisterous entry into a literature of analytical and introspective psychology, Sous le soleil de Satan (Under the Sun of Satan), aroused applause in many quarters and was singled out for the annual prize of the French Academy.

The protagonist, Father Donissan, is a weird, self-martyrizing ascetic, who sees Satan lurking everywhere around him. He exorcizes a hysterical girl, Mouchette, then tries to bring her back to life with the Devil's complicity. Like the monk in Anatole France's Thaïs, he is visited by images, not of animals, but of men. Other temptations threaten him: of the undermining conviction of his own unworthiness as a priest, who might clumsily ruin souls instead of saving them, and of despair at his own inadequacy. He has vainly attempted to save Mouchette, the fierce, stubborn girl who at sixteen had become pregnant by a selfish marquis, and who had killed a deputy who was her other lover because he planned to forsake her. Instead of saving her, the priest drove her to suicide. Her mother became insane. The end of this wilfully disconcerting novel is a heavy handed assault against Bernanos's *bête noire,* Anatole France. 'My choice was between trying to convince or to seduce. I chose to convince and not to please,' wrote the novelist apropos of his first novel. He does not succeed altogether, but some scenes are unforgettable.

L'Imposture, his second novel (1928), is even stranger. Again, a priest is the arena of conflict in which Satan deals the strongest blows. A few scenes here and there are vivid and intense hallucinations. The poor whom the abbé Cénabre encounters and the abbé himself are the only characters endowed with any life. Their behavior defies all verisimilitude. When Bernanos imposes his visionary creatures upon us for a fleeting moment, he can achieve full suspension of disbelief. Often however, he fails and the novelist in him then yields to an overeloquent, wrathful pamphleteer. *La Joie,* in 1929, treats another stage on the road to saintliness. The character thus blessed with aspirations to holiness, or with the will thereto, is no longer a priest, but a woman, Chantal de Clergerie. Her father is a wretched and worldly Catholic writer, mentally half sick; her grandmother is frankly insane. The girl is disarmingly naïve and defenseless, like Dostoevski's *Idiot,* who must have been Bernanos's favorite character among the Russian novelist's creations. Her purity works havoc in the household. Her father, aghast at having such a scandalously innocent daughter, consults a psychiatrist, who, like all those who attempt to guide themselves according to intellectual standards, is the butt of Bernanos's sarcasms. Chantal experiences a fit of ecstasy which is powerfully conveyed in the lyrical prose of the author. She has visionary glimpses of Judas and of the tree on which he hanged himself. She is then, inexplicably, murdered by the Russian chauffeur of the family, who himself commits suicide near her (there is a recurrence of suicides in Bernanosian fiction). A recreant priest who had talked with Chantal is brought back to faith by that death. The few scenes of rare power fail to redeem the novel from its cascade of unbelievable incidents and ludicrous buffoonery.

After several ventures in polemical literature, which was more and more to be the vehicle for his indignation, Bernanos wrote in 1934 the first draft, entitled originally 'The Dead Parish,' of the novel which he was to publish at last in 1946 as *Monsieur Ouine* (*The Open Mind*). No other work by him arouses such a clash of opinions: some critics, among whom is Albert Béguin, a Swiss who became an ardent convert to Catholicism, rate it as the masterpiece of the author and a masterpiece of modern French fiction. Others, with whom this writer chooses to concur, are dismayed by the mixture of melodrama and of polemics in a story with one or two murders, insanity, two suicides, a scene of lynching, endless tirades by the language teacher M. Ouine, who revels in indecision, always saying 'oui' and 'non,' and balks at clear involvement. The satire is directed at Gide, the perverter of the youth, the sower of 'those dark, ferocious forces which the charming little dilettanti issued from Gide's pocket caress in impunity with their dainty fingers.' The unconvincing and corrupting teacher is made to recognize his worthlessness before he dies.

The *Journal d'un Curé de Campagne* (1936), which as a splendid French film has been popular in a dozen countries, is, in our eyes, Bernanos's one undoubted great novel. The nameless, awkward, sickly hero officiates as a country priest in a village in northern France. The country people are materialistic, wily, and suspicious of this priest who is devoid of all glamor: his parents were poor farm laborers, who transmitted to him an alcoholic heredity; he is tormented by a stomach cancer, made worse by lack of care, bad food, cheap, sour wine, and poverty. He does not preach, he seldom prays, he confesses to his diary, and, on the eve of his gloomy death, he takes refuge at a friend's from seminary days, an unfrocked priest living with a woman, who gives him absolution. The other members of the Church distrust and scorn him: they sense in him a mystic, a rebel against the Catholic hierarchy and tradition, a foe to prudence and to the reasonable wisdom perhaps inevitable in clerics who are also administrators. He himself has harsh words for the stupidity of clerics, 'even more irritating than feminine stupidity, from which it sometimes seems to sprout.'

The daughter of the haughty nobleman who lives in the castle near by, Chantal, has discovered that her father, whom she worshipped, is making love to her private schoolmistress. His wife is aware of it; but, ever since her little boy died, she has rebelled bitterly against God. She hates her daughter, who is obdurate, sly, and tempted by suicide. The priest engages in a duel of pride against the countess; he succeeds in humbling her arrogance and in persuading her to repent as the only way for her to be reunited with her dead son in another world. He wins, she confesses, and she dies during the following night. The country priest, more than ever suspect to the count and to the villagers, perishes soon after. Desperately alone, weak and weary, he has at least refused all compromise and remained true to his vocation: to answer the call which bids a priest give all of himself to those whom he must save and manifest to others a little of that presence of the divine which may illuminate their otherwise sordid lives.

The narrative is monotonous and moves slowly. It resorts to no surprise, no accumulation of incidents, no variety or affluence of characters. But rarely has human aloneness been conveyed more forcefully than in that lugubrious diary. The fight between two prides, that of the countess and that of the man doomed to holiness, is dramatically rendered. So is the despair of the daughter, one of those creatures whom Bernanos loves, but who is hunted, possessed by a devilish presence, engulfed in darkness, yet athirst for purity. Like Mauriac, Bernanos denounces two enemies relentlessly: sex or concupiscence, the mask of pleasure which is so close to that of anguish, and 'le ramollissement du cœur,' the insipid softening of our selves which is even more lamentable than vice; the latter, at least, may occasionally 'storm the kingdom of heaven' promised, in St. Matthew, to the violent ones. From the apathy of a timid Pharisee's heart nothing may be expected.

The last published fictional work of Bernanos is Les Dialogues des Carmélites (The Fearless Heart in the strange title of the inadequate English translation of 1952). It is not a novel, but a play, the idea of which was borrowed from the German writer Gertrude von der Fort. The protagonist, Blanche, an aristocratic lady with the indomitable soul of a Joan of Arc, the prioress of a Carmelite convent in Compiègne during the days of the Terror, does not lack courage and spiritual energy; but she fears the pride which can contaminate the search for spiritual integrity. She also frantically dreads fear itself, to which she knows she might fall prey, as Bernanos as a child used to be seized with fear of death. She is heartened by the thought of the Mother Superior, dying on the scaffold with her fifteen nuns at the end of the Terror, not immune to fear but aware of the need for martyrs in tragic times and rejoicing in the sacrifice of the innocents as the one compensation for the crimes of the unjust. Martyrdom and saintliness alone can bring about the redemption of lost souls. Bernanos himself throughout his life was, half consciously, seeking his true vocation as a martyr—as have, on a less lofty plane, Céline and even Sartre. Martyrdom, saintliness, and a secular but at the same time spiritual grandeur remain the unavowed temptation for a number of compatriots of Father de Foucauld, of Pétain, and of De Gaulle in the most bourgeois country of Europe. Francis Poulenc did much for Les Dialogues des Carmélites (first given as a play in 1952) and for Bernanos's posthumous fame in composing a striking opera on that theme in 1960.

That passionate heart was not joined to a very lucid head, no more than was Céline's, to whom he is often compared and contrasted, or than was the case with Barbey d'Aurevilly, Veuillot, and Léon Bloy, three Catholic masters of vituperation among his predecessors. Such men can also betray with passion any cause put forward in a manner that is not in accord with their own chimerical ideal. In 1936, Bernanos, until then a champion of the conservative and royalist cause and yearning for a renewed alliance between the altar and the throne, happened to be in Majorca, drawn there by the allegedly lower cost of living, when the Spanish Civil War broke out. He witnessed the ghastly slaughter of Republican prisoners murdered with the approval of priests, of the local archbishop blessing the machine guns and approving the execution of Spaniards who had deserved punishment since only fifteen per cent of them had attended Easter Mass. The whole fabric of his traditional faith in the Church as the vessel of honor in our century crumbled. Courageously, alienating his supporters and readers among the French Right, Bernanos related what he had seen and what he felt in an ardent but overlong volume, *Les Grands Cimetières sous la lune* (1938). Disgusted with the capitulation of Munich in 1938, then with that of France in 1940, Bernanos attempted to live with his family in Paraguay, then in Brazil. He multiplied eloquent but tediously verbose polemical appeals to the English and to the French from his exile, was hailed as a great patriot by the Free French, and was even mistaken for a statesman. His work as a novelist, however, was completed. 'No one,' he had declared, 'is less than I a devotee of art for art's sake, no one is less of an amateur.' At the conclusion of World War II, he repeated: 'The *métier* of writer is no longer a *métier*. It is an adventure, and primarily a spiritual adventure. Every spiritual adventure is a Calvary.' Up along his Stations of the Cross Bernanos fiercely climbed, distrusting intellectual values more and more, but trusting words and art as propaganda more and more. 'Nothing is more monotonous than passion and repeats itself more wretchedly,' he warned in a posthumous book, *Un Mauvais Rêve* (*Night is Darkest*). Alas! that is just as true of political and intellectual passions as it is of sexual ones. Bernanos's novels have moments of intense visionary beauty, few and far between; but ponderous irony, sneers of hatred, tireless hammering of a few passionate convictions encumber them. His characters are often little more than ghosts, feebly catching a few glimpses of what eludes them in the mysterious workings of Satan among us, tools of destiny and of grace. The plots are successions of disconnected episodes. The ideological digressions, unlike those which were no less intrusive in the fiction of Balzac, Tolstoi, or Dostoevski, seldom express a very deep mind.

The *Diary of a Country Priest* alone shuns the faults which Bernanos perversely accumulated throughout his other novels. A few detached scenes here and there in his other books should be rescued from oblivion, and the most unforgettable ones invariably have to do with a double theme which obsessed him. The first is the omnipresence of evil, or rather of 'Satan trismegistes,' as Baudelaire called the thrice very great prince of darkness and annihilator of 'the rich metal of our will power.' To Bernanos, as to the anti-Catholic Dostoevski, and to France's modern Catholic novelists, the world has become the kingdom of Satan; the artist is the Devil's most sedulous accomplice. But his mission is to dramatize the conflict between passions and faith, between the perdition most safely incurred through reliance on the intellect and the salvation, which a writer who has the vocation of a martyr must effect. The world of sin and of boredom (the latter the most insidious of all the wiles of Satan, like Baudelairian spleen) is opposed to that of grace. Bernanos, it is reported, fought that one endless fight to his dying hour when, ready to encounter the Archenemy at last, he exclaimed: 'Now, let's have it out.'

But the source of fresh poetry which never dried up in Bernanos's heart was his nostalgia for the loveliness and the purity of childhood. The omnipresence of that theme of childhood in a country which, until Rousseau, had seldom taken account of children in its literature is a surprising reversal. It has inspired their finest pages to Proust and Gide, to Alain-Fournier and to Saint-Exupéry, to Anouilh and to Julien Green. It is the only lost paradise that we wish to recapture. Bernanos was prone to dividing all grown ups between those who have obstinately reneged the divine grace of childhood, the pharisees and the complacent bourgeois, and the saints, the naïve and awkward priests, the hardhearted, peevish adolescent girls who long to maintain the spirit of childhood in themselves. Childhood to Bernanos meant also solitary wanderings along the roads of northern France, the search for the enchanted land of heart's desire, as for Alain-Fournier's hero, the enticement of the path across the countryside which had taken Rimbaud's unwearied steps across Europe. The country priest, enslaved to the sordid platitudinousness of his parish, repeatedly voices his nostalgia of the roads to nowhere which might lead to freedom and to purity. Even more than for Proust, Bernanos's vocation as a novelist and as a poet in a broad sense had stemmed from his yearning to recover the visions, the scenery and even the language of his childhood. In a diary which he kept while in Brazil, in 1940, later published as *Les Enfants humiliés,* he confessed: 'I write in order to justify myself in the eyes of the child that I had been.'

If preposterous claims were put forward by some fanatical admirers of Bernanos, even more exaggerated ones (also first launched by the same royalist extremist, Léon Daudet) maintained that Céline should be revered as a Rabelaisian epic novelist, a renovator of language, and a 'sacred monster' whose cult should displace all the academic fake demi-gods of literature. It is doubtless salutary that such demented and ranting exhibitionists (Léon Daudet was himself one of them and Marcel Jouhandeau and Jean Genet maintain the tradition) should periodically appear in the would-be 'classical' literature of France to remind us of the country's perennial bent toward 'démesure' and fierce hatred of reason and of wisdom. The weird power of the grotesque, the poetry of ugliness, the intoxication with scatology were not absent from medieval letters and art, nor from the exuberant Renaissance, not even from the age of Diderot or from that of Balzac. 'Les charmes de l'horreur n'enivrent que les forts' asserts a line in Baudelaire's 'Danse macabre.'

Unfortunately, writers like Céline are often cursed with a coterie of weaklings whose inveterate anemia attempts to conceal itself under uncritical acclaim of brutality. Many a reviewer, unsure of his own judgment, deficient in imagination, eager for cheaply assumed originality as a mask for his inner emptiness, jumped on the bandwagon of Céline, who wrestled with his pallid ghosts and produced the illusion of a tough giant. The monotony of Céline's inspiration, the artificiality of his language and the 'pompiérisme' of his tawdry sentimentality should have become blindingly manifest after his second novel, when he specialized in anti-Semitic vituperation even more sorely devoid of intelligence than that of Hitler. Some, however, stubbornly refused to be disillusioned. Even after the lamentable display of Céline's later pamphlets of insane eructation, some reviewers maintain that he should be granted a place among the chief novelists of our age. But Céline is as artificial in his own way as any of the précieux writers of this century, Giraudoux, or Gide at his most effete, as wily in his speculations on the public's gullibility as any concocter of detective stories, and more commonplace as a mind than even the proverbially despised French concierges.

Not only is Céline an exhibitionist, he is also a mythomaniac. Like a number of men of letters, he became unable to separate the semi-fictional characters whom he had projected in his books from his own self. More and more, he became his peevish, shouting, and debunking hero and attributed to himself the picaresque adventures and the grudges of his Bardamu. He wished to assume the figure of a man from the lower classes, talking the language of the underprivileged, in revolt against the oft-indicated selfishness of bourgeois society. If we disregard this pose, and his pseudonym, we find Louis-Ferdinand Destouches to be a typical 'petit bourgeois' of Paris. His anti-Semitism and loud railing against the government, the state, and all organized authority is exactly that of many little tradesmen who cling to their narrow view of things, who vote for Poujade and other demagogues, and who blame the Jews for their own failure to modernize their shops and their minds. His ancestors belonged to the lesser Norman nobility, Destouches de Lentillère. His grandfather also married into the lesser nobility and taught literature at the lycée of Le Havre, where Sartre was later to discover his writer's vocation while teaching. His father had married a shrewd woman who sold ancient lace to choice customers and had a comfortable trade; he held a degree in letters and sold insurance, owned a villa by the Seine near Paris and spent his Sundays, as many a Parisian likes to do, as a patient, if hardly complete, angler. There was neither poverty nor divorce or squabble in the ménage, a prosperous and loving one. Céline was so embarrassed at having wickedly caricatured them in the grotesque picture of his childhood in *Mort à crédit* (*Death on the Instalment Plan*) that he begged his mother, then the only survivor of the couple, not to read the volume.

When in his teens, Céline was sent by his parents to Germany, then to England, to acquire, as he did, a mastery of foreign languages and a taste for trade. His precocious sexual development involved him in trouble and on his return he was placed as an apprentice in several shops; but his turbulence, and not any patriotic enthusiasm as his partisans have hinted, caused him to enlist in the army at eighteen. He was exactly twenty when World War I broke out. He was serving in the cavalry, was wounded early in the war, not in the skull as he liked to hint; according to those who knew him best as a soldier and then as a medical student,[1] the legend that he had undergone a trepanation was entirely of his own making. He was wounded in the right shoulder by a shell, hospitalized for a year, and decorated with the highest honor in the French army, the 'médaille militaire.' He decided soon after to study medicine at Rennes, married the rich daughter of a well-known surgeon in that city, and served at an American mission then located in Rennes trying to combat tuberculosis. He proved successful in research in Roscoff's Breton labora-

---

1. Notably Marcel Brochard, whose precise account of Céline's parents and youth, in *L'Herne*, No. 3 (1963), pp. 13–17, is the only reliable one.

tory, propounded some interesting views and, in 1924, did his doctor's thesis on the Austro-Hungarian physician Semmelweiss (1818–65), the inventor of prophylaxis against puerperal fever. That discovery had saved the lives of numberless pregnant women; but Semmelweiss, a lone and cantankerous man, was unrecognized by his colleagues, thought himself persecuted by them, and he died insane, committing suicide. Céline's medical thesis received a prize and caused some stir in 1924. Retrospectively, it is easy to read in it premonitions of some of the future obsessions of the doctor turned novelist: aloneness of great men, complex of persecution, anarchic temperament, and attraction to madness and to death. 'In the endless march of time, life is nothing but a delirium. The truth is Death,' proclaimed the young author of that strange medical dissertation.

Céline tried to settle as a doctor in a dispensary in Clichy. He was not apparently a very successful doctor, although a kindly one. He was sent by the Rockefeller Foundation on missions to Africa, at a time when efforts were being made to extirpate sleeping sickness there. He concentrated on his writing at night. He had then divorced his wife and was living with an American woman, a dancer, Elizabeth Craig, whose aristocratic long legs he raved to all his friends about and to whom his first novel, *Voyage au bout de la nuit* (1932), is dedicated. The long, unwieldy manuscript was first accepted by Denoël and Steele, the Belgian and the American who then ran a publishing firm in Paris. Léon Daudet and two or three other critics acclaimed the book, which narrowly missed the Goncourt Prize. From then on, Céline's concern was to continue writing and making much money. He gloated over the huge sums which his publisher paid out to him for manuscripts, sight unseen. His avarice became as proverbial in literary circles as that of André Gide and of Jules Romains. He clung to his accumulated gold coins buried in Denmark as Rimbaud in Abyssinia had done to his. The thundering success of the first novel encouraged Céline to publish *L'Eglise*, a play he had written earlier and which was only staged once, in Lyons, and failed lamentably. His anti-Semitic gibes already revealed him in that comedy, which appeared in 1933, the very year in which Hitler came to power in Germany and proclaimed the extermination of the Jews as his aim. *Mort à crédit*, in which Céline worked backward from the man to the child in his fictional and mythical autobiography, was published, also at Denoël's, in 1936. *Bagatelles pour un massacre* (1937), a shrill and long cry of hatred for the Jews and an appeal to their massacre, followed. For most readers, who cannot stomach the endless strings of coarse insults and the crude rhetoric of a half insane author, the first two novels, his only books that may claim to belong to fiction rather than to pamphleteering, are all that has anything to do with literature in Céline's fiction.

Le Voyage au bout de la nuit is a rambling and ranting odyssey of six hundred pages in which a restless hero, perpetuating the romantic archetype of the wandering Jew, intent upon his own ruin, successively shouts his hatred of war, of the middle classes all conspiring against him, of Africa and its Negroes as well as its colonists, of America the land of automats, fed on statistics and accounts. Nothing ever redeems the sordidness of that inferno. (Strindberg at least, who did write an Inferno, had voiced yearnings for understanding and tenderness and maintained some faith in the redeeming power of love.) The truest ancestors of Céline in literature are Jules Renard with his bitter sarcasms and Courteline with his coarse barrack-room humor and small business clerk mentality. Indeed, one could go back to the Jansenists and even the Fathers of the Church. Céline's systematic debasement of love is indeed akin to the most ascetic aspects of Jansenism. When, after the success of his first novel, Céline undertook a trip to Russia (with the avowed intent of collecting and spending his Russian royalties there), he came back embittered and full of venom again, which he poured out in Mea Culpa (1936). His error had been to have almost believed that man could be happier under another political regime and in a different social order. 'The very claim to happiness is the hugest of frauds. . . . There is no happiness in this life of ours, only misfortunes. Those who are most assured of being damned are those who think they are happy. . . . The superiority of the great Christian religions lay in this: they did not attempt to sugarcoat the pill.' And Céline gleefully endorsed Jules Renard's quip, 'It would never suffice to be happy. We have to know that others are not.'

From Zola and the naturalists, on the other hand, Céline felt remote. They perceived poetry in the sordid reality which they described and created out of it an art of epic stature. The speech which his friends persuaded Céline to deliver as a tribute to Zola in 1936 lays bare his inanity as a judge of literature and his dismal dearth of any critical ideas—not a word, naturally, on Zola's fight for Dreyfus, not a hint that the future could be made better by the denunciation of the universal corruption of today. America was Céline's pet hatred, although most of the professional help he received came from that country and the women who gave him most happiness were American. One being Molly, the sentimental prostitute of Detroit, portrayed in his first novel as the only character who does something to redeem the inferno of mankind. 'I do not believe in men,' Céline confided to the kindest of all his French correspondents, the doctor and art critic Elie Faure. 'They are and will always remain filth.' Medicine is scorned as 'cette merde,' a gigantic imposture. To any beauty in women or in art, Céline's characters know only one response: masturbation.

The few pages in which Céline displays any real power are those in which he depicts characters cornered by physical fear, an emotion which from all accounts he had often experienced himself and which, except for other hunted men like Julien Green, has been all too seldom rendered in modern literature. But those few pages, to be found chiefly in the section on World War I in the *Voyage* and in the caricatural sea journey to Africa on the phantom ship 'Admiral Bragueton,' are few and far between. The rest is endless wallowing in all that is coarsest and basest in the scatological nightmares of an adolescent who never could outgrow his nostalgia of excremental filth. The *Voyage* is woefully unstructured and Céline already suffered in it from his congenital inability to end, or even to know when to stop. When he reviled Proust as 'Talmudic, tortuous, arabescoid and a disordered mosaic,' the foe of Semitic literature in Céline was in effect characterizing his own writing. Along with that incapacity to order his experience into an artistic pattern, Céline's vulgar sentimentality, of the kind which the French like to attribute to concierges, is the second greatest artistic flaw in those novels. Those loose stories of flight from himself and from death by a character who masochistically enjoys being a perpetual victim are not, as Céline once asserted, quests for love. What the paranoiac fugitive mistakes for love is the tawdriest kind of sentimentality (in the scenes with the Detroit prostitute) and what he calls, when relating a prolonged visit to a New York urinal, 'its joyous communion of filth.' Among all the visions of America in modern French literature, from Paul Morand to Georges Duhamel and Jean Cocteau, Céline's is the least flattering and the most hateful. The public, which eventually hailed his books and provided him with the two or three most favorable critics of his works,[2] was depicted by Céline as 'depraved by tam-tam, bluff and artificiality . . .

2. Milton Hindus and Rima Drell Reck, both, strangely enough, of the very culture or 'race' which Céline revelled in denouncing. See the bibliographical notes at the end of this chapter.

the stupidest on earth.' As late as 1950, while he was attempting to find haven in the United States, he wrote to the Swedish critic and student of style, Ernst Bendz: 'All that is American or English . . . is altogether alien to me and indigestible, and disagreeable. I see in it nothing but disorder, chaos, bombast, big useless din and hollow effects. . . . Nothing which could satisfy my taste which after all is *classical.*' Strange is the undying covetousness of the title 'classical' among the least organized and restrained of French rebels!

In one respect alone Céline may have seriously entertained the belief that he might hold a position of historical consequence in French literature: as an influence on language. He boasted repeatedly of his affinities with Rabelais, who had undertaken to write as one speaks (sic!) but who, in the evolution of French style, had regrettably lost to another sixteenth-century writer, Amyot, and thus to a clear, refined, allegedly aristocratic French language. In truth, neither Saint-Simon nor Diderot nor Balzac nor Michelet could be called 'artistocratic' or 'clear,' nor a score of other masters of French prose. But Céline liked to contend that slang was born of hatred: hatred of workmen for their employer, of schoolboys for their teacher, of soldier for the sergeant, of petty officials for the State. He defined his purpose as one of endowing language with a new sensibility, so that it would palpitate instead of reasoning, speak to our ears with the rhythm of the spoken tongue, and eschew all literary artifice.

It seems likely that Céline's language will in fact be judged the most artificial element in novels, which themselves rank among the most deliberately contrived and the most self-conscious of the present age in French. Few scholastic exercises will prove easier for students of style than to dissect Céline's tricks and mannerisms, as Leo Spitzer did in a very shrewd essay in *Le Français moderne,* in 1935, reprinted in *L'Herne,* vol. V. Céline was far from sure of his stylistic effects even after his first book, *Voyage,* in which he had hastily unburdened himself and hit upon a 'poncif,' a caricature of Parisian folk language, bejewelled with four-letter words at the rate of a dozen per page. 'He hesitates. He is searching for his style,' confessed his publisher to a member of the Goncourt Academy, Phillipe Hériat. There is indeed no unity of tone in the language of the book, unless it be an inveterate love of rhetoric and of paroxystic bombast. The Parisian pimp, apache, or prostitute has never spoken as in Céline's highly artificial transposition. Grammarians in 1965 are already dissecting Céline's use of argot as a quaint, very literary mixture of sophisticated reflections by the novelist himself with the kind of slang which may have been occasionally heard in 1930 and is now already archaic or forgotten. There is a flavor of death, as everywhere in Céline, in the systematic resorting to a slang which is doomed to be forgotten ten years hence. In their hatred of the classics, whose imposing presence blocks their way to fame and imposes too exacting standards upon them, the users of highly stylized slang such as Jean Genet, Raymond Queneau, and Céline condemn themselves to premature death and sure oblivion in an obscure niche among the minores of literature.

The volumes by which Céline attempted to pursue his literary career after the outbreak of World War II have been only feeble repetitions of his rhetorical devices and of his universal hatred of the Jews, of the French, of all mankind. A few visionary pages of some forcefulness might, at best, be extracted from *Guignol's Band* (1952), *Féerie pour une autre fois* (1952), and *Nord* (1960), all of which Céline regarded as ballets of foul words and obscene eructations: they could by no stretch of the imagination be called novels. Page after page of mechanical prattle, punctuated with hundreds of exclamation and suspension dots, repeat that man is but a wicked beast and can never become otherwise. A dwindling number of reviewers heroically endeavored to display fairness to an author who insulted them regularly and for whom they felt more pity than resentment. Men of literary polish themselves, they gazed in awe at a monster in his cage who seemed to embody the revolt against the very concept of literature, a revolt paradoxically typical of the present age, surfeited as it is with literature, and of the country which always adulated men of letters. It irks respectable, ageing critics to admit that they are morally shocked by the extreme muckraking of Céline, Genet, Henry Miller, and William Burroughs. They fear not to be up with the avant-garde any longer and to be dismissed by teenagers as old fogeys. They would however gain the respect of the young, and their own self-respect more securely, if they did not abdicate their role of cultured men with a sense of tradition and awareness that literature in past centuries teemed with authors like Herondas, Petronius, Martial, the author of *Fanny Hill,* and the grossly overrated and tedious Marquis de Sade himself, whose obscenity did not save him from insignificance and boredom.

Céline, who had pretended that he stemmed from the lower strata of society and spoke for those who had not yet gained a place in literature, proved to be their betrayer. He had only scorn for the working classes and apparently never understood them. Leon Trotsky (in an article which appeared in English in *The Atlantic Monthly* of October 1935) and a doctor who had been a genuine and generous friend of the poor, Elie Faure, were for a brief while duped by what they took as Céline's sincerity. The first must have been disillusioned when he watched Céline turn into a supporter of the worst ranting of Nazi anti-semitism; Céline rewarded Faure, who had humbly wished to help him and to interpret him, by hinting, after his death, that he must have been one of the hated race of Jews. When the Germans occupied France and established an Institute for the Study of Jewish Questions on rue La Boëtie in Paris, in a gallery which had belonged to the picture dealer Rosenberg, Céline wrote several letters to recall to them that he had been one of the pioneers of anti-Semitism and that his books against the Jews ought to be displayed more conspicuously in the exhibitions. These displays were the prelude to a slaughter of one hundred thousand French Jews, one-third of those who lived in France between two world wars. In 1942 or 43, he deplored, in a Nazi-subsidized newspaper, the taking over of the Southern Zone of France by the German occupant, for France should once and for all throw overboard all her population south of the Loire, made up of Jews and Arabs. He fled with the Germans in 1944, when the courageous gesture would have been to stay behind and face those whom he had insulted from a position of immunity, even if it meant the firing squad for an author who had posed for a man of courage and a martyr.

Céline's savior and most helpful good samaritan, in the years after his transfer from Germany to the safety of Denmark, was Milton Hindus, the Brandeis professor who felt a boundless pity for him and heard in his works 'the voice of the little man in Europe amplified a thousand times.' This American Jew went to Denmark, lavished presents and kindness on the ranting prisoner who poured obscene insults on the Germans (it seems that he had asked to be naturalized as one of them when they were victorious), on the Danes, and on the Americans. He soon noted in his diary that 'Céline is as tightly packed with lies as a boil is with pus,' that 'Céline is a viper and in the end he is bound to suffer the viper's fate, as it is told in Aesop.' He was dismayed by Céline's moral hideousness, his greed for money, and 'his lack of respect for the art which he practices. What he says is true of women is certainly true of himself——he will sacrifice anything to secure an effect.' [3] Céline grossly berated his publisher Denoël, who had been assassinated by angry Frenchmen, apparently for having published Céline's works of hatred. When Milton Hindus showed Céline the notes on their meeting, in which sympathy wins over repulsion, the crippled giant threatened to sue him for libel and wrote to the president of the university where Milton Hindus taught to denounce him as a spy, accuse him of not knowing French or Latin properly, and of being 'crass with ignorance and pretentiousness.' In July 1961, Céline died, forgiven by the French and by the Jews, in his suburban villa at Mendon. The line of Boileau, valid for prose writers as well as for poets, should be the most apposite epitaph for one whom his compatriots are already embarrassed at having taken too seriously:

Le vers se sent toujours des bassesses du coeur.

Julien Green's place among today's outstanding French novelists is controversial in an altogether different sense. Even more than Mauriac, he has been content with a traditional technique; even more than Martin du Gard, he has had the courage to tell a story with smooth continuity and to do so in a deliberately equable tone and an almost colorless style. Technical devices, farfetched reversals of chronology and surprise effects, interior monologues, author's invocations to his characters in the second person singular, ingenuously ingenious contrivances calculated to upset the reader's expectations are disarmingly absent from Green's classical, almost Victorian, novels. Their author could have been a contemporary of Hawthorne and of Emily Brontë. If the interest of a novel lies primarily, as a few naïve critics would like to have us believe, in experimental new devices so as to make that branch of literature ever more demanding for the reader, Julien Green might be viewed by posterity as having counted for less in the evolution of that literary genre than the first practitioner of the interior monologue, Edouard Dujardin, or Valéry Larbaud, or Jules Romains, or Michel Butor perversely waylaid in the labyrinthine ways of Degrés. Such appears to have been the reasoning of a number of American critics of fiction, always on the lookout for innovations in technique and ideological attitudes to emerge from France, and unwilling to concede that these might come from an American-born writer. It took many years for American teachers of literature to admit that Faulkner might not be unworthy of the American classics and that Dos Passos

3. Milton Hindus, The Crippled Giant (New York, Boar's Head Books, 1950), pp. 69, 70, 87.

could have fertilized the French fiction of the nineteen-thirties; they have refused to recognize the setting of *Mont-Cinère* (*Avarice House*), *Moïra*, or *Chaque Homme dans sa nuit* (*Each in His Darkness*) as bearing any resemblance to any scenery in the United States.

The French, on the other side, perhaps over-attentive to a style which does not rise to the lyrical or rapturous beauty of Mauriac, of Malraux, and of Gide at their most poetical, have been cool to Julien Green. The homage which he paid their language and their literature by choosing French as his medium touched them less than the wierdness of his dream world, which they dubbed at once 'Anglo-Saxon.' Even his Catholicism seemed shot through with Protestant obsessions; the French province in which he set the scene of *Adrienne Mesurat* (*The Closed Garden*) or of *Léviathan* appeared to them as an insane universe, insulting to the land of Descartes and of the conservative and nostalgic dreamers of an Arcadian dream among them. Little did they reflect that Balzac and Zola, and the portrayer of *Madame Bovary* himself, had likewise been generally pronounced to denigrate French peasantry and to place ships of fools along the Loire and the Seine. It is an outrageous evidence of chauvinism not to have offered to Green, hardly less French than Henri Bergson, Henri Troyat, or Joseph Kessel, also born of non-French parents, an honorary French nationality and a seat in the French Academy.

Julien Green, it is true, has chosen to be a solitary writer, and not to parade his nonconformism as Cocteau or Montherlant has gained publicity in doing. He was, from his most tender years onward, the dweller of a private universe of his own, in which he alternately delighted and felt stifled. Of all the writers of his time, Proust and Mauriac included, he was least the 'professional man of letters,' the farthest removed from the playful dilettantism of Giraudoux or of Cocteau. He was convinced that, much like Rilke and Kafka, he had to write fiction or to perish, like many of his characters, from insanity or suicide. Of several of his novels he confided in his diary, as he did when he was composing the most perfect of his novels and one of the finest of this century, Moïra: 'This book helps me live, helps me breathe.' An interior necessity sways the lives of his characters. They are as far away from average creatures as are the heroes of Balzac and of Dostoveski. Yet we soon acquire the conviction that they had to be as they are, pursued by an implacable fate. The author does not allow them to yield to God. 'I was not able to put my own faith into my books,' he avowed. 'Until Moïra, the believer in me has not written.' His earliest volume, a polemical 'pamphlet against the French Catholics' published under a pseudonym when he was barely twenty-three, ventured the confession that the idea of Hell is far more intoxicating than that of paradise; it alone endows some of our sins with a superhuman dimension and makes them inexplicable to us, and makes us proud of having perpetrated them. The obsession with sin, with the flesh lusting against the spirit and, in the words of the Epistle to the Galatians, of the spirit lusting against the flesh, along with the emotion of panicky fear, constitutes the constant theme of Green's powerful novels. Of the writers of fiction in French in our century he is one of the most original.

Two volumes of recollections, *Partir avant le jour* and *Mille Chemins ouverts* published in 1962 and 1964, as Green (born in 1900) marched on toward the age of three score years and ten, have illuminated at times too glaringly what had only dimly shone in his long diary and been magnified in his novels. More posthumous revelations, and private letters, may some day supplement our knowledge of one of the most solitary and mysterious writers of this age. He was born in Paris, of parents who came from Virginia and Georgia. His father was the representative of a Southern cotton company in France, a kindly and broad-minded Presbyterian; his mother belonged to the Episcopalian faith and was more rigid in her attachment to the Bible and to the Protestant traditions. He likes to hint that he was the product of a complex ethnic blend and may have owed his lifelong anguish and his brooding on predestination to his Scottish ancestors, his sense of mystery and his fitful belief in metempsychosis to his Irish blood. Most of all, his mother's teaching permeated him with Southern traditions. He never saw the American South as a child, but he was convinced of the superiority of the Southern culture that the victors in the Civil War and the carpetbaggers who followed them had wrecked. It was early impressed upon him that he belonged to a vanquished nation. It was just as clearly hammered into the little boy, with five sisters older than himself, that all that pertained to sex was evil. He worshipped and feared his mother, but he also dreamt of the flesh (of a statue, of the picture of a nude in an art book, of his own body when furtively contemplated) with passionate longing. His dream life was intense. At school, the handsome boy that he was felt strangely drawn to other handsome boys and masculine beauty sent him into raptures and dreams, while he remained shy and fearful in the presence of any women: they appeared to him like inferior images of his adored mother.

His mother, exhausted by the care required by a large family of very

modest means and ceaselessly lamenting the passing of the affluence
which might have been theirs in Georgia half a century earlier, died in
1914, after becoming a convert to Catholicism. His father also converted
secretly, although he was hardly of an impulsive or mystical nature.
Julien himself espoused the Catholic faith in 1916, and was tormented by
the impulse to become a monk and escape once and for all the temptations of the flesh. These loom large in the notations of his diary and in
his novels, and of several of them he was to note later that they uttered
a long shout of horror for sexual instinct. Peace, however, did not come
to him easily and perhaps he did not covet it. 'Does there exist a novel
without sin? Can one plunge into the world of sin, as the novelist must,
and not be tainted by it?' The volumes of his free, often humorous and
extremely revealing memories of childhood and adolescence have shown
Green as anything but 'a pagan suckled in a creed outworn,' but also as
anything but a saint or a creature who ever could have been long satisfied with serenity. He remained, long after the middle of his life and
the inevitable chastening of desire, far more frail and torn than Gide,
Mauriac, and probably Malraux, incapable of the exhibitionism which
delights other Catholics also dwelling in Sodom, like Marcel Jouhandeau.

All his works, except for one volume of happy memories and very minor
pieces, were written by Green in the language which he had learned as a
child at the Lycée Janson-de-Sailly and not in his mother tongue in
which his mother dutifully annotated the family Bible for him. He was
sent as a young man to study at the University of Virginia, where he
filled his eyes with visions of the Southern landscape, eagerly observed
his classmates, and read Southern history. He never could have written
fiction or confessions in English, however. 'I have always spoken English,'
he remarked, 'but whenever I attempt to write it, I feel as if I were trying
on a coat that has not been made for me. . . . Clarity of thought: that
is in effect what France gave me. The great English and Russian novelists
are full of confusion; the French never. The French have no objection
to one's treating obscure subjects, provided the treatment of those be
crystal clear.' French clarity may well be a myth, as many French scholars
hint, and it is in any case an acquired virtue, instilled into the French
by years of rhetorical and grammatical teaching. But Green obscurely
felt, as have a number of students who emigrated from Russia and Germany to the United States during the years 1930–45, that only through
the language and the cultural traditions of France could they recover a
spiritual balance and reconcile their split selves. Green studied painting

and his remarks on painting and music evince an unusual degree of insight and of expertise. He could have been a critic of talent, one of the most sensitive of his age. He read a good deal of English and American literature and wrote brief essays on Hawthorne, Blake, Charlotte Brontë, and Charles Lamb: the choice is revealing and all those authors were 'wits to madness near allied.' But his true affinity is to Balzac and Flaubert. Proust meant less for him than for Mauriac; Gide alternately seduced him and repelled him. Maritain's influence over him has been more apparent in the novels of his latter years, after he drew Green back to Catholicism in 1939.

Those are in our opinion the best. It would be idle and false to categorize them, as French critics like to do, as 'Catholic novels.' There is not an ounce of preaching in them, not the slightest intent to argue or to demonstrate that Christianity is the truth or helps us live. Very occasionally, and in incidental asides which are closer to Voltaire than to St. Francis, Green offers a question like this one in *Le Visionnaire* (*The Dreamer*): 'I wonder at times what ferocious beasts we would become if a little religious hypocrisy did not intervene to temper our evil instincts.' André Blanchet, the Jesuit priest who, of all his critics, wrote most piercingly and most favorably on him (in *La Littérature et le Spirituel*, vol. II), concludes with much fairness that his novels 'have not been conceived in a Christian climate,' yet that 'only a Christian could write them since, as Pascal contended, one must know Christ to fathom human misery to its utmost depths.' Green was profoundly marked in his youth by the assiduous reading of Pascal, but it is doubtful that he would himself have hinted that human misery had not been fully probed by Homer, Sophocles, or Lucretius. The Catholic sensibility of this convert, like that of Maritain himself and of Newman, always retained traces, and perhaps some nostalgia, of his Protestant upbringing. Religion enters as a burning temptation in his novels, but also enhances the insidious appeal of the other temptations, especially those of male friendships and of the flesh. More than once, Green applied to himself the phrase of his contemporary and fellow-Puritan in revolt against Puritanism—'we are crucified in sex.'

Green first tried to locate one of his earliest novels in the country of which his mother had told him longing stories, enhanced by remoteness of time and place, and by her Paris exile. *Mont-Cinère* (*Avarice House,* 1926), relating the atrocious avariciousness of a woman in a Virginia mansion, hating her own daughter, hated by her, with their hatred finally climaxing the willful setting on fire of the country house, was too impossible to command suspension of disbelief. The characters seemed to come straight from one of the black novels of Ann Radcliffe or 'Monk' Lewis, whom the French surrealists were then discovering. *Adrienne Mesurat* followed a year after and *Léviathan* appeared in 1929: they have been taken, outside France, for faithful portrayals of life in France; the second of those two novels, with its unleashing of the Biblical monster which gives it its title, its accumulation of rape, murder, and suicide usual with Julien Green, was even selected in some American universities during World War II as required reading for American officers then trained to take over the administration of provincial France. The faithfulness of these novels is comparable to the rendering of American customs and moods to be studied in *Desire Under the Elms, The Great Gatsby,* and *Wild Palms* by a foreign observer. Green's vision of provincial France and, in *Epaves* (*The Strange River,* 1932—the most desolate of these novels), of Paris and the mournful banks of the Seine, is one of solitude and boredom. An hysterical and sequestered old maid percipitates her tyrannical father down the stairs to his death. An average man, Guéret, in *Léviathan,* hates his ugly wife, becomes mad with lust for the cheap servant girl at a restaurant, Angèle, lashes her with the branch of a tree when he attempts to rape her, and kills a man out of sheer anger; Angèle. as in a film or like Lady Anne in *Richard III,* becomes strangely drawn to the man who wanted to hurt her and flees with him. Another equally weird woman, who also loved the most unattractive Guéret, takes her own life out of jealousy. For some beings yielding to their insensate greed is more essential than life itself; they would sooner murder themselves and, in Blake's phrase, an infant in its cradle than nurse unacted desires.

Le Visionnaire (*The Dreamer,* 1934) and *Minuit* (*Midnight,* 1936) followed in close succession. Their titles betray the growing hallucinatory obsessions of the novelist. The light of day was always hardly bearable to him; he only begins to live in darkness and under melancholy's black sun. The dread which he makes prey upon his characters then causes them to tremble in convulsions. Any of their eerie dreams seems possible. For they are all visited by the conviction that the life they and others lead is unreal. 'And nothing is but what is not,' as is said at the beginning of *Macbeth*. Many times in his own life, Green became overpowered with an immense bliss which obliterated surrounding reality and brought him the certitude that another world exists, that one may communicate with it. The readers who had mistaken him for a traditional and minutely realistic painter of provincial life discovered the true face of Green in *Le Visionnaire*. The world is nothing but a visionary abode, as it could be for an English romantic poet. Its dwellers are all hunted and hallucinated creatures, driven by their anguish, in which an impossible carnal love and the lure of death are married, as they were for Edgar Allan Poe. All of them, like the protagonist of *Le Visionnaire*, experience the only respite from the fate which drives them when they destroy the world around them to conjure up another one. Love never affords any quietude; there is no more relief from its fulfillment than in Dostoevski, none of the tenderness and of the mutual understanding which, in D. H. Lawrence, may result from carnal ecstasy. *Le Visionnaire* and *Minuit*, however, suffer from being cut up into episodes which break up the mounting effect of horror sought by the novelist. The imagined world and the real one are forcibly juxtaposed, but poorly joined with each other. The compensatory castle in which Manuel lives in his imagination and imposes upon the belief of his cousin, one of the girls hated by their mothers who populate the Greenian world, fails to be similarly imposed upon the reader. *Le Grand Meaulnes* and Cocteau's *Enfants terribles* managed to conquer the reader's faith more triumphantly in this regard.

The two or three years preceding the surrender of Munich and the invasion of Poland, then of France, by the Germans filled Green with agonies of anguish. He spent the war years in the United States, served in the American army for a time when the United States entered the fight, but was soon found to be better suited to information service broadcasting in French or English. Of all the émigrés from France then, including Saint-Exupéry who was anxious to resume his active career as flyer, none suffered more than this American citizen Julien Green from being severed from all that he loved in the sky, the streets, the art, and the people of Paris. His anxiety over the fate of Western Europe was multiplied by a harrying religious restlessness. Green studied Hebrew in order to read the Old Testament in the original, pondered over predestination, and even more over the transmigration of souls. He read eagerly on Buddhism, and often the conviction gripped him that he had lived here or elsewhere earlier and that man was but a passing and recurring traveler on this earth (*Le Voyageur sur la terre* was the title of his second fictional attempt). The Buddhist influence was, rather strangely, most conspicuous in the novels between *Minuit* and *Moïra*. Their titles are

Varouna (*Then Shall the Dust Return,* 1940) and *Si J'étais vous* (1947),
but of all Green's works they are the least successful, coming the closest
to some sort of didactic and allegorical message. Those years were precisely those in which, early in 1939, the novelist had returned whole-
heartedly to his Catholic faith. But he eschewed religious themes in his
fiction and he was in dread of becoming tainted by the complacency and
the moralizing bent which he had observed among fellow-converts, even
in the critics Charles du Bos and Albert Béguin. His diaries of the war
years are, like the earlier ones, replete with contradictions. The carnal
temptations repel and still fascinate him; but he would not side with
those stern doctors who denounced concupiscence everywhere. 'They forget only one thing,' he wrote in the fourth volume of his *Journal* in 1943;
'that the sexual instinct comes from God.'

After his return to France, Green attempted to free some of the demons
that had always wrestled in him by impersonating them in dramas. Gide
had once proceeded likewise in *Saul* and was, after 1945, experiencing a
new vigor in literary activity through adapting for the stage his *Caves du
Vatican* and Kafka's *Trial*. Montherlant was, as Giraudoux had done
earlier, discovering that the stage enlarged a hundred- or a thousandfold
the public which they had reached through their novels—strangely static
and overwritten novels, to be sure. But the drama could not prove an apt
vehicle for the secretive allusions to unfulfilled and upsetting attractions
between two males which recur in Green's works; nor could the drama
convey the subtle presence of 'the invisible,' which lurks behind the
behavior and the probing of the characters; and the invisible has been
the one constant concern of the novelist who stated peremptorily in his
Journal III: 'There is no verity or no absolute except in the invisible.' *Sud*
performed in 1953 at the theater of L'Athénée and *L'Ennemi,* in 1954, at
the Bouffes Parisiens, although artistically staged, scored but a *succès
d'estime. L'Ombre,* two years later, lacked dramatic progression and even
more markedly emotional appeal. The greatness of Julien Green, in the
second half of his career which may be said to have begun in 1939, shines
in his last two novels to date, *Moïra* (1950) and *Chaque Homme dans sa
nuit* (*Each in His Darkness,* 1960). A third one, *Le Malfaiteur,* not quite
accurately entitled *The Transgressor* in Anne Green's translation, appeared in 1956, but was an earlier work staging what T. S. Eliot terms
the one thing that never does change: 'the perpetual struggle of Good
and Evil.' It is much less powerful.

Moïra was created out of Green's imagination and of his own struggles with himself, like all intensely personal novels from which the first person singular is nevertheless banned; and of the memories of his years at Charlottesville as a student. At the university which Green knew well, a young man from the hills, uncouth, unsophisticated, handsome in a rough way with his flaming red hair, Joseph Day, has registered in order to study Greek, and thus to read the New Testament in the original. He is deeply religious, intolerant of the laxity of his friends, furiously determined to save them from sin. He tears up his copy of *Romeo and Juliet* as a lewd and coarse play; he fights with one of his classmates who is mysteriously drawn to him and who remarks ominously that his adversary has the big hands of a murderer. In the boarding house where he had rented a room, Joseph Day happens to hear that his bed had recently served for Moïra, the landlady's adopted daughter. He is repelled and pursued by the thought of that daughter of destiny, as yet unseen. Joseph's friends practise a cruel joke on the fanatic. They lock Moïra, a girl of rather easy virtue, in his new room. Horrified, he at first bids her leave while he stays fiercely silent. When she does attempt to leave, he throws himself on her, lewdly, and sleeps with her. On waking up the next morning, he strangles her and buries her body under a tree. The young man who had wrestled with him offers to help him escape. Joseph Day declines, surrenders to the police, and accepts the penalty for his sin. The marriage of heaven and hell is accomplished. The Devil has won the wager against God in the young stallion from the Virginia hills. The birth of sexual desire in Joseph Day's hitherto dormant senses has violently silenced his sense of horror at infringing the moral law. But both he in his crude brutality and the prostitute who could have become a repentant Maria Magdalena are delineated with delicacy and sympathy by the convert Julien Green. In them there is a dim insight into the mysteries of the flesh, and of the soul; while the other students, sophisticated and promiscuous cynics or self-righteous young preachers of abstinence, are incapable of exploring human nature to its depths. The novel is told with restraint; it unfolds with the inevitability of tragedy and its emotional and sexual conflicts in awkward teenagers are rendered with no incumbrance of psychological and clinical analysis. The author's touch, in contrast to that of Theodore Dreiser and of Thomas Wolfe, remains delicate. Only the suicide of Simon, a sophisticated youth attracted by Joseph Day's physique and by his imperious violence but rejected by him, sounds, like the many suicides in Greenian fiction, a jarring note of conventionality.

Chaque Homme dans sa nuit is but the first of an alexandrine line of Victor Hugo which ends 's'en va vers sa lumière.' But Julien Green is the foe of such a light, symbolic or real. He noted somewhere that, to him, sunlight inevitably connoted tragedy. The novel is more devious and misleading than *Moïra;* the incidents and the characters are more numerous than in the earlier story, the setting is far more unreal (the city could be Baltimore, Richmond, or Atlanta, transfigured into a city of dreadful night), the religious theme of a sinner's eternal salvation is played too heavy-handedly. All the threads of a mystery story are there, deftly woven; but the minor characters are too summarily presented and their meek bowing to the spiritual sway of the clumsy protagonist, a younger brother of the humble hero of *The Idiot,* fails to convince the reader. These sexually obsessed sinners striving for purity amid their greed and frustrations, and radiating a sanctifying influence on others while unable to become saintly themselves, have tended to become stock characters of Catholic novelists such as Mauriac, Graham Greene, and Bernanos. Dostoevski, who abhorred Catholicism, reigns over the creation of their tortured Western imaginations.

Wilfred Ingram, a twenty-four-year-old lad, shy, hardly educated, hopelessly awkward, belonging to the impoverished branch of an old and proud Southern family, takes a job in a haberdashery store. His trade is a constant humiliation for him; but male customers are strangely drawn to him, and so is his cousin Angus. He remains indifferent to their approaches. He desperately wants to live as an obedient Catholic, turning to the Crucifix in his bare room for help, but also profanating it and his faith through his secret life as a débauché. His Uncle Hector, the only Catholic close to him, has been disowned by the conventional, strait-laced, Protestant family. Hector is dying. He has summoned Wilfred to his death bed, bequeathes to him a few securities, some treasured love letters and faded photographs of a former mistress. Among the other relatives are James Knight, a stern puritan, Wilfred's cousin, who however becomes fascinated by the strange young man and forgives him his occasional insolence and awkwardness. His wife, Phoebe Knight, with an angelic face, an ethereal innocence, senses that Wilfred has fallen in love with her. She reciprocates the strange adoration for the poor, sinful, impulsive cousin of her husband. Their love will never be consummated, hardly expressed; but it will lead the young sinner to his redemption.

The store at which Wilfred sells ties and underwear, the bars where he pursues cheap pleasure at night, the churches where he kneels down in fitful and tortured remorse are conjured up by Green with visionary power. A young clerk at the store who had out of bravado risked his first experience of sex, dreading the disease which he naïvely fears might follow as his punishment, poisons himself. Wilfred, who was too clumsy to save him, baptizes him *in extremis*. A demoniacal character, Max, has observed Wilfred praying at a Polish church; he visits him insistently, attempts to force the would-be saint to fall with him into his hell of crookedness and self-debasement. He shoots him in the end and Wilfred almost seeks and welcomes that death. He had struggled in vain to free himself from God's clutches. He consents to his symbolic crucifixion at the hands of a devil's apprentice. Which of us, James Knight had said when discovering that Wilfred wanted to seduce his own wife Phoebe, is not a Judas ready to betray Christ? The novel accumulates unlikely incidents and presents characters such as few of us have ever encountered in American cities. The duel between corruption and faith, the greed for self-destruction and that for salvation, is too neatly dramatized; Green's Catholic heroes appear to have heeded Luther's strange precept: sin with force, believe with greater force still. The women's characters, all either angelically pure like Phoebe or devastating and domineering mothers who would not disfigure a Tennessee Williams play, are crudely drawn. Physical violence holds a weird fascination for Green, in real life the meekest and least Nietzschean of men; and his idea of the enticement of sexual pleasure is such as may only have been dreamt by seminary recluses or hermits in their Thebaïd of old. Yet the opening scenes, the death of the saintly sinner, and occasionally his pangs of self-doubt and of morbid shyness, rise to a pitch seldom achieved in contemporary fiction.

The originality of Julien Green lies in his total disregard of literary trends and fashions and in his aloofness from all groups, theories, and schools. He is one of the most cultured of contemporary novelists, at home in the world of painting and of music, in love with English and French poetry, a student of religion. His *Journal* may well some day rank above that of Gide for its psychological penetration, for its spiritual profundity, and for the incisiveness of literary opinions modestly offered on writers of the past and, more discreetly and never in a spirit of slander or cant, on contemporary writers. The struggles that he sustained in his vain attempts to curb certain tendencies in himself were more tragic, if less provokingly dramatized, than those of *Si le grain ne meurt* and *L'Immoraliste*. Green's familiarity with two or three fictional tradi-

tions could have induced him to write volumes of aesthetic criticism in
the craft of fiction as Mauriac, Robbe-Grillet, Nathalie Sarraute, Michel
Butor have done. He preferred silence and solitude. He has been punished for his aloofness by critics who have written relatively little on
him, although never in a derogatory or hostile mood. The Catholics,
except for the very eclectic and generous critic of the Jesuit periodical
Etudes, Father André Blanchet, have as a rule been embarrassed by that
strange brand of Catholicism which has disdained security, intellectual
comfort, and made light of creeds and dogmas.

Julien Green ranks among the dozen French novelists of the years
1930–60 who have succeeded in creating and in imposing their own
universe. Like Mauriac, he has imprisoned himself in narrow precincts,
geographic, social, and psychological. Frightened and persecuted little
girls, atrocious middle-aged women, young men whose charm recalls the
handsomest and most mysterious noblemen of Bronzino, but who are
desperately searching for the key to their own torn selves in the ghosts
which elude them, older men whose gradual detachment from the flesh
brings them closer to a mystical communion with mysteries: these are
Green's favorite characters. Many of them are secretive, wily, wickedly
sadistic. Nevertheless Green's sense of humanity is not relentlessly
dragged in the mud as in Céline or derided as it is by the ferocious Voltairian sarcasm of Marcel Aymé.

The atmosphere in which Green bathes his creatures is sultry and
ominous. His novels often begin like those of Thomas Hardy. A bleak
provincial public garden, a 'vague' uninhabited area near a factory yard,
the banks of the Seine where human waifs wander at nightfall, a lugubrious and decrepit country house in the American South haunted by
ghosts of the past are the kind of scenes that make up the setting of
those novels. An insurmountable 'ennui,' such as Baudelaire night-
marishly depicted, or Gide in a tragic page of his minor *récit, Isabelle,*
hovers over all the stories of Green. Men are the prisoners of a routine
that they resent one day as no longer bearable. Green records in his
Journal many a moment of extraordinary elation, of joy which invaded
him as it invaded young Wordsworth or Shelley when the 'Spirit of
Delight' visited them in their childhood and adolescence; but he did not
attempt to introduce it into his novels. The revelation of existence, which
startles an otherwise Greenian character from the gloomy routine of his
provincial city in Sartre's *La Nausée,* affords no impulse to endow a
meaningless life with a deliberate significance in Green's fiction. 'The

mere fact of being alive is oppressive and men only tolerate it by performing stupid chores. I, however, could no longer bear existing.' That aside of one of his characters is typical of all of them.

Out of those weary, flat, and unprofitable occupations which men invent in order to live, there is but one way: desire, greed, lust, in which, as in Racinian heroines, hatred has an even larger share than love. Passion is essential to those lamentable characters, even though they know beforehand that it cannot be fulfilled. For a moment, when they fall prey to their carnal loves, they forget the boredom of living. There are no erotic of risqué episodes in those austere novels; love is treated too seriously for the novelist to play at it or tease his readers with any cerebral analysis of sex. In *Journal* V, at the date of June 14, 1946, Green confessed:

'Carnal lapses [the word 'fautes' which is neither errors nor mistakes nor sins is one of the most difficult to render] teach some people what they never could have known otherwise, and I mean this not only in an erotic, but in a broadly human sense. The experience of physical love goes infinitely farther than the body. It embraces a world which it is precious to have known and in which much good is blended with much evil.' Christian moralists had long been aware of it and St. Augustine had long ago warned us that love is spiritual even in the flesh and carnal even in the spirit. Like Bernanos and Mauriac, Green gives flesh and concreteness to the abstraction denounced by preachers of all faiths.

It seems to Green's characters, made unto puppets of desire and lechery, as if another person, their double, has entered into them. For a time, they are magnetically driven by that invisible man in˙themselves. They bow passively. Nothing is of any moment any more. Green's perennial subject in novel after novel, as he himself remarked, is the hunted and haunted creature who leaps headlong into the very abyss which it dreads. No characters in the land of Corneille and Balzac have been delineated with so little will to resist or to fight. They are desperately alone, certain beforehand that neither in love, always unfulfilled, nor in friendship, banished from the Greenian world, will they ever be able to communicate with others. The writer tries that more determinedly than other men. But he too is doomed to failure. Words betray. Would-be 'sincere' confessions betray most blatantly of all. 'For it is the body which speaks in them and takes up all the room; or else it is the soul which gags the body and speaks for it.' (*Journal* V, October 1948)

Green's fiction oscillates between an impossible love, often ashamed of itself, and fear and death. Many other novelists in our age, and Proust foremost among them, have proved deeper explorers of love. Death, not heroically courted as in Malraux and Saint-Exupéry, but loved mystically as the ultimate and only solution to the vicissitudes of desire and remorse, and often sought half amorously by the many characters in Green who see no exit to their anguish but self-slaughter, is omnipresent in his fictional universe. But even more ubiquitous is the emotion of fear. Green is among the moderns the supreme master of dread. In the first volume of his *Journal,* he confided some of the anguished fears which had been his throughout his life and which he lent to several of his characters; he quoted approvingly the casual remark of R. L. Stevenson in 'The Suicide Club' (*New Arabian Nights*): 'People trifle with love. Now I deny that love is a strong passion. Fear is the strong passion. It is with fear that you must trifle, if you wish to taste the intensest joy of living.' Greenian heroes are incessantly pursued by their anguish, ready to flee from a dismal absence of love, but ever the captives of their nightmares. Their creator was blessed with a happy childhood and parents who understood and spoiled him. But his portrayal of family life and of the solitude of human beings is as starkly despondent as that of Kafka. He is indeed the closest counterpart to the author of *The Castle* in the French literature of this century. The monotony of his vision and the weirdness of his universe have palled upon some critics, as has the lack of *éclat* and of lyricism in his style. Others, among them Father Blanchet, hail his work as 'one of the most original and most profound series of novels of our age. . . . He is perhaps the one who will longest command attention.'

Bibliographical Notes

On Bernanos, a diversity of essays have been grouped together in *Etudes bernanosiennes* (*Revue des Lettres modernes,* VIII, 1961–62) and *L'Herne* (1961). The most valuable books of criticism are those of Albert Béguin, *Bernanos par lui-même.* Seuil, 1954; Luc Estang, *Présence de Bernanos.* Plon, 1947; Gaëtan Picon, *Bernanos romancier.* Marin, 1948. Neither Henri Deblue, *Les Romans de Bernanos ou le défi du rêve* (Neuchatel: La Baconnière, 1965), nor Peter Hebblethwaite, *Bernanos* (Cambridge, England: Bowes and Bowes, 1964), proves of much use.

The most valuable works on Céline are the two bulky volumes of biographical and critical essays published by *L'Herne* and the strange volume by his American admirer (later disillusioned), Milton Hindus, *The Crippled Giant* (Boar's Head Books, 1950). Michel Beaujour wrote coolly and lucidly on him,

'Céline artiste du laid,' *The French Review*, XXXVIII, 2, December 1964, 180–190. Truly critical appraisals of Céline's imagination and language are still missing. Marc Hanrez is far from impartial in *Céline* (Gallimard, 1961). David Hayman, *Céline* (Columbia University Press, 1965), is summary but fair.

The best monographs on Green are those of Antoine Fongaro, *L'Existence dans les romans de Green*. Rome: Signorelli, 1954, and Samuel Stokes, *Green and the Thorn of Puritanism*. New York: King's Crown Press, 1955. Excellent essays supplementing these books are those of André Blanchet in *La Littérature et le spirituel*, Aubier, vol. 2, 1960; Charles Koella, 'La Puissance du rêve chez Green,' *P.M.L.A.*, LIV, June 1939, 597–607; Charles Moeller, *Littérature du XXe siècle et Catholicisme*. Paris and Tournai: Casterman, 1953; Gaëtan Picon, in *Fontaine*, No. 55, October 1946, 443–454.

VIII

André Malraux

The detached observer, who is able to look at the contemporary European novel without being dazzled by its prestige or its temporary appeal, may well decide that until 1930 or 1940 it proved deficient in audacity. For a while, it toyed with technical innovations: reversed the slavery to time, shifted the storyteller's point of view; and penetrated into the interior monologue. But it failed to renovate the very substance of fiction. Although the French and English novel of the last decades has thrown some light on individual psychology and patiently unwound the mechanism of falling in and out of love, it has usually kept to a narrowly monotonous setting.

Meanwhile, the man of the twentieth century has been gradually engulfed by metaphysical and social preoccupations that scarcely found expression in the novels of 1910–30, not even in those of Proust, Joyce, and Mann. The originality of our age lies in a tragic conception of philosophy, and Pascal, Kierkegaard, Nietzsche, Unamuno, Sorel and Heidegger (to cite men of very unequal stature) are its most influential prophets or exponents. It has dawned on many of us, in the course of two world wars, that revolution, intense and chaotic action, violence, torture, and sadism are the climate of modern man, a climate to be found, for those who had lived through some of the horrors of the years 1936–45, in the novels of Balzac, Dostoevski, and Faulkner. André Malraux ranks close to such geniuses. He broadened the setting as well as the spirit of French fiction and boldly assailed the enigmas of man's fate.

Malraux is not a clear and easy author. His writing spurns the conventional storytelling technique, with its continuous narrative leading to a climax and a denouement and its gradual presentation of characters with the focusing of interest on a few of them. He avoids the description of scenery and seldom deigns to enlighten his reader on the complex historical and political background of his many-sided plots. His style is elliptical and jerky, rich in aphorisms and in imperious utterances on the meaning (or the meaninglessness) of life, some of which will appear to many readers as brilliant *non sequiturs*. 'All art rests on a system of ellipses,' Malraux once posited as an assertion essential to him. His own elliptical art demands much from the reader and allows no nonchalant dreaming.

Malraux's themes are universal; his tone is one of metaphysical anguish, which has become the new *mal du siècle* of our neo-romantics; the stress of an intense personal suffering underlies his stories of violence. Malraux is obviously not an Anatole France smiling with detachment at man's insoluble contradictions nor a jesting Pilate amused by the diverse follies of human puppets under exotic skies. He is engaged in the struggle that he depicts. He has, in Pascal's terms, gambled his whole life on the causes for which he successfully fought. But he has never failed to do justice to his adversaries, and his novels have the artistic irony that envisages the two opposite sides as impelled by noble and metaphysical motives. The acrimonious partisanship of the Catholic Bernanos or the Communist Aragon or that of many former and disillusioned Communists turned propagandists is never present in Malraux as an imaginative writer. He has turned to political action and to art criticism since 1941. Many regret it. But it was a sign of unusual courage in a writer who, emerging as a hero from the war and the resistance and surrounded by the admiration of the youth as Gide and Barrès had been in their day, might have attempted to repeat his earlier literary achievement and would perhaps have been only a shadow of himself. This constant seeker after fraternity has once more preferred solitude.

Malraux, the explorer of remote lands and fighter for revolutionary causes in Asia was born in Paris. He came from the bourgeoisie and apparently from a family that enjoyed financial ease. His studies at the Lycée Condorcet, which Proust had attended some thirty years earlier, were chiefly humanistic in character. Art and archaeology soon fascinated him, and his ambitious *Psychology of Art* is the outcome of long observation and reflection. As a very young man, Malraux, whose brilliant intellect dazzled his elders in a country wont to admire intelligence and

conversational talent, edited some little-known texts by Charles Baudelaire, Edouard Corbière, and Jules Laforgue and, in 1920, wrote a
brief article on the origins of Cubist poetry (Max Jacob, Pierre Reverdy,
and Blaise Cendrars) in a magazine entitled *La Connaissance*. His
earliest imaginative attempts were two strange fantasies in poetical prose,
which already pointed to some of the constants in his future work and
to a fascination with wars, cruelty, and tragedy: *Royaume Farfelu* (1920)
and *Lunes en papier* (1921).

Except for these very brief essays, Malraux did not rush into print, as
many young men were then doing in the literary upheaval that shook
Paris as soon as the Treaty of Versailles had been signed. Malraux
wisely chose to gain some experience of the world in time and space
before composing a novel. He sensed the peril of beginning a novelist's
career by the usual introspective volume.

In 1923, the young archaeologist left for Asia. He undertook excavations
in Indo-China, which soon brought him into conflict with the French
Department of Antiquities in Hanoï and with the scrupulous bureaucracy
of colonial administration. It was widely rumored that the young archaeologist was more an adventurer than a legally minded museum curator
and that he was impatient to appropriate some of his finds. He was, in
any case, accused of carrying off some of the Khmerian sculpture that
he had been instrumental in discovering and was probably sentenced to
imprisonment. His wife, a German woman, Clara Goldschmidt, from
whom he was to separate in the thirties, called upon Malraux's Parisian
friends to stand guarantors for his integrity, and he was released—not
without some fear of imprisonment, which he lent to several of his characters. In 1925, Malraux seems to have gone to China to work with the revolutionary committee of the Kuomintang. He acquired prominence in organizing conspiracies and in directing revolutionary propaganda. His
exact whereabouts have not been ascertained by his biographers, and he
prefers to be surrounded by a mysterious halo of legend rather than to
provide inquisitive historians with facts and dates.[1]

---

1. His first wife, Clara, wrote a delicate and pleasant volume of her memoirs, *Le
Bruit de nos pas* (Grasset, 1963). André Vandegans has disproved the legend which
made Malraux a graduate of the Ecole des Langues Orientales or of the Sorbonne
(*Revue des Langues Vivantes*, XXVI, 5, 1960, 336–340). He published in 1964 at
Pauvert's an extraordinarily precise volume on Malraux's beginnings as a man of
letters: *La Jeunesse littéraire d'André Malraux*. Walter Langlois unearthed much
new documentation on Malraux's courageous revolutionary action in Indo-China
from the local press which he consulted in Viet Nam. An article by him appeared

The account adopted by journalists and critics has it that Malraux soon became prominent in revolutionary circles in China and that he was, in 1926, one of the twelve leaders entrusted with organizing an uprising in Canton. When, in 1927, Chiang Kai-shek brutally turned against his Communist allies, Malraux left the Kuomintang and seems to have gone back briefly to archaeology. In 1934, he was reported to be flying over Arabia, in the hope of discovering ancient ruins from the air (some said, the palace of the Queen of Sheba). But he had by then made a name in literature.

Europe had meanwhile become ready for revolutions. With the advent of Hitler to power in 1933, the era of postwar bourgeois complacency was clearly over. A showdown between facism and communism seemed inevitable. Malraux apparently never belonged to the Communist party, but he had sided with communism and defended Dimitrov at the Berlin trial which followed the Nazi-fomented Reichstag fire. The Bolshevik authorities looked askance at a writer who showed little regard for Marxist orthodoxy and must have appeared temperamentally closer to Trotsky than to any other Communist leader. The French Communist party avoided making too much of Malraux; the French right did not attack him as venomously as they did other leftists. The liberal Catholic philosopher Maritain spoke with respect, in 1936, of the 'tragic feeling and of the spiritual quality of Malraux's work,' and Mauriac, the following year, in his *Journal II* looked with both fascination and envy at the ardent novelist then campaigning in Spain.

Malraux's service with the republicans in Spain was outstanding. He commanded the squadron *España* in the republican air force, rallied faltering energies, and exerted himself to teach the ill-united forces fighting for Madrid and Barcelona the value of organization. He stayed in the war until the fall of Málaga. Injured in service, he then came to America, in February 1937, and attempted to collect funds for the republican cause and to explain 'the value to literature of active political careers by its creators.' Engagement was not yet the fashionable motto for men of letters, but Malraux was campaigning for it and asking American intellectuals to leap forward to a heroic life or death. 'If they lived,' said he, according to *Time* (November 7, 1938), 'their writing would be better for the experience gained in the fight; if they died, their deaths

in *P.M.L.A.*, LXXXI, 1, March 1965, 111–122, followed by a volume listed in our bibliographical notes. Charles Roedig had a brief article on 'Malraux in Asia' in *The American Society of the Legion of Honor Magazine*, XXXII, 3, 1961, 145–163.

would make more living documents than anything they could write if they remained in ivory towers.'

The republican cause was doomed by the indifference of the democracies, the perverse blindness of many Catholics and conservatives, and the Spanish lack of aptitude for disciplined and united fighting; and the course of history was changed thereby. But some artists and writers had proved more foresighted than diplomats and professional strategists. 'The bloody manoeuvers preceding the European war had begun,' noted Malraux in *Espoir*. While he wrote that feverish book, literally on the battlefield, he made a film, also on the spot, that is a document charged with emotion.

His Spanish experience was to haunt Malraux. If revolution still appeared to him as the myth of the modern world, for he is not one to subscribe to any established order, he became aware of the usual aftermath of revolutions: one tyranny is replaced by another one, perhaps worse. No revolution can be effected without the great dynamic hope called by him the 'apocalypse.' But no revolution can survive without rushing into organization and order, police, and a repressive bureaucracy. Thus comes the crystallization, or perhaps the strangulation, of the revolutionary impetus. Malraux began to appear suspect to many orthodox Communists.

When the war actually broke out in Europe in 1939, Malraux was not to be found among those European writers who elected to live in New York, California, or Mexico so that, as they put it, some of the torchbearers of European culture might survive. Along with former antimilitarists like Louis Aragon and André Chamson, he volunteered for the hardest missions. He fought in 1940 in the tank corps and was taken prisoner in the French debacle. He was able to escape before the Germans, who had reason to fear the author of *Le Temps du mépris*, had recognized him. He worked for a while in Roquebrune, on the Mediterranean coast, on his volumes on art and on a life of T. E. Lawrence, whose personality seems to have impressed him powerfully. He saw his war novel, *Les Noyers de l'Altenburg*, through its first edition in Switzerland. The Germans occupied the whole of France in 1942, and Malraux then plunged into the underground movement. Under the name of Berger, he commanded a group of partisans in central-western France with the rank of lieutenant colonel. He maintained a close liaison with the British fliers who parachuted arms to the French guerillas.

Once again, wounded in the leg, he was captured by the Germans, and it is said that he paraded as a British officer to avoid being summarily shot. The French partisans raided the Saint-Michel prison in Toulouse, where the Gestapo held him, and set him free. He soon resumed fighting and became a colonel in the Alsace-Lorraine brigade, which he had helped organize. He served in Alsace during the hard winter of 1944–45 and answered his many admirers who wished him back in Paris at that time, 'I am fighting for my ideas as I have always done, and I shall not write one line until Fascist and Nazi methods are annihilated.'

After the German army surrendered Malraux found himself estranged from his former revolutionary friends. The death of his second wife in a railroad accident on the very day of the liberation, and the death of his own brother in the war had grievously affected him. He subsequently married his brother's widow. De Gaulle and he were drawn to each other by some similarity in their views and a common conviction that they were both men of destiny, impersonating forces doomed to triumph in the general decadence of politics around them. De Gaulle appointed Malraux as his minister of information in the short-lived cabinet that he constituted after the elections of October 1945. In January 1946, De Gaulle resigned abruptly to meditate on the reform of the party system, and of the constitution which he hoped to propose to France. Malraux became one of the directors of his propaganda organization. His gifts of rapid intelligence and of nervous, staccato eloquence fascinated audiences. He has repeatedly interpreted the latent philosophy of the Gaullist regime to French and to American audiences. In 1958, he became a Minister of State in charge of cultural affairs and he achieved much in the realm of the theater, architecture, museums, and reform of artistic education. He delivered impassioned speeches to the French Parliament on France's cultural and mystical vocation and on the reform of mass media.

Malraux is hardly a systematic or a logical thinker; his mind works far too swiftly to submit to the shackles of pedestrian rationality. But he does not indulge in vagueness. He can be eloquently sumptuous in his style; but he is less close to Chateaubriand and to Balzac than he is to Stendhal and at times to Barrès. He belongs to the generation of the postwar youth that, in 1920, had survived the great slaughter. The presence of death alone seemed capable of enchancing man's determination to live with purposeful intensity. And the contemplation of history, of old stones and mysterious inscriptions, and of civilizations that had been mortal, as Western civilization seemed itself to be, pathetically, in 1920, filled young men with a strange ardor to seek a means of defense against omnivorous Death.

Malraux is not the traditional or the conventional novelist, not any more than Proust or Kafka. He does not describe places or manners; he does not build love plots or tell a smooth story; he does not weave his intense tragic crises into one dramatic conflict. Yet Malraux is primarily a novelist, and even his volumes on art, perhaps lauded to excess, are those of an imaginative creator who molds reality anew rather than those of a historian or a philosopher. He overflows with ideas. But he does not invent puppets to exemplify them. He is not superior to his characters, but at one with them. He preaches no doctrine. He obviously could not linger long in communism, which became intolerant of any literature and art not at the service of the party line. He courageously pointed out, in 1935, the weakness of modern Russian literature, which had, after Dostoevski, failed to be both psychological and pathetic. The year before, in a speech delivered in Moscow and published in *Commune* (September–October 1934), he had warned the Communists of the disappointment of all their friends who failed to find power and truth in Soviet letters:

> Beware, comrades, of assuming that one necessarily creates a powerful literature because one expresses a powerful civilization; do not readily believe that, from the photographing of a great age, there will automatically spring a great literature . . . Art is not a submission but a conquest: a conquest of sentiments and of the ways of expressing them . . . a conquest over the unconscious, almost always; over logic, very often. Marxism is the consciousness of the social; culture is the consciousness of the psychological . . . The cultural motto of Communism must be that of Marx: 'More consciousness.'

Such an avidity for an increased consciousness sets Malraux's characters outside and above ordinary humanity. They seek neither money nor property nor do they, like Stendhal's, set out every morning hunting for happiness. Their quest is metaphysical and moral. At the very moment when they raise their arm to kill with a dagger, or are blown up by a bomb, they seize in a flash the essential meaning of life. The 'fraternity of death' lays bare to them the purpose for which they were living. The highest form of love is, to Kyo and May in *La Condition humaine*, to lure the loved one into death. Malraux rejects the static introspection of many French novelists. 'Man is an unknown animal,' he wrote, reviewing Matveev's *Les Traqués*, 'who thought he could know himself in quietude.

Let drama intervene and he discovers his powers of dream, his specific madness.'

But Malraux's man does not surrender to the forces that would engulf his lucidity and his will power. He directs them and unceasingly ponders over the moral issues raised by tragic life: How can, how must man guide his fate? Of what is he capable? One recognizes Nietzschean questions, carried over to an age that has unfortunately fulfilled some of Nietzsche's prophecies. To them, Malraux adds another preoccupation, which has become that of a whole generation deprived of God and unable to bear its loss: Is it possible for a man who thinks and who has the will to act to escape from the implacable solitude of tragic heroes? Can he reach solidarity with his fellow beings, whom he wants to love and serve?

Along with Nietzsche, who permeated his thought and influenced even his style, Dostoevski is obviously the master whom Malraux recalls. But he has never discussed and probably never studied his Russian predecessor with especial concentration; his technique owes little to him. Trotsky's powerful intellect held Malraux under its spell when orthodox Communist literature repelled him. Trotsky was indeed one of the few who praised Malraux's first novel as having dared to seize the great modern theme, revolution. As an artist, however, Malraux must be placed in the French tradition, which he pursues while transforming and extending it.

He voiced his distaste for Flaubert's rhythmic prose and carefully balanced novels. Flaubert's fiction appeared to him, perhaps wrongly, as imprisoning and debasing man. Malraux wants to exalt man, through his challenge to the mediocrity of life. He has no affinities with Zola, although some literary historians, strangely misled by their partiality for labels, have occasionally classified *La Condition humaine* as 'a proletarian novel.' Masses do not appear in Malraux's scenes of conspiracy. Stendhal is clearly the novelist most dear to him. He was the first, Malraux remarked, 'to see that the most powerful means of expression of the novelist lay in the ordering of facts.' He drew a similar lesson from the American novelists whom he has admired most: William Faulkner, of course, but also John Steinbeck and especially Dashiell Hammett. He borrowed nothing from their technique. But he was attracted by the melodramatic violence of their stories, by their disregard of regular arrangement of material, and by their graphic rendering of gestures, attitudes, and objects. In one of his few pronouncements on his own literary views, Malraux, who had set out in life as an explorer of Asia, prophesied the development of an Atlantic culture, as distinct from the former great Mediterranean heritage. He hailed the achievement of American fiction, more concerned with the fundamental man than the English, and observed shrewdly: 'To my mind, the essential characteristic of contemporary American writing is that it is the only literature whose creators are not intellectuals . . . The great problem for that literature is to intellectualize itself without losing its direct approach.'

Malraux's first significant work is not a novel but a brilliant ideological debate between two lobes of his brain and between two poles of modern thought and sensibility. The title itself, *La Tentation de l'Occident* (1926), is ambiguous, since it designates both the temptation of the West for some Easterners, and the far more potent attraction, after World War I, of the East to Western men. It came out at a time when Europe, led by a defeated Germany, which saw in her collapse the metaphysical portent of the collapse of Western civilization, was taking stock of those elements in the West that could withstand the Eastern invasion and an inner disintegration. To many Frenchmen, the East included Bolshevist Russia and extended as far as the Rhine; the phrase coined by Jules Michelet to designate Germany, which he admired, 'the India of Europe,' had enjoyed great fortune. Hermann Keyserling was at that time interpreting the wisdom of Asia, as his facile mind had absorbed it during his travels; Morand, Giraudoux, Huxley, and other literary travelers were toying with the opposition of East and West. Romain Rolland led the discouraged band of those who, despairing of the West doomed to mechanization and to warfare, turned longingly toward Asia.[2] Of all these men, Malraux proved the least partisan and the least superficial.

La Tentation de l'Occident is a series of letters supposed to have been exchanged by a Frenchman living in China and a Chinese visiting France. The Frenchman refrains from generalizations and is content with sketching a few vignettes of Eastern scenery and Chinese life, vividly expressed. The Chinese visitor to Europe is less easily carried

2. We have mentioned other features of that debate in a brief article on 'East and West in Contemporary French Literature,' *The Dial,* LXXXIV, 5, May 1928. Malraux, very early, was eager to determine what the European West was bringing to Asia which would ultimately effect a thorough intellectual as well as technological upheaval in that continent and shape the future. In an essay, 'Jeune Chine,' in *Nouvelle Revue Française,* XXXVIII, 1, No. 220, January 1931, 5, he asserted: 'The function of European thought is the transformation of the world by man. Any European thought may therefore be reduced to 'a secret of manufacture.' Provisionally, the two great secrets are Comte and Marx, the secret of the cure from metaphysics and the secret of history.'

away by what he sees. His letters constitute an unflinching diagnosis of the sickness that afflicts Europeans. Cities, museums, machines, hygiene, and books hardly concern him. He sets out to analyze a more subtle element—European sensibility. Europeans appear to him as weary of themselves and weary of their crumbling individualism, having built their lives upon a structure of negations. They act feverishly, often heroically, their 'soul's joy lies in doing' and in rushing to generous self-sacrifice. But they do not find underlying reasons for their activity. Boredom is their constant fear. They must resort to pastimes to escape it. Art is one of these and eroticism is another.

Malraux's Oriental mouthpiece ponders, in Malraux's disconnected, enigmatic fashion, on eroticism, as the characters in the novels will repeatedly do. The closing scene of *La Voie royale*, the episode in *La Condition humaine* in which the banker Ferral is humiliated by Valerie and vexes her in revenge, the latent drama of Kyo and May, tormenting each other in their love, which they had imagined to be above conventions and above sentimentality, reveal in sudden flashes the significance of the theme in Malraux's virile universe. Here is clearly one of the keys to the understanding of Malraux's psychology; but the author's reflections on the subject are too fragmentary to allow any construction that would substitute a systematic view for his occasional pronouncements. It is to be hoped that some day Malraux may express himself more fully on the subject than he has done in his essay on Laclos and in his five-page preface to the French translation of *Lady Chatterley's Lover*.

Malraux's conception of love stands at the opposite pole from D. H. Lawrence's, for it stresses the cerebral aspect of love more than the physical. It is Proustian in the sense that it is imprisoned in subjectivity. 'One only possesses what one loves,' says a character in *La Voie royale;* and again in *La Condition humaine:* 'One possesses of another being only what one changes in that being.' Appeasement of their senses or of their mental anguish seldom follows the brief and usually venal sexual experiences of Malraux's characters. They remain desperately alien to the woman whom they have just caressed. Of all of them it could be said, as it is of Ferral: 'He never slept with anyone but himself.' They will only be aroused by feeling some opposition in their partner, by a conquest to be made. 'There is eroticism as soon as to the notion of pleasure is added that of coercion,' declared Malraux.[3] He stresses the

3. That constraint may be persuasion rather than force, as in Laclos, on whose eroticism Malraux wrote a curious essay in *Tableau de la Littérature française,*

eroticism of men who want to humble the woman, to treat her as an object, to demand gratitude for the pleasure she has received and the shame she may have experienced. But they are no conquering Don Juans. Their eroticism exists almost independently of the person loved or desired, and their pleasure springs more from their tortured brain than from any physical fulfillment, from imagining themselves in the place of their partner. Their inner solitude is in no way alleviated by their ecstasies, which ignore tenderness, humiliation of male pride, and affection.

The Chinese observing the West, who prefigures Malraux's characters in the novels, is haunted by two other themes: the absurdity of life, and death. The life of the Western man is absurd, for he pursues goals he does not enjoy reaching. The loss of Christianity's hold upon the European man appears to Malraux as irretrievable. God is dead, as Zarathustra had shouted in his bitter exultation; but now man also is dead, and we seek his successor whom we might entrust with his legacy. Malraux will, in his last novel and his volumes on art, attempt to reconstruct the basis on which a renewed concept of Western man might be established. In his first volume, he was intoxicated with the wild despair of his youthful negations.

Upon all our joys the prospect of ultimate death sits as a curse. It impels Malraux's characters to seek violent action, to seize power, to rush to pleasure or to lose themselves in the creation of art, as if they were thus averting the sting of death. They will cherish death when fearing it most. In thus projecting his own obsession into his heroes, Malraux is voicing one of the preoccupations of many modern minds faced with a huge void inside and around them and powerless to fill it.

Gallimard, 1939. It may also be a desperate refuge against human aloneness, as in D. H. Lawrence ('Lawrence and eroticism,' *Yale French Studies,* No. 11, Spring 1953), although in Malraux's characters, it is, if anything, an intensification of their profound and incurable solitude: Perken, Kyo, Ferral. They do not encounter the tenderness which might follow the appeasement of physical desire, as in Lawrence. Their cerebral imagination exacerbates the carnal lust which then can no longer be satisfied. Like Dante's she-wolf, their greed grows after being fed: *E dopo il pasto ha piu fame che pria* (*Inferno,* I, 99). Women characters are only granted a very insignificant role in Malraux's fiction, as if the males feared the perils into which they might ensnare them. Nietzsche had written that 'the man worthy of that name loves only two things: danger and game. That is why he loves woman, the most dangerous of all toys.' Strangely enough, the only good studies of eroticism in Malraux have been done by women: Rima Drell Reck, in *Forum,* III, 9, Winter 1962, 44–46, and Micheline Herz, 'Passion and Intellect; or André Malraux,' *Yale French Studies,* No. 18, Winter 1957, 7–19, article on 'Woman's Fate.'

In order to destroy God, and after destroying Him, the European mind has annihilated all that could be opposed to man: having reached the goal of his efforts, like Rancé [4] in the presence of his mistress' body, he finds nothing but death . . . Never was discovery more disquieting.

Les Conquérants (1928) is a very different book. It is less finished in structure and less polished in style than its predecessor and therefore more promising, for in it Malraux no longer recalls poetical masters of prose, such as Barrès or Gide. He is elaborating a technique of his own, which is purposely disconcerting to the usual fiction reader. The characters are plunged into action and reflect only as they act.

Again the title is ambiguous. It may designate revolutionary agitators plotting against European imperialism, or Asia in ferment and one day enabled to turn against Europe, or the strong men who galvanize the masses, or even disease and death, the ultimate conquerors of men of action. There is hardly any unity to the book, little progression, and no organized plot. Malraux, one of the first among the writers of the present time, wants to utilize and rival a journalistic technique. Dispatches are flashed in the text, and events are reported as they happen, with the suspense of a still uncertain outcome, not embraced and weighed by the comprehensive eye of the novelist who controls their unfolding. The scene is laid in China, but not in the picturesque China described from the outside by travel books or by thrillers. There is no description of nature, no evocation of swarming crowds, no respite from the jerky, feverish action. The reader is plunged into a confused turmoil and shown a few episodes as disconnected as scenes in a newsreel. Whether such a method leaves the reader with a stronger impression of reality faithfully rendered is doubtful; there is even more artifice in the author's effort not to organize and not to intervene in his abrupt chapters than in the traditional device that, grasping the reader's interest, allows the author to be forgotten behind his narrative.

4. Rancé is the famous seventeenth-century Frenchman who, after a not very edifying youth, reformed the monastery of La Trappe. Hearing that his mistress, the Duchess of Montbazon, had just died, he rushed to her house to see (so the story goes) that the men come to bury her, unable to fit the body into too short a coffin, had sawed the head off and placed it in the oblong box alongside the body. Chateaubriand related Rancé's career in a small volume, in 1844. The theme of death pervades much of modern literature between 1920 and 1950: Rilke's *Notebooks* and his poems, Thomas Mann, Malraux, Charles Morgan, the *Overtures to Death* of Cecil Day Lewis, and others.

The setting is in Canton, where the Chinese, incited by Russian agitators, have decreed a general strike. The danger of insurrection threatens Hong Kong. Malraux has not attempted to exploit the epic possibilities of such a theme: East against West and the rise of Communists against Europeans. He has focused the light on the different factions and methods among the revolutionaries, and on the leaders, almost excluding the masses. The protagonists are not, but for one, men of the East; there are practically none of them in Malraux's fiction. They are European adventurers, to whom the author has liberally lent his own problems: How turn the absurdity of life into meaningfulness? How challenge disease and death through action? How reconcile what is most precious in individualism with the exigencies of a collective task that requires the sacrifice of the present and of the nuances dear to the intellectual? How accept the means required in order that the end imposed by the anonymous party line be ruthlessly achieved?

One of the characters, Borodin, borrowed from history, is a man of action, determined to devote all else to the obedience demanded by his party. He welcomes fanaticism, without which the order of tomorrow would never dawn. Garin, who stands in contrast to him, is more complex and more like his creator, though Malraux is too much of an artist ever to paint only in black and white. Garin was born in Geneva of a Swiss father and a Russian mother. He was molded by French ideas, deserted from the Foreign Legion, and mixed cynicism and idealism in his attitude. He never subscribed to any body of ideas, not even to Marxism in which he saw only a powerful incitement to the tension of the will. He is enough of an individualist to be repelled by what he terms 'the doctrinal farrago' of Bolshevism. He is less concerned with the lack of justice in society than with his deep anarchy. 'I am a-social as I am an atheist, and in the same fashion.' He is ready to devote his life to the cause of the people, but he has no love for them; and he hates the middle class, from which he sprang, even more. Those who possess defend their possessions with such stupid principles that they deserve no respect.

This strange, semi-Nietzschean revolutionary is an organizing genius. He helped Chiang Kai-shek reform the military academy, and he organized a good deal of Communist propaganda in China; but he has not abdicated his individual intelligence. Sooner or later, he will be liquidated by the very cause whose triumph he will have furthered. He cares little. For years he has been afflicted with paludism and dysentery. He hardly condescends to cure his sickness. A strange exaltation comes over him, when he contemplates the absurdity of any social order and of all that is human. Revolution had provided a means of escaping temporarily from that absurdity; for it had afforded some men a little more hope, and 'man's hope is his reason for living, and for dying.' Garin-Malraux has found one of the themes of all his meditations: 'No strength, no true life without the certainty and the obsession of the vanity of the world . . . The only defense is in creating.'

Les Conquérants, with its contempt for the ordinary devices of story-telling and of character presentation, with its bitter, if constructive, pessimism, was not likely to be a popular novel. It suffered from obvious faults. Its imperious dialogues, formulating the essential preoccupations of the author, were not skillfully merged into the action. The protagonist was analyzed independently of the plot. The characters tended to be types. The style was too elliptic in its incisiveness. But these were original and promising faults, asserting a haughty temperament, too rich to be tamed too soon by any readily accepted order. Leon Trotsky praised the novel in an acute article in *La Nouvelle Revue française,* No. 211, April 1931, 488–500, only regretting that Malraux failed to have any sympathy for the revolutionary masses. Malraux replied to him, *ibid.,* 501–507. Edmund Wilson praised the book as an expressionist novel, not unworthy of *Wuthering Heights* or *The Karamazovs* (*The Shores of Light.* New York: Farrar, Straus and Young, 1952, pp. 566–574).

La Voie royale, which followed in 1930, is in some respects more conventional. It is the smoothest of Malraux's novels, with a dramatic build-up of the reader's curiosity and several thrilling moments. The protagonists are again intellectuals. They are characterized with greater individuality than in the earlier novel; and their language is less uniformly that of their creator.

The title alludes to the unexplored expanse of the Indo-Chinese jungle, where old tombs and stupendous sculptures have been overgrown by the vegetation of several centuries. Claude, a young archaeologist with many features of the author, has long hoped to discover these carved stones, both for the aesthetic thrill of it and for the profit of trading them. The French institute in Hanoi, suspecting his purpose, refuses to lend him any assistance in his dangerous expedition, which will take him through the area of savage tribes. A Danish adventurer, Perken, whom he met on the boat, will be his companion.

Perken would be a Byronic hero but for the cynical bluntness of his talk, which contrasts with the affectation of Byron's mysterious and ever-

eloquent corsairs. He fascinates Claude by his scorn for established values
and by his passion for action, linked with his conviction that action,
like everything else, is vain. Both are obsessed with death and convinced
that courting it with a lover's zeal sets them above other mortals, who
cling to a life they do not know how to enjoy. Old age is to them the
worst calamity that can befall man, for it represents to them cowardice
and semi-impotence. But suicide is a fallacy; he who kills himself runs
after a complacent image of himself. These lovers of death are most
avid for life, and Perken voices Malraux's favorite views in neat aphorisms: 'I have staked my life on a gamble greater than myself.' 'I think
of death in order, not to die, but to live.' 'The exaltation which springs
from the absurdity of life when you face it as you face an undressed
woman.'

The two men, exchanging such formulas in their daily conversation,
set out on their expedition. They succeed in reaching the Royal Way and
in loading enormous sculptured stones on their ox-drawn chariots. But
their guides betray them when they announce their determination to
pursue their way to a remote village where Perken hopes to find a
former comrade, Grabot. Grabot, a gambler against fate, had also fled
from the conventionality of European life. He had sold arms in Thailand,
dreamed of erotic experiences with native women, of power over the
unruly tribes. But the man who would be king had ended as a wretched
slave. The natives had blinded him and tied him to a treadmill; like a
camel or a donkey, he turned round and round in a narrow cabin,
covered with dirt, a bell dangling around his neck. He had not even lost
his reason in the process. When, after a long search, the two explorers
discover their compatriot in that abject decay, he could only utter one
discouraged word—'nothing.'

After elaborate negotiations with irate tribesmen, the Frenchmen succeed in buying back their companion. Their march amid dangers is told
like a thriller. Malraux could indeed have become a writer of lurid stories
of violence. But adventures in themselves do not interest him long—
only as a means of showing how low man can sink when afflicted with
suffering and how intense can be the lucidity gained when death is felt
to be near. Perken, while returning, has been wounded by the poisoned
splinters planted by the natives on their warpath. He knows that he is
doomed. He will enjoy a last experience of physical love, coolly and
precisely described, and then accept his end.

La Voie royale showed Malraux's growing mastery over the mold of the novel. But he would not repeat that easy success. *La Condition humaine,* which followed in 1933, is a more ambitious work. It is one of the striking novels written in any language during the fourth decade of the present century. The atmosphere is still that of Malraux's earlier works, but his tenseness is somewhat relaxed. There are philosophical conversations, sections that verge on tenderness but just miss it at the last minute, and even scenes of comedy when Clappique, the tragic and farcical mythomaniac, appears. After the first few pages, the reader accepts Malraux's world unquestioningly, and this is the most telling tribute one can pay a novelist. In one of his very revealing and pregnant annotations to Gaëtan Picon's little book on him, Malraux had written in one of the margins that the novelist's affair is to create, not characters, but, like any other artist, a coherent and particular world. He succeeded in this novel. The characters are endowed with individuality and with the quality most sought after by Malraux: intensity. But they all bring to the novel what Malraux singles out as the prerogative of the art of fiction: they make it 'a privileged medium for the expression of the tragic in man.' In the second half of our century, dominated by events occurring in Asia, many readers will feel that they are reliving scenes from Malraux's novels.

La Condition humaine is not a novel of ideas, although it forces one to think. It is even less a novel of propaganda. The Chinese revolution in Shanghai provides it with a general theme, but it is in no way dependent upon a historical framework for its major interest. Balzac would have described the city of Shanghai, its geography and appearance, its motley crowd of natives and foreign traders, its smells, and some of its shops and houses. Tolstoi might have written at length of the great and small causes that had brought about the revolt and of the way in which events had been determined. Malraux's method, like that of most moderns, makes greater demands on the reader's brain. Nowhere is the confused skein of factions and assassinations and plots unraveled for his benefit. The irrational disorder of history is scrupulously respected. Malraux relates the struggle as an actor in those events and not as an omniscient and reflective spectator. The contemporary public, which has lived through one or more wars and is learning daily, through the press and the radio, how disconnected and futile are most of the events in which they are forced to take an interest, do not balk at the efforts they are asked to make. They know too well that men are not heroes curbing fate at will and that betrayals, contradictions, and dissonances are the common occurrence of any war, civil or foreign.

It takes no great subtlety to discern a pattern and a structure in the novel and the seven parts or sections into which it is unevenly divided. The revolution is the center. It is first prepared by Ch'en securing the weapons, Kyo and Katow, the other chief actors, getting psychologically attuned to the gigantic event, and Gisors, more remote, and Clappique, theatrical, looming in the background. In sections two, three, and four, the revolution appears as it strikes diverse characters: Ch'en the terrorist and Ferral the banker; Kyo the leader confronted, during a trip to Hankow, by the dilemma of political expediency imposed by higher orders as against individual action. The attempt to bomb Chiang Kaishek, whose betrayal the revolutionaries foresee, fails. Ch'en dies in the process at the end of Part Four. Meanwhile, the individual struggles, within each of the main characters, have been presented: Gisors, while fearful for the fate of his son, extracts the philosophical and social significance of the fight; Ferral's sexual frustrations parallel his financial and unscrupulous deals; Hemmelrich is pitifully enslaved to a poor, ailing family; Kyo, Gisors's son, and his wife May torment each other through honesty, shyness, nobleness, and because it is difficult for human beings to seek happiness with a simple soul.

The descent from the climax begins with Part Five. Clappique's weakness causes Kyo to be captured by Chiang Kai-shek's police. Torture will follow for him and for Katow. Death triumphs in Part Six, and yet virile fraternity vanquishes death's horror. A brief final chapter adds a note of irony, with Ferral's attempt to receive his financial reward in Paris, and of tenderness, with May's devotion to the memory of Kyo. All through the varied episodes, the themes of revolution, death, eroticism, fraternity, and the fate meted out to man, as well as that which he can control and make for himself, recur as the unifying themes of the book.

The old unities of tragedy are respected, after a fashion, in that comprehensive and often baffling volume. All the action, or almost all, takes place in Shanghai. It is concentrated within a very few days, grouped around March, then April, 1927. At first, Chiang Kai-shek is still the ally of the Communists. The general strike is declared; the movement spreads; it may fulfill its unbounded hopes, free the country from foreign domination, and initiate agrarian reforms. Then failure threatens. Chiang Kai-shek, bought by European finance, betrays his Communist allies; he escapes the bomb. The higher revolutionary authorities, inspired by Moscow, do not support a revolution they judge to be premature. The organizers of the revolt are thrown alive into the fireboxes of locomotives;

labor unions are dissolved; liberation is indefinitely postponed. But the abortive revolution has served one of its purposes: it has woven together individual lives and provided the violence necessary for intense thought.

It would have been an artistic fault of the author to weld the varied scenes and episodes of his book into an organic whole at the expense of the impression of jerky, scattered, and futile truth, which he wanted to produce. The real unity of the novel lies in the parallel but always separate preoccupations of the characters. More than any other motive, the consciousness of their implacable solitude drives them to common action. Those reckless revolutionaries constitute a motley gallery of tragic heroes, not without affinities with Saint-Just, Robespierre, or Lenin, eagerly molding a new world in Asia and haunted by the ultimate vanity of power, of greatness, even of all action. Ch'en, the first to appear on the scene, is the most pathetic. He is not fit for his role of murderer, and his determination to plunge his dagger into the sleeping man, with the city lights flooding the room and a cat weirdly observing him, is that of a diffident intellectual steeling his weak nerves for action. A sense of sin lingers in him, from his upbringing in a Lutheran environment; he is deeply insecure, doomed to solitude even in his loves, dissatisfied by the collapse of his childhood faith. Killing is to him an atrocious means of reaching a certainty, almost a substitute for a wild merging of his whole self in sexual passion. The opening scene of Ch'en's murder of the sleeping man, then his descent in the elevator in a state of trance, then his two vain attempts to bomb Chiang Kai-shek, and, finally, his desperate suicide are unforgettable scenes in the book. He, who had first killed like a stern priest offering a sacrifice, sacrifices himself to his own gods, as desperately alienated from mankind and from himself as the hero of *Crime and Punishment*.

The end of another conspirator, Katow, is no less superbly handled. He had already faced torture and death as a Russian revolutionary under the czars and had served a term in Siberian jails. He cannot forget or forgive. When the revolution is betrayed and crushed, and while Kyo dies by his side, he meets death by swallowing the cyanide he always carried in his belt. Two other prisoners lie beside him, young men who tremble before the end that awaits them in the fireboxes of the locomotives. Katow soon resolves to make the supreme sacrifice. He cuts his poison in half, hands it to the two young men, depriving himself. Their hands drop it clumsily; then, groping for the treasure that will shorten their pain, they grasp Katow's hand. A soft feeling of fraternity comes over him at that handshake. Death alone could provide 'that absolute friendship.' 'It is easy to die when one does not die alone.'

Kyo is the third hero of the book. He is the son, by a Japanese woman, of Gisors, an opium addict, a meditative dreamer, and a professor of sociology, who has powerfully influenced his disciples and even Ferral. To Gisors, Malraux has lent several of his favorite thoughts and he alone is loosely linked to the action, though essential to a novel that turns about man's difficulty in bearing his human fate. Kyo is no philosopher himself. A half-caste, he has early been wounded in his pride, and revolution is partly his revenge. He is relatively passive and more an organizer than a fighting hero. But he desires action as a means to forget his solitude. May, his wife, has thwarted his desire for tenderness and feminine understanding, and hurt him. He is not just the terrorist, like Ch'en, who concentrates on his immediate action. He believes in the revolution as a great cause, which alone can instill a sense of their own dignity into the millions of Chinese now perishing from slow starvation. 'There is no possible dignity, there is no true life for a man who toils twelve hours a day without knowing what he is toiling for.' When the chief of Chiang Kai-shek's police, the former German König, questions his prisoner Kyo, the latter will not jeopardize his dignity as a revolutionary idealist to save himself from torture and death. 'What would have been the value of a life for which he would not have been ready to die? . . . Dying could be an exalted act, the supreme expression of a life to which this death bore a strong resemblance.' Since the Renaissance heroes intoxicated with Roman Stoicism and at times by their own eloquent histrionics, few characters in literature have sung such hymns to meaningful death.

> The stroke of death is as a lover's pinch,
> Which hurts, and is desired,

whispered Shakespeare's Egyptian queen, kissing the asp. Malraux's heroes had looked in vain for those proud mutual caresses through which other tragic lovers boasted of 'standing up peerless' against challenges of fate and of death. Except for May, the women who gave a fleeting sense of companionship to these men were venal or semivenal professionals of love. Unable to learn humility or tenderness, these feverish rebels were only thrown back, unappeased, upon their own desolate solitude. Thus Malraux's universe, once again, recalls Pascal, but without God and with-

out charity. Men forever pursue a diversion that will intoxicate them and
make life bearable until the potion that soothes once and for all is quaffed.
Gisors explained his disillusioned view to Ferral: 'China has opium, Islam
has hashish, the West has women . . . Perhaps love is chiefly the means
by which the Western man tries to shake himself free from man's fate.'

La Condition humaine won a resounding success. It was one of the few
truly good choices of the Goncourt Academy, the best, perhaps, since
the crowning of Proust in 1919. The critics from all parties hailed it.
Abroad, where French literary prizes have very little influence on opinion, the book was praised as one of the more cosmopolitan and universal
French novels. If devoid of superficial charm and undoubtedly a difficult
book, indeed one calculated to repel the conventional woman reader as
publishers unfairly picture her to their authors, it had meat, vitality, and
boldness in it. The world, torn between the American depression, the
ominous rise of Hitlerism, and the abject appeasement policy of the
Western democracies, was realizing around 1934 that the time for effete
entertaining literature and an ostrichlike fear of fear would have to come
to an end. Malraux loomed as the prophet of the new era.

But he was a prophet for the few, for the middle classes, whom he
treated scornfully, and the literati, whose circles he had fled. The working
classes, as they are called, seldom opened his novels. They would have
been puzzled by the difficulty of the style, by the lack of apparent continuity and traditionally lighted focus, and by the pitiless soul-searching
to which the characters yield in the midst of action. Malraux's Communists may well be found to have stood closer to reality than any others
depicted thus far in fiction, much as their cynical egotism and their ruthlessness may have dismayed the idealistic admirers of communism in the
'thirties. At a time when Coriolanus, performed at the Comédie Française,
almost provoked a revolution in Paris, René Lalou aptly quoted the
words of Brutus, which seem especially fitting to Malraux and to most
of the revolutionaries in La Condition humaine:

> You speak of the people
> As if you were a god to punish, not
> A man of their infirmity . . .

Malraux's next novel was much less detached from the fate of the
common man, far more vitally 'engaged,' as the word now goes. Between
1933 and 1935, the crisis had deepened in Europe. The question was no
longer that of winning part of Asia to the revolutionary cause, but

whether western Europe itself could withstand the counterrevolution. 'Revolution! All that is not revolution is worse,' had exclaimed Malraux in *Les Conquérants*. It now had to be defended at home. *Le Temps du mépris*, translated as *Days of Wrath*, showed both an increased fervor in Malraux's faith and an original attempt at renovating his technique instead of repeating some of the devices that had succeeded brilliantly in *La Condition humaine*.

The book is less ambitious than any other work by the same author, more condensed, simpler, moved by feverish anger but tempered by humanity and even by pity. It is practically the novel of one single character, Kassner, engaged in one action for which even the name 'plot' would be a misnomer. A leader of Communist trade unions in Germany when Hitler has come into power, Kassner falls into a trap set by the Gestapo. He chews and swallows the revealing list of his party comrades, which the Nazis had hoped to seize, and he steels his will to resist torture and the weakness of the flesh, which might lead him to speak. The first part of the novel is a vivid and subtly contrived picture of the prisoner's mind. The guards torment him, question him harrowingly, starve him. He emerges from a daze into dim childhood memories, flashes of his past career as a Communist soldier in Russia, and disconnected and lurid nightmares. The threat to his reason frightens him. He would rather, as his last lucid act of will, commit suicide and rest assured that the silence of death would save his comrades from being betrayed.

But the first act of the closely knit novel, swift and ardent as a tragedy, closes when Kassner is saved from his solitude and his vagrant sick mind. He hears knocking at the wall of his cell. He is aroused from his preying loneliness and, after hard mental effort, he deciphers an alphabet in the unequal knocks. 'Comrade, take courage' are the words he has time to spell before the guard discovers his neighbor's device. The message binds him to another man. He emerges from the slough of despondency. Then, as in a tragedy, a surprising vicissitude occurs. Another Communist, judging Kassner's life to be essential to the cause of the party, gives himself up as Kassner, and the real Kassner is freed. Another comrade agrees to fly him, in bad weather and before the Nazis discover their mistake, to Czechoslovakia.

The danger is over, the storm is vanquished. The released prisoner reaches Prague and meets his wife. Unlike Malraux's other characters, he behaves toward her with simplicity, directness, and a tender consciousness of the anxious strain to which his revolutionary activity condemns her. She has not a word of reproach, and, hinting at his next mission, she comforts him implicitly by the fortitude with which she will bear her fate. The drama is resolved with a serene restraint rare in Malraux. Malraux refrained from political dialogues and reflections on life's significance in the face of annihilation. He stripped the book bare to a long short story and reserved the message with which he wanted to accompany it for a separate preface. The chief character, exceptional for Malraux, is not an intellectual.

The preface, apparently written after the novel had appeared serially, is the most important text penned by Malraux on his faith and on his artistic intentions. In it, he defined (neither geometrically nor logically) his conception of tragic fiction, reduced, like ancient tragedy, to a very few characters: man, the crowd, the elements, woman, and destiny. He took issue with the nineteenth-century conception of fiction and opposed to it his own, thus strikingly formulated: 'One may wish the word Art to mean an attempt to give men a consciousness of their own hidden greatness.'

Art, for Malraux, was never equated with propaganda and never was assigned the purpose of demonstrating anything. But, says the author in his fervent preface, it can also impoverish itself by systematically ignoring or belittling the brotherhood of man, or by that contempt for one's fellow-beings which is the surest mark of a fascist mentality. In noble language, Malraux added a few elliptical but pregnant sentences, which clear much of the misunderstanding raised by the imperious Nietzscheism of his earlier novels:

> The individual stands in opposition to society, but he is nourished by it, and it is far less important to know what differentiates him than what nourishes him. All psychological life is an interchange; the basic problem for the living individual is to know upon what he intends to feed . . . It is difficult to be a man. But it is not more difficult to become one by enriching one's fellowship with other men than by cultivating one's individual peculiarities. The former nourishes with at least as much force as the latter that which makes man human, which enables him to surpass himself, to create, invent or realize himself.[5]

L'Espoir (1937, translated in America as *Man's Hope*, in Great Britain as *Days of Hope*) comes near to being a great book on a great theme; but

5. The translation is, but for very slight changes, that of Haakon M. Chevalier, quoted through the courtesy of Random House (*Days of Wrath*, New York, 1936, pp. 6–8).

we would not be ready to agree with Malraux who declared to Ralph Butes that he thought it his best book.[6] The novel is instinct with a warm quality of sympathy for men of all parties and with a welcome gift for personifying philosophical views in living and moving characters. Malraux no longer seems to look upon revolution as a personal opportunity to live tragically and escape from dull, prosaic pursuits. His own faith is deep and sincere. The style itself has sloughed off some of its flashy brilliance; it occasionally submits to reposeful dialogues and relates some incidents with patience and humble fidelity to events as observed. *L'Espoir* stands as a powerful work inspired by the most productive (on the literary plane) of recent wars—the civil war in Spain; and it deserves the preference granted it by most critics and students over *For Whom the Bell Tolls*. Yet we doubt whether any but a very few scenes and the characters actually remain impressed upon the reader's memory. Malraux purposely played against several self-imposed difficulties. It is not certain that he won.

For one thing, the volume is very close to the events it describes. It respects their confusion, takes us alternately to Barcelona, Madrid, Toledo, Guadalajara, and multiplies scattered scenes of fighting and of cruelty, interspersing them with conversations now humorous, now enigmatic and perhaps profound. While reality may indeed have been irrational and disorderly, as Malraux depicts it, and while it is true that the republican cause in the Spanish war counted an unusually large number of intellectuals and thoughtful debaters among its defenders, it may be questioned whether Malraux did not violate some conventions of the art of fiction, only to be punished for his transgression. Even Stendhal's celebrated Waterloo episode and Tolstoi's admirable war diary of Sevastopol respected a pattern of unity more than does *L'Espoir,* and they had fewer pages. The very variety that Malraux wanted to embrace in his several scenes turns into monotony when the reader perceives that they all bear the imprint of the author's vision and style. The reader expects a sense of progression of interest, which the novelist refuses to satisfy.

Such a criticism may seem unfair since it tends to take an author to task for not having achieved what he deliberately refused to undertake. But the question recurs again and again to the mind of the reader: Is not Malraux clinging to a musical composition or, as it might rather be termed, to cinematic devices of disconnected scenes through some de-

6. *The New Republic,* November 16, 1938.

ficiency of his imaginative power? Is he not naïve in his sophisticated attempt to respect literal truth and to reject the synthetizing power of invention, co-ordinating the scattered debris of reality into a living order? The sparkling exchanges of ideas in which all those exceptional soldiers indulge might have become superfluous if Malraux had made his characters live those truths in action and had refrained from voicing their reflections in his own words. The novelist's task is to make us believe in truths that need not be translated into neat formulas.

Malraux similarly defied the conventions of the novelist's art when he refused to focus the interest on one or more heroes. He valiantly attempted to violate our expectation that a novel must be enacted by a few outstanding characters who will engross our attention. It is true that the republican cause in Spain did not create or find its representative men, its Mirabeau, its Lenin, or it Bela Kun. But the reasons for this failure, the psychological dramas within some of the individuals tormented by the gulf separating reality from their ideal, would have been worthy of concentrated exploration. Malraux preferred the divergent novel in which centrifugal forces constantly move away from an elusive center. His novel consequently demands from the reader that he reconstruct in his own imaginative memory the scattered data laid before him. For that exceptional reader alone does the book take on full significance.

L'Espoir is an intellectual epic, critical and lyrical at the same time, on the great hope of the revolution. Seldom has a revolutionary creed been more alien to materialistic aims. Other leaders have held out promises of more comfort, more justice, better hygiene, and less poverty. Malraux's revolutionary fighters are all alike in this, but their hope in the victory of their cause does not preclude understanding their adversaries and realizing that the same men who shoot at each other could, in different circumstances, have been comrades at arms. They are not sentimentalists. Malraux never was squeamish about scenes of cruelty, and some of his episodes of horror are worthy of Goya's brush. 'The highest duty of the soldiers,' one of the characters remarks, 'is to do one's utmost so that shreds of iron will riddle human flesh.' But those fighters are also intellectuals, bent on absorbing with their sensibilities and analyzing with their minds a momentous experience. Malraux, fighting in Castile, is a true son of Montaigne, Descartes, and Stendhal when he coins some of those formulas that sum up and guide a life. 'Tell me, Major, what is, in your opinion, the best thing a man can do with his life?—To transform as wide as possible an experience into consciousness.'

The true tragedy in *L'Espoir* is indeed of an intellectual order. The implicit unity of the novel lies in the anguished questions it poses about the revolution as it was envisaged and enacted by men of thought. These strange fighters flocked to Spain from several countries, after being trained in art and books, after pursuing the nuances that make truth complex and fascinating. They plunged suddenly into the world of action. They realized that 'action is Manichean, and pays a tribute to the devil.' The most dearly cherished part of their being had to be offered in sacrifice on the altar of a better world, in which their hope seemed at times rather dim. They had to learn action, fanaticism, and organization.

There lies the rub. Revolutions, to be sure, are a poetical myth or, as Malraux prefers to say, an apocalypse. They exalt men above the present, in an *élan* comparable to the Messianic hope of the Jewish people or to the religious aspirations of the early Christians. 'Men will only die for what does not exist,' that is, for sublime but half-fallacious hope never to be fulfilled. And there will never be any dearth of youths eager to risk their lives for an abstract cause. In fact, all modern wars are fought for abstract causes (democracy, a way of life, the cause of peace) and no longer to capture or recapture a province or a colonial island or to protect one's trade.

But the willingness to die is not enough. Malraux soon learned in Spain that intellectual anarchists may provide martyrs and warriors but that Spain needed men who would fight first and then organize their victory. Revolution and war canot be justified by the fact that they afford an opportunity for intense living and meaningful dying. The word 'organize,' dampening as it is to the rash hopes of mystics of the revolution, becomes the burden of Malraux's mournful song. 'Courage is a thing which must be organized; it has to be kept in good condition, like a rifle'; or 'A popular movement, a revolution or even a rebellion, can hold on to its victory only by methods directly opposed to those which gave it victory—sometimes even opposed to the feelings from which it sprang.'

Hence the unresolved and insolvable conflict in the book and in Malraux's soul. In the past, the man of thought or the artist could afford to stay aloof and to avoid or ignore practical politics. He prepared action in undisturbed meditation; he observed it detachedly, meted out praise and blame, and retained unsullied an ideal of pure justice. He was the cleric who did not betray.

But during and after World War I, the world changed. New political leaders claimed to control the minds and the souls of their subjects—subjects who had often willingly and in mass hysteria elected them to un-controlled power. At the same time, military service claimed all men, even those intellectuals who once were left alone provided they cele-brated the beauties of war and the greatness of the sovereign's conquest. Hence the revenge taken by the war literature of Erich Maria Remarque and Henri Barbusse, of John Horne Burns, who wrote *The Gallery,* Norman Mailer, and James Jones. A thinker or an artist was no longer left free to reap the benefits of a social order in which and for which he took no risks and which he often scorned as impure. He had to take sides in a Pascalian wager.

And as sincerity had meanwhile become part of his ethics as a writer, Malraux had to realize that, as Goethe expressed it in *Wilhelm Meister,* to think is easy, to act is less easy, but to act according to one's thought is the most difficult thing in the world. The whole twelfth chapter of Part Two, Section two in *L'Espoir* is concerned with that crucial problem. The intellectual plunged into war and revolution must consent to the hardest sacrifice for him—*il sacrifizio dell' intelletto.* He is constantly faced with a dichotomy. Malraux has sketched it more than once. There are two types of revolutionaries: the individualist or the anarchist, who will not renounce his freedom of thought and lives intensely in the present (Garin, Tchen, Scali, and the Negus in *L'Espoir*), and the organizer who accepts and imposes discipline, silences his scruples, and suppresses all else for the sake of a better future (Borodin, Kyo, Kassner, and in *L'Espoir* Garcia and Manuel). Between the two, Malraux, deep down, has never made the final choice. As much as Gide though less compla-cently, he is *un être de dialogue.* His present political alignment may not be his last.

The very dilemma in which he writhes is that of his age. Around him in many lands, men are wavering between the revolutionary apocalypse and the inevitable and ruthless organization of the apocalypse; between the nuances necessary to thought and Manichean action; the sanctity of the individual and the inevitable sacrifice of the most precious in him to the collective good. The international revolutionaries whom Malraux has gathered on the Spanish battlefield symbolize the tragedy of modern man at his crossroad. Their dialogues can hardly sound natural, under the buzz of airplanes. But they voice the hope and also the forebodings of the modern man, willing to help the advent of a future he hopes may prove brighter, yet conscious of all that is irreplaceable in the art and culture of the past. 'For a man who thinks, revolution is tragic,' says

Garcia. 'But for such a man, life, too, is tragic . . . There may be such a thing as a just war, but there is no such thing as a just army . . . There is a politics of justice, but there is no just party.'

L'Espoir revolves around another dilemma still, no less tragic for the twentieth-century revolutionary who can no longer believe that an uprising of the people and the raising of barricades will bring about the triumph of a generous cause. The republican forces in Spain had met with defeat because they were not assisted from outside, but also because they had not found leaders. Malraux soon observed it, and understood that any popular movement that fails to evolve leadership is doomed. Power corrupts or intoxicates; most revolutions have been known to end in a stronger centralized authority, a more repressive police, a more rigid bureaucracy than had the regime they overturned. But, unless leaders emerge from the masses, a rebellion will soon flounder into anarchy; and a reactionary and militaristic tyranny will replace it.

Malraux's novel does not give a glowing picture of the leader whom he sees as indispensable. His dialogues comment sadly upon the solitude of the chiefs, whom authority and efficiency make daily more alien to the men whom they command. *Misereor super duces* could be one of his mottoes. For the task of a chief is exacting. He must be loved because he is just and efficient but not because he courts popularity. 'An officer must never seduce . . . To be loved without seducing is one of the highest feats of man.' And again: 'There is more nobleness in being a leader than in being an individual: it is more difficult.'

The role of the chief, who is himself condemned to solitude, is to develop 'virile fraternity' in his men. The phrase is among the most striking coined by Malraux; the passage in his books where characters reach that fraternity, when threatened by death, are the summits of his art as a novelist. In *L'Espoir*, the Spanish peasants carry down the mountain paths the stretchers of wounded airmen. In both the book and the film, the scene is rendered with a sobriety and an emotion not often achieved by Malraux. Without any unanimist theory, without any of the moralizing that tempted Saint-Exupéry, without the reasoning about their all-embracing responsibility indulged in by some existentialists, Malraux makes fraternity a living and moving force.

Soon after *L'Espoir* appeared, the Munich crisis, then World War II burst upon Europe; and the novelist's prophecies of a world in which sadistic cruelty and mass brutality would reign were fulfilled. Malraux had even foreseen that, parallel to wars between nations striving for power and impelled by hatred, implacable rivalries between ideologies and parties would henceforth rend nations internally. Malraux was much read and often quoted in the years 1940–44. The scene in which Kyo refused to betray his cause and his honor before the chief of police was often re-enacted in the underground movement and before the Gestapo. 'Human dignity . . . is the contrary of humiliation.'

Malraux did not then capitalize on the timeliness that his ideas and his writings had assumed. He acted, and wrote little. He avoided publicity. He published only one novel in Switzerland, in a limited printing of fifteen hundred copies, in 1943: *Les Noyers de l'Altenburg*, as the first part of a longer work with the title, evidently an allusion to Jacob's struggle in Genesis, *La Lutte avec l'ange*. As an artistic achievement, the book is not satisfying. Its long ideological discussion is badly integrated into the plot, and there is hardly any semblance of a plot. The characters are too clearly the mouthpieces of the author's own anxiety. Yet several passages rise perhaps higher than anything Malraux had previously written; and they are free from the obsession with lurid violence and with death, which harried Malraux in his earlier novels. Edmund Wilson was right, at the time, when, in a thoughtful critique, he called the novel 'the most impressive and the most exciting piece of literature . . . inspired by the war.'[7]

Les Noyers de l'Altenburg derives its title from the peaceful setting of an old abbey in Alsace, shaded by walnut trees. The novel is made up of three parts of unequal length and purposely disjointed, but in each the same question is asked. The hero in the first part is a young French Alsatian, Vincent Berger, who, in the battle of France in 1940, was taken prisoner by the Germans and thrown with thousands of other captives into the nave of the Cathedral of Chartres. The naïve hopes of his fellow prisoners and their bewilderment are rendered with human pity and with power. The young Alsatian, in the next part, then meditates upon his father's experiences, which he has pieced together from a set of notes found after his father's death. The bulk of the volume is devoted to that tale of the elder Berger's career and to philosophical meditations connected with it.

Berger's father, whose life was lived mostly before 1918, was of German nationality. He combined intense scholarly curiosity and adventurous action. The East lured him. He had served with the German mission in Turkey, dreamed of a movement uniting all the people of Turkish

7. *The New Yorker*, September 8, 1945.

origin, and had been disillusioned after a stay in Afghanistan. He then took part in the serene Altenburg colloquies in his native Alsace. There, immense problems were stirred up by a few thinkers: Nietzscheism, Hegelianism, Pan-Germanism, and anthropological observation of primitive people. Nietzsche's shadow hovers above the talks, and his madness is depicted in vivid pages by the narrator's great-uncle, who had been a friend of the philosopher. Malraux's criterion for a great work, to which he has himself frantically tried to live up, is Nietzschean: a work is great through its ability incessantly to question the validity of the world, *par son aptitude à remettre le monde en question*.

During World War I, the elder Berger took part in an attack against the Russian lines, in which the Germans experimented with poison gas. The scene is reminiscent of Malraux's most violent and dramatic moments. The German soldiers, following up their gas shells, stand horrified at their own murderous success. They rush to help their dying enemies and feel seized with revulsion against the modern methods of warfare. In the last part of the book, the scene shifts to World War II and to young Berger fighting with the French and defeated. He relives in his memory his last fight before he was captured. He was, like Malraux, serving in the tank corps. While he was leading his tank against the Germans, it fell into a trap where death was a certainty. He waited for it, horror-struck. Miraculously, the German shells missed him. He and his crew crawled out of their ditch, reached a village, and escaped from the jaws of death into the rediscovery of life.

If *Les Noyers de l'Altenburg* probably does not succeed as a novel, even in Malraux's own opinion, it reveals much about its author, in an earnest and passionate tone. His youthful obsession with hatred, eroticism, and action for the sake of action has disappeared. His early rhetoric and his Byronism have been transformed and raised to a plane of universality. This war book, completed while the French were fighting the occupying German forces in the underground, is devoid of partisanship. The very choice of heroes of Alsatian origin, with a name as much German as French, is significant. In the middle of the most atrocious fight, the wish of one of the characters is that of the author and many of his countrymen during World War II: 'Ah! May victory come to those who have fought the war without loving it.'

For the true subject is not war, but man's fate, his struggle against it and his acceptance of it. Repeatedly, and more than ever in his books on art, Malraux has played striking variations on the theme of fate and paraphrased, never clearly, the significance of the word. The word holds for him an undying fascination. 'It owes its special accent,' he says, 'to the fact that it expresses our dependence, and the mortal lot of all that imposes upon man the consciousness of his nothingness, and first of all of his solitude.' Thus, in his third volume on art, Malraux continued his search for a world intermediate between the absolute world of God, which he considers dead, and the ephemeral world of men, which fails to satisfy his anguish. Malraux's heroes, and all men as he sees and pictures them, are creatures conditioned by the privilege that has been bestowed upon them; man is 'the only animal which knows that it must die.' [8] His joys are poisoned at the source by the realization that he is not to be immortal. But the awareness of death awaiting him urges man to action. He seeks beauty in a frail world in which his stay will be brief, or creates beauty in order to triumph over death, the ephemeral, and the relative. After looking death straight in the face, the characters in *Les Noyers de l'Altenburg* find 'Life more inexhaustible than Death.' Malraux the negator does not look for an easy refuge against the contemplation of man's weakness; he remains a tragic pessimist, as Nietzsche and Pascal, and the Greeks before them, had been. But there is hope indeed in his fight against the angel, or against the gods. In one of his most Pascalian sentences, he exclaims in his last novel: 'The greatest mystery is not that we should have been thrown here below at random between the profusion of matter and the profusion of the stars, but that, from our prison, we should draw from our own selves images powerful enough to negate our own nothingness.'

'What is man capable of?' was one of the Nietzschean interrogations, which echoed in Malraux's earlier work. In action and adventure, in eroticism and an anguished but vain quest for identification with his partners in love, in shaking audiences and political parties to the depths through his nervous eloquence, and in courting and vanquishing death, Malraux had attempted to push further the boundaries of man's capabilities and of his self-knowledge. With *Les Noyers de l'Altenburg* and his subsequent books on art, his tone has ceased to be one of jerky and passionate questioning. A positive faith is formulated. It rests on the central issue raised by Malraux's studies in ethnology and anthropology, as well as by his confrontation of East and West, past and present. On

8. The remark was a commonplace of eighteenth-century philosophy. Rousseau defines man, in his *Discourse on inequality*, as outgrowing the animal condition when he begins to know that he must die.

what basis can the notion of man be founded? Are there unity and continuity in men's successive and isolated efforts to challenge fate? Is the experience of men cumulative or do cultures appear and die as detached cycles, all doomed to tragic failure and leaving nothing but a few sculptured stones around which 'the lone and level sands stretch far away,' as around Ozymandias's shattered visage?

The colloquy in *Les Noyers de l'Altenburg*, and even more the contemplation of the serene and aged walnut trees shading the house in which facile thinkers exchanged ideas always born from other ideas and not originating in facts, already showed Malraux as transformed by his experience of revolution and war. Fraternity is a noble ideal, though a difficult one to live by in everyday existence; our affection for our fellow-beings has to withstand severe jolts when daily confronted with men's greed, cowardice, and superstition. But the realm of art provides Malraux not with an escape but with the means of a transfiguration. For if the pre-eminent role given to interrogation constituted the best in Western civilization, art, with Leonardo and Rembrandt, with Cézanne and Picasso is, or has turned into, 'an interrogation of the world.'

Malraux's works on art, collected in a one-volume edition, reorganized and somewhat clarified, as *Les Voix du silence*, may well remain his greatest achievement and one of the significant books of our century. They negate history and disregard the filiation of schools and of ideas. They are hardly concerned with technical discussion of the pictorial elements in painting. They discuss the art works, not in themselves, but in reference to the culture which underlies them. They throw at us a cascade of ideas, some of which may have been borrowed from Worringer, Focillon, and Elie Faure. But they force upon the reader a broadening of his Greco-Roman-western European perspective by letting African masks, Oceanic idols, and Chinese and Indian temples and sculptures intrude incessantly upon his secure, shrunken vision. Malraux's attempt to redefine man reflects his concern and that of the moderns; unless the Asiatic and the African men are integrated into, but not summarily merged into, our broadened concept of man, modern Western humanism is a ludicrously complacent fallacy. The 'museum without walls' has made such an integration possible. Photography enables us to familiarize ourselves with the art of all times and of all nations, and the juxtaposition of heterogeneous works of art in modern galleries allows us to compare and to set up new systems of relations or of metaphors in the original sense of constant 'carrying over' from one culture to another.

Parallel examples drawn from many lands and forty centuries converge around a few lessons, which Malraux lived in his own fiction before he rediscovered them in the great creators of the past—who all assume the mask of Malraux's characters. Every artist is a lonely hero, set by his genius at a wide distance from ordinary mortals. He is a rebel against fate, a living revolt against history. He is more sensitive to his own universe, the universe of art, than to that of other men, into which he happens to be thrown. He is driven to painting or to sculpture by an inner daemon that impels him to oppose, to works of art that their predecessors had created, new or future works of art that they must create in their turn, as rivals of nature and not transcribers of it. Borrowing, probably without knowing it, a notion Croce had once developed, Malraux proposes a pattern to which he submits every style and every individual artist. According to that pattern, every creator begins by imitating former artists; then he breaks away from his early models and turns ungratefully against them. Writers and artists regularly started from other writers and artists, never or seldom fom nature. Their originality is, in terms dear to Malraux, an annexation of the achievement of others and an imperious conquest.

Thus is some continuity in our civilization established, and some degree of universality, underlying varied cultures and different continents, asserted. Modern times have, according to Malraux, witnessed the end of the absolute. Religion survives with undoubted fervor in many of us. But it has lost the character of an unchallenged belief in another world, which it once possessed; it no longer conditions our daily lives, as it did in the Middle Ages. In his essay on European youth, written in 1927, Malraux had remarked that Christianity is like a scar imprinted deeply in our very flesh, and we, who are no longer Christians, are still forced to perceive and to decipher the world through a Christian code. Nostalgia for a new absolute plaintively breathes through the pages of Malraux's volumes on art; it may well some day bring the former Nietzschean negator to a religious conversion. He cannot rest content with the acceptance of the relative and the worship of history, which, since the late seventeenth century and even more since Hegelianism, have expelled the absolute from our philosophies. He is concerned about the dissatisfaction and the anxious despair that are reflected in modern art. But he unstintingly admires the modern artists who struggle against fate, as El Greco and Tintoretto once did, and are not content with adorning and prettifying life. 'Civilization is not sweetness, but consciousness and mastery of man.' In the very last sentence of his long excursus through the art of several continents, Malraux lyrically exclaims: 'O scattered world, ephemeral and eternal world which, to survive itself instead of repeating itself, stands in such need of men.'

Malraux's message, like that of Giraudoux, of Giono, of Gide, and of Cocteau, is a message of humanism. To have become a man without the help of the gods, such is, to Malraux, man's chief claim to greatness. Such humanism is superficially antireligious. But it voices one of the most eloquent protests against the debasing of man, which has been systematically practiced in our century by internecine wars, ideological hatreds, tyrannies of the mind, and much literary obsession with all that is low. Malraux's fiction answers in the affirmative one of the most tragic questions asked by Nietzsche: *Ist Veredlung möglich?* Is it possible to ennoble man?

Bibliographical Notes

The following novels by Malraux have appeared in English translation: *The Conquerors,* translated by Winifred Stephens Whale (Harcourt, Brace & Co., 1929; and London: Jonathan Cape, 1929); *The Royal Way,* translated by Stuart Gilbert (Smith and Haas, 1935); *Man's Fate,* translated by Haakon M. Chevalier (Smith and Haas, 1935; and as *Storm in Shanghai.* London: Methuen, 1934); *Days of Wrath,* translated by Haakon M. Chevalier (Random House, 1936; and London: Gollancz, 1936); *Man's Hope,* translated by Stuart Gilbert and Alastair Macdonald (Random House, 1939; and as *Days of Hope.* London: Routledge, 1939). The three volumes on art have been published in New York by Pantheon Books as *The Psychology of Art,* translated by Stuart Gilbert, and *The Voices of Silence* was published in 1953 by Doubleday. The early volume, *La Tentation de l'occident* (Grasset, 1926), appeared in English translation as *The Temptation of the West,* Vintage Books, in 1961. To the important volumes on art should be added *Saturne: Essai sur Goya* (Gallimard, 1950: *Saturn.* Phaidon-Garden City, 1957). A number of Malraux's forceful book reviews (of Keyserling, Bernanos, Arland, Matveev, Gide, Guilloux, *et al.*) appeared in periodicals and should some day be collected, as should Malraux's prefaces and his remarkable speeches on cultural subjects, on Leclerc, on Jean Moulin, delivered since he has been one of De Gaulle's ministers.

An unusually large number of volumes of criticism and of articles have been devoted to Malraux. The most important are:

Bespaloff, Rachel, *Cheminements et carrefours.* Vrin, 1938.
Blanchet, André, 'La religion de Malraux,' *La Littérature et le Spirituel,* II, Aubier, 1959, 191–232.

Blend, Charles, *Malraux, Tragic Humanist.* Columbus: Ohio State University Press, 1963.

Blumenthal, Gerda, *Malraux, The Conquest of Dread.* Baltimore: Johns Hopkins Press, 1963.

Boisdeffre, Pierre de, *André Malraux.* Editions Universitaires, 1952.

Delhomme, Jeanne, *Temps et destin.* Gallimard, 1955.

Fitch, Brian, *Les deux univers romanesques de Malraux.* Lettres modernes, 1964.

Frank, Joseph, *The Widening Gyre.* New Brunswick, N.J.: Rutgers University Press, 1964.

Frohock, Wilbur, *Malraux and the Tragic Imagination.* Stanford: Stanford University Press, 1953.

Goldmann, Lucien, *Pour une sociologie du roman.* Gallimard, 1964.

Hartman, Geoffrey, *Malraux.* London: Bowes and Bowes, 1960.

Langlois, Walter, *André Malraux, The Indo China Adventure.* Praeger, 1966.

Ollivier, Albert, 'Mythologie de Malraux,' *Critique*, No. 6, November 1946, 483–503.

Picon, Gaëtan, *André Malraux.* Gallimard, 1945.

————, *Malraux par lui-même.* Seuil, 1953.

Righter, William, *The Rhetorical Hero.* London: Routledge and Kegan Paul, 1964.

Savane, Marcel, *André Malraux.* Masse, 1946.

Simon, Pierre H., *L'Homme en procès.* Neuchâtel: La Baconnière, 1950.

Stéphane, Roger, *Portrait de l'aventurier.* Sagittaire, 1950.

Vandegans, André, *La Jeunesse littéraire d'André Malraux.* Pauvert, 1964.

See also Janet Flanner, *Paris Journal.* Atheneum, 1965, *passim* and her biographical articles in *The New Yorker*, November 6 and 13, 1954, and the special numbers of *Esprit*, 1950, and *Yale French Studies* (*Eros*, No. 11, Spring 1953, and *Passion and Intellect*, No. 18, 1957).

IX

Existentialism and French Literature: Jean-Paul Sartre's Novels

Existentialism is a metaphysics, a psychology relying upon phenomenology, a sociology of literature, a therapeutics, and, probably more than anything else, an ethics. Clouds of confusion, due in part to the complexity of the issues and to a failure to agree on clear definitions of words, but in part also sedulously thickened by the rival high-priests of existentialism, have turned it into a myth, surrounded it by a cult, but created in others a bitter animadversion. Far too much publicity, not always sought by the German or French champions of that philosophy, has surrounded the movement. Many among the early detractors of existentialism in France, even more in Britain and America where the movement was branded for ten or fifteen years as a systematic debasement of all values and as obscene scatology, have tried to discredit it as erotic titillation and delight in coarseness.[1] After two or three decades of discussion, we may not necessarily be much clearer as to the meaning of existential-

1. Claude-Edmonde Magny in *La France Libre*, 15 December, 1945, 96–102, and *Les Sandales d'Empédocle* (Neuchâtel: La Baconnière, 1945), 105–172, Gabriel Marcel in many reviews, Jean Wahl with far more objectivity, Pierre Boutang in *Sartre est-il un possédé?* (Editions La Table ronde, 1946) and Raymond Las Vergnas in a little book which does not rank among his best, *L'Affaire Sartre* (Haumont, 1946), have criticized or satirized Sartre's ideas. The *Times Literary Supplement* has had many reviews of Sartre, some of the early ones not very understanding, others (July 12, 1957; May 5, 1961; July 23, 1964) overgenerous. In America, Marjory Grene, James Collins have taken issue with Sartre. Walter Lowrie, in 'Existence as understood by Kierkegaard and Sartre,' *The Sewanee Review*, LVIII, 3, Summer 1950, 379–401, attributes Sartre's popularity to his affection for 'vomit, offal, and carrion.'

ism. There will never be a consensus among philosophers as to what 'existence,' 'nothingness,' 'the absurd,' 'a project,' or our moral duty as discovered by our own derelict self and still valid for other men, may signify. But it is possible to relate existentialism to its precursors, to its age, and even to assess, as Croce did for Hegel and as has been done for other philosophy, what in that system is dead or moribund and what, from it, is likely to survive.

The general context in which several of the existentialist moods and ideas appeared antedates World War II. Indeed, like much that permeates the second half of the twentieth century, it can be traced back to the general failure of reason's claims to explain the world, around 1910–15, and to the growing lack of faith in science as affording absolute certainties. The earliest printed expression of Sartre's anguish is probably found in an 'Enquête auprès des étudiants d'aujourd'hui,' reported in *Les Nouvelles littéraires* on February 2, 1929. Sartre, then at the Ecole Normale and preparing for the Agregation of Philosophy (where he was to be admitted number one that very year, after having failed the previous year for inadequate knowledge of history of philosophy), said: 'At the bottom of the human creature as at the bottom of nature, I see sadness and boredom. . . . Good and Evil, ideas of man working on man: vain ideas. Vain also is that determinism which strangely attempts to effect the synthesis of existence and of being. We are as free as you wish, but powerless. . . . There is no will to power. All is too weak: all things tend to die. . . .' Comparing his generation, which regarded itself as sick with 'le mal du siècle,' to previous generations, Sartre concluded, at twenty-four: 'We are more unhappy, but more "sympathiques."'

Soon after, an economic and social depression was to darken the prospects of Western man. Unemployment was to grow catastrophically. Nationalism became resurgent in Europe and tyrannies ruled over half of its area. Traditional humanism had become inadequate. Faith in the future had collapsed; so had faith in fraternity and faith in the moral and sexual liberation which, after Freud and the breakdown of old taboos, had seemed to promise happiness. Man felt desperately alone and knew he would have to rely upon himself, a derelict. 'Leave us alone without books, and we shall be lost in confusion at once, had written Dostoevski, then eagerly read in France. 'We are oppressed at being men, men with a real individual body and blood. We are ashamed of it, and we try to continue being some sort of impossible generalized man.' Another Russian, who lived in Paris and who is often called a Christian existentialist (he was an Orthodox, but the friend of many French Catholic thinkers), Nicholas Berdiaev, wrote in *Solitude and Society* (1938): 'Sex is one of the chief causes of human solitude. Man is a sexual being, that is, half a being, divided and incomplete.' The comfort which the young people of France had derived first from the philosophy of Bergson, mostly influential between 1905 and 1925, then from that of Maritain, appeared of little avail to the intellectuals of 1935–38. Disappointed with Stalinist Russia, estranged from the new Messiah (which the surrealists, André Gide and others had naïvely hoped to hail in 'Cette grande lueur à l'est,' as the French title of Romains's *Men of Good Will*, volume 19, puts it), they were seeking elsewhere. Bergson, it is true, had sketched a distinction between the 'deeper self' and the 'superficial self' that was to be formulated anew and with greater rigor by the existentialists when they contrasted the authentic with the inauthentic self. But he had not stressed the recoiling before anguish which led man to take refuge in the inauthentic. Moreover he tended to explain man by what had preceded him, an *élan vital* of which God was the prime mover, and he had declared the notion of nothingness to be unthinkable. Not without much injustice to the moving developments of *Les Deux Sources de la Morale et de la Religion* (1935), the existentialists, in their claim to hold a monopoly over anguish, resented Bergson's apparent serenity. Merleau-Ponty, however, made amends to Bergson in his inaugural lecture at the Collège de France, *Eloge de la Philosophie*, in 1953.

The existentialists were attracted by phenomenology, of which Merleau-Ponty, for many years a close friend of Sartre and his collaborator at the helm of *Les Temps Modernes*, was the chief exponent in France. Husserl, its founder, conceived it as a method which, in presence of an object, seizes only the appearance according to which we think it and which it assumes in our consciousness, and a method which remains unconcerned with the reality which may not correspond to that appearance. Such a method, intent on grasping the meaning of the world directly, would resort to literary description as preferable to abstruse and abstract speculation. It sought an ally in fiction and drama and another one in political and social 'engagement' or involvement. 'The world is not what I think, but what I live,' declared Merleau-Ponty, echoing Kierkegaard. Sartre, like him a professional metaphysician, but one who is equally at home in the novel, the drama, polemics, and criticism, stated: 'Metaphysics is not a barren discussion on abtract notions which lie beyond the reach of experience; it is a living effort to embrace, from the inside, the human condition in its totality.'

The later volumes of Sartre and of his friends have been acclaimed in the Anglo-American world. A skillful but minor masterpiece, *Les Mots*, was rapturously over-praised in 1963–64. *Time* and *Newsweek*, which had at one time mocked him as decadent, devote respectful articles to him. *Playboy* publishes reverential interviews with him, and grave essays by him. Camus has had more worshippers in the United States than any writer since Harriet Beecher Stowe and was mourned upon his death as a saint. Simone de Beauvoir ventured to suggest, after one of her trips to this country, that America was *the* land for existentialism *par excellence;* the youth of the United States has certainly, since 1960, been far more drawn to that ethics of freedom and of action than that of France, and more philosophical and literary volumes on Sartre and on Camus appear in the United States than in the whole rest of the world. Some of the Sartrian formulas ring like echoes of pragmatist compatriots of William James and of John Dewey: 'To understand the abstract concretely'; 'The world is not what I think, but what I live'; or 'Freedom is nothing else than a choice which creates for itself its own possibilities.' Even Sartrian professions of atheism have failed to dismay Unitarians, Episcopalians, or the Catholics of 1965 who are advised by the Ecumenical Council to understand atheism and to learn from it. 'If you admit God,' said Sartre, 'it is because you are afraid to be what you are, simply men, and to be self-sufficient. I say: God is not, man is sufficient unto himself'; or (in *Action*, on December 29, 1944), 'A motto for man: to do and through doing, to "do" himself [*Faire et en faisant, se faire et n'être rien que ce qu'il s'est fait*] and to be nothing but what he has made of himself. . . . True optimism is to be glad to count on oneself alone, and to act alone for the good of all.' The change in Anglo-American opinion reflects a deeper transformation in the moods of the English-speaking nations. During and just after World War II, the Anglo-Saxon allies, spared invasion or bombing of their own lands, holding high their courage and determined to save the rest of the free world, looked down upon the oppressed and demoralized Europeans of the continent as doomed to misery for years, unable to solve their problems and therefore seeking an escape in grandiose abstract speculations. They compared their weakened allies whom they were rescuing to the Germans who, in 1917–18, sensing that they were going to lose the war which they had at first hailed as 'fresh and joyous,' concluded that their collapse was a gigantic 'Decline of the West.' Many an American commentator then contended that existentialism, a philosophy of decadence emanating from a Europe that had lost all faith in herself and in the future, was as such discredited and would never seduce a healthy and optimistic New World. Such however was not the case. Much of what is significant in that philosophy was already latent in the nineteen-twenties and 'thirties, not only in Germany but in an early volume by Malraux and in Sartre's first philosophical writings, which antedated and did not foresee the capitulation of Munich and the collapse of the ruling classes in France in 1940. However, even if the subsequent formulation of existentialism, on the absurd, on the necessity for anguish, and on the need for man to formulate his own immanent values himself and to conquer his own freedom, had been inspired by the catastrophes which shook Europe in 1940, by the gas chambers, and by the bombings of civilian populations, such a lived source for emotions and ideas would in no way impair the validity of that philosophy. It would, on the contrary, be revolting that thinkers could have then ignored the breakdown of values around them, could have polished words and systems as Goethe had done, singing wine, women, young men, and the delights of art in his *West-Östliche Divan* while Napoleon was trampling Germany under foot, and could indeed have remained deaf to the clamor of oppressed people who then hoped in vain to hear clear and militant encouragement from the Pope or from their religious and academic leaders. The existentialists then lived their ethics with courage. They bid farewell to universals and chose to concentrate on the way in which traditional and general truths presented themselves to them *hic et tunc*, then and there.

Sartre, like Camus, like Genet whom Sartre has ironically transfigured into a saint, and like the leader of surrealism, Breton, before him, considers moral issues alone as important and has said so in the presentation of his own ethical thought by his friend Francis Jeanson. But a moralist is not a teacher of lay Sunday school precepts for obedient little boys. Somewhat provokingly, and as a part of his anti-bourgeois obsession, he has sought to give some jolts to the decorum of middle class ethics; because of this some of the Parisian reviewers of his novels even classified him with the naturalists of the last century. Their perspective was faulty and Sartre is certainly no Zola. His occasional incursions into scatology in one or two of his short stories and in the second volume of *Les Chemins de la liberté* (*Roads to Freedom*) are more the 'canulars' or practical jokes of a 'Normalien' and of a bachelor dwelling among books and ideas than a systematic attempt at portraying the lower realities of life. There is no doubt a negative aspect to Sartrian philosophy, and with it some reveling and wallowing in the mud. But, as Leibnitz and Renan liked to assert, any philosophy is false in what it negates and true in what it asserts. With a perspective of several decades, we may now safely disregard the few negative, superficial, and ephemeral aspects of Sartrian existentialism and assert that his most lasting contribution may well lie in the psychological acuteness of his descriptions of moods and states of consciousness (of the *café* waiter, the caress, the 'inauthentic' and frigid woman in *L'Etre et le néant*, of the Spanish soldier afraid of death in *Le Mur*, and of the schizophrenic couple in *La Chambre*), in his search for an ethics, in his achievement as a novelist, and, at his best, as the most superb essayist of our age.

Existential thought was more profound perhaps in Kierkegaard, certainly in Husserl, who remains the primary and the earliest advocate of a return to things ('Wie wollen auf die Sachen selbst zurückgehen') and of the project (or intentionality) as being the very nature of consciousness. Heidegger was probably not known to Sartre when he began elaborating his own system of thought in the early nineteen-thirties and there always remained many differences between his thought, called in French *existentiale*, and that of Jaspers, dubbed *existentielle*. Heidegger himself always carefully separated his own doctrine (or successive doctrines) from French existentialism and deplored Sartre's dualism, as radical and ill-founded in his view as that of Descartes. His own ambition is to restore a link between the object and the subject: his concern is with existence, or, as he puts in the Latin plural in *existentialia*, in what is. But the originality and the force of French existentialism is that it did not stay enclosed in university seminars of philosophy and wrapped in abstruse language. As an English commentator of that French literature has called it, it was from the start 'literature as philosophy' (Everett Knight) and the work of the 'Novelist as Philosopher' as another Englishman, John Cruickshank, entitled his volume.

The movement of ideas, derived in part from German predecessors and, to a lesser extent, from Pascal, Kierkegaard, Nietzsche, and Unamuno, made a momentous commotion in France and elsewhere, shaking most of the branches of literature, our response to poetry, painting, and music, and affecting the lives of thousands of individuals. As had been the case once with Cartesianism, then with the Enlightenment and with Bergsonism, philosophy sprang to a new life in attempting to seize the individual and the concrete. It coincided once again with life, fulfilling the wish formulated by Kierkegaard when he took issue with Hegelian philosophy turned obstinately backward: 'We live forward, but we understand backward.' This correspondence between philosophy and an *Erlebnis,* a lived experience, proved a boon to literature. The latter could no longer be reduced to seductive stories, skillful comedies, and pleasing garlands of imagery and of words. Such literature has been treated contemptuously by Sartre, even when it was written by his former close friend, Camus, or (as he repeated in *Les Mots*) by himself. The French readers of 1940–60 insisted upon literature facing the anguish of modern man. Everything had crumbled down around them and they knew that all had to be called in question, with the feeling—termed by the poet Henri Michaux the most precious asset of modern man—'irrespect.' That literature of years of distress had to attempt what Marx had defined, in his *Critique of Hegel's Philosophy,* as being radical: going to the very roots. And, Marx added, the root of everything is in man himself.

The importance of a movement, ideological, aesthetic, and even political, cannot be measured clearly by the number of persons who present themselves as belonging to it, but by the quality of their sensibility and the power of their ideas. Surrealism has influenced scores of painters, sculptors and poets, in and outside France, from René Char to Giacometti and Arshile Gorki, who never bowed to the iron rod of André Breton. There may well never have been more than sixty existentialists or sixty surrealists; nevertheless those movements constituted the marching wing of French literature for several decades. None rivaled them in importance. The years 1940–65 may well be labeled, in future histories of taste, the existentialist era. Nor does it seem of much consequence to debate at length on who was, or was not, a genuine existentialist, or an authentic surrealist, or a true romantic. Existentialism never constituted a chapel, or a school, from which a heretic or an unruly child is expelled: it is a mood. Camus repeatedly refused to be labeled an existentialist; but in spite of his technical differences on the respective role of essence and existence and on the meaning of the absurd, or his attitude toward concentration camps in Russia or toward the Algerian war, Camus nevertheless grew up in the same climate of sensibility, acclaimed the same masters (Dostoevski, Kierkegaard, Nietzsche, Kafka), fought the same battles as other existentialists; the very bitterness of his later quarrel with Sartre and Jeanson testifies to his closeness to his 'frères ennemis' and to the passionate dialectics required to distinguish him from his former allies. Along with Camus, and besides the high-priestess of existentialist altars, Simone de Beauvoir, the leading French phenomenologist Merleau-Ponty, from whom Sartre became estranged and on whom he wrote a moving essay after his friend's death in *Situations IV*, played a significant role in existentialism. Jean Genet, Violette Leduc, J.-M. Le Clézio, even Robbe-Grillet (reluctant as he would be to be thrust into a pigeonhole with other phenomenological doves), Colette Audry, and others have been or are close to existentialism. So are a number of critics and moralists, such as Jean Pouillon, Francis Jeanson, and Bernard Dort. Unlike Breton, Sartre has never attempted to imprison any disciples in his own system or to impose his technique to them. He is too intelligent not to be aware of the danger of epigoni, who would soon degrade his most original artistic devices by turning them into mere tricks. The chief existentialist review, *Les Temps Modernes,* after bidding fair to renovate literary life in the nineteen-fifties, has become monotonous, obsessed with a few political and sociological themes and remote from literature and art. It has been too long under Sartre's exclusive control and has failed to draw outstanding young talent. But if a movement is worth as much as its leader is, existentialism remains very considerable. Sartre stands out, 'above the rest proudly eminent,' as the most extraordinary intelligence of his generation, as a novelist and storyteller of the first order, as a successful playwright, as a brilliant essayist and critic of literature, art, life, even as a political thinker, and, of course, as a psychologist and as a philosopher. Like Voltaire and Diderot, he unites an amazing variety of gifts in one person; and he has occasional flashes of insight into poetry and into religion, of which his eighteenth-century predecessors had not proved capable.[2]

2. Those French thinkers who profess Christian existentialism (as well as Karl Jaspers and Paul Tillich) have not very clearly distinguished their attitude, except on the question of God's existence, from the agnostic existentialists. This is not to suggest that their philosophy, stemming from Kierkegaard's 'I exist, and therefore I think,' from man's need for God as in Pascal, and resting on phenomenology, is not just as valid existentialism as that of the atheists. Catholic thought is rich and influential in France today as it has never been since the classical age (Maritain, Simone Weil, Teilhard de Chardin, the Belgian A. de Waehlens, Jesuit fathers De Lubac and Blanchet, etc.). But no very considerable Catholic existentialist literature has been inspired by that philosophy. Gabriel Marcel is better in his early philosophical treatises or in his *Philosophical Journal* than he is as a dramatist. Interesting Catholic novelists like Jean Cayrol, André Lesort, Loys Masson, or poets like Jean-Claude Renard and Jeon Grosjean, have not been influenced by existentialism.

'A fictional technique,' Sartre wrote, 'always sends us back to the novelist's metaphysics. The critic's task is to elucidate the latter before appraising the former.' The assertion may lead to erroneous conclusions if all literature comes to be interpreted as nothing but philosophy in another form. But since so much confusion has clouded the few vital principles that existentialism has upheld, it is useful to state the fundamental points which Sartre and his friends put forward. But the imaginative works of Sartre preceded his most important philosophical treatises. So did *Caligula*, in an earlier version, *L'Etranger*, and the essays in which Camus voiced his pagan lust for life, which all came before the murky dissertations of *Le Mythe de Sisyphe* and of *L'Homme révolté*.

The first notion stressed by existentialism is that of nothingness. That notion was discarded by most philosophers, and again not long ago by Bergson, as untenable. But the existentialists stress it, at least negatively, and, outdoing or contradicting Pascal, they establish a colloquy with the absence of God. We experience, according to Heidegger, the utter nothingness of not being; existence (*Dasein*) is steeped in it. Sartre contends that the concept of nothingness comes into the world through man.[3] Why do I exist? Why does anything exist? Why is there not just nothingness? If the idea of nothingness does not lend itself to analysis, it can at least be experienced in fear and trembling. The *Angst* or anguish, of which Kierkegaard made so much, is the starting point of a personal philosophical reflection. Thanks to it, we pass from the superficial level of conventions lazily observed to the deeper level of individual reflection which accompanies man's awareness of his dreadful freedom.

Man facing nothingness undergoes the revelation of the absurd. No word has been more misinterpreted, partly through lack of a neat definition of what was meant by it on the part of Kafka and Malraux, who first threw the notion among us, then through the same indefinition on the part of Sartre and Camus.[4] The word itself has retained in French its Latin meaning of 'dissonant,' 'discordant' (*ab* intensifying *surdus*, deaf or insufferable to the ear), 'inharmonius,' hence 'foolish' and 'unreasonable.' For Kafka, man is surrounded with mysterious signs which he cannot

3. See an article by Victor Bentata, 'La Question du Néant,' *Revue de Métaphysique et de Morale*, April–June 1965, 193–198.
4. A confused and youthful little book by Manuel de Diéguez, *De l'Absurde*, Le Triolet, 1948, and an article by R. Verneaux, 'De l'absurde,' in *Revue de Philosophie*, 1946, 165–197, hostile to atheistic existentialism, were among the early French attempts to clarify the idea of absurdity. Sartre's very important statements on the point appeared in his early 'Explication de L'Etranger,' in *Cahiers du Sud*, February 1943, often reprinted and translated, and in an interview given to *Paru* in December 1945.

decipher and which appear to be hostile to him. For Sartre, the absurd is what in a being is 'given,' injustifiable, the weight of all that is contingent and makes man feel 'de trop,' superfluous, unwanted. But Camus made the most of the notion of absurdity which, to him, lies in a relationship between man and the world which is jarringly dissonant. Man is athirst for rationality yet he continually stumbles upon irrationality. He harbors in him 'a wild need for clarity' and he is confronted with darkness and confusion. He wishes happiness but the conditions of life seldom or never bring happiness within his reach. He would like a presence to watch over him and guide him through perils, but the eternal silence of the heavens fills him with dread. 'Men die and they are not happy' is the realization which prompts Caligula to commit his insensate crimes. The absurd is the conflict between human nostalgia for a reasonable order and the ubiquitous presence of the irrational.

That lag between man's wild wishes and 'reality's dark dream,' as Coleridge called it, fills the brain and the stomach of the existentialist with nausea. His temptation at first is to resort to what Camus, after Novalis, calls the only truly philosophical gesture, suicide. But suicide would merely amount to doing away with the one element, rational, courageous, and capable of clarity, that protests against the absurd irrationality of a blind universe: man. Camus rejects suicide, anxiously but with a little of the same sophistry with which Schopenhauer had eluded it. He welcomes the paradoxes that Kierkegaard, in his *Journal* for the year 1838, had lauded as the true privilege of intellectual life and the hallmark of great thinkers, the ability to proclaim the truths of tomorrow. Sartre and Camus will not, as did Kierkegaard, resort to the leap of faith to reach 'the absolute paradox, Christianity.' Their move of transcendence will not be toward a nonexistent God, but toward the world, other men, and toward the future.

Atheism is the third postulate. Existentialists waste no time attempting to prove a negative, which is deemed impossible in logic. What is gratuitously asserted may, in any case, be just as gratuitously negated; as old logicians ruled, 'quod gratis asseritur gratis negatur.' Their placid assumption is that everything takes place as if God did not exist, and they drive the famous Nietzschean 'death of God' to its consequences. They spurn the facile solaces of deism ('the deist is he who lacks the nerve to be an atheist,' said the French Catholic writer, De Bonald) and of pantheism, the latter being one of the most glittering diamonds in that jewel-case of synonyms that Renan hinted the modern had substituted for

God. For too many moderns, God is merely a convenient symbol to whom we transfer the burden of our problems in order to evade solving them ourselves as religious thinkers, grateful to atheistic existentialism for its forthrightness, have pointed out.[5] 'Man is a being that projects to be God. . . . Man loses himself as man in order that God may be born. But the idea of God is contradictory and we lose ourselves in vain. Man is a useless passion': thus concluded the philosopher of *L'Etre et le néant*. Let us transcend ourselves, not vertically, seeking a heaven above, but horizontally, like the doctor and his friend in *La Peste*, assume our human condition fully and, most difficult of all, our freedom. Existentialist philosophy has been praised by its devotees as a liberation, albeit a frightening one. There is indeed more stoicism and optimism (or 'muscular and constructive pessimism') in existentialism than there is apathy or irresponsibility. Again and again, its partisans have stressed their difference from Kirilov who, in Dostoevski's *The Demons* (or *The Possessed*), exclaimed: 'If God does not exist, everything is allowed.' In their view, on the contrary, man must unflinchingly assume his duties to himself and to his fellow-beings. Since God does not exist, or since everything happens as if He did not exist, nothing is permitted. Man will set himself up as the creator of values, in the place of an absent or silent God. It is up to him to create his own essence and accept his total freedom.

The fourth credo of the existentialists is the well-known assertion that existence precedes essence. Man was not created according to a preexisting mold or pattern, like a table or a paper-knife. He is not just one sample of a general entity pompously dubbed 'human nature.' He is not a shadow in Plato's cave, aspiring to the noble and stable Idea. He was thrown into the world, a derelict; he exists. No properties were assigned to him beforehand. He is what he conceives himself to be and what he makes of himself; but he does not have to fulfill any pre-established plan. Only as he is here and now, does anything begin for him. He enjoys a 'morose delectation' in feeling thus forlorn, a prey to care or *Sorge*, shorn of God and of a Redeemer. From his very dereliction he will draw audacity. He will create his own human nature and his own values, through transcending the past and the present, throwing himself into the future

5. In America, Dean Samuel H. Miller, of the Harvard Divinity School, at the Commencement speech of the Princeton Theological Seminary, June 6, 1961; in France, Father de Lubac and Jean Lacroix in *Le Sens de l'humanisme athée*, Casterman, 1958, a collective volume, *L'Athéisme, Tentation du monde, Réveil des Chrétiens*, Editions du Cerf, 1963.

and pursuing his project. 'One is nothing else but one's own life.' Man, thrown into this world through a sudden and random *Geworfenheit*, does not long dwell in gloom. He accepts himself and looks forward. Sartre summed up his ethical message as 'You are free. Choose, that is to say, invent.'

Subjectivity is the obvious starting point for such a doctrine, and here again the ancestor is Kierkegaard. *Sum* has become the foe of *cogito*. *Sum, ergo cogito* proposed the disgruntled Hegelian from Denmark, who added: 'A thinker cannot prove his existence through thought, for insofar as he thinks abstractly, he forgets precisely this: that he exists.' Man is a subject with a self to acquire, and not an object to be known. The literature of existentialism does not proceed through generalities about man, nature, passions, the world. It attempts to seize man in the quick, to grasp him in the irreducible uniqueness of his existence. Man is described *en situation*, in certain conditions that happen to constitute the framework of his existence, and in his project. He fulfills himself, through living, in a world and with a consciousness inextricably welded to each other. *Sein* is *Zeit* for him.

The fifth postulate is man's freedom, fundamental in Sartre's view of things and totally unproved, but a necessary postulate. Man has the freedom to become free. He chooses and projects himself toward his choice. He does not want that freedom, which is a heavy burden; the creature who has realized how momentous his freely assumed burden is becomes seized with dread. But that freedom also constitutes man's greatest single asset. It entails involvement, the duty of bringing a similar awareness of man's potential and dynamic freedom to others, through political, journalistic, and literary action. That freedom is always in danger of being lost and must incessantly be reconquered.

The individual, thus nondetermined, condemned to be totally free, does not turn into an anti-social anarchist, intoxicated with his individualism—or so Sartre assumes. He chooses the good and rejects vice, crime, oppression. He would not treat any person as a thing. Existentialism, gratuitously, almost mystically, considers freedom as the basis for responsibility and formulates what amounts to a new categorical imperative. The free person avoids becoming the mere captive of former decisions, for the irreplaceable quality of individual existence would then be dried up, and he must also heroically extend his responsibility to the awakening of placid unprivileged mortals who have not yet assumed the burden of their freedom. One of the favorite existentialist maxims is none other than the declaration in *The Brothers Karamazov:* 'Everyone is responsible for everything before everybody.'

The awareness of his freedom and of his boundless responsibility comes upon the hitherto uncommitted individual with the illuminating unpredictability of a religious conversion, and it transforms him into a proselyte: such is the case for Orestes in the drama *Les Mouches,* for Mathieu in the second and third volumes of *Les Chemins de la liberté,* for the Parisian journalist Rambert stranded in Oran in *La Peste.* Suddenly the character thus blessed with that burden of a nondivine and purely human grace frames and lives his values. He passes from the complacent *en soi* to the more creative *pour soi.* He is not only his own master, but also his own providence. His anguish is enhanced further, but it is the sign of the mission which he must fulfill.

Before he became involved in tortuous philosophical expositions several thousand pages long, in 1944–48, Sartre uttered a number of cogent and unambiguous statements which will some day receive a place among the noblest moral sayings in French. Thus in a short-lived weekly, *Action,* in 1944: 'Much pharisaism would be required for us [or our critics] not to detect in anguish itself the formidable mission which is entrusted to each of us.' And again:

> Every one of our acts has, as its stake, the meaning of the world
> and the place of man in the universe. Through each of them, whether
> we wish it or not, we set up a scale of values which is universal.
> And one would want us not to experience dread and anguish in the
> face of such a momentous responsibility!

Existentialist dramas and novels have not been afraid of displaying inverts, weaklings, idle drinkers committed to talk and absinthe rather than to the cause of freedom, promiscuous women, and men urging their mistresses to resort to an abortion rather than assuming their responsibilities as fathers. Sartre himself has been charged with encouraging his followers to fight (or not to fight, hence to reject being drafted for anti-colonial wars) while remaining prudently at home himself or parading as a talkative guest of Mao Tse-Tung and of Castro, instead of exposing himself to danger in the front lines. But he was not a coward during World War II and the resistance, and his essays on 'La République du silence' and 'Paris sous l'occupation'[6] will remain as the classical texts, austere, concise,

6. The first of those essays appeared in *Lettres françaises* in 1944, the second in *La France libre* in 1945: the latter is translated in *Playboy,* XIII, 1, January 1966. Both are reprinted in *Situations III,* Gallimard, 1949.

tersely striking, to which historians of World War II will have to resort. In most of those pronouncements, Sartre appears primarily as a moralist advocating the resolute assumption by man of his duties to others and to himself. *Qu'est-ce que la littérature?*, in *Situations II*, translated as *What Is Literature?* in the Philosophical Library in 1949 is rich in vibrant declarations such as this one: 'There is no such thing as a given freedom. One must conquer oneself over passions, race, class, nation, and one must conquer other men along with oneself.' For many years, Sartre has hinted that he was working on a formulation of his ethical views and preparing a *traité de morale*. Many questions raised by his postulates of man's boundless and frightening freedom and of his responsibility might be cleared up in such a treatise, if Sartre would eschew some of the barbaric language of his later philosophical volumes and recover the restraint and the clarity which he displayed again in *Les Mots*, in 1964.[7] Sartrian ethics is primarily an ethics of sincerity and authenticity, hunting out bad faith and assuming that man chooses the good. But the good can be conceived in conflicting ways. Sartre has defined evil as a pure luxury, a gratuitous activity, which presupposes much vigilance and a constant inventiveness akin to genius. One thing is clear: no ethics can legitimately tell men how to behave under any circumstances without an outrageous hypocrisy. Treating man as an absolute end is a worthy ideal; but pretending that it is possible to do so in society today is an utter impossibility.[8] Commitment is a fine motto to offer to men of letters who have taken it for granted, throughout a hundred and fifty years, that they could reap all the advantages of living in a comfortable bourgeois and capitalistic society but run no risk whatever in rising against its injustice. But, as applied to literature and to the arts, it can never guarantee the aesthetic value of a work or contend that only commitment to the left is moral in France today. Literature written by partisans of colonialism and even by Fascists could conceivably be, and probably has been, as deserving aesthetically as anti-

7. 'Sartre n'est pas en bons termes avec les mots' was, ironically enough, the title of an article by Jean Paulhan in *La Table Ronde*, No.35, November 1950, 9–20; an English commentator, John Mander, in *The New Statesman*, October 8, 1960, went so far as to assert: 'How unFrench Sartre is! How exceedingly German! Tortured, compulsive, overbearing, long-winded' and he alluded to the German blood running in the veins of Albert Schweitzer's great nephew. But Sartre's father hailed straight from the indubitably French province of Périgord, near Thiviers (Dordogne), where Sartre's grandfather had been a country doctor and had married a girl from Corréze. On his father's side, Sartre was a compatriot of Montaigne.

8. See an essay by a Los Angeles psychotherapist, Thomas C. Greening, 'Existential fiction and the paradox of ethics,' *The Antioch Review*, Spring 1963, 93–108.

colonialist and democratic writing. With all his talent for dialectics, perhaps unmatched since Plato, and his virtuosity as a defender of his paradoxical political attitudes, Sartre, as a moralist, as a political thinker, and (in his *Critique de la raison dialectique*) as a neophyte in economics, is the living embodiment of multiple contradictions. If logicians may blame him for it and practical politicians disregard him, readers of his literary works can rejoice. Pascal, Diderot, Balzac, and Nietzsche were no less fertile in unresolved internal clashes. Sartre is sincere when he explains that his existentialism is a humanism and when he defines his professed aim as raising man above his preliminary nausea and hopefully, through man's own free choice, toward heroism. But attaining heroism, as he acknowledged, is no easy affair and is not achieved upon command from some mentor. One must first face evil with open eyes. The pages which Sartre seems to have written with the greatest gusto are tinged with the poetry of evil and sound a melancholy knell: in *Les Mots,* in *Le Diable et le Bon Dieu* (*The Devil and the Good God*), in the occasionally profound but more often indigestible disquisitions on *Saint-Genet,* in the mournful scenes in *Le Sursis* (*The Reprieve*) which draws together two pitiful disabled beings amid foul smells, in *L'Enfance d'un chef* (*The Childhood of a Leader*). In these and elsewhere, Sartre, who called his own inspiration in his dramas 'Jansenist,'[9] expressed a horror of the flesh and an obstinacy in seeing in sex an irretrievable defilement which are closer to the Jansenists or to Ramon Lulle than to the pagans. Even if we take into account the implied existentialist contention that life has constantly to be lived under the threat of disintegration, we may grow weary with Sartre's acceptance of all that is viscous, moist, and lush, and with his assimilation of human flesh to crawling slugs. Malraux, Saint-Exupéry, Camus have proved more responsive to the message voiced by Nietzsche which Mauriac admired and endorsed: 'In man, there is matter, fragment, excess, clay, mud, folly, chaos; but in man there is also a creator, a sculptor, the hardness of the hammer and the divine contemplation of the seventh day.'

Sartre's nausea, however, is, or should be, a temporary *ascesis,* an inverted mystical experience or a visitation from outside, which upsets the selfish quietude of a life and forces the mind to start abruptly again and to revise all its values. While very concrete and specific, that experience is generalized and the hero has soon become a type. 'In every purpose

9. See Sartre's remarkable essay, 'Forgers of Myths, The young playwrights of France,' *Theatre Arts,* June 1946, 324–332.

there is universality,' said Sartre on his ethics. *La Nausée* (*Nausea* in the American version and, rather infelicitously, *The Diary of Antoine Roquentin* in the British version, which preceded the American) is not a philosophical novel nor a *roman à thèse;* but it is replete with the philosophical implications of what Sartre had been thinking since 1931 or so. The revision of all his values undertaken by the protagonist is not like Descartes's dreams which led to his methodical doubt. The veneer of falsehood, which concealed authenticity in things and persons, is scraped off. From mere existence, the victim, who is also the victor, of the bout with nausea passes on to being and reaches toward his own essence.

The revelations provided by Simone de Beauvoir, who had passed the *agrégation* of philosophy the same year as he had (1929) and saw much of him in the succeeding years (*La Force de l'Age*), and Sartre's own reminiscences in *Les Mots* have thrown light on the slow elaboration of *La Nausée*. Sartre first wrote a manuscript, more philosophical in character, in 1930–31, which bore the title of *La Légende de la vérité;* a subsequent and tentative title was *Melancholia*. When the *Nouvelle Revue Française* declined to publish the novel serially in 1936, Gallimard suggested the present title: *La Nausée*. The novel appeared in 1938 and was immediately successful.[10] 'I was Roquentin,' declared Sartre in *Les Mots*. He was, in the same sense as Flaubert had stated that Madame Bovary was he. Like his hero, he had been impressed, and profoundly depressed, by the notion of contingency, hammered into him by the contemplation of the 'vain proliferation' of a tree. He moreover drew the character of Annie from life: she has several features, or mannerisms, of a young woman, Camille Jollivet, whom Sartre had known well in his twentieth year. Bouville, the city of mud, is naturally Le Havre, where Sartre taught philosophy after his military service. Like Roquentin, Sartre was a bourgeois in revolt against the bourgeoisie; but his very hostility, as Simone de Beauvoir stated, was individualistic, hence 'bourgeoise.' In the years preceding the publication of the volume in 1938, Sartre had been impressed by Céline and chiefly by the American novelists: Dos Passos was then rated by him above any writer and exercised a lasting influence on him. The novel in Sartre's final version (even if disillusioned he speaks slightingly of it in *Les Mots*), is a milestone in twentieth-century fiction. Its impact on the creators of 'the new novel' was powerful. Critics and students have heaped up commentaries on its meaning and on its style. It has the fresh

10. See 'La Nausée revisited,' by A. James Arnold, *The French Review*, XXXIX, No. 2, November 1965, 199–213.

impetuousness of a youthful work, the joy of an adolescent revolt against the sham values of one's environment; it audaciously mingles philosophy and fantasy, poetry and comedy.

The novel is the diary of Antoine Roquentin in Bouville, a scholar with a meditative temperament, who has not yet at thirty achieved much. He has some money of his own, he is red-haired and rather unprepossessing; he is a bachelor and he has a capricious and tenderly scornful but lively mistress, Annie, whom he visits in Paris at the end of the story. Like not a few excellent novels, *La Nausée* is an ironical work. It includes a virtuoso's satire on Proustian privileged moments, of the personal novel and of the journal à la Gide, even of classical funeral orations and of the celebrated galleries of ancestors' portraits in Hugo's *Hernani*. All the parts are harmonized in a slow moving and undramatic but skillfully composed novel. More aptly than the Proustian novel, it could be compared to a symphony, with unforgettable pieces such as the Sunday afternoon walk of the Bouville bourgeois, and the epic tour of the provincial museum climaxing in the famous cry: 'Farewell, lovely lilies, elegantly enshrined in your painted sanctuaries, good-by, lovely lilies, our pride and our reason for living! Good-by, you bastards [*salauds*].' Several of the more concrete scenes, such as the meditation on the bluish suspenders of the *café* waiter, the fake, pompous strutting of the self-taught man in the local public library, the personality of the dreary provincial boulevard, all setting off the unauthentic bad faith in which one is bogged down, are equal to anything in Flaubert and Zola.

Little happens outwardly and little need happen. Roquentin is working on a historical biography of some obscure character who traveled in Russia in the eighteenth century, but he never becomes engrossed in it; he occasionally goes to bed with the coarse woman who owns his favorite *café;* he meets in the library the self-taught man, a farcical creature, who is a cruel caricature not only of Flaubert's Pécuchet but of any scholar who has been professionally deformed to the extent of never entertaining a single idea that is his own and of resting content only if it has already been expressed before by some revered name. He acquires culture voraciously, through asking for all the books in the library, one after the other in alphabetical order. In the end, his grotesque comedy is exploded: he is discovered by the Corsican employee, who has all along resented handing down the books to him, to be a pederast, making advances to young visitors to the sanctum of dead knowledge.

But the drama lies in Roquentin's sudden experience of nausea. A sickening feeling takes hold of him when a new aspect of objects is suddenly unveiled for him: their opaque, absurd existence. He realizes that we cannot receive any consciousness of the outside world except as a projection of our own minds. He is oppressed by the slimy viscosity of things, of people, of his own flesh reflected in a mirror, of his eyes, like fish scales, of all that is like a repellent polyp in him. The veil that seemed to prettify things has been torn open. Everything now seems meaningless, in the way, gratuitous, *de trop*. He, too, is *de trop*. He, and all that is, appears contingent, superfluous. His own irreversible past stretches as a mere disconnected succession of events. He is seized, not with fear of objects, but with the anguish with which his immense responsibility overwhelms him. Blessed with such an inverted 'mystical' ecstasy, he returns to the world of man as if he were alienated from him, like a crab or some crawling beast. He knows the meaning of existence.

> I too wanted to be. I wanted nothing else. I now see clearly
> through the apparent disorder of my life. At bottom . . . I only
> wished to banish existence out of me, . . . Then the pitiful fellow
> that I was has understood and opened his eyes . . . He thought:
> I am a fool. Just then, on the other side of existence, in that other
> world which one can see from afar but never come close to, a little
> melody ('Some of these days, you're gonna miss me, honey') began
> to dance and sing: 'You must be like me; you must suffer in tune.'

Sartre's next volume, though of more limited range and closer to phenomenological description than to any metaphysical revelation, is also a masterpiece of storytelling and of humor. For, contrary to what blind or prejudiced critics of Sartre have contended, he is no exception to the saying that no great intelligence is devoid of the comic spirit. The five stories that make up the volume *Le Mur* (*The Wall*) have become classics, collected (with a few expurgations) in college anthologies. There are few, if any, short stories in French since those of Balzac to match them.

The most moving is 'La Chambre,' which concretely displays the bad faith of Pierre, the husband, who went a few steps further than Roquentin and voluntarily deluded himself into perceiving things in a way different from that of 'normal' people. He is crazy. He lives with his favorite visions in a room; and his wife, Eve, though aware that Pierre in no way needs her, insists upon playing up to him and sharing his schizophrenic existence, out of stubborn pride. Sartre has gone very deep into the psychology of a paranoiac, attempting desperately but vainly to restore a link between the world and his own sick consciousness.

'Le Mur' is a masterly treatment, achieved in a dry, restrained, Hemingway-like manner, of the attitude of man toward death, a theme that is one of Sartre's concerns in his philosophical *Summa*. A Basque, captured by the Spanish soldiers of Franco, does not analyze himself or meditate when faced with execution. He knows no big words like immortality, regret, suffering. In a graphic manner, he witnesses and describes the future that is being obliterated, the essential absurdity of everything. He does not try to behave heroically but, playing a trick on his torturers, he gives them a false lead, which ironically proves to be true and brings about the arrest of his companion, for whom they were hunting.

'Intimité' is probably the most successful and the most entertaining interior monologue in French literature. Lulu, an empty-headed Parisian girl, married to an impotent but good-looking husband, quarrels pathetically with him, leaves him, on the advice of a girl friend, who insists upon making her heroic, to join a lover, becomes remorseful and, as far as she is capable of it, anguished, and returns to her weak and pompous husband. All of the characters are glaring illustrations of bad faith: the husband because he will not accept himself for what he is; Lulu because she vacillates and will not confess that an impotent husband is, to her (half Lesbian), more restful and safer than a possessive and carnal lover; the lover because he is a bourgeois at heart and dares not confess that he would be bored were he to elope with Lulu and break with the safe routine of life with his mother and father.

One senses more strain and some artificiality in 'Erostrate,' the story of a weakling who tries to become a gratuitous criminal in order to live in the memories of men, like the ancient who, to attain glory, set fire to the temple in Ephesus.

There is more crudity, but an unrivaled satirical gift in 'L'Enfance d'un chef,' a mock biography of an ambitious and vain middle-class character, who espouses all the literary fashions and all the vices of the years 1920–40. Unlike Roquentin, he flees his own nonexistence and joins anti-Semitic and fascist groups in order to delude himself that 'he belongs' and that there is more in him than gelatinous amorphousness.

Three volumes of *Les Chemins de la liberté* (*The Roads to Freedom*) have appeared, the first two, *L'Age de raison* and *Le Sursis,* in French in 1945, the third, *La Mort dans l'âme,* in 1949. They have all been translated, the first two by Eric Sutton, and the third by Gerard Hopkins [11] under the title *Troubled Sleep*. While they met with considerable success, especially in Europe, it is our conviction that the superb skill of the author and their immense significance as sheer literary works have been underrated by many hasty or hostile reviewers. Two easy escapes were offered to critics, who could not remain unaware of Sartre's immense importance in world letters: one was to brand him as immoral and pessimistic, whereas no great writer has perhaps been more concerned with the formulation of moral values. His outlook on life has been called, by a very lucid critic, Oleg Koefoed, from a Protestant, earnest, and 'bourgeois' country, Denmark, 'the most rashly optimistic humanism which our generation has produced.' The other was to acknowledge Sartre's triumph as a dramatist (and it is indeed dazzling), but to add in the same breath that, as a novelist, he was a failure. Our conviction is that not only *La Nausée* but *Les Chemins de la liberté* tower above most European fiction of the years 1935–55.[12]

Even in his hatred of the flesh and in his cruder pages, Sartre has remained a moralist and, as the French say, *un grand timide*, whose psychoanalysis would doubtless reveal him as an unusually sensitive orphan, hurt, like Baudelaire and Hamlet, by his mother's second marriage and wounded in his early idealization of women by his lack of facile grace and of superficial 'good looks.' The sound and the fury raised by some outraged Pharisees about Sartre's unromantic delineation of love have too easily blinded some readers to the highly perspicacious analysis of love and of sexuality in his works. The pages on love, desire, hatred, and sadism (pages 431 and following) in *L'Etre et le néant* go very deep and take for granted the truth that man is originally and fundamentally a sexual being, and aware of it, just as he is the only animal

11. Published in New York by Alfred A. Knopf, in 1947 and 1951.

12. Even so, a great many cultured American readers and students, admitting that the two early dramas by Sartre were great achievements, will treat with condescension *Morts sans sépulture*, which is in no sense a sensational melodrama but a masterly study of pride, as one of the masks of bad faith, in the tortured resistance fighters. They pour out their scorn upon *La Putain respectueuse*, in which the Americans, who, since Tocqueville remarked upon it, have always been mortified at being misunderstood in Europe, have insisted in seeing a crude treatment of the Negro problem. Sartre intended nothing of the kind. The prostitute, Lizzie, and the innocent Negro are, in the eyes of the author, the true villains of the play. They lack the courage to revolt, to assume their responsibilities. They bow to prejudices through sentimentality, inadequate intellectual force, and the same fear of freedom that crushed Electra's early passionate revolt in *Les Mouches*.

with the awareness that he will die (or so we claim). Love must be free, that is, without tyranny or sadism. The lover cries:

> My existence is, because it is called for. In so far as I assume it, it becomes pure generosity. I am because I give myself lavishly . . . Instead of feeling ourselves as superfluous [*de trop*], we now experience that our existence is prolonged and willed in its slightest details by an absolute freedom that, at the same time, it conditions, and that we want to deserve through our own freedom. In this lies the deepest element of our joy in loving, when it exists: that we feel justified in existing.

It is well-nigh impossible to summarize Sartre's novel, because its center is to be found neither in the plot or plots nor in the characters in the traditional sense. The protagonist is, once again, a professor, as was the case in the very early story written and published by Sartre at the age of eighteen, 'L'Ange du morbide.' Ever since he had broken a beautiful ancient vase at the age of seven as a gesture toward freedom and then, upon reading Spinoza at twenty-one, had decided to be in nature 'not like a subject, but like an empire within an empire,' reversing Spinoza's formula, Mathieu had been yearning for freedom. But he is no man of action or of determination. He has little will power, and he analyzes and ponders every problem, displaying his own flabbiness pitilessly. The others, however, respect him and cannot conceal their awe in the presence of a philosophy teacher who attends all their parties, lives unconventionally like them, but all the while pursues elusive freedom.

He has had a mistress, Marcelle, for several years. She appears in the book as not particularly attractive and as unusually sedate and weakwilled. She is now pregnant and, having few illusions about her lover's passion for remaining unattached, free from responsibility, and available for the visitation of freedom devoutly wished for by him, she is hardly surprised when he advises her to have an abortion. Mathieu, however, is disturbed by his act and by the little creature whom he will thus keep from ever existing. He silences his scruples and gets the money needed for a first-class clandestine 'operation' from his disciple Boris, who steals it from his mistress. But he is nonplussed when a friend of his, Daniel, offers to marry Marcelle and act as father to the child.

Mathieu wallows in bad faith and unauthenticity, merely enjoying a mockery of freedom. Daniel lives in worse falsehood still: he is a homosexual who has not been able to accept himself for what he is. A concealed shame, hence a tormenting hatred for himself and for others, rules his every act. He is the ideal sado-masochist, who looks in vain for his own redemption in his 'generous' offer to Marcelle, who cowardly accepts it. Lola, a singer, a passionate and tragic woman whose mellow ripeness fills her with a desperate fear of losing her very young lover, Boris, and Ilich, also of Russian origins, an intelligent, peevish, unpredictable girl, not far remote from Xavière in Simone de Beauvoir's L'Invitée (She Came to Stay), are the other women portrayed. Mathieu feels attracted by Ilich, emulates her semimystical and masochistic gesture when, at a party, she pierces her hand with a knife, and is fascinated by her adolescent coldness, yet he refuses her when at last she offers herself to him. Boris, Ilich's brother, an admiring student of Mathieu, is a caricature of the disciple, like the famulus of Goethe's Faust, but a caricature delineated with warmth by Sartre; he has more ebullience and more naturalness than most of the other characters in the volume.

The actors in the dramatic fresco of L'Age de raison (The Age of Reason) seem to wade hopelessly through the marshes of the prewar world. Only one of them, the Communist Brunet, has resolutely decided for engagement, for abdication of any further choice through affiliation with the Communist party and support of the Spanish republicans. Mathieu, as he himself confesses, sedulously tills the inner garden of his freedom, mistaking availability to any future whatever for freedom, awaiting, like Orestes in Les Mouches (The Flies), the ideal free act, his own freely elected deed, which would dispel his dreary complacence in his wasted Parisian years. He is now thirty-four; he has kept shy of political ties, of ideological affiliations, of patriotic élans, of any velleities of reforming the world, and of course of marriage. But, as Dr. Johnson said long ago and as Kafka has echoed, if marriage has many pains, celibacy has few joys. Mathieu is aware of his own desiccation, and, having read Hegel on the unhappy conscience, he has diagnosed the gnawing worms in him: bad faith and cowardice.

Le Sursis, which displayed Sartre's virtuosity in handling, better than John Dos Passos himself, the simultaneous technique of Manhattan Transfer and U.S.A. is astonishingly clever. The reader wonders whether Sartre, like Picasso—Sartre and he have the same cool mastery in handling the new and the unpredictable, the same tantalizing knack for carrying off successfully tightrope acrobatics—has not starved his genius to feed his talent and his greed for experimenting. But Sartre's attempt was not that of the effete traditional novelist, laboriously building up characters whose dreary continuity seems unaffected by the momentous events in which they are immersed. He has vehemently repudiated the convenient faith in a stable, universal human nature, entertained by the classical writers of France, and has stressed man's perpetually fluid behavior.

His purpose was to embrace the variegated and discordant unity of Western Europe in the tragic week of September 1938, which preceded the surrender of Chamberlain and Daladier at Munich. Few of those who lived through those days and nights of anxiety and shame and saw the abject intellectual dishonesty of men who deluded themselves into believing they had achieved peace in our time will refuse to proclaim the truth and the power of Sartre's portrayal. Unanimism is at play here, far more felicitously than anywhere in Romains's works; the actors or the puppets in the tragicomedy of Europe are delineated with a concrete vigor and a skill in vivid dialogue that make many of the pretentiously symbolic and cerebral novels of the present time appear unreal and sham.

Daniel has hardly changed since the crisis in the first volume in which he attempted to drown his cats before his contemplated suicide, then toyed with the idea of mutilating himself so as to be free forever from his pederastic urges, and finally justified himself in his own eyes through playing the archangel for Marcelle. He will emerge fully in the third volume, when the reign of evil has spread over France with the defeat. And heroism might have saved him too, when, in the fourth volume, Sartre was to portray the resistance to the Germans. Charles, a paralytic from Berck, evacuated under gruesome conditions with a whole train-load of invalids, 'rising' to a disgusting and yet pathetic copulation with another human wreck, is a bold and powerful character. The adolescent, Philippe, even Mathieu's sister-in-law at Juan-les-Pins, and other episodic characters compel belief, as do the boisterously comic adventures of the illiterate shepherd from Prades, Jean-Louis. The humble fellow will never understand what the mobilization was all about or why he was buffeted by a fate personified by malicious men, greedy prostitutes, and the blind machinery of the army. But he rings truer than any heroes of Maupassant or of Courteline, and he provides the proof, if one were needed, that Sartre can depict people far removed from professors, phenomenological introspectives, and idlers of Montparnasse *cafés*.

The hydra of war reaching over men, aghast and powerless, enables Mathieu to cast a backward glance, ironically bitter, at his vain search for a false freedom. He had thought he could treasure up his leisure, his comfort, and his refusal of all family, party, and other social bonds. But, like a sponge, life had perfidiously absorbed the slimy semblance of freedom he had cultivated. In a classical meditation on the Pont-Neuf, at the end of *Le Sursis,* he realizes his error. His liberty has been there all along, at hand; he was *it.* It does not descend upon one like an illumination of delight, a tongue of fire. Freedom does not come laden with comforting presents; it is grave and massive, 'a plenitude.' 'Freedom is exile and I am condemned to be free.'

War is only delayed by the reprieve of Munich, and, when it comes, Mathieu will not turn overnight into a flamboyant warrior. The path to freedom and perhaps to heroism is an arduous one. (Sartre, remembering Gide's and Mauriac's warnings about the impossibility of portraying noble feelings and saints, must have been pondering lengthily his fourth volume, long overdue.) *La Mort dans l'âme* still resorts to the devices of simultaneity bewilderingly used in *Le Sursis.* But there is more continuity within each chapter, and more concessions are thus made to the reader's laziness. Moreover, while Munich impressed western Europeans as Sartre depicts it as a senseless shake-up of all illusions, in which placid and selfish beings like Mathieu were nothing but peas suddenly mashed up in the crushing of a big can, the defeat of France stressed again the barriers behind which countries sought to convince themselves that the wretched fate of France could in no case be theirs. A Spanish republican in New York, who represents the attitude of some of the European refugees in America, is aware that the events of June 1940 mean defeat for all liberals and for civilization, yet he sees in the oppression of France a punishment for her betrayal of the Spanish republicans and the Czechs. Boris has become a determined fighter. Mathieu has witnessed, as a participant, the disorderly retreat. He now stirs up other French soldiers to reorganize and to shoot the approaching Germans. It will be of no avail and he knows it; the armistice is then being signed. But through the ordeal of fire he will emerge a new man.

Sartre has been accused of lacking warmth and sensibility. But sensibility need not be declamatory and does not necessarily lie at the opposite pole to the superb intelligence, one of the broadest since Goethe and Renan, which marks the existentialist leader. Though cold and insensitive, the man who wrote 'La République du silence,' 'Paris sous l'occupation' in the third volume of *Situations,* the impassioned evocations of torture and injustice in *Qu'est-ce que la littérature?,* and the chapters in the third volume of *Les Chemins de la liberté* devoted to the Communist Brunet, bolstering up the morale of his companions in a German prison camp, has produced some of the most moving passages in modern fiction. (Sartre had a firsthand acquaintance with prison camps in 1940–41, until he was released because of his deficient eyesight; he then engaged in the resistance movement.) We do not believe there is anything more telling, more restrained and, since the word must be used in spite of Sartre's *pudeur,* more noble in spirit in the abundant literature devoted by the French to the ordeal of captivity.

Sartre's fiction is original on many counts. First of all, his mastery of the language is extraordinary. And few significant works of our age, since Joyce and Mallarmé, can afford to ignore the problems and the pitfalls of language. The flashes of poetry in prose, which illuminate the novels of Malraux and of Giono, are absent from Sartrian fiction. Metaphors are scarce, but they are precise, convincing, and sharply delineated. Sheer adornments are spurned by him, as well as the music of prose. But the great moments when the characters, suddenly aware of their existence or of their nascent freedom, seem to be favored with a gift of second sight are impregnated with a severe and precise beauty, not unlike that of Stendhal, without his fondness for revery. Above all, Sartre's mastery is conspicuous in some of his dialogues, in an interior monologue purified of much of the irrelevancy and insignificance of the genre, and in his unorthodox use of the spoken language. With less artificiality than Céline or than Queneau, Sartre has successfully broken with the romantic illusion that interposes a pretty screen of words between the reader and the scene represented. His language welcomes slang, profanity, and obscenity. It catches up with the least conventional spoken language, as written words had not done for a whole century, in spite of Wordsworth's rebellion against poetic diction and of Hugo's *mettant un bonnet rouge au vieux dictionnaire.* Not only does it thus translate an individual, specific, and concrete reality without betraying it and without imprisoning it in abstract categories, it revivifies French through integrating into the written style all the fluid and picturesque, or malodorous, wealth of the language of the common people.

Then, in spite of many assertions to the contrary, Sartrian fiction avoids most of the dangers of philosophical literature, and it gains, in our opinion, far more than it loses, in paralleling an arresting philosophy. Sartre's early novel, *Défaite,* written in his teens and destroyed for lack of a publisher, his early story, 'L'Ange du morbide,' and even *La Nausée* seem to indicate that he was, even in terms of chronology, a literary artist before he was a philosopher. Whatever philosophy there is in his fiction

and in his plays is not artificially and didactically placed there, as might
be said to have been the case with Balzac and Tolstoi, and even more so
with Bourget and Romains. He creates and endows with autonomous life
his own universe. The main postulates of Sartre's philosophy are to a
certain extent present in his fiction. But they are no longer assertions di-
alectically presented; they are lived situations. There are no essences, and
therefore no types, no general categories, no universal human nature, no
harmonious consistency in man. There is no determinism, and man is not
to be 'explained' ponderously by all the shackles that bind him to his
environment and to his past. Freedom alone, slowly and painfully conquered, can consitute an exit from a world that would otherwise be a
purposeless, loveless, derelict abode of viscousness and cowardice.

The novels of Sartre thus stand in reaction both to naturalism and to
intellectual analysis. Existentialism as conceived by Sartre, despite some
superficial similarities with the stories of men adrift, dear to Zola and the
early Huysmans, despite the dreary humiliation of sex lengthily described
by the same writers in *Pot-Bouille* and elsewhere, is a revulsion from the
materialistic and deterministic novel of Zola, Maupassant, Dreiser, even
of Hardy and Heinrich Mann, to the extent that they might be called
naturalists. For Sartre, man is not determined by heredity and environment, and only to a very limited extent by his past. He himself is his own
Prometheus, as Michelet would have put it. He always remains unpredictable, free to break with what he has been and to elect a new path.
Within each of Sartre's characters there is indeterminacy and the possibility of accomplishing a new action, which will stand totally unconnected
with previous actions and inconsistent with other features of the characters as they had previously appeared. In a revealing interview, granted on
November 24, 1945, to Mme Dominique Aury and published in *Les Lettres Françaises,* Sartre declared:

> Every one of my characters, after having done anything may still
> do anything whatever . . . I never calculate whether the act is cred-
> ible according to previous ones, but I take the situation and a free-
> dom chained in situation . . . In Zola, everything obeys the strictest
> determinism. His books are written in the past, while my characters
> have a future . . . With Mathieu, for example, the situation which
> he slowly created for himself is of consequence. He is bound hand
> and foot by his mistress and by his culture. He himself forged his
> own links. He is much too clearsighted for psychoanalysis to be of
> any usefulness to him; this is moreover true for all intellectuals . . .
> He is still waiting for God, I mean for something outside him to

beckon to him. But he will only have the cause which he will have
decided to be his own.

Proustian analysis is treated with no less severity, and Mauriac's technique of leading his heroes by a leash to God come up for even harsher
criticism. Such analysis appears to Sartre as the luxury of a select leisure
class, trained in self-contemplation and cherishing every nuance of its
enjoyment of nature, of food, of art and of the delicious 'reciprocal torture' of love. It went as far as it could go with Proust, Joyce, and Mann;
it perhaps even became lost in a blind alley. But this analytical literature
no longer fully answered the demands of a new and less cultured public
and of a generation that had endured the material and spiritual agonies
of World War II and German concentration camps. Many young men
discovered that Dostoevski, Malraux, and Faulkner had a truer ring for
them. The French, who had hitherto constituted the ideal audience for
the novel of analysis, went over to the side of the unanalytical novel of
action and violence translated from the American. Sartre proclaimed how
significant to him and to his generation the discovery of Dos Passos,
Hemingway, and Faulkner had proved. His own novels tend to set off the
truths that man perceives when he least expects them and when a new
quality in objects is suddenly revealed to him.[13]

Lastly, much has been written, often glibly, on the pessimism of existentialist fiction. There is far more pessimism in Thomas Mann's stories of
decrepitude and of the inevitable unbalance of genius, in Cesare Pavese's
and in Alberto Moravia's novels, indeed in almost all modern Italian literature, and in three-fourths of American letters, Mark Twain and John
Dos Passos not excepted, and William Faulkner himself included in spite
of his official speeches, than there is in recent French literature. There
was infinitely more obsession with decadence and death in Flaubert and
his contemporaries, between 1850 and 1870, than there has been in our
own age.

To be sure, some form of pessimism is rampant around us today. But it
is, we believe, a very different pessimism from that of the nineteen-
twenties, much less cynical and complacent, more courageous and more

13. Similarly, in a remarkable manifesto, 'Forgers of Myths: the Young Playwrights
of France,' Theatre Arts, June 1946, Sartre declared that, for the existentialist dramatists, 'man is not to be defined as a "reasoning animal" or as a "social" one, but
as a free being, entirely indeterminate, who must choose his own being when
confronted with certain necessities . . . we wish to put on the stage certain situations which throw light on the main aspects of the condition of man and to have
the spectators participate in the free choice which man makes in these situations.'

constructive. The men and women of 1920–30 had tried to forget a war they considered as a huge mistake and to resume, freed from all remnants of Puritanism and from bourgeois morality, a search for happiness, often conceived as mere pleasure, once hampered and then interrupted. Their literature refused *engagement* and closed its eyes to tragedy. It took the American depression, the advent of Hitler in Germany, the vogue of Russia as the new land of promise, and the threat of an impending new war to arouse the writers of the early 'thirties out of the shallow optimism of the preceding years. The Spanish civil war and the defeat and occupation of France were then the two great creative events in thought and literature. Catastrophes had not been forestalled. They had to be lived through.

Existentialism does not ignore despair. But it attempts to lead away from it after having drunk from its cup to the dregs. 'The gravest form of despair,' said Kierkegaard, 'is not to be desperate, not to be aware of one's despair.' Faith in a divine providence is rejected. Faith in progress is rejected likewise, or at least critically re-examined. Faith in the innate goodness of man has been exploded by the spectacle of wars, of concentration camps, of man's inhumanity to man. Fear is with us, and it has spread to the New World, once immune from it. Like the conscience in existentialist doctrines, it gnaws like a worm in the fruit, at our unequaled prosperity and at our worship of science, education, and good neighborliness.

The usefulness of existentialist literature, regardless of its aesthetic value, is in its rejection of the delusions through which modern man often attempts to forget the duties he must assume. It is deliberately modern, and, as Sartre put it in a famous manifesto, one must write for one's own time. It thus spurns the easy escape of many scholars who, heirs to a nineteenth-century tradition, seek the explanation of the present in the past and of modern man in the study of primitive societies—the matriarchate among the Polynesians, incest among the Amazon tribes, or the swaddling clothes of Russian babies. Existentialism is a socially conscious literature, which fights with equal ardor communism on its left and the middle class on its right; the one has abdicated critical spirit and freedom, the other suffers from a Hegelian bad conscience and dares not face the future; it is pitiful in its good will and in its maze of contradictions, but it is sterile. 'The freedom to write,' Sartre asserts in his remarkable *Qu'est-ce que la littérature?*, 'presupposes the freedom of the citizen. One does not write for slaves. Prose-writing is bound up in solidarity with the only regime in which prose retains a meaning: democracy . . . To write is another way of wanting freedom.' Marxist materialism has been dealt grievous blows by Sartre and Merleau-Ponty, for the existentialists reject the acrobatics through which good and evil play off against each other in the dialectical pursuit of the synthesis. But they stand equally firm against the easy solace of religion or the comfort of philosophical idealism, for which evil is merely a shadow necessarily accompanying the good. If elsewhere Sartre may be charged with excessive *virtuosité* and even with sophistry, he has written, in *Qu'est-ce que la littérature?* and in *Réflexions sur la question juive,* some of the most moving and most definitive pages of our age. Better than any other French writer since Bergson, or earlier still, since Renan and Voltaire, he has combined clarity and depth, a tragic feeling for life and the conviction that man has not yet said his last word. Through revolting against God, or against one of the successive conceptions of God that man has made for himself, the modern hero who has plumbed the depths of absurdity and of anxiety and discarded the illusions of mechanical progress teaches and practices self-reliance and holds out a beacon in the night, which threatens, or lures, us today.

In words that aptly render the moral attitude that was then Sartre's as well as his own, Camus has stated the existentialist position, deprived of all philosophical subtleties and expressed with forthrightness and nobleness.

> We refuse to despair of man. Without having any exaggerated ambition to save him, we hold at least to the idea of serving him . . . To the last we shall reject a divine charity that would deprive men of the justice which is their due.

And elsewhere, after defining his position:

> Is this pessimism? No. This is an honest effort to determine what is wanted, what is unwanted . . . We, young Frenchmen, label as pessimists those who say that all goes well and that nothing changes human nature. We call them pessimists, because they are among those from whom nothing can be expected. *They* will be to blame if the world indeed never changes. But there are among us enough men of decision pledged to do all that is within their power to cure the world and themselves of their present sickness.[14]

14. Sartre protested convincingly against the charge of 'blackness' in a revealing conversation, reported in *Paru,* No. 13, December 1945, 5–10. He also stressed there the indeterminacy of his characters, each of them seeking his own salvation in his own way, inventing his own path, free to do so, and anguished because he is con-

Bibliographical Notes

A whole library has accumulated on French existentialism and on Sartre, in a dozen languages. Only the essential titles on existentialism as philosophical literature and on Sartre as a novelist need be listed here.

Barnes, Hazel, *The Literature of Possibility. A Study in Humanistic Existentialism*. Lincoln: The University of Nebraska Press, 1959, and London: Tavistock, 1961.

Barrett, William, *Irrational Man*. Doubleday, 1958.

Campbell, Robert, *Sartre ou une littérature philosophique*. Ardent, 1945.

Champigny, Robert, *Stages on Sartre's Way*. Bloomington: Indiana University Press, 1959.

Cohn, Robert G., 'Sartre versus Proust,' *The Partisan Review*, 1961, No. 5–6, 635–645.

Collins, James, *The Existentialists: A Critical Study*. Chicago: Henry Regnery, 1952.

Cumming, Robert D., *The Philosophy of Sartre*. Random House, 1964.

Douglas, Kenneth, *A Critical Bibliography of Existentialism*. Yale French Studies Monograph, No. 1 (1950).

Grene, Marjorie, *Dreadful Freedom*. Chicago: University of Chicago Press, 1948.

Greene, Norman N., *Sartre*. Ann Arbor: University of Michigan Press, 1961, and London: Cresset Press, 1961.

Harper, Ralph, *Existentialism: A Theory of Man*. Cambridge, Mass.: Harvard University Press, 1948.

Jeanson, Francis, *Le Probléme moral et la pensée de Sartre*. Myrte, 1947.

———, *Sartre par lui-même*. Seuil, 1955.

Kaufmann, Walter, *Existentialism from Dostoevsky to Sartre*. Meridian Books, 1956.

Knight, Everett, *Literature Considered as Philosophy*. London: Routledge and Kegan Paul, 1957.

Murdoch, Iris, *Sartre*. Cambridge, England: Bowes and Bowes, and New Haven: Yale University Press, 1954.

Salvan, Jacques, *To Be and Not To Be: An Analysis of Sartre's Ontology*. Detroit: Wayne University Press, 1962.

Tody, Philip, *Sartre*. London: Hamish Hamilton, 1960.

Waehlens, A. de, *Une Philosophie de l'ambiguité: l'existentialisme de Merleau-Ponty*. Université de Louvain, 1951.

———, *Existence et Signification*. Louvain: Nauwelaerts, 1958.

Warnock, Mary, *The Philosophy of Sartre*. London: Hutchinson, 1965.

scious of that very freedom. A similar point is stressed by Frederick Will, 'Sartre and the Question of Character in Literature,' *P.M.L.A.*, LXXVI, 3, September 1961, 455–460.

Wild, John, *The Challenge of Existentialism*. Bloomington: Indiana University Press.

Yale French Studies, No. 1 (1949); No. 16 (1956); No. 29 (1964), all special issues on Sartre and existentialism.

On *La Nausée*, see more particularly: Arnold, A. James, '*La Nausée* revisited,' *The French Review*, XXXIX, 2, November 1965, 199–213; Champigny, Robert, 'Sens de la Nausée,' *P.M.L.A.*, March 1955, 37–46; Jameson, Fred, *Sartre. The Origins of a Style*. New Haven: Yale University Press, 1961; Koefoed, Oleg, 'L'Oeuvre littéraire de Sartre,' *Orbis Litterarum*, VI, 1949, 209–272, and VII, 1949, 61–141; Oxenhandler, Neal, 'The Metaphor of Metaphor in *La Nausée*,' *The Chicago Review*, XV, 4, 1962, 47–54; Poulet, Georges, '*La Nausée* et le cogito cartésien,' *Studi Francesi*, No. 15, September–December 1961, 452–462, and *Le Point de Départ*. Plon, 1964, pp. 216–236; Walker, Margaret, 'The Nausea of Sartre,' *The Yale Review*, 42, Winter 1953, 251–260; Weightman, John, in *The Novelist as Philosopher*, edited by John Cruickshank. Oxford University Press, 1962, pp. 102–127.

On the short stories of Sartre: Braun, Sidney D., 'Source and Psychology in Le Mur,' *Criticism*, VII, 1, Winter 1965, 45–51; Simon, John K., 'Sartre's Room,' *Modern Language Notes*, 79, 5, December 1964, 526–538.

On *Les Chemins de la liberté*: Aury, Dominique, *Les Lettres françaises*, November 24, 1945, 5–6; Blanchot, Maurice, 'Les romans de Sartre,' *L'Arche*, No. 10, October 1945, 121–134, and *La Part du Feu*. Gallimard, 1949, 195–211; Fowlie, Wallace, 'Existentialist hero,' *Yale French Studies*, 1, 1947, 53–61; Lichtenstein, Heinz, 'On *L'Age de Raison*,' *Philosophy and Phenomenological Research*, IX, 1, September 1948, 148–153; Magny, Claude-Edmonde, 'Les romans existentialistes,' *Poésie 46*, No. 29, January 1946, 58–67; Picon, Gaëtan, *Confluences*, V, 8, October 1945, 883–890.

On *Les Mots*: Bensimmon, Marc, 'D'un mythe à l'autre,' *Revue des Sciences Humaines*, No. 119, July–September 1965, 415–430; Girard, René, 'L'Anti-héros et les Salauds,' *Mercure de France*, No. 1217, March 1965, 423–449; Josa, Solange, 'Les Mots,' *Esprit*, 32, April 1964, 654–659; Peyre, Henri, 'Les Mots,' *The Yale Review*, 53, 1965, 241–248.

X

Feminine Literature in France: Simone de Beauvoir

'Feminine literature.' The phrase sounds even more patronizing, slyly ironical, or condescendingly complimentary in English than it does in French. Yet even in France women have lately come to resent it. A man who composes a sonata or a play, who writes a novel or an ode, does not tell himself: 'I am going to express my own male self, prove my literary or artistic virility and champion man's fate.' Must a woman necessarily feel as a woman when she composes an imaginative work, any more than other women who chisel an abstract piece of sculpture, contrive and watch a scientific experiment, write a scholarly dissertation? The rights of a woman whose career is in literature have been bravely and brilliantly vindicated in our age by Virginia Woolf and by Simone de Beauvoir. The fight is won today. The very many women writers of contemporary France have ceased to carry a feminine chip on their shoulders. Not a single prohibition stands in front of them, not a single taboo daunts their boldness. How are they availing themselves of their exhilarating freedom?

No other history is probably as rich as that of France in remarkable women: saints, queens, courtesans, favorites, tyrannical mothers, warlike heroines. Down to the eighteenth century, there flourished also more women writers of the first rank in France than in Italy, Spain, or Britain. Marie de France has no equal in any other medieval literature; nor have Mme de Sévigné and Mme de La Fayette or the prolific and passionate letter writers of the age euphemistically dubbed 'age of reason.' George Sand and Mme de Staël were, in the romantic era, the last great survivors of a long series of great women writers, who lived through their novels even while writing them. The former is a far more acute psychologist than is often admitted, and it is deplorable that the turbulent story of her life should have overshadowed her fiction and her remarkable *Histoire de ma vie*. The latter sowed probably more ideas, true and false, in the French nineteenth century than any other writer's work, and her insight as a political thinker reflecting on the French Revolution may well have been matched only by Tocqueville.

During the hundred years or more which elapsed between 1800 and 1930, while three at least of the best novelists in England were women (Jane Austen, Emily Brontë, George Eliot) and Elizabeth Barrett Browning and Christina Rossetti were not unworthy of the good, if not the best, poets among Englishmen, France was strangely devoid of feminine talents. Mme de Noailles may be rehabilitated some day, but at present the fulsome praise lavished upon her by Maurice Barrès and Marcel Proust appears to us as one of the classical examples of complimentary mundane condescension to womanhood. The symbolist movement should, it seems, have counted many a woman poet: Henri de Régnier, Albert Samain, composed many an *odelette* or an elegy which might have been signed by a feminine name. But women may not be so apt as men imagine at singing ethereal purity and the chastity of idealized Beatrices or blessed and uncorporeal damozels leaning on the bar of heaven. Renée Vivien preferred darker abysses of loneliness. The one woman writer who, up to a few years ago, would have been claimed by most Frenchmen as the glorious paragon of literary talent, if not of genius, was Colette. Our own conviction is that she was always grossly overrated and that she may well, more than any other cause, be responsible for the sad plight of feminine writing in France up to the fourth decade of the present century.

Her skilled workmanship is of course not to be denied, even if it was ridiculously overpraised by gallant French critics whom Glenway Wescott echoed in this country when he hailed her in 1952 as 'the greatest living French fiction writer.' She could chisel swift, sensuous sentences admirably, convey the color of an adolescent girl's eyes or the earthy fragrance of rain-soaked gardens, the lusciousness of pears or peaches melting in the mouth. She possessed the classical art of omission. Gide, who defined classicism by all that was left out in a finished work and by the effective use of litotes, congratulated her thus on *Chéri:* 'What I like most of all in your book is what is cut out and taken away from it: its nudity.' But even that nudity is adorned and, with affected simplicity but in truth with expert coquetry, casts knowing glances at those who are expected to admire it. Colette, like Proust with whom she has not a few points in common, hunted the adjective, 'the chatoyant, evanescent, entrancing adjective,' as she calls it somewhere in an adjectival triad worthy of Proust. She could conjure up the very special taste of tears gliding down a powdered cheek or the feel of male muscles pressing on a pliant body. But she seldom reached that naturalness in style which has obliterated effort. She seldom prefers her prose and its sobriety to the pleasure of displaying her skill in welding it expertly. Too many women writers in France have been lured by her example into a new preciosity. She and Giraudoux may well appear some day as the most insidious corruptors of taste in our age and as antediluvian writers cherishing allusions and quaint, far-fetched comparisons. Voiture and Mlle de Scudéry were their ancestors.

Antediluvian, Colette also is in the subject of her stories. She is at her best when she harks back to her childhood and to her roots, and she and many a critic have erred, or led us into error, by dismissing the early *Claudine* volumes as youthful sins inspired by her first husband. Even as a little girl, Colette was already experienced, adorned, mature, and attracted by naïveté, as slightly corrupt sensibilities can be. She entertained our grandmothers through her insolent boldness and the audacity with which she rent the veils covering 'those pleasures that are lightly called physical. But her implicit ideals never endangered bourgeois values. She reveled in stories of marriages arranged by prudent families, of aging roués caught in the contrivedly naïve nets of a cool-headed girl, in courtesans aping the women of the middle class, and in interiors which are as respectable, as stuffily rancid as in any 'nineteen hundred' novel for model 'jeunes filles.' Her world is one of boudoirs and of bedrooms, with no genuine joy and no tenderness ever emanating from those unconvincing love gymnastics attempted by Antoine and Minne at the end of *L'Ingénue libertine* or by Léa and her child lover, Chéri. It is typically a pre-World War I microcosm, in which outward nature itself appears adorned and powdered as in some Alexandrian tale retold by Pierre Louÿs. The only men who are loved are brainless gigolos who would not be so relentlessly pursued, 'loved they honor a little more.' In a volume on her laborious sentimental and professional education entitled *Mes Apprentissages,* in 1936, Colette made a melancholy avowal: 'I have not come near those men whom others call great. They have not sought me.' It is not surprising that many males should refuse to recognize themselves in those men who have little brain and less heart and whose introspective

life is so elementary. 'I do not like you to be subtle. [*fin* is hardly trans-
lateable.] You are subtle only because you are unhappy,' the woman
remarks to her partner in *Duo*. It is hardly less surprising that French
girls of 1966 should feel totally estranged from those creatures who were
all slightly venal, never forged bonds of comradeship with men, never
discussed politics, ideas, ethics, aesthetics with them, never tried to found
a loving relationship on candidness and on loyalty, and accepted deceit as
the condiment to their love life. 'There is a pleasure,' Colette wrote in
La Retraite sentimentale, 'in the attachment we feel for those who deceive
us, who wear lies like a richly adorned gown and open it only because of
voluptuous pleasure in nudity. I loved Renaud no less while he was jilting
me.' In her Proustian volume, where the jealousy of the senses is not far
from reaching an anguished greatness, Colette epigrammatically collected
the ashen bitterness which drops from her exquisite but artificial flowers:
'There are two kinds of love: unsatisfied love which renders you odious
to everyone else, and satisfied love, which renders you idiotic.'
(*L'Entrave*)

Life, meanwhile, was changing fast after World War I, even if Colette
and a few of her followers who turned out piquant and glittering feminine
prose failed to be aware of it. Girls invaded the *lycées* and the universities, women entered careers in growing numbers and rivaled men as
teachers, lawyers, doctors, managers, still insisting on being treated courteously and gallantly by the very men whom they challenged in the
citadel of the office, not forsaking coquettishness, the use of cosmetics, or
the art of dressing seductively. But they would no longer be treated as
smiling and empty-headed dolls. Dowries disappeared, inherited furniture
and embroidered trousseaux were relegated among antiquated customs
for provincial 'white geese,' marriages ceased to be arranged for con-
venience sake. Most surprisingly of all, the century-old reluctance of many
young French mothers to bear several children vanished and the birth
rate, especially in middle class families and even where the woman had a
career, became one of the highest in Europe. Women asserted their rights,
not only to be loved, but also to loving actively, and to experiencing
pleasure thereby. Thirty years before British wives were allowed to read
D. H. Lawrence's novel in which an aristocratic lady proclaimed her right
to sensual satisfaction (the gamekeeper's pleasure did not seem to interest
Lawrence quite so much, and perhaps he compensated through talking
profusely), French girls nonchalantly perused that all too famous story,
prefaced by André Malraux in its French translation. But sex, even in its
French version, is very far from being the exclusive or the chief concern

of the best women writers who followed Colette and preceded the greatest of them all, Simone de Beauvoir. Among those who have disappeared from our midst, three women stand out and vindicate feminine literature (in all its nobility) between 1930 and 1945: Marcelle Sauvageot, Paule Régnier, and Simone Weil.

All were single women, and the single woman, like the cuckold, has long ceased to serve as a pretext for cheap jesting and salesmen's stale humor, in our age which detects tragedy everywhere and stands in awe before that badge of greatness which modern theologians revere as 'Angst.' Balzac's tale *La Vieille Fille* is perhaps his masterpiece among his shorter novels. But the single woman writing on herself with no rancor, no self-pity, is a rarity in a literature which had heretofore counted no Jane Austen, no Emily Dickinson. Almost every French woman writer, since the medieval and somewhat cantankerous Christine de Pisan (who was Italian and was left a widow with several children), was blessed or afflicted with husband and lovers, or held suitors at bay like the celebrated Marquise who preferred to vent her possessive passion on her daughter. The admirable quality of those three women, and of many more around them such as the dramatist Marie Lenéru and the novelist of *Les Allongées,* Jeanne Galzy, is unflinching clearsightedness in their analysis of themselves married to an artistic restraint which gives the lie to those who equate feminine literature with declamatory self-pity.

Commentaire, Marcelle Sauvageot's slim volume, was published posthumously thanks to Charles Du Bos who wrote a moving preface to the book, in 1934 (and reprinted with a few essays on art, in 1936). The author was a Lorraine girl born in Rimbaud's city, in 1900, who had fled the German invasion in 1914, had studied subsequently at the Sorbonne, passed the *Agrégation* and taught at Charleville. Her portrait reveals a delicate and rare beauty of outline and of expression. She loved and was loved. But in 1930 she was stricken by a lung disease and spent some time in a sanatorium where she wrote those pages whose title suggests 'mens,' meditations of a mind which watches the heart beat and feel. The man whom she loved then turned elsewhere, sedulously avoided 'I love you' during their few meetings, then sent the usual hypocritical letter of the male: 'I am getting married . . . but our friendship survives and will be truer now that it will be purer.' Marcelle Sauvageot was not taken in. Balzac had remarked somewhere that 'women's friendship is superior to their love.' The few among them who do rise to friendship seem indeed to have banished all vulgarity and all selfishness from it. The young woman who, in her nursing home, had opened the letter offering friendship as a substitute for love, wrote:

> Do you know what friendship is? Do you believe it to be a more lukewarm feeling which can be contented with remnants and with small services which one cannot avoid rendering? Friendship is, I believe, a stronger and more exclusive love . . . but less 'vociferous.' Friendship does know jealousy, expectation, desire.

She rereads the letter which, like many a song, began 'You whom I loved so much . . .' and continued as if accompanied by a guitar 'I would not have known how to give you happiness.' And she jotted down a meditation on happiness worthy of the most acute of French moralists between Montaigne and Joubert. Happiness is a physical euphoria and a sensuous exaltation, a fulfillment of ardent feelings. But intellect must participate in it as it never does in Colette. And the most beautiful of all the substantives in the French language, lucidity, cannot be absent from it, for a woman who will not any more give up watching herself than La Jeune Parque does.

> Still to have a small corner of consciousness which always knows what is happening, which, because it knows, allows the whole intellectual and reasonable being also to enjoy, every second, something of the happiness which comes, to have that small corner of consciousness which slowly appreciates the evolution of the joy, follows it to its extreme ends, is not that happiness? There is a corner which does not vibrate, but that tiny corner stays a witness to the joy that is felt. To it is left the role of remembering and of whispering: I have been happy and I know why. I consent to lose my head, but I want to watch the very moment when I lose my head and to drive awareness down to the deepest recess of the consciousness which abdicates. One must not be absent from one's happiness.

Marcelle Sauvageot's obsession was that of Gide, of Jacques Rivière, and of Charles Du Bos himself: the obsession of utter sincerity and of never forcing the expression of one's feelings and thus betraying one's inner self. Her *Commentaire* never once exhales fear, self-pity, revolt against the absurdity of fate which struck her as it struck Albert Camus in his student days, about the same time. She is very remote from the sonorous complaints of women wailing their betrayed love or pathetically calling for the forsaking lover, of which literature and opera have been fond. 'What hurts me,' she states, 'is not so much the death of our love as the death of a truly living being which the two of us had created, which perhaps I alone had created . . . That being was a union of you and me, such as we both wanted to be.' Four years after writing these pages, Marcelle Sauvageot died at Davos, on January 6, 1934.

Passionate lucidity and relentless self-analysis also characterized Paule Régnier, who belonged to the generation of Saint-John Perse. No woman could be more remote from Colette, and none could be more French, in the same way as Valéry and Claudel, the most antithetic of poets, were produced by the same country and admired the same masters. She may well have composed the best 'feminine' novel of the first half of the present century in France, *L'Abbaye d'Evolayne* (1933), and one of the rare novels which is not autobiographical and in which the protagonists are men. A lovely and passionate girl, Adelaïde, has married a doctor, an agnostic, a fanatic devotee of science to whom World War I, however, revealed the pathetic inability of science to alleviate human misery and to cure human folly. Like the doctor in Camus's *La Peste,* he chose a life of action and of sacrifice to his fellow beings.

The doctor and his wife, vacationing in Belgium, happened to be close to the abbey of Evolayne where a college friend of his was a Benedictine monk. Husband and wife attended mass. Before long, the agnostic husband became a convert. Jealous, like Pauline in Corneille's drama, of that happiness which her husband finds elsewhere than with her, Adelaïde also becomes a convert. Both decide to enter the Holy Orders and thus to live apart. But the exigencies of religious life proved too demanding for the woman in her nunnery. Remorse, desire, solitude harried her. Through her husband alone could she reach God. She asked to be relieved of her vows, left the convent, took refuge in Savoy where she refused a love which was offered to her. Obsessed by the memory of her husband, she went to visit him, hoping to disturb his serenity. She took poison under his very eyes and died. Her monk-husband would not even attempt to confess her, for she whispered dying: 'What is the use . . . I would take you as my God.' She had only entered the cloister to serve his chosen vocation, secretly adoring nothing and no one but him. The death scene, without a single jarring note, restrained in its tragic and blasphemous end, is one of the most moving in modern fiction.

Both the *Revue des Deux Mondes* and the *Revue de Paris* refused to publish the novel serially, alleging that no libertine or erotic novel would frighten their readers as surely as a story involving religion would. It did nevertheless receive the Grand Prix du Roman of the French Academy in 1934. The author was then forty-six. She was one of the four daughters of an army officer and grew up in Versailles. She was afflicted with an infirmity and hunchbacked. She grew up cheerfully but was not prepared by her conventional education for any career and after Colonel Régnier had died and the family was swindled out of its fortune by a dishonest broker, the unmarried daughter had to live in poverty and by her pen alone. She had an immense capacity for love and an intense eagerness to be loved; but, like Leopardi, whom her pessimistic jottings in her diary often recall, she was also convinced that she was exiled from love. Her literary admiration went to Hugo 'the well nigh absolute master of my religious thought,' as she declared in her letters of 1936 to Elémir Bourges and to Paul Claudel, and the only great poet who spoke nobly and charitably of monsters. But Claudel rebuked her harshly when he read her novel which he thought as revolting as Zola's *La Faute de l'Abbé Mouret.* 'Your hero,' he wrote her, 'is hardly appealing, your heroine unbearable, your monks are impudent criminals. I shall always take the side of *le bon Dieu* against crazy sensibilities and unhealthy imaginations. Your heroine would have done better to have babies.'

Such disappointments repeatedly afflicted Paule Régnier, who had no protector in the world of letters, no 'salon' in which to shine and be courted, no cénacle to advertize or to encourage her. She loved intensely one of the most promising writers of her generation, a genuine poet, Paul Drouot. He appeared to return her love and his esteem for her was boundless. Paul Drouot was killed on June 9, 1915, on the front in Artois. He left a manuscript first entitled *Pour Votre Altesse,* then rechristened *Eurydice deux fois perdue,* whose lyrical prose is worthy of Nerval's *Aurelia* and superior to the best of Barrès. Paule Régnier published it posthumously and never ceased to mourn his memory. Her love was possessive and voracious. To her *Journal,* on June 9, 1928, exactly thirteen years after Drouot's death in battle, she confided:

> I am unable to understand how people manage to live when they love. I do not believe that human love can have the slightest sweetness. Even if he had loved me, I would not have tolerated for him to have a friend, man or woman.

Rightly could the editor of her *Journal,* Jacques Madaule, hint that Paule Régnier's lineage was that of the Portuguese nun, of Julie de Lespinasse or of Jeanne la Folle, who went insane because of her inconsolable grief after the death of her husband. But these heroines of love had actually known the raptures of a love that had, momentarily at least, been shared. Paule Régnier had not. Long after Paul Drouot's death, his mother, dying from cancer, entrusted her with her son's letters. In that bundle of mail and manuscripts, Paule Régnier discovered that the man whose love she had hoped to win had felt pity, admiration, affection for her, but had actually been in love with another woman. She experienced the depths of solitude and of despair. She realized how deceitful her romanticism could be, how rash her illusions. In spite of her Catholic faith (many of the letters in the volume of letters published in 1955 are addressed to the priests who counseled her), the temptation of suicide haunted her. Late in 1950, her latest novel having been refused by the readers of the Plon publishing house, despairing of ever reaching self-mastery through lucidity, she prepared three letters, to her sister, to Mme Charles Du Bos, to a priest. 'Death is not lucid, nor is life,' she wrote in one of them. On November 30, 1950, as Virginia Woolf had done, as an admirable French woman, a high-priestess of letters, Adrienne Monnier, was later to do, she committed suicide.

Simone Weil, who also courted or devoutly wished the consummation of death, has, since her end in London on August 23, 1943, been projected in a limelight of fame which would have horrified her. Her most ephemeral notes have been published; literary prizes have been bestowed upon her; her most erratic pronouncements on political or social thought, on the need for roots, on the Greeks metamorphosed into anticipators of the Christian revelation, have been published and naïvely pondered over. This arch-rebel has lately been in danger of being turned into the prophet of a new orthodoxy. She may still be canonized some day, although she never did become a Christian, more in fidelity to her beloved Greeks who were relegated to limbo by the Church than to her Jewish ancestors, whom she abhorred. Her rebellious soul, inhabiting a body hardly blessed by feminine charm, was one of those violent ones of whom St. Matthew declared that they seize by force the Kingdom of Heaven, which is conquered through violence (xi, 12).

Her biography has been told, with an objectivity helped by psychological insight and taste, by a French scholar in America, Jacques Cabaud, in L'Expérience vécue de Simone Weil (Plon, 1957, followed by an even richer volume in English: Simone Weil, New York: Channel Press, 1964). Reminiscences of her friends, analyses of the complex and baffling paths which that woman in search of total certitude trod during the ten years of her adult life (she died at thirty-four) will long appear in France and elsewhere. Her influence on religious thinking, Catholic and Protestant, was doubtless second to none in the years 1948–60 and is only now being assimilated and perhaps weakened. It may well have

FRENCH NOVELISTS OF TODAY

acted more powerfully on agnostics than upon orthodox Christians, and some clerics, like Charles Moeller, have uncharitably denounced the dangers of her views. She made the most determined attempt perhaps in our age to sever the New Testament from the Old and the humility of Christ from the Jewish myth of a people chosen by an exclusive God. 'Humility is the root of love,' she noted in *La Connaissance surnaturelle*. 'God would be inferior to us if, in the person of Christ, he had not been humiliated.' While feminine literature with Colette, Germaine Beaumont, and a score of skilled chiselers of style and employers of magic lanterns of sensation dwelt on the epidermic pleasures of life, her unceasing concern was for depth and a spiritual striking for roots. The most fiercely dogmatic beings have often belonged to the sex whose name is supposed to be frailty. With a monumental rigidity, Simone Weil fired questions at priests, scored the many errors of the Church and on that account punished Christianity by refusing to enter the gates of Catholicism. She confidently asserted that the Apostles had misinterpreted Christ's teaching, instead of teaching the varied peoples of the earth (especially those Greeks whom St. Paul discoursing on the Areopagus failed to understand) how to add the Christian message each to its own religion. She spurned any compromise with the modern world, as Mother Angélique or Pascal's own Jansenist sister once did. She rejected what she considered as the superstition of history and upbraided Hegelianism in a Kierkegaardian manner. She blamed Christianity for having introduced the heresy of progress, its poison, into the modern world and for thus 'dechristianizing it.' Hellenism and Buddhism would more than once appear to have been the secret poles of her oscillations. Yet no one wrote on the love which must be redirected toward grace and away from the *pesanteur* (the weight which draws us downward), on the need to immolate our will in order to contemplate the providential order of the world with an inspired passiveness, as forcefully as she did. If feminine literature often gravitates around autobiography and egotism, Simone Weil constitutes an impressive exception. 'To say I, is to lie,' that Pascalian soul exclaimed. Amid glittering and petulant stylists of either sex who swarmed around Giraudoux, Cocteau, Giono, she reduced style to its nudest simplicity and wanted the writer to be as accurate a recorder of her thoughts, unadorned and unemotional, as a translator from a foreign tongue has to be.

With Simone Weil, another philosopher among women, Simone Pétrement, and a third one, Simone de Beauvoir, whose novels and ideas are treated below, French women challenged man in the gravest realms of philosophical meditation and of literary creation. Claude-Edmonde Magny, for a few years the best critic in France, was another one of those women born around 1910, who stormed the bastions of the most masculine of *agrégations* and outshone the feminine thinkers of any other land. Nor are Marguerite Yourcenaar, Marguerite Duras, and Nathalie Sarraute novelists who could be accused of levity and of thinking merely with their hearts. The three of them should be included in any listing of the thirty finest French writers of the present time, and to their names should be added, in our opinion, three others whose talent is equally eminent: Françoise Mallet-Joris, Colette Audry, and Dominique Rolin. Nor is Françoise Sagan to be dismissed so perfunctorily as her ridiculous fame has caused her to by disgruntled or fastidious critics. Her stories lack substance, her characters are sketchy, her plays are charmingly fanciful but brittle and when she attempts to report on Cuba, Algeria or to express political ideas, she allows herself to be sadly misled by her desire for remaining in the public eye. But her skill as a restrained and perspicuous prose writer and her austere and uninviting description of bored and unselective girls and of cool-headed and whisky-warmed bed hoppers are not contemptible; she will some day be included by literary historians among the new Jansenists in our midst, of whom Sartre will be the Grand Arnauld, and will occupy a niche in the album of sex fashions of our age.

With those women thinkers and writers, gone is the prejudice long fostered by males who treated women as incapable of profound abstract thinking and of the sustained effort of composition required by fiction (*Les Mandarins, Les Mémoires d'Hadrien, Martereau* gave the lie to that contention), or of the creation of characters which would be other than projections of their own selves: the portraits of the adolescent heroine, of her Belgian father and of his Russian mistress in Françoise Mallet-Joris's *Le Rempart des Béguines* (successfully rendered as *The Illusionist, The Loving and the Daring* and *Into the Labyrinth,* all three unfortunate titles) can victoriously stand comparison with any character delineation attempted by men novelists in their teens or their very early twenties, as the author was when her first book appeared. Virginia Woolf's specious argument concerning *A Room of One's Own* which would allegedly be unavailable to women, has not been seriously endorsed by the women writers of France, who are free to compose amid the bustle of *cafés* just as many men do. Nor would the new feminine French authors feel resentfully alienated from a men's world or hampered because all the values of life, hence the order imposed by the novelist upon his material, are masculine, as the same Virginia Woolf claims in the essay 'Women and Fiction,' reprinted in her posthumous *The Agate and the Rainbow* (1958). The cyclical influences to which her life is for many years submitted, the expense of attention and of energy which has to be given to husband and children during the twenty most creative years of a person's life, impede woman's literary and artistic work more materially. Probably also, if she is more egotistic in some of her writings, woman is less selfish than her male companion and does not, like him, enjoy the capacity of total obsession with the private universe he carries in him and with the need to impart his obsessions to readers, his accomplices. If the genius, as Baudelaire liked to say, quoting Emerson, is 'he who is immovably centered,' a woman accedes with more difficulty to that monstrously selfish but creative concentration than the man.

All is not uniformly grave and loftily moral in French feminine literature today, and the myth of French levity may well die hard. It may be that it proved easier for women to rival men in academic professions, in medicine and in psychology, in editing and publishing, even in politics, than in writing. In poetry they have failed to achieve eminence and as a playwright even Simone de Beauvoir encountered failure. Colette Audry is perhaps the only one who, with a powerful and restrained drama on a political theme, *Soledad* (1956), rose to something not far remote from the best in Sartre and probably superior to Camus's *Les Justes*. The same Colette Audry had mastered her craft through vivid and tender short stories, thin in content but ingeniously suggestive, *On Joue perdant* (1946). Short stories and *récits* could easily become the preserved shooting ground of women writers, but they have as a rule chosen in preference the ampler scope of the novel. Fluent storytellers such as Elsa Triolet, Louise de Vilmorin, Lise Deharme, Clarisse Francillon, Anne-Marie Soulac abound among them. More audacious ones, like Lucie Marchal in *La Mèche*, have challenged Mauriac. Nicole Vedrès, of Russian birth like Zöe Oldenbourg, Nathalie Sarraute, and Else Triolet, has brought intellectual vigor to a tale of adventure, of love and life under the German occupation, *Les Cordes rouges* (1953). Célia Bertin, who now seems to have turned to sociological writing, is the author of two novels of note, *Les Saisons du Mélèze* (1949) and *La Dernière Innocence* (1953), a gruesome struggle between a possessive widow and her two daughters at war with each other. Still, if honorable, these novels are not likely to count among the dozen or so by which the last fifteen years may hope to survive in fiction.

The public has been more attracted by the feminine invasion of semi-erotic literature. Men, condescendingly at times, also with a sly curiosity which led them to pry into the sensuous or sexual secrets of the other sex, have drawn the public attention to those 'ouvrages de dames' in a jocular mood. True, some of these works are too blatantly sensational, such as Christiane Rochefort's expert but grossly overpraised novel *Le Repos du guerrier* and books clearly aiming at giving the readers a thrill or a shock: *Judith Albarès,* for example, by Simone Jacquemard (1957). The first of those volumes, however, daringly posed some of the problems which arise from woman's newly won total sexual independence. The feminine partner leads and orders, in those strange sex relations, bountifully 'watered' with whiskey; and the male, a misfit of an artist tempted by suicide, accepts sex and drink instead of the death for which he had tried, but rejects the hypocritical sentimentality which his female savior would like to embroider around their bed. Christiane Rochefort's next volume, *Les Petits Enfants du siècle* (1961), gave evidence of a rare humorous and satirical talent, displayed at the expense of the welfare state and of modern love mores. Simone Jacquemard is more ambitious, more involved, and desperately and joylessly in earnest; her prize-winning novel in 1962, *Le Veilleur de nuit,* translated as *The Night Watchman* (1964), reads like a pretentious parody of William Faulkner and of Claude Simon. Dominique Rolin is a novelist of greater power who takes passion seriously and depicts its ravage in a family or in a couple; *Le Souffle* (1953), translated in England as *The Pulse of Life* (1953), like an earlier book, *Les Marais* (1942), which mirrored the bitter despair of an era, is a strong 'masculine' novel, embracing a whole family and not just the adolescent crisis of a girl torn between childhood and the threshold of a life of care. In *Les Quatre Coins* (1954), she returned to a poetical portrait of a fourteen-year-old girl, suddenly plunged into drabness and bewildered by the promiscuity of inhabitants in poor Paris districts, 'la jeune Parque des faubourgs' as the book's advertisement put it. Monique Wittig, in 1965, returned, with much skill and charm, to the favorite theme of women novelists in *L'Opoponax* (1964), the evocation of childhood. The strange word is that of the plant which symbolizes for the little girl emerging from childhood all that opposes and defies her.

One of the freshest of feminine talents since Françoise Sagan's ap-

pearance seems to be that of Michèle Perrein. She comes like Marguerite
Duras from the region around Bordeaux: one of her earlier books, an
original series of long letters, some imaginary, some self-exploratory,
presumably written by the heroine or by two men between whom she
hesitates, *La Sensitive* (1956), revealed a singular gift of analysis. The
protagonist was a girl student at the University of Bordeaux, hardly more
preoccupied with her studies than Françoise Sagan's heroines with theirs,
courted imperiously by a male student with a reputation as a great hunter
of hearts, yielding and alternately denying herself to him. The man,
clearly unbalanced and much less self-assured than he pretended to be,
after idling his student years away in his search for a tenderness which
he did not know how to inspire, more skilled at tormenting inexperienced
girls than at loving any of them for her own sake, committed suicide.
There can be much morality of a strange kind in these stories of promiscuity, drug addiction, half-consented rape, and lesbian delicacies, told by
the liberated women novelists of France. *Le Repos du guerrier* and Noelle
Loriot's *Eve*, the boldest of them, may well have driven disheartened
readers to Pascal, Bossuet, or to Madame de Ségur!

Michèle Perrein is a lively storyteller and a gifted stylist, with more
humor and comic power of observation than most of her sister novelists,
as she showed in *Le Soleil dans l'oeil* (1957) and in *Barbastre* (1960).
The heroine of the latter is a girl who has set out on a vacation trip with
two young men: one, Lupesco, lacks aggressiveness, or even taste for
women, and watches amusedly the vertiginous progress of intimacy between his friend Armand, a painter, and the girl Marianne. After twenty-
eight pages of their travel adventures, Marianne courteously understands
Armand's desire and coyly asks: 'Should I take off my dress or do you
prefer to do it yourself? . . . and the electric light, do you want it on?'
They vacation cheaply, dally at *café* terraces, and entertain few illusions
about romantic love. A lesbian friend of Marianne whose advances that
healthy and candid girl has spurned, imparts to her her knowledge of
men thus: 'The secret is the Stendhalian fiasco . . . All in all, there are
two categories of men, those who are sure of being able to always function, and those who do not feel certain of it.' Nothing could be simpler.
But, in a France which is economically and industrially resurgent, where
engineers, technicians, economists and even parachutist officers or political fanatics appear, according to newspapers, to constitute the energetic
part of the younger generations, it is entertaining to find that literature
has renounced the portrayal of 'arrivistes' and ambitious upstarts and

power-greedy Balzacian youngsters of the kind depicted in the nineteen-twenties and 'thirties. Girls do not place many hurdles between men's desire and fulfillment; most of them have a trade or a profession and are ready to earn their living, and that of their mates as well. But young men are more interested in their female companions and partners than they are in materialistic greed. They set out, like Stendhal, every morning to hunt, not for venal gain, but for happiness, and they do not conceive of happiness without the participation of the sex which knows how to adorn it and how to make it last.

Have French women profoundly changed in the last twenty years, as those who are fond of viewing literature as a mirror to life might be led to believe? They are certainly much more candid in their dealings with men and less easily taken in by romantic myths of love. They have freed themselves from conventional repressions and from many an age-old taboo. Planned parenthood is within their reach and they lucidly have chosen to bear more babies than their more fearful and probably more hypocritical grandmothers and mothers had done. They feel less doomed to aloneness in their love life than once may have been the case when pleasure and marital duties or procreativeness were disassociated. They undoubtedly have become more virile or rather the core of firmness, of reasonableness, of solid 'masculinity' which woman always had in herself while she had to appear feminine outside—this firmness is now less often concealed by her. Man, in reverse, in life perhaps and certainly in litera-ture, allows himself to reveal the femininity inside him, once disguised or covered up by his male pose. So many men come to women when they are wearied of being strong, tired of trying to be at their best, and stand in need of encouragement, perhaps of pity. The picture of man as he appears in most of these feminine novels may be that of an expert in the physics of sex, but it is hardly an edifying one otherwise. There are not many heroes in the eyes of women writers.

A number of sociological inquiries have lately appeared in France on the two, once inseparable, subjects of love in modern society and of woman's condition: *Problèmes de la sexualité* (1937) by several writers, including a Protestant pastor and a German thinker, Peter Wust, on 'the metaphysical mission of woman'; a very remarkable special number of the review *Esprit* on sexuality (November 1960); a volume on the promo-tion of woman in modern society, rather perfunctory and superficial, by Célia Bertin, *Le Temps des femmes* (1958); another one on *La Française et l'amour* (1960), by Jacques Rémy and Robert Woog (not on love-

making, but on what French women think about love and connected
questions) and *La Française aujourd'hui*, by several women writers, a
number of *La Nef* (October–December 1960). These studies are impressive and they owe much to the very seminal volumes of Simone de Beauvoir on *Le Deuxième Sexe*. There are probably more women today holding positions of responsibility (in teaching, in medicine, in social work,
in legal careers, in commerce, in politics, in journalism) in France than in
the United States, in Britain, or in Germany. The conditions enjoyed by
the working or the career woman, as required by law, are substantially
better. The feminist movement, having never been so aggressive as in
Anglo-Saxon lands and having profited from the gains made by women
elsewhere, has also not been afflicted with the same disappointing flagging of energy. The small part played today by American women in politics, in diplomacy, in the upper echelons of scholarly and scientific careers, in the directing bodies of enterprises or of labor unions, is a severe
disappointment to the feminists among men. A British commentator remarked on 6 August 1960 in *The Economist* that in Australia, once known
for the energy and resourcefulness of its women, there are practically no
women occupying senior jobs. Their world would seem to be bounded by
Kinder, Küche, Kirche. They are content thus. And a book entitled *Do
You Want To Be an Australian?* placidly, and not even with cynicism or
irony, observed:

> It is not true that ordinary Australians fail to recognize the value
> of women. Any man will tell you that they are indispensable for
> packing picnic baskets and for keeping other women company while
> you are drinking with their husbands.

An English woman writer, Barbara Wootton, in the *New Statesman* of
24 December 1960, gravely concerned with the same trend in feminism,
or rather by the resigned abdication of modern Anglo-Saxon women,
wrote thus:

> It used to be said that men must work and women must weep. 'Eman-
> cipated women,' however, must now do both: and they weep from
> the sheer strain of always trying to do two jobs at once—one at home
> and one outside. For this reason one cannot wonder, though one may
> sometimes regret, that some of the younger women of today are dis-
> posed to turn their back on the opportunities so hardly won by their
> forbears, and even to adopt an aggressively 'I-am-not-a-feminist'
> attitude. For unlike many of those forbears, they are not supported
> by staffs of reliable servants and virtually self-regulating households.

It is impossible, after all, long to probe into the condition and the morale of modern women without encountering the servant problem, next to sex, and perhaps to parking, the heaviest source of anxiety and of neurosis in our civilization. Men, proclaiming all the while that women were the victors in the battle of the sexes and ready to die of heart attacks at fifty to prove that they had become the soft-hearted sex today, were insidiously surrounding themselves with plentiful and decorative secretarial help and leaving the wives to struggle in forlornness with deep freezers, waxing machines, cellophaned carrots, peanut butter sandwiches and other varieties of wax, diapers, and children's questioning.

Feminine literature, even more than that which men have long taken as their empire, may probably conjure up what is not rather than what actually is, and voice the dreams of women thinking back to their childhood, of the private world of dolls, of nature, of girlish solitude which they planned to offer some day to a charming prince. Or else it resorts to the idealization of men, or to the idealization in reverse which through a compensation for the inevitable monotony of married life, imagines sex prowesses and extra-marital revelations perhaps accompanied by the desacralized language of love used by D. H. Lawrence's Mellors and by many a male protagonist in French women's fiction. French women today are probably going through the two or three decades which will remain as the Golden Era of French feminism. Their total liberation only dates back to 1930–50, to their turning their backs on the Colette kind of boudoir literature and to their facing and assuming their situation squarely. As often happens after a revolution, social or political, new layers of people, heretofore without any voice of their own, are suddenly endowed with an autonomous personality and with self-expression. As in Britain, the United States, Australia, and probably Russia, this golden age may not last more than a quarter of a century. The whole of man should be the domain explored by these women now flocking to literary careers, and the whole of woman. They have convincingly displayed their mastery of erotic literature. Let them write on the deeper and more tragic subjects which have as yet hardly been touched; maternity, the anguish of motherhood, the rivalries of mother and daughter; or the solitude of the single woman, the dilemmas of the working woman and of her who desperately insists upon combining a career and a home; the intellectual and sentimental divorce between women and men once children have been raised, sent to school or college, and the gulf of their aloneness at reaching middle age; the new realm of tenderness and loyalty and fidelity in the relationship between the sexes which remains to be conquered by Western women whom Freud, D. H. Lawrence, Kinsey, and a host of French libertine writers have at last endowed with their full rights to sexual freedom but who dread not coming up to the new expectations thus aroused in their mates and in themselves. The fear of frigidity, of aridity of heart, of being incapable of total abandon, haunts more liberated women today than it ever did their underprivileged grandmothers. And it is not a fuller picture of women which modern readers hope to discover in feminine literature, but also a truer portrayal of men as seen, understood, judged by women. A rosy opportunity is now within the reach of the women who create. None had envisioned it more hopefully than, exactly ninety years ago, two prophetic authors whose own proclivities were not directed to the other sex but who could praise women disinterestedly and reframe them in their fervid imaginations: one is Walt Whitman, in his *Democratic Vistas* (1871) dreaming of a literature which would achieve 'the entire redemption of women out of these incredible holds and webs of silliness, millinery, and every kind of dyspeptic depletion.' The other, also in 1871, was the teenager Rimbaud, announcing in his 'Seer's Letter':

> When the infinite serfdom of woman is broken, when she finally lives for and by herself, man, hitherto abominable, having then released her, she too will be a poet . . . She will discover strange, unfathomable, repulsive, exquisite things.

Easily half of the talents in French fiction and short story, since 1930 or so, have been women. Still the French males hint that, if their female rivals possess qualities of 'charm,' 'graceful elegance,' 'deftness,' they tend to produce only pleasant 'ouvrages de dames.' No French woman writer as yet has probably risen to the stature of Jane Austen or of Virginia Woolf, of Willa Cather, perhaps even of Edith Wharton. The exception, towering above all other women writers, may well be Simone de Beauvoir. She has not been daunted by the male conspiracy. Feminine charm has not been denied her; her intuition can be as piercing and her touch as delicate as those of women writers who never mastered Spinoza or Hegel. With *Le Deuxième Sexe* (*The Second Sex*), she has achieved, however, in spite of some needless display of pedantry and crudeness, the most formidable vindication of woman's rights since Mary Wollstonecraft, and she has, in her *Ethics of Ambiguity*, given the best exposition to date of existentialist ethics. She ranks, with Merleau-Ponty and Sartre, as one of the three best philosophers of French atheistic existentialism. And two of her novels are among the finest fictional accomplishments of that militant group that has invaded the drama, the short story, and critical and polemical writing, as well as the novel and philosophy. The third, *Tous les hommes sont mortels*, is an artistic failure such as the most intelligent writer will sometimes perpetrate, and needs no mention here, except as a reminder of the author's dangerous bent, in which her qualities melt into faults: too clear an awareness of her purpose and too obstinate a zeal in building a work of fiction around an idea.

L'Invitée (*She Came to Stay*), published in 1943, was, along with *L'Etranger*, the most penetrating revelation of the war years in French fiction. The epigraph from Hegel boldly advanced the claim of transposing a philosopher's notion into a concrete situation: 'Every conscience seeks the death of the other.' But the first pages arouse the reader's curiosity in the old-fashioned manner of novelists (What will happen? How? Why?) and strike him with the novelty of the psychological analysis. Every object or person perceived by us is a reminder that there is more than ourselves in the world. The experience of otherness, or as the French existentialists call it, of *altérité*, comes first as a shock. A fine page in the sixth chapter, which anthologies of the future will certainly collect, describes the first impression of solitude and of anguish experienced by the heroine as a little girl, when, alone in the house, she gazed with earnest sympathy at an old coat thrown on the back of a chair. The worn coat could not complain, could not even notice her, it existed and was not aware of it, and she could not identify herself with it, translate its sadness, speak for it. For others, each of us is often likewise a limited, alien, cold object. We dread to accept as valid the vision of others, and especially spiteful or envious rivals, may entertain of us. We may be driven to the extermination of such a vision.

The heroine, Françoise, is thirty and is proud of the mature wisdom and of the directness that set her apart from some of the women around her, either younger and girlishly coquettish in their devious calculations or frustrated in their life and loves, unstable, and lying to themselves. When the story begins, she looks wistfully at Gerbert, a rather inarticulate young man, handsome and awkward, who has worked all evening with her at their theater. She feels an urge to tempt his naïve and admiring youthfulness, but she resists the temptation easily.

For several years, Françoise and Pierre have lived a model liaison; they share every thought, they esteem, respect, and love each other. Pierre would confess to her, and thus justify in her eyes, a passing whim for another woman, which sometimes waylaid his imperious nature. She feels secure in her conviction that he would, of himself, always return to the almost virile and fraternal comradeship he had formed with her eight years before. Pierre, the director and leading actor of a Parisian theater, a Dullin or a Jouvet, is returning that night from an absence. Their company will then rehearse and produce *Julius Caesar*. Françoise watches the theater lobbies and, backstage, the dressing rooms, deserted and unused that night. Through her, these objects and places assume an existence. She reflects, interprets, and thinks of the sweetness of that lovely hour.

Pierre and Françoise have invited Xavière, a girl whom they met in Rouen, to come to Paris, stay at their expense in the hotel where they live, and find her way into some career. Xavière's dream was to act, but she conceived of the theater romantically and was disappointed when she saw Françoise and Pierre, producers at the head of a vanguard stage, living regularly and prosaically, succeeding by dint of hard work, and observing effortlessly a code of mutual loyalty. Xavière is lazy, unable to organize her life, totally ignorant of punctuality, capricious, and nervous. How the older couple could bear with her after a few weeks astonishes all their friends, and the reader. She obviously takes a malicious pleasure in filling the function Claudel attributes to women, that of complicating life incessantly.

Françoise, like most human beings, has the instinct of a teacher. She wanted to train and to mold Xavière and to launch her into Parisian life, imagining her at first more manageable than the little provincial girl turns out to be. She would thus satisfy some instinct for domineering in herself. Xavière held little interest for Pierre until he, accustomed to being the admired and obeyed boss, never questioning the assumptions on which his life rested, and serene in the security of his union with Françoise, suddenly discovers, in Xavière, 'the other.' Her petulance, her unpredictability, and her blunt questioning of the placid semimarital order of his life with Françoise amuse him at first. He becomes interested in Xavière, eager to instruct the inexperienced girl in literature and acting and in the mysteries of Parisian night life. In the presence of this other one, whose values upset theirs, whose youthful vision is fresher, Françoise witnesses the sudden collapse of the artificial world that she and Pierre had thought they were building on authenticity and a freely accepted order. Jealousy, which she had imagined banished from her life (for she has a direct and virile nobleness of soul, akin to Corneille's Pauline), now stings her venomously. She is ill for some weeks, and, during her absence in a clinic, Pierre is drawn closer to Xavière. The 'other' couple becomes crystallized, and Françoise is a stranger to it.

Heroically, she tries to maintain remnants of her dream. Pierre, who is a little callous in matters of sentiment and does not realize how cruel telling the truth that hurts can be, does not conceal from Françoise that he now loves Xavière. Generously, Françoise tries to integrate her into a trio. Her very nobleness humiliates Xavière, who delights in inflicting suffering upon Pierre. The girl gives herself to young Gerbert after a drinking orgy, is peeved at her own conduct, hates Françoise for still sharing the thoughts and the professional interests of Pierre, and blames herself morbidly amid scenes of sulking in her room and of insulting Françoise. The war breaks out. Pierre is mobilized. The two women attempt to patch up their differences. Françoise has done her best to live truly and frankly, avoiding the banality of the usual adulterous trio, maintaining seriousness and loyalty above all other values. She has failed. Neither Pierre's sentimental seduction and physical possession nor the more subtle fascination that Françoise, as an older woman, with moral and intellectual qualities, exercised on the young girl, proved successful in achieving the impossible: knowing and controlling the consciousness of the other one. Françoise, in the end, is reduced to contemplate, aghast, the picture that Xavière has of her, that of a domineering, mean woman, prosaically jealous of a younger person, lying to herself in spite of all her claims to utter sincerity. She turns on the gas in the room where Xavière is asleep and thus achieves the death of the other one.

The novel suffers from one fault: it is too long, too leisurely in its pace, and too tolerant of sinuous ups and downs, which are no longer necessary once the atmosphere has been created and the central issues formulated. But it is in other respects a remarkably incisive psychological portrayal of the conflict opposing, as in a classical tragedy, three characters whom a fatal logic sets apart. The life of a Paris theater, the meetings and excited conversations in the *cafés* and *dancings* of Montparnasse, the sense of the preciousness of every hour in the face of the threat of World War II, and the parting of Pierre from Françoise, when he dons his uniform and leaves for the *Gare de l'Est,* are rendered with superb mastery. The triumph of the author is not only in the new nuances of psychology she renders but also in very expert dialogue, never wordy, abstract, or unnatural, and in the impressionistic touches through which the unceasing change in the consciousness of the characters is faithfully revealed. *L'Invitée* is a philosophical novel made fully concrete.

It is also one of the ablest delineations of women attempted by a woman novelist. *Jeunes filles* have become a rarity in contemporary French fiction; and very few of them, certainly neither Montherlant's, who exist only for and through the man, nor Giraudoux's, too idealized and too sweetly reasonable, attain the convincingness of selfish, capricious, fierce little Xavière. Rare are the women novelists who have depicted women as other than passionate and sensuous, enthroning love as the cynosure of their lives. Françoise, fully feminine and somewhat maternal, embodies reasonableness, straightforward loyalty, devotion to a professional task lucidly undertaken and intelligently pursued, and tender affection, which are seldom portrayed in literature and frequent in actual life. The heroine of *L'Invitée* is a woman capable of friendship. Her final crime is gradually and subtly made to appear inevitable and almost justified. At the same time, both she and Xavière and episodic women in the book are feminine to their fingertips and are portrayed smoothing their hair, concealing or betraying the drawn weariness of their features, expert in making up their complexions or their eyes, analyzing mercilessly the blouses, the tailored suits, or the gait of other women, and piercing cruelly the mask of steady composure under which their sex conceals their fear of aging and of loneliness.

Le Sang des autres (*The Blood of Others*), published in 1945, is not unequal to *L'Invitée*. It has less classical concentration on the inner life of a very few characters and it offers more variety as a fresco of the moods and problems of French youth before and during World War I. It, too, incarnates a philosophy and illustrates a problem, but with no lack of concreteness and restrained emotion. The emphasis in Simone de Beauvoir's thinking is twofold: on ethics rather than on metaphysics, and on the peculiar situation of women in the world and especially in the world of literary creation. On ethics, she expressed herself fully and clearly in her volume *The Ethics of Ambiguity* (published in translation by the Philosophical Library, New York, in 1948, one year after its appearance in French). Ambiguity is the inevitable condition of man, and the disbelief in God, which existentialists take for granted, only serves to make that ambiguity more tragic and a courageous way out of it more necessary. Man tries to expand and enrich his life, to act as if an indefinite future were assured for him, but he knows that there is one end to it and that is death.[1] Man is conscious of a world yet part of that world, confronted and oppressed at times by the consciousness of others. Man is a subject and also, for others, an object. Freedom is his one safe privilege. But he can only make that freedom meaningful if he outgrows the attitude of children as yet unaware of it, the despicable attitude of slaves abdicating it, the conventional cowardice of the 'serious man' preferring security, and the domineering passion of those who want to possess and control others and do not respect their freedom. Engagement is inevitable but hedged around with pitfalls, which Le Sang des autres conjures up vividly.

The position of a woman of letters is especially arduous. She enters a world fashioned by man and has to meet standards set by him. She has to live imaginatively in an artistic and literary universe created by man to complete, replace, or interpret the real one. She tends to be restricted to one domain: that of woman's existence, where the search for love and for man's caresses, for the family comfort of children, a home and a tenderly tilled garden, and refuge in childhood memories are the main themes. Simone de Beauvoir is determined to meet successfully the challenge often thrown by male critics to female letters and to pass from the particular truth of women, which they alone can express in their subjectivity, to a universal truth. From the desolate solitude of a consciousness set apart from others, she passes on to the interaction of several conscious beings upon one another, hence to the eventualities of responsibility, risk, and guilt faced by the characters in Le Sang des autres.

An epigraph from The Brothers Karamazov has been popularized by existentialist literature: 'Everyone is responsible for everything before everybody.' It stresses the claim of existentialist ethics to rival the Christian ideal of charity and solidarity and to evolve a communion of saints and sinners, in its own way. There is no escape into solitary contemplation or forbearance from participating in political and social action, which lured the writers of the symbolist and postsymbolist era, from Mallarmé to Valery, who dreamed of Axel's castle. Through the mere fact that we exist, we act upon other people. We had better face our interdependence and our far-reaching responsibility unflinchingly from the start. 'Live—

1. Simone de Beauvoir treated the subject of action, adventure, and projecting oneself incessantly into the future in an essay of intelligent popularization, Pyrrhus et Cinéas (Gallimard, 1944). Her long novel, Tous les hommes sont mortels (Gallimard, 1947), revolves around the theme of death as giving value to life. Immortality, far from constituting a desirable goal as it does to the Christian, would deprive immortal men of the privilege of giving their life to a cause and of loving someone or something usque ad mortem.

our servants can well do that for us,' exclaimed the author of *Axel*. The protagonist of *Le Sang des autres*, sixty years or so later, strikes another tune, closer to Voltaire and Diderot: 'We exist only if we act.'

Jean Blomart was born in a comfortable middle-class family. His father, the owner of a big printing establishment acquired solely through his own merits, embodies the conventionality and unimaginativeness, but also the honesty, the frugality, the assiduous and conscientious virtues of the middle class. But Jean suffers from scruples that keep him from enjoying his privileged position in society. He is attracted to workmen and to revolutionary action in their ranks. It is difficult, in continental Western Europe, as Sartre and other well-meaning intellectuals have found out, to 'go to the people' without also going to communism; and Communist workers eye with suspicion a bourgeois who joins their party and obviously does not want his own liberation, as every one of the workers thinks he does, but theirs. A friend of Jean Blomart remarked to him: 'There will always be a gulf between a workingman and you; you choose freely a condition which he did not choose and has to endure.' Jean, however, soon becomes a leader in the trade-union movement and in syndicalist agitation. He has drawn to the cause a friend and admirer of his, Jacques. In one of the riots between Communists and royalist agitators, which preceded World War II, Jacques, to whom Jean had lent a pistol, is killed.

Jean is harried by remorse and by the sense of his responsibility. He will henceforth renounce direct action and refrain from influencing others and limit himself to supporting only the professional claims of the unions. A girl, Hélène, engaged to a workman, Paul, who is a friend of Jean Blomart and a colleague of his in the trade-union movement, meets Jean, in an entertaining scene, described with much freshness, in which she has tried to involve the men in the theft of a bicycle. She falls in love with Jean, who treats her like the peevish, romantic, and fickle young girl she is and refuses to listen to her declarations. He is not interested in her. He is solely concerned with his self-assigned mission, and he will remain loyal to his friendship for Paul.

Hélène is stubborn. She breaks with her fiancé and, vexed by Jean's spurning of her advances, gives herself, in one night of desolation, to an unworthy and unscrupulous man. She becomes pregnant and must arrange for an abortion. She asks Jean to lend her his room for the very night when the gruesome operation is to take place. Jean, taken aback, consents, assists her timidly and clumsily, takes pity upon her, and gradually feels for her a tenderness akin to love. We are responsible also for those who love us.

The great tragedy of Europe in 1937–39 now engulfs the more limited drama in which Jean is an unwilling but inextricably involved actor. The Spanish republicans are being crushed, and Jean had contended that the French working classes could do nothing for them. Austria and Czechoslovakia are invaded. It dawns upon Jean Blomart that he may have erred in avoiding his responsibility to others, to the whole world. 'I have not created the world. But I re-create it through my very presence at every minute. And all that happens to it seems to happen through me.' The war comes to France, and Jean is mobilized. Hélène tries desperately to have him withdrawn from dangerous positions. She defies army regulations, suspicions which mistake her for a spy, and her own weariness to visit him in the village where he is stationed. The scene, related in Chapter Eight, is one of the most vivid narratives of World War II. But Paris falls. Hélène at first, ranking Jean's life and her own happiness with him above all else, comes near to collaborating with the Germans. But Jean has worked out the problem of his responsibility to others. He joins the resistance movement, and Hélène freely follows him. The choice entails Cornelian dilemmas. Blowing up trains and shooting a few German officers in dark streets may appear as vain gestures and will surely cause the deaths of many innocent French hostages. Yet it must be accomplished; for only through the ruthless German retaliation on French civilians will the French patriotic conscience be aroused and the fight against the invaders be resumed some day.

Jean now truly loves Hélène, and they are fighters in a common cause. The sight of little Jewish children carried away by the Germans moves her to the depths. She is now ready to face death, as Jean had explained to her, so that life may retain a meaning. She joins the resistance network directed by Jean. Once again he, as the chief, sends others to risk their lives, while he stays relatively secure, organizing the fight. Hélène, lucidly, volunteers for a perilous mission and is gravely wounded. She dies and has only words of gratitude and solace for Jean. One must pay with the blood of others, heart-rending though it may be. Jean embraces her as she dies, while his comrades are pressing him to give the signal for the next attack by the *maquis*. Without any outburst of emotion or of eloquence, Jean moves on to the battle, silencing his sorrow and his scruples. He knows that responsibility can never be eluded and that he has fought all along for 'that good which saves every man from all others and from himself: freedom.'

It would be neither correct nor fair to maintain that *Le Sang des autres* is the demonstration of a thesis or the imparting of a message. The artistic and technical merits of the novel are in no way subservient to the moral thinking that informs the tale. The characters are concretely and unpredictably alive. Hélène, at first selfish and light and girlishly immature, then determined to win the man whom she fails to understand but admires and loves because she *wants* to love him, is a very true person. So is Mme Blomart, the distressed mother who, torn and powerless, watches her son standing against his father, rejecting the bourgeois order he was to inherit and preserve, living on a workman's wages, and then courting death in the resistance. The atmosphere of the strikes of 1936, of the political debates, then of the awareness of the national peril overshadowing the social struggle, and the unfolding of the gradual growth of the moral conscience in the French people, at first dazed by their defeat, are rendered with more simplicity and naturalness than in perhaps any other French novel since 1944. The past is merged with the present without any technical jugglery. Blomart is at the bedside of Hélène, who is dying, and relives his past life. He moralizes occasionally, but that is in keeping with his character and with the situation in which he finds himself, anguished at the deaths he has caused by paying with the blood of others, desperately seeking a moral justification for his acts.

Simone de Beauvoir does not cultivate emotional effects and does not utilize the violence, the coarseness, or the surprise that have been frequent in recent fiction. She also shuns the relative facility (for French authors steeped in that tradition) of the psychological novel in the first person singular. Although everything is seen and related by Jean Blomart, it is not colored by his own spectacles, and events are never a pretext for introspective delving. The forte of the author, indeed, is dialogue. Through their earnest desire to face each other with full frankness, the characters lay bare and discover what is truest in them, in brief, clashing sentences. They talk too well, to be sure, and with a neat firmness of phrasing that is part of the stylization of the novel. One never quite forgets the author, who has planned and governed every incident with a lucid intellect and an inflexible will. There is more mystery and less docile obedience in the truly living and haunting characters molded by the very great masters of fiction.

In her memoirs, when telling the story of her life during the German

occupation and of her literary debut, Simone de Beauvoir expressed herself with little leniency on *Le Sang des autres.* With the cool objectivity
of an austere and combative suffragette, as she was called in the British
press, she did not hide from herself the charges to which her two early
novels would be exposed. The most damaging is the perennial reproach
of didacticism. An immense portion of literature, and not in the Middle
Ages alone or in the novels of Richardson (and perhaps of Laclos and of
Sade, or so they asserted), has been and still is didactic. The purists
among literary critics may object, often because they would like to retain
the monopoly of sermonizing for themselves. Many a reader does not, who
agrees with Horace that the utmost skill in literary art may well lie in
blending 'utile dulci.' An impressive portion of Balzac, Tolstoi, and Proust
would have to be thrown out of their fiction if all their didactic and
philosophical passages were to be excised. The common contention has it
that the characters should first obsess the novelist's imagination or haunt
his memory, and the ideas which they subsequently express or symbolize
should only emerge from the living characters.

In truth, however, the secret of creation is far more complex. The
greatest among the novelists (and some of the greatest among the poets,
Milton, Shelley, Hugo, and, of course, Virgil among them) started with a
deliberate intent to justify the ways of God to man, of acting the role of
a reforming sovereign to reluctant farmers, or of showing the man of
today who was to be redeemed into the progressive man of tomorrow,
freed from tyrants. George Eliot and Zola preached likewise, and the
former at least put less consistency between her private life and her
moralizing than did Simone de Beauvoir. Few of the novelists of the past
who were didactic happened to be as good philosophers and as consistent
in their views as the authors of *The Roads to Freedom, The Plague,* and
The Blood of Others. The crudeness of Balzac's developments, of Tolstoi's
ponderous historical theses, of Zola's demonstrations of how experimental
the novel should be (and fails to be) are probably rendered more palatable to the fastidious critic by his realization that he thinks more consistently and more clearly than those great creators did. It would be a
paradox if, in an age of ideas when even our international wars have
become ideological ones and when most of the fictional heroines are university graduates, ideas were banished from fiction. Many an American
reader has been heard to lament the absence of momentous philosophical
and political issues in the vital American fiction of 1920–60, where too
many of the favorite characters are idiots, perverts, or falsely innocent

adolescents of the two sexes: Malcolm, Candy Christian, or Salinger's
schoolboy. The 'new novelist' of the 'sixties in France may some day appear as thin and unsubstantial as the poets of Art for Art's Sake or those
of effete symbolist cénacles do to us today: for, in an age of immense developments in science and in social studies, they have severed themselves
from all that might have looked like a dramatization of metaphysical, social, and political issues.

Simone de Beauvoir is occasionally over-explicit in her display of the
philosophical ideas which her characters evolve, live by, or demonstrate.
A male prejudice makes some of us balk at a woman writer who knew so
very clearly what she wanted to do and appears so cool in her mastery of
her material. But her first two novels were not, in our judgment, lacking in
warmth and in emotional appeal. The characters of Françoise and of
Xavière are living creations, and there are not many women in Malraux,
Camus, Sartre, or Robbe-Grillet who could be compared to them. The
dialogue is very skillfully used, as is the creation of suspense even in a
novel which, like Le Sang des autres, moves backward, in a series of
flashbacks, from the deathbed of Hélène and Jean's remorse of conscience.
Both novels are relatively short, an uncommon merit in a generation of
writers, and presumably of readers, who, as Diderot said of Richardson,
seem never to have enough of a good thing and want their novels (and
now their films) long and tedious enough to give them their full money's
worth.

Les Mandarins, published ten years later (1954), was more loudly
acclaimed by the critics and the prize-giving boards: it was given the
Goncourt award that year, translated immediately under the same title,
and judged by many to be the best existentialist novel since The Stranger.
This critic for one disagrees and believes that it will eventually be
eclipsed by its predecessors. Much of the curiosity which it aroused was
extra-literary. The book was immediately declared by those who were in
the know in Paris to be a roman à clef. And many English-speaking
literati did not want to be left behind Paris in their ability to identify the
models for the half-imaginary portraits. Simone de Beauvoir vehemently
denied, in the third volume of her memoirs, La Force des choses (1963;
Force of Circumstance, New York, Putnam, 1965), that Dubreuilh was a
portrait (not a flattering one at that) of Sartre, that Henri could be identified with Camus; and she hinted that there was at least as much of herself
in Henri as there was in Anne. Her denials are sincere; but she could not

keep herself from transposing into features of Henri some of Camus's attitudes that arose when he had to leave his newspaper, *Combat,* and when he turned against Communist Russia. It is even clearer that Anne's mournful love affair with Lewis Brogan is a thinly veiled narrative of her own affair, since bluntly discussed in her memoirs, with Nelson Algren. Proust and Gide likewise borrowed much from real persons when writing their novels; but they remarked, as many novelists have done, that their invented characters always rang more true than those whom they had in part imitated from actual models.

The faults of *Les Mandarins* are the unjustified length of the novel arising from the author's stubborn wish to be overexplicit. Nothing is left for our imaginative ability to supplement or is lightly and mysteriously suggested. With equal stubbornness, Simone de Beauvoir appears determined to use a colorless, pedestrian prose that is tantamount to a refusal of style. But style, even if at times insincere, can also create a vividness and display a communicative power which constitutes a new type of literary sincerity. She attempted to present confused events and a relatively large number of characters and of episodes, with less mastery than she had attained in her earlier novels where she focused the interest on two or three protagonists caught, as in classical tragedy, in the grip of one momentous crisis. Finally, the sex scenes, especially those where Nadine, the young girl who had been unwanted and unloved by her mother, is described in her unhappy pursuit of passion and those in which Anne belatedly hopes to find total fulfillment with her American novelist, seem as callously crude and as deliberately intrusive as similar love episodes in Jules Romains's *Hommes de bonne volonté.*

But, while lacking the intensity, and the art, of a novel which might have been destined for survival, *Les Mandarins* will be valuable to the readers eager to understand the peculiar problems of French and other Continental European intellectuals just after World War II. The ironical title designates the persons possessing both knowledge and a spiritual cast of mind who enjoy living and thinking in secure isolation from the masses. The German occupation and the grave moral issues posed by the war of 1939–45 had brutally forced men of letters to take sides; the collapse of the ruling classes (political, military, scientific, and ecclesiastical) in 1940 in France had suddenly entrusted poets, novelists, and philosophers with a new and august function. Their mission, as they viewed it, was to save man and to build a new world. They conceived

chimerical schemes for a new constitution, a purer press, more democracy and social progress, and a stable international peace built upon the
end of power politics.

Liberation came and with it atomic explosions, the nuclear race, and
imperialistic rivalry between the two powers newly aware of their enormous strength. Most of the intellectuals felt more attracted to Russia
than to America. Few were Communists. But many were those who
dreamed of a non-Communist left which would preserve the fraternity
of which industrial workmen were a part during the war years. Then
the news of Russian labor camps, only slightly different from the hated
German concentration camps, leaked out. For Sartre, Camus, Rousset,
and Simone de Beauvoir, the dilemma became a harrowing one. Should
writers side with the 'American imperialists' who were not supposed to
be able to understand the deprivation and the socialist hopes of an
underprivileged world by nature and tradition distrustful of capitalism?
Should they join with the Communists in spite of their ruthlessness and
thus abdicate their right to dissent, to protest, and to strive for their
ideal? Or, in the bitterness of their disillusionment, were they to choose
silence, disinterest in politics, and to enjoy selfishly the intellectual comfort of mandarins, renouncing all political influence?

The problems then hotly debated by the French intellectuals were not
those of a frustrated and impoverished nation, incapable of reforming its
institutions and finding an escape in idle talk or abstract issues. They
could again become the problems of Germany and of Britain; they are
posed by the vocal protests of Russian literary men after they were
liberated from the iron hand of Stalin; they have become those of a
growing segment of American writers, professors, and students during
the Viet Nam wars. Simone de Beauvoir's claim to our respect is that she
had the audacity to treat those questions with impartiality and dramatic
irony, as Malraux did when writing fiction on the Chinese revolution
and on the Spanish civil war. Cynics may scoff her naïveté when she,
and Sartre, expound their remorseful doubts whether one has the moral
right to compose fiction while thousands of people on our planet are
dying from hunger and lack of care. They may suggest more efficient
ways, resorted to by the scorned 'affluent capitalists,' to assist the poor
and to feed the hungry. Still, such concern, which was that of Michelet,
Dickens, Hugo in their day, is not only morally admirable; felt in anguish, it should constitute as fitting a subject for great fiction as personal
love affairs, drug addiction, greed for money or for power, or the preser-

vation of an old family manor. Dostoevski's *The Demons* was also a novel centered on the philosophical and political debates of intellectuals. Simone de Beauvoir's relative failure, due to a lack of imaginative intensity and perhaps to an excessive closeness to the events depicted, which harmed her inspiration, should not hide from us the courage of her attempt. Her failure was far more laudable than the mere successful repetition of an earlier success would have been. The oft-heralded sickness unto death of the modern novel might indeed be more than a mere pretext for mournful critical prophecies if the twentieth-century novel did not dare to confront the momentous problems of our time, which are political and ethical. It was especially heroic of a woman to make the attempt.

Simone de Beauvoir has scored a more resounding success in Britain and America with her more sensational and, in this writer's opinion, far less original volumes of memoirs and of anthropological sociology on 'the second sex.' Much in her ponderous volumes on the condition of woman is needlessly pedantic and fails to go to the heart of feminine problems: maternity, the need for talented women writers to cling to a man (a need which her own lifelong dependence on Sartre emphasized, in contradiction to her rigid theories), the urge for one or several 'grandes passions.' Still, Simone de Beauvoir encouraged her successors among women writers to renounce a number of limited subjects to which feminine memoir and fiction writers had timidly limited themselves. Her satire of some arrogant contemptors of 'the leprous ones,' as Montherlant called women, is done with marvelous verve.

Simone de Beauvoir's book on the United States, *L'Amérique au jour le jour* (Morihien, 1948, reissued in 1954 by Gallimard, translated as *America Day by Day*, New York: Grove Press, 1954), was on the contrary received with unjust severity by the country that the French existentialist high-priestess admired and attempted to understand. True, she traveled hastily, met chiefly writers, college professors, and students, visited bars and slums, but ignored the business and industrial life of the country, the philosophers and, more astonishingly, the women of America. Her diagnosis of this country, as the ideal land for the spread of existentialism, was nevertheless very shrewd and has been confirmed by the extraordinary interest taken, in the 'sixties, by American youth in existentialist ideas. In a thoughtful article in the *New York Times Magazine* of May 25, 1947, she stressed the chief pragmatist elements in her creed, which many Americans may feel they have been living by all these decades: 'Man is man only by his refusal to be passive, by the urge which throws him from the present toward the future, which thrusts him toward things with the aim of dominating and shaping them; for him, to exist is to remake existence, to live is the will to live.' Man's freedom is only real if it strives to effect some change in the world. One should judge a man, not by what he is, but by what he does. Man fulfills himself by his will to realization, by his 'project' in the world.

At the same time, while praising the splendid sense of fraternity of Americans and voicing unbounded faith in the youth of the United States, she pointed to the danger of worshipping objects isolated from the subject and making an idol of the thing itself. She also and very lucidly denounced the peril inherent in a faith in progress which regularly sacrifices the present to the future and which tends to scorn the past. 'To transcend is also to preserve; if uprooted, the movement toward the future becomes an indefinite flight. . . . If we regard the present as the annihilation of the past, as the bearer of the latter's death sentence, then we condemn the present also. . . . What was done ten years ago is already worthless. Then, what is done today will be worthless ten years from now.' That obsession with moving forward fast puts a flavor of death in American existence.

Bibliographical Notes

The novels of Simone de Beauvoir are *L'Invitée*. Gallimard, 1943 (*She Came To Stay*, London: Secker and Warburg, 1949; and New York: World Publishing Co., 1954); *Le Sang des autres*. Gallimard, 1945 (*The Blood of Others*. London: Secker and Warburg, 1948; New York: A. Knopf, 1948, and Popular Library, 1948); *Tous les hommes sont mortels*. Gallimard, 1946; *Les Mandarins*. Gallimard, 1954. Her fine philosophical essay, has come out in translation, *The Ethics of Ambiguity*, at The Philosophical Library in 1948; *The Second Sex* at A. Knopf's in 1953. The first two volumes of her memoirs have also been published as *Memoirs of a Dutiful Daughter*. London: Deutsch, Weidenfeld and Nicolson, 1959; New York and Cleveland: World Publishing Co., 1959; *The Prime of Life*, ibid., 1962. The French titles of the others are *La Force des Choses*. Gallimard, 1963, and *Une Mort très douce*, Gallimard, 1964, on her mother's death, which has recently appeared as *A Very Easy Death* (Putnam, 1966).

On Simone de Beauvoir, see 'Ethics and Art,' by Gwendolyn Bays, *Yale French Studies*, I, 1, 1948, 106–112, and 'Memoirs of a Dutiful Existentialist,' by René Girard, ibid., No. 27, Spring–Summer 1961, issue on women writers, and 'Simone de Beauvoir and the Related Destinies of Woman and Intellectual,' ibid., 26–32. Georges Blin had an early and valuable essay on her in *Fontaine* (No. 45, October 1945, 716–730); M. Merleau-Ponty discussed her novels in his chapter, 'Le Roman et la Métaphysique' of his volume *Sens et non-sens*, Nagel, 1948, 51–82. *Les Mandarins* was reviewed most penetratingly by Dominique Aury in *La Nouvelle Revue Française*, December 1954, 1080–1085, and by Rima Drell Reck in *Yale French Studies*, No. 27, Spring–Summer 1961, 33–40. Small volumes have been devoted to Simone de Beauvoir by Geneviève Gennari, Editions Universitaires, 1959, and by a cleric, A. M. Henry, O.P., *Simone de Beauvoir ou l'échec d'une chrétienté*, Fayard, 1961. An American monograph by Konrad Bieber is due to appear at Twayne Publishing Company. An excellent essay in English is that of Maurice Cranston in *The Novelist as Philosopher*, edited by John Cruickshank, Oxford University Press, 1962. Two other books on Simone de Beauvoir appeared in 1966: one by a lawyer, Serge Julienne-Caffié, Gallimard, the other by a Dominican, A. M. Henry, subtitled 'L'Echec d'une chrétienté,' Fayard.

XI

Albert Camus: Moralist and Novelist

It is questionable whether Camus (or Saint-Exupéry, or Sartre himself) will remain for posterity one of the masters of the art of fiction. But few are the French writers who would not prefer the title of 'moralist' to the glory of being a novelist, a dramatist, a philosopher, or even a poet. The word is often misunderstood outside Latin countries, since it is well-nigh untranslatable. It is very far from designating a preacher of morality or a teacher of ethics. It is often used to allude to the authors of maxims and isolated thoughts who flourished chiefly in the classical age, between the time of Montaigne and Diderot. Few moderns have, as warmly as did Camus, admired those classical moralists of France, their wisdom nurtured on the experience of life and directed toward the practice of living. Just after the war, on November 15, 1945, as he was working on *La Peste*, Camus declared to *Les Nouvelles Littéraires:* 'I know but one revolution in art, the exact appropriation of the form to the subject matter, of language to the subject. From that point of view, I only love, and very deeply, the great classical literature of France.' There were moralists in France after the century of classicism: Vauvenargues, Diderot, Chamfort, even Laclos in the eighteenth, Joubert and Baudelaire in the nineteenth. Leopardi, Schopenhauer, Nietzsche, and some Spaniards today like Ramón Gomez de la Serna have convincingly showed that the pointed and lucid aphorism is not the sole monopoly of the French language. English literature, by contrast, does not appear to favor this genre of writing, just as it eschews another original art of prose writing which has been dear to the French and to German writers such as Hermann Hesse and Rilke: the prose poem.

Camus, however, except in his posthumous *Notebooks,* did not usually sum up his wisdom in those somewhat bitter pills of disillusion of which authors of maxims are fond. He is a moralist in another sense: in his novels and in his short stories, one senses the presence of a man who is looking for reasons for living, tormented by the concern to lead men to the elusive goal of more happiness; he is obsessed by the need to justify his characters' behavior, indeed to justify literature itself, which he is perpetually calling in question. Little did he care for the elaboration of a system of abstract and logical thought. It is easy to refute each of the intellectual attitudes which he adopted and to take issue with the ambiguity of his positions (on existentialism, on his criminal Christ-figure Meursault, on the sarcastic narrator of *La Chute,* on the Algerian problem). Any meditation which would not lead to action would hold scant value in his eyes. Epistemology per se is futile for him, even more than for Sartre, and he indulges elaborate dialectics far less than the author of *Critique de la Raison dialectique.* In a sense, this Pascal without Christ, as Camus was called in the Jesuit monthly *Etudes,* who spurned all the advances of the orthodox believers, might have echoed Pascal's contemptuous assertion that 'the whole of philosophy is not worth one hour's trouble.' Like the existentialists, he aimed at understanding the abstract concretely, through placing his fictional and dramatic characters in a situation where rights and duties entered into conflict. Any literature worthy of the name must attempt to 'change life,' as Rimbaud proclaimed, hence to change man through assisting him.

The novelist who is also a moralist (as were Gide, Montherlant, Malraux, and the early Giono, all of whom influenced Camus) acts like a psychologist relentlessly bent upon seeing clearly into his fellow men, unveiling their sophistry or their cowardice, but also revealing to them their potentialities for an upward thrust and toward 'the repose of the seventh day' which, as Nietzsche put it, coexists in them with mud and clay. He chastises in order to correct, he analyzes in order to improve, and he is often tempted to supplement his writing with ethical and even political action. The moralist in him is not long remote from a prophet. Prometheus, the rebel and savior, is secretly dearer to his heart than haughty and discouraged Sisyphus. The peril is great for the teller of tales not to be able to prefer his tale to himself and to his message. Symbolic and even allegorical meanings may prove more tempting than the unrestrained involvement in a carnal world or in a visionary one, where creatures live and move and have their being. But, in an age such as our post-atomic one, in which the readers of Europe and of America seem to be desperately yearning for a literature of salvation, and for guidance in the labyrinthine forest of decision-making, moralists among imaginative writers have been the father confessors and the guides to a multitude of bewildered men of good will. Perhaps since Victor Hugo and Dostoevski's death in the early eighteen-eighties, no man of letters was in our century mourned with such deep sorrow as was Camus when an absurd blow of destiny put an end to his life on 4 January 1960.

The art and the thought of Camus are closely bound up with his life, with circumstances which provoked some statement by a man who was attentive to every event, irked by any contradiction which he judged to be mean or unfair, a journalist of the very highest order and a polemicist in the noblest sense, that is, a loyal adversary of all that struck him as false, base, or nefarious. He was predestined to become a rebel against injustice, a fighter in the ideological and ethical controversies of his age, and first of all by his origins. He was French, doubly so for having risen to culture and to the wielding of a magnificent prose amid many handicaps; and yet he felt alien to much that was narrow, conventional, gloomy, and, as he would say, sunless in the traditions of France. Several times, after he had come into his glory, he would apply to himself, and to man in general, the two adjectives in which one letter alone differs: 'solitary' among other French writers and impatient of any party, yet 'solitary' of his compatriots, of his own age, and of men. There are many men of letters in our time who have thus felt impelled to assume the condition of an alienated individual in the country in which they lived: Jewish expatriates from Nazi Germany or Austria, exiles from Russia or from Spain, a Rumanian or an Irish dramatist finding his own vocation as a French playwright, Czechs like Kafka communicating through the German language, American expatriates like Henry James, Edith Wharton, and T. S. Eliot, or Irishmen and Englishmen like James Joyce, D. H. Lawrence, Aldous Huxley, W. H. Auden, and Lawrence Durrell choosing to live away from Britain as their romantic predecessors had once done. The aloneness and the alienation of modern men have been strikingly dramatized by those solitaries and by their characters. Those who remained in their own land, obsessed by its poetry or by its secret corruption, Proust, Mauriac,

Faulkner, Giono have hardly been less solitary, or more leniently disposed to forgive and to admire.

Camus was born of a father from Alsace who had emigrated to Algeria and was killed at the battle of the Marne when his son was one, and of a Spanish mother of very little culture to whom her son always remained devoted. He came into the world in Algeria, where he was educated at the primary school, then on a scholarship at the lycée and at the University where he specialized in philosophy. He was 23 when for the first time he crossed the sea to visit France, after having caught a glimpse of Spain and of Italy. Italy had filled him with exaltation through her marriage of Pagan love for life with Florentine gravity. Greece was all along his spiritual home.

The ominous wind which heralded an inevitable war was then blowing over Europe. In the face of the ascent of Nazism and of the vociferous provocations of Mussolini directed toward Abyssinia, Albania, and France, Western nations were divided, frightened, and internally torn between right and left, disturbed at finding themselves through the force of events the allies of Stalinist Russia. A latent civil war fostered disunity and hatred among the French parties and blinded them to the threats from outside. Camus, passionate for health and happiness since his childhood (but declared by doctors, as early as 1930, to be tubercular), already aware of the talent which had been lodged in him, experienced with anguish the rift which was then rending apart Europe, a continent proud but also weary of its long past and addicted to internecine feuds. 'Do you realize,' he asked later in one of the articles collected in *Actuelles*, 'that within twenty-five years, from 1922 to 1947, seventy million Europeans have been uprooted, deported or killed? Such is the plight of the land of humanism which, despite all protests, must be termed ignoble Europe.' Camus's own Algerian land was, some fifteen years later, to become in its turn the stage of a furious civil war which would fill the French with shame and remorse. He himself, the most famous of all North African writers, refused to condemn either side and to play the part of a lamenting prophet or that of a penitent-judge.

The land which was the setting for Camus's childhood and youth had once upon a time provided Christianity with very great names: the Tunisian Tertullian in the third century who had described as the greatest joy for the blessed that of watching Roman emperors burn in hell; then the Bishop of Hippo (today Bône), St. Augustine who oriented Christian theology toward original sin. Their remote descendant considered that,

after too many fratricidal wars, persecutions, and too much lust for
wealth and power, Christian religion had been betrayed. Early in his
career, and to the end, he protested in the name of paganism.[1] Father
Bruckberger, in the number of the *Nouvelle Revue Française* devoted
in March 1960 to Camus, stated that his ideal was 'the Hellenic man. . . .
He was engaged in an anti-Christian undertaking, . . . trying to find a
substitute body for Christianity.' In the same number, Jean-Louis Barrault
descried two faces in him: that of 'a secular monk, all streaming with a
God whom he dared not name' and the other facet which, 'more secret,
revealed a voluptuous love for life.'

Some of the most sumptuous pages of prose written by Camus between
1937 and 1940 are indeed those of a pagan moralist, intoxicated with light,
with love, and with the warm and fragrant nature of Southern climes.
His first volume *Noces* (1938) celebrates the wedding feast of the sun,
the wind, the Mediterranean land and sea. With less affectation than in
the *Nourritures terrestres* of the liberated Protestant André Gide, with
less verbal flamboyance and epic transfiguration of reality than was found
in Giono, Camus sings the glory of a life untainted by original sin. 'I have
never been able to understand the meaning of certain words, sin for example' Camus was to declare. The first piece, from which the youthful
volume draws its name, 'Noces à Tipasa,' shows the author treading on
the fragrant herbs called wormwood or absinth:

> We are walking to a meeting with love and desire. We are not
> seeking any lessons or the bitter philosophy which may be asked
> from greatness. Except the sun, kisses and perfumes, all seems to us
> futile. . . . Here I understand what is called glory: the right of lov-
> ing immeasurably. There is but one love in this world. To embrace
> a woman's body is also to preserve close to oneself that strange joy
> which descends from the sky toward the sea. . . . There is no
> shame in being happy. But nowadays the fool is sovereign, and the
> fool is in my eyes he who is afraid of enjoyment.

The whole volume reverberates 'that invincible sun' which Camus says
elsewhere illuminates the core of his work. But it is not a series of
majestically orchestrated descriptions such as Chateaubriand was fond
of painting. These lyrical essays are rather the reflections of a moralist.
The burden of the song is the 'hic et nunc' of a Pagan who refuses to

1. We have developed the point in several essays, notably in 'Camus the Pagan' in
Yale French Studies, No. 25, Spring 1960, 20–25. Camus's hellenism is more
ardently felt than either that of Giraudoux or Valéry, about which too much has
been written. Neither of them was deeply 'Greek.'

sacrifice the present to the future, the concrete possession of a rich experience to mere hope. The thought of death intrudes in these pages. But it is not an obsession; it is not wooed as it was by Shakespeare's Cleopatra comparing its sting to a lover's kiss, or by the characters of Rilke and of Malraux. It is ugly, as it also disease which the young author had sensed to be prowling around him:

> I do not choose to believe that death opens out on another life. To me, it is a closed door. I do not deny that it is a step someday to be taken; but I do say that it is a ghastly and sordid adventure.

Such a determination to prefer joy to sorrow, shared also by Giono, and to make that joy lasting, was all the more courageous as, to Camus, joy had not proved easy of access. He was born in the midst of poverty, if not of utter destitution. His father had been a humble mason; his mother had been forced to take employment as a charwoman in order to raise her two children. In the home were a grandmother afflicted by a cancer of the liver, and a paralyzed, ever grumbling uncle. In his earliest book, *L'Envers et l'endroit,* written in 1935–36 but only published in 1958, which another moralist, Brice Parain, whose childhood had been surrounded by poverty, prefers to all of Camus's other works, he recalled that misery which marked his early years. It could have made him envious and bitter, full of hatred for the rich like Jules Vallès; or proud of his lowly origins and of his merit in rising above them, like Michelet, Péguy, or more recently Giono and Guéhenno. He might have sided with revolutionaries intent upon the subversion of an unjust order which protects vested interests and the inequities of birth. If for two years (1934–35) he belonged to the Communist party, from which he was then ejected, and then belonged for a time to the anticlerical French freemasonry, he did not subsequently advocate revolt in the political or social realm. He considered that the Algerian sun and sky had abundantly consoled him for the hardships around him. 'My passions as a man have never been "against." The beings whom I have loved have always been better and greater than I.' In that earliest of his collection of essays and reminiscences, he nobly proclaimed:

> Poverty never was for me a misfortune. It was always counterbalanced by the riches of light. Poverty kept me from judging that all was well in the world and in history. The sun taught me that history was not everything. . . . Fear or discouragement, I may have known; bitterness, never.

And again:

> There is a solitude in poverty, but a solitude that grants each thing its true price. At a certain stage of wealth, the sky itself and a night studded with stars may seem like a natural gift. But at the bottom of the ladder, one finds the sky regaining its full significance: that of a priceless boon of grace. Summer nights, mysteries amid the crackling of the stars. Behind the child that I was, there stretched a stinking corridor; his broken little chair collapsed under him. But once he raised his eyes, he drank from the purity of the stars.

Camus did not, unlike others and notably his early friends the existentialists who have reached the age of reminiscing about their past, indulge in any detailed narrative of his experiences and his moods during his formative years. Even from his posthumous *Notebook*, little is to be gleaned on the novelists whom he most avidly read, the influences he underwent, the political reformers by whom he was attracted, or the Christian theologians who may have antagonized him and whom he depicted harshly in the chaplain who visits Meursault in his prison or in the Jesuit preacher Paneloux. He was drawn to the theater, as a producer rather than as a dramatist at first, and because of the fraternal and communal work which it entailed. He and his friends staged, on an amateur stage, Aeschylus' *Prometheus Bound, La Celestina* and other Spanish dramas, a French version of Synge's *Playboy of the Western World*, and a dramatization of Malraux's *Days of Wrath*. Malraux and Dostoevski he always admired. Kafka impressed him. He never intimated that the American novelists then (1936-42) immensely popular in France—Hemingway, Dos Passos, and Faulkner—had impressed him much; critics, always fond of detecting parallels and influences unnoticed by less learned readers, have grossly exaggerated any impact of Hemingway upon *L'Etranger*. There was no calculated attempt in Camus, whose generosity as a writer was great, to hide any debt he may have owed to others; rather a classical restraint and a *pudeur* which made him eschew the display of his own self and any romantic exuberance, and even of the technical means through which a style is perfected or a book composed. In a lucid passage of *L'Eté*, pages 131-2, he protested against the romantic conception of the artist necessarily portraying himself in his work. 'It is not at all ruled out, on the contrary, that an artist is first interested in other men, or in his own age, or in familiar myths. Even if he happens to depict himself at times, only exceptionally does he write on his real self. Works of art often trace the history of our nostalgias or of our temptations, almost never our own history, especially when they claim to be autobiographical.'

Facets of Camus have inevitably been included, usually transfigured, exaggerated or even caricatured, in Meursault, Dr. Rieux, and most of all perhaps in the monologuist of *La Chute*. But his own conceptual message as a moralist he unambiguously imparted in those essays, scattered through newspapers and magazines, where he spoke in his own name. He steadily nurtured an ideal which, he thought, had been first proposed by the Greeks. In a very fine article, 'L'Exil d'Hélène,' first published in a special number of *Les Cahiers du Sud* in 1948, he upbraided his contemporaries, unequal to the model offered by the citizens of Athens: 'like those buffoons in Dostoevsky, who boast of everything, ascend to the stars and end up by displaying their shame in any given public place, we lack that pride in man which is fidelity to one's limits, clearsighted love of one's condition.'

Noces, first published in Algiers, aroused little attention in the years preceding World War II, nor did then the first version of *Caligula*, that haughty and enigmatic drama in which the demented emperor is shown proving the absurd through his obstinate logic. Strangely, the warmth and the passionate interest taken by Camus in real or imaginary characters somehow failed to pass into his plays. They retain something cool and geometric, perhaps too deliberate in intent and too sumptuous in execution, which keep audiences from being moved or convinced. Camus's drama will probably, like that of Montherlant, be occasionally read and respected but seldom performed. He adapted plays from Lope de Vega, and dramatized novels by Faulkner and Dostoevski with modesty and generosity and he would probably, had he lived, have become an original theatrical director and an acute and very personal critic of the authors whom he admired. In an unknown essay which came out in a short-lived review, *Spectacles*, in March 1958, he recorded what a revelation Dostoevski's discovery had been for him as a young Algerian student of twenty; he added:

> Very soon, as I was living the drama of my own age more cruelly, I loved in the Russian novelist him who lived and most profoundly expressed our historical fate. To me Dostoevski is, long before Nietzsche, the author who read into contemporary nihilism. He defined it, predicted its monstrous or demential consequences, and tried to point to the way to some salvation. His main subject is what he himself terms 'the profound spirit, the spirit of negation and of death.'

Camus, in the years which preceded World War II and during the German occupation of France, grew close to the group which had then replaced the surrealists as the pole of attraction for the younger generation always dissatisfied with the literature which precedes them. Sartre, Simone de Beauvoir, and their friends welcomed him and were the first to praise him, aware all along that Camus was never fully to espouse their dialectics and that political as well as philosophical disagreements would soon draw them apart. *L'Etranger* appeared in 1942 and *Le Mythe de Sisyphe* in 1943. Sartre was the first to write an 'explanation' of Camus's novel, the acuteness of which has not been matched by the score of commentators who have since dissected every sentence of that *récit*. The more rigorous philosophical minds of Sartre and his friends and their metaphysicians' or psychologists' ambitions probably aroused in them dissent from the loose and less professional assertions accumulated in *Le Mythe de Sisyphe*. Fundamental differences in their attitudes and their conception of art were to widen a rift between Camus and Sartre. Not unsurprisingly Camus, raised in poverty and one of the few European writers to have risen from the lowest social strata, was the one whom Sartre and Simone de Beauvoir, an officer's son brought up amid comfort and a 'jeune fille rangée' raised in intellectual security and in affluence, were to charge with 'embourgeoisement.'

Specialists will argue, probably inconclusively, whether the label of existentialist should be applied to Camus. The point is of small moment. Camus did not stress freedom forcefully; he did not subscribe to the ontological and chronological precedence of essence over existence; a determined atheist himself, or at least more vocally anti-Christian than the existentialists, he did not parade his negation of God overmuch and, contrary to Rousseau and Robespierre who thought atheism to be aristocratic, pagan Camus found it slightly vulgar. He kept away from the terminology of the 'en soi' and 'pour soi.' As early as September 1945, in an article in *Combat* reprinted in 1950 in *Actuelles*, he stated: 'I do not much relish the celebrated existentialist philosophy and, to put it candidly, I believe its conclusions to be false. But it represents nevertheless a great adventure of thought.' The same year, in December, in a conversation with the editor of a monthly, *Paru,* Sartre casually, and lucidly, elaborated on the point:

> Camus is not an Existentialist. He does refer to Kierkegaard, Jaspers, Heidegger, but his true masters are the seventeenth century French moralists. . . . His pessimism is solar, would I say, recalling

what is black in the sun. Camus' philosophy is a philosophy of the absurd, and, for him, the absurd springs from the relation of man and the world, from the reasonable demands of man and the irrationality of the world. . . . I do not see any absurd, in the sense of scandal and deception, where Camus does. The thing which I call absurd is, in my eyes, a very different affair. It is the universal contingency of the being which is, but which is not the foundation of his being. It is what in the being is given, unjustifiable, which always comes first.

In many respects and in spite of technical differences in their views of the absurd, Camus and those existentialists who were his friends in those early nineteen-forties had then much in common—certainly in what they all opposed, and in their passionate acclaim of the same masters. They were indeed much closer in their networks of affinities than ever were those to whom we give the inclusive label of 'romantics,' 'realists,' 'symbolists,' and even 'surrealists.' It was fortunate for his imaginative creation, however, that Camus's thought always remained contradictory, ever confused, and never could be whipped together into a system. His novels were endeavors to elicit some clarity from the chaos of his contradictions and dilemmas. He came to distrust all ideologies, especially as they ended in a sophistry which justified oppression, conquest, or killing. No one would call Sartre a clear thinker. Contradictions between his anti-Marxist polemics and his subsequent advocacy of a personal brand of Marxism, altogether arbitrary distinctions between poetry and prose (the latter as merely expository, hence bound to submit to 'engagement') in *Qu'est-ce que la littérature?*, innumerable sleights of hand in his dialectical and polemical writings abound in his 'chaos of clear ideas,' to use a phrase coined for Voltaire. But Sartre's doctrinal views and aesthetic theories obtrude more blatantly in his novels and in a few of his plays (fortunately less so in his short stories) than they do in Camus.

Rightly or wrongly (and the misunderstanding, if it be one, is not altogether the public's fault, since Camus made much of the absurd in his first theoretical, and in truth lyrical, essay on his hero Sisyphus), Camus has become associated with the absurdist movement in contemporary letters. The notion has proved richer in dramatic, and even in comic, effects than it has been useful in fiction. Camus did not invent it. It is the logical crowning development of a long process of resistance to Cartesian rationalism, driven to its utmost consequence by Hegel's assertion that the real is rational and the rational is real. Marx, in a famous pronouncement, has hinted that it would be easier, and preferable, to change the world

than to understand it. Bergson, in *L'Evolution créatrice,* had calmly submitted that 'intelligence is characterized by a natural inability to understand life.' Gide, after many others, had yearned in his early *Nourritures
terrestres* for a deliverance of his mind from the heavy shackles of logic.
Realism, which implicitly assumed that the real could be faithfully described as it was, and thus made some rational sense, had lost its appeal
in France and elsewhere in Western Europe by 1910 or so. The advances
of psychology and of physics, the theories of Freud, and those of Jung on
the ancestral myths controlling us or living again in us, had dealt hard
blows to a formerly arrogant rationalism in the very years when Camus
appeared. World War I added to the universal bewilderment. Soon after,
the surrealists aimed their sarcastic arrows at the once sacrosanct principle of identity in logic. Kafka, alienated in his own culture, deeply Germanic in spite, or on account, of his Jewish and *Ausländer* origin, portrayed men of good will, eager to be model bureaucrats and perfect
officials, avid for respectability and bowing to orders, baffled in all their
endeavors to belong, and eventually bowing to a punishment which they
failed to understand. Camus found valid reasons, in his own life and in
the disease which afflicted him, to experience the absurd without having
to find the notion in previous writings by others. His immense success
was due to the fact that he came at a time when, after a world depression
and during a senseless massacre, audiences were ripe for his questions
and yearned for some answer.

The word 'absurd' has been misinterpreted by those readers who first
branded Camus as a nihilistic pessimist, then were relieved that a declared agnostic could be such a moralist and propose an ethics which
reassured the Christians, or those who were just as agnostic as he, but
still clung to the rites and language of Christianity. In 1920, the word
'tragic' and in 1945 the adjective 'absurd' were taken by many journalists
in the United States to denote something un-American and sinister, only
fit for corrupt and weary Europe. By 1960, they had become, along with
the substantive 'anxiety' and the phrase 'human condition' the password
to graduation from every high school and a convenient theme for commencement addresses. With a Latin like Camus, the word 'absurd' was
closer than seems to be the case in English to the etymology. *Absurde
canere* means to sing out of tune and *absurditas* is a discordance, a jarring note, a lag. Hence in science and logic an absurd assertion is that
whose consequences seem so utterly impossible (to our reason) that it

must needs be rejected. The turning point in the use of the word occurred when Camus declared: 'It is absurd that this should be—yet so it is.'

It is neither the irrationality of the world nor man's insistence upon a logical and comforting answer which revolts Camus, but the relation between the two. Man wants and needs immortality, yet he is faced by an unjust death. Caligula's naïve phrase can also be tragic: 'Men die and they are not happy.' Man yearns for justice, but, as Job centuries ago mourned, the wicked is often favored over the good and God-fearing person. He desperately wishes to find some rationality in the world which surrounds him, but the order of things and the order of thought fail to correspond. 'What I do not understand is without reason. . . . The world is but an immense irrational.' Lastly, man (or the Frenchman) wants clarity; however, 'nothing is clear, all is chaos, and man only retains his clearsightedness and the precise knowledge of the walls encircling him.' Absurdity springs from that confrontation between the 'pathetic call of man and the unreasonable silence of the world.' The romantics had perceived it and deplored it, and voiced their self-pity. Baudelaire had relished a bitter irony in finding himself 'a false discord in the divine symphony.' Sisyphus, more stoically, chooses to cherish his absurd doom, 'and calm of mind, all passion spent' to triumph stoically over it. 'Absurdity is a passion, the most heart-rending of all.' Elsewhere in the same youthful essay, Camus voiced his original disillusioned optimism. 'Life will be lived all the better for its being devoid of meaning.' To him Man is not a surplus quantity, *de trop,* unwanted in the universe. He endows the universe with some significance at least and he is the one element which can utter a protest against the senselessness of it all. But there is no easy way out of the conviction of the tragic absurdity of conditions imposed upon creatures who have ceased to have faith in reason. Camus never rested in any haven of intellectual comfort, as his sneers in *The Fall* remind us. In a cryptic but symbolic notation of 1945 in his *Notebooks,* he had jotted down: 'The sole contemporary problem: can we transform the world without believing in the absolute power of reason?'

A writer can hardly transform the world, even if he wields a journalist's pen with the skill and the contagious sincerity which Camus possessed. At other moments, Camus had declared his goal to be less ambitious: 'What characterizes this century of ours is not so much our having to rebuild the world as our having to rethink it.' By thinking, Camus, even though he held a degree in philosophy from Algiers University, did not mean erecting a system of abstract propositions; he meant rather, with regard to phenomenology, to learn how to see and feel afresh, to direct one's attention vividly and to search for one's own values, gropingly, tentatively, distrusting the doctrines which seem to explain everything and appear to take over from us a burden which is ours to carry.

That 'tabula rasa' or that spiritual 'ascesis,' as the French are fond of designating it with the Greek noun, was imaginatively practiced by Camus in his first short novel, *L'Etranger*. Almost at once, it became a classic, on account of its deceptive facility and polish, of its simplicity of vocabulary and syntax, and of the easy identification which teenagers of any land can achieve with the protagonist, a new romantic hero who defies society and dies persecuted by it. It seemed natural at first that young Frenchmen, turned cynical by a confusing era of successive allegiance to Daladier, Pétain, Laval, De Gaulle, of alternating party approval and indictment of the Russians or of the Western Allies, emerging from the turpitudes of a black market era, should have recognized themselves for a time in the pagan hero Meursault. It proved more of a surprise when the success of that minor masterpiece became even more widespread and more lasting with the American youth of the postwar years. But it is regrettable that far too many teachers of French and critical commentators should have summed up all of Camus in that early work and buried it under naïvely ponderous pages of exegesis on the systematic use of the *passé composé* as a tense retaining the past enmeshed in the present, on the omission of all co-ordinating particles between the sentences, and on the somewhat strained conciseness of a style which smacked, with less irony, of Voltaire and Mérimée even more than of Hemingway. The manner came as a relief from the rich draperies of Proust, Giono, and Mauriac. But a lament on the disappearance of the adjective should be sung by some lover of prose, or by anyone who deplores the dearth of qualifying and evocative sensuousness in the manner of writing, tainted with artificiality, practiced in many of our magazines. Camus's natural, or early bent, as evinced in *Noces* and *L'Eté* was for a vibrating and romantic prose in the tradition of Chateaubriand and Barrès. He imposed upon himself almost impossible restraints in his novels in order to pare down all that might be superfluous flesh and caressing resonance to his voice. When successful, his style reached a muscular sparseness which is in the truest lineage of the classical moralists. At times, however, its sobriety verges on dryness. The romanticism preliminary to any classical pruning and softening was perhaps not strong enough to be overheard through the novelist's fear of orchestration. The finest pages of writing by Camus are to be found else-where than in his three novels and six short stories.

The emphasis on the technical mastery of *L'Etranger* has been stressed to excess; its structure, whether made up of two or of three parts, its discreet suggestion of symbolic prolongations of some details, its con-trolled use of the past tense (Robbe-Grillet hinted that Camus had simply intended to write a story in the *passé composé* which he then padded with a murder, just as some poets undertake to compose an ode or a hymn merely to try a certain verse form) have been overanalyzed. They are but means to an end, and the end was a catharsis. Into that imaginary diary, not kept day by day but somehow reconstituted after the protagonist's death, Camus poured his obsession with what he con-sidered as the absurd, his rebellion against conventionality and his ques-tioning of 'bourgeois' or 'capitalist' or, more generally, human justice. Because he felt personally involved in his creation and, like any creator, became his own protagonist more and more as he was instilling life into him, he sedulously banished all that might seem theatrical or sentimental, both tenderness in sexual relations or in friendship or repentance tinged with Christian undertones. Meursault, in truth, is hardly a three-dimensional character. He has no past and no links with any past: neither his mother's nor childhood memories, no memory of the race or sense of belonging to a culture, no interest in his work, no affection for the Arabs among whom he has grown. Nor has he any 'project,' ambition, or desire for any future, still less, obviously, for an afterlife. He is more intelligent than Billy Budd, in a sense his successor (probably not known to Camus when he wrote *l'Etranger*), and possesses less contrived innocence than James Purdy and other American novelists like to lend to their falsely naïve heroes, Malcolm, Purdy's entertaining and empty-headed rapist, or Southern's Christian Candy. French novelists would keep shy of the simpletons whom Americans have attempted to present as their innocent Adams on a new land; the Shakespearean phrase 'a tale told by an idiot' is admired by them when dramatized by William Faulkner but would hardly be glamorous, or bearable, in a story in French.

The incidents of Meursault's uneventful life are few. A clerk in a small commercial firm in Algiers, he leads the drab existence of many characters in naturalist fiction. His mother dies, in a home for the aged where he had placed her three years before for the simple reason, as he states it, that they had nothing more to say to each other. He attends the burial, unable to shed a tear or to feel any emotion and unwilling to magnify an almost nonexistent feeling by translating it into words. The very next day he goes swimming, meets a girl, Marie, goes to the movies and then to bed with her. He sees her again the following weekend, and at lunch time she asks him if he loves her. The question was meaningless to him; he answers that he doubts he does. She then asks if he would marry her and since he does not care, he answers yes. He then goes with a not-too-respectable neighbor, for whom he again cares little, to a friend's bungalow on the beach. They eat a big lunch. After lunch, he takes a stroll with his friends and they get into a brawl with some Arabs. The sun and the sand are hot and dazzle him. Meursault, in the course of the brawl, sees the glint of the Arab's knife and pulls the trigger of the revolver which his friend had asked him to carry. He kills the Arab (he fires several shots), for no reason whatsoever, except the glare of the sun and because he did not care enough one way or the other not to do it.

He is thrown into jail, and the usual investigations are started about his private life to unearth some motives for his behavior. The investigators are puzzled and ill-disposed, for the Stranger had failed consistently to show normal social reactions. It is taken as a bad sign that he evinced no grief after his mother's death. The examining magistrate asks him if he loved his mother; he answers casually 'like everybody else, yes.' He never analyzed his reactions and he is sparing of words; he can only state the actual facts dryly, while others seem to live in a world of conventional patterns of emotion and according to myths. God has never meant anything to him. His clumsy though frank and naïve defense antagonizes the gentlemen of the jury. The verdict is soon issued. He will be guillotined as guilty of premeditated murder.

Back in his prison cell, he grows a little more self-awareness. He does concede, when finding the whole proceedings rather ludicrous, 'after all, I was the criminal.' His reaction mounts to angry indignation when the chaplain visits him and proffers the conventional solace of religion. He is unconcerned about another life and about God, but he loves this life as he had known it. His one regret is that he had broken up the harmony that wedded him to nature. (If the narrative were not attributed to the protagonist, Camus would have said that he has, with *hubris,* gone beyond the limits which Fate, or wisdom, imposes upon men.) His last wish, when facing his death sentence, is that there may be a huge crowd of onlookers when his execution takes place, so that he will feel less lonely.

The symbolic suggestions which have been read into the story add little depth or mystery to it. Man is an outsider also in an alien world, and perhaps to himself. A moment's nausea, as in Sartre, an inverted epiphany or revelation may at any time and suddenly unmoor us from our conventional values and habits, and the meaninglessness of it all flashes upon us. We become, as Sartre put it, like observers watching dancers and their mechanical evolutions from behind a glass door, or a man gesticulating and laughing in a telephone booth. Nowhere does the author uphold his stranger as a model or as a typical hero: he is too shrewd an artist to offer a thesis. After all Meursault has committed a murder, firing several shots, and not all the guilt can be passed on to the sun. And while justice in France and in Algeria has never been above reproach, the picture presented of it in the story is an impossible caricature of it. After the book, unpretentiously written in 1940–41, had gained the status of a classic, Camus wrote rather portentously on it, in a preface to the American school edition published in 1955: 'He [Meursault] is far from being totally deprived of sensibility, for he is animated by a passion, profound because it is tacit; the passion for the absolute and for truth. It is still a negative truth, the truth of being and feeling, but a truth without which no conquest of the self and of the world is possible.' More daringly still and more confusingly, he added, apropos of his unheroic murderer: 'He is the only Christ whom we deserve.' Camus's Christology was always eccentric, as a British commentator, A. J. L. Bussy, remarked. He insisted on the need for all of us to feel guilty, as Meursault and later Clamence invite us to do. But he stressed even more the guilt of Christ, always and gloomily mindful of the slaughter of the Innocents for which he bore indirect responsibility. He noticed that Christ never laughed; nor does Meursault.

The Stranger is a minor masterpiece of restraint and of effectiveness: but too much is lacking for the protagonist to rise to tragic stature. There is some trickery in the author's stacking all the cards against Meursault and emptying him of will power, of anger, passion, even of psychological substance. The romantic condemnation of a 'bourgeois' society whose judges sentence a murderer too harshly is a little facile. But the young Camus had thus to begin by setting himself against the world as he found it; before he could discover how to change it or how to rethink it, he had to depict it as unsatisfactory. The starting point of any ulterior message had to be found in the solitude and the clear sightedness of Meursault.

Between 1942 and the years in which he polished his second novel, *La Peste* (1947), the success of which was sudden and immense, Camus wrote his most decisive essays as a moralist, collected in *Actuelles* and the noble letters to a German friend, perhaps his masterpiece of grave and

vibrating prose. He was then the object of many advances from the most
liberal groups of Catholics, as he was, after his death, to be drawn into
the sermons of many Protestant pastors outside France. Jean du Roustu,
in the Jesuit review *Etudes* (October–November 1945), envisaged him as
a Pascal perhaps ready for a sudden illumination. The Dominicans invited
him to a frank debate in the course of which Camus did not minimize his
differences. A Belgian member of the Church, Charles Moeller, very hard
on Simone Weil, Julien Green, and Bernanos, and other Christians,
proved paradoxically very lenient on Camus the inveterate Pagan. 'He
had no need of baptism; he has grace,' another member of the Church
quoted in *L'Express* of January 7, 1960, declared.

It is nevertheless improbable that, had he lived, Camus who would
have become an Academician, an official personage of the French Republic, an organizer of State spectacles as Goethe once had been at Weimar,
perhaps even an author of lapidary (if seldom profound) inscriptions on
monuments and of eulogies of artists and writers of the past, would also
have joined the ranks of churchgoers. Malraux's attitude, imbued with the
feeling for the tragic but contemptuous of the security of faith, was his
most admired model. With a rare lucidity, as early as April 1943, writing
in *Les Cahiers du Sud* on Father Pouget, a Lazarist (or member of the
order of St. Vincent de Paul) more than half-blind and then in semi-
disgrace, Camus had pronounced:

> Contemporary incredulity no longer leans on science, as at the end
> of the last century. It denies both science and religion. It no longer
> is the skepticism of reason concerning the miracle. It is a passionate
> unbelief.

The formula pointedly expresses the attitude of contemporary critics
who, in France in particular, reject religious orthodoxy and ask from
Christianity that it be more demanding in its ethics, less lenient to mundane conventions and to selfish hypocrisy. They indict it in its ethics and
its morality and often feel morally nobler than most believers, and almost
as self-righteous. In the same article, Camus submitted that, 'to sum it all
up, the heretics might be called those who want to go faster than God.'
His reasoning apparently is that Christianity errs in soothing us with the
hope of another life (the great stumbling block, for, as great Catholic
writers like Charles du Bos and François Mauriac confessed, it is the
hardest thing to conceive), a life in which we would be relieved from
our body's presence. Present life is thus envisaged as a mere transitory
stage, a gloomy vale of tears and of despondency. Alfred de Vigny, of

whom the reader of *La Peste* is more than once inevitably reminded, had anticipated Camus when he noted in 1834 in his *Journal d'un poète:* 'The religion of Christ is one of despair, since it despairs of this our life and pins its hopes on eternity.'

For Camus, hope, which remains last at the bottom of Pandora's box in the meaningful Greek myth, is the blackest of our miseries; for it is tantamount to a resignation to our ills and to the absurdities of this life. 'To live is not to be resigned.' During the years of gloom which witnessed the ascent of Mussolini, Hitler, Franco, it had been tempting for Church dignitaries to render up to Caesar what was seized and appropriated by Caesar and to dwell in passive resignation until some belated redressment might occur. In a vibrant and wrathful article of *Combat* of December 26, 1944, Camus stigmatized the silence of the Papacy during the years following 1935 when Franco proclaimed himself a soldier of the faith and concentration camps were established in Germany. In his introduction to *Actuelles* (1950), Camus remonstrated with Christians haughtily, refuting once more the unfair charge of pessimism flung at the existentialists.

> True despair does not arise in the presence of obstinate misfortune or of exhaustion in an unequal fight. It comes from one's not knowing one's reasons for struggling, or even whether, precisely, one must take up arms. The following pages very simply state that, difficult as the struggle may be, the reasons for putting up a fight are at any rate always clear.

The second article of faith of Camus as a moralist, also apparent in *La Peste* and yet more maturely and obliquely proposed there than in *L'Etranger,* is more easily understood if replaced in its French context than when transposed into English: it is summed up in the other slogan formulated by Camus: the need for revolt. The truly moral man has the duty to revolt against his condition and to refuse to bow supinely to injustice or to the ununderstandable. Camus, and all the moderns who have been marked by Nietzscheism, would spurn the lessons voiced in the book of Job, where the Lord, answering Job's complaints out of the whirlwind, all too easily silences him: 'Where wast thou when I laid the foundations of the earth? . . . And said, Hitherto shalt thou come, but no further' to the ocean.

The man in revolt, like the Greek of yore, faces up to such scornful reproaches with the equanimity of a humanist. He stands for justice, which presupposes revolt, Camus insists, while 'Christianity . . . is a doctrine of injustice. It is founded upon the sacrifice of the innocent and upon the acceptance of that sacrifice.' Camus takes over the three small Latin words by which we are urged in the Gospels not to delay preparing for here and with haste man must see clearly into his condition and undertake to assist others, perhaps to save them without recourse to faith. The concluding message of *La Peste*, 'the most anti-Christian of his books' as he said in an interview given to Claudine Chonez in *Le Monde*, advocated ideals of solidarity and of fraternity parallel to those of the Christians. Camus was not afraid of incurring the charge of didacticism in a novel. But why should not a novelist who thinks allow his thinking to enrich his tale, if the tale remains imaginative? Do not his convictions deserve being voiced through some objective correlative or some symbol, thus firing other men? Balzac, Tolstoi, Dostoevski, Zola, Proust, all didactic novelists after a fashion, had not proceeded otherwise. But they were endowed with more power to create a world.

La Peste is an allegory, as are many novels of our time—Joyce's *Ulysses* and its rich progeny of characters starting on a quest to retrieve their past, Kafka's stories, or Butor's *L'Emploi du temps*. All that normally makes fiction attractive to readers, imaginative escape, love adventures, seductive women characters, surprise in the invention of incidents, is excluded. Camus felt still too close to the events symbolized in his fiction to relate them and to elicit their moral purport otherwise than with a Jansenist severity and a haughty nobleness. The style of the volume is deliberate and restrained, almost dry. The romantic, perhaps the Spanish, facet of Camus's personality was obscured there. He felt profoundly that the French novel has a special mission, which sets it apart from the other great fictional literatures of Europe. That mission is, thanks to a very limited number of situations, to express and illustrate a certain conception of man. The primary role belongs to intelligence, which rules over the conceptions of such a novel and imposes upon it 'a marvellous economy and a sort of passionate monotony. . . . To be classical means to repeat oneself and to know how to repeat oneself,' as he put it in his essay of 1943 on 'L'intelligence et l'échafaud.' The texture of the novel strives after monotony. There are hardly any touches of humor, no superfluous adornment, and very few evocations of scenery to appeal to our senses: all takes place in the dullest of provincial cities, with no lurid scenes of horror, which the subject might easily have seemed to call for.

Camus likewise curbed his imagination in his approach to the subject. There are celebrated evocations of the plague in literature in Thucydides and Lucretius, in Gregory of Tours and Boccaccio, which come to us dressed in awesome magnificence. Camus chose to place his under the aegis of the barest, dryest of them all: Daniel Defoe's *Journal of the Plague Year*. His own narrative is an unpassioned matter-of-fact diary of the plague at Oran, kept by Dr. Rieux, one of Camus's mouthpieces. It is clear from the outset that the epidemic that strikes an average and banal Algerian city is an allegory. To his French readers, the allusions to the plague were taken to refer to Europe under the German occupation. War was clearly alluded to, with the separations and the prison camps, the cowardice of some, the deliberate heroism of others, and the feeling of stoic solidarity that it fostered in the best. Under the duress of those age-old evils like plague and war, nothing less than man's fate was called in question. More imaginative power would perhaps have been needed to expand the allegory into a myth and make the book more nearly comparable to *Moby Dick*, *Ulysses*, or *The Trial*.

As in a classical tragedy, a given situation (the epidemic afflicting the city of Oran) is powerfully depicted in the opening scenes. The question then turns on the reaction of the characters to the plague, their inner torments stemming from their obstinate will to rest their actions upon some moral justification. There are those whom Camus ridicules or pities, who establish themselves in the abnormal conditions inflicted upon them and even rejoice at them, because, like Cottard, they can thus take refuge from some past misdeed and, in the midst of the exceptional, escape the attention of the police. There are the seekers of 'diversion' in the Pascalian sense who concentrate their misplaced energy on the endless repetition of some meaningless gesture. One spits from his balcony on cats every day at the same hour. Another has taken up as his hobby the study of railroad timetables and dreaming about impossible travels. A third crazily hopes to write: year after year he polishes the same sentence, adding, then erasing an adjective or refining a cadence. All, enacting the picture of the human condition already sketched by Pascal and Vigny, are prisoners sentenced to death who, in order to forget their doom, weave straw in the courtyard of their prison.

The Christian attitude (or, in truth, an ironical and unfair caricature of it) is illustrated by a learned Jesuit, Father Paneloux. He has devoted his life to archaeological research. The catastrophe moves him to address packed Sunday audiences in two notable sermons. The dilemma posed by the plague is, for the Christian, that of justifying the catastrophe through transcending it; of negating the absurdity and the injustice of evil through appealing to a higher significance. Can a Kierkegaardian leap do away with the harrying doubt raised by the epidemic? Paneloux's first answer is that which was heard in some French cathedrals under the Pétain regime: the catastrophe was willed by God as a punishment for the sins of men. But Paneloux, leaving his scholarly pursuits, watches the concrete suffering in the city of Oran and particularly the most revolting of all deaths, the death of innocent children. The slaughter of the Innocents, Paneloux reminds his audience, is commemorated by the Church calendar. Such a criminal absurdity is a challenge which most men prefer to disregard. In his second sermon, the Jesuit takes the 'leap': we must will the suffering of children since God wills it. 'One must either believe all or deny all. Who among you would dare deny all?' The ultimate logic of his position brings him to reject the assistance of a doctor and to refuse to alleviate evil, just as the Church, two centuries before, had banned vaccination. Camus, in driving the position of a minority of Christians to its harsh logic, states his own secular message. He will not consent to a view of creation which accepts and appears to condone the slaughter of the innocent ones. The fight against evil will be more determined if the belief in God is thrown out.

Rambert, a journalist from Paris who was caught by the plague in Oran, felt for a long time that the misfortune of a besieged city to which he did not belong was none of his concern. He would remain an isolationist in the face of the scourge. He at first attempted to flee and return to the woman he loved. All was prepared for his escape. At the last minute and on further reflection, he chose to stay and fight against the evil, along with Dr. Rieux and his friend Tarrou. Strangers, foreigners, all human beings became bound in the same solidarity.

The two protagonists, both embodying elements of their creator's personality, are Tarrou, who kept nôtebooks and recorded his tragic moral concern during the plague, and Dr. Rieux, who is revealed at the very end as being the narrator. Camus, who valued *pudeur*, a sense of restraint and a distrust of sentimentality and of big words, above most other virtues, gave few commentaries on his works: in the one revealing interview which he granted to Claudine Chonez of *Le Monde*, he explained that he felt some sort of sympathy for Paneloux, a man with a vocation, after all. But his standard-bearer was the doctor who spurned any transcendence and who attempted to cure evil then and there. 'Since the order of the world is ruled by death, it is perhaps better for God that we do not believe in Him and that we fight with all our might against death, without lifting our eyes toward a Heaven where He is silent.' Tarrou, the son of a prosecutor general, had been profoundly impressed when, as a boy, he had heard his father requesting the death of an accused man whose guilt was clear. He had watched the frightened criminal, listened with horror to his father's passionate rhetoric indicting the man in the name of society. The thought of his father having to rise early the next morning to watch the execution long disturbed him. Must social order rest on legalized murder? (Camus's last and zealous crusade was for the abolition of the death penalty.) One thing alone remained certain for him: There are on this earth plagues, tormentors, and executioners, and there are victims. Never would he align himself with the first group. The one essential question is: Can one be a saint without God? After organizing the fight against the plague, Tarrou dies from the disease, without illusion and without hope as he had lived.

As powerless he was watching Tarrou die, Dr. Rieux received the news that his wife, whom he had sent to a nursing home in the country, had passed away. The glimpses the reader gets of Rieux's mother, a shriveled old woman of few words and of patient devotion, are among the most moving in the book. With admirable modesty, Rieux refused to resort to notions or words like charity or saintliness or heroism, which have been dragged into the service of too many unworthy causes. 'Honesty' is the one word he will tolerate, or 'sympathy,' to denote the devotion he has unstintingly given to the care of the sick. He spurns rewards and honors after the plague has been vanquished. He is aware of the limitations of reason but will not lightly have reason abdicate before fanaticism and stupidity. If there is any worthwhile transcendence, it is only toward other men and for them. He sides with 'those for whom man and his poor and terrible love suffice.' When relief and joy have at last re-entered the long besieged city, he declares: 'There are in men more things to be admired than things to be scorned.'

Naturally such an ethic may seem somewhat negative and, with all its devotion, too prudent: there is not enough bold risk connected with it. Gaëtan Picon remarked upon the limitations of the message and of the novel, in the best article inspired by *La Peste,* in *Fontaine* (September 1947) reprinted in *L'Usage de la lecture* (1960). The peril of an allegory is that it makes things too clear: a plague is an unmitigated evil. But in the face of social injustice, oppression of the poor by the rich, the threat of a foreign war, the scourge of a propaganda poisoning the minds and of party spirit, does an ethic of non-violence and of melancholy devotion suffice? Once the battle against the plague is won, once France is liberated after 1945, what positive message will be offered so that the freedom then assured, the life recovered in its fullness, may be enjoyed and pursued? Against the tyrannies of racism or nationalism, the evil mixed with much good in colonialism, the lure of communism, the elements of nefarious fanaticism and complacency and those of charity and goodness in religion, is there a set of examples or of precepts which a moralist can offer?

It was almost inevitable that, after *La Peste*, Camus should appear to many of his readers, perhaps eventually to himself, as the prophet of a new era who would propose a new message to war-weary nations eager to strike a middle road between communism and the American way, judged by Europeans to be too conservative, only fit for a rich nation and not concerned enough with the inner life of idealistic individuals. Like many Europeans who had witnessed the gruesome results of German efficiency, he distrusted a quality which stresses means rather than ends. His yearning, shared by a number of earnest men in Western Europe in the years 1945–55, was for the emergence of a non-Communist Left. Everywhere it was soon to prove an idle dream. A controversy divided French intellectuals after *La Peste*, and was prolonged by the publication of *L'Homme révolté* in 1951, a confused and, in our opinion, unconvincing attempt to found a positive ethic upon the notion of revolt. Camus was particularly angered by those of his compatriots who then tried to legitimize violence in the name of an ideology. He earnestly contended that no ideal could be pursued which could only be fulfilled through another war. Against his friends who then advocated communism, he argued that they became the accomplices of a revolution founded upon violence. He preferred to incur the accusation, usually dreaded by men of letters, of favoring the bourgeois and of being a sentimentalist. At the end of some very revealing avowals made to an American interviewer,[2] he explained his ambiguous position and his timidity at assuming the role of political moralist that had been thrust upon him by his many admirers:

> I know that my political horizon is rather limited, if not narrow.
> I can't believe in radical and sudden changes any longer. . . . The
> greatest political achievement I can conceive of today would be that
> we succeed in letting the younger generation grow up in peace. . . .

2. Nicola Chiaromonte, 'Albert Camus and moderation,' *The Partisan Review*, XV, 10, October 1948, 1142–1145.

The controversy with Francis Jeanson and Sartre which followed *L'Homme révolté* did little credit to the three men. Sartre, a master of polemics, scored a few points against his former friend's lack of philosophical rigor, and against his readiness to defend the social classes which were then acclaiming him and would soon applaud him as a Nobel laureate. Camus's noble refusal to become sectarian and to be enmeshed in the political sophistry to which Sartre has had to resort ever since he praised communism as the lesser of two evils, evinced a warmth and a directness which won admirers to his position, even when it was a halting and an ambiguous one. His last novel, *La Chute*, was to bear the imprint of the wounds inflicted by the break of an old friendship and also of the pitiless self-analysis which Camus, reluctant to become a complacent preacher and to pass for a saint, practiced. 'What else can I wish,' he pathetically remarked, 'than to exclude nothing and to learn how to weave with a white thread and a black thread the same tight rope tense to the breaking-point?'

La Chute (1956) is the most complex, and not the least baffling, of the author's three novels. It disappointed those who expected in Camus an evolution toward faith, or at least toward para-Christian ethics. The sarcastic tone and the use of Christian allusions in a spirit of blasphemy (the very title, the names of Jean-Baptiste Clamence, suggesting both the prophet who prepared the coming of Christ and the *'vox clamantis in deserto,'* of the third chapter of St. Matthew) seemed to denote a return to Camus's early nihilism, from which he had emerged with *La Peste*. 'It is from ironical philosophies that passionate works spring,' Camus had remarked. There is both irony (indeed brilliant wit also, and striking epigrammatic thoughts) in *La Chute*, and there is passion. As a work of art, this long monologue which recalls Diderot's *Le Neveu de Rameau* and some of Robert Browning's 'apologies' is even more successful than *L'Etranger* as a virtuoso feat of writing.

Clamence had enjoyed professional success as a Paris lawyer who specialized in pleading for the underprivileged and enjoyed a reputation for generosity. There was another side to his life, as there was to Camus's own. 'Is not woman all that is left to us from the earthly Paradise? Camus, whom death interrupted when he was contemplating a book on Don Juan, liked to ask. Another one of his questions was: 'Why should one love but seldom in order to love much?' Clamence had had a number of feminine adventures, which satisfied his ego. Suddenly, he was seized with remorse and restlessness. One evening, while walking on a bridge of the Seine, he failed to rescue a girl who was plunging to her death in the river. He could probably have achieved but little by jumping from the bridge. Still he was remorseful not to have tried. The revelation that his own life, and that of most men, rested on lies, that the selfishness of a secure and successful man is only matched by his monstrous vanity, descended upon him. He left Paris, not for the Southern lands loved by Camus, but for the misty harbor of Amsterdam.

He opened a low class bar there and became a 'judge-penitent,' pouring out his confession garrulously to a silent listener who, like Coleridge's Wedding-Guest, cannot choose but hear. He then multiplies self-incriminating questions to denounce the good conscience that had once stifled his scruples. He lays bare his own ignominious complacency and cherishes his newly discovered guilt feelings. Meursault the murderer was innocent of such introspective self-torture Clamence, whose guilt was slight, by indicting himself indicts all men thereby. He merges his own guilt into the universal guilt and makes all others his accomplices—not unlike the man of letters who, through his art, leads his readers to imagine that they, also, might have committed the errors or the crimes of Baron Hulot, Emma Bovary, or the Mayor of Casterbridge. By dint of repeating his self-accusation, while he is not much worse than the average among us, he puts forward a sweeping and caustic 'J'accuse.' He likes to repeat that we cannot vouch for anyone's innocence, but we certainly can assert the guilt of us all.

The long, vivacious, epigrammatic monologue, laden with allusions and systematically sardonic, provides a portrait 'not of an individual, but the aggregate of the vices of our whole generation' unrelieved with hope or charity. The words just quoted are a quotation from Lermontov, with which Camus chose to prefix the English translation of La Chute. Clamence has indeed some features in common with Pechorin, the character in Lermontov's A Hero of our Time, published in 1840.[3] It would have been too easy for Camus to sound self-righteous and to appear to brand his character as a demonic individual symbolizing the vices of others or the faults of those with whom he had ceased to agree. The récit may be read as a satire on the existentialists and their claim to being denouncers of the bad conscience of the bourgeois society. It is no more charitable

3. The use of Lermontov's story and the similarities between the two characters have been ably studied in an article by Marilyn K. Yalom, in The French Review, XXXVI, No. 2, 1962, 138–145.

to the Christians (nor is the most striking of the stories in *L'Exil et le royaume* entitled 'The Renegade,' which portrays a priest who betrayed his faith with even more ferocious bitterness). The indictment is doubtless most sweeping of the men of letters whom society adopts as its moralists and who purge themselves of all that may be sordid in them by confessions 'à la Gide' or 'à la Julien Green' or by declamations 'à la Céline.' They secure the complicity of their readers while exorcizing their own demons. Most of all, especially as the style lent to Clamence is clearly Camus's own, the satirical portrait must be interpreted as partly the author's. He had some reason to incriminate himself for not having always observed the commands of marital fidelity, and even more reason to fret inwardly at the figure of a professor of moral idealism which he was cutting in the world. The trade of a man of letters is indeed a perilous one. He can seldom resist becoming a public figure, a savior of souls, a man concerned with and involved in the problems of his time, hence inflating his own person with a monstrous egotism.

Camus however was denouncing the egotist which he might have become in order to avoid ever becoming it. Death cut short the promises of more mature achievement at the very time when Camus was meditating most intensely on the position and duties of a man of letters in the modern world. In a polemic reported in the second volume of *Actuelles,* he had modestly declared that he was no philosopher, as he had declared earlier in an interview given to the *Revue du Caire* that he was not a Christian. 'Nothing,' he added, 'authorizes me to speak with condescension of an age with which I feel altogether solidary. . . . But I do preserve the right to say what I know about myself and others, provided it does not add to the intolerable misfortune of the world.' He would not hide his anger when self-righteous Christians or unthinking and conventional magazine articles branded him as a pessimist. He retorted that his detractors were those who had long subscribed to 'the terrifying formulas of the curse of God, . . . of "nemo bonus" and the damnation of the unchristened children.' To him, evil was 'that which obscures people to one another, dims ourselves to ourselves.'

Camus is not likely to remain among the supreme novelists or the most gifted of imaginative writers. Fiction to him was a convenient mold in which to elucidate his own conflicting doubts; it was also a medium for judging himself with objectivity while avoiding the dryness which preys upon the abstract thinker or the complacent coiner of moral aphorisms. To his art he always expressed his unconditional loyalty. He declared it in noble terms in his Nobel Prize acceptance speech in 1957. He had said it even more forcefully soon after the end of World War II in the most convincing statement of our age on the function of the writer and the artist as a witness to freedom, retorting to those who charged the artist with being a mandarin untouched by the turmoil and the misery of the world:

> The misery of the world! I am not adding anything to it. Which of you can say as much? . . . The artist has chosen a profession which, in the midst of a world withered by hate, enables every one to say in all peace of mind that he is no man's mortal enemy. True artists are on the side of life, not of death. . . . Artists bear witness to that in man which refuses to die.

Bibliographical Notes

The essential writings of Camus are available in French in the two volumes of the Pléiade collection, *Théâtre, Récits, Nouvelles,* and *Essais,* edited, with valuable notes, by Roger Quilliot in 1963 and 1965. The three novels have appeared in translation at Alfred A. Knopf and so have most of the significant articles on ethics and politics in *Resistance, Rebellion and Death,* 1960, and *Notebooks,* 1965. *The Myth of Sisyphus,* Alfred A. Knopf, 1955, and *The Rebel,* Alfred A. Knopf, 1961.

There are two outstanding volumes in English on Camus: those of Germaine Brée, *Camus,* new edition (New Brunswick: Rutgers University Press, 1961), to which should be added: *Camus: A Collection of Critical Essays* (Englewood Cliffs: Prentice-Hall, 1962), which she edited, and John Cruickshank, *Camus and the Literature of Revolt* (New York and London: Oxford University Press, 1960). John Cruickshank also edited a very valuable volume, *The Novelist as Philosopher* (London: Oxford University Press, 1962), which contains a very perceptive chapter on Camus, pp. 206–229. Thomas Hanna, *The Thought and Art of Camus* (Chicago: Henry Regnery, 1958) is less remarkable. A thorough study by Emmett Parker, *Camus, the Artist in the Arena* (Madison: Wisconsin University Press, 1965), explores the novelist through his articles as a journalist and has a valuable bibliography. Philip Thody, *Camus* (New York: Grove Press, and London: Hamish Hamilton, 1959), is perceptive. In French, Robert Champigny's monograph on *L'Etranger, Sur un Héros païen* (Gallimard, 1959), and Paul Ginestier's *Pour connaître la pensée de Camus* (Bordas, 1964), are the best complete volumes on Camus, but do not come up to the studies in English. In an appendix Ginestier has recorded Camus's answers to several questions, which clarify his affinities with and his differences from existentialism. G. P. Gélinas, in *La liberté dans la pensée de Camus* (Fribourg: Editions Universitaires, 1966), is solid but too systematic. Other books by Henry Bonnier, *Camus* (Lyon: Vitte, 1959); Jean-Claude Brisville, *Camus* (Gallimard, 1959); Johanna Gadourek-Backer, *Les Innocents et les coupables* (The Hague: Mouton, 1963); Léon Thoorens, *A la Rencontre de Camus* (Brussels: La Sixaine, 1947), and even Roger Quilliot, *La Mer et les prisons: essai sur Camus* (Gallimard, 1956), offer less interest.

Articles on Camus have been extremely numerous since *La Peste*, 1947, and even more so since the Nobel Prize was awarded to the author and after his death. A highly selective list only can be given here:

Allen, Louis, 'La Chute,' *The Downside Review*, Exeter (England), 1957, 259–274.

Ayer, A. J., 'Camus,' *Horizon* XIII, 75, March 1946, 155–68.

Bespaloff, Rachel, 'Le Monde du condamné à mort,' *Esprit*, No. 163, January 1950, 1–26.

Bieber, Konrad, in *L'Allemagne vue par les écrivains de la résistance française* (preface by Camus). Geneva: Droz, 1954.

Blanchot, Maurice, 'Le *Mythe de Sisyphe*' and 'Le Roman de *L'Etranger*,' in *Faux-Pas*. Gallimard, 1943.

Blin, Georges, 'Camus ou le sens de l'absurde,' *Fontaine*, No. 30, 1943, 553–62. and 'Camus et l'idée de révolte,' *Fontaine*, No. 53, 1948, 109–17.

Boudot, M., 'L'absurde et le bonheur dans l'oeuvre de Camus,' *Cahiers du Sud*, No. 315, 1953, 291–305.

Brombert, Victor, 'Camus and the Novel of the Absurd,' *Yale French Studies*, No. 1, 1948, 119–23; *The Intellectual Hero*. New York: J. B. Lippincott, 1960.

Chiaromonte, Nicola, 'Camus and moderation,' *The Partisan Review*, No. 25, October 1948, 1142–45; 'La Résistance à l'histoire,' *Preuves*, No. 110, April 1960, 17–20.

Doubrovsky, Serge, 'Camus en Amérique,' *Nouvelle Revue Française*, No. 98, February 1961, 292–96; 'Le Monde de Camus,' *Preuvès*, No. 116, October 1960, 39–49.

Fraisse, Simone, 'De Lucrèce à Camus, ou les contradictions de la révolte, *Esprit*, No. 3, March 1959, 437–53.

Girard, René, 'Camus' Stranger retried,' *P.M.L.A.*, LXXIX, No. 5, December 1964, 519–33.

Mason, H. A., 'Camus and the Tragic Hero,' *Scrutiny*, December 1946, 82–9.

Mohrt, Michel, 'Ethics and Poetry in the Work of Camus,' *Yale French Studies*, No. 1, 1948, 113–18.

Mounier, Emmanuel, 'Camus ou l'appel des humiliés,' *Esprit*, No. 163, January 1950, 27–66.

Ollivier, Albert, 'Camus ou le refus de l'éternel,' *L'Arche*, No. 6, October–November 1944, 158–63.

Peyre, Henri, 'Camus: An Anti-Christian Moralist,' *Proceedings of the American Philosophical Society*, 102, No. 5, October 1958, 477–82.

Picon, Gaëtan, 'Remarques sur La Peste,' *Fontaine*, No. 61, September 1947, 453–60; *L'Usage de la Lecture*, Mercure de France, Vol. 1, 1963.

Rossi, Louis, 'Camus: The Plague of Absurdity,' *The Kenyon Review*, 1958, 399–422.

Roustu, Jean du, 'Un Pascal sans Christ: Camus,' *Etudes*, October–November 1945, 48–65 and 165–77.

Roynet, L., 'Camus chez les Chrétiens,' *La Vie Intellectuelle*, April 1949, 336–51.

Saint-Aubyn, Frederick, 'Camus and the death of the other,' *French Studies* (Oxford), XVI, 2 April 1962, 124–41.

Sartre, J. P., 'Explication de *L'Etranger*,' reprinted in *Situations I*, Gallimard, 1947, 99–121.

Shattuck, Roger, 'Two Inside Narratives: *Billy Budd* and *L'Etranger*,' *University of Texas Studies in Language and Literature*, IV, 3, Autumn 1962, 314–20.

Simon, P. H., *L'Homme en Procès*. Neuchâtel: La Baconnière, 1950; *Les Témoins de l'homme: de Proust à Camus*. A. Colin, 1951.

Viggiani, '*L'Etranger*,' *P.M.L.A.*, LXXI, No. 5, December 1956, 865–887.

Yalom, Marilyn, '*La Chute* and *A Hero of our Time*,' *The French Review*, XXXI, No. 2, December 1962, 137–45.

Useful and varied series of studies may be found in J. H. Matthews, *Camus: Configuration critique*. Lettres modernes, 1961; and *Yale French Studies*, No. 25, Spring 1960.

XII

Main Trends since World War II. The 'New Novel'

The preceding chapters have obviously not attempted to encompass the whole varied range of French novels written in the last half-century, not even to the point of presenting a survey of all the novelists who may be considered as the best or the ones most likely to survive. A volume of criticism should differ from an enumerative dictionary of authors. It aims at informing and enlightening its readers and at stirring up debates around the works of art. The writer of such a book reserves the right to treat those novelists with whom he feels in greater sympathy or whom he believes to be most significant. Among the novelists whose achievement has come close to that of others who were selected here for more detailed treatment, seven or eight have failed to convince this particular observer that they are likely to survive as fiction writers of consequence. Those whom it has been most embarrassing to leave out are Valéry Larbaud and Jean Giraudoux, both original in their technique and in their sensibility, but lacking the power to impose their creations upon our memory. André Maurois is a far more skillful biographer than he is a novelist and Paul Morand a superb master of the short story, but one whose breath never seemed long or deep enough to sustain him through a full fledged novel. The ironical novel, of which Morand, like Giraudoux, has proved a master, is perhaps destined never to rise to very great heights, unless, as in Cervantes, the irony is blended with sympathy. Some perverseness in the reader will not let him enjoy feeling inferior to the novelist's condescending smile or to his display of mocking préciosité. Marcel Jouhandeau, Jacques de Lacretelle, and Henry de Montherlant have been left out of our panorama much less regretfully: none of them has done a single work of fiction of more than ephemeral significance and each of them, after his fortieth year, has spoilt the promise of his earlier achievement through lapsing into monotony, sterile officialdom, or, in the case of Montherlant, prolonged boyishness and woeful inadequacy of theme to a masterful style. Roger Peyrefitte is in that respect not far remote from Montherlant and never, after his early *Amitiés particulières*, could he muster up enough force and substance to do more than amuse us and shock us mildly. There is more sensibility, less egocentrism, and a more determined attempt at striking for roots in their native Cévennes, Brittany, or Valais in André Chamson, Louis Guilloux, and Charles F. Ramuz, three relatively unacknowledged or unstudied writers, at least outside French-speaking lands. They may well be substituted by our successors for Duhamel, Romains, Giono, or Saint-Exupéry, who have received attention in this volume. Others still, who have enjoyed widespread sales and even the dubious accolade of having their novels adapted for the stage or the screen, Maurice Druon, Marcel Aymé, Henri Troyat, even Hervé Bazin who for a time promised to upset complacent traditions in French fiction, appear to us to have lacked the ability to grow. Their achievement remains respectable but hardly lasting. On all these men, and a number of others whom it is not our purpose to assess summarily here, a very brief statement is offered in the appendix to this volume.

The purpose of this final chapter is not to classify the multifarious modern novel of France into a number of overly neat categories: novel of manners, novel of adventure, feminine novel, psychological novel, etc. Categories, movements, and trends amount ultimately to nothing but what a few individuals make of them. We choose rather to direct the reader's attention to a few themes or points of view, singled out as especially significant for our purpose: the impact of American fiction upon the French novel; the novel of comedy and of fantasy; after surrealism, and then existentialism, had made their influence felt upon literature, the emergence of what was for a time to be termed the 'new novel'; the temper of the French people as interpreted through their fiction. In every case, generalizations will have to be attempted. But if generalizations are proverbially said to be dangerous, they are equally inevitable and probably more valid, when all is said, than excessive timidity at venturing conclusions.

The notion of influence is among the most misleading in comparative literature. It seldom happens that an idea, a mood, an art form, a technique 'flows into' another mind or group of minds which are not already prepared to receive it. It happens even more rarely that the individual undergoing the influence fails to transform it altogether into 'something rare and strange,' which becomes unrecognizable to the originator of the so-called influence.

There are nevertheless tides of fashion, and external impulses, which are experienced by a literary genre or by a whole literature, and which sway development or make suddenly clear to authors what they were heretofore only vaguely aware of. French literature has at many periods of its history influenced English Augustan literature or Russian symbolism, German decadentism or American naturalism. It has also absorbed many such impulses from the Italian Renaissance and from Spain, from the eighteenth-century English novel, and then from the Russian. Ever since 1930 or so, the most dynamic impact has been produced by American fiction. No account of the French novel after 1930 can afford to ignore it. Indeed the French, often known for their cultural nationalism and for their unconcern with what is being said or written about their literature in other lands, have in this case overstressed their admiration for and their debt to American novelists. Their debt to the recent English novel has, in comparison with the transatlantic one, been light since *Ulysses* and the death of D. H. Lawrence. None of the writers from Britain, from the veteran E. M. Forster and Evelyn Waugh to Graham Greene and to the picaresque but unconvincing stories of Angus Wilson, John Wain, and Kingsley Amis, has left any imprint on the French novel of 1940–65. From the German-speaking lands, Thomas Mann, then Hermann Broch, and Robert Musil have enjoyed the warm esteem of an elite; but Kafka alone has been an influence and even an obsession with the French. Little has come out of Russia since Gorki, Chekhov, and Bunin that could match the extraordinary sway of Dostoevski over the French imagination just before and just after World War I. American novelists alone, between 1930 and 1950, fascinated the French, the Italians (Vittorini, Pavese), some Germans, subsequently, and often through French intermediaries, the Spaniards, and the South Americans.

The drama and even the poetry of the United States have also been acclaimed, at times translated or adapted by the French, though seldom truly naturalized in France. American painting has met with more resistance. American architecture, American music, and even the Hollywood movies (except for a few names revered by European aesthetes, Charlie Chaplin, John Ford, Orson Welles) have not been warmly appreciated in France. The *élan* toward American fiction was most keenly felt in

France when the United States was in the throes of a depression and had
not revealed its immense power by its intervention in World War II, or
its prestige by assuming the burden of putting war-exhausted Europe
back on its feet. Indeed the admiration for American letters subsided at
the very moment when that country was enjoying unprecedented prosperity and became the protector and leader of the free world. Its influence ceased to be important around 1955-60.

Naturally, as it is to all influences, the reaction in France has been
partial and arbitrary. The French have stressed the present but often ignored the past, or only very slowly proceeded from the contemporaries to
Hawthorne, Melville (on whom French scholars have produced remarkable studies), then Stephen Crane. The cult of Edgar Allan Poe, even that
of Walt Whitman, has lost its fervor, and the European fondness for Jack
London, or for Upton Sinclair, has long ago died out, these writers having
been derided by sophisticated American critics and even more by those
of Great Britain. Henry James has been respected by a few, actually read
by even fewer on the continent, and has been dismissed as lacking in the
qualities of vitality, brutal energy, and primitive behavior which the rest
of the world likes to ascribe to Americans. Naturalism, even in Sinclair
Lewis or in the least crude and turgid works of Theodore Dreiser, novels
now underestimated in America and probably improving with translation,
has seemed *passé* to the French for whom the classic was Zola. Thomas
Wolfe, because of his lack of restraint and formlessness, and Thornton
Wilder, perhaps because of his too refined culture and of his fastidious
art, have somehow done much less well in France and other Latin countries than in Germany.

The great names of American fiction for the French were therefore
Hemingway, Steinbeck, Faulkner, and Dos Passos. It would hardly be an
exaggeration to hint that the Nobel prizes awarded to the first three were
due more to their prestige in France and Western Europe than to their
American fame, which the academics and intellectuals of the United
States were slow to promote. Scott Fitzgerald was only revealed to the
French later as the precursor of that group. Erskine Caldwell was for
some time rated on a par with the prestigious four. Then came Carson
McCullers, Truman Capote, Norman Mailer, Robert Penn Warren, James
Jones, Nathaniel West, Horace McCoy, J. D. Salinger, Richard Wright,
and James Baldwin. The last and rather warm *succes d'estime* in the early
'sixties was that of William Styron. The Beatniks, William Burroughs,
John Cheever (perhaps because his irony presupposes some familiarity
with the American scene), and John Updike, probably too sophisticated

as Mary McCarthy would also appear to Europeans, have been read, but remained uninfluential. *Traduit de l'américain* has ceased, since 1960, to be the magical label which it had been fifteen years earlier.

The sociological and aesthetic phenomenon which that American impact constitutes should lead to a few comments of relevance both to the French novel at mid-century and to the European view of American letters.

Geographically, the region of the United States that is brought to the fore is no longer New England, once the abode of culture in the New World. It is not even New York. The literary map of America, as pictured in the minds of millions of foreign readers, draws, in sharp outlines, the country of Steinbeck, the California of James Cain, the setting of *Desire Under the Elms,* and the proud solitude of Carmel and Point Sur, dear to Robinson Jeffers. It also emphasizes the importance of the Middle West, from which have sprung Sherwood Anderson and Hart Crane (Ohio), Vachel Lindsay, Carl Sandburg, Edgar Lee Masters, and Archibald MacLeish (Illinois), T. S. Eliot and Marianne Moore (both from St. Louis, Missouri).

But the most original American works have since 1930 been inspired by the South. The most active critics have been linked with the Southern periodicals: the defunct then reborn *Southern Review,* the *Virginia Quarterly Review,* the *Sewanee Review,* occasionally the *Southwest Review.* Allen Tate, John Crowe Ransom, and Robert Penn Warren had even dreamed of building up in the South a new economy as the basis for a better-balanced culture, and French periodicals have occasionally treated that movement of 'the Fugitives.' James Branch Cabell, Ellen Glasgow, and Willa Cather were Virginians. Thomas Wolfe and Margaret Mitchell have popularized other parts of the South, which they love. William Goyen, Truman Capote, and half a dozen other writers of note, since 1945, also came from the Deep South. Negro writers, at least two of whom have been warmly admired in France, the novelist Richard Wright and the fine poet Langston Hughes, have added to the literary prestige of the South. Above all, Erskine Caldwell in Georgia and William Faulkner in his Yoknapatawpha County in northern Mississippi have done for those states what Thomas Hardy had done for Wessex and Walter Scott for Scotland, Giono for Provence and Mauriac for the French Bordelais. They have annexed new provinces to literary geography and won for their native districts an epic glamor, which is already attracting pilgrims.

Such is the magic of literary creation. The South, vanquished in the

Civil War, left behind in the economic struggle, the depressed area of the United States in the eyes of many Americans, has had its revenge; it has won the literary battle of America. Through the South, the immense continent seems to have gained a consciousness of tradition and a sense of history. Through the South also, it has acquired a sense of tragedy, which haunts Southern novelists (Wolfe in *You Can't Go Home Again* and Faulkner in *Absalom! Absalom!*) like a curse; but this sense of history and of tragedy was probably necessary to the growth of American literature, since its expansion beyond Concord and Boston and Baltimore. Faulkner, like Hardy in England and Mauriac in France, has tapped the richest source of fictional themes for a novelist: the excessive concentration of life in a restricted provincial environment, the jealous spying of family upon family, the bitter struggle between dispossessed traditional heirs and brutal newcomers. Above all this, he has conjured up the ghost of slavery, which hovers over his novels and for which the South must still atone. The fascination of the American South has proved so great for several younger writers of France who have never crossed the Atlantic that they have unwittingly transplanted that setting into their own novels of French life; one hears Negro spirituals in the Pyrenees or drinks Jamaica rum in Burgundy to exorcise ancestral spirits, the fields are planted with cotton or with corn, and the smell of sassafras perfumes the countryside. Thus the mechanical imitation of much admired American novels has played upon some French writers the same literary trick of which American poets had been victims in the early nineteenth century, when they conscientiously composed hymns to skylarks and odes to nightingales without ever having heard or seen those European birds.[1]

Strangely enough, the natural scenery of America, which now populates the imagination of European readers, is no longer that of Mayne Reid or Fenimore Cooper, not even that of Jack London's stories. It is seldom that of New England or of the Mid-western plains, for neither Robert Frost's verse nor evocations of *American Beauty* attempted by Edna Ferber or LeGrand Cannon, neither Ruth Suckow's descriptions of Iowa nor Willa Cather's Nebraska scenery in *One of Ours* have succeeded in bringing those sections of America vividly to foreign eyes. The Far West and its

---

1. Indeed, it is seriously advanced that the widespread reading of Southern writers has led the French agronomists to turn the Rhone Delta, the once arid Camargue, into rice fields, and the region south of Montpellier, once exclusively planted with vines, into a cotton-growing district. Some success seemed to have crowned their efforts, which the development of irrigation financed by the Marshall Plan helped also.

colorful canyons, the splendors of Nevada, Arizona, and Colorado, and the bays and mountains of Washington and Oregon have had thus far little or no place in American literature; the superb rivers and trees, unequaled on the European continent, have apparently beggared description or daunted the powers of writer and painter alike. As a result, the most familiar local color for readers of American works is the dreary expanse of Georgia or Mississippi, humanized by deeply rooted traditions and apparently better attuned to the tragic sensibility of literary creators.

The second feature that marks the American novels selected by the French for translation is their violence. The day now seems remote indeed when Flaubert and Zola were deemed too brutal for English-speaking readers! The compatriots of Proust and Céline apparently find their own literature too tame, for they plunge with the delight of exotic discovery into the improbable scenes of American letters. Desertion occurs in almost every war novel, in Dos Passos's remarkable *Three Soldiers* and in Hemingway's *A Farewell to Arms* for instance. Rape, next to incest, might be judged, from several of these novels, to be a favorite pastime of Americans. O'Neill, Jeffers, even Faulkner seem haunted by incest. Only homosexuality seemed, again judging from literature, to find more favor with the French than with the Americans, until a new generation of American novelists rose to redress that 'defect' in their national heritage. John W. Aldridge, in his *After the Lost Generation,* listed a number of novels touching on that burning theme. Some recent French plays even take place in an American setting, so as to enjoy, one suspects, the advantage of a dramatic lynching scene.

But the amusement and amazement of French readers have been especially aroused by the drinking and loving habits that they find described in American fiction, heightened, of course, by the intensity or the stylization of art. Heroes of *The Sun Also Rises,* of *The Iceman Cometh,* of Salinger, Hammett, and others seem endowed with a superhuman capacity for imbibing, at which the French marvel all the more as they would inevitably have to pay for such orgies with liver troubles and dreary Vichy 'cures.'

As to sex, the French feel vaguely humiliated by the descriptions of American fiction, which are throwing many of their own love stories into the tepid category of Sunday-school reading! Hemingway's evocations of love as the most glamorous of sports next to bull-fighting, Caldwell's *Journeyman* and *God's Little Acre,* and Steinbeck's *Wayward Bus* are a veritable orgy of love. Edmund Wilson's *Hecate County* has not ravished

French critics. But the greatest uproar was caused in 1946–47 by Henry Miller. This disciple of Céline and Lawrence found himself the cynosure of literary life in 1946. Critics, reporters, and moralists aligned themselves for or against him; his books were deemed so perilous to virtue that they were brought to trial, while admirers of *Tropic of Cancer* and *Tropic of Capricorn* compared their hero to Christ flagellated by jealous or narrow-minded Pharisees! Sober commentators remarked that it had taken an American (long steeped in the most malodorous aspects of Parisian life, to be sure) to make Céline appear more innocent than a choirboy and Casanova an impotent weakling.

The entertainment derived from the debauchery of violence in American fiction is accompanied by some feeling of silly complacence among the inheritors of an old culture who like to think of North America as populated by young barbarians. The interest taken by Europeans in the United States has not ceased, since the *Jesuit Relations* and Rousseau, to be an aspect of their taste for primitivism. Few Frenchmen, however, are naïve enough to take the murders, the sexual prowess, and the drinking bouts of American fiction as a faithful copy of American life. Rather they admire in that violence a healthy, if brutal, reaction against the monotony and standardization of conditions prevailing in America. Many of them heave a sigh of relief, after imagining American life as an 'air-conditioned nightmare,' in which cleanliness reigns supreme, efficiency crushes individuals, and conformity is the law, when they discover that there are also the itinerant destitutes of *The Grapes of Wrath*, the non-conformists of *Tortilla Flat*, the human waifs of *Tobacco Road*, and the idiot, whose masterly monologue in *The Sound and the Fury* is already a *locus classicus* of French criticism.

Their esteem for America is in no way impaired by contemplation of the seamy side of things. Only Nazi Germany (and perhaps Stalinist Russia) has insisted upon displaying in their literature nothing but the clean, efficient, moral—and lifeless—face of their country. Robust and adult nations like the United States and France know fully well that there is more to their civilization than the Champs Elysées and the Riviera hotels, than Fifth Avenue and Miami Beach. They are not afraid to emphasize the uncomely sights of their country in their plays and novels. Only a few superficial observers will see in this a proof of French corruption or American brutality. Behind unusual aspects of the United States, the French readers of American works seek something deeper, of which they are in dire need: a message of vitality and a freshness of vision, which raise violence and vice to the stature of the epic.

The literature of Europe, however expert in technique and subtle in psychological dissection, lacks vigor and knows it. Kafka and Proust, Huxley and Gide, Auden and Rilke are supremely endowed with intelligence and sensitiveness; but they lack imaginative power to re-create life, that is, an intense grasp on the concrete. They are unequaled in self-conscious delineation of moods of frustration and repression, in polished irony, and even in searching exploration of the recesses of the ego. But their readers detect signs of excessive maturity in their overrefined works and yearn for the uncouth youthfulness that Steinbeck, Hemingway, and Caldwell seem to have in abundance. The splendid promise of American letters, to be sure, is seldom fulfilled; the last touches that would assure true greatness, the tranquil recollection that might sublimate and prolong the shock of immediacy, and the depth of thought that has seldom marred good novels are often lacking. But Europeans who dip into *Sanctuary*, *God's Little Acre*, even *The Big Money* are relieved to discover characters who take hold of them and plots in which the authors seem to have earnestly believed. We may imagine their thrill of discovery, after having lived too long in the rarefied atmosphere of Proust and become weary of the effete irony of Maurois or E. M. Forster, the unconvincing and laborious synthesis of Jules Romains, the impalpable halo into which Virginia Woolf dissolves her heroines, and the elaborate philosophical discourses of Thomas Mann's mouthpieces.

The ambition of the novel has been, since Balzac and Tolstoi, to take the place left vacant by the disappearance of the epic. An element of willful intensification of life has always been necessary to the epic. The power to move heroes through ordeals and battles and to relate adventures with convincingness have been attributes of the epic creator. In this sense, the American novel of today, at its best, comes near to the epic. Dos Passos in *U.S.A.*, Steinbeck in his admirable *In Dubious Battle*, which is a greater achievement artistically than *The Grapes of Wrath*, and Faulkner in *As I Lay Dying* rank among the epic novelists of our age.

Jean-Paul Sartre, whose prestige is second to none with the contemporary French public, said aptly: 'What we looked for above all in the American novel was something quite different from its crudities and its violence.' It was nothing less than a renewal of the setting, the subject matter, and the technique of the traditional French novel. The recent vogue of American letters was excessive; some of its manifestations were at times ludicrous and will pass away, as the waves of enthusiasm for Byron, Poe, and Dostoevski ebbed away. But they left French and other European literatures profoundly transformed.

The French are the unchallenged masters of the *roman d'analyse*. From *La Princesse de Clèves* to Marivaux and Laclos in the eighteenth century, then from Benjamin Constant's *Adolphe* and Stendhal to Proust and Mauriac, their vocation in fiction has been to probe searchingly into the workings of man's mind and soul, to bring to light the hidden motives of actions and the complex nuances of feelings. Proust has gone as far as seems humanly possible in that direction. Nothing was left for French novelists to do, after him, but to break away from an introspection that was becoming static and artificial. Since 1925 or 1930, French fiction, led by Malraux, Saint-Exupéry, and Giono, has aimed at capturing the mysteries of man in action and not at rest, at substituting a synthetic perception of human nature for an analytical dissection. While they were seeking new paths away from a valuable but exhausted French tradition, they hit upon Faulkner and Dos Passos and even upon Dashiell Hammett, Damon Runyon, Raymond Chandler, and writers who were lesser artists than themselves but from whom they were ready to learn. In an important interview given in January 1945, to the English review *Horizon*, Malraux declared: 'To my mind the essential characteristic of contemporary American writing is that it is the only literature whose creators are not intellectuals . . . They are obsessed with fundamental man . . . The great problem of this literature is now to intellectualize itself without losing its direct approach.'

Malraux converted elder writers like Gide, who, himself more gifted in abstract analysis of man than in concrete evocation of man's behavior, had nevertheless felt the need of more 'raw meat' in French literature, which was addicted to dressing and softening its fare. Gide went so far as to proclaim his admiration for the superior detective stories of Dashiell Hammett (*The Thin Man, The Maltese Falcon,* and *The Red Harvest*). The most refined of French novelists then discovered with eagerness *Miss Lonelyhearts,* the cruel and very able story by Nathaniel West, whose untimely death at thirty-six is one of the gravest losses of modern American literature; John O'Hara's skillful rendering of the atmosphere of the 'twenties in *Appointment in Samara;* James Cain, Horace McCoy, Damon Runyon, and other 'poets of the tabloid murder,' as Edmund Wilson once called these novelists of the hard-boiled school.

This is not only contagion of literary fashion. The French have realized lately that their excessively analytical literature was too narrowly addressed to an 'unhappy few': the few thousands in any country who are capable of introspection and enjoy the leisure required by such soul-searching. Millions of other potential readers, untrained in such examinations of conscience and often inarticulate, were never reached by the traditional novel of analysis. These readers had to resort to the coarser type of murder stories. Why not do for them what Poe and the author of *Crime and Punishment* had already done, cater to their legitimate craving for sensation and the thrill of violent action, while fulfilling many of the requisites of art?

This taste for synthetic as against analytical psychology, for sensations powerfully evoked as against elaborate disquisitions on hidden motives, has been apparent in France since Malraux, Giono, and Saint-Exupéry succeeded Proust and Gide in popularity, in 1930 or thereabouts. It became more marked with the war years. The vision of brutality and swift, cruel, illogical action presented by American novels then became an all-too-real nightmare in the countries invaded by Germany. Any attempt to understand rationally a baffling apocalypse or to philosophize about events seemed ludicrous. For the men and women summarily arrested by the Gestapo, huddled together into concentration camps, and for the youth exposed to the hazards of the *maquis,* American books assumed a prophetic character. They proved to be the ones best attuned to a tragic era of incomprehensible violence and brutal sadism.

To be sure, the French readers, when some semblance of normality was again enjoyed, could not fail to be sensitive to the lack of art, which characterizes much American literature. Very soon the most gifted followers of Dos Passos, such as Sartre, of Hemingway, such as Camus, and of Faulkner, such as Mouloudji, Des Forêts, and Magnane, were much more preoccupied than their models by the problem of discovering a form for their functional attempts. But the form will be a richer one for having known a few variations from the older, and outworn, French mold. The writers of the New World have taught the French a refreshing disregard for composition, a total detachment from such rules as unity of plot, a youthful freedom from artistic restraint. Theirs was a type of writing that aimed neither at pure art nor at eternal values and that cared little for posterity or even for survival. To compatriots of Flaubert and Mallarmé, whose sin was to deify literature, the contrast was salutary.

The best among modern French writers are not content with imitating their American models. Camus, in *La Peste*, and Sartre, in *Le Sursis*, have beaten Hemingway and Dos Passos at their own game. Elsewhere they have out-Faulknered Faulkner. With more art than their masters, they have used their devices: Faulkner's reversibility of time, Dos Passos's simultaneous action, the 'punch' of Caldwell's dialogue, Steinbeck's vivid narrative, and Hemingway's 'eye on the object.' The coarseness and orgy of sex and lust, which entertained the French public for a time, will soon be forgotten; but the lessons of concreteness and effectiveness, learned from American writing and substituted, in the canon of literary qualities, for abstractness and beauty, are likely to remain. American fiction has brought to European artists a new accumulation of materials.

Another characteristic of modern American books fitted them peculiarly to the days of wrath through which Europe had been living. Their implicit philosophy is one of pessimism. Their pessimism may be a constant and deep-seated feature of the literature of America, for, with the exception of Emerson and possibly Whitman, it has characterized most of the important writers of the 'young country': Mark Twain, Poe, Hawthorne, Melville, Emily Dickinson, Henry James, Stephen Crane, Edgar Lee Masters, Theodore Dreiser, and all our contemporaries, including American-born Julien Green, the gloomiest of present-day French authors. The most disillusioned books about World War I came from the writers of the country that was physically least affected by it: *The Enormous Room, Three Soldiers, What Price Glory*, and *A Farewell to Arms*. The sharpest revulsion against mechanical civilization, the bitterest satire of businessmen and of ladies' clubs, of the good fellowship of Rotarians and of standardized religion have been expressed by O'Neill and Steinbeck, by the authors of *Elmer Gantry* and of *Journeyman*, even by James Branch Cabell and the Thornton Wilder of *Heaven's My Destination*.

But America need not blush at this literature of despair. Its pessimism is not the sterile mockery of cynics nor the decadent need to soil the beauty of the world. It is the expression of sincere idealism, of lucid faith. It asserts with eloquence that all is not well with the world, but that, by facing realities boldly, we could make life more worthy of being lived. If American literature today has scaled epic heights more courageously than any other, it has also plumbed the depths of tragedy. André Malraux, as early as 1933, prefacing the French translation of *Sanctuary*, called Faulkner's book 'the intrusion of Greek tragedy into the detective novel.' Few writers, since Emily Brontë and Thomas Hardy, have a more just claim to continuing in the tradition of Sophocles than has Faulkner.

The reasons for this tragic pessimism of American writing are complex. They are in part social and reflect the isolation of the artist in a society in which money values are paramount, which esteems him no more than a flute player. They are in part religious, for the fatality of original sin haunts Faulkner as it did his truest predecessor, Hawthorne. O'Neill revives the Catholic doctrine of man's guilt, and Jeffers the wailing of the Jewish prophets about the vanity of everything under the sun. One of the great American poets of the century, Hart Crane, was driven to suicide. Henry Miller, with all his obscene eroticism, is far remote from any cheerful enjoyment of life; his torrent of words hardly conceals an abyss of inner emptiness.

But this tragic pessimism of American writers is to be explained chiefly by their acute perception of the gulf that divides man's power to transform the world through science and technology and his powerlessness to change himself. A similar gulf lies gaping between man's proud assertion of his freedom and his bondage to the fatalities that flesh is heir to. His official philosophy bids the American citizen practice the pursuit of happiness, and as soon as he stops working, he is oppressed by boredom and must drink a few cocktails so as to endure his leisure hours. He claims to live without tragedy, and he is driven to seek substitutes for tragedy in drinks, sex, or murder stories. He stares several times a day at advertisements that proclaim that women are lovely, pink-cheeked creatures, with immaculate hair and alluring stockings, intent upon welcoming husbands in the cleanest of modern homes—and no literature is more deeply obsessed than his by misunderstanding and antagonism between the sexes. Seldom has woman been hated and love reviled, in fiction or drama, as it has been in *Desire Under the Elms, Tamar, Men without Women,* and *Miss Lonelyhearts.*

But this pessimism is virile. It is probably the deep manifestation of the influence that movies have had upon American letters. Through the shallow conventionality of its films, their sickening happy endings, and their fear of the realities of life, Hollywood has driven many of the best American writers to emphasize what the screen has left unsaid: the seamy but authentic and robust aspects of modern life. In so doing, American novelists have provided their countrymen with a healthy psychological outlet. They have been led to eschew sentimentality and to reach for

great subjects. Their pessimism and violence conceal a virile quality of
warm humanity. Foreign observers have seen it perhaps more acutely
than many Americans. The critic of a French weekly, *Action*, wrote, on
October 6, 1944: 'The American novel is well suited to teach us the road
to a healthy, powerful literature which finds, in a broad contact with the
world, essential reasons for faith in itself.' Others lauded plays drawn
from American novels and acted with phenomenal success in Paris—*Of
Mice and Men* and *As I Lay Dying*—because their humanity had helped
the French live through the darkest days of the war and the postwar
years. Sartre, who is the influential prophet of a new French generation,
paid a debt of gratitude when he declared in 1946:

> The greatest literary development in France between 1929 and
> 1939 was the discovery of Faulkner, Dos Passos, Hemingway, Cald-
> well, Steinbeck . . . To writers of my generation, the publication of
> *The 42nd Parallel, Light in August, A Farewell to Arms* effected a
> revolution similar to the one produced fifteen years earlier in Europe
> by the *Ulysses* of Joyce.[2]

The fascination which the American novel held for the French has
not been accompanied by an excessive number of slavish imitations:
those writers whose talent was weak, like Yves Berger in *Sud* (1963), have
only offered caricatural imitations of the exterior features of Southern
novels laid in the French south. The very skillful ones, like Sartre in *Le
Répit*, made almost a game of playing with the Dos Passos technique of
simultaneous events and carried it off triumphantly. The one Frenchman
who had the audacity to imitate Faulkner, Claude Simon, soon shook
off some of the borrowed elements and asserted his own originality, the
most marked perhaps of all the 'new novelists.' The most beneficent
result of the shock given by the discovery of another fictional universe
was to force the French novelists to give up the complacency which had
caused some of them to believe that no other literature experimented
with a new technique or offered a fresh vision. A number of pessimists

2. The bibliography of French writings on recent American literature is immense.
The essays by Sartre (on Dos Passos and on Faulkner) collected in *Situations*,
volume I, have become classics. Camus has been more discreet on the American
writers. Claude-Edmonde Magny did a very good volume on *L'Age du roman
américain*, Editions du Seuil, 1948. Cyrille Arnavon, Roger Asselineau, Maurice-
Edgar Coindreau have written penetratingly on contemporary novelists from Faulkner
to Kerouac. Among the many special numbers of reviews devoted to the subject,
those of *L'Age nouveau* (Nos. 74, 75, 76, June–August 1952), of *Fontaine* (Nos.
27, 28, August 1943), and *Yale French Studies* (No. 10, 1952) are especially useful.

among the critics and even among the weary practitioners of the novel asserted that the death of the novel was at hand, since the bourgeois class itself was on its way to disappearance. Why and how the public reading fiction or portrayed in it should be more identified with the bourgeoisie than that for the theater, the cinema, or the concert hall has never been made clear. Under a very thin veneer of socialism, France, like Italy and West Germany, is probably more bourgeois today than it has ever been, and America herself has become reconciled to the fact that she is not a classless society. In any case, predictions of the decline and imminent death of the art of fiction have only served to incite new practitioners to attempt something more audacious. Joyce, Mann, Broch, Moravia may all have entertained the thought that they had put an end once for all to the art of the novel. After every false death, however, a rebirth has come. The French, like the English, enjoy the advantage of having several traditions behind them: they may always exchange one, temporarily sterile, for another one, which has happened to lie quiescent for a generation or two.

The trend which diverges most sharply from the American influence, which so impressed the French between 1930 and 1945, is that which has produced a number of ironical *récits*, highly intellectual, often dry, too self-conscious and distrustful of naïveté to allow either the reader or the author to be taken in by the hastily sketched characters. That *récit*, distinguished from the short story by its greater interest in psychology, less dramatic and tense than the briefer and more objective form, usually grants less attention to the description of the setting and much more to the self-analysis practiced by one or more characters to whom the author has lent much of himself. The ancestor and model is Benjamin Constant in *Adolphe*. Few of Constant's successors, however, have matched the cruelty of his analysis or the tragic vacillations of his impotent will. Their ironical self-consciousness often reminds us of Stendhal; like him, many French novelists seem to fear being taken in by creatures of their imagination and multiply warnings to the reader who might too spontaneously identify himself with the fictional characters. Stendhal, the most poetical of French novelists before Proust, could proceed thus while still surrounding his characters with a halo of youthful illusions and of romantic tenderness. His irony and his shy self-defense against his public acted as a corrective to his wildly romantic leanings. But the sobriety of his successors is often too easily achieved, with no romantic exuberance to restrain: hence the excess of clarity in their *récits* and an ever present control of the story and of the characters by an intellect which is reluctant to leave anything to chance. Belgian-born Félicien Marceau and the late Roger Vailland have greater staying power than most other storytellers who seem to align themselves with that witty, ironical, entertaining tradition (Jean Dutourd, Jean d'Ormesson, Bertrand Poirot-Delpech). Their ever alert intelligence and the incisiveness of their style, purified from all sentimentality and free from rhetoric and metaphysical pretentiousness, are a delight to the readers from other countries, who are reassured to find their conventional notion of the French as sons of Voltaire, Laclos, and Mérimée confirmed by these moderns. One of the purposes of literature is to entertain us and to sharpen our own wits through the contact with authors who take their revenge upon some of the more irrational aspects of life through irony. World literature, with the Russian, the American, and even the Spanish novel having become ponderously realistic, overabundant, and pretentiously anguished, would be poorer without those open-eyed and cynical French writers of novels which read like expanded but lightly controlled long short stories. The austere critic, usually a professor of literature, who attempts to anticipate the verdict of posterity, tends to be a little irked by these light works because they fail to provide their students with a message and lectures with material rich enough for them to discuss elaborate structure or an existential problematics on the condition of man.

Critics, and ultimately the posterity of readers, likewise appear to resent the novelists who have attempted the most difficult of all tasks, as Molière once termed it: that of making them laugh. Comedy has well nigh disappeared from the stage in this century of ours and French companies have, since World War II, fallen back upon such jaded authors as Labiche, Feydeau, and even Courteline when they wished to offer their audiences some relief from the cosmic or political anguish preying upon them in the outside world and from the sway of tragedy on the contemporary stage. Yet never perhaps has the need for satire at our philosophical pretentions, at our economic and sociological jargon, at our political oracular prophets, at our social hypocrisy been greater. The jokes of the *Canard enchaîné* and of a few Montmartre cabarets are too repetitious and too innocuous to represent by themselves the quality which Meredith used to praise as the 'magnificent French boyishness' and the Gallic ability at drawing a source of comedy from the very midst of misfortune. With first a Marshall of France at the helm during the Vichy era, then a tall and earnest general presiding over its renaissance, the country seems to have been bent upon wrecking once for all the old myth of French levity. Malraux was seldom comic in his novels and Camus even more rarely. The practitioners of the 'new novel' take themselves and their readers desperately seriously.

The few worthwhile attempts at allowing laughter to be reintroduced into the fiction of Rabelais' compatriots have been made by women novelists, at times half-wittingly, by virtuosos of language, and by a few champions of the picaresque. Among the first, Christiane Rochefort appeared as the most promising with her novel, ironically called after the phrase used by Nietzsche to define woman's role, *Le Repos du guerrier* (1959). The book sold generously, entertained widely, shocked no less violently and was soon translated in America as *Warrior's Rest*. Naturally it stands as far as can be from the *roman de jeune fille* which once was intended to preserve the virtue of the French girl up to the wedding night revelation. A man, rescued from suicide by a girl of the French middle class, is at once selected by that young lady as the male who might have been a hero of the Kinsey report. He drinks as much as he makes love, and with the same zestful nonchalance. He also beats his savior-lady with vigorous conviction, and it is rumored that those scenes of correction of the female by the male won a number of feminine readers to this best-seller, which was crowned with the 'prix de la nouvelle.' As some of those ladies confessed in a subsequent questionnaire on women's aspirations today, if the woman does not exactly wish to be beaten, she likes to be reassured that her male companion would at least be up to ministering a few solid blows, if he had to. In the end, after a melancholy orgy, the woman brings her warrior to rest from whisky, and probably from sex—through marriage. Then, clearly, they can be unhappy ever after in exemplary fashion. The book lays no claim to profundity; but it is not devoid of social significance for those who wish to explore the strange forms assumed by feminine sexuality in our time. It is told with winning naturalness.

The same could not be said of another best-seller of the same year 1959, the first genuine success scored by a writer then nearing sixty, Raymond Queneau, who had, up to then, been greatly admired only by a small élite of connoisseurs. There was a contrived and highly self-conscious humor in some of his earlier volumes, *Loin de Rueil* (1944, translated as *The Skin of Dreams*), *Le Dimache de la vie* (1951), too wry and too geometrically calculated to arouse generous laughter. The author is immensely learned and the organizer and editor of several encyclopedias published since World War II in the Pléiade collection by Gallimard. Not unlike Joyce, he has for years centered his meditations on language, and, not unlike Wordsworth in his famous preface, he has attempted to bring the French language 'near to the language of men.' Respect for their polished, perspicuous, often stylized language, laden with nuances which reveal the class stratification of the country, is the only cult which had survived the shattering downfall of most idols for the French people during the propaganda era of World War II. Queneau's words are artfully printed as they may be spoken by the unrefined and supposedly naïve common people of Paris. The effect is entertaining for a while, then soon palls upon the reader as it becomes monotonously mechanical. The characters are all wooden puppets and the teenager, Zazie, is a vulgar and would-be innocent little girl, about as tedious as the Lolita of the New World.

A similar fate, it is to be feared, may befall another virtuoso of language and intrepid striver after comic effects, Boris Vian, dead before his fortieth year. Alfred Jarry, rather than James Joyce, is his literary ancestor; but Vian was steeped in the American literature of 1930–50 and his best sales with the French public came with pastiches of the more violent American novels published under the pseudonym of Vernon Sullivan. *L'Ecume des jours* (1947) and *L'Herbe rouge* (1950) allow a latent tragic bitterness to emerge through the ludicrous dialogue and the picaresque and improbable incidents.

The wish to recover in fiction something of the boisterous illogic and of the impetuous action which had once entertained our ancestors in the Spanish, French, and English picaresque novels has spurred several Englishmen and a few Frenchmen to attempt a revival of the genre among us. André Gide, with characteristic ambiguity, had advocated, when he was working at his *Faux-Monnayeurs,* both a purification of the novelist's art from all stress on descriptive details ('the novel démeublé' as Willa Cather had called it in a parallel reaction to Balzac's saturation of his novels with things) and a return to the raciness and toughness of 'raw meat,' which he hailed as the privilege of English fiction. Russian-born Romain Gary, soon after he made a startling entry into literature with one of the most moving books written about the underground in eastern Europe, *Education européenne* (1945), declared to a literary weekly, *La Gazette des lettres,* on October 12, 1946: the 'modern novel will be picaresque or it will not be at all. Picaresque, like a fresco teeming with adventures, motion and swarming characters, and also with optimism.' He had seen action as an airman during World War II and had embarked upon literature as one of his careers (diplomacy being the other) as a protégé first of Malraux, then of Sartre. He was determined to reintegrate laughter into fiction. Even more than his plea for the preservation of African elephants, *Les Racines du ciel,* which blended some symbolic didacticism with a vitality not unworthy of Alexandre Dumas, he succeeded as a humorous writer of fiction in his imaginative autobiography, *La Promesse de l'aube* (1960), one of the few entertaining and vigorously healthy books written in France since World War II. Romain Gary apparently altered the course of his talent after his reaching the perilous 'mezzo del camin' of his life (he was fifty in 1964) and his later books have failed to evince a deepening or an enrichment of his talent. His only potential rival in the picaresque genre, Roger Nimier, who had raised great hopes with his comic and insolent novel, *Le Hussard bleu,* in 1950, died prematurely in 1964. An admirer of Bernanos and Retz, the most cynical and yet the greatest literary talent among all French cardinals, Nimier related with verve the riotous conquests (over German women) and the droll military experiences of a twenty-year-old conscript serving in 1945 in occupied Germany.. The experience of battle, brutality, and sex galore gained by these untrained young recruits made them subsequently unfit for readaptation to the prosaic, disciplined life of peacetime. Nimier was one of the few virile and exuberant talents who represented in France what John Horne Burns, Norman Mailer, then James Jones portrayed in America of World War II and its liberating demoralization. Politically, for his bitterest satire is unleashed against those who stood for liberalism in politics, he was one of that typically French confraternity: Catholic anarchists of the extreme right, and hard-boiled sentimentalists. One of his volumes, *Amour et néant* (1951), is a hymn to love, erotic and tenderly jealous, as the one force able to cope with the temptation of nothingness.

English and American critics, accustomed to the dubious privilege of their literature having inspired much critical disquisition on imagination as distinguished from fancy and as contrasted with reason, have taken some pity on the poverty of French discussions of imagination before Baudelaire; and Baudelaire himself, when he lauded that 'queen of all the faculties,' was echoing Edgar Allan Poe and through him, perhaps, Coleridge. Since the advent of surrealism, soon followed by Sartre's volumes on imagination and 'the imaginary,' French criticism has made up for its lag. Naturally there had been many a fantastic tale in French much earlier: Charles Nodier, Balzac, Flaubert's 'Légende de Saint Julien L'Hospitalier,' and a number of other romantics and post-romantics who have lately been studied in monographs by Pierre Castex and Marcel Schneider.[3] As in the gracefully reasonable fairy tales of Charles Perrault and the playfully logical fables of La Fontaine, several nineteenth-century practitioners of the fantastic novel in France had their feet solidly fixed on the ground. Théophile Gautier remarked, on the occasion of a translation of Hoffmann's tales in 1836, that 'the wildest fantasy demands a framework of reason, a certain pretext, an outline, characters and some control.' Prosper Mérimée repeatedly and half-cynically offered recipes for the fiction which plays with the supernatural, in letters to Delessert and in his studies on Russian literature: he recommended multiplying details on material reality, a very meticulous description of objects as a starting point, then a gentle passage from the quaint to the marvellous so that the reader can hardly realize that the real world has been left far behind him. Maupassant practiced a similar technique, and so have many moderns who have been determined, in their estrangement from realism, to obliterate all frontiers between the known and the unknown, the watchful state and the oneiric one.

It was one of the professed purposes of the surrealist movement to liberate dreams and to fulfill Gérard de Nerval's prophecy that they would be allowed to flow into 'real life.' Much of the attention of André Breton and of his early followers went to strange coincidences and to registering with great precision cases of what they called the workings of 'objective chance'—le hasard objectif. André Breton's Nadja (1928) can hardly be called a novel or even a tale; it is closer to a series of poems in prose blended with records of weird experiences. Louis Aragon's Anicet, published as early as 1921, before surrealism had truly appeared as a group or as a cult, has some features of a 'fantastic novel.' Breton, later, hailed the novels of Julien Gracq, a teacher of geography who is also a master of elaborate prose, as among the few works of fiction inspired by surrealism. Their deft suggestion of a weird atmosphere reminds the English-speaking reader of Horace Walpole's Castle of Otranto and of Mrs. Radcliffe's 'black' novel. They fail to be compelling, in either story or character. In truth, surrealism, which has left a deep and durable imprint on French poets (long after they had divorced themselves or

3. For these titles and others, alluded to here, see the bibliographical note at the end.

been expelled from the group), and a hardly less deep and less beneficent one on painting and decoration, appears to have failed completely to have marked French fiction. The best among the devotees of the imaginary in French novels and tales since 1945 or thereabout have had only tenuous links, soon severed, with surrealism. They, even more than poets like Paul Eluard, Pierre Reverdy, Henri Michaux, and René Char, who had to stay aloof from surrealism or to break away from its orthodoxy in order to strike their own individual note, could only write fiction if unhampered by the ideology of surrealism.

If any label could be affixed upon them, it would be rather that of neo-romantics; none of them however possesses the exuberance, the visionary power or the ability to take himself with pompous seriousness which the most Promethean of the romantics, Balzac or Hugo, assumed with no qualms of modesty. Like a surprising number of Frenchmen today, they hark back rather to Musset, to Nerval, with a sprinkling of Alain-Fournier's *Sehnsucht* and nostalgia for lost childhood, and of Apollinaire's eroticism. Louis Pauwels is the least well known of those men abroad; his *récit, Saint Quelqu'un* (1946), is a tender story of a man whose happiness is absurdly wrecked through a misunderstanding with his wife, which causes her and their son to commit suicide. The short novel is not annoyingly didactic and it is written with restraint and smoothness. Louis Pauwels, in collaboration with Jacques Bergier, subsequently published, in 1960, a long and surprisingly modest and clear volume of semi-mystical philosophy, *Le Matin des Magiciens,* the subtitle of which is 'an Introduction to fantastic realism.' With the help of science, of modern psychology, and the writings of the strange and perhaps charlatanic Gurdjieff, on whom he also wrote a book, Louis Pauwels in a manner parallel to that of Teilhard de Chardin and in no way unworthy of him, explores some of the unorthodox paths on which modern man might pursue his quest for transcendence. His fastidious scrupulousness and perhaps his overgenerous resort to the philosophical and scientific views of others seem to have impaired his confidence in his power to tell concrete stories.

Noël Devaulx is not too remote from him; but, at the age of twenty-nine, in 1934, without shaking off his haunting disquietude, he chose to find a haven in the Roman Catholic faith. He excels at sketching characters watching themselves fall into the traps of weird adventures (somewhat like those in Henri Bosco's fiction), analyzing themselves lucidly all the time, and exorcizing thereby some of their demons. Around them, death prowls. An exotic setting, in Italy or Spain, lures the reader to the wished-for suspension of disbelief. Noël Devaulx, however, can be called a novelist only by stretching the meaning of the word. He is in fact chiefly a writer of short stories, collected in volumes entitled *L'Auberge Parpillon* (1945), *Le Pressoir mystique* (1948), *Sainte-Barbegrise* (1952), and *La Dame de Murcie* (1961).

André Dhôtel, in contrast, is an inveterate writer of full novels. Born in 1900, published repeatedly in *La Nouvelle Revue Française* and by Gallimard, he has not yet been translated into English, although he is familiar with this country. He has taught in Greece, then near Paris, but he is basically and obstinately a man from eastern France, whose novels are never laid south of the Loire. He is, since Giono and Bosco, the finest painter of nature in French fiction, always laying the mysterious adventures of his heroes along the banks of pale rivers and canals, in the glades of forests, on the moors of Champagne or of his native Ardennes. One of his titles, *Le Pays où l'on n'arrive jamais* (1955), might be apt for all his eight or nine novels, recalling Yeats's 'Land of heart's desire' and Alain-Fournier's 'nameless country.' The favorite characters of Dhôtel are teen-agers or young men, hardly convinced of their own existence, dreamers ill-adapted to real life, seekers of adventure; but their dreams of purity in girls, of fidelity to an impossible ideal which makes them unfit for stark reality, are too beautiful. Like Jean Anouilh's characters, they spurn compromise and adaptation to the sordid calculations of life, which would betray their fierce rejection of this corrupt world. They cling to their childhood. When their yearning for the fantastic has been frustrated by the tragic occurrences of life, they vanish away at the end of those long, eerie, unstructured but winningly poetical novels: *L'Homme de la scierie* (1950), *Bernard le Paresseux* (1952), *Mémoires de Sébastien* (1955).

Among the many champions of the fantastic and adventurers into the impossible who have arisen in France since the impact of surrealism, the one novelist who has reached a wide audience and been translated into English is André Pieyre de Mandiargues. It would be hypocrisy to deny that part of his success, and of his charm, has been due to a skillful use of eroticism. The word used to conjure up shades of Sade, Sacher-Masoch, or, closer to us, of Henry Miller; it has become a cerebral obsession with D. H. Lawrence, Malraux, and Lawrence Durrell, and is one of the most ponderously austere subjects on which every undergraduate in college now writes a few essays as his initiation to steady dating and preparation for his future paternity. The French writers who were at one time connected with surrealism, however, have domesticated the oneiric and the

sexual obsessions which the movement, in its early years, shared with
Freud. The prose volume by Pieyre de Mandiargues (born in 1909, he
first wrote brittle and evocative poetry in verse and prose and he has
remained a poet to this day) which most entertained his French and his
English and American readers is *La Motocyclette* (1963). Within its limits, this *récit* reaches a sort of perfection. The heroine, Rebecca Nul (born
Res), married to a dull scholarly husband, sets off in the early morning
along the roads of Alsace, then of Germany and Switzerland to meet her
lover. She rides her roaring machine with the same voluptuous delight as
horsemen in English novels used to ride their mares. The trip is a fitting
preparation for the encounter with the man who gave her the motorcycle
and who is depicted as an accurate and masterly lover. Her communion
with her 'black bull,' which she embraces and controls like an ancient
goddess, matches her other two loves (for her nice and prosaic husband
and for her athletic lover) in intensity. She will perish through her erotic
intoxication with speed. There is not one coarse sentence in the novel, no
ponderous stress on symbolism. The strangeness of the world there and
elsewhere (in *Le Lis de mer*, 1956, his other masterpiece, and in collections of superb stories, *Feu de braise*, 1959, and *Porte dévergondée*, 1964)
created by the author is accepted very naturally by the reader. The very
slight uneasiness, when we slip from reality into fantasy, is soon dispelled.
His talent is such that we submit even to his slight mannerisms. His elaborate love ceremonial, before the jeunes filles who people his *récits* surrender to Great Pan, only enhances the romantic ecstasies which follow
and are precisely but discreetly evoked. Pieyre de Mandiargues, who
appears to have been attracted, as several surrealists were, to Brentano,
Eichendorff, Achim von Arnim, and E. T. A. Hoffmann, has ravished a little
of their strangeness and of their charm. With him, surrealism has become
a gently formalized classicism.

Surrealism had attracted by its exhibitionist manifestations and its imperious theories much of the attention of the literary world between 1930
and the breaking out of World War II. Existentialism, acting much more
drastically upon the novel and the drama, filled the ten years which
followed the liberation of France. Neither of the two movements was
disposed, after 1950–55, to be silently buried and replaced by newcomers.
Surrealism, the more dogmatic of the two, proved more inimical to the
new movements and the fiction which has been produced in France since
the middle of the century owes to it little more than a fondness for the

fantastic tale and for a poetical delineation of gracefully mysterious women. The founders of existentialism, on the other hand, have not attempted to exclude or to combat the promoters of the 'new novel' as it was soon to be called. Sartre first sponsored Nathalie Sarraute's fiction, praised Michel Butor generously and loudly, and offered but minor objections to the kind of novel which Robbe-Grillet practiced and unabashedly advertized. A direct line of descent relates the novelists of the nineteen-sixties to the two works from which much of their achievement stemmed: La Nausée and L'Etranger.

By the years 1952–56, however, the novelty of existentialism had worn off; the postwar era, with its material difficulties, the sense of economic inferiority in war-impoverished France, but also the dreams and illusions of its philosophers and writers, had come to a close after the mystical number of eleven years, one-third of a third of a century, had elapsed since victory; as the post-World War I phase had then yielded to another mood of disappointment after 1929. The country, while not yet launched on its road to political stability and to Gaullist isolation, and still in the throes of post-colonial wars in the Far East and in Africa, had rebuilt its economic structure with conspicuous success. But its literature failed to reflect its optimism or a placid contentment with a newly won affluence. It is unlikely that future historians will ever speak about a Gaullist era in literature. The leaders of existentialism were approaching their sobering fiftieth year and innovations were eagerly desired. Teachers of French the world over, and particularly in the United States where the emphasis is laid more strongly on the very modern period and sometimes on the latest fads, were watching Europe intently for any signs of a new movement which they might be the first to study. By a fortunate coincidence, Robbe-Grillet's Les Gommes, in 1953, was hailed as a striking herald of a fictional revolution by some critics (Roland Barthes, Maurice Blanchot); and L'Emploi du temps, by Michel Butor, was admired by philosophical minds when, three years later, it appeared. Novels by slightly older writers (Samuel Beckett, Marguerite Duras, Nathalie Sarraute) which had received little attention up to then were lumped together with those of the newcomers, to whom Claude Simon, Claude Ollier, the Swiss Robert Pinget were soon added. An informing number of the monthly review Esprit, in July–August 1958, established 'le nouveau roman' in the public eye. Parallels with the 'new wave' in the cinema were loosely hinted at. A 'new eroticism' was at the same time asserting itself which, in some cases, argued for the recognition of the new novel as a radical departure from the past. For another ten years a rejuvenated and bellicose vanguard was to shift the world's attention to France, at the very time when both Britain and America seemed to be lamenting a dearth of young literary talents.

Like all groups, that of the 'nouveaux romanciers' is artificial and loose. Butor has very little in common with Robbe-Grillet, and the latter is immensely different from Nathalie Sarraute. Claude Simon is far closer to Faulkner than he is to any of his compatriots. Jean Cayrol should never have been linked with them. Contemporary with the 'new novelists' such as Violette Leduc or younger, are many robust talents, like J. M. Le Clézio, whose achievement may well outlive that of such a pseudo 'school' (also called 'L'Ecole du regard') and who are more widely read; for the 'new novelists' have had the courage to court not only difficulty, but sheer boredom. Joyce and Proust and, in more leisurely times, Richardson and Rousseau also defied boredom and conquered. The gamble is, however, a risky one and it is hard to say when the reader will feel that his persistent good will has, or has not, been rewarded. It was probably inevitable that publishers should step into the literary debates aroused by the new fictional attempts and organize loud publicity around the books they championed for literary prizes. Most of the practitioners of the new fiction have been writers of utmost discretion and their sole means of capitalizing on the fashion which had thrown them to a pinnacle of literary fame was their acceptance to lecture about their work and their readiness to visit American universities, where their most ardent commentators occupied teaching positions. Robbe-Grillet's critical manifestoes, like those of Eugene Ionesco on the new 'anti-theater,' have not eschewed insolent dogmatism, and it is up to his readers to receive them with more than a few grains of salt. Adversaries of the new fiction, meanwhile, have not remained silent. The literary critics of *Le Monde,* of *La Revue de Paris,* some professors eager to distrust tides of fashion, and disgruntled novelists of another bent have expressed their distrust of loudly advertized innovations and denounced a number of devices which had become facile tricks. The few positive gains scored by the best of the new novelists may well not be sufficient (they are not, in our opinion) to compensate for what, in their determined asceticism or *amaigrissement,* as it has been styled, they abandon. But not the least of their merits was to step into the literary arena in France at a moment when Mauriac, Céline, Giono, Bernanos, Malraux, Cocteau had given up the writing of fiction. Against the prophets of doom, who have been glibly announcing the death of the novel for decades, they staged a lively rebirth of the genre. A special and narrow mode of poetry, with a fixed form, a ballad or a *rondeau*, conceivably even the ode or the sonnet, might die; so may the epic which was bound by narrow definitions and shackled by conventions and assumed a recognizable form; so might perhaps the historical novel or, in the future, the very personal and solipsistic French novel of analysis. But the novel in general, so free from traditions and conventions, so infinitely flexible that any creator may remold it at his own whim, consumed equally by rich and poor, the purveyor of the cinema, of the television, often enough of the theater, is assured to outwit all the gloomy forecasts of its early death in our culture.

A vital change had been occurring, since the end of World War II, from which much gain, at least in the form of discussion by the public, accrued to the 'new novel': it received the assistance of an equally and determinedly 'new' group of critics. All the leading novelists of the nineteenth century in France, from Stendhal to Zola, had found the critics, from Sainte-Beuve to Anatole France, aligned against them. They had fought back fiercely or, like Flaubert, chafed and fumed in their letters, but remained uninfluenced by critics who would not accept them as they were. With the era opened by the conclusion of World War I, criticism and creation, in literature and in the arts, appeared to be reconciled. Proust, Gide, Mauriac, Larbaud, Malraux, elsewhere Joyce or Virginia Woolf were admired, analyzed, elucidated, at times obfuscated by commentators in newspapers, magazines, and on the radio. Newcomers to fiction, assured in advance that they will seldom be the butt of outrageous denunciations from critics, have little reason to view them as foes. All their animadversion goes against the tradition of earlier novelists, from whom they strain every nerve to differ.

Most of those novels of mid-century have thus been directed against the tradition established by their predecessors. Their authors have claimed either to ignore or to repudiate Proust as well as Joyce, Lawrence as well as Broch or Musil. The ambitious frescoes of social and political life which had been attempted by writers (Jules Romains, Roger Martin du Gard) who wanted to understand how their world could have drifted into the war of 1914 failed to strike the imagination of their successors. World War II, Nazism, the social issues of 1933–39, the dilemmas which tore so many families during the resistance might just as well have occurred on another planet as far as Robbe-Grillet, Michel Butor, or Nathalie Sarraute are concerned. What life says or seems to say hardly concerns them. The techniques of the cinema applied to fiction, of the interior monologue perfected by their predecessors, and even their pre-occupation with the adolescent or with the solitude of lovers imprisoned inside their solipsism do not interest them. Their revolt seemed for a while so radical that the famous and dangerously convenient phrase 'the anti-novel' was coined for its fictional expression.

Sartre coined the phrase in an acute and prophetic essay which he wrote in 1957 as a preface to Nathalie Sarraute's *Portrait d'un inconnu* and later reprinted in *Situations IV* (1964). The anti-novel preserves the outline and the appearance of a novel. But, at the very moment when its author appears to be erecting a work of fiction, he destroys it and uses the fictional form to question fiction itself. It takes an ironical attitude toward the facile devices of the ordinary mystery story, while making full use of them. It implies a rejection of the novelist's bad faith. Nathalie Sarraute, as Sartre analyzed her intentions more lucidly than she did herself, refuses to take her characters either from the inside or from the outside, 'because we are, for ourselves and for others, both wholly outside and inside at the same time.' The meeting ground is the commonplace, which 'belongs to every one in myself and is in myself the presence of every one.' Behind the banal words uttered by the characters and their gestures, a constant flight away from oneself toward daily chores, mediocre tasks, insignificant thoughts, and all forms of inauthenticity is attempted. The reader often feels that he is on the verge of some momentous happening which never does occur: the puppets lapse back into the commonplace. An elusive inauthenticity, such as Sartre was fond of denouncing, into which human cowardice, fleeing from the assumption of freedom, takes refuge: such was the new motive which lurked behind the brief, ironical sketches of *Tropismes* and behind Nathalie Sarraute's second novel.

She is the dean of the novelists who have been, arbitrarily and against their own protests, forced into a 'school' and she is approximately of the same age group as Sartre (she was born in 1902). Claude Simon is the only other author whose fame emerged after World War II and who, like her, was born before the First World War. Sarraute's Russian family set-tled in France in 1910. Her father was a chemist and her mother wrote. She studied at the Sorbonne, learned English and read much English literature. She married a lawyer and has three daughters, one of whom writes criticism. Her first, and perhaps her best book, written as early as 1933, received no attention when it appeared in 1939; it was however the subject of very thoughtful articles, mentioned at the end of this chapter, when it was reprinted after Nathalie Sarraute, then praised in Sartre's magazine, *Les Temps modernes,* had extended her inspiration, perhaps overextended it, in novels. Her theoretical ideas, discreet and judicious, free from all aggressiveness, had then given her the role of the thinker among the new novelists—an ungrateful role, no doubt, for her intentions have not been conspicuously fulfilled in her fiction and her acute intellect has not been helped by a powerful imagination.

She was determined from the outset, having read much Dostoevski, Proust, Kafka, and several of her English contemporaries (she has been much more impressed than most continental Europeans, and more than many Englishmen, by the skill of Ivy Compton-Burnett and by Henry Green's dialogues), to differ from her predecessors and to be 'a rebel in a world of platitudes.' Such was the title given by the *Times Literary Supplement* on June 10, 1960, to an essay devoted to the rejection of clichés and ready-made ideas. Her thesis was that a writer must completely impregnate himself with the works of the past, and then forget them in order to feel with freshness. 'While studying the admirable implements forged by his predecessors, he must never forget that these implements could only be used by them. If he fails in this imperative requirement, he ceases to be a writer, he disappears into academicism.' Later, at a literary congress held at Leningrad in the summer of 1963, Nathalie Sarraute stressed all that separated her from another French participant, Alain Robbe-Grillet; but she insisted upon sharing with him and others a determination to repudiate traditional literature. Her respect for the novelists of the last hundred years is great, and she proclaimed it, as Sartre did at the same congress, against the Russian detractors of Proust and Flaubert as bourgeois. But the reality which they depicted has long ago lost its mystery. It was once invisible; their art made it visible. Her own intent is to convey a new vision through a renovated technique, appropriating Paul Klee's classic saying that 'art does not express the visible; it makes the invisible visible.'

To Flaubert, she owes a debt of gratitude for having been the first to introduce inauthenticity into literature, in order to denounce it. Like Sartre and less ambiguously than he, she is irked, yet fascinated by the nineteenth-century novelist. She is more severe on the limitations of introspection as practiced by Proust and contends that he failed to reach the ultimate depths, that his analysis appears to her laboriously self-conscious and imprisoned in snobbery, when compared with the desperate urge of Dostoevski's characters to establish contact. Dostoevski is, in her eyes, far greater, for he penetrated more deeply into subterranean psychological moves, discarding or ignoring the so-called motives: he presented the antics of his tragic and ludicrous buffoons, without claiming to explain them. But our age is the 'era of suspicions' prophesied by Stendhal. We distrust everything; invention, plot, character. The character with a neat label affixed, warning us that he is the miser, the lover, the jealous, the upstart, used to be the meeting ground of author and reader; 'he has now become the converging point of their mutual distrust.' Along with others today, she has declared war against him. Her aim is to explore those tenuous states, similar to those of the particles of modern physics which a feeble ray distorts. She gives the name of tropisms to those microscopic movements of attraction and repulsion that lie beneath the level of consciousness and defy analysis. They can only be deftly, poetically, elusively suggested.

Like most of the practitioners of the recent or new novel in France, Nathalie Sarraute is austere. She demands much from her readers. The mere device of refusing even to ask the Shakespearean question 'What's in a name?' and of designating the agents, or passive, half-sickly observers, as 'he,' 'she,' 'they,' inherited in part from Faulkner's confusion of names given to several characters and from Kafka's half-anonymous men, erects a hurdle of dubious value between the book and the reader. Descriptions 'à la Balzac' are derided by Nathalie Sarraute, as they had already been by Gide and Virginia Woolf; and circumstances of the extremely tenuous action are omitted. All is fake and inauthentic, and must therefore be banished: order, causation, logic, self-analysis, language all are deceptive. As a starting-point for a new fictional enterprise and the antechamber to some new palace of art, the therapeutic cure advocated by Nathalie Sarraute could probably prove beneficial. *Tropismes,* her earliest volume, consisting of casual talks between ladies in a tea room, of insignificant conversations between a decrepit old man and a polished little girl, is a clever series of sketches, somewhat between Aloysius Bertrand's so-called prose poems and Henri Monnier's reproductions of pointless conversations among vulgar individuals in his early, and much more realistic, *Scènes parisiennes* (1830). Behind the empty or seemingly harmless chitchat, tropisms faintly appear; enmity and cruelty, envy and suspicion, never thus termed and never analyzed, are discreetly suggested by the author. Those sketches, which never assume the integrated solidity of short stories, were relieved with irony and were varied and short enough not to weary the reader's patience. Her novels, however, do. Professional technicians of the art of the novel, chiefly Bernard Pingaud, have discovered profundities in them, which are only perceptible to professionals. Others, who insist upon not divorcing literature completely from emotional, intellectual, and social life, may not feel adequately rewarded by those technical feats. Proust refused any hint that his tool was the microscope and insisted that it was rather the telescope, through which other worlds were descried and explored. Nathalie Sarraute does use a symbolic microscope to discover what we may perceive at a glance but cannot, she submits, render into words: 'an entire human being with its myriads of little movements which appear through a few things said, a laugh, a gesture.'

Portrait d'un inconnu (1949; *Portrait of a Man Unknown*, as it was translated in the Braziller edition of 1958) and *Martereau* (1953) do not lend themselves to any analysis of plot or structure: events do not count, characters are not characterized, tension hardly mounts and certainly fails to grip the reader. The storyteller alone has some inkling of the sense, if any, of the book. Some semblance of tension mounts when a father and his daughter face each other in a scene of bitterness and violent admonitions. But they consent to a silent though rancorous compromise of mutual toleration after the daughter challenges her father through her decision to become engaged. Behind the deliberate triteness of the conversations, we sense some venomous alienation of the actors from their own family. But we are neither impelled nor even invited to share in their feelings. *Martereau* is only a trifle stronger or clearer. An unnamed young orphan, sickly, would-be or would-have-been artist, watches a rather insignificant family which has accepted him in its midst. An outsider, the only one with a name, Martereau, swindles the family and is perhaps the wife's lover (love and sex are cruelly absent from this novel). The apathetic observer does not discover anything and does not judge. Much subtlety and much stylistic skill are expended by the novelist on thin and brittle material in which this reader, and probably many like him, refuse to be concerned. French wits, waxing impatient at so much garrulous talk around trifles, unmindful of the serious psychological purpose of the author, have disparagingly called them 'sarrauteries,' or innocuous society dances or 'sauteries,' during which mothers, keeping an eye on their daughters and the husbands whom they might lure through their wellbred simpering, embroider their 'ouvrages de dames.'

Le Planetarium (1959) has been the one novel by the author which has been moderately praised. There can but be calculated irony in the title, conjuring up an artificial heavenly vault which shows the motions of stars and planets. The story is certainly laid in stuffy claustration; never a touch of nature and never an intruder from the masses. Even in Proust, servants and elevator boys brought a touch of country life and appeared to be doing something with their hands. The same apathetic, vaguely sickly intellectual, here called Alain, irked at being called lazy by his wife's family, persuades his wife, Gisèle, that he is at work on a literary work of promise and that a prestigious woman writer, Germaine Lemaire, has faith in him. An old aunt, Berthe, who had been neurotically obsessed with some damage inflicted by clumsy workmen upon an oval oaken door which she had just bought for her apartment, agrees to let Alain and Gisèle occupy her flat. Amid so much triviality and the invading triteness today of the theme of literary impotence (whole novels, diaries, and even plays are woven out of an author's incapacity to receive inspiration and of his distrust of language as a betrayal), some satire of the noble laziness of the leisure class and of literary life in general may be read between the lines. The publisher, to forestall the common reader's impatient reaction, warned him in one of those helpful notices which are designed to provide critics with their leitmotif, distributed a prospectus explaining that 'the anecdote is but a thin thread which makes it possible to cluster the psychological movements around several themes and keeps them from being scattered all over.' The purpose of Nathalie Sarraute was to portray the 'facticity' of those private universes in which we complacently imprison ourselves, while sketching the idle dream of wanting to escape from them.

Les Fruits d'or (1963; *The Golden Fruits,* 1964) is even more totally devoid of plot, character, and motion. The reader has to work his misty way among dim and gloomy alleys. The only external events consist of a man holding a shawl for a lady, an umbrella being annoyingly forgotten, the asinine acclaim of a novel entitled *Les Fruits d'or,* and equally superficial and ludicrous attacks against the novel by others, or by the same persons who have espoused another snobbery. As a satire of the would-be 'ins' in literary fashions, and of their pompous and sibylline oracles, it arouses a faint smile on our lips now and then. Snobbery, however, deserves a sounder thrashing; from La Bruyère to Proust, French satirists of pretentious fakery had accustomed us to more robust fare. 'He that drives fat oxen must himself be fat,' Dr. Johnson ironically quipped. She who intends to portray insignificance and tedium should probably not banish all humor, forcefulness, and even exaggeration from her books and incur the one unforgivable charge in literature: that of unshakable dullness. Even microscopic tropisms need to be magnified to conquer a place in literature.

Alain Robbe-Grillet has also been vocal and entertainingly dogmatic in his indictment of previous literature, but much less coherent in his delineation of his own intentions. His theories, formulated in reply to reporters and to professors who like to sum up an author in some formula or to link him to an ideological system, are, as the polite word used by those who remain unconvinced has it, 'provocative.' A convenient publication of his collected articles in pocketbook format, *For a New Novel*, and even more the sophisticated enigmas of his *Last Year at Marienbad* on the screen, have won for Robbe-Grillet the most eminent place among the novelists of the new wave. He and Michel Butor will be the first of their generation (they were born respectively in 1922 and 1926) to come to terms with the establishment and to sit among the Paris 'Immortals.' Neither of them takes himself quite so seriously as their critics take them, and their laudators among those critics have chiefly been in the United States: the three full length and awe-struck volumes studying Robbe-Grillet to have appeared by 1965 were all by scholars in American colleges. The French, by contrast, have remained skeptical. Not altogether fairly, they have hinted that these novelists, whom they charged with dehumanizing literature, were discussed more than they were actually read. The public has not resigned itself to do half of the work for the author, as that so-called 'cafeteria' or 'help yourself' type of fiction requires him to do, reconstructing events and enacting the roles of furtive and passive anti-heroes.

The Bretons, among whom Robbe-Grillet was born in Brest, are said to be a dreamy and poetical Celtic race, fond of vagueness, and haunted by tales of love and of the supernatural. But Robbe-Grillet has little of Chateaubriand, Renan, or Villiers de l'Isle Adam. He was trained at the Paris Agronomic Institute as an agronomist and a statistician, then assigned to international food organizations where he became a specialist in exotic fruits. In 1953, he puzzled and conquered a few expert readers with *Les Gommes* and, two years later, received the Prix des Critiques. His next two novels scored an even more marked success and were promptly translated into English: *Le Voyeur* (1955) and *La Jalousie* (1957). Later ones have been inferior to those and disturbed those of his admirers who had hailed him as the phenomenologist conquering fiction. Irked as he was by the inevitable parallels which the early reviewers of his work sketched between the newcomer and the giants of the past (from Balzac to Kafka), Robbe-Grillet fought back and asserted, as all innovators have done, that the past had to be transcended, perhaps rejected, and that he was riding the wave of the future. Raising a respectful hat to Flaubert and to *The Counterfeiters* (where the novelist and his reflection on the novel were introduced inside the work, not without much artifice), Robbe-Grillet submitted that, from now on, 'it is the novel which thinks itself, questions and judges itself; not through the means of the characters developing superfluous commentaries, but through an incessant reflection, at the level of the narrative itself, of each element upon itself: gesture, object, situation' (*L'Express*, November 8, 1955).

The clarity of the author's formulas is deceptive, and he is more adept at deriding the critics who cling to the past than at defining his own purpose. Few would complain of it. It is through creating and unfolding his stories that a novelist reaches clarity about his aims most securely. If he started with a full awareness of his intentions, like Jules Romains, the reader would be deprived of the needed impression of finding his way and of being overpowered by living creatures, which the novelist should produce. A few points in Robbe-Grillet's reflections on his art stand out. He wishes to banish the story and all anecdotes more or less pertaining to it, as had been already the dream of Flaubert and that of Joyce: with those stalwarts of art for art's sake, Scheherazade ceases to stand as a symbol of fiction-writing; or rather the interest of curiosity is titillated through the tricks of the detective story manipulated by an expert who, his tongue in his cheeks, pulls all the wires and contrives coincidences and encounters which should have ravished André Breton. In *La Maison de rendez-vous* (1965), Robbe-Grillet, forsaking all pretense of being a thinker among novelists or a psychologist competing with Flaubert and Nathalie Sarraute, even condescended to facile tricks of erotic literature and evocations of local color in a luxury prostitution establishment of Hong Kong not unworthy of the once famous Claude Farrère. Robbe-Grillet, however, discards the naïve assumption of his predecessors that the adventures alluded to had actually happened to real characters, hence that we lived in a coherent universe which the novelist was able to decipher. He is no advocate of the absurd, which amounts to the most blatant form of anthropomorphism: complaining that the world does not suit man's conveniences. To him, the world is, and that is all. Man's function is in no way to force a meaning upon it.

Robbe-Grillet aims many barbs of his irony at the second idol of dramatic and fictional literature: character. He laughs at the conventional reader's demand that the actors of a novel should have a name, a pedigree, a profession, certain material possessions, and should belong to a social and human category; even more ludicrous is our insistence that there be some inner logic in their make-up and that they be 'human.' His irony at character, that mummy just good enough to be discarded, is entertaining; but even if it were true in theory that the creation of character, that sacrosanct requirement of criticism, can be dispensed with, the desire of the reader to have the novelist impart some life to his personages cannot be so easily dismissed. And it is doubtful whether the jealous husband-narrator of *La Jalousie,* the soldier turning around and writhing in his labyrinth, the peddler in watches and alleged rapist and murderer in *Le Voyeur,* and the painstaking and solemnly childish detective in *Les Gommes* have struck many of us as alive and as likely to survive for even a few years in our memories. It may be heroic to attempt to sever oneself altogether from the outdated storytelling, character-creation, chronological sequence, and three-dimensional perspective of past fiction. It takes ingenuity to substitute anti-heroes, or insignificant people like the phantom-like lover in *La Jalousie* and like the little boy, the woman, and the soldier wading in their labyrinthine snows, for the boldly outlined characters of Zola and of Proust. But the role of a pioneer is an ungrateful one for some day, like Edouard Dujardin when he experimented with the interior monologue to be picked up by James Joyce, he may be followed by more powerful talents than his own. His fortunes with posterity are likely to be brighter when he has not been seized upon too early by a chorus of explicators and followers. The flabby generalization that a name, a face, a social position, a profession and possessions have ceased to count in our topsy-turvy world of 1950–70, and fiction should consequently relinquish those to Madame Tussaud's wax museum, requires more gullibility in this era of triumphant bourgeois materialism than most of us are gifted with. Paradoxical aphorisms such as 'the true writer has nothing to say but he has only a manner of saying' are about as valid as those which Oscar Wilde used to flip.

Symbols and metaphors are among the ingredients of the traditional novel which the impetuous Robbe-Grillet proclaimed as doomed. Symbols, however, are not lacking in *Les Gommes:* the eraser itself, for which Wallas meticulously looks and which, rather obviously, suggests the desire to erase time and its deeds; then the heavy-handed allusions to the most childish of the ancient myths, that of Oedipus. Behind the systematic use of the present indicative, of which the author makes much, and his reduction of everything to a flat surface, lurk memories of his predecessors: Ellery Queen, Kafka's *Castle*, Simenon's *Quai des Brumes*, and even Baudelaire's petrified architecture in his strange poem, 'Rêve parisien.' The canals, dykes, draw-bridges, and store windows, neatly measured with their angles and rectangles, might conjure up a harbor in Brittany or Holland; but Robbe-Grillet's universe is colorless, odorless, and tasteless, impeccably hygienic and deprived of the mystery which Lorrain or Vermeer might have allowed to suffuse such scenes. The complicated narrative of an unmotivated crime, first bungled, then committed by the clumsy detective Wallas who had tried to buy an eraser of a certain type and listened to the sphinx-like riddle proposed by a drunkard, may entertain intellectual decipherers of laboriously contrived enigmas.[4] To those who ask from literature some psychological substance and who will only be interested in a murder if the victim first had enough reality and substance to warrant a reader's curiosity, *Les Gommes* may well remain a skillful tour de force by an engineer trying his hand at literature.

Le Voyeur (1955) takes place in a setting which, in the author's fashion, is never precisely localized, but which appears to be an island off the coast of Brittany. In it, Robbe-Grillet has shed some of the useless means of deception by which the contriver of a detective story throws his readers on the wrong track. The plot is simple and some anguished fear in the protagonist, not unworthy of Edgar Allan Poe or of Julien Green, is imparted to the reader. The title, replacing an earlier one, *Le Voyageur*, designates one who, like Robbe-Grillet's reader in this novel and in *La Jalousie*, looks at the characters solemnly practicing their wiles or preparing their crime as if they were beasts in a cage; he takes no part in the action, he does not even understand it; he seizes fragments which it is his task, not the novelist's, to piece together, separated by gaps in time or in logic which no one attempts to fill. The actor of the drama, Mathias, is a traveling salesman in wristwatches who returns to the Breton island where he once lived. He is struck, on landing, by the shape of an horizontal symbol for an eight (∞) which appears in the flight of seagulls, in a bit of string lying on the wharf, and naturally in the eyes or in the spec-

4. The most careful unraveling of the plot is provided in Bruce Morrissette's volume on Robbe-Grillet (chapter on 'Oedipe ou le cercle fermé') mentioned in our bibliographical note. The earliest and most laudatory, if not necessarily clear, appraisal of the novel was offered by Roland Barthes in 'Littérature objective,' *Critique*, Nos. 86–87, August 1954, 581–591.

tacles of him who sees. A few pictures and posters representing a girl strangled by a man, another one offering herself as a victim, convey a lurking sense of anguish and the obsession of a rapist in the peddler in watches. A thirteen-year-old shepherdess, whom the villagers knew to be an independent and rebellious child, disappears soon after. The next day, her body, torn and pecked by seagulls, is found among the rocks. She has been the victim of a sadist. Mathias must be the murderer, although he is never identified as such. He overhears conversations in a *café* about the crime, conceals his embarrassment and is never really suspected, except by a little boy who knows his alibi to be fake, but says nothing. Mathias misses his ship, nevertheless leaves the island the next day unharmed.

The novelist's mastery of his devices is perfect here. All the details, sensations, gestures, childhood memories, or vague projects of Mathias, expressions of fear in his behavior, are presented from the outside; even if they refer to the past or the future, they are given in the present indicative. The reader is made to borrow the eyes of Mathias throughout the story and there are thus two voyeurs, the reader and the rapist-murderer. But the former is afforded no insight into the dark recesses of the killer's desires or fear. His imagination is nowhere stimulated, his sensibility is not touched; the obliteration of both past and future makes the perpetual present very thin. The proliferation of exterior details drowns the attention of the reader-voyeur. Such elimination of all poetry about objects, scenery, human beings, man's sensations of nature impoverishes fiction. Reductionism in literature proves enjoyable only for a few undaunted ascetics; those who are neither saints nor snobs will not so readily consent to being deprived of all refined pleasure.

La Jalousie (1957) is a marvelous clockwork, which owes little or nothing to detective stories or to the suspense of an impending murder but lets psychology enter through a back-door. The title plays upon the twofold meaning of the word in French, but the definite article unfortunately has to be dropped in the English translation: Venetian blinds through which the sparse words of the protagonists and the jealous husband's tense gestures are watched, and the suspicious anguish of the latter. While next to nothing happens and the tricks of repetition soon wear off their obsessive force and merely pall on us, an effect of tenseness is eventually contrived. We can hardly resist the temptation of drawing a diagram of the cage in which those human monkeys come and go in silence, in the same way as we share in the game practiced by the solemn actors in the film *L'Année dernière à Marienbad*. In the two works, we are left similarly wondering, if it ever mattered to us, whether the woman and the 'lover' have actually given the gloomy husband cause to be jealous, or whether the jealous one is merely a neurotic carried away by his imagination.

No portrayal of jealousy such as Proust and Mauriac had offered in their unforgettable pages is to be looked for in Robbe-Grillet. Since any such portrayal was bound to pale in comparison, their successor sought originality elsewhere. The scene is somewhere in the French Antilles, in a large plantation house surrounded by geometric rows of banana trees. The description is done over and over again with the dry meticulousness of a land surveyor or of an auctioneer. 'The veranda is a wide, covered gallery surrounding the house on three sides. Since its width is the same for the central portion as for the sides, the line of shadow cast by the column extends precisely to the corner of the house . . . ; just now the shadow of the outer edge of the roof exactly coincides with the right angle formed by the terrace and the two vertical surfaces of the corner of the house.' A few details, perceived through the eyes of the husband-narrator, who however does not use the first person singular, recur obsessively: the voluptuous hair of the young woman, A.; her blue writing-paper, of which a sheet is seen by the husband being folded in the pocket of Franck, his neighbor and perhaps his wife's lover; the hands wielding knife and fork at the table, some (Franck's hands) with ominous energy denoting self-assertiveness and male vigor, others with sly hesitation; a centipede crawling on the wall, clearly symbolic of the neurotic husband's obsession and probably the messenger of sexual connotations, for symbols, even anthropomorphic ones, are not altogether absent from those pages even if they are written by a foe of symbol, metaphor, and psychology. A. takes a trip to the neighboring town with Franck; a real, or an invented, breakdown of their car detains them overnight in a hotel while the husband silently fumes and rages. On A.'s return, the couple sit down to their meals as if nothing had happened. Franck presumably will resume his visits, leaving his own wife, Christiane, at home; all we know of her is that she is wearied by the tropical climate and concerned about the health of their child, and is too weak to fight against radiantly healthy A. to recapture her husband. The jealous husband appears to dream of his rival's wished-for death in an automobile accident, revolves in his sick mind the incident of the centipede squashed by Franck (mentioned some seventeen times in the book). The total impression is one of emptiness (the word is actually used), of solitude (not mentioned), and of total lack of communication between the characters, as isolated as they could be in their hieratic

solemness as in a painting by Seurat. The novel is an ideal one for professors to elucidate ingeniously in a classroom, through all its tricks: such as
the gaping zone of darkness at the center (are Franck and A. actually
lovers?, a favorite question pondered over by biographers and critics).
All the novelist's skill is spent on the objective measurement of things and
on repetitions multiplied in those tales of eternal recurrence. The bewilderment of the trapped reader grows as the very precise details around
him no longer seem real and turn the meticulously surveyed setting into a
phantasmal scene.

'Kafkaesque' is the adjective which comes to mind when we read
Robbe-Grillet's novels, and the comparison naturally belittles the French
novelist, whose expertly used devices never seem to unfold with the inevitability of the events in *The Castle,* or in some of Faulkner's novels.[5]
James Joyce and his theme of a wandering anti-hero pursuing his quest
for a never stated goal also come to mind. But the intensity of that metaphysical pursuit of an undecipherable meaning, which oppresses us in
Kafka, has given way to a series of traps into which the more playful and
wily Frenchman lures us. *Dans le labyrinthe* (1959) drove even further
that disturbing sense of an author playing cat and mouse with his reader.
A brief warning, in the way of preface, notifies the reader that no allegorical value is to be looked for and that gestures, words, events as they
are related have no more nor less significance 'than his own life or his own
death.' The very title of a Labyrinth comes down to us, nevertheless,
laden with mythological and symbolical associations. A soldier wanders
aimlessly along snowy streets, dimly looking for an address which he has
forgotten. A waif from a defeated army, vaguely expecting to be seized
and shot by enemy patrols (as he is indeed at the end), he has been asked
by a dead soldier who was his friend to take a box to the latter's widow.
Was he secretly wishing to console and perhaps to love that widow? We
are never told, or rather we are told not to ask. After the messenger has
been shot and dies at the house of the widow to whom he has never
spoken, the box is opened and found to contain love letters, a watch, and
a dagger: in spite of the novelist's admonitions not to read any ulterior
meaning in any details, we are bound to wonder why those were selected

5. Robbe-Grillet does not separate Kafka's from Faulkner's fiction in his recognition
of predecessors whom he prefers to much-abused Balzac. See interview with André
Bourin in *Les Nouvelles Littéraires,* January 22, 1959. Olga Bernal, who quotes
that interview, rightly remarks that Faulkner's luxuriant prose and Robbe-Grillet's
ascetic leanness stand, however, at opposite poles. The American novel's lesson to
the French was the temporary avoidance of psychological analysis.

and whether they do not connote love, time, and death. Or else, if no further meaning is anywhere implied, our involvement in the images dimly glimpsed at through the play of a magic lantern becomes non-existent and our interest wanes altogether. The stress on a picture hanging on the wall of a dingy *café*, which duplicates exactly the scene laboriously described in the story (soldiers emerging from a defeat, a little boy hold-ing a box, in snowy weather) produces tedium rather than curiosity in the reader if he is forbidden to look for some meaning in it. Not a word is devoted to analyzing, or merely to stating, what the unhappy and totally uninteresting soldier feels or thinks. The novelist's purpose is to cease being, as in Balzac or Mauriac, a god aware of all that takes place inside the skulls and the hearts of his creatures, but to act only the cool observer of their exterior behavior. All links with reality are cut off in that strange realism: the novel must be erected, like an object or a pure and cold art work, outside life, in a rarefied empyrean. The novelist is a virtuoso engi-neer, but it is too easy to take all his clever mechanisms to pieces and then to be left with little but naïve wonderment at his skill. Man feels super-fluous, *de trop*, in that artificial world and far more of a derelict than in Sartre's universe.[6]

The practitioners of the 'new novel' have for the most part been cosmo-politan authors, like the champions of the antitheater. Nathalie Sarraute and Samuel Beckett were born in Russia and in Ireland; Michel Butor who hailed from the most northern region of France lived in Egypt, Britain, Germany; Robbe-Grillet, a son of the westernmost part of France, has worked in far distant lands; Robert Pinget is a Swiss, Claude Ollier lived in Africa. Claude Simon, on whom the impact of foreign literatures has been greatest (Dostoevski, Conrad, Joyce, most of all Faulkner, as he has proclaimed in several interviews), is a stay-at-home Frenchman. He comes from the district of Perpignan, near the Spanish border, and, having written close to ten novels and one play up to 1967, he still lives there as a vine-grower. His father was a cavalry officer. He started his career as a painter and he envisaged the problem of writing fiction as not dissimilar from that of the painter: to convey, not a succes-sion in time and a sense of duration, but simultaneousness; to transpose one dimension into another and organize images which coexist in memory.

6. *La Maison de rendez-vous* (1965) adds nothing to Robbe-Grillet's reputation and only brings out more blatantly the artificiality of many of his devices. It has much in common with a James Bond film. It provided the opportunity for clever statements made by the author to an interviewer, Thérèse de Saint-Phalle, in *Le Figaro littéraire*, October 7–13, 1965.

Hence his inordinately long sentences, meandering over several pages, and his dismissal of all punctuation. His demands upon the reader's attention are cruelly exacting and not a few critics have refused to accede to them. He himself confessed that he could only emerge from the chaos of his simultaneous composition and of his thickly colored 'baroque triptychs' (such is the subtitle of *Le Vent*) through writing with colored pencils and assigning a different color to each character and each theme. As to the public, Claude Simon, who nowhere attempts to outwit his readers with detective story trickery, firmly asserts that it can be disregarded by the novelist, as it was by Van Gogh and Picasso: the primary duties of a creator are to himself.

Simon's early books, including *Le Sacre du printemps* (1953), written in rich and sensuous poetical prose which recalls Giono, lacked a theme and a solid structure. His play, *La Séparation*, staged in March 1963 at the Théâtre de Lutèce, whose substance was drawn from one of his novels, *L'Herbe*, proved that neither his vision of the world nor his language could be transposed from lyrical fiction to the stage. *Le Palace* (1962, translated in 1964) evinced a decline in the author's power of vivid evocation of places and people. A nameless Frenchman who served with the loyalists in the Spanish Civil War returns to Barcelona after fifteen years. He revisits a former palace hotel, converted into a labor union center, then into a bank; he gazes mournfully at that decay, symbolic of the loss of his youthful enthusiasm. He describes lengthily both his memories brutally belied by the passing of years and his own present experience. Unlike Robbe-Grillet, he does not size up and report the configuration of objects with 'geometric moroseness,' as that belabored inventory of some new novelists has been called; Simon retains the love of color of a painter and the rhythm of his sumptuous sentences has a Dionysian tempo. Nothing happens in the novel, made up of shadowy dialogues and Proustian reminiscences. The unnamed visitor to the disaffected Catalan palace in the end kills himself in a public lavatory. There is no attempt at rendering or at suggesting any reality in such a book. The chief concern of the novelist, who no longer relates a story or presents images of real people, is to devise a language which may be true to his purely subjective vision. Like recent French critics, the author of such a work of fiction from which anything fictional is banished wishes to call into question literature itself and austerely, but not without a debauchery of verbal fireworks, to indict or, as the fashionable verb puts it, to 'contest' language itself. As the new media like television are taking over some of the traditional functions of literature, the novelists, abdicating any imperialism, consent to see themselves reduced to a shrunken and half-deserted territory, which they jealously cultivate for a chosen few.

Le Vent, in 1957, and *L'Herbe* (1959), both translated into American by Richard Howard, had more humanity and the reader of traditional fiction was half reassured, in the midst of his Faulknerian bewilderment at a deluge of words and at the tampering with chronological succession, to encounter vividly portrayed individuals in conflict. The southern wind rages over the southern French city in its disorderly abundance; all the senses of the onlookers are tosssed about like corks on a turbid pool. Montès, a sailor, has returned to the windswept city to recover some vine-planted acres of soil which once belonged to his family. He is submerged in a welter of lawsuits, ancillary loves, semi-paternal feelings for the children of his servant-mistress. But his speech is inarticulate and his answers to the teacher who pieces together the semblance of a story are befuddled. Clarity is eschewed. The idiots of Dostoevski and of Faulkner have at last invaded the fiction of the nation which used to pride itself on 'seeing clearly into its heart.' Simon's endeavor is to watch the chaotic and swarming becoming of something which never actually assumes a clear-cut shape—the becoming and not the being. No author could stand at a more directly opposite pole to Paul Valéry and to the sculptor Maillol, who came from the very same region of southern France, between the Pyrenees, the Mediterranean, and the Rhône.

L'Herbe receives its title from an epigraph from Boris Pasternak: 'No one makes history, no one sees it happen, no one sees the grass grow.' The growth which is watched and reported by a cold-blooded witness is that of death's dominion over a decaying body. The French title of one of Faulkner's greatest novels, *Tandis que j'agonise*, would have been more apt and less enigmatic. The raucous gasps of Aunt Marie, the paralyzed person in her agony, in a solitary room, are reported by her nephew's wife, Louise, to her lover, by whose side she is lying outside, on the grass. She comes and goes between her weirdly fascinated lover and the patient's gloomy room, and also between the anguishing present (the process of dying lasts ten days) and the sordid, irretrievably bygone past.

Nothing emerges clearly at first, except the haunting rhythms of the sobs and shivers of human flesh struggling against the inevitable end. Gradually, some significance is elicited by the reader who hears in those gasps the mournful sobs of mankind and the voice of a silent, stoical resignation. Aunt Marie and her sister Eugénie, a country schoolteacher, had deprived themselves of all the gratification that money and success can bring, in order to pay for the education of a younger brother, Pierre. That brother turned into a fat, pampered, ungrateful man, a heap of repugnant flesh, who married a hideous girl addicted to drink, a bejeweled and painted doll. Their son Georges turned out no better; a coward and a spendthrift, the nephew of the dying aunt is the cuckolded husband of the narrator. Those contemptible characters are all dismally isolated from one another; no dialogue, no mutual trust ever unites them. The tone is that of an incessant solo, punctuated with 'the terrible rattle escaping from the lungs of the dying woman . . . slow and endless bellows resounding like the trumpets of the Last Judgment.' Outside, it is the time of the defeat of France in 1940. Through cascades of parentheses and interminable sentences, the author conveys an obsession with the repulsiveness of all flesh, preyed upon by corruption, and with all passion being desiccated into dust. Claude Simon conjures up glimpses of the beauty of exterior nature and caresses words with sensuousness; but like Sartre, Beckett, and others of that generation in Europe, he well deserves the name of a Jansenist.

His next novel, and the one in which he displayed his gift of a baroque master of prose to the fullest, *La Route des Flandres* (1960), is likewise haunted by death and by the corrosion of 'time which takes survey of all the world.' The last sentence epitomizes the story of the confusion and absurdity of the defeat of 1940 in Flanders, which Simon had witnessed as one of the participants in the vain struggle: 'the incoherent, nonchalant, impersonal and destructive work of time.' There is no punctuation; present participles, which the author especially affects, roll in cascades; parentheses follow each other, paragraphs are not resorted to, for they would break into the ceaseless back and forth motion between the present and the past. The technique is wielded masterfully and the language is hauntingly rich, probably too rich and too gratuitous, like a romantic or baroque painter's medium which submerges pallidly drawn figures. Simon, who confesses candidly that he has little imagination, revealed that he was still pursued by a few images: of the chaotic defeat of 1940 in Flanders; of a captain whom he then saw dying and whose death might have been a suicide; of an ancestor of his whose suicide had been reported to the novelist when he was an impressionable child; of women and horses and mobs of peasants on the cluttered roads. 'I was haunted,' he said, 'by two things: by discontinuity, the fragmentary aspect of the emotions we experience and which are unrelated to one another, and yet by their contiguous place in our consciousness.' [7]

The cavalry officer who rides into an ambush with the will to perish, De Reixach, had suffered from his wife's infidelities with a jockey, Iglesia, and with Georges, whose turbid monologue fills the novel. But the incidents are immaterial. The recapturing of the past, as in Faulkner, and the reliving of ancestors' sins by descendants fascinated by them are the felicitous elements of that chaotic and labyrinthine novel in which the collapse of 1940 in northern France is powerfully rendered. Along with other experimenters among recent novelists, Claude Simon attempts to bypass literature in communicating an experience directly and with an immediacy such as painting could have; but few styles are more consciously literary than his. The overall impression is that he possesses the greatest gifts of any prose writer among the modern French since Huysmans and Giono, but hardly those of a writer of fiction, if fiction must engage and maintain a reader's interest. Poets, since Mallarmé and George, have eventually created a limited audience of fervent lovers of their poetry and influenced philosophers, fiction writers, painters, and musicians. It is more doubtful whether novelists can likewise relinquish the spacious realm which once was theirs, cultivate an impossible purity, and survive. The history of the artistically written novel, from Chateaubriand to Walter Pater and George Moore, is strewn with mishaps.

Butor's is the finest mind among those who have undertaken to renovate the novel since 1950—the only one who at times recalls the density and the complex orchestration of the Proustian saga fiction or whose universal intellectual and artistic curiosity grants him a place in the literature of the last third of our century comparable to that of Sartre at mid-century. He received Sartre's blessing and he himself has been generous as well as clear-sighted in praising the avatars of Sartrian thought since 1960. Up to 1960, when *Degrés* appeared and discouraged those of his admirers who had become accustomed to his earlier manner, and especially with a number of perversely noble rather than successful experiments with literary collages and with a risky use of sound and of spoken words in descriptive prose (in two volumes laid in the American scene, *Mobile* and a Niagara Falls typographical and cinematic montage), Butor was among the new novelists the favorite of critics and of philos-

7. Interview given by Claude Simon to Claude Sarraute in *Le Monde*, October 6–12, 1960.

ophers. His early collection of travel sketches, *Le Génie du lieu* (published only in 1958), and his two volumes of *Répertoire* show a rare and modest intellect at play. Born on September 14, 1926, in the north of France, educated first by Catholic ecclesiastics, then drawn to the study of philosophy and becoming a teacher in Egypt, England, and Switzerland, Michel Butor made his entry into literature at the age of thirty with *L'Emploi du temps* (1956; *Passing Time*, 1960). On that volume and on his one truly popular novel, *La Modification* (1957; *A Change of Heart*, 1959), his position as a novelist must for the present rest. An earlier attempt at fiction, *Passage de Milan* (1954), was an ingenious but overlabored experiment over which he progressed with surprising speed. Like many of Butor's titles, it revealed the author's fondness for ambiguities, since Milan is both the north Italian city and the kite, a cruel bird of prey (the word 'butor' itself means a marshbird, the bittern), and the 'passage' in question is the small street or alley in Paris where two priests, a large family, and other people lead a banal existence. The plot is almost non-existent, as in Nathalie Sarraute's static and deliberately empty novels, and the irony too gentle to arouse the reader's interest.

L'Emploi du temps is far more powerful and complex and its play on several superimposed planes is carried off with mastery. Through a series of counterpoints, alternating between the past as lived six months earlier and the present time when Jacques Revel keeps a diary in which he records the past, the narrator endeavors to come to grips with the British city of Bleston (*alias* Manchester), which had threatened to stifle his personality in rain and soot and gloom. His liberation can only result from his understanding all that happened to him in that labyrinth and devouring minotaur of a city. His only friend for a time was a Negro, like him an exile who revenged himself against the hated city through lighting fires in its desolate hovels. Symbols, somewhat too obviously stressed, punctuate the gradual recovery of past time by the young Frenchman: a stained glass window of the cathedral depicting Cain's murder of Abel; a detective novel inside the novel on a similar theme, whose author nearly falls the victim of a plotted accident; in the museum, a tapestry of Ariadne and the Cretan labyrinth which encourages Jacques Revel to find his own thread and escape unscathed from his own past which he had been in danger of losing in the dreaded metropolis of fog and mud. The atmosphere of a melancholy England, similar to that of *Silas Marner* or of *Mark Rutherford*, engulfing all joy and annihilating any will to resist, is hauntingly rendered by Michel Butor. His hero, or *alter ego*, does recapture his past through recording it and raising it to the plane of art; meanwhile he has let the possible rewards of the present, love for Rose, one of two sisters, and the love borne for him by the other one, Ann, slip by. The two separate series of events, one occurring during the first seven months of his stay, the other in the present of the next five months during which he struggles desperately to shake off the obsession of the mournful past, clash in the end. There is no easy triumph, as in Proust, through the enshrining of the past in a work of art which preserves its fragrant essence. Technically, the novel admirably succeeds in the attempt also made by Proust, by Gide in *Les Faux-Monnayeurs*, by Sartre, of inserting a reflection on the novel inside a work of fiction. The remarks on the detective story and its philosophy, on the novel which endeavors to be 'not a simple flat projection of a series of events, but the restitution of their architecture, of their space, for they present themselves diversely according to the position occupied, relatively to them, the detective or the narrator' are only a trifle pedantic. Now and then, the symmetry with which the few events in the plot are contrived borders on artificiality. But the novel is remarkable as a technical feat and as a poetical attempt to suggest in fiction the mysterious substructure of reality instead of portraying the material appearance of things or the psychological atomization of consciousness which an earlier century had stressed.

La Modification (1957), rendered in Britain as *Second Thoughts* and in America as *A Change of Heart*, both clumsy betrayals of the French title, is less rich than *L'Emploi du temps*, but more striking as a successful renewal of the author's manner, and as a paradox sustained through two hundred and thirty pages without artificiality or weariness. The stark simplicity of the theme and the unities of time and place, the stillness in the midst of motion, are arresting. A middle-aged man who represents an Italian typewriter firm in Paris has grown weary of his wife and children. He thinks he has decided to divorce her and to marry his mistress, Cécile, who lives in Rome. He will find a position in Paris for Cécile and he will start a new existence; he meditates on his scheme while traveling overnight on the train from Paris to Rome. He had once met Cécile on a similar train journey and the ride is rich in fond memories and in poetical dreams for him. He observes his fellow passengers or the rain dripping along the windows; he conjures up dim visions of the Grand Veneur in the forest of Fontainebleau, the legendary Master of the Hunt who blew his horn across the glades calling 'Do you hear me?' a portent of the vague remorse about his wife in Paris who has done him no wrong and to whom he is held by more links than he admits to himself. The thought of being divided between Rome and Paris and of the change of direction which he plans to give to his life reminds him of Julian the Apostate, to whom we owe the earliest extant description of ancient Paris, or Lutèce, in Greek: he too is plotting a sort of apostasy, half aware that he lacks the nerve to see it through.

All the while, the traveler expresses his gradual inner change and records his view of the night world perceived from his carriage, not through an interior monologue but through an original device: the second person singular. In an interview given to *Le Figaro littéraire* on December 7, 1957, Butor explained: 'The narrative absolutely had to be told from the point of view of a character . . . I needed an interior monologue beneath the level of the character himself, with a form between the first and the third person. The *vous* allows me to describe the situation of the character and the manner in which language emerges in him.' The drawbacks of the *je* (imprisonment inside the closed consciousness of the narrator) and of the *il* (with its pretense that the narrator could be detached from the observed reality) are thus eschewed. An advantage of the second person singular or plural is moreover that the reader himself feels involved and he, like the narrator-confessor, is under indictment. The device, however, becomes somewhat monotonous and the immobile position of the one actor and reporter of the entire fiction tends to atrophy the book.

But before he reaches Rome, the traveler, after having dreamed of the Italian city and vaguely understood that it was only a myth for him, has suddenly come to terms with his own duplicity. Cécile, associated with the fountains and the monuments and the trattorie of Rome, would prove out of place in Paris; forsaking his wife and children is a more momentous step than his vacillating and timid nature would be ready to take. The meditative businessman, who has watched images of the Roman city pass before his mind's eye for an entire night and morning will finally return to Paris without even seeing his mistress. He consents to his own demise and, a changed man from the lover he had hoped to become, he decides to write his banal adventure without having lived it.

Butor's talent reached its highest point in this eventless book. Critics have glibly used the phrase 'classical tragedy' to describe it, since the novel is encompassed in such narrow limits and contains hardly more action than *Bérénice* or Constant's *Adolphe*. Butor, however, in no way aims at recalling Racinian tragedy or the traditional personal novel of the French. His novel is rather a triumph of elaborate structure and offers original solutions to questions asked by Henry James, Joyce, Proust, and Gide: From what angles and through what devices can reality be studied and made a part of a work of art? Like *Les Faux-Monnayeurs*, with less intellectual self-consciousness and complacency, *La Modification* is a novelist's novel. It is a solidly, almost discouragingly earnest book, ponderously weighed with conjunctions and formulas of reasoning with which the narrator indicates that he is a slow-paced logician rather than a poet. In one of the debates in which Butor generously agreed to define his intentions, the novelist, in his allegiance to Mallarmé, stressed the difference between reading for information and the artistic reading which fiction, like poetry, demands. In the latter, 'the words on the page are but milestones on the path of the reader. Through them, he calls up characters, objects, landscapes in his imagination.' The one grave weakness of *La Modification*, which has aged the book prematurely, is the heavy-handed repetition of adverbs and of explanatory conjunctions and logical formulas. Proust and Faulkner appear like light-winged poets in comparison.[8]

A number of other novelists have, between 1950 and 1967, been more or less loosely grouped with the renovators of the French novel. Some of them have a very minor talent and their publishers attempt to have their volumes ride the wave of favor (with the critics, though hardly with the public at large) which appears to carry the 'new novel' forward: Jean Ricardou, Marc Saporta, Jean Lagrolet. Two others, highly intelligent men in love with difficulty and enigmas, Jean-Pierre Faye and Philippe Sollers, have flown into rarefied air after having, at least in Soller's case, written a story of winning and traditional charm. Marguerite Duras, born in 1914, has won fame through her skillful scenarios and cinematic adaptations of her novels, but is hardly likely to occupy more than a very modest niche in any history of the modern novel; nor will the Swiss author of *L'Inquisitoire* (1962), Robert Pinget, who has far more substance and depth, but strives heroically to confuse and discourage

8. Butor's fourth novel, *Degrés*, considered by this critic as a failure, even as an exercise in the technique of fiction, is omitted from this account as best ignored by readers who wish to do justice to the most cerebral and the most modest of the practitioners of the 'new novel.' For another view of that elaborately experimental book ending in utter tedium, the two warmest American admirers of Butor should be consulted: Léon Roudiez and F. S. Saint-Aubyn. See the bibliographical note at the end of this chapter.

readers. On those and others, summary indications are offered in the appendix to this volume. A strange result of the perverse determination of many recent novelists in France to be systematically esoteric and to discard any desire to entertain, please, or instruct is the conquest of readers' imagination by less ambitious authors, who are less exclusively concerned with technique. On the one hand, esoteric novelists write for each other, for a few critics, and for an audience of professors in America and Japan who await any innovation from France so as to be the first to publish articles on works as yet unrecognized by their timid European colleagues. On the other, the public's fictional imagination remains molded by more superficial and traditional writers who continue to tell a story, to believe in character portrayal, to embrace real events and to blend either autobiography or history with their fiction, and thus to preserve for literature an audience which might flee to television, movies, or sports events: Henri Troyat, Maurice Druon, Louis Aragon, Henri-François Rey, Violette Leduc, J. M. G. Le Clézio.

To the two last of these some attention may well be granted in a survey of the French novel brought up to date in the late nineteen-sixties, for each of them published the most remarkable volumes of the years 1964–65 next to Sartre's *Les Mots*. Violette Leduc's *La Bâtarde* (1965), translated under the same title the same year, was by no means the first book by this already middle-aged woman. It might be called a long *récit* of an autobiographical nature, rather than an imaginary invention of events and attempt to give life to fictitious characters. But it is also stranger than most fiction and far more instinct with life than much straitlaced and strictly controlled novelistic literature recently written by fanatics of technique. Far from calculating hard so as to avoid faults, it multiplies them: especially the lack of concision (Diderot praising Richardson, along with Rousseau, Balzac, Tolstoi, Proust, and not a few American novelists had, after all, taken it for granted that a novel is never too long) and the absence of that restraint which the French call *pudeur*, that 'wrapping of the body by the soul,' in the phrase which Nietzsche admired, and stole from another woman of scant restraint, the mystical Mme Guyon. Still this garrulous confession of an inveterate Lesbian is nowhere designed to titillate the pruriency of readers. It is a work of art as well as a courageous if uninhibited self-revelation.

The story, mixing truth and probably a good deal of *Dichtung*, is that of the first forty years of the author's life. She grew up without her father having acknowledged the daughter whom he had had, somewhere in northern France, by an intelligent but rancorous woman who never show-ered much affection on her daughter. 'I was born the bearer of your mis-fortune as one is born a libation bearer,' she tells her mother at the outset of her story. At school, other girls mocked her as 'la bâtarde.' Moreover she was ugly and aware of it. She felt atrociously alone in the world as a child, when she most needed understanding and consolation. She grew sour, cynical, rebellious, but at the same time she desperately yearned for beauty in music, poetry, nature. She sought the love of other girls and occasionally attracted strangely innocuous males longing for an intel-lectual camaraderie. Intoxicated with literature, profoundly in love with the works of Romains, Gide, Cocteau, and Green, she was not long in discovering that she had an unusual talent herself. Her long narrative is a weird mixture of burning, naïve, lucid, and unadorned sincerity, and of a poetic inner monologue.

Time and again she invokes the reader, her grandmother to whom she was attached, her women friends, in high-flown passages, but in a far less contrived way than in Butor's systematic use of the second person in *La Modification*. She displays her emotions unabashedly, and the public as well as the critics (and her sponsor, Simone de Beauvoir) welcomed such directness, and the analysis of a genuine and coherent character, as a relief from much disembodied, over-technical fiction. She first discovered the raptures of cerebral passion with one of her classmates at school, then with a music teacher who was dismissed when her 'irregular liaison' was discovered. She encountered strange men in Paris, voyeurs, timid but undaunted pursuers, one of whom she eventually married, then di-vorced. She finally met the man whom she was to adore: Maurice Sachs, the author of a brilliant and cynical autobiography, *Le Sabbat*, a Jew and a homosexual, who encouraged her to write. Forced to hide from the Germans when France was occupied, Sachs went to live in a farm in Normandy, close to, but never quite with, the author of *La Bâtarde*, pre-ferring his own sex to that of a romantic Baccha. The episodes of her ac-tivity on the black market, when she walked or bicycled miles to feed herself and the man whom she revered, are among the most vivid por-trayals of some aspects of life during World War II, equal to the best stories of Marcel Aymé. Sachs then chose to serve the Germans in a factory in Hamburg, became suspect to his employers, and was shot by them in the course of a forced march when his captors had to flee the advancing Allies. That pitiful if picturesque wretch lives touchingly in the last chapters of this baroque, flowery, rambling, and gripping *récit*.

In the bright revival of feminine literature since 1945, Violette Leduc occupies a position which is not far from the very top. Almost alone among the authors of fictional memoirs, at a time when the existentialists preferred to reminisce with mournful remorse about the sins they had not committed or the people they had failed to save, Violette Leduc recovered a zestful tone of joy at having lived, and relived her past when transmuting it into semi-biographical fiction. 'I came into the world and swore to have the passion for what is impossible,' she confesses. Perhaps such romanticism is not amiss indeed in the novel, a genre which notwithstanding many a facile assertion, owes far more to the romantic urges of the last century than to that same century's dubious urge to copy and to exalt the bourgeoisie through realism.

Le Clézio is the only one of the French novelists to have reached eminence with three volumes before the age of twenty-six, and to have been born in 1940, after *La Nausée* and also long after *La Condition humaine* had appeared. His father, an Englishman, was a medical officer in Nigeria who retired to Nice; there the boy, whose mother is French, grew up. He studied at the local lycée, wrote an essay or 'diploma' for Aix University on 'Solitude in the Work of Henri Michaux,' spent some time in Bristol and in London between twenty and twenty-one, and dreamed of becoming a painter. He still hopes to complete a thesis on Lautréamont and teach. Of all the newcomers into the gardens and forests of French fiction, he is the one on whom the loftiest hopes are set. His third volume dangerously stressed his mannerisms, but did not betray any flagging of his young powers. His first novel, *Le Procès-verbal* (1963, inaccurately rendered as *The Interrogation*, 1964), having just missed the Goncourt Prize because of timid voting by the Academy, was vindicated at once by the award of the Renaudot Prize, given by more adventurous journalists. Clamorous praise was poured upon the young winner through all the high-powered channels of literary publicity in France; but, judging from interviews which the *Revue de Paris* (May 1966) and *L'Express* (May 9-15, 1966, no. 777) secured from him, Le Clézio has remained modest and wisely reluctant to imitate Robbe-Grillet or Ionesco by evolving a philosophy of literature dismissing the legacy of the past.

There is no plot in this novel and hardly any character study in the traditional sense: the protagonist alternately speaks of himself as 'I' or as 'he.' His long monologue is interspersed with fragments of a diary altogether non-introspective, bits of letters totally unliterary and crude, addressed to a girl with whom he occasionally copulates on the floor or on a billiard table, jerky dialogues, and, in the end, questionings by the staff of a psychiatric hospital. The one anti-hero, Adam Pollo, is a young man of some culture, who has read the mystics and a few philosophers, and probably been fascinated by Antoine Roquentin of *La Nausée* and by Camus's Meursault. He wanders around the parks, the *cafés*, and the beaches of Nice, always meticulously conscious of his body, as characters of Le Clézio will all be: nothing of what takes place in their lungs or their stomachs, or of the aching sensations of an ailing tooth or a migraine headache, escapes them. They walk unweariedly, indifferent to the commonplace life around them, with Byronic haughtiness or rather, like Adam, surveying their earthly abode with wonder and estrangement.

Adam Pollo settles in an abandoned house by the sea, rapes a half-willing girl who subsequently denounces him to the police, murders a white rat with billiard balls, at once sadistic in his systematic destruction and strangely fascinated by his victim. Like a prophet leaving his solitude to indoctrinate men, he delivers long, incoherent speeches to a listless crowd. Picked up by the police and sent to a psychiatric ward, he parries questions skillfully and manages to return to his own visionary's private world. This strange novel, if it carries an unobtrusive message, appears to be an indictment of reality, of psychological science, and of society in general. There are glaring faults of style and even of grammar, displays of pedantry and tricks taken over from the cinema and from detective fiction. But the young author has an uncanny gift of psychological description and a power to move and to obsess readers which has not often been encountered since Camus's *La Chute*.

His second volume, a collection of some long short stories entitled *La Fièvre* (1965; *Fever*, 1966) is even more remarkable and is to date his masterpiece. The nine weird stories, laid in a concrete and placid setting, all revolve around a series of physical or mental accidents: a man harried and anguished by his unbearable toothache, another one a prey to a delirious fever caused by a sunstroke, a third one, abandoned by his wife, endlessly walking, a fourth one a passenger on a train registering all that flits before his eyes. The most moving of all, perhaps the finest story written in French since Sartre's 'Le Mur,' is that of Martin, a hydrocephalic boy of twelve and a genius of erudition and mental powers, tortured by other children as cruel and inhuman as those of *Lord of the Flies*. The humanity portrayed by Le Clézio, and the city where those characters evolve, Nice, the sunniest in France, all seem whirling in a state of vertiginous disintegration. Men and things spiral down irretrievably to a black nothingness, not philosophically analyzed but concretely described. Maddened by physical pain, by isolation, by the overpowering sense of the débacle of the physical world around them, and by the betrayal of those whom they attempted to love, Le Clézio's characters struggle for a while with a haughty irony, then collapse. Unlike the existentialists, they do not assert their will to freedom or acknowledge a responsibility to others. *Le Déluge* (1966) is the most sombre of the author's three volumes. The deluge is one of words which Le Clézio unleashes, words of despair in a man whose girl friend has left him the tape of her last and vain struggle against suicide and who himself welcomes a ghastly death in his turn.

The preposterous claims put forward by critics who have made themselves the heralds of the 'new novel,' encouraged by the publishing firms supporting the newcomers, or by the partisan spirit of one literary circle belittling its rivals, have taken in a portion of the reading public and antagonized an even larger share of it. Almost any method of criticism, if not of publicity, is valid which stirs up discussion around the work of art and helps books be read by those most likely to appreciate them. Unfortunately many of those 'new novels' have been talked about more than actually read and the pedantry and philosophical pomposity of many of their critical advocates have kept naïve readers of good will, but diffident of jargon, at a distance. The argument that Balzac and Proust had been valid for their own times (Stendhal and Zola are seldom mentioned by the new novelists and apparently fail to arouse them) but that they must now be transcended and slightly pitied, constitutes a strange application of the notion of progress to literature. Many vociferous claims to novelty and rejections of the past have ended in being but excursions into blind alleys which have hardly altered the main course of literary evolution, whatever that is; and similar claims that the novel must today radically differ from that of the past on the pretext that society has changed, that the ruling class is no longer the bourgeoisie, that individualism and hence heroes have disappeared from our midst, have rested upon unproved assumptions and then been relegated to ridicule. The will to achieve something new at all costs, proclaimed by Robbe-Grillet and by Nathalie Sarraute (*New York Times Book Review,* April 24, 1966), has more than once sounded puerile to the next generation: the truest revolutions in art have often been accomplished by those who believed they were pursuing the work of their predecessors and who were original without having to proclaim it, or without being aware of it.

In truth, the attempts of the new novelists to link themselves with either phenomenology or new ethics, even with the speculations on language to which philosophy likes to confine itself, have convinced only a small group among the critics and readers.[9] The few solid features common to the recent novelists and to our age can be very briefly summed up.

First, a general conviction that, contrary to the Hegelian assertion that the real and the rational are one and the same, it is utterly impossible to establish an adequate link between our mind and reality. Realism is but a fallacy; it fails to explain the world or to elicit a significance in it. 'If the world signifies anything, it is that it signifies nothing,' peremptorily declares the sovereign portrayer of life as a downward march to a meaningless death in modern fiction, Claude Simon. The void fascinated a number of nineteenth-century minds, Edgar Allan Poe, Baudelaire, and Mallarmé among them. Flaubert repeated his desire to do a book on nothing, without a subject. Edmund de Goncourt claimed in his answer to the inquiry of a journalist, Jules Huret, in 1891, that 'he had done all he could to kill the fictional [le romanesque].' With the novelists of the nineteen-sixties in France, even more than with Joyce, absence, nothingness, the void has been promoted to the role of central elements in fiction as in poetry. The boring done by the worm in the fruit and the holes in gruyère cheese are their most succulent relishes.

The second characteristic is an urge to objectivity. Henry James, André Gide, most of all J.-P. Sartre in his all-too-famous criticism of Mauriac and in his philosophical treatises, have impressed upon our contemporaries the urgency of denouncing bad faith as the supreme adversary. To outwit bad faith, the novelist must not consent to any duplicity; he must not be both inside, and outside, his characters. He renounces introspection which merges subject and object traitorously into one. 'There is no such thing as inner man,' wrote the French exponent of phenomenology, Merleau-Ponty. 'Man is in the world, he knows himself there.' Objectivity will be one of the goals of the new novelist's description. No

9. The most determined and the most talented of those attempts concerns Robbe-Grillet's novel and has been made by a professor at Vassar College, Olga Bernal. Other American professors, John K. Simon for Robbe-Grillet, F. S. Saint-Aubyn for Butor, Léon Roudiez with more discreetness for Butor, and others, have expended conspicuous ingeniousness on efforts to rest the new novel upon a phenomenological basis. See our bibliographical note.

longer will the novelist organize the world around man, lording over everything like an omniscient god.

The tone will rather be that of a gradual discovery, the journey of a man lost in a labyrinth or turning in a circle, pursuing a goal which eludes him or that he is not even aware of. The novelist slowly unveils a plot, borrowing devices from detective fiction—with him, the reader inquires, deciphers, is baffled and in the end must reconstruct by himself some puzzle which the author will not reveal to him. Mallarmé had stated that 'the poem is a mystery, the key of which must be sought by the reader.' The novel likewise demands from the reader that he meet him more than half-way; the pure, ethereal, Flaubertian story becomes an object (Butor is much concerned with physically establishing the book as an object standing by itself) and a thing of beauty, remote and cold, 'pinnacled dim in the inane sublime.'

Finally such a novel, its practitioners and advocates assert, unconcerned with plot and with the creation of coherent characters, banishing fictional invention, implies and translates a certain way which a man has of 'being in the world.' It refuses to explain, to analyze, and, as Flaubert had already warned it, to conclude. Hence its cold atmosphere and the anonymity which it sedulously cultivates. Characters have no surnames, just initials; they talk at inordinate length, caring little to communicate. Isolated and desperately incapable of linking with other men, they passively wander about in their labyrinths.

The resistance to the vogue of the 'new novel' has been vigorous in France, where even academic critics deem it their function to engage in polemics and where writers, young and old, will fight stubbornly for the ideas they hold dear.[10] Mauriac, slightly nettled by the advocacy of new movements and of 'l'alittérature' of his son, Claude, a mediocre novelist himself, stood up for characterization and poetry in fiction, against Nathalie Sarraute and what he terms her polypi of sensations deprived of any support or substance. Against her conventions or those of Robbe-Grillet, he maintains his own, time-proved, one. 'What if the only element worthy of surviving in the memory of mankind were those confused motions of sensibility, which are recreated according to an idea they

10. In English-speaking countries, the sanest essay on the subject, diffident of many of the publicity claims of French writers, appeared in an excellent Australian periodical, *Essays in French Literature* (Nedlands, Western Australia), I, ii, November 1965, pp. 1–14, 'Le "nouveau roman" in France.' The author, J. M. Cocking, is professor at the University of London.

entertain of man's destiny? Why should there be fictional truth only at the lowest level, and indeed the most hypothetical one?' Simone de Beauvoir, probably supported by Sartre, who had been responsible for launching Nathalie Sarraute's anti-novel, took issue with her books in a bitterly acrimonious tone in *La Force des choses* (1963, pp. 648–49). She denounced, in the dehumanizing conventions of the new novel, an even more radical expulsion of man than in the old naturalist fiction. More passionately still, she vituperated against novels like *Le Planetarium* and *Les Fruits d'or* in which 'the paranoiac attitude of the petty bourgeoisie is minutely studied as if it constituted the immutable nature of man . . . The world of enterprises and struggles, of need, of work, the real world vanishes away . . . One of the constants of that literature is boredom: it takes away from life its salt, its fire, its *élan* toward the future.' Among the critics proper, Pierre-Henri Simon in *Le Monde*, Jean Bloch-Michel in a slim volume, *Le Présent de l'indicatif* (1963), J. B. Barrère in a brochure deriding *La Cure d'amaigrissement du roman* (1964), Pierre de Boisdeffre, Françoise Mallet-Joris, several others have in various ways deplored the obstinacy of the new novelists to imprison themselves in an ascetic stylization and in a voluntary diet of poverty that betrays an absence, or a terror of, imagination. Françoise Mallet-Joris, who received in 1964 the Grand Prix littéraire of Monaco and herself then hardly thirty-five years old, declared, for those reasons, the new novel already dated and pronounced it a timid escapism voluntarily cut off from life.

The apparent concern of many novelists today to call in question literature in general, language itself, and fiction, which, they insist, has at last come of age and must 'contest itself' at every step, entails a serious consequence: the literary genre which had for centuries been fortunate in not being theorized upon and ruled over by critics has now become their favorite hunting-ground. The novelists, like the tragic writers of old who dug the grave of tragedy, and not unlike a number of modern poets who wonder anxiously what is the essence of poetry, have now become the master theorists of modern letters. A century ago or a little more (on February 28, 1860), Sainte-Beuve had not unwisely given to Champfleury, who had asked him to collaborate in a review devoted to fiction, a warning which we believe to be still timely:

> The novel is a vast field for experiment which is opening up to all forms of genius, to all manners of writing. It is the epic of the future, probably the only one which modern times can have. Let us not shrink it. Let us not make the theory of it overmuch, let us not or-

ganize it. Let each novelist on occasion express his own views, to be
sure. But let us never, on account of manifestoes and apologies, lose
one single good novel which the author might meanwhile compose!

The team of novelists which had claimed to eliminate philosophy and
ideas, anthropomorphism and sentiment, imaginative and emotional style
from the novel has in effect, with Simon and Butor, reintegrated many of
those elements into fiction under another guise. Or, as in the case of
Robbe-Grillet, Claude Ollier, and Robert Pinget, it has impoverished that
literary form to the point of stripping it of all psychological and sensuous
appeal. To make literature thus simple in an increasingly complex world
may be worthwhile as a health cure or as a purge, provided new authors
follow those austere geometricians and theorizers and undertake once
again, starting from a new basis, to make life more significant and richer.
The assumption of much that has preceded, in the present volume, was
that the novel, of all literary genres, is liable to lose most grievously if it
abdicates that function which makes it a mirror to the manners, the
moods, the social and political history, and the individual and collective
passions of the people. Technical innovations seldom survive or matter
unless they reflect for the people concerned a deeper change in the vision
and in the way of apprehending reality. Interior monologues, kaleido-
scopic action as presented by John Dos Passos and Sartre, dissolution of
objects into an effulgent halo as in Virginia Woolf, abrupt dialogues un-
encumbered with any sense of the past as in Hemingway, ironical allusions as in Giraudoux: these and other technical innovations have seldom
proved of lasting value in fiction. Criticism of fiction ages fastest in proportion to its pedantry and to its pseudo-scientific ponderousness. Not
many novelists and even fewer lovers of novels would disagree with the
following typical answer made by an expert craftsman of fiction, Louis
Guilloux, to an interviewer in *Les Nouvelles littéraires* of December 21,
1935:

> There is no technique of the novel properly speaking. There is a
> technique appropriate to each novel and it is not transmissible. The
> novelist must incessantly invent his technique, and this means that
> the work he has just completed teaches him, as a rule, very little
> about the way in which he will write the next. The novelist is a man
> who is obsessed: What are the means of making the objects of his
> obsessions visible? . . . If there existed a technique of fiction, the
> writing of novels could be taught.

The American novelist and critic, Robert Penn Warren, was even more outspoken when, to the *Paris Review* questioners, he equated the phrase 'experimental writing' with 'an élite word for flop.' Another English-speaking teller of tales, Frank O'Connor, after having faced the academics of a great American university, all engrossed by the analysis of technique as a key to the secret of the novelist's art, rose at last exasperated to conclude: 'I'd like the students to remember that writing is fun.' Indeed, few things appear more naïve today than the technical experiments so diligently devised by the authors of *Point Counterpoint, Les Hommes de bonne volonté, Le Sursis,* and *Degrés.* A regrettable development in French (and other European) fiction since 1940 is that its range has shrunk; spiritual, ethical, and social conflict do not appear to attract its authors, and the most creative minds choose, even in the realm of literature, other pursuits.

No explanation for the temporary weakening of the French novel in the seventh decade of the twentieth century need be sought in economic or political causes underlying it, and still less in the effects of a moral censorship, which, in fact, if it has made some absurd mistakes when public morality was deemed to be at stake or when the Chief of State could feel insulted, has not frightened away or stifled any literary talents. Immediately after World War II, the intellectual élite of the country did harbor a complex of guilt about its own partial collapse and that of the managerial classes in France in 1940. The words of Renan assessing, after 1871, the reasons for his country's demise, were then quoted approvingly by some austere diagnosticians of their land: 'In the struggle which has just taken place, France's inferiority was mainly intellectual: the head, and not the heart, is what proved deficient in us.' It seemed then, between 1945 and 1955, that the French would never emerge from the instability of party rule, the weakness of their executive, their chronic deficit and corroding inflation, their inability to reform education at home and to put an end to colonization abroad. Literature, with its favorite themes of anxiety, disquietude, self-incrimination, 'nostalgia for the mud,' from Sartre's *Nausée* to Beckett's 'Fin de Partie' was pronounced to be the corollary to the woeful decline of the country's *élan vital.* Erudite debates then took place among political scientists and historians of the United States, Switzerland, and Britain to assess the extent of that lack of will and of self-reliance.

A quarter of a century after World War II, the French intellectuals are, if anything, even more disillusioned with their government and, half-heartedly, they claim to belong to a political opposition whose platform and aims are undefined and perhaps undefinable. But the country is astonished to have enjoyed years of stability, of financial security, to find itself heeded and even feared in the councils of the world, spending itself rich, rid of its colonial worries, and with a bourgeoisie more self-assured in its triumph and in its enjoyment of the welfare state than it had been under Louis-Philippe, convinced that whole layers of the former prole-tariat are being won over to 'embourgeoisement' every year. The old nightmare of terror of a Germany twice as populated as France has vanished. The loss of nerve of a middle class, which used to look up to the Fascist state and in some cases to the much publicized strength through joy of the Germans and which, earlier, had hailed books on the reasons for Anglo-Saxon superiority has, after 1960, changed to some condescension to France's neighbors and partners. The faith of the French in the future of their growing population, of their rebuilt cities, of their decentralized cultural life is probably more ardent than it has been since the Consulate, or at least since the Second Empire. The 'capitalist anar-chy' branded by Marx, the unrestricted monopolies, the pauperization of the proletariat have been drastically remedied since 1936 or 1945, mostly through the lessons learned from Communists and socialists in other lands. The revolutionary left has been deprived of its slogans. The intel-lectuals and the scientists have lost, with the liberation of Algeria, their last idealistic cause, recalling the 1848 moves to free Poland or the South Slavs.

The novel, however, refuses to give a voice to such prosperity and complacency. It dreams of erecting a structure immune to the turbulence of life, geometrically contrived and hygenically odorless, as untouched by the contingencies of the misery in Asia and of the atomic age elsewhere as Mallarmé's 'Hérodiade' and Valéry's 'Jeune Parque' once were. The spirit of fraternity and of crusading salvation for mankind through litera-ture, which Malraux and Camus vibrantly expressed, has not died. But its flame burns today behind a veil of irony and of artistic detachment. Much harm has been done in our century by literature which set itself at the service of a cause, and by the evil use to which fanatics put elo-quence and emotional appeal. If a generation of novelists cultivates de-tachment, gently cynical lucidity, and single-minded devotion to its art for a number of years to come, in a mood which evokes that of Flaubert and Gautier disillusioned by the victory of the middle class after 1852, the lasting spirit of French literature remains that which was voiced by Saint-Exupéry, Malraux, Giono, Bernanos, Sartre, and other writers who have been discussed in this volume. Camus puts it unforgettably when he declared: 'To live is not to be resigned,' and ended *La Peste* nobly: 'We refuse to despair of men.'

Bibliographical Notes

Gide's essay on what English literature had meant for him appeared in *Verve*, I, No. 2, Spring 1938.

On American influence on the recent novel in France, see note 2, p. 350.

On the comic novel, see Dorothy Brodin, *The Comic World of Marcel Aymé* (Debresse, 1964); Andrée Bergens, *Raymond Queneau* (Geneva: Droz), 1963; David Noakes, *Boris Vian* (Editions Universitaires, 1964); *Les Vies parallèles de Boris Vian* in *Bizarre*, nos. 39–40, February 1966.

On the fantastic and visionary novel, Pierre-Georges Castex, *Le Conte fantastique en France de Nodier à Maupaussant* (José Corti, 1951); Marcel Schneider, *La Littérature fantastique en France* (Fayard, 1964); notices on Noël Delvaux and André Pieyre de Mandiargues in *Contes et Nouvelles d'aujourd'hui* (Harper and Row, 1966); articles on Pieyre de Mandiargues by Mark Temmer, *Yale French Studies*, No. 31, 1963, 99–104, and by Stirling Haig, *The French Review*, XXXIX, No. 2, November 1965, 275–280. André Breton's *Nadja*, Gallimard, 1928, was translated by Richard Howard and published at the Grove Press in 1960. On Aragon's novels, consult Yvette Gandine, *Aragon prosateur surréaliste* (Geneva: Droz, 1966).

On Nathalie Sarraute, Yvon Belaval, *Nouvelle Revue Française*, VI, No. 62, February 1958, 335–37 (on *Tropismes*); Claude Mauriac, *Le Figaro*, May 27, 1959 (on *Le Planetarium*); Anne Minor, *The French Review*, XXXIII, No. 2, December 1959, 107–115; Gaëtan Picon, in *L'Usage de la Lecture*, *Mercure de France*, Vol. 2, 1963; Bernard Pingaud, 'Le Personnage dans l'œuvre de Nathalie Sarraute,' *Preuves*, No. 154, December 1963, 19–34; Helen Watson-Williams, 'Etude du Planetarium,' University of Western Australia, *Studies in French Literature*, I, i, November 1964; Gerda Zeltner, 'Nathalie Sarraute et l'impossible réalisme,' *Mercure de France*, No. 1188, August 1962, 593–608.

Robbe-Grillet has been a favorite novelist with ingenious critics who have taken his mechanisms to pieces with great gusto and treated his theoretical paradoxes with much earnestness. Among them, the following stand out: Didier Anzieu, 'Le Discours de l'obsessionnel dans les romans de Robbe-Grillet,' *Les Temps modernes*, No. 233, October 1965, 608–637; Roland

Barthes, in *Critique*, Nos. 86–7, July–August 1954, 581–91; Olga Bernal, *Alain Robbe-Grillet: le roman de l'absence.* Gallimard, 1964; Maurice Blanchot, 'Notes sur *Le Voyeur*,' *Nouvelle Revue Française*, July 1955, iii, 31, 105–112; Germaine Brée, 'New Blinds for Old,' *Yale French Studies*, No. 24, Summer 1959, 87–90; Bernard Dort, in *Les Temps modernes*, June 1957, 198–9; Melvin Friedman, 'The Neglect of Time,' *Books Abroad*, Vol. 36, Spring 1962, 125–30; Gérard Génette, in *Tel Quel*, No. 8, Winter 1962, 34–44; Bruce Morrissette, *Les Romans de Robbe-Grillet.* Editions de Minuit, 1963, and several articles in *Critique*, No. 146, July 1959, 579–608; *Saggi e Ricerche di letterature francese*, Milan, 1961, 267–298; *Evergreen Review*, III, No. 10, November–December 1959, 103–190; Maurice Nadeau, 'Le Nouveau roman,' *Critique*, August-September 1957, 123–124, 707–722; Roy Jay Nelson, 'Vers une esthétique de l'absurde,' *The French Review*, XXXVII, 3, February 1964, 400–410; Dominique Penot, 'Psychology of the Characters in La Jalousie,' *Books Abroad*, Vol. 40, Winter 1966, 5–16; Jean Ricardou, 'Description et infraconscience chez Robbe-Grillet,' *Nouvelle Revue Française*, November 1960, 890–900; Ben F. Stoltzfus, *Alain Robbe-Grillet and the New French Novel.* Southern Illinois University Press, 1964; J. C. Weightman, 'Robbe-Grillet' in *Encounter*, XVIII, 3, March 1962, 30–40 (reprinted in *The Novelist as Philosopher*, edited by John Cruickshank, Oxford University Press, 1962).

On Claude Simon, interviews in *L'Express*, November 10, 1960, and January 12, 1961; Michel Deguy, on *Le Palace*, *Critique*, No. 187, December 1962, 1009–1032; Edouard Morot-Sir, *Bulletin de la Société des Professeurs français* (New York), 1962, 5–8; Jean Ricardou, on *La Route des Flandres*, *Critique*, No. 163, December 1960, 1011–1024; Bernard Pingaud, 'Sur *La Route des Flandres*,' *Les Temps modernes*, Vol. XVI, No. 178 (February 1961), 1026–1027; Léon Roudiez, 'Claude Simon,' *The French Review*, Vol. XXXIV, No. 6 (May 1961), 593–594.

On Michel Butor, R. M. Albérès, *Butor.* Editions Universitaires, 1964; Pierre Deguise, 'Butor et le nouveau roman,' *The French Review*, XXXV, No. 2, December 1961, 155–162; Marius Guyard, 'Butor,' *Etudes*, CCXCVIII, September 1958, 227–237; Michel Leiris, 'Le Réalisme mythologique de Butor,' *Critique*, No. 129, February 1958, 99–118; Monique Nathan, 'Un Roman expérimental: *L'Emploi du Temps*,' *Critique*, No. 116, January 1957, 17–21; Jean Pouillon, 'A propos de *La Modification*,' *Les Temps Modernes*, Vol. XIII, No. 142, December 1957, 1099–1105; Jean Roudaut, 'Butor, ou le livre futur,' Gallimard, 1964, and his article in *Critique*, No. 158, July 1960, 579–590; Léon Roudiez, *M. Butor.* Columbia University Press, 1965; Frederick St. Aubyn, 'Butor and Phenomenological Realism,' *Studi Francesi*, No. 16, 1962, 51–62, and 'Entretien avec Butor,' *The French Review*, XXXVI, No. 1, October 1962, 12–22.

On the 'new novel,' the following items will be useful: Anon., 'The Philosophy of the New Novel,' *Times Literary Supplement* (London), May 4, 1962;

Georges Blin, Pierre-Henri Simon *et al.*, 'Formalisme et Signification,' *Cahiers internationaux du Symbolisme*. Havié-les-Mons, Belgium, 1966; R. M. Albérès, 'Aux sources du nouveau roman,' *Revue de Paris*, March 1962, 74–86; J. B. Barrère, *La Cure d'amaigrissement du roman*. Albin Michel, 1964; Pierre de Boisdeffre, 'Où va le roman?' *La Table ronde*, No. 164, September 1961, 15–27; Jean Bloch-Michel, *Le Présent de l'indicatif, Essai sur le nouveau roman*. Gallimard, 1963; Germaine Brée, 'The New Novelists of France,' *Meanjin Quarterly* (Melbourne), XXII, No. 94, 1963, 169–278; J. M. Cocking, 'The "nouveau roman" in France,' *Essays in French Literature* (University of Western Australia, Nedlands), I, ii, November 1965, 1–14; Bernard Dort, 'A la recherche du roman,' *Cahiers du Sud*, No. 334, April 1956, 347–64; Jean-Pierre Faye, 'Surprise pour l'anti-roman,' *Les Lettres Nouvelles*, March–April 1965, 5–27; *Esprit*, special number with a rich variety of articles, the essential document on the subject, July–August 1958; Alfred Fontenilles, 'Reflections on the New Novel,' *The Colorado Quarterly*, XII, No. 2, Autumn 1963, 165–176; Michel Foucault, 'Distance, aspect, origine,' *Critique*, No. 198, November 1963, 931–45; 'Débat sur le roman' (with J. P. Faye, Claude Ollier *et al.*), *Tel Quel*, No. 17, Spring 1964; Matthieu Galey, 'Vie et mort du nouveau roman,' *Revue de Paris*, September 1963, 122–127; W. J. Harvey, *Character and the Novel*. London: Chatto and Windus, 1965; Jacques Howlett, 'Thèmes et tendances d'avant-garde dans le roman d'aujourd'hui,' *Les Lettres Nouvelles*, February 1963, 139–149; Ludovic Janvier, *Une Parole exigeante*. Editions de Minuit, 1964; Henri Lemaître, 'On demande des créateurs,' *La Table ronde*, No. 169, February 1962, 31–38; Laurent Lesage, *The French New Novel; An Introduction and a Sampler*. Philadelphia: Pennsylvania State University Press, 1962; J. H. Matthews *et al.*, *Un Nouveau Roman? Recherches et traditions, Revue des Lettres Modernes*, 1964; Bruce Morrissette, 'Narrative "You" in Contemporary Literature,' *Comparative Literature Studies* (University of Maryland), II, i, 1965; Léon Roudiez, 'Character and Personality: the Novelist's Dilemma,' *The French Review*, XXXV, No. 6, May 1962, 553–62; Philippe Sénart, 'Jalons pour le nouveau roman,' *La Table ronde*, No. 169, February 1962, 105–111; John K. Simon, 'Perception and Metaphor in the New Novel,' *Tri-Quarterly* (Evanston, Illinois), 4, 1966, 153–182; Philippe Sollers, 'Le Roman et l'expérience des limites,' *Tel Quel*, No. 25, Spring 1966, 20–34.

Panorama of Present-Day Novelists

The reader will find grouped in this appendix, in alphabetical order, the names of French novelists who have been conspicuously successful or promising since 1940 or thereabouts and are likely to be the authors of significance through the nineteen-sixties and 'seventies. Succinct information about their works and a candid and summary judgment of their merits, as they appear to us, are presented in each case.*

Abellio, Raymond (b. 1907). The author who writes under this pseudonym started his career after World War II, after varied and stormy experiences that compromised him into collaboration with the Germans and landed him in exile in Switzerland. There was a great deal of publicity about his position and the strangeness of his books, which are full of political digressions and mystical interpretations of the Old Testament. They can be called 'novels' only through a painful stretch of the mind or of the definition of a novel. *Heureux les pacifiques* (Le Portulan, 1946) is a tortuous intellectual auto-biography of a man who, between 1934 and 1944, embraced, successively, opposite parties, as well as several women. *Les Yeux d'Ezéchiel sont ouverts* (Gallimard, 1950) is an even more disorderly and pretentious book. The main events, violently dramatic, take place in December 1945 and are told with undeniable vividness. An undercurrent of prophetic mysticism runs through the book. A Spanish priest, whom the protagonist had helped during the Spanish civil war, repays him with endless prophecies supposedly interpreting the Bible. (Abellio is also the author of *La Bible document chiffré*.) The gist of it all is that murder, evil, and bloodshed are a prerequisite for our salvation and that a chosen band of a few superior persons, depositories of spiritual energy and technocratic secrets, will alone save a world sunk deep in evil. The author writes with occasional power. He may some day either become a literary figure of note or end in an orgy of unreason.

Aragon, Louis (b. 1897). Became best known as a poet during and after World War II, but is most likely to go down to posterity as a virtuoso master of prose and as a novelist. *Le Paysan de Paris* (1926), following two youthful autobiographical *récits*, is an excursion into the marvels of everyday life in

* Here and in the following section, the place of publication of the original books is Paris unless otherwise specified, and of the English translations New York.

398

Paris and a projection of the author's self. *Les Cloches de Bâle* (1934) and *Les Beaux Quartiers* (1936) are more ambitious in their creation of character and portrayal of a symbolic reality. After *Les Voyageurs de l'impériale*, published during the war years (1942), Aragon wrote another long and meandering novel of tender love and of prolonged adolescence, *Aurélien* (1944). He received more praise for his picaresque historical reconstruction of the Hundred Days of 1815, superficial, colorful, verbose (1958). The last and most ambitious fictional attempt of that inveterate sentimentalist was *La Mise à mort* (1965), the flamboyant and symbolic tale of a writer who becomes jealous of the character whom he created and whom he must kill in the end. A small volume by Pierre de Lescure, *Aragon romancier* (Gallimard, 1960), and a thesis by Yvette Gindine, *Aragon prosateur surréaliste* (Droz, 1966), have studied the beginnings of Aragon's career as a novelist. His extraordinary facility has led him more than once into sentimentality and formlessness.

Arland, Marcel (b. 1899), cut a figure among the young men who, soon after World War I, turned against their elders and proclaimed themselves the generation of anxiety afflicted by a new *mal du siècle*. He won the Goncourt Prize with his long chronicle of a generation, *L'Ordre*, in 1929. He then became a critic of note, a subtle appraiser of contemporary fiction for the *Nouvelle Revue Française*, which he directed, and a restrained and delicate storyteller. He made a second entry into imaginative literature in 1965 with *Le Grand Pardon*, an organized and stately procession of twenty serious stories of provincial France, stressing the grief and the omnipresence of death consecrating humble lives. Those tales, like chapters of a disconnected fictional ensemble, have a melancholy unity of tone and are among the few French works of imagination of these years which evince real sympathetic insight into the lives of peasants.

Aymé, Marcel (b. 1902), has scored some triumphs on the stage since 1945. He composed some excellent short stories during World War II (*Le Passe-muraille*, Gallimard, 1945) and a bitter satire of the mores of a small town during the years of German occupation, in which Aymé's political distrust of enthusiasm and of reforming impulses is translated into boisterous comedy in *Uranus* (Gallimard, 1948; *The Barkeep of Blemont*, Harper and Brothers, 1950). *Le Confort intellectuel* (Flammarion, 1949) is ponderous, and its characters are papery puppets, mocking the literary vogues of the day. His best work since 1939 is, in our opinion, *La Belle Image* (Gallimard, 1941; *The Second Face*, Harper and Brothers, 1952), whose fantasy and use of the supernatural win the reader's admiration. But, as is often the case in such tales, credibility is smoothly achieved in the first hundred pages but not long sustained. The claims of some of his admirers, who see in Marcel Aymé an unacknowledged genius, seem to us unfounded. He approaches power, but somehow, in his novels at least, he misses it, and he does not reject facile or cheap effects. The word genius, which has been glibly used by some of his American admirers since 1950, seems a strange aberration. The translation of his Rabelaisian story, *La Jument verte* (1933; *The Green Mare*, Athenaeum, 1963), added little to his fame in English-speaking countries. A good study, *The Comic World of Marcel Aymé* by Dorothy Brodin (Debresse, 1964), stressed the human kindness behind his humor rather than his occasional savage cruelty.

Badiou, Alain (b. 1936), a *Normalien* and a teacher of philosophy, poured allegories, linguistic experiments, geometric and musical speculations, and much else into an unwieldy first book, *Almagestes* (Seuil, 1964), which he prefers to call 'an experience in thinking' rather than a novel. He impressed a small coterie and he may some day write a less pretentious and less juvenile work.

Bastide, François-Régis (b. 1926), whose training was in music and who has lived in Germany and Sweden, won a prize for his critical work on *Saint-Simon* in 1955 and the Prix Femina in 1956 for his novel *Les Adieux* (Gallimard). It is a melancholy and not very eventful story of a Swedish girl who came to Paris to teach and study languages and of a Russian émigré who kills himself after having deceived her, and all his acquaintances, through his charlatanry. A skillful, humorous but unconvincing novel.

Bazin, Hervé (b. 1918), made a resounding entry into the literary world with *Vipère au poing* (Grasset, 1948; *Viper in the Fist,* Prentice-Hall, 1951), then with *La Tête contre les murs* (Grasset, 1949; *Head Against the Wall,* Prentice-Hall, 1952), *La Mort du petit cheval* (Grasset, 1950), and *Lève-toi et marche* (Grasset, 1952; *Constance,* Crown Publishers, 1955). His success was due in part to his being the scion of a very conservative family from western France, nurtured in the strictest Catholic traditions, who revolted against his class and exploited a relatively untouched subject, the hatred of one's mother. But the literary merits of the young writer were obvious: he had a lively style, handled cruelty and sarcasm with elegance, and did not fall in with the vogue of philosophical anguish or of ponderous self-pity. He told a bitter story and sketched characters or caricatures mercilessly. His second book was hardly a novel, and it shunned emotion and even naturalness to the point of artificiality. It was a pamphlet against French mental hospitals, close to journalistic reporting. *La Mort du petit cheval* followed and turned out to be a better book, full of dash and of calculated nonchalance, on the subject of family hatreds and of son against mother—a subject that began to wear thin however. Bazin, who has been hitherto a French equivalent to Evelyn Waugh or an acrid successor to Jules Renard, changed his tune in *Lève-toi et marche*. The heroine is a paralytic young woman whose family has been killed in a bombardment. She frets against her enforced idleness and her worsening malady, and she tries to help friends and neighbors. But her own bitterness and the venom that rankles under her impulse toward goodness bring about woeful results. The total impact of the book is uncertain, but the intelligence, the gift of vivid characterization, and the stylistic verve of the author are beyond doubt. He may become an important novelist. *L'Huile sur le feu* (Grasset, 1954) contains some of the best writing of Hervé Bazin. It is less voluntary and strained, less consistently hostile to all feelings of family affection than his earlier books. The strange character of the father, a wounded veteran of the war, cruelly treated by his wife and admired by his daughter, who turns into a maniacal arsonist and ends in suicide amid the fire that he has lighted, is skillfully delineated. The daughter is the first convincing woman in Hervé Bazin's fiction; and the tone of the book is more natural. *Qui J'ose aimer* (Grasset, 1956; *A Tribe of Women*, Simon and Schuster, 1958) showed a change of manner, but a loss of originality. Once again, a contemptible male who has seduced his own step-daughter fails to rise to the stature of an energetic criminal and is expelled by women stronger than he is. *Plumons l'oiseau* (Grasset, 1966) attempted, not very brilliantly, to restore farcical humor into fiction.

Beck, Béatrix (b. 1914), has written two novels (*Barny*, Gallimard, 1950, and *Une Mort irrégulière*, Gallimard, 1951) superior in many respects to her winner of the Goncourt Prize of 1952, *Léon Morin, prêtre* (Gallimard, 1952). The author was the daughter of one of Gide's friends, had served as the secretary of the aging writer, and learned from him how to prune and omit, and even how to banish sentiment and rhetoric. *Barny* is one of the very few good, imaginary autobiographies of a little girl. Her second novel told of the early days of the war and of the suicide of her Jewish husband, who was serving in the Foreign Legion. *Léon Morin, prêtre* is the sketch of a city occupied by the Germans and a description of the increasing attraction of religious faith for the heroine. Not Christ, however, but a handsome, courageous, at times slightly vulgar priest, Léon Morin, is the conqueror of Barny's atheism. The priest, sensing the peril of that violent and rebellious convert, who is more than half in love with him, is transferred elsewhere. Béatrix Beck, a rather arid and strained storyteller, strangely lacks the tenderness and the poetry commonly associated with feminine literature. She does not seem to us destined to a much higher fame than she has now achieved. Her next volume, *Des Accommodements avec le ciel*, published in the *Revue de Paris* in July and August 1954, shows no renewal of her manner and no deepening of her talent.

Beckett, Samuel (b. 1906), an Irishman, has become a French writer, like Julien Green and the Hungarian Dormandi. He sprang to glory with *Molloy* (Editions de Minuit, 1951), which attracted readers to his earlier *Murphy* (Bordas, 1947) and to *Malone meurt* (Editions de Minuit, 1951). Beckett's play, *En attendant Godot*, which is remarkable, was a signal success in the spring of 1953. While he is very much of an Irishman and deeply influenced by Joyce (as well as by Kafka), Beckett 'belongs' to the French literary climate: his themes are the total absurdity of everything, the worthlessness of love, of life, and especially of literature and language, ludicrously vain representations of a meaningless world. Humor abounds, but it is bitter and 'black.'

Molloy is an epic of nothingness about a sick man, whose memory has been destroyed and who rides on a bicycle to visit his dying mother. He will never reach his goal, like Kafka's surveyor. He gets lost in a forest, falls into a ditch, and stays there, mumbling to himself. Meanwhile, a man and his son have been asked to go after Molloy, of whom they had never heard. Both become afflicted by paralysis, are separated, involved in a murder, and reduced to the lowest level of degradation. The voluntary obscurity of the novel has spurred commentators to ingenious exegeses. The underlying assertion, if one may use such a term for a literature of total negation, seems to be that everything and everybody is in a state of disintegration and that yielding to some abject nirvana is perhaps the only relief from anguish and absurdity that man can seek. *L'Innommable* (Editions de Minuit, 1953; *The Unnameable*, Grove Press, 1958) not only provides a key to Beckett's other work but must rank as his greatest novel: it is one of the starkest expressions of the yearning for utter sincerity in silence and ultimately in death in the whole range of literature. What the hero or anti-hero fails to realize is that there is anything to know. *Comment c'est* (Editions de Minuit, 1961; *How Is It?* London: John Calder; New York: Grove Press, 1964) drives the dismal conclusion even more rigidly to its desolate logic. The difficulty of interpreting Beckett's novels and the sense of superiority in those who succeed in elucidating (or in obscuring) them have stimulated several gifted American critics to write important monographs on Beckett: Hugh Kenner (1961), Ruby Cohn (1962), Josephine Jacobsen and William Mueller (1964), Raymond Federman (1965). He will soon be, next to Camus, the most prolifically commented on writer of his generation.

Berger, Yves (b. 1933), scored a success in 1962 with a novel, *Le Sud* (Grasset), which was soon translated into English (as *The Garden*, Braziller, 1963) after being awarded the Prix Femina. It is the impossible tale of a landowner in southern France who, disgusted with the modern world, builds up a world of make-believe in which he forces his daughter and his son to live. They both grow up in an atmosphere of 'Sud,' that is, of the American South carried into Provence. The daughter, suitably called Virginie, attempts, through initiating him to love and other means of tender persuasion, to educate her brother out of that American fantasy. But the boy, somewhat like Alain-Fournier's hero, refuses to become reconciled to adult existence.

Bertin, Célia (b. 1921), is one of the most steadfast and imaginative builders of a plot and creators of dramatic tension among present-day women novelists. She does not balk at crude language and at stories of free exchange of partners by persons of her sex. *Contre-champ* (Plon, 1954) was confused and did not escape dullness. *La Dernière Innocence* (Corrêa, 1953; *Last Innocence*, London: Gollancz, 1955) has a well woven plot: in the South of France, where most of Mme Bertin's stories take place, a love affair develops between the daughter of the hostess and the latter's brother-in-law. But through it the sham of her mother, who devoted her widowhood to the cult of her husband, a painter, is exploded. Her writing often reminds one of English women novelists such as Elizabeth Bowen. *Une Femme heureuse* (Corrêa, 1955) attempted a loftier theme: the universal responsibility of human beings in the presence of suffering. The 'happy' heroine is one who resigned herself not to be happy and found grave consolation therein.

Blanchot, Maurice (b. 1907), one of the three or four acute critics in France today, is also the author of several difficult works of fiction, in which a few philosophical readers see one of the deepest symbolic portrayals of our age. One cannot summarize Blanchot's novels, for in them he unequivocally rejects imitation of life and reality; he rejects all that is not ambiguous and allegorical. The themes that obsess Blanchot, as novelist as well as critic, are the loneliness of man, the even greater solitude of the artist who must communicate through language and begin by making language over again so that it will be authentic, and death, which is the beginning and the end of all meditation for Blanchot. The conditions of his creation force a rarefied and unreal atmosphere upon the novelist, as in *L'Arrêt de mort* (Gallimard, 1948), where 'death pauses,' somewhat as in the myth of Orpheus. There are monotonous, yet inevitable, repetitions in the novel. The name Kafka has often been heard in connection with Blanchot, but he is in truth far closer to a Mallarmé who might have translated into fictional form his aspiration toward silence, his denial of gods, and his weird fantasy. *Thomas l'obscur* (Gallimard, 1941) is the most accessible of Blanchot's novels, *Le Très-Haut* (Gallimard, 1948) the most esoteric, and *Aminadab* (Gallimard, 1942) probably the least successful. Blanchot is not a critic or a philosopher who has turned novelist. Fiction is to him the fittest means of expression, or rather of the dissolution into an imaginary form, of all the details that normally obstruct our perception. He will never be read by more than a few, but those few prize his gifts of imagination and style as singularly original. See the essay on him by Geoffrey Hartman in *The Novelist as Philosopher* (ed. John Cruickshank), Oxford University Press, 1962.

Blanzat, Jean (b. 1906), showed a delicate sense for the suggestion of silence in nature and in human beings, of discreet love in the valley of a small river, the Gartempe, in western France, during the years of World War II: *La Gartempe* (Gallimard, 1957). *Le Faussaire*, in 1964, marked a change in his inspiration which won him the Prix Femina: the dead came back for a day among the living, worked havoc in their safely rebuilt lives and the visionary atmosphere, usually more easily suggested in poetry than in fiction, was touchingly evoked. *L'Iguane* (Gallimard, 1966) was another venture into the supernatural, but so disconnected in the narrative, so stilted as prose as to disappoint those who had hailed Blanzat as an arresting novelist.

Bloch-Michel, Jean (b. 1912), wrote a concise analysis of the bad conscience of a young man who, having acted twice like a coward, cannot silence his belated scruples, an approximation to a more analytical *Lord Jim*. He relates his own failures unflinchingly and becomes his own witness. After this first and very effective *récit*, entitled *Le Témoin* (Gallimard, 1949; *The Witness*, Pantheon Books, 1949), and a colorless collection of essays (*Les Grandes Circonstances*, 1949), the author's second novel, about a family carried away in the debacle, *La Fuite en Egypte* (Gallimard, 1952), fails to do justice to the great themes which the exodus of 1940 and the gradual attraction of the underground should have offered to French novelists. The tone is too monotonous and stylized (*The Flight into Egypt*, Scribner's, 1955).

Blondin, Antoine (b. 1922), published five novels between 1949 and 1963 and many articles: the second one *Les Enfants du Bon Dieu* (La Table ronde, 1952) brought him a measure of fame and *Un Singe en hiver* (La Table ronde, 1959; *A Monkey in Winter*, Putnam's, 1960) sold widely in spite of a gloomy theme: the search for fraternity and understanding on the part of an alcoholic. The humor and the picaresque liveliness of this book offset the dismal picture of a joyless addiction.

Boisdeffre, Pierre de (b. 1926), an impetuous young critic, attempted the novel of collaboration (a theme that is likely to be long exploited) with *Les Fins dernières* (La Table ronde, 1952). His hero has been sentenced for siding with the enemy and relates everything retrospectively before his imminent execution. He blames the society that has made him what he is (he came from a family of officers, worshipped Maurras, and so forth) as much as himself. The book is thin, in every sense, and declamatory, but does not preclude more genuine fictional writing by the author, misled in part by his admiration for Stendhal announced in the epigraph. The author is far more gifted for literary criticism and occupies a position of importance in the literary world which should eventually be consecrated by a seat among the 'Immortals' of the Academy.

Borel, Jacques (b. 1925), up to then known as a teacher of English and a Verlaine scholar, won the Goncourt Prize in 1965 with his first novel, *L'Adoration*. It is a long and rich romantic novel, blending autobiography and invention, prolix but delicately and tenderly poetical. The story is that of an orphan son deeply attached to his mother, then initiated into love by an older woman and finally marrying. His initiation to literature is even more moving than his sentimental education. The novel is as different from the objective and phenomenological 'new fiction' of the nineteen-sixties as could be imagined and, if anything, closer to Proust.

Bory, Jean-Louis (b. 1919), won the Goncourt Prize in 1945 with a pitifully mediocre story of the German occupation, *Mon Village à l'heure allemande* (Flammarion, 1945). *Fragile ou le panier d'œufs* (Flammarion, 1950) has a little more sprightliness and humor and lauds moderate, everyday happiness, an uncommon theme today. Still the future of the writer, who is a professor, as are many recent writers, seems doubtful as a novelist. He has written, however, a remarkably lively biographical and historical volume on Eugène Sue.

Bosco, Henri (b. 1888), started publishing as early as 1924. His early work, written while he taught Italian in southern France, was gracefully poetical and fragrant with the herbs of Provence. The author was then transferred to a teaching position in Morocco, from where his novels *Hyacinthe* (Gallimard, 1940) and *Le Mas Théotime* (Algiers: Charlot, 1945) won sudden and wide fame. His subsequent works, *Monsieur Carre-Benoît à la campagne* (Algiers: Charlot, 1947), *Malicroix* (Gallimard, 1948), *Un Rameau de la nuit* (Flammarion, 1950), and *Antonin* (Gallimard, 1952), betrayed some monotony and he creates an atmosphere that is not without artificiality. In our opinion, *Le Mas Théotime* is both the most successful and the most typical of Bosco's novels. The plot owes much to detective stories, but the mystery is unnaturally kept up through an abnormal capacity for silence displayed by the narrator, a cultured farmer named Pascal. He welcomes into his house, without a single question, his cousin Geneviève, whom he loves in silence. She has left her husband who, by mistake, killed a neighbor with whom he was on bad terms, instead of killing Pascal, as he had probably intended to do. Through some unexplained confusion, Pascal inherits the estate of the murdered man. The whole novel hinges on the obstinacy of the characters in keeping their lips sealed and in coming and going mysteriously and mutely. Such behavior is not a little surprising in normally garrulous farmers from southern France, but it is necessary to the frail plot, whose assumptions would collapse at once if the characters ever explained themselves to one another. The solitary, gruff character of *Malicroix*, roaming fiercely about his native Camargue, magnified into a wild South American jungle, is, like Giono's heroes, a man of mystery and of gigantic stature, who strains our power of belief. But the author succeeds in creating a visionary and chaotic world out of the clear outlines and normally ironical and sensible Provençal peasants. Bosco, living away from publicity and academies, received the Renaudot Prize for *Le Mas Théotime* and later the Grand Prix National des Lettres. His gently satirical novel, *Monsieur Carre-Benoît à la campagne* has been translated into English in 1956 (London: Staples Press) as has *Un Rameau de la nuit* (*The Dark Bough,* London: Staples Press, 1955); by far the best study on Bosco, acute and admiringly discerning, is by R. T. Sussex, *Henri Bosco, Poet-Novelist,* Christ Church, New Zealand, 1966.

Boulle, Pierre (b. 1912), an electrical engineer by training, worked as a planter in Malaya in 1936, served in Indo-China, where he was taken prisoner by the Japanese. He became well known as a writer of absorbing stories of adventure and of love, with some philosophical implications, with *Le Pont de la Rivière Kwai* (Julliard, 1952; *The Bridge over the River Kwai,* Vanguard Press, 1954), where the portrayal of the muddle-headed officer was especially skillfully drawn. *Les Voies du salut* (Julliard, 1958; *The Other Side of the Coin,* London: Secker and Warburg, and New York: Vanguard Press, 1958) was another thrilling story of escape and terror in Asia interspersed with ironic comments on an American woman baffled by the Eastern mentality. *La Face* (Julliard, 1953; *Face of a Hero*, Vanguard Press, 1954) is a novel about a trial within a trial in which Pierre Boulle leans more heavily on his scientific turn of mind and contrives incidents and thrills with too sure a mastery. So does he in *Contes de l'absurde* (Julliard, 1953). *Le Sacrilège malais*, published in Belgium in 1955, has also been translated by Xan Fielding as *Sacrilege in Malaya* (London: Secker and Warburg, 1959), as has *La Planète des singes* (Julliard, 1963; *Planet of the Apes*, Vanguard Press, 1963).

Bourbon-Busset, Jacques de (b. 1913), a *Normalien* who occupied a high position in the French Foreign Office, gave up diplomacy for literature. He is the author of six or seven short novels, introspective, austere, a little solemn, written with classical restraint in exact, polished prose. *Antoine mon frère* (Gallimard, 1956), *Fugue à deux voix*, and *Moi César* (both 1958) revealed a rare talent for introspective analysis; *La Grande Conférence* (1963) is more humorous as a satire of diplomats dehumanized by protocol. There is more dramatic irony and lively dialogue in *La Nuit de Salernes* (1965), but the author is at his best in a thoughtful diary, *La Nature est un talisman* (1966).

Bourniquel, Camille (b. 1918), one of the leaders of the monthly *Esprit*, was already the author of four volumes which had reached only a limited audience when his novel *Le Lac* (Seuil, 1965) was widely praised by critics. It conjured up a small world of the inhabitants of a lake shore near Paris, the passing of time between 1914 and 1960, intimate dramas as are encountered in Chekhov, and a sentimental love discreetly lived. An unfashionable and grave novel of inner life.

Brasillach, Robert (1908–45). His prewar novels just missed the Goncourt Prize twice and deserved some esteem, but they were unduly overpraised by the author's fanatic friends of the extreme right. He was subsequently executed for collaboration with the enemy, and some of his followers have tried to present him as a martyr. His posthumous works include mediocre poems and a novel, *Six Heures à perdre* (Plon, 1953), which is his freshest and most human book. A French officer released by the Germans from his prison camp describes wartime Paris, as he finds it and relates the life of a young woman who, once married to a brutal husband, killed him point-blank during the confused and thrilling years of the black market and of universal conspiracy.

Brincourt, André (b. 1920), was one of the most promising among the prewar talents. His *Vert Paradis* (La Table ronde, 1950; *The Paradise below the Stairs*, Duell, Sloan and Pearce, 1952) ranks among the most revealing imaginative portrayals of the cruelty, viciousness, and essential naïveté and repressed sentimentality of adolescence. *La Farandole* (La Table ronde, 1952) paints a more poetical and more analytical picture of love and friendship at odds within a man, who ends by preferring the friendship of his mistress's husband to her love. The novel, very deftly constructed and perfumed with the atmosphere of southern France, is also an attempt to dissociate sentiment and eroticism in love, along the lines indicated by the author's master, Laclos. It also presents a disturbing picture of the uneasy fear that love for a career woman, too lucid and too practical, stirs up in a male. Brincourt seems to have given up fiction writing for criticism.

Cabanis, José (b. 1922), who hails from southwestern France, made his literary debut with a solid and winning novel, L'Age ingrat, in 1952. There is no symbolic or philosophical message in it, no calculated obscurity. It revealed only the brilliant abilities of a storyteller, who sang the praises of desire and of normal, unfettered love and provided scathing observations of bourgeois hypocrisy. The author combines the crudities of certain naturalists with a gift for pitiless and ironical dissection of human frailties, which marks him as another admirer of Stendhal and Laclos. The theme is the sensual education of an adolescent in a provincial city of the south of France, recorded without monotony and with a keen sense for comic situations and, incidentally, for the caricature of the pompous complacence of some of the supporters of Marshal Pétain. The novel, with its distrust of sentiment, pales a little in the second half. But it reveals technical mastery. Cabanis must be either a magistrate or a professor-author. (The protagonist becomes a teacher.) The second novel by Cabanis, L'Auberge fameuse (Gallimard, 1953), portraying two children exposed early to the vices of grown-ups and preferring death, heralded a more sympathetic understanding of life's tragedies. Cabanis has been repeatedly drawn to the theme of a child deprived of happiness, not with much originality in L'Age ingrat (Gallimard, 1952), more felicitously in Le Fils (Gallimard, 1956), a series of three episodes on the pursuit of erotic pleasures by a son whom his father had not known how to love. His next novel, Le Bonheur du Jour (Gallimard, 1960), betrayed some wearying in his inventive power. He has since written pleasant critical impressions, Plaisir et lectures (Gallimard, 1964), and narrowly missed the Goncourt Prize in 1966 with La Bataille de Toulouse (Gallimard).

Cau, Jean (b. 1925), better known as a journalist and for several years Sartre's secretary, won the Goncourt Prize in 1961 with a novel which inevitably was to be compared to Huis-Clos: La Pitié de Dieu (Gallimard, 1961; The Mercy of God, Atheneum, 1963). In contrast to the author's earlier and flimsy fictional attempts, such as Le Coup de barre (Gallimard, 1950), it is a solidly structured novel. All the events take place before the story opens and the setting is the bare and unchanging one of a prison. Four prisoners, all apparently having once committed one or more murders, haunted by their past and considering themselves as almost innocent, relate the whys and wherefores of their crimes. They also dissert, somewhat pompously, on the significance of punishment and on God's mercy, which they decide in the end to have deserved. The reader agrees with them.

Cayrol, Jean (b. 1911), has a voice and a tone that are distinctly his own and conjures up a misty, melancholy, and overlyrical, but authentic, fictional world. He is one of the sad southerners, more numerous than is commonly

thought. He was born in Bordeaux, and, after courageous activity in the
Resistance, he spent three trying years in German concentration camps, and
then emerged as a poet and a poetical novelist. He is the author of a trilogy,
Je vivrai l'amour des autres (Editions du Seuil, 1947–50: 1. *On nous parle*,
2. *Les Premiers Jours*, 3. *Le Feu qui prend*), and of a smoother and more
restrained story, *La Noire* (Editions du Seuil, 1949). The earnestness of the
author, his profound pity for poverty, misery, and dereliction, and his attempts to picture the sudden invasion into daily life of a superreality, which
is reminiscent of surrealist ambitions, arouse sympathetic emotion in the reader.
Yet, and again in *Le Vent de la mémoire* (Editions du Seuil, 1952), Cayrol
seems to drown his vision in a deluge of would-be poetical words and to
lack the vividness and the sharp outline that might give more compelling
reality to his evocations of a wretched Lazarus in our midst. The reader, and
perhaps the author himself, bogged down in the marshes of this *romanesque
lazaréen*, seem to wait in vain for the advent of a resurrected Christ. Cayrol's
next *récit*, *La Gaffe* (Seuil, 1957), was again the story of a wretched character
at last reconciled with life through a woman's love. *Les Corps étrangers* (Seuil,
1959) is the more moving interior monologue of a murderer, always a stranger
to himself, unable to grasp his past or to discover why he killed his mistress—
a pathetic creature in search of his own identity, and perhaps of God. *Midi
Minuit* (Seuil, 1966) is another portrayal of a confused character, a woman.
Too poetical in his style, too sombre in his manner, Cayrol has failed to win
a sizable audience outside his own country.

Cesbron, Gilbert (b. 1913), after several indifferent novels, reached a wide
public and aroused much discussion with his book on the *prêtres-ouvriers*,
Les Saints vont en enfer (Laffont, 1952). This gives a vigorous picture of the
misery, even more spiritual than physical, of the French and North African
Communist workmen of the Paris suburbs and of the priests who endeavor,
against heavy odds, to bring Christ's message to them. It does not seem,
however, that either his technique and style or the quality of his vision and
imagination promise Cesbron a great future as a novelist. Cesbron attempted
another social novel, *Chiens perdus sans collier* (Laffont, 1954), on the problem of juvenile delinquency. He succeeded in creating living individuals out
of two adolescents who were not raised by a family and, yearning after a
happiness they never knew, wandered into revolt before finally recovering
confidence in men. The novel was rendered into English as *The Innocents of
Paris* (Boston: Houghton Mifflin, 1956). The author is also a director of radio
programs and a playwright.

Chamson, André (b. 1900), belongs to the generation of Malraux, with whom
he was associated during the resistance, of Saint-Exupéry, and of Queneau.
A Southerner and a Protestant from the Cévennes, a keeper of archives and a
museum director by profession, he established himself between the two world
wars as one of the most original novelists of France. His best inspiration came
from his native province, which he portrayed with love through its humblest

workmen of the last century in *Les Hommes de la route* (Grasset, 1927; *The Road*, Scribners, 1929) and in the Protestant rigor of some of its stern men of duty in his finest book, *Le Crime des justes* (*The Crime of the Just*, Scribners, 1930). A moralist and an historian who has not been afraid of commitment in political and patriotic struggles, he was drawn to the baffling question of Franco-German friendship among factory workers at the very time when Nazism began to blight those hopes: *L'Année des vaincus* (Grasset, 1935) was a solid and thoughtful novel on that theme. Since World War II, his fictional work has consisted mainly of brief *récits* of an autobiographical character, laid in the Cévennes region: among these are *Adeline Venissian* (Grasset, 1956), published when the author had just been elected to the French Academy. He later did a very striking story of the decrepitude, through the corroding influence of the war, drink, and laziness, of a gifted friend of the author's youth: *Comme une pierre qui tombe* (Gallimard, 1964). Chamson lacks the imaginative force and the inventive fertility as well as the original view of life and of nature which have brought greater fame to Malraux, Giono, and Camus; but he ranks not far behind them and he has not received his due in America among critics and students.

Colin, Paul (b. 1920), was awarded the Goncourt Prize in 1950 for his one novel, *Les Jeux sauvages* (Gallimard, 1950; *Savage Play*, E. P. Dutton and Company, 1953). The book is uneven. The first part, which describes, in the form of a diary, the wild and cruel play of three children in the Sologne region, has vivid freshness and beauty. The author sings hymns to nature and to woman's body, which are not often heard in recent fiction. The second part, in which the adolescents studying in Paris are unable to outgrow the splendor of their radiant childhood, seems strained and too long. The third ends in tragedy. Paul Colin is talented but inexpert as yet. But he has the romantic sense of wonder and the gift of profusion, which are of good omen in a young novelist.

Cordelier, Jean (b. 1912), a Breton doctor who spent five years in a German prison camp, scored some success with *Les Yeux de la tête* (Editions du Seuil, 1953). His book, which describes, in a manner reminiscent of John Dos Passos, life in German cities as seen by a prisoner of war enjoying a good deal of freedom as a doctor, is much too long and too monotonous. But several scenes, depicting with extraordinary sympathy German women in love with war prisoners, are vividly written and very revealing as documents with only a veneer of fictional arrangement. The hero dies when he tries chivalrously to protect one of his German mistresses from rape by a Russian.

Curtis, Jean-Louis (b. 1917), born in the Pyrenees near the Basque province, became a teacher of English, fought in Alsace and Germany at the end of World War II, and won the Goncourt Prize in 1947 with *Les Forêts de la nuit* (Julliard; *The Forests of the Night*, Putnam's, 1951). The novel offers an unflattering but vivid picture of a small town of southwestern France during the war years: a family torn by discord and vice, and hypocrisy and cowardice among the inhabitants. A gift of satire was the novelist's chief asset. It turned to caricature in subsequent and scathing portrayals of St.-Germain des Près and its literary snobs (Les Chers Corbeaux, 1953) and to acid portrayal of amoral postwar Paris in Gibier de potence (Julliard, 1949; Lucifer's Dream, London: John Lehmann, and New York: Putnam, 1953). Les Justes Causes (Julliard, 1954) was another attempt at sketching a broad fresco of several layers of French society demoralized by the occupation and the black market. There is less cynicism reminiscent of Aldous Huxley and more playful and poetical sympathy for young men in Cygne sauvage (Julliard, 1961): the hero is a sentimental and naïve French student who falls in love with the attractive mother of an American friend of his. The lady, one of the sanest characters in French fiction, succeeds in fending him off through naturalness and humor. With La Quarantaine (Julliard, 1966), Curtis returned to an unpedantic and solid sociological novel, devoid of optimism but stopping short of tragedy: one of the many works which ignore the 'new novel.'

Des Forêts, Louis-René (b. 1918), is the author of striking and formally impeccable short and long short stories, Le Bavard (Gallimard, 1946) and La Chambre des enfants (Gallimard, 1960). His affinities are with the objective and meticulously descriptive 'new novel,' but in one of the stories, 'Une Mémoire démentielle,' the author makes an original and probing attempt to reconstitute his childhood memories.

Deharme, Lise (b. 1902), sensitive, easily hurt by reality, felt, as she records in her diary of the war years Les Années perdues, thrown into the world of the marvelous. There indeed she dwelt, encouraged by the example of her surrealist friends, Eluard, Aragon, and Gracq. Her novels, La Porte à côté (1949), Eve la blonde (1952), Pierre de la mer morte (1962), are visited by the mysterious presence of women who have retained all their girlish naïveté and charm in adult life. They are close to graceful and old-fashioned fairy tales.

Del Castillo, Michel (b. 1933), born a Spaniard, related, in Tanguy (Julliard, 1957; Child of Our Time, Alfred A. Knopf, 1958), the tragic story of a Spanish boy equally mistreated in his native country and in German concentration camps. He followed it up with La Guitare (Julliard, 1957; The Guitar, translated in London by Humphrey Hare, Rupert Hart-Davis, 1959). His talent as a novelist does not come up to the tragic greatness of the themes or of the experience of the writer. The second novel was weakened by its themes of dereliction and solitude, but the first, describing the horror of concentration camps from the point of view of a child, was forceful.

Déon, Michel (b. 1919), after the usual law studies, began a journalistic career during World War II on the Action Française, traveled, wrote several nonchalant and intellectual novels of little weight and in 1956 succeeded in putting more solid content and some tragic tension in Les Trompeuses Espérances (Plon, 1956).

Devaulx, Noël (b. 1905), fervently admired by a few, stands for the maintenance of a poetic tradition in the French novel, attracted since 1940 by philosophical and existential speculation. His short stories (for he has written no continuous novel as yet), collected as *L'Auberge Parpillon* (Gallimard, 1945) and *Le Pressoir mystique* (Editions du Seuil, 1948), give evidence of a graceful touch and an ability to feel and suggest mystery that are worthy of Kafka. Like Blanchot and other moderns, Devaulx (who joined the Catholic Church in 1934) seems obsessed by the omnipresence and the significance of death, envisaged without morbidness but with visionary innocence. His *Sainte-Barbegrise* (Gallimard, 1952) was more strained than his earlier tales. He proved more natural in the stories collected in 1961 as *La Dame de Murcie* (Gallimard). See our last chapter.

Dhôtel, André (b. 1900), who teaches in a secondary school at Coulommiers, near Paris, and once wrote studies on the logic underlying the visions of his compatriot from the Ardennes, Rimbaud, became a very fecund novelist in the years 1948–52 when he published, in rapid succession, *Le Plateau de Mazagran* (Editions de Minuit, 1947); *David* (Editions de Minuit, 1948); *Les Chemins du long voyage* (Gallimard, 1949); *L'Homme de la scierie* (Gallimard, 1950); *Bernard le paresseux* (Gallimard, 1952). The surrealist adventure of the nineteen-twenties left him with a passion for mystery and for the marvelous inserted into daily life. He surrounds his half-real characters with a halo of poetry and an obstinate elusiveness, which bewilder most readers. There is no structure, no solidity whatever to his stories, no progression, only gratuitous fireworks of tender poetry amid rolling layers of clouds. *Bernard le paresseux* seems to have more psychological density, through the delineation of the bonds of unexplained hatred, stronger than love, between Bernard and a woman who finally is drowned with him in a frozen river. *Pays natal* (Gallimard, 1966) is another fictional plea for the privilege of dreaming. In our opinion, too much has been made of Dhôtel's gifts as a novelist, but he stands among the inheritors to the graceful and brittle charm of Giraudoux and Alain-Fournier among existentialists and geometricians of objective fiction. See our last chapter.

Drieu La Rochelle, Pierre (1893–1945), had appeared, after a fine soldier's record in World War I, as one of the most representative talents of the nineteen-twenties, along with Malraux and Aragon, who resembled him. He searched for political convictions throughout his life, which ended in a dramatized and dramatic suicide, and for a literary mold into which he might have poured the anxiety, the corroding pessimism, the rootlessness, and the desperate need for women which pursued him. His *récits* in *La Comédie de Charleroi* (Gallimard, 1934) are among the most remarkable ones inspired by World War I. *Gilles* (Gallimard, 1939), with its subsequent and revealing preface of 1942 on his fictional work, is the least unsatisfying of his novels between the two wars. Since his death, *Les Chiens de paille* (Gallimard, 1964), and even more the unfinished *Mémoires de Dirk Raspe* (Gallimard, 1966), in which Drieu reveals much of himself under the mask of an imaginary painter very similar to Van Gogh, have brought new fame to the writer perhaps most typical of the lost generation in the years after 1919. The most searching interpretation of this significant figure has been offered by Frederic Grover in *Drieu La Rochelle and the Fiction of Testimony* (Berkeley: University of California Press, 1958) and in several other studies.

Druon, Maurice (b. 1918) tried, with some robustness and workmanship, but with otherwise undistinguished gifts, to revive the portrayal of a French family, more or less decadent. His stories do not stand out among many others of the same kind, which have preceded them and which will doubless follow. Their titles are *Les Grandes Familles* (Julliard, 1948), *La Chute des corps* (Julliard, 1950), and *Rendez-vous aux enfers* (Julliard, 1951). They sell widely and they easily adapt to the screen and brought their author to the French Academy in 1966.

Duras, Marguerite (b. 1914), published a first and rather undistinguished tale, *Les Impudents*, in 1941, then a remarkable *récit* of country life in southwestern France, told in the first person by a girl naïvely attached to her brother and then to a friend of his, who loves her, *La Vie tranquille* (Gallimard, 1944). It has no plot, nothing but childish happenings, but it shows the nascent talent of an expert writer. *Un Barrage contre le Pacifique* (Gallimard, 1950; *The Sea Wall*, New York: Pellegrini & Cudahy, 1953) is written in the same objective jerky style but shows more ability to frame characters involved in the semblance of an action. It takes place in Indo-China and relates the pathetic and frustrated efforts of a destitute French woman to erect a wall against the ocean to protect her meager holding. The adventures of her daughter, courted by a wealthy but incredibly stupid young Frenchman, whom she rejects obstinately, and the behavior of her lazy and shrewdly simple-minded brother Joseph provide the comic element. The novel is clearly modeled after Steinbeck and, especially, Caldwell and the action might almost have taken place among poor whites in America instead of poor whites in a French colony. It is not without flaws, but the author has a vigor that is not common among feminine novelists. *Les Petits Chevaux de Tarquinia* (Gallimard, 1953), entitled after a famous Etruscan fresco, which French tourists in Italy are expected to visit, is a very discreet and subtle novel about human relations and the obstacles to sincerity and to communication, even in love. The world-wide success of Alain Resnais's film for which she had written the scenario, *Hiroshima mon amour*, then of another film drawn from one of her novels, *Moderato Cantabile* (Editions de Minuit, 1958; Grove Press, 1958), brought fame to Marguerite Duras. She became, rather hastily, hailed as one of the practitioners of the 'new novel,' with which she has in fact nothing in common; and, because her *récits* were brief, written with simplicity and purity, harmless in their subjects (as compared with the sexual boldness favored by other women novelists), they became read by pupils in French classes in the United States. *Moderato Cantabile* is built ingeniously according to a musical technique suggested by Diabelli's sonatina learned on the piano by the heroine's child; its vague and delicate tale of a woman dreaming of love 'strong as death' which she knows she cannot have is instinct with emotion and restrained tragedy. *Le Square* (Gallimard, 1955; *The Square*, John Calder, 1959) and *L'Après-midi de Monsieur Andesmas* (Gallimard, 1962; *The Afternoon of Mr. Andesmas*, Grove Press, 1962) are stripped of action, of psychological depth, and of stylistic brilliance. More and more, in *Le Ravissement de Lol V. Stein* (1966) and *Le Vice-consul* (1966), the author, obsessed by the impossibility of communication, sketches a fiction of silence and of the show lapse of time engulfed in vacuity which recalls the 'theater of silence' of the nineteen-twenties and is destined to be forgotten just as fast. See on her work a pamphlet by Jean-Luc Seylaz in 'Archives des lettres modernes,' Minard, Paris, 1963, and a fine introduction by Germaine Brée to Marguerite Duras's *Four Novels* (Grove Press, 1965).

Dutourd, Jean (b. 1920), after some early and pale attempts at the humorous novel (*Le Complexe de César, Le Déjeuner de lundi*), won a larger public with his entertaining and bitter story of a metamorphosis, *Une Tête de chien* (Gallimard, 1950; *A Dog's Head*, Simon & Schuster, 1953). The sad plight of a boy born with a dog's head, his misfortunes in the army, then in love, his fortune, made on the stock market, and the sudden flattering advances made by men and women to a man of wealth, and his sorry end after he has married a beautiful but crazy wife are told with incisive humor reminiscent of a Voltairian *conte*. *Au bon beurre* (Gallimard, 1952; *The Best Butter*, Simon & Schuster, 1955), the story of the social ascent of a butter-and-egg merchant, leans too heavily on Balzacian social description, but it has verve. The author promised to be one of the good minor talents of his generation and one of the rare entertaining writers of an age that prefers to wallow in its anguish rather than to laugh at it. His risqué treatise of seduction, *Le Petit Don Juan* (Laffont, 1950), is entertaining and healthy. *Les Taxis de la Marne* (Gallimard, 1956; *The Taxis of the Marne*, Simon & Schuster, 1957) and *Les Horreurs de l'amour* (Gallimard, 1963) have not revealed any deepening in the story-teller's talent. He is at his best in chatting with his readers about Stendhal or about the foolishness of love's illusions.

Emmanuel, Pierre (b. 1916), better known as a poet and for his very out-spoken, yet tactful, autobiography, *Qui est cet homme?* (Egloff, 1947), invaded the field of the novel with a very personal—at times embarrassingly so —love story, *Car enfin je vous aime* (Editions du Seuil, 1950). It is the poetical and rapturous record of a brief encounter in America, with the two partners soon recovering their clearsightedness and knowing when and how to break off what might have degenerated into prosaic dullness. The book has occasional poetical beauty but shows little evidence of fictional mastery.

Estang, Luc (b. 1911), is commendable for his virtues of earnestness and steady zeal and his touchingly good intentions. Yet his first novel, *Les Stig-mates* (Editions du Seuil, 1949), disturbed Catholic orthodoxy; it presented a man who, a prey to evil in all its forms, still drew some drops of grace from his sea of corruption and redeemed himself, after a fashion, through bringing the son of his mistress to religious faith. The same plunge into evil, fascinating to a Catholic novelist who, coming after Bernanos and Gide, must believe in the positive reality of the Devil, constitutes the substance of *Cherchant qui dévorer* (Editions du Seuil, 1951). The novel depicts a college for future priests who seem more 'devoured' by anguish and shame at the sins of their parents than inspired by faith. The book fails to spring to life.

Etiemble, René (b. 1909), a university professor and an ebullient and bellicose critic, showed no mean courage in choosing the themes of his first novel, *L'Enfant de chœur*, published before his thirtieth year and reprinted by Gallimard in 1947. A note of venomous revenge against his mother (incest sprawls unashamedly in the book) and against his education and society sounds throughout the novel, which is replete with vivid dialogue and caricatural sketches of human, and especially provincial, stupidity. The long novel of his youth and the Parisian circles in which he lived as a student, entitled *Peau de couleuvre* (Gallimard, 1948), did not fulfill the promises of the more compact, more spontaneous earlier book. It suffers from stuffy laboriousness. Polemics and combative criticism may be the author's most felicitous bent.

Faye, Jean-Pierre (b. 1925), is a philosophical mind, a determined partisan and theorist of a rather disembodied type of 'new novel,' and clearly a person of rare and objective intelligence. He is closely associated with the group of the magazine *Tel Quel*. His novels, however, cultivate allegory, vagueness, rarefied allusions and deliberately confuse the reader. *Entre les rues* (Seuil, 1959) and *L'Ecluse*, which received the Renaudot Prize (Seuil, 1964), are marvels of skilled contrivance and of allusiveness, but stand little chance of winning an audience.

Gadenne, Paul (1907–56), is another professor who, after talking his *agrégation* and starting teaching, was struck down by disease and had to live, a semi-recluse, in the provincial cities first of Gap, then of Bayonne, in a more suitable climate than that of the north of France, where he comes from. A creeping sadness, some fondness for northern mists and the barriers separating souls, even a bold but perilous challenge to tedium, in which tedium occasionally gets the better of the author and reader, characterize his novels. Yet Gadenne occupies an original place among contemporary novelists: he is one of the least superficial of them, unconcerned with ephemeral vogues and publicity, and one of the most successful in evoking inner life. *Siloé* (Julliard, 1941), then *Le Vent noir* (Julliard, 1947), were tenacious explorations of the mysteries of individual life, by a novelist who had mastered the lessons of Thomas Mann and of Franz Kafka, without losing his originality. In *Le Vent noir* especially, the character of the protagonist, living passionately for the sake of a few meetings with the girl he loves, is reminiscent of the Proustian narrator, torturing himself through his insatiable search for knowledge and tormenting those whom he pursues with such intellectual passion. Gadenne's aspirations are for a spiritual, perhaps an inhuman, love. *L'Avenue* (Julliard, 1949) had a similar density; the hero, a sculptor driven by the war to southern France and exploring an avenue leading to a mysterious building, has grave meditations on art and on all human effort. *La Plage de Scheveningen* (Gallimard, 1953), entitled after Jacob van Ruisdael's picture, is more concrete and revolves around a man's insistent pursuit of his past, of a former friend who had collaborated with the Germans and was shot, and of a woman, Irene, who has ceased loving the over-introspective narrator. Gadenne's novels are neither easy to read nor joyful; they grant too much to symbolism and to style, but they are important, and among the few truly deep novels of our age. Gadenne, who had struggled for twenty years against disease, died on May 1, 1956. He had written some of the wisest reflections on the present state of fiction in France, which have been praised by his best critic, R. T. Sussex, of the University of Canterbury in New Zealand.

Gary, Romain (b. 1914), whose name was Romain Kacew, has traveled extensively, fought in the Free French Air Force during World War II, served in the diplomatic service, observed and reflected. His first book, *Education européenne* (Prix des Critiques, 1945; *A European Education*, Simon & Schuster, 1960), rested on a firsthand acquaintance of eastern Europe, since the author was born in Wilno, and on a deep sympathy with the Polish underground which is depicted in vignettes alternately tender and brutal. It is one of the few unforgettable books on World War II. *Tulipe* (C. Lévy, 1946) which followed was a pretentious allegory. *Le Grand Vestiaire* (C. Lévy, 1948) is a more acute study of adolescents in the demoralized and unbalanced war and postwar years, blending pity and comedy, satire and sentiment. *Les Couleurs du jour* (Gallimard, 1953; *The Colors of the Day*, Simon & Schuster, 1953) is again of uncertain merit, hesitating as it does between satire and a deeper and more sympathetic attitude of the author toward his weak-willed movie actor. Gary's gift for the picaresque and his facile inventiveness, allied to unabashed sentimentality, were best manifested in his novel about African elephants, *Les Racines du ciel* (Gallimard, 1956; *The Roots of Heaven*, Simon & Schuster, 1958), depicted as the last great individualists in the world and champions of freedom; but the book, while winning the Goncourt Prize for 1956, was criticized by purists for the author's occasional slipshod writing. *Lady L.* (Gallimard, 1963) is a clever satirical fantasy of an old English lady, in the manner of Paul Morand, but too paradoxical. *Pour Sganarelle* (Gallimard, 1966) is a good-humored attack against the gloom of unsexed and sedulously tedious modern fiction. Gary's best recent volume is his fictional autobiography, *La Promesse de l'aube* (Gallimard, 1960), humorous and cheerful but also rich in emotion. It was translated as *Promise of Dawn* (London: Michael Joseph, and New York: Simon & Schuster, 1962) and even turned, unsuccessfully, into a play.

Gascar, Pierre (b. 1916), Pierre Fournier being his real name, won fame in
1953 when his two *récits* published in one volume, *Les Bêtes* and *Le Temps
des morts* (Gallimard, 1953), were awarded the Goncourt Prize, an award
which aroused less dissent than usual among French critics. The author drew
on his experience as a prisoner of war in the disciplinary camp of Rawa-
Ruska, called Brodno in the book. The hero is entrusted with the grim task of
digging graves in a cemetery for deceased prisoners. The tone is objective
and documentary, but the effect is powerful without stressing the macabre.
The stories which compose *Les Bêtes* are equally effective, especially the first
about horses watched by a frightened soldier and escaping in a mad rush to
freedom when starved during the early days of mobilization. The style of
Pierre Gascar is at times needlessly pretentious and involved and his pessimism
rings too familiar a note. But his talent is great. It shone to best advantage,
free from mannerisms, in an autobiographical story, *La Graine* (Gallimard,
1955; *The Seed*, Boston: Atlantic-Little, Brown, 1959) and in the stark and
dramatic stories collected in translation as *Women and the Sun* (Boston:
Little, Brown, 1965). Most of those stories had appeared as *Soleils* (Gallimard,
1960). Two other books, less striking, have been published by the same American firm: *The Coral Barrier* in 1961 and *The Fugitive* in 1964.

Gautier, Jean-Jacques (b. 1908), has a vivacious talent, journalistic in the
best, although too often derogatory, sense of the word, and ingenious. He is
neither better nor worse than the average Goncourt Prize winner (he won it
in 1946), and his *Histoire d'un fait-divers* (Julliard, 1946) shows skilled
workmanship and some overworking of tenuously thin material. He followed
it with *M'auriez-vous condamné* and *La Demoiselle du Pont aux anes* (Julliard, 1951). The latter is an entertaining, though cruel, satire of theatrical
manners and of an ageing writer imprudent enough to fall in love with a dry-
hearted candidate for the stage. Conviction, penetration, and emotional content seem to be too deficient in Gautier's stories for him ever to rise to the
rank of an true 'creator.' He has shown insight and laudable severity as a
dramatic critic. However, in *Si tu ne m'aimes pas, je t'aime* (Fayard, 1960),
he hit upon a theme—a divorced couple meeting after fifteen years' separation
and experiencing a new love, doomed to a new failure—which lent itself to
his fine gift of portrayal.

Genet, Jean (b. 1907), is probably the most controversial writer to have
risen to fame since 1940. The differences of opinion concerning him are partly
attributable to considerations of morality and taste, but also to the permissible
anger of broadminded readers who will not be browbeaten by the contention
of a few elect that only homosexuals have any literary talent. The atmosphere
of coterie, which surrounds Genet, is regrettable, for his books are bought if
not read (for they are not easily digestible) on account of the legend surrounding their author. The publication of the *Oeuvres complètes* of Genet (the
second and third volumes, the first being Sartre's unwieldy and abstract
exegetic *Summa*) by Gallimard (1952–53) may help dispel that aura. Whether

Genet is a novelist or a poet is an idle question—his most magnificent gift, however, is that of poetic style. Next to this is his ability to conjure up a universe of 'evil' that compels our belief, and to forge a new language. Last is Genet's success in extracting the universal significance of his stories of thieves, traitors, and sodomites. The outlaws and the hunted men of all ages are his subject. His 'transvaluation of all values' endows the wretched creatures who, with relentless monotony, people his world of prisoners and perverts with a weird, erotic, and saintly beauty. His talent is greater in the drama and in the realm of autobiography (*Journal du voleur*, Gallimard, 1949; *The Thief's Journal*, Grove Press, 1964) than in what may perhaps be called fiction: *Notre-Dame des fleurs* (*Our Lady of the Flowers*, London: Faber and Faber, 1965; New York: Grove Press, 1963), the poetical story of a country boy who becomes a homosexual prostitute in Paris and *Le Miracle de la rose* (Lyon: L'Arbalète, 1946; London: Anthony Blond, 1966; and New York: Grove Press, 1965) in which Genet returned to autobiography. There are some who, impressed especially by Sartre's ambitious and pedantic exegesis of 'le cas Genet,' like to speak of Genet's genius. He is at any rate a master of language. See Joseph McMahon, *The Imagination of Jean Genet* (1963), and the essays by John Cruickshank in *The Critical Quarterly* (Autumn 1964).

Gorz, André (b. 1926), Austrian in part, lived in Switzerland, adopted French as his language and existentialism as his philosophy when, as a child from an underprivileged Jewish family, he felt ashamed of men's passivity in the presence of evil. He wrote a remarkable autobiography, *Le Traître* (Seuil, 1958; *The Traitor*, Simon & Schuster, 1959), which Sartre introduced and praised in a long preface. It is an extraordinarily intelligent work—a dramatic interior monologue on man's sickness and on the tedium of living that drives mortals to realize that they exist and thus must think. It borders on fiction and read as such it is one of the few successful existentialist novels.

Gracq, Julien (b. 1910), whose real name is Louis Poirier, is a professor of geography who has been hailed by André Breton as the great hope of surrealist fiction. He writes beautifully, though with affectation and some pomp. He pursues Celtic mysteries through the modern world and is a devout worshipper of the Grail legend, whose multiple meanings lend themselves best, he feels, to the expression of our unquiet dreams. We must declare that his novels appear to us as unbearably pseudo-romantic, as fake rehashings of Mrs. Radcliffe and Monk Lewis. *Au Château d'Argol*, first published on the eve of World War II, was reprinted by Corti in 1945, when the same publisher launched *Un Beaux Ténébreux* (*A Dark Stranger*, W. J. Strachan, Norfolk, Conn.: New Directions, 1949). The latter, depicting a pretentious young man who transcends himself in death, through an ostentatious suicide after refusing the love of the beautiful Christel, is the least unconvincing of his novels. *Le Rivage des Syrtes* (Grasset, 1951) stirred up more attention, since, for the first time in French annals, its author was granted the Goncourt Prize against his will. It is a solemn allegory, which strains the reader's patience and brings him scant reward. *Un Balcon en forêt* (Corti, 1958; *Balcony in the Forest*, London: Hutchinson, and New York: Braziller, 1959) on the author's experience with French soldiers in the Ardennes region during the first uneventful months of World War II has little of the tragedy of war in it, and little of a novel grasping real life. Gracq also wrote a play on the Grail theme, *Le Roi pecheur* (Corti, 1949), and a volume of acute critical essays, *Préférences* (Corti, 1961). Louise Varese translated *Au Château d'Argol* as *Castle of Argol*, for New Directions in 1951.

Guérin, Raymond (1905–55), stormed French literature with a book so full of crudities, indeed obscenities, that some lines had to be excised by the censor: *L'Apprenti* (Gallimard, 1946). The author, it is true, might have had his eroticism exasperated by four years of captivity in Germany. The strange hero of this epic of modern corruption is a servant in a low-class hotel, employed at washing dishes and perfunctorily cleaning bedrooms, who peeps through keyholes and seems fascinated by what he observes. But Guérin shows an immense power over words and of making his reader share in the unsavory atmosphere of his book. Had it been less morbidly weighted down with obscenity, *L'Apprenti* might have been a novel of true vigor. *La Confession de Diogène* (Gallimard, 1947) explores too slim a subject, the backstage activity of contemporary literature, and it failed to arouse interest. *Parmi tant d'autres feux* (Gallimard, 1950) is a volume of sprawling length—eight hundred pages—which could just as easily have gone on for two thousand more. A middle-aged man, after remembering at length his youth in Bordeaux in a corrupt circle of addicts to varied vices, marries. The loving bride, who had made advances to him, soon turns into a persecuting demon. Her death opportunely relieves him, and he may now relapse into his commonplace immorality. The volume evokes a dull boredom seldom equaled in literature, even by Sade or Henry Miller. *Les Poulpes*, the author's next venture, does not fulfill his promise. Guérin died on September 12, 1955.

Guersant, Marcel (b. 1913), was launched with some fracas in 1953 as the author of a bulky novel, *Jean-Paul* (Editions de Minuit). It is the story of a son of the upper bourgeoisie, severely educated, who discovers himself to be homosexual. He tries in vain to be won to the other sex, falls into the public pursuit of young men, is arrested and, having been gravely wounded by a bully who rejected his advances, he is hospitalized. An intern converts him to Catholicism. After some relapses, followed by remorse, confession, and a deeper faith, Jean-Paul is saved. The book, which is fearlessly crude in its first half, is presented as a moral and religious work likely to save sinners. The author is clearly a convinced Roman Catholic who poured too much too soon into a novel and could not resist moralizing inopportunely.

Guilloux, Louis (b. 1889), had in 1935 conquered the literary world of Paris with *Sang noir* (Gallimard, 1935; *Bitter Victory*, Robert McBride, 1936), a powerful delineation of a rebellious but weak intellectual, asphyxiated (hence the title) by his stifling Breton surroundings and by his own passionate anger. The book remains as one of the precursors of Sartre's *La Nausée* and of many novels of social and metaphysical revolt of the period following World War II. Unlike many other French novelists, but like Green, Guilloux is deeply concerned about his heroes and his inner world; his novels are not just intellectual pastimes and technical displays. His long and unwieldy *Jeu de patience* (Gallimard, 1949) is a purposely confused projection of many lives, with the distinction between the past and the present, what is actual and what is remembered by the characters, obliterated. It is also a unanimist record of the life of a small town through two world wars, with all social classes represented. The tone of social revolt and of revolutionary hope, which was heard in Guilloux's earlier work, has given way to gloomy acceptance of futility. The gruesome allegory of two Scandinavians vainly seeking an unhappy girl in Venice and remaining captives of some northern evil spirit, which Guilloux entitled *Parpagnacco ou la conjuration* (Gallimard, 1954) added little to the author's stature. Guilloux has been praised warmly as the novelist of poverty and of justice by Albert Camus, especially for an early book, *La Maison du peuple* (Ferenczi, 1937) and has received attention from two American critics, Eleanor Clark in 'Death of a Thinker,' *The Kenyon Review*, Summer 1941, and Victor Brombert, *The Intellectual Hero*, Philadelphia: J. P. Lippincott, 1960.

Hardy, René (b. 1911), a railroad engineer, served heroically during the German Occupation sabotaging the railroads then used by the Germans. He was arrested by the Gestapo in 1943, escaped his captors, and, after the war, was indicted in a famous trial for having allegedly collaborated with the Germans and betrayed his co-workers. He was in prison three years, then again three more years, but acquitted in the end. He wrote a striking novel on the Indo-China war, *Le Fer de Dieu* (Laffont, 1953; *The Sword of God*, London: Hamish Hamilton, 1954). The plot is involved and the technique is imperfect. But the ambitious theme lays bare the inevitable corruption of war, in which the men of good will and of heroic intent become contaminated by their torturers.

Hougron, Jean (b. 1923), is one of the novelists of adventurous life who have set themselves in determined opposition to the surfeit of symbolism, frustration, and nothingness, which they deplore in recent French fiction. He is also one of several who have discovered the opportunity of exploiting the war in Indo-China for imaginative literature. *Tu récolteras la tempête* (Domat, 1951; *Reap the Whirlwind*, Farrar, Straus and Young, 1953) is neither introspective nor elaborately constructed. It shows no conventional heroism and does not conceal the brutal murders that mark the war of ambush and treachery in the rice fields and jungle of Vietnam. The novel develops with impetuous energy, and the author is likely to become one of the popular successors of the adventure novelists of an earlier generation, Joseph Peyré, Roger Vercel, or even Henry de Monfreid. He can see and narrate breathlessly. The French Academy singled him out for its 1953 Prix du Roman. The next novel in Hougron's Indo-Chinese cycle, *Mort en fraude* (Domat, 1953), followed fast upon the previous one, and was in turn followed by *Les Asiates*. In *Mort en fraude* the author deserted the world of traffickers and opium addicts of the European colony to attempt a powerful picture of the native villagers terrorized by the Communists. The creation of atmosphere is very successfully achieved. The events of the 'fifties in Indo-China have brought forth other novels of note laid in that country: *Un Barrage contre le Pacifique*, by Marguerite Duras; *Les Chemins de la révolte*, by Nguyen-Tien-Lang (Amiot Dumont, 1953), an intelligent and peaceful Buddhist of Indo-China who suffered arrest and persecution at the hands of the Viet-Minh; *La Bataille dans la rizière*, by Jules Roy (Gallimard, 1953), a chivalrous flier and dauntless French patriot. Jean Hougron himself published another stirring story shortly before the American involvement in the Indo-Chinese peninsula, *La Terre du barbare* (Del Duca, 1958; *Barbarian's Country*, Farrar, Straus & Cudahy, 1961). He succeeded even better in three tense short stories, striking in their economy of means and not unworthy of Maupassant, *Les Portes de l'aventure* (Domat, 1954). His *Histoire de Georges Guersant* (Stock, 1964), a long and slow moving *Bildungsroman*, is less original. Critics have been severe to the author who, although a law graduate and for a time a philosophy student, prefers the adventures and the thrills of an inventive fiction writer to the aesthetic and contrived planning of an intellectual adept of the 'new novel.'

Huré, Anne (b. 1918), attracted some note through *Les Deux Moniales* (Julliard, 1962), a lurid story of life in a convent, in which she had for a time been a cloistered nun, a 'moniale.' She was probably, like Catherine Sarrazin, jealous of Jean Genet's success. The novel revealed a genuine gift of storytelling and a sophisticated mind. Some scandal was attached to it when it was revealed that the author, who had spent some seven years in jail earlier, had again been imprisoned for theft.

Husson, Jean (b. 1923), coming of age during the war years, did a number of varied manual trades, attempted fiction with moderate success three times before he was brought to the fore in 1965 by *Le Cheval d'Herbeleau* (Seuil, 1965) which was awarded the Prix du Roman by the French Academy. The story is traditional: an old farmer has parted from his horse which is sent to a slaughter house: he is fraternally and mystically attached to the animal, pursues it to the city to recover it, but finds it dead. Behind that quest, a symbolic meaning is implied: a revolt against ugliness and cruelty in the world of men. But the author's gift is that of a concrete and robust storyteller, who can arouse breathless curiosity in the non-sophisticated reader and puzzle the philosophical one.

Ikor, Roger (b. 1912), a *Normalien* and another professor, has none of the features often associated with academic novelists. Of Russian origin himself, he is an abundant and flowing storyteller, somewhat like Henri Troyat, another Russian, little encumbered with problems of technique or with the enigmas proposed by 'human condition.' His traditional qualities in *Les Eaux mêlées* (Albin Michel, 1955) were rewarded by the Goncourt Prize. He has since pursued a cyclical 'roman-fleuve' of which *Les Murmures de la guerre* (Albin Michel, 1951) constitutes the best section. *Les Eaux mêlées* was translated as *The Sons of Avrom*, Putnam, 1958.

Jacquemard, Simone (b. 1924), had one novel, *Le Veilleur de nuit* (Seuil, 1962) which, selected by the journalists for their annual Renaudot Prize for 1962, received some praise from the literary vanguard and was published in English as *The Night Watchman* (Holt, Rinehart and Winston, 1964). It is written in stilted language, interminable sentences, pedantic and symbolic allusions, and the adventures of a night watchman, who is also a thief, a torturer, and a learned criminal, read like a caricature of Robbe-Grillet and Claude Simon joined into one labyrinthine and dark underworld.

Jouhandeau, Marcel (b. 1888), has long been one of the unclassifiable outsiders of French letters. He emerged in 1919 from the war years, during which he was far from heroic, with a limited but fervent circle of admirers, who tried to present him as Gide's successor and as one of the leading lights in the world of the novel. But Jouhandeau has a knack of disrupting all endeavors to raise him on a pedestal, through his own inordinate conceit and the tactless publicity around his books and his marital troubles, which he apparently condones. He has, since 1945, published far too much; he is repetitious and he has shown little attempt to deepen or renew his inspiration. Although he has remarkable introspective gifts, he has not succeeded in making his *Essai sur moi-même* (Lausanne: Marguerat, 1946) a probing autobiography. Nor has he found forcible expression for his sincere love of animals (*Animaux familiers*, Gallimard, 1947) and for his eleven-year-old pupils in a Catholic school in Paris, whom he has taught for years (*Ma Classe de sixième*, Editions de Flore, 1949). The best of Jouhandeau's work appeared around 1930, and little more can now be expected from him, except variations on his marital chronicles and perhaps, as death approaches, a more haunting obsession with the Devil and with the threats of hell. Claude Mauriac entitled his book on Jouhandeau *Introduction à une mystique de l'enfer* (Grasset, 1938). His chief works were a scathing picture of Chaminadour, an imaginary name for the small provincial town of Guéret, where Jouhandeau's father was a butcher; a bitter comedy of small-town life, *Les Pincengrain* (Gallimard, 1924), short stories that introduced the characters Véronique and Monsieur Godeau, who are Jouhandeau's truly great creation. His splendid economy of means, his incisive cruelty, and the Catholic undertones of his novels, in which God and the Devil are always struggling, have brought to Jouhandeau a few very warm admirers who, like the late Havelock Ellis, have hailed him as a modern Cervantes.

Kessel, Joseph (b. 1898), was already famous between the wars as a writer of novels of action and adventure. Born of Jewish parents who went to France first, then to Argentina where Baron Hirsch had founded an agricultural colony for *émigrés*, he studied in Paris, fought in World War I, steeped himself in

Russian as well as in French literature, and wrote one of the best novels on aviation, *L'Equipage* (Gallimard, 1924). He did some superb reporting from London during World War II and found full recognition (and then membership in the French Academy in 1962) after the age of sixty. For mysterious reasons or due to mere chance, Kessel has not been widely translated or read in the United States, although *Le Lion* (Gallimard, 1958), located in Kenya, a story about a lion and a European child who are curiously fond of each other, was translated as *The Lion* (Alfred A. Knopf, 1959).

Klossowski, Pierre (b. 1905). Opinions differ as to the claims of this writer (the brother of Balthus, *alias* Balthasar Klossowski, the painter) to be called a novelist. He has written on Sade, translated the *Aeneid*, blended in very provocative mixtures metaphysics and eroticism, brutality and abstruse meditations on language. His earlier volumes which might be called esoteric and semi-poetical fiction reached a limited audience: *Roberte ce soir* (Editions de Minuit, 1953) and *La Révocation de l'Edit de Nantes* (Editions de Minuit, 1959). *Un Si Funeste Désir* (Gallimard, 1963) was more revealing and a strange novel, historical, poetical, and symbolic, *Le Baphomet* (Mercure de France, 1965), was extolled by a few and damned by others. Our conviction is that he would be more at home in philosophical speculation than fiction.

Lagrolet, Jean (b. 1914), a Frenchman from the extreme southwest, made a name in the nineteen-fifties, when he was aligned by critics with the 'new novel,' through two works: *Le Pire* (Gallimard, 1953) and especially *Les Vainqueurs du jaloux* (Gallimard, 1957). The second of these is a slow-moving and meandering search by a man of sixty for the protagonist, who is eighteen. He observes the younger man and his girl friend, is drawn to him by genuine affection, but is irrationally jealous of him and of all happiness. He analyzes and lays bare all that is mean in him with a morbid masochism. The expression, often stilted, and the monotonous use of the first person in a perpetual monologue, mar the genuine psychological interest of the volume.

Laurent, Jacques (b. 1919), began, like a few determined Frenchmen, with a huge novel of sprawling length (one thousand and sixty-eight pages), *Les Corps tranquilles* (J. Froissart, 1949), to prove to others and to himself that he had what is called a novelist's temperament. His potentialities are undeniable. There is imagination, verve, cynical and satirical portraiture, humor, a burlesque talent, and thought in his book, but there is also a deplorable confused accumulation of extraneous matter, which makes one pray for slender and selective *récits*. A few critics declared that their patience had been rewarded and that this first novel was a great book. The author might still become an original novelist, especially in the humorous rendering of the foibles and inconsistencies of men.

Le Clec'h, Guy (b. 1917), is a refined, introspective, and melancholy novelist, who is only gradually learning the technique of his trade but who has it in him to become one of the finest portrayers of inner life and of moral dilemmas. *Le Témoin silencieux* (Albin Michel, 1949) is a meditation on death, by a young man who, having just lost his father, examines and rejects the religious explanations or justifications for death and finally kills himself. (There is an epidemic of suicides in the contemporary novel.) The book offered promises that the author's second novel, *Le Visage des hommes* (Albin Michel, 1950), disappointed. *La Plaie et le couteau* (A. Michel, 1952), entitled after a line of Baudelaire and conjuring up a Dostoevskian atmosphere, is far more impressive. An exasperatingly weak, self-tormenting young man, Jacques, who likes to blame the 'out-of-joint' time in which he has to live for his own lack of will, becomes madly jealous of the happiness that a friend of his, Richard, has won for himself through loving and thus curing a paralytic young woman. He kills her and indirectly brings about the death of his friend. He regrets all the while, as we do with him, 'man's inability to kick himself in the pants.' *Le Défi* (1955) and *Une folle Joie* (Grasset, 1961) attempted, in vain, to be humorous and joyful novels. Guy le Clec'h was better inspired when he portrayed and analyzed his generation in *Tout homme a sa chance* (Albin Michel, 1957).

Le Clézio, Jean-Marie (b. 1940), born of an English father in Nice, lives there and lays the scene of his novels around that city. His first novel, *Le Procès-verbal* (Gallimard, 1963; *The Interrogation*, Atheneum, 1964) was one of the most acclaimed literary debuts of the last two decades. See Chapter XII for a brief commentary on it. The series of *récits* entitled *La Fièvre* (Gallimard, 1965; *Fever*, Atheneum, 1966) is even more remarkable for its psychological accuracy and its warm emotion. *Le Déluge* (Gallimard, 1966), with several good chapters, smacked of haste and repeated some of the mannerisms and devices of *Le Procès-verbal*. The young author's mastery over his rich and concrete language is prodigious.

Leduc, Violette (b. 1910), had written novels which were embarrassingly autobiographical, such as *L'Affamée* (Gallimard, 1949), about an ugly woman who has long hated herself and the mirror image that others seem to present to her of herself; long unloved, the heroine encountered love in the end. Such is again the theme of a brief *récit* published in 1965 (Gallimard), *La Femme au petit renard*, published in English as *The Woman with the Little Fox*, tr. Derek Coltman, Farrar, Straus and Giroux, 1966. But she treated the subject more amply, very intensely and stirringly, in *La Bâtarde* (Gallimard, 1965; translated under the same title by Derek Coltman, London: Peter Owen, and New York: Farrar, Straus and Giroux, 1965). The qualities of the book, one of the best feminine novels of the decade, are briefly characterized in our last chapter.

Leiris, Michel (b. 1901), is the author of one of the most searching and truthful autobiographies of our age, *L'Age d'homme* (Gallimard, 1936; *Manhood, a Journey From Childhood into the Fierce Order of Virility*, Grossman, 1963), which could well have been one of the best *romans d'analyse* in

French. His restrained, exact prose recalls that of Benjamin Constant and his cold, anxious, masochistic study of himself (he attempted suicide) arouses more emotion than most novels. All his work, including *Brisées* (Mercure de France, 1966), is critical and autobiographical.

Lesort, Paul-André (b. 1915), is much admired by a small group of serious-minded Catholic critics, among whom are Gabriel Marcel and Jacques Madaule. He has reflected with originality on the technique of the novel and, in *Les Reins et les cœurs* (Plon, 1946), elaborating ideas evolved while he was a prisoner of war and preferring a 'perspectivist technique' to the interior mono-logue, judged artificial, he wrote an original work on a grave subject. *Le Vent souffle où il veut* (Plon, 1954) attempted an even loftier theme, defined by Mauriac as 'a spiritual drama closely bound up with the drama of a couple': a husband, almost resentful of the quietude and of the affection provided by his loving wife, is tormented by the quest for another love. He seeks God; he finds Him while a prisoner in Germany. The writing is often pedestrian and too slow-moving. The feverish prose of Mauriac or the ardent poetry of Claudel might have done better justice to an ambitious duel between two loves.

Limbour, Georges (b. 1902), became appreciated for a story of charming and ingenuous fantasy, *Les Vanilliers* (Gallimard, 1938). He followed it up with a mild and uneventful tale, *L'Enfant polaire* (Fontaine, 1945), and in 1963 he made an attempt to enlarge his limited circle of readers with *La Chasse au mérou* (Gallimard). A surrealist atmosphere of weirdness and of oneiric illogic is created by the author; but he remains a novelist for the courageous few.

Malaquais, Jean (b. 1908), a Pole by birth, was launched like many young novelists through Gide's praise, lavished somewhat excessively on *Les Javanais* (Denoël, 1939; translated as *Men from Nowhere*, Fischer, 1943). His *Planète sans visa* (Pré aux clercs, 1947; *World without Visa*, Doubleday and Company, 1948) is a picture of the frustrated Europeans without a country awaiting an American visa. The two works have some solidity and weight, but, in our opinion, lack of originality and even life. The author's next fictional attempt, *Le Gaffeur* (Corrêa, 1953), is a clever fantasy but too obviously in the manner of Kafka. It is less cruel than Aymé's satirical fiction, of which it is reminiscent. The author has since written specialized works of philosophy and taught at several American universities, apparently interrupting his novelist's career.

Mallet-Joris, Françoise (b. 1930), a Belgian-born young woman duplicated Radiguet's feat of writing, before the age of twenty, a novel of uncanny maturity and of impeccable workmanship: *Le Rempart des Béguines* (Julliard, 1951; *The Illusionist*, Farrar, Strauss and Young, 1952). The novel showed a frighteningly precocious insight into life: the daughter of an industrialist in

Bruges felt drawn to her father's mistress and became her lesbian lover. The story was never coarsely told; it was poetical and artistic and provided one of the keenest revelations on the psychology of that most undecipherable of characters, according to Balzac: the 'jeune fille.' At the age of thirty-five, Françoise Mallet-Joris had been married, divorced and married again, had had four children and published seven or eight novels and several *récits*. *La Chambre rouge* (Julliard, 1955; *The Red Room*, London: W. H. Allen, 1956) and *Café Céleste* (Julliard, 1958; *Café Céleste*, Farrar, Straus and Cudahy, 1959) were attempts at an altogether different kind of novel, realistic, brutal, with spineless characters crushed by fate, as in Zola. *Les Mensonges* (Julliard, 1956) revolved around money, as in Balzac, and implied a disillusioned view of life and of love: the characters in those books passively accept their degradation. The author has since attempted a sort of historical fiction; *Les Personnages* (Julliard, 1961; *The Favourite*, London: W. H. Allen, and New York: Farrar, Straus and Cudahy, 1962), revolving around Louise de La Fayette, the passionate friend of Louis XIII in his youth: the favorite was drawn to religion as the author herself then came to be and the book is an indirect confession. Françoise Mallet-Joris confessed more directly but much less movingly in a confused and disturbed *Lettre à moi-même* (Julliard, 1963; *A Letter to Myself*, London: W. H. Allen, and New York: Farrar, Straus, and Giroux, 1964). With *Les Signes et les prodiges* (Grasset, 1966), she returned to a well composed, ethical, and humanistic novel (very much anti-'new novel') on wretched and anguished characters who should be looking for a religious key to life's miseries. The book is long, ponderous, and only fitfully vivid.

Mamméri, Mouloud, in *La Colline oubliée* (Plon, 1952), exploited the newly discovered subject and background of North Africa and the conflict between ancestral traditions (Berber or Kabyl, in his case) and the breakup with which they are threatened by modern life and French culture. There is earnestness and concentrated power in the novel, which is of good omen. Mamméri is one of a number of French writers (often of partly Spanish descent, or wholly of Arab or Berber origin) born and trained in North Africa. who have lately brought new vigor into French fiction. The names of the best known among the others are: Jean Amrouche, Albert Camus, René-Jean Clot, Mouloud Feraoun (author of *La Terre et le sang*, Editions du Seuil, 1953), Mohammed Dib (who received the Fénéon Prize for *La Grande Maison* in 1952), Albert Memmi, Marcel Mouloudji, Robert Merle, Emmanuel Roblès, Jules Roy, and Michel Zéraffa. The influence of the American novel has been especially strong on them. Since Algeria won her independence from France, Mamméri has fought for Algerian writers who choose to write in French. Their characters, as in his second novel (*Le Sommeil du juste*, Plon, 1955; *The Sleep of the Just*, London: Cresset Press, 1956, and New York: Beacon Press, 1958), are Arabs or Kabyls torn between the old world of their childhood and the impending future which, although colonization is portrayed in a lurid light, is bound up in the authors' eyes with the language and literary traditions of France.

Marceau, Félicien (b. 1913), studied at Louvain, served on the Belgian radio during the war, which cost him a sentencing to hard labor in 1946. He then adopted French nationality, changed his name (he had been born Albert Carette), and published several novels before winning fame on the stage with *L'Oeuf* in 1957. He is a very intelligent judge of fictional technique, an admirer of Balzac, a humorous teller of tales. *Bergère légère* (Gallimard, 1953) is an entertaining and fresh fantasy; *L'Homme du roi* (Gallimard, 1952) was a more ambitious story of a character grappling with the world like a Balzacian hero and taking on the airs of a Nietzschean superman. He was awarded the 'prix interallié' for *Les Elans du cœur* in 1955 (Gallimard): the story is that of a provincial family caught in the webs of intrigue, decay, and shabbiness, but it is relieved by wit and an agile prose.

Margerit, Robert (b. 1910), impressed a few critics by the naïvely overstrained eroticism of his first novel, *Montdragon* (Gallimard, 1946), the story of a servant employed in a French castle to tame horses. He seduces the lady of the castle, then tries to pervert her daughter and her maid. He is finally killed by the daughter. Laclos (*lui, toujours!*) is obtrusively present here. He has not totally effaced himself in *Le Dieu nu* (Gallimard, 1951), the author's best novel, which celebrates the naked god of love. Many conventional elements encumber the novel. The characters ride on horseback around provincial chateaux, reminiscent of Victor Cherbuliez and Georges Ohnet, and they are restrained by family traditions and outmoded conventions. The beauty of the women always beggars description, and they all act unpredictably. Yet, to modernize his themes, Margerit has deftly added just a soupçon of lesbianism and an even fainter one of a too-ardent attachment between brother and sister. The book is a novel of romantic passion that is frustrated to the end by the prejudices and the excessive prudence (or is it fear of love, or even lack of taste for the male sex?) of the beloved women. 'Ardent and chaste,' thus bracketed together, are the two key adjectives of the author. Margerit and Gracq, who sponsored him, Emmanuel, Brincourt, Dhôtel, and Gadenne seem to be the champions of a new romanticism in French fiction. In *La Femme forte* (Gallimard, 1953), Margerit attempted the theme of a masterful woman who runs a newspaper and enters into professional and emotional conflict with masculine rivals.

Mauriac, Claude (b. 1914), has written stimulatingly on A. Breton, the new novel, and what he termed *L'Alittérature*, but without the acumen or the conviction of a gifted critic. His novels, purposely very different from his father's, follow the fashion of a later generation. They are ingenious, technically curious, but in our opinion altogether lifeless: *Le Dîner en ville* (Albin Michel, 1959; *The Dinner Party*, Braziller, 1960) and *La Marquise sortit à cinq heures* (Albin Michel, 1961; *The Marquise Went Out at Five*, Braziller, 1962). The author is not endowed with what is called a novelist's temperament and his stories seem to revolve around characters who, like a Gidian hero, wonder how they will ever write a novel.

Memmi, Albert (b. 1921), published, first in *Les Temps Modernes*, then at Corrêa, in 1953, an arresting novel, *La Statue de sel*, one of the five or six truly outstanding ones in a yearly production. It is a document rather than a cleverly arranged and elegantly adorned story. It rests upon an intensely personal experience of misery, injustice, and war. The hero is a Jewish son of a poor family in Tunis. He is entranced by French culture, which was revealed to him at school, and he turns in revolt against his Jewish background, the rites of his religion, and even his half-illiterate parents. The war and the German occupation of Tunisia deprive him of his position and of his hopes for an academic career. He suffers from being a stranger everywhere, unwelcome to the French controlled by Vichy, hardly at one with the backward Arabs, distrusted by the orthodox Jews. He falls into stark despair, then decides to emigrate to Argentina. With earnestness and solidity, at times with some ponderousness, Memmi has hit upon and treated one of the significant problems of an age that has uprooted and alienated thousands of its most gifted men. The author is a teacher of philosophy. He published in 1962 a volume, *Portrait d'un juif* (Gallimard, 1962) in which he stressed the allegedly irreducible differences between a Jew and a non-Jew: the thesis angered many people who prefer to deny all such differences and the very notion of race, even acquired 'race.' The author expects to seek remedy for that alienation of the Jew in modern societies in two future volumes, also of sociology, *L'Impasse* and *L'Issue*.

Merle, Robert (b. 1908), is another Algerian and another professor. His *Week-end à Zuydcoote* (Gallimard, 1949; *Week End at Dunkirk*, Alfred A. Knopf, 1951) reveals his close acquaintance with the modern American novel. It was criticized as brutal, tough, and artificial, but wrongly so in our estimation. It is one of the few true, convincing, and even moving novels written as yet on the catastrophe of 1940. The evacuation at Dunkirk had, as it happens, caught up with the violence of American novels, and the author conveys it truthfully. His next work of fiction, on a German bureaucratic torturer in concentration camps, *La Mort est mon métier* (Gallimard, 1953), on the contrary, sounds false from beginning to end and would be better forgotten. The author's most conspicuous gifts lie probably in the realm of the drama and in the adventure novel. *L'Ile* (Gallimard, 1962; *The Island*, New York: St. Martin's Press, and London: Humphrey Hare, 1964) is such a story of adventure, reminiscent of Melville and of the Bounty mutineers. Whites and Pacific Ocean natives are opposed a little too conventionally to each other. A too obvious ideological or ethical message mars the otherwise robust storytelling.

Mohrt, Michel (b. 1914), is a delicate, sensitive, and intelligent novelist, who began with a light but cheerful account, in Stendhalian fashion, of his war experience on the Italian front in 1940, *Le Répit* (Laffont, 1945). (There was, however, far more than nonchalant egotism in Stendhal the novelist, a fact that Stendhal's admirers often overlook.) The author touches upon the subject of collaboration in *Mon Royaume pour un cheval* (Albin Michel, 1949) and reaches a more felicitous blending of lucid analysis and of poetry in *Les Nomades* (Albin Michel, 1951), which describes European exiles in America and the obstinate sentimental education of the protagonist. The novelist seems to have fought shy of tragedy and of suffering, with a resulting thinness in his material. Perhaps, as he remarks in his third novel, 'the supreme sin is in failing to believe in one's passions.' He wrote a far more credible story of adventure and of irony in *La Prison maritime* (Gallimard, 1962), one of the few truly entertaining novels of the decade, wholesomely sensual and highly intelligent. *Campagne d'Italie* (Gallimard, 1965) is briefer, disenchanted, but fragrant with the nostalgia of the author's army career and feminine conquests of his youth.

Molaine, Pierre (b. 1906), after earlier pale attempts, such as *De blanc vêtu*, impressed the public and the committee of the Renaudot Prize, with *Les Orgues de l'enfer* (Corrêa, 1951; *Strange Laughter*, Roy Publishers, 1953). The scene is laid in an insane asylum, whose inmates, buried alive, cry out their love of life and cherish in vain the dream of freedom. The wife of one of the patients persuades the doctor to admit her as a nurse. She and a former anarchist agitator, temporarily an inmate of the asylum, fall in love with each other but dare not betray the mad husband. The latter, after a hair-raising escape, is captured and confined once again. The events related in the novel have all the weirdness of a hallucination. The style is too labored and too rhythmic, but the classical structure of the novel contrasts felicitously with the disorderly minds of the madmen. Molaine succeeded honorably in this attempt, after courting many difficulties. His book is anything but commonplace.

Mouloudji, Marcel (b. 1922), was hailed as one of the revelations of the years 1944–45, when he received the Prix de la Pléiade for *Enrico* (Gallimard, 1944) and soon after published *En souvenir de Barbarie* (Gallimard, 1945). The whole arsenal of tricks borrowed from American novelists is displayed in these two books. The young North African and itinerant actor clearly knew of no other literary tradition but the recent American one. The themes are as sordid as can be imagined: the repellent misery of the poorest eastern quarters of Paris, the squalor of stuffy rooms in which a whole family lives, sleeps, and raises rabbits, and a gruesome abortion, which the girl Barbarie undergoes. There is skill, but a derivative and imitative skill, in the broken-up narrative and the disjointed interior monologues. Mouloudji's talent has not developed since, and *La Grande Sortie* (Gallimard, 1951) may be dismissed as the most insipid of pretentious allegories (purporting to symbolize German occupation of France). *La Guerre buissonnière* (Gallimard, 1965) is an ironical tale of an adolescent who tried in vain to enlist in 1939–40 and ended the war ingloriously. It lacks forcefulness as well as novelty.

Nimier, Roger (1925–64), clearly belongs to the family of minds of the French right, which has never lacked verve, robust use of hearty language, *élan,* and cynicism, and which, while claiming to be realistic, has also been fooled by its own slogans and has wistfully looked backward. He showed, in two volumes of essays, that he was no profound thinker. *Amour et néant* (Gallimard, 1951) is verbose and confused and succeeds in making most aspects of love, except perhaps jealousy, appear dull. *Le Grand d'Espagne* (Table ronde, 1950), which mentions Bernanos, is an organized attack against liberals, humanists, republicans and, most of all, Jacobins. It is full of zest and of wit, but negative and, as political thought, trite. Nimier the novelist happily knows how and when to throw the weight of ideas overboard. His early volume, *Perfide*, on fifteen-year-olds, is thin and cheaply cynical. *Le Hussard bleu* (Gallimard, 1950; *The Blue Hussar*, 1953, Julian Messner, 1953) is a brilliant book. A French soldier serves in 1945 with the troops occupying Germany, maneuvers with skill among decrepit, vicious, or selfish officers, conquers a more than willing German lady for whose senses two French soldiers are hardly adequate fare. She kills one of them, however, at the behest of her brother, a Nazi without conviction. The nonchalance and the insolent dash of the book are its main charm. However, the author suffers from the serious sin that makes men attractive but novelists unconvincing: he never takes himself or his characters seriously and does not even lend any of them an individual style. Nimier can be exasperating, but he counts. Unfortunately he forced his talent in *Les Enfants tristes* (Gallimard, 1951), in which he tried his hand at the psychological analysis of the insipid amours of the modern fashionable youth. He died prematurely in 1964.

Nizan, Paul (1905–40), a *Normalien* and close friend of Sartre, who wrote touchingly on him in *Situations IV*, was for a time a Communist. Killed on the battlefield in 1940, he might have become the best intellectual novelist of his generation. *Les Chiens de garde* (Rieder, 1932) was a virulent onslaught on the teaching of philosophy in France; *La Conspiration* (Gallimard, 1938) is hardly a novel, rather a portrayal of an anguished age group, drawn to leftist causes through generosity.

Nourrissier, François (b. 1927), is the author of several volumes of essays, then of a novel, *Le Corps de Diane* (Julliard, 1957) on jealousy, poisoning, and destroying love. He then embarked on a fictional trilogy, the first two volumes of which appeared in 1958 respectively at Grasset and Fasquelle: *Bleu comme la nuit* and *Portrait d'un indifférent*. Both were insolently scornful of sentiment and reveled in clear-sighted cynicism, in the tradition of Montherlant. The third volume, *Une Histoire française* (Grasset, 1965), is equally intelligent, but closer to an autobiography, very thinly veiled, than to a novel. Like many others of his generation, he has much pessimistic condescension toward life and little imagination.

Oldenbourg, Zoë (b. 1916), born into a Russian family of scholars and journalists, has lived in France since 1925. She is well versed in history and her novels are among the few successful examples of the new historical novel in French today. *Argile* (Gallimard, 1946, subsequently entitled *Argile et Cen-*

dres; The World Is Not Enough, Pantheon, 1948) took place during the Crusades. *La Pierre angulaire* (Gallimard, 1953; *The Cornerstone,* Pantheon, 1955) continued the story with greater psychological insight and with marked stylistic ease. She then devoted several novels to the Albigensian crusade and to the most cruel slaughters of French history: *Les Brûlés* (Gallimard, 1960; *Destiny of Fire,* London: Gollancz, 1961); *Le Bûcher de Montségur* (Gallimard, 1960; *Massacre at Montségur,* London: Weidenfeld and Nicolson, 1961) and *Les Cités charnelles* (Gallimard, 1961; *Cities of the Flesh,* Pantheon, 1963). She has a wide audience and there are many who regret that the Goncourt Prize was not bestowed upon her. She did however receive the Femina award.

Ollier, Claude (b. 1922), is the closest to Robbe-Grillet among the novelists who have come to the fore since 1958: he won the Medicis Prize that year for a remarkable novel, *La Mise en scène* (Editions de Minuit). Sedulously, the author eschewed anthropomorphism, emotional communion with the reader, psychological or philosophical significance. An engineer in the Algerian desert, refusing adventure, recorded with perspicuous objectivity all that he observed and gradually reconstituted the murder of his predecessor and other crimes. But the complex threads of that lurid affair of love and jealousy are not unravelled. The next novel, *Le Maintien de l'ordre* (Minuit, 1961), cultivated the photographic eye and the scientific description with the same zeal, but with less deliberate aridity of form. The setting was also in Africa and the detective story plot was slightly more human and clearer. *Eté indien* (Minuit, 1963) was more intricate in its structure and far more sophisticated in its parallel recreation of space and of style, but also more remote from the average reader. Ollier has since participated in learned discussions on the 'new novel' as recorded in *Tel Quel* (Spring 1964, No. 17). He declared there: 'If I write, it is to invent another world, a second one which balances the visible world . . . My primary goal is to establish a valid world parallel to that of our experience, not necessarily as a counterweight to the existing one, but also to compare one to the other.'

d'Ormesson, Jean (b. 1925), son of an eminent diplomat, *Normalien* and *agrégé*, chose a career as a cultural officer in international institutions. He wrote an entertaining and, in the end, tragic novel in the Stendhalian tradition about three young people who, out to enjoy life and casual love out of boredom, discover jealousy and the death of one member of the trio: the one who had taken love seriously. The title is ironical: *L'Amour est un plaisir* (Julliard, 1956). His next novel, *Au revoir et merci* (Julliard, 1966) is even more insolently cynical and entertaining: a portrait of a disillusioned generation.

d'Otremont, Stanislas (b. 1899), is to be ranked among the conservative and even the conventional novelists. He recalls *Dominique,* the minor masterpiece of Eugène Fromentin and, what is worse, some of the effete stories of Victor Cherbuliez and Jules Sandeau. His *Thomas Quercy* (Gallimard, 1953) is a long canticle to love and purity. A young businessman, whom disease has induced to live in a country retreat and to analyze himself, falls in love with a radiant *jeune fille*, then, after her death, with her friend. Thanks to his romantic passion, he triumphs over disease and death. The author, a Belgian lawyer, has narrative gifts and stages a return to a well-built, romantic novel. Unfortunately, he spoils his best chapters through lengthy and unconvincing philosophical developments.

Pauwels, Louis (b. 1920), published a superb *récit*, *Saint-Quelqu'un* (Editions du Seuil, 1946) on a clumsy workman, who bungles the happiness he should have enjoyed placidly with his wife and family and who involuntarily drives his wife and son to suicide. The gray, softly poetical style, the gentle sadness that suffuses the book, and the discreet religious implications of the title contribute to make a modest and moving work. The mysterious author seems to have remained silent after that striking debut, except for an essay, *Les Voies de petite communication* (Editions du Seuil, 1949). He contributed to *Gavroche*, then to *Combat* and *Arts*. See our last chapter for some of his subsequent and strange work.

Perec, Georges (b. 1936), won a literary prize in 1965 for a story, *Les Choses: une histoire des années 60* (Julliard, 1965), which has none of the traditional elements of fiction and resembles rather a laborious, and tedious, sociological survey of the daily life, worries, and joys of a middle-class couple. The dry manner and the dehumanized description read like a caricature of Robbe-Grillet's technique.

Perrein, Michèle (b. 1929), an able storyteller, unpretentious, natural, equally at home in ironical, light-hearted stories of couples exchanging partners and in depicting serious passion, morbid jealousy, and suicides of jilted adolescents. Her first novel, *La Sensitive* (Julliard, 1956), impressed Colette; it takes place among students in Bordeaux, the author's city, and the heroine tries hard to live after her models, Medea and Antigone of another Bordeaux author, Jean Anouilh. *Le Soleil dans l'œil* (Julliard, 1958) tried too hard to be modern in its portrayal of adultery as a refuge against boredom in today's marriages. *Barbastre* (Julliard, 1960) tells the vacation adventures of a trio: a girl, who thinks she can only love Barbastre, an imaginary or an absent character, but she submits with no fuss to the desire of one of her two male friends, requiring from him expertness in love alone; the other one is the inevitable pederast of most novels these days. The dialogue has naturalness and the few events are related entertainingly.

Perret, Jacques (b. 1901), is not too remote from Nimier, though less youthful and less promising. After a brilliant war career as an escaped prisoner and a *maquisard*, he recorded or re-imagined his experiences in a war book that is good but hardly of enduring worth, *Le Caporal épinglé* (Gallimard, 1948). His next novel, *Le Vent dans les voiles* (*The Wind in the Sails*, London:

Rupert Hart-Davis, 1954; and New York: Norton, 1955), on nautical life,
shows no deepening of his talent. *Bande à part* (Gallimard, 1952) is even
more disappointing. *Le Machin* (Gallimard, 1955), a series of short stories,
evinces chiefly verbal exuberance.

Perry, Jacques (b. 1921), is not a man of action, like Perret, but an introspective writer, haunted by man's helplessness. The protagonist of his novel
L'Amour de rien (Julliard, 1952) is determined upon suicide, and he casts a
patient, backward glance at his lonely life. One hardly feels sorry about the
oncoming death, for he had certainly failed to endow his life with significance. *Le Mouton noir,* published in *La Table Ronde* in 1953, then by
Julliard (*The Black Sheep,* London: Gollancz, 1955), is a very acute portrayal
of a cruel childhood. A father, whose wife died of grief at the profound
wickedness of her boy, spares no effort of devotion and comradeship to bring
his son back to a decent life. An unexplained instinct for evil carries the boy
away. The theme of the child irresistibly lured by evil is one of the most
timidly approached themes in fiction. Here it is attacked frontally, and the
novel, in spite of a few weaknesses, is effective, until the end, which ceases to
carry conviction. *La Vie d'un païen* (Julliard, 1965) and its sequel, *La Beauté
à genoux* (Julliard, 1966), showed the same zest for living and relish in
adventurous life. Perry's books are novels with a content and much ardor, and
some fragrance of the lavender which their author cultivates in Dordogne.

Peyrefitte, Roger (b. 1907), is a genteel humanist, a devotee of pagan antiquity, and an elegant stylist who has not conspicuously succeeded in the novel,
a genre for which he is poorly equipped in imagination and sensibility. His
ironical *récit* of the death of his mother, *La Mort d'une mère* (Flammarion,
1950), was entertaining but very thin and strained. The author's travel books
on his beloved Greece and Sicily show him at better advantage than his attempts, and failures, at fiction writing. But, in 1945, Peyrefitte encountered a
subject on which he felt deeply and venomously, and which enabled him to
tap his childhood memories and to portray the dubious and tender age of
adolescence with heartfelt sympathy. *Les Amitiés particulières* (Vigneau,
1945; *Special Friendships,* Vanguard Press, 1950) cannot be taken at its face
value as a document on Catholic colleges or on the young men educated there,
for the author depicts them as monsters of hypocrisy and deceit, unable to
control their animal urges. But it is a very talented distortion and re-creation,
and one more striking novel on the fashionable theme of pederasty. Another
volume, a *récit* rather than a full-fledged novel, *Jeunes Proies* (Flammarion,
1956), has charm and even delicacy in spite of its unpleasant subject: the
resigned, then joyful acceptance of a night of heterosexual love by a man
whose tastes are of another sort. Peyrefitte's subsequent books are picaresque
and often crude satires of diplomats, Knight Templars, the Vatican, more and
more striving after the sensational and as devoid of fictional interest as they
are of truth. A long and tedious volume on the Jews in 1966 brought only

ridicule to the author. Sensationalism has spoiled a talent which at one time was great.

Pieyre de Mandiargues, André (b. 1909), became known for his *Musée noir* (Laffont, 1946), a surrealist story influenced by Lautréamont, and especially for his collection of fantastic tales, *Le Soleil des loups* (Laffont, 1951), which received the Prix des Critiques. The author is a man of wide culture, interested in archaeology, whose vast knowledge has not dried up a rich gift for inserting the marvelous into daily life. His tales are very skillfully contrived, but far more poetical than Maupassant's visionary stories, less crude in their effects than Poe's, far superior, in our opinion, to the *Contes de l'absurde* (Julliard, 1953) by Pierre Boulle (b. 1912), which are addressed to scientifically minded readers. He is a poet in the surrealist tradition of 'apprivoiser le sinistre,' taming the weird and frightening element of life, celebrating both dreamy purity and carnal sensuousness (*L'Age de craie*, Gallimard, 1962). Eroticism, in his tales, is formalized and thus subdued, precisely and richly cool. His best *récits* which may be called novels are *Le Lis de mer* (Laffont, 1956), *La Motocyclette* (Gallimard, 1963; *The Motorcycle*, Grove Press, 1965) and a collection of tales with some underlying unity, *Porte dévergondée* (Gallimard, 1965). See our last chapter.

Pilhes, René Victor (b. 1934), published in 1965 *La Rhubarbe* (Seuil, 1965), an entertaining, fanciful first novel about a 'bâtard' who discovers by chance his sister (who is legitimate) and attempts, through varied and vivid series of incidents, to live in imagination the life which would have been his, in the region of the Pyrenees, amid fields of rhubarb, if his father had acknowledged him.

Pingaud, Bernard (b. 1923), a *Normalien* and primarily a literary critic of rare seriousness and zeal, is devoted to interpreting the novels of his more imaginative and less melancholy contemporaries. He directed the compilation of a valuable anthological and critical dictionary, *Ecrivains d'aujourd'hui: 1940–1960* (Grasset, 1960). His two novels, *L'Amour triste* (Table ronde, 1951) and *Le Prisonnier* (Table ronde, 1958), the latter inspired by a meditation on a serious painting by La Tour, are works of a moralist.

Pinget, Robert (b. 1919), has aroused enthusiastic admiration among the most advanced and dogmatic partisans of the 'new novel' and left most readers of lesser courage unconcerned; for he is primarily an experimenter with technique, highly intellectual and scornful of any concessions to his public. *L'Inquisitoire* (Minuit, 1962), his eleventh novel, is made up, through five hundred heavy pages, of questions and answers around a detective story plot. The narrator who attempts to answer questions is old and deaf and apparently uninformed on the disappearance of a male secretary around whom the questioning revolves. It eventually dawns upon the reader that the two aged owners of the castle in which the crime occurred are queer homosexuals. Not many will have the patience to pursue the difficult work to make such a common discovery. In 1965, Pinget received from the Femina committee their annual prize for *Quelqu'un* (Minuit, 1965); it is a meticulous, very slow, and very tedious search, by the narrator who is a writer, for a bit of paper. No plot, no progression, no character, and hardly any new tropisms explored. An earlier book by Pinget, *Le Fiston* (Minuit, 1959), was ably translated into English by Richard Howard and published by the Grove Press, 1961. Of all the 'new novelists,' Pinget is, along with J.-P. Faye, the most esoteric. His characters perpetually and aimlessly wander in the labyrinth of their identity crisis, asking themselves, like American students but long after the age of studying, 'Who am I? What am I doing? Whither am I going?'

Poirot-Delpech, Bertrand (b. 1929), is the author of a clever first novel, *Le Grand Dadais* (Denoël, 1958), a teenager at first too closely held by his mother who sows his wild oats generously, and with no little cynical scorn for the girls who are his partners, and stumbles into a broil in which he kills a man without ill will or premeditation. He writes his story from prison. A second novel, *La Grasse Matinée* (Denoël, 1960), has a no more admirable protagonist, a man of forty who abandons his responsibilities, has several tiresome affairs and is caught by love in the end. The author, like many of his compatriots, is intelligent, cynical, alert but hardly a teller of convincing tales.

Ponchardier, Dominique (b. 1917), is likely to remain known as the author of one book, *Les Pavés de l'enfer* (Gallimard, 1950). He poured into it his thrilling experiences as one of the hardest fighters in the French Resistance. Unlike Remy or Guillain de Benouville, Ponchardier, a former Navy officer, preferred to organize his recollections in the form of a novel. The tone is smooth and unemotional, the adventures related are hair-raising, and the sadness felt by the hero when faced by the collapse, after the war, of the lofty hopes cherished during the dark years for a renovation of the country are, without effort, imparted to his reader.

Prévost, Jean (1901–44), had the qualities of a critic and of an interpreter of other lands rather than those of a creator of characters and an inventor of plots. He wrote one of the four or five best volumes on America, *Usonie* (Gallimard, 1939), and one of the finest autobiographical studies of a young man from the masses, a socialist and a rebel among the *Normaliens*, *Dix-huitième année* (Gallimard, 1929). He was killed in the Vercors maquis in 1944, leaving behind him a well constructed 'populist' novel, *Les Frères Bouquinquant* (Gallimard, 1930), and an intelligent portrayal of the struggle between generations, with a Stendhalian title and many Stendhalian overtones: *La Chasse du matin* (Gallimard, 1937).

Queffélec, Henri (b. 1910), is a *Normalien* and professor. He began his literary career with a violent and cynical story in the fashion of the time, *Journal d'un salaud* (Stock, 1944). *Un Recteur de l'Ile de Sein* (Stock, 1945; *Island Priest*, E. P. Dutton & Co., 1952), an indifferent novel, won acclaim in the movies as *God Needs Men*. The following stories by Queffélec, notably that of a schoolmistress fighting against politics, administration, and pupils in a remote district of Brittany, *Au bout du monde* (Mercure de France, 1949), do not throb with life. *Tempête sur Douarnenez* (Mercure de France, 1951) is more moving and brushes aside much of the literary sentimentality about Breton fishermen. The author is not conspicuously adroit or poignant in creating living beings. But one character is alive and overpowers the book—the sea. *Un Homme d'Ouessant* (Mercure de France, 1954) shows Queffélec growing in stature as a creator of powerful characters. It is brief and tense, written with rare concreteness and evocative power. It takes place on a primitive island off the Brittany coast during the reign of Louis XVI and lends life to stubborn, superstitious yet magnificent fishermen, far different from Pierre Loti's sentimental Bretons, defying the law of their king and the teaching of the Church. *Un Royaume sous la mer* (Presses de la Cité, 1957) was translated as *The Kingdom under the Sea* (London: Arthur Barker, 1959).

Queneau, Raymond (b. 1903), is perhaps not a great novelist but he is a great writer and an incomparable virtuoso of style. His chief concern seems to be re-creating language through effective use of colloquial speech, of slang and of many of the devices of rhetoric, entertainingly used. But he owes as much to Charlie Chaplin as he does to James Joyce. His *Pierrot mon ami* (Gallimard, 1942), which relates the hero's vicissitudes in an amusement park, in a truck in which he rides with apes, and his frustrated love affairs, is a masterpiece of hilarious comedy, as was his first and perhaps best novel, *Le Chiendent* (Gallimard, 1933). *Le Dimanche de la vie* (Gallimard, 1952) has excellent parts on naïve and winning fools at odds with wily women and escaping scot-free, like Chaplin or even like Dostoevski's idiot, from the ordeals of modern life. The stumbling blocks for Queneau are probably his immense store of knowledge, rivaling that of Joyce and occasionally intruding into the tale as pedantry, his total disregard of the structure of his novels, hence some monotony in the 'flat' comic characters, and an ending usually unequal to a brilliant beginning. *Zazie dans le métro* (Gallimard, 1959; *Zazie*, Harper, 1960) is in our opinion a strained and artificial *tour de force;* like many of the comic attempts by the author, it seems to have been synthetically contrived by a geometrician versed in philology. Two excellent volumes by American professors have appeared on Queneau: Andrée Bergens (Geneva: Droz, 1963) and Jacques Guicharnaud (Columbia University Press, 1965).

Réage, Pauline. The secret of this writer's identity is well guarded, although most people suspect the author of the preface, aged academician Jean Paulhan, notoriously fond of paradoxes and of assuming several personalities, to be responsible for *Histoire d'O*, published first and then again at J. J. Pauvert in 1954 (*Story of O*, Grove Press, 1965). It can be variously described as an erotic book in the manner of the eighteenth century or, as has often been suggested of the works of Sade, as the work of a moralist. The heroine consents to slavery, humiliation, prostitution, and torture. The book is not coarse and its art is impeccable and fastidious, even solemn. It avails itself of many of the tricks of the 'black novel' and its French commentators have been too inclined to underplay its virtuosity and to acclaim mystical and portentous implications in this clever masterpiece of eroticism.

Rebatet, Lucien (b. 1903), after a political career without honor as a collaborator with the Germans and a fierce anti-Semite, is putting his energy and his violent temperament to better use. He published a novel of inordinate length in two volumes of over five hundred pages each, *Les Deux Etendards* (Gallimard, 1951), from which politics is banished. It portrays a double religious vocation, in a young man and a young woman, who join the Jesuit order and a convent. A friend of the young man falls in love, in mystical exaltation, with the young woman who will soon be a nun. He fails to receive the gift of faith and elopes with the novice to whom the prosaic human love thus accepted will never bring spiritual peace. Rebatet's power is real but overabundantly displayed, yet, amid so many novels that lack substance and a theme, he has handled a tragic dilemma. Rebatet's next novel, *Les Epis mûrs* (Gallimard, 1954), is the story of an imaginary musical composer of genius, killed in World War I. It shows insight into artistic creation and avoids conventionality, so common in the fictional delineation of genius. The author stresses the obstacles in the path of genius which a vulgar democratic society, according to him, accumulates.

Régnier, Paule (1890–1950), is a novelist of the era between the two world wars; but she has received more attention since 1950 and especially after the publication of her letters in 1955. Her life was pathetic; hunchbacked and plain, she loved ardently, only to discover that the man she loved (Paul Drouot, the author of a beautiful poetical tale, *Eurydice deux fois perdue*, killed in World War I) had in fact loved another woman. An ardent Catholic but also a solitary pessimist like Leopardi, she found a refuge in her writing and finally took her life in 1950. She had published a novel, *L'Abbaye d'Evolaynes* (Plon, 1934), far superior to her other novels and strangely moving to this day in its profound seriousness. A lovely and warm young woman married a doctor who, up to then an unbeliever but deeply disturbed by his experience in the war, becomes a convert while vacationing near a Benedictine abbey in Belgium. He decides, with his wife's consent, to become a monk and she agrees to become a nun. But while he finds serenity, she tortures herself with jealousy of his God and in the end takes poison in his presence. Paul Claudel scolded her for such a picture of faith and bluntly wrote her: 'Your heroine would have done better to have children.' But the novel is one of the most dramatic written by any woman on the theme of love *versus* religion.

Régnier, Yves (b. 1914), received the Prix des Critiques for a rather tepid philosophical *récit* on an imaginary quietist utopia, *Le Royaume de Bénou*

(Grasset, 1957). He proved a more vigorous writer on the traditional triangle, with the woman, freshly sensuous and entertaining no illusions, confessing that all men being the same as far as pleasure goes, a shrewd girl should select hers for either money or brain. The novel, entitled *Le Sourire* (Grasset, 1960), is graceful and the young hero, Narcissus-like, loves himself in others and smiles to his own smile.

Reverzy, Jean (b. 1914), a physician with a fine record in the Resistance, solitary and obsessed by suffering and by death, obsessively introspective, turned to fiction and his first book, *Le Passage* (Julliard, 1954): the story is that of an incurably sick man who, returning from Polynesia to die in France, exchanges thoughts on death with his doctor, also a man of gloom. *Le Corridor* (Julliard, 1958) is an even more anguished novel, a true modern 'danse macabre.' In a *récit*, *Le Silence de Cambridge* (Les Lettres nouvelles, 1960), he came down to a more earthy plane in relating a sordid story of greed. His writing is not only austere but heavy and his small but ardent group of admirers is courageous as well as discriminating.

Rey, Henri-François (b. 1920), does not experiment with esoteric devices or conceal the trend of his plots. He writes abundantly, too much so, but with a picturesque talent and an evident relish in his tales. Two of his novels are important and enjoyable: *Les Pianos mécaniques* (Laffont, 1962), a picture of corruption and of fear in people weary with their own selves and with the facility of promiscuous love, and *Les Chevaux masqués* (Laffont, 1965). Love, drink, masochism, pederasty, and flagellation are blended with mystical yearnings. An American in a weird boarding school in southern France attempts to discover the mystical woman loved by two abnormal men, one of them her husband. Precocious and cruel, the child is surrounded by several other unsavory characters. The vividness of the narrative and the humor of the novelist impose a lurid and decadent world upon the reader.

Roblès, Emmanuel (b. 1914), the son of a mason in Oran, became one of the leaders of the brilliant literary group that, during World War II, gathered in North Africa. He published *Travail d'homme* (Algiers: Charlot, 1942), *Nuits sur le monde* (Algiers: Charlot, 1944), and *L'Action* (Algiers: Charlot, 1946), three dramas of marked power. His first important novel is *Cela s'appelle l'aurore* (Editions du Seuil, 1952), from a sentence in Giraudoux's *Electra*. Its moral qualities have been warmly praised, because they stood out against the background of eroticism and of homosexual bad conscience in many contemporary novels. But the nobleness of the book is achieved through painful struggles against hypocrisy, narrow-mindedness, and cowardice. The book does not preach; but it implicitly revaluates true love and friendship. The hero is a doctor in Sardinia devoted to his wretched village and married to an insignificant wife. He falls in love with a superior woman, Clara. He struggles to maintain his loyalty to his wife and gives refuge to a murderer whom he knows to have acted madly out of grief for the loss of his own wife. The doctor's

wife fails to understand him, while his mistress maintains her love for him
and spurs him to his deeds of abnegation and devotion. Roblès, who was unsuccessful in weaving a novel out of North African resistance, *Les Hauteurs
de la ville* (Charlot, 1948), has here composed one of the few haunting books
of the early nineteen-fifties. It was translated as *Dawn on Our Darkness* (London: Messner, 1953 and New York: Collins, 1954). *Le Vésuve* (Seuil, 1961)
is, along with *The Gallery* by the American John Horne Burns, the most vivid
evocation of the war in Italy and of the mixture of squalor, demoralization,
brutality, and desperate need for tenderness in the face of danger which
appears to have characterized the Allied occupation of Naples in 1943–44.
It deserves to be translated and admired in America. So does Roblès's next,
and rather more conventionally mysterious novel about a professor turned
rebel, criminal, lover of his victim's mistress, and finally saved through love
for her: *La Remontée du fleuve* (Seuil, 1964).

Rochefort, Christiane (b. 1917), received the much advertized Prix de la
Nouvelle Vague for *Le Repos du guerrier* (Grasset, 1958; *Warrior's Rest*, New
York: David McKay, 1959). The unconvincing but humorous story of a 'nice'
French girl, rescuing a man from suicide, taking him to her bed, pampering
him with whisky and feminine submission, finally marrying him after he had
beaten her, comfortably shocked, entertained, and was dutifully and ponderously scanned by sociologists and critics. The novel showed a fine mastery of
restrained and ironical style. *Les Petits Enfants du siècle* (Grasset, 1961) is
also entertaining, but treated a graver theme: the absurd and immoral growing
up of the new youth in city blocks and the hard-boiled attitude of parents
considering the advent of a new baby, in the welfare state, as the opportunity
for a frigidaire or a television set. The cynicism is not without charm. *Une
Rose pour Morrison* (Grasset, 1966) is a lighter attempt in the same vein.

Rolin, Dominique (b. 1913), a granddaughter of Léon Cladel, was praised
first as the author of *Les Marais* (Denoël, 1942), a debut whose promise, in
our opinion, *Le Souffle* (Editions du Seuil, 1952) hardly fulfilled. She had
failed also in attempting a story of half-mystical mists and undefined characters, *L'Ombre suit le corps* (Editions du Seuil, 1951). But *Moi qui ne suis
qu'amour* (Denoël, 1949) is one of the most ardent novels of carnal and pagan
love written by a woman, from the point of view of a woman who became,
in adultery of course, 'the prey of Venus.' *Les Quatre Coins* (Seuil, 1954) on
a teenage girl, her terror of the sordid loves she observes in a Paris suburb,
between the four corners of gates and walls which imprison her roaming, was
vivid in parts; but the chief character, there and again in *Artémis* (Denoël,
1958), lacks depth.

Rossi, Jean-Baptiste (b. 1931), is the author of one book, *Les Mal Partis* (Laffont, 1950; *Awakening*, Harper and Brothers, 1952), whose skill and discreet
deftness in handling the most perilous of subjects were, in a lad of nineteen,
literally disconcerting. An adolescent falls in love with a nun, ten or twelve

years older. She defies her own scruples and her true purity, her convent and society in order to live a passion that fulfilled some claims of her maternal instinct but could only bring her grief and misery. The adolescent is soon taken away from her and placed in a religious school. Rossi was widely compared to Radiguet whom he has, in several respects, transcended in insight and narrative skill.

Roy, Jules (b. 1907), has at least two homonyms in contemporary letters, Claude Roy, an incisive and combative critic of Communist affiliation (once a royalist), and Jean Henry Roy, an able reviewer in *Les Temps Modernes*. Jules Roy, the son of a policeman and a peasant woman from Rovigo (North Africa), is, like Roblès his compatriot, one of the champions of loyalty to one's task, of fraternity, even of heroism. He gave brilliant service as a flier with the Royal Air Force, which his *Vallée heureuse* (Charlot, 1946) describes modestly. The euphemism, as is (or was) well known, designated the Ruhr Valley. It is hardly a novel, but it is one of the few good books devoted to aviation since Saint-Exupéry, whom Roy worships. The author, who had begun his literary career by writing poetry and delicate essays, published an essay, reminiscent of Vigny, *Le Métier des armes* (Gallimard, 1951), and attempted to master dramatic form with *Beau Sang* (Gallimard, 1952). The essay is probably a more fitting medium for him than imaginative creation; he has since written chiefly books of reporting and polemics. But *Le Navigateur* (Gallimard, 1954; *The Navigator*, London: Turnstile Press, and New York: Alfred A. Knopf, 1955), while embarrassingly reminiscent of *Night Flight*, is a good, concise story on the profession of aviator. *Le Femme infidèle* (Gallimard, 1955), still vibrant with the memory of the author's experiences and meditations during the war, was thin.

Sabatier, Robert (b. 1923), is better known as a refined and harmonious poet. He keeps aloof from fashions and coteries and his novels have only reached a few. The latest one to date, *Dessin sur un trottoir* (Albin Michel, 1965), tries to be like an intricate pattern drawn on the pavement, on a quay of the Paris Left Bank. The love affairs, in which an American girl, an American artist, the storyteller and a friend take part, serve chiefly as pretexts for meditative conversations and reflections on life. The author does not seem to be overpowered by his characters and he fails to win his readers.

Sachs, Maurice (1906–45). The moot question of whether Sachs is a novelist should probably be answered negatively, if one excepts from fiction fairy tales, such as his *Abracadabra* (Gallimard, 1953), which is of mediocre quality in any case, and picaresque autobiography. *Le Sabbat* (Corrêa, 1946; *The Day of Wrath*, London: Barker, 1953), the first part of a meandering and entertaining autobiography of a Jewish youth who was killed by Allied bombing while serving as a civilian in Germany, is brilliantly written. Its success was due in no small degree to its frankness in recording love experiences (chiefly, though not solely, of homosexual nature) and to its cruel portraits of well-known literary figures. The author was an insolent scoundrel, a shameless *arriviste*, an exhibitionist, and a pretentious rival of Rousseau in his urge for confessions, but nevertheless an entertaining, a brilliant, and, at times, a pathetic writer.

Sagan, Françoise (b. 1935), whose real maiden name was Françoise Quoirez, at the age of nineteen scored the most surprising literary triumph of the year 1954 with *Bonjour, Tristesse* (Julliard, 1954; *Bonjour, Tristesse*, Dutton, 1955). The title is drawn from a pretty poem by Paul Eluard which has thus become a classic. The story, which a million readers had devoured within a year, is that of a girl of seventeen, naïve and sophisticated at the same time, raised in a totally amoral way by a father who treats her as a friend and confides his own feminine adventures to her. When he seems disposed to marry one of his mistresses, by whom his daughter is fascinated as well as intimidated, the teenage girl contrives a plot to break the marriage. The father's mistress seeks death in an automobile accident. Gloom and a foretaste of the vanity of all pleasure creep into the life of the girl, up to then free from care and from remorse. The plot is slim, the characters sketchy, but the style restrained and a trifle dry. Much was expected from her after Sagan had thus become world-famous. Her following novels, or *récits*, depicted the same monotonous world of boredom, drink, sex, vague pursuit of pleasure ending in sorrow. They are almost indistinguishable from one another and their titles hardly matter. *Un Certain Sourire* (Julliard, 1956; *A Certain Smile*, London: John Murray, and New York: E. P. Dutton, 1956) is the least unsubstantial, *Aimez-vous Brahms . . . ?* (Julliard, 1959; E. P. Dutton, 1960) the thinnest and most papery. Françoise Sagan's admirers and publisher have attempted to repeat her early success in praising *La Chamade* (Julliard, 1965), but the characters who make up the eternal triangle never take on any reality. The skillful authoress (who has also had three plays produced) has showed neither depth nor the ability to acquire it.

Saporta, Marc (b. 1923), published two or three novels in rapid succession in 1960 and 1961: they impressed a few persons, avid for novelty, by their tricks, but none of them amounts to a serious work of imagination, of psychology, or of style. They are exercises in technique: *Composition No. 1* (Seuil, 1960) is in the form of a pack of cards to be sorted out by the reader. *La Distribution* (Seuil, 1961) combines interior monologues, stage directions, experimenting with tense, erotic pursuits, none of them of much interest to the reader or, presumably, to the author. *La Quête* (Seuil, 1961) follows the fashion of that year for objective description and utilizes the techniques of the camera and of the detective story combined. It all seems obvious and quickly turns tedious.

Sarraute, Nathalie (b. 1902), born of Russian parents like Gary, Troyat, and Elsa Triolet, came on the literary scene with *Tropismes* (Denoël, 1946), artful brief stories or unpoetical poems in prose. Sartre's preface to her first real novel, *Portrait d'un inconnu* (Marin, 1948; *Portrait of a Man Unknown*, Braziller, 1958), christened a typical 'anti-novel,' brought her fame. All her novels have been translated, as has her challenging and overpraised volume of ingenious critical theory, *L'Ere du soupçon* (Gallimard, 1956; *The Age of Suspicion*, London: John Calder, and New York: Braziller, 1963). See our last chapter. She is a serious but hardly an inventive or revolutionary novelist, whose fine intellect has won admiration among American professors.

Sarrazin, Albertine (b. 1937), was, as a writer, discovered by the enterprising publisher Pauvert, who bought the novel she had written while in jail (where she has spent a good deal of time), *La Cavale* (1966), and *L'Astragale* (1966) on her escape, her stay in a hospital with a broken ankle bone, and on other adventures in rather crude surroundings. The two volumes have been over-inflated by publicity, on account of the author's unusual career and the jail slang she uses. She has a fine sense of comedy and a genuine talent as a stylist. The two novels on the thought of escape (*se cavaler* is to escape) and on escape are at times thrilling. It cannot yet be assured that she has it in her to write more on other, more sedate, subjects. She is now married and free, though still under police surveillance.

Schneider, Marcel (b. 1913), a teacher in a Paris *lycée*, is a cultured, discreet, and highly polished teller of tales impregnated with the charm of Alsace and the poetry of childish loves. He has already written much, and his volumes emerge only faintly from an evanescent and glimmering light, which blurs all outlines and characters. His affinities seem to be with the authors who cannot resign themselves to outgrowing too splendid a childhood (like Alain-Fournier, Robert Francis, and Julian Gracq) and with the surrealists. *Cueillir le romarin* (Table ronde, 1949), his third novel, is a girl's confession, delicately portraying solitude and the intimate joy of suffering. *Le Chasseur vert* (Albin Michel, 1949) is a more robust evocation of a family in Alsace, whose most original member, dressed in green, shot but also loved and tamed birds. A half-humorous story of twins, *La Première Ile* (Albin Michel, 1950), struck us as strained and somewhat childish. *Le Sang léger*, which followed, played with the fantastic in narrating a New Year's Eve in Paris during which time became reversible, the two heroes were plunged backward through several centuries. Schneider has his devotees, who place him at the very top of the authors now writing fiction that is truly fictitious.

Schwarz-Bart, André (b. 1928), wrote the most moving novel about the martyr-dom of the Jews, not only at the hands of Nazism, which comes only at the end of the book, but through the centuries. The Legend of the Just Man has it that the first Just Man was martyred in York, England, in 1185. For his descendants suffering is a sign of election. The novel, *Le Dernier des justes* (Seuil, 1959; *The Last of the Just*, London: Secker and Warburg, 1961, and New York: Atheneum, 1960), won the Goncourt Prize in 1959 and aroused a controversy in Paris, where the author was ridiculously charged with having

borrowed some of his material. A Polish Jew himself whose parents and three
of his brothers and sisters were cremated by the Nazis, he clearly is a deeply
spiritual person and his novel, humorous and terrifying, loosely organized and
too long, has the courage to approach some of the most disturbing questions
of our age and of the history of Christianity. Among many light episodes of
flirt and sex, it treats a great subject with warmth and generosity.

Semprun, Jorge (b. 1923), won the Prix Formentor in 1963 with *Le Grand
Voyage* (Gallimard; *The Long Voyage*, London: Weidenfeld and Nicolson, and
New York: Grove Press, 1964). He is not a subtle artist and his technique does
not come up to the tragic theme. The novel clearly rests upon a direct and personal experience: a young Spaniard fleeing from the Spanish nationalists joins
the French Resistance, is caught by the Germans, and exposed to the squalor
and horror of the harrying trip to Germany. The picture of his tormentors is
done dispassionately but luridly, with realism and at times too much eloquence.

Simenon, Georges (b. 1903 in Liège, Belgium), is the prodigious author of
hundreds of novels. He was famous long before World War II and is now read
in schools and occasionally treated seriously by critics and authors of dissertations. *Les Anneaux de Bicêtre* (Presses de la Cité, 1963) and *Le Petit Saint*
(Presses de la Cité, 1965) have been praised as marking a new departure in
the fecund novelist's career. The earlier ones, more expert at conjuring up
atmosphere, were, in our opinion, much better. None of them is likely to
survive.

Simon, Claude (b. 1913), has written some ten novels between 1946 and
1966, but only came to the fore with *Le Vent* (Minuit, 1957; *The Wind*,
Braziller, 1959) and *L'Herbe* (Minuit, 1959; *The Grass*, Braziller, 1960).
La Route des Flandres (Minuit, 1960; *The Flanders Road*, London: Cape,
1962, and New York: Braziller, 1961) on the 1940 débacle placed him in the
forefront of today's novelists. *Le Palace* (Minuit, 1962; Braziller, 1964) overstressed the author's mannerisms: long sentences, deluge of words. He is not
widely read in France and can hardly expect to be, and his success in translation, in countries where he recalled Faulkner too closely, has been scant. But
he may well be the novelist of the nineteen-sixties most likely to endure. See
our last chapter.

Simon, Pierre-Henri (b. 1903), is well known as a moralist, as a Christian
champion of heroism and of nobleness in literature, and as the grave and
influential literary critic of *Le Monde*. He is also a gifted novelist. *Portrait
d'un officier* (Seuil, 1959; *Portrait of An Officer*, London: Secker and Warburg;
and *An End to Glory*, New York: Harper, 1961) dramatizes the problems of
conscience of a professional army officer, well read and meditative, in the age
of Indo-Chinese and Algerian wars; there is more conversation than action
in it. *Histoire d'un bonheur* (Seuil, 1963) explores provincial society in an era
of change but again poses a moral dilemma. *Le Somnambule* (Seuil, 1961)

had more direct emotional force in the conflict of love and moral scruples which it illuminated. The author was elected to the French Academy in 1966.

Sollers, Philippe (b. 1936), another grave and melancholy Southerner (from Bordeaux), scored an early and deserved success with *Une Curieuse Solitude* (Seuil, 1958), the story of a teenager who, like Radiguet's hero, discovers freedom and love with a Spanish woman. The tale had freshness and poetry, and showed a precocious mastery of style. The author could not repeat such a success and, with *Le Parc* (Seuil, 1961), he disappointed most critics and alienated the mass of readers in giving a deliberate, cold, obscure 'new novel' with no subject and no characters. The experimental skill of the book is, however, striking. *Drame* (Seuil, 1965) throws even more of a challenge to the conventional novel: the book diabolically attempts to bewilder, astonish, and remain impenetrable to the reader. More and more the young author appears to have become preoccupied with extremely ingenious questions of technique and of criticism. He brought out a remarkably sensitive volume of essays, *L'Intermédiaire* (Seuil, 1963), and his articles in *Tel Quel* in 1965–66 on the intents of the coterie of novelists to which he belongs evince intelligence, haughty scorn for the writers who condescend to please, and not a little sophistry.

Stil, André (b. 1921), may deserve mention, since Communist novelists have been more scarce in France than Communist painters and poets. He received the Stalin Prize in 1952 for his two-volume novel, *Le Premier Choc* (Editeurs français réunis, 1952), on the 'occupation' of a French port, presumably Bordeaux, by Americans in peacetime and on the wrath of French workmen in being humiliated by the 'imperialists' from overseas. The book plods conscientiously, portrays workmen's lives and feelings with honest application, but has neither insight nor life.

Thomas, Henri (b. 1912), is one of the most original French writers today. He is a very delicate poet in verse and in prose, an admirer of Melville and, above all, of Rimbaud. He, like several other French novelists of the years 1940–50, testifies implicitly to the profound impact of surrealism on French imagination. His heroes pursue a superhuman moment of exaltation, an invasion of the whole being with an ineffable joy and a sense of purity. Through such ecstasies, the anguish and the weight of solitude, which crushed these pilgrims of an *éternité retrouvée*, are swept away. *Le Seau à charbon* and *Le Précepteur* (Gallimard, 1940 and 1942) first revealed the extraordinary climate of purity and strangeness in which Thomas lived and plunged his creations. *Les Déserteurs* (Gallimard, 1951) is even more haunting. It has elements of a psychological detective story. An officer, after simulating accidental death, has started life again under a new name in Corsica. He is discovered through a doctor who had once known him and who leads toward him a young woman who is fascinated by his recognition of the metamorphosis that overwhelms human beings when, at thirty-five or so, they allow the energy accumulated in them to explode. The women in Thomas's novels are perhaps the purest and most mysterious for their unpredictable simplicity in France since Giraudoux. Thomas creates his own universe, which recalls that of some German writers. He had translated one of Ernst Jünger's books during World War II and has been haunted by Hölderlin. *Le Promontoire* (Gallimard, 1961) and *John Perkins* (Gallimard, 1961), the latter preferred to Simon's *La Route des Flandres* by the judges of the Prix Médicis, blend mystery and poetry felicitously. John Perkins is an American of the Boston region against whom his wife and a woman friend whom he admires plot ruthlessly. The dénouement is deliberately shrouded in obscurity; the novelist offers two possible conclusions, between which the reader is free to choose. In spite of some artificiality, the reader's interest is whetted and he admires the discreet skill of a poetical novelist. *Le Parjure* (Gallimard, 1964) again presents a resident of America, who went there as a professor writing a thesis on Hölderlin, but became a bigamist and lost his eyesight; it is a milder tale.

Triolet, Elsa (b. 1903), the Russian-born wife of Aragon, of whom he sang rapturously in his wartime poems, is a gifted storyteller whose best achievement remains her four stories on the French Resistance entitled (after the mysterious phrase that signaled to the French in June 1944 that the Allies had landed and that the underground could unleash its full strength) *Le Premier Accroc coûte 200 francs* (Denoël, 1945). 'Les Amants d'Avignon,' which had already appeared in the clandestine *Editions de Minuit*, is the best of them. All of them are a little unreal, as many of the events described seemed to be, yet they convey the atmosphere of conspiracy and breathless confusion of Lyon during the war. Tender passion had its place among heroism and some cowardice in these adventures. Elsa Triolet's later books have proved very inferior to her vivid and attractive, if not profound, volume on an era that she lived and felt intensely.

Troyat, Henri (b. 1911), Russian-born (whose name was Tarasov) also endowed with superb facility as a storyteller, has won several of the literary prizes of France. *L'Araigne* (Plon, 1938), which came after two earlier novels of some distinction, brought him a wide audience. The person whom Troyat compares to a venomous spider is a despicable intellectual who, out of spite and nihilistic wickedness, becomes the tormentor of his mother and his three sisters. (Europeans seem to depict tyrannical males, while Americans prefer domineering and stifling mothers.) Troyat's novel, however, lacks passion, psychological depth, and also renewal of the suspense presented too fully at the very beginning. His more ambitious trilogy, *Tant que la terre durera* (Table ronde, 1947–50; the first volume has been translated as *My Father's House*, Duell, Sloan and Pearce, 1951), describing a boyhood in southern Russia, lengthy adventures through the Russian-Japanese war and anti-Tsarist riots, and finally exile after the Bolshevik victory, is eminently readable and smoothly told in a manner reminiscent of Gogol and Tolstoi; yet, when all is said, it suffers from its smooth facility and fails to move or to strike the reader.

La Neige en deuil (Flammarion, 1952; *The Mountain*, Simon & Schuster, 1953) is briefer, more concentrated, and built like a thriller. Two mountaineers search for a wrecked plane in the Alps, one out of greed, the other out of kindness and also because he is intimidated by his malicious younger brother. It is to be deplored that the author turned his vigorous story into a parable, with a beautiful lady from India, one of the travelers in the wrecked plane, symbolizing the rather obvious moral. Henri Troyat has consistently just missed satisfying those readers who want more from the novel than charm and escape, just as has another Russian-born writer of lesser talent, Kessel. He has won many prizes, election to the French Academy, and is one of the most popular of French writers as well as one of the most productive. But he has not convinced fastidious critics that he is more than a pleasant and often conventional spinner of overlong historical romances. His success abroad has not paralleled his inflated reputation in France.

Vailland, Roger (1907–65), was another of the literary talents revealed in the admirably rich year 1944–45. He had been much impressed by the surrealist clean sweep, then he became a Marxist and a courageous member of the resistance. He has portrayed himself, unfavorably, in Marat, the hero of *Drôle de jeu* (Corrêa, 1945), one of the earliest novels, and the best, on the French underground, a book full of destructive humor. Vailland diverged more and more from surrealist orthodoxy when he rejected the worship of love and insisted that, as another French novel has put it in its title, *l'amour n'est qu'un plaisir*. His three idols are Laclos, Sade, and Stendhal (the latter being, in our opinion, thus misrepresented as a cerebral sensualist). His subsequent novels never recaptured the vitality and the controlled frenzy of *Drôle de jeu*. *Les Mauvais Coups* (Corrêa, 1949) reads too much like a didactic debunking of *l'amour-passion* and like a story of demoralization in the Laclos vein. *Bon Pied, bon oeil* (Corrêa, 1950) is equally frank in its claims for a liberal and unsentimental ethics of sex, but naïve in its idealization of Communists. *Un Jeune Homme seul* (Corrêa, 1951) is a poor novel but a clever demonstration of a social 'ascent,' contrasting with the one Paul Bourget used to depict. In Vailland's novel, a middle-class engineer, feeling unhappy and consciencestricken among the bourgeoisie, chooses to go to the people and espouses Communism. Vailland's promise was great, but it has not been matured by his following a desiccating master, Laclos, and by his Communist orthodoxy. The question asked by Sartre when, in November 1938 he reviewed in the *Nouvelle Revue Française, La Conspiration*, the novel of a Communist intellectual Paul Nizan, killed in 1940, is still a timely one: 'Can a Communist write a novel? I am not convinced that he can; he does not have the right to make himself the accomplice of his characters.' Vailland's political convictions, however, weakened after the middle nineteen-fifties. The author became afflicted with a disease from which he was to die in 1965. But he maintained a tone of cheerfulness in the zestful novels which he wrote then and which enlarged his audience. *La Loi* (Gallimard, 1957; *The Law*, London: Cape, and New York: Alfred A. Knopf, 1958) won the Goncourt Prize in 1957 and

conjured up the atmosphere of an impoverished city of southern Italy with
rare skill. 'The law' is nothing but a *café* game which gives the winner the
right to humiliate the losers, even and particularly if they are the representa-
tives of officialdom. The conventions and the poetical and satirical picture of
the good-humored anarchy prevailing there are as imaginary as those of *La
Chartreuse de Parme*, but the novelist has the skill to make us believe in them
uncritically. *La Fête* (Gallimard, 1960; *The Sovereigns*, London: Cape, 1960;
Fête, New York: Alfred A. Knopf, 1961) tells a much thinner story and is in
truth a long short story, with little tension, parading as a novel. It is a sophisticated tale on the trite theme of successful love-making as a basis for a
deeper love. D. H. Lawrence, however, would have been horrified at so little
seriousness and so much intellectual analysis put into a mere search for
pleasure.

Vercors, pseudonym of Bruller, Jean (b. 1902), was known to a few artists
before World War II as an etcher and decorator. He became famous overnight
for his *récit* of silent resistance to the German enemy, *Le Silence de la mer*.
The short novel was a minor masterpiece of restraint and did much to encourage the literature of the Resistance. Vercors then wrote other *récits* of a
moralist tormented by problems of political ethics and attracted to liberal
causes. His real bent is toward didactic literature. *Les Animaux dénaturés*
(Albin Michel, 1952; *You Shall Know Them*, Boston: Little, Brown, 1953)
is a none too successful allegory. *La Liberté de décembre* and *Monsieur
Prousthe*, joined in translation as *Paths of Love* (G. P. Putnam, 1961), is
frankly unpleasant as well as technically awkward. *Sylva* (Grasset, 1961;
Sylva, G. P. Putnam, 1962) is a philosophical tale of a bachelor who rescues
a she-fox and metamorphoses her into a human being; but that new Pygmalion
does not succeed and the woman returns to her original animal nature. The
novel, Vercors's best, is one of many which ask today the monotonous question: what is man? Later allegories with an anti-American flavor by Vercors
have only confirmed his lack of grasp on sensations, images, and the concrete.

Vian, Boris (1920–59), one of the many *enfants terribles* of French existentialism. He had assimilated superbly and caricatured the tricks and the tone
of the toughest American novel and had concocted the story of an American
colored man hunted by the whites after committing a string of thefts, rapes,
and murders: *J'irai cracher sur vos tombes* (signed Vernon Sullivan, Editions
du Scorpion, 1946). His *L'Ecume des jours* (Gallimard, 1947) is entertaining,
witty, and jocular, but it is decidedly unsubstantial and unconvincing. The
comic devices are too threadbare and facile. *L'Arrache-cœur* (1953, published again by Pauvert in 1963) and *En Avant la zizigue* (1959) were
equally cold, satirical, and funny, somewhat in the manner of Queneau. The
author, an engineer by training, then a trumpet player in cabarets, a *chan-
sonnier* and a born anarchist, was surrounded by a legend in Saint-Germain
des Prés. His talent was brilliant but brittle. But he was threatened by disease

and he died in June 1959 while filming one of his least good novels. He has enjoyed surprising sales since his death in part due to the public's weariness with the austere 'new novel,' in part also to an excellent little book on him written by an American scholar for a Columbia dissertation: *Boris Vian* by David Noakes (Editions Universitaires, 1965).

Wittig, Monique (b. 1937), till recently unknown, attracted attention with her novel, *L'Opoponax* (Minuit, 1964). It is a subtle and warm picture of the passing from childhood to adolescence of a girl from the country. The touch is deft and just; the manner is not overly poetical and is clearly influenced by the precise and objective manner of writers of the Editions de Minuit, where the author is a proof reader. The title is a word invented by the girlish heroine to designate anything or anyone who is annoying, fractious, and deserves to be cursed by the petulant child. A light novel but one of the few which presents the world of childhood without sentimentality and without making it perverse or brutal. The novel appeared in English in 1966 (London: Peter Owen, and New York: Simon and Schuster).

Yacine, Kateb (b. 1929), whose first name means 'writer' and whose family, in the region of Constantine, was a highly cultured one, was arrested by the French authorities in Algeria in 1945, then lived and wrote for a time in Paris; he is a poet, a playwright, but his novel *Nedjma* (Seuil, 1957) is the best constructed work of fiction in French by a representative of Arabic culture, in which structured novels have never been the vogue. Four men who have all loved one woman, Nedjma (who is a real and concrete creature, but also the Algeria made up of Arabic sources and of French influence) are fascinated by the complex mystery for which she stands. The several planes on which the story is told and the characters seen are very ingeniously interwoven.

Yourcenar, Marguerite, is the anagram of Mlle de Crayencour. She has an immense cultural background, has written on Pindar, translated Henry James, and taught literature and art. After several volumes that brought her the esteem of a limited circle, she won general attention with a novel that made no concession to fashions or to facility, the imaginary memoirs of Emperor Hadrian, *Mémoires d'Hadrien* (Plon, 1951). The aging ruler looks back over his career, records the lessons of his life for young Marcus Aurelius, and, having known the joys and sorrows of power and of passion, he faces death serenely. The book, impeccably documented, steers clear of all the pitfalls of this type of historical fiction. It is neither overwritten and anachronistic nor addicted to facile local color; it has more truth and more simplicity than *Salammbô* or *Marius the Epicurean*. It crowns worthily an author's career, up to then obscure. The volume was translated into English with the collaboration of the author as *Memoirs of Hadrian* (London: Secker and Warburg, 1955; and New York: Farrar, Straus and Young, 1954).

Zéraffa, Michel (b. 1918), was warmly praised for his first novel, *Le Temps des rencontres* (Albin Michel, 1948). It is a work of solid and ingenious craftsmanship, portraying five characters of varied backgrounds thrown together in a corner of the Alps, then following their fortunes through the Resistance, collaboration, and the confusion of the war years. The author had not yet learned the art of omission and of going deeply into his chosen themes. *L'Ecume et le sel* (Albin Michel, 1950), which followed, deals with the scuttling of the French fleet in Toulon. It sets off the lurid and cruder sides of the people affected by the event and seems to seek brutality needlessly. *Le Commerce des hommes* (Albin Michel, 1952) shows progress in the author's portrayal of character and more naturalness in the invention of incident. A young man is desperately lonely (solitude is the obsession of all of Zéraffa's heroes) and remorseful after the murder of his brother in 1944. He watches with disgust his stepmother and her abject Russian lover, who, tired of the mother, makes love to her daughter as well and is shot by the jealous elder woman. The discouraged young man (a teacher, like the author) leaves for the New World. Zéraffa has more vigor than delicacy, and the behavior of his characters often lacks the inner compulsion that would make them truer to life or truer than life. But he has many of the gifts of a novelist. (Zéraffa's first novel appeared in 1953 in New York as *The Living and the Lost;* Roy Publishers.)

Novels with Titles of English Translations *

Aragon, Louis. *Aurélien,* Fribourg: Egloff, 1944; *Aurelien* (Eithne Wilkins), London: Pilot Press, 1946; Duell, Sloan & Pearce, 1947. *Les Beaux Quartiers,* Denoël & Steele, 1936; *Residential Quarter* (Haakon Chevalier), Harcourt, Brace, 1938. *Les Cloches de Bâle,* Denoël & Steele, 1934; *The Bells of Basel* (Haakon Chevalier), Harcourt, Brace, 1936. *Les Voyageurs de l'impériale,* Gallimard, 1942; *The Century Was Young* (Hannah Josephson), Duell, Sloan & Pearce, 1941; also *Passengers of Destiny,* London: Pilot Press, 1947. *La Semaine sainte,* Gallimard, 1958, which inaugurated Aragon's new manner, was translated as *Holy Week* (Haakon Chevalier), Putnam, 1961.

Aymé, Marcel. *Autres Contes du chat perché,* Gallimard, 1950; *The Magic Picture. More about the Wonderful Farm* (Norman Denny), Harper, 1954. *La Belle Image,* Gallimard, 1941; *The Second Face* (Norman Denny), Harper, 1952. *Le Chemin des écoliers,* Gallimard, 1946; *The Transient Hour* (Eric Sutton), A. A. Wyn, 1948. *Le Confort intellectuel,* Flammarion, 1949. *Contes du chat perché,* Gallimard, 1934; *The Wonderful Farm* (Norman Denny), Harper, 1951. *Le Moulin de la sourdine,* Gallimard, 1936; *The Secret Stream* (Norman Denny), Harper, 1953; London: The Bodley Head, 1953. *La Table aux crevés,* Gallimard, 1929; *The Hollow Field* (Helen Waddell), Dodd Mead & Co., 1933. *Travelingue,* Gallimard, 1941; *The Miraculous Barber* (Eric Sutton), Harper, 1951. *Uranus,* Gallimard, 1948; *The Barkeep of Blémont* (Norman Denny), Harper, 1950. More recent translations are: *La Jument verte,* Gallimard, 1933; *The Green Mare* (Norman Denny), London: The Bodley Head, 1955. *Les Tiroirs de l'inconnu,* Gallimard, 1960; *The Conscience of Love* (Norman Denny), Atheneum, 1962; and two collections of short stories from several French volumes of stories by Aymé, *Across Paris and other Stories* (Norman Denny), Harper, 1958; London: The Bodley Head, 1957 (mostly from *Le Vin de Paris,* Gallimard, 1947) and *The Proverb and Other Stories,* Atheneum, 1961, drawn in part from *Le Passe-Murailles,* Gallimard, 1942.

* Names of translators are enclosed in parentheses. Also included here are the titles of recently published works not as yet translated but which are in the opinion of the author deserving of translation. N.t. means that no translator's name is given.

Bazin, Hervé. *L'Huile sur le feu*, Grasset, 1954. *Lève-toi et marche*, Grasset, 1952; *Constance* (Herma Briffault), Crown, 1955. *La Mort du petit cheval*, Grasset, 1950. *La Tête contre les murs*, Grasset, 1949; *Head against the Wall* (W. J. Strachan), Prentice-Hall, 1952. *Vipère au poing*, Grasset, 1948; *Viper in the Fist* (W. J. Strachan), Prentice-Hall, 1951. A secondary novel, *Qui J'ose aimer*, Grasset, 1956, appeared as *A Tribe of Women* (Richard Howard), Simon and Schuster, 1958.

Beauvoir, Simone de. *L'Invitée*, Gallimard, 1943; *She Came To Stay* (Roger Senhouse & Yvonne Moyse), London: Secker & Warburg, 1949; Cleveland and New York: The World Publishing Co., 1954. *Le Sang des autres*, Gallimard, 1945; *The Blood of Others* (Roger Senhouse & Yvonne Moyse), Knopf, 1948. *Tous les hommes sont mortels*, Gallimard, 1946; *All Men Are Mortal* (Leonard M. Friedman), Cleveland: World Publishing Company, 1955. *Les Mandarins*, Gallimard, 1954; *The Mandarins* (Leonard M. Friedman), World, 1956.

Beck, Béatrix. *Léon Morin, prêtre*, Gallimard, 1952; *The Passionate Heart* (Constantine Fitzgibbon), J. Messner, 1953.

Bernanos, Georges. *Un Crime*, Plon, 1935; *A Crime* (Anne Green), Dutton, 1936. *La Joie*, Plon, 1929; *Joy* (Louise Varese), Pantheon, 1946. *L'Imposture*, Plon, 1927. *Journal d'un curé de campagne*, Plon, 1936; *The Diary of a Country Priest* (Pamela Morris), Macmillan, 1937; London: Boriswood, 1937. *Monsieur Ouine*, Plon, 1946; *The Open Mind* (Geoffrey Dunlop), London: John Lane, 1945. *Sous le soleil de Satan*, Plon, 1926; *The Star of Satan* (Pamela Morris), Macmillan, 1940; also *Under the Sun of Satan* (Harry L. Binsse), Pantheon, 1949. *Un Mauvais Rêve*, Plon, 1951; *Night is Darkest* (W. J. Strachan), London: The Bodley Head, 1953. *Mouchette* (J. C. Whitehouse) appeared in 1966 at Holt, Rinehart and Winston.

Bloch-Michel, Jean. *Le Témoin*, Gallimard, 1948; *The Witness* (Eithne Wilkins), Pantheon, 1949. *La Fuite en Egypte*, Gallimard, 1952; *The Flight into Egypt* (Frances Frenaye), Scribners, 1955.

Blondin, Antoine. *Un Singe en hiver*, Table ronde, 1959; *A Monkey in Winter* (Robert Baldick), Putnam, 1960.

Bosco, Henri. *Malicroix*, Grasset, 1948. *Le Mas Théotime*, Charlot, 1945; *The Farm Theotime* (Mervyn Savill), London: Aldor, 1946; as *Farm in Provence*, Doubleday, 1947. *Un Rameau de la nuit*, Flammarion, 1950; *The Dark Bough* (Merwyn Savill), London: Staples Press, 1955.

Boutron, Michel. *Hans* (taken over by Editions André Bonne, 1951); *Hans* (Robin Graham), London: Verschoyle, 1952.

Brincourt, André. *La Farandole*, Table ronde, 1952. *Le Vert Paradis*, Table ronde, 1950; *The Paradise below the Stairs* (Herma Briffault), Duell, Sloan & Pearce, 1952.

Camus, Albert. *L'Etranger*, Gallimard, 1942; *The Stranger* (Stuart Gilbert), Knopf, 1946 (also Vintage Books, 1954); *The Outsider* (Stuart Gilbert), London: Hamilton, 1946. *L'Homme révolté*, Gallimard, 1951; *The Rebel* (Anthony Bower), Knopf, 1954. *La Peste*, Gallimard, 1947; *The Plague* (Stuart Gilbert), Knopf, 1948. *La Chute*, Gallimard, 1956; (Justin O'Brien), Knopf, 1957. *L'Exil et le royaume*, Gallimard, 1958; *Exile and the Kingdom* (Justin O'Brien), Knopf, 1958.

Cau, Jean. *La Pitié de Dieu*, Gallimard; *The Mercy of God* (Richard Howard), Atheneum, 1963.

Céline, Louis-Ferdinand. *Bagatelles pour un massacre*, Denoël, 1937. *La Bande de Guignol*, Denoël, 1944; *Guignol's Band* (Bernard Frechtman and Jack T. Nile), New Directions, 1954. *Mort à credit*, Denoël, 1936; *Death on the Installment Plan* (John Marks), Boston: Little, Brown, 1938; New Directions, 1947. *Voyage au bout de la nuit*, Denoël, 1932; *Journey to the End of the Night* (John Marks), Boston: Little, Brown, 1934; New Directions, 1949. See the chapter on him.

Cesbron, Gilbert. *Chiens perdus sans collier*, Laffont, 1954. *Les Innocents de Paris*, Corrêa, 1944; *The Innocents of Paris* (Marguerite Waldman), Boston: Houghton Mifflin, 1946; London: Collins, 1946. *Les Saints vont en enfer*, Laffont, 1952; *Saints in Hell* (John Russell), London: Secker and Warburg, 1953; Doubleday, 1954.

Chamson, André. *L'Année des vaincus*, Grasset, 1934. *L'Auberge de l'abîme*, Grasset, 1933; *The Mountain Tavern* (Edwin Granberry), Holt, 1933. *Le Crime des justes*, Grasset, 1928; *The Crime of the Just* (Van Wyck Brooks), Scribners, 1930. *Le Dernier Village*, Mercure de France, 1946. *La Galère*, Gallimard, 1939. *Les Hommes de la route*, Grasset, 1927; *The Road* (Van Wyck Brooks), Scribners, 1929. *Les Quatre Eléments*, Grasset, 1935; *A Mountain Boyhood* (John Rodker), London: J. Lehmann, 1947. *Roux le bandit*, Grasset, 1925; *Roux the Bandit* (Van Wyck Brooks), Scribners, 1929.

Cocteau, Jean. *Les Enfants terribles*, Grasset, 1929; *Enfants terribles* (Samuel Putman), Harcourt, Brace, 1930. *Le Grand Ecart*, Stock, 1923; *The Grand Ecart* (Lewis Galantière), New York and London: G. P. Putman, 1925. *Thomas l'imposteur*, Gallimard, 1923; *Thomas the Impostor* (Lewis Galantière), Appleton, 1925. *Les Enfants terribles*, Cocteau's only real novel, appeared also in London as *Children of the Game* (Rosamond Lehmann), Harvill Press, 1955.

Colette. *Le Blé en herbe*, Flammarion, 1923; *The Ripening* (Ida Zeitlin), Farrar & Rinehart, 1932. *La Chatte*, Grasset, 1933; *The Cat* (Morris Bentinck), Farrar & Rinehart, 1936. *Chéri*, Fayard, 1920; *Cheri* (Janet Flanner), Boni, 1929; London: Gollancz, 1930. *Duo*, Ferenczi, 1934; *Duo* (Frederick Blossom), Farrar & Rinehart, 1935. *L'Entrave*, Librairie du livre, 1913 (subsequently Flammarion); *Recaptured* (Viola Garvin), London: Gollancz, 1931; Doubleday, 1932. *La Fin de Chéri*, Flammarion, 1926; *The Last of Cheri* (Viola Garvin), London: Gollancz, 1933; G. P. Putnam, 1932; also in *Cheri* and *The Last of Chéri* (Roger Senhouse), Farrar, Straus & Young, 1951. *Gigi*, Ferenczi, 1945; *Gigi, Julie de Carneilhan, Chance Acquaintances* (Roger Senhouse), Farrar, Straus & Young, 1952. *L'Ingénue libertine*, P. Ollendorf, 1909; *Gentle Libertine* (R.C.B.), Grosset & Dunlap, 1931. *La Naissance du jour*, Flammarion, 1928; *A Lesson in Love* (Rosemary Benét), Farrar & Rinehart, 1932. *Mitsou ou comment l'esprit vient aux filles*, Fayard, 1919; *Mitsou or How Girls Grow Wise* (Jane Terry), Boni, 1930. Since Colette's death in 1954, several other translations have appeared: *Claudine in Paris* (Antonia White), Farrar, Straus and Cudahy, 1961; *Break of Day* (*La Naissance du jour*) (Enid McLeod), Farrar, Straus and Cudahy, 1961; *La Seconde*, Ferenczi, 1929; *The Other One* (Viola G. Garvin), Cosmopolitan Book Corporation, 1931, also (Roger Senhouse and Elizabeth Tait), Farrar, Straus and Cudahy, 1960; *La Vagabonde*, Ollendorf, 1910; *The Vagabond* (Enid McLeod), Farrar, Straus and Young, 1955; also *Earthly Paradise: An Autobiography Drawn from Colette's Lifetime Writings* (Herma Briffault and others), Farrar, Straus and Giroux, 1966.

Colin, Paul. *Les Jeux sauvages*, Gallimard, 1950; *Savage Play* (Alfred van Ameyden van Duym), Dutton, 1953.

Curtis, Jean Louis. *Les Forêts de la nuit*, Julliard, 1947; *The Forests of the Night* (Nora Wydenbruck), G. P. Putnam, 1951. *Gibier de Potence*, Julliard, 1949; *Lucifer's Dream* (Robin Chancellor), London: J. Lehmann, 1952; G. P. Putnam, 1953. *Les Justes Causes*, Julliard, 1954. *Cygne sauvage*, Julliard, 1962. *Un Saint au néon*, Denoël, 1956; *The Neon Halo: The Face of the Future* (Humphrey Hare), London: Secker and Warburg, 1958.

Del Castillo, Michel. *Tanguy*, Julliard, 1957; *Child of our Time* (Peter Green), 1958. *La Guitare*, Julliard, 1957; *The Guitar* (Humphrey Hare), London: Hart-Davis, 1959.

Drieu La Rochelle, Pierre. *Le Feu Follet*, Gallimard, 1931 and 1963; *The Fire Within* (Richard Howard), Knopf, 1961.

Druon, Maurice. *Alexandre la grand*, Del Duca, 1958; *Alexander the God, A Novel* (Humphrey Hare), Scribners, 1960. *La Fin des hommes*, Julliard, 1948–51; *The Curtain Falls, A Modern Trilogy* (Humphrey Hare), Scribners, 1960.

Les Rois Maudits, Del Duca, 1955–59; *The Accursed Kings* (Humphrey Hare), Scribners, 1956.

Duhamel, Georges. *La Chronique des Pasquiers:* (1) *Le Notaire du Havre,* Mercure de France, 1933. (2) *Le Jardin des bêtes sauvages,* Mercure de France, 1934. (3) *Vue de la terre promise,* Mercure de France, 1934. (4) *La Nuit de la Saint Jean,* Mercure de France, 1935. (5) *Le Désert de Bièvres,* Mercure de France, 1937. (6) *Les Maîtres,* Mercure de France, 1937. (7) *Cécile parmi nous,* Mercure de France, 1938. (8) *Le Combat contre les ombres,* Mercure de France, 1939. (9) *Suzanne et les jeunes hommes,* Mercure de France, 1940. (10) *La Passion de Joseph Pasquier,* Mercure de France, 1941; *The Fortunes of the Pasquiers* (Samuel Putnam), Harper, 1935, contains vols. 1, 2, 3; *The Pasquier Chronicles* (Beatrice de Holthoir), London: Dent, 1937; also Holt, 1937, contains: (1) *News from Havre* (also trans. as *Papa Pasquier,* Harper, 1934), (2) *Caged Beasts* (also trans. as *Young Pasquier,* London: Dent, 1936, as *Fortunes of the Pasquiers,* Harper, 1934), (3) *In Sight of the Promised Land* (included in *Fortunes of the Pasquiers,* Harper, 1935), (4) *St. John's Eve,* (5) *The House in the Desert. Cecile among the Pasquiers* (Beatrice de Holthoir), London: Dent, 1940 (American title *Cecile Pasquier,* same translator, Holt, 1940), contains: (6) *Pastors and Masters,* (7) *Cecile,* (8) *The Fight against the Shadows. Suzanne & Joseph Pasquier* (Beatrice de Holthoir), London: Dent, 1946 (American title *Suzanne and Joseph,* same translator, Holt, 1949), contains vols. 9 and 10.

Civilisation, Mercure de France, 1918; *Civilization* (E. S. Brooks), Century, 1919. *Vie des martyrs,* Mercure de France, 1917; *The New Book of Martyrs* (Florence Simmonds), Doran, 1918; London: Heinemann, 1918. *Vie et aventures de Salavin:* (1) *La Confession de minuit,* Mercure de France, 1920. (2) *Deux Hommes,* Mercure de France, 1924. (3) *Le Journal de Salavin,* Mercure de France, 1927. (4) *Le Club des Lyonnais,* Mercure de France, 1929. (5) *Tel qu'en lui même,* Mercure de France, 1932; *Salavin* (Gladys Billings) G. P. Putnam, 1936, contains: (1) *Confession at Midnight,* (2) *Salavin's Journal,* (3) *The Lyonnais Club,* (4) *End of Illusion. Le Voyage de Patrice Périot,* Mercure de France, 1951. *Inventaire de L'Abîme* and *Biographie de mes fantômes,* Hartmann, 1945, have been translated in one volume as *Light on My Days* (Basil Collier), London: J. M. Dent, 1948.

Duras, Marquerite. *Un Barrage contre le Pacifique,* Gallimard, 1950; *The Sea Wall* (Herma Briffault), Pellegrini & Cudahy, 1952. *Les Petits Chevaux de Tarquinia,* Gallimard, 1953; *The Little Horses of Tarquinia* (Peter Duberg), London: Calder, 1960. *Le Square,* Gallimard, 1955; *The Square* (Sonia Pitt-Rivers and Irina Murdoch), Grove Press, 1959. *Moderato Cantabile,* Minuit, 1958; *Moderato Cantabile* (Richard Seaver), Grove Press, 1960.

Dutourd, Jean. *Une Tête de chien,* Gallimard, 1950; *A Dog's Head* (Robin Chancellor), Simon & Schuster, 1953. *Au bon beurre,* Gallimard, 1952; *The Best Butter* (Robin Chancellor), Simon & Schuster, 1955. *Les Taxis de la*

Marne, Gallimard, 1956; *The Taxis of the Marne* (Harold King), Simon & Schuster, 1957.

Gary, Romain. *Les Couleurs du jour*, Gallimard, 1952; *Colors of the Day* (Stephen Becker), Simon & Schuster, 1953. *Education européenne*, C. Lévy, 1945; *Forest of Anger* (Viola Garvin), London: The Cresset Press, 1946. *Le Grand Vestiaire*, C. Lévy, 1948; *The Company of Men* (Joseph Barnes), Simon & Schuster, 1950. *Le Mangeur d'étoiles*, Gallimard, 1959; *The Talent Scout* (Joseph Markham Beach), Harper, 1961. *Les Racines du ciel*, Gallimard, 1956; *The Roots of Heaven* (Jonathan Griffin), Simon and Schuster, 1958. *Education Européenne* also appeared as *A European Education* (Viola Garvin), Simon & Schuster, 1960.

Gascar, Pierre. *La Barre de Corail*, Gallimard, 1958; *The Coral Barrier* (Merloyd Lawrence), Boston: Atlantic-Little, Brown, 1961. *Les Bêtes, Le Temps des morts*, Gallimard, 1953. *La Graine*, Gallimard, 1955; *The Seed* (Merloyd Lawrence), Boston: Atlantic-Little, Brown, 1959. *Le Mouton de feu*, Gallimard, 1953; *Lambs of Fire* (Merloyd Lawrence), Braziller, 1965. *Soleils*, Gallimard, 1960; *Women and the Sun* (Merloyd Lawrence), Boston: Atlantic-Little, Brown, 1965.

Genet, Jean. *Journal du Voleur*, Gallimard, 1949; *The Thief's Journal* (Bernard Frechtman), Grove Press, 1964. *Le Miracle de la rose*, Lyon: L'Arbalète, 1946; *Miracle of the Rose* (Bernard Frechtman), Grove Press, 1965. *Notre-Dame des Fleurs*, Lyon: L'Arbalète, 1948; *Our Lady of the Flowers*, London: Faber and Faber (Bernard Frechtman); Grove Press, 1963.

Gide, André. *Les Caves du Vatican*, Gallimard, 1914; *The Vatican Swindle* (Dorothy Bussy), Knopf, 1925. *Dostoievsky d'après sa correspondance*, Imprimerie Jean & Berger, n.d. (1908) (from an article in *La Grande Revue*, 25 May 1908, pp. 289–315); *Dostoevsky* (n.t.), London: J. M. Dent, 1925; Secker & Warburg, 1949; Knopf, 1926; New Directions, 1949. *Les Faux-Monnayeurs*, Gallimard, 1926; *The Counterfeiters* (Dorothy Bussy), Knopf, 1927; also The Modern Library; as *The Coiners*, London: Cassell & Co., 1927. *L'Immoraliste*, Mercure de France, 1902; *The Immoralist* (Dorothy Bussy), Knopf, 1930; also Vintage Books, 1954; London: Cassell & Co., 1930. *Isabelle*, Gallimard, 1911; *Isabelle* (Dorothy Bussy) in *Two Symphonies*, Knopf, 1931; London: Cassell & Co., 1931. *Les Nourritures terrestres*, Mercure de France, 1897; *Fruit of the Earth* (Dorothy Bussy), Knopf, 1949; London: Secker & Warburg, 1949. *Paludes*, Librairie de l'Art Indépendant, 1895; *Marshlands and Prometheus Misbound* (George D. Painter), New Directions, 1953; London: Secker & Warburg, 1953. *La Porte étroite*, Mercure de France, 1909; *Strait Is the Gate* (Dorothy Bussy), Knopf, 1924; London: Secker & Warburg, 1924. *La Symphonie pastorale*, Gallimard, 1919; *The Pastoral Symphony* in *Two Symphonies*. *Thésée*, Gallimard, 1946; Pantheon, 1946; *Theseus*

(John Russell), London: *Horizon*, 1948; also in *Two Legends: Theseus* and *Oedipus*, Knopf, 1950; London: Secker & Warburg, 1950.

Giono, Jean. *Batailles dans la montagne*, Gallimard, 1937. *Le Chant du monde*, Gallimard, 1934; *The Song of the World* (Henri Fluchère and Geoffrey Myers), Viking, 1937. *Colline*, Grasset, 1929; *Hill of Destiny* (Jacques LeClerq), Viking, 1929. *Le Grand Troupeau*, Gallimard, 1931. *Le Hussard sur le toit*, Gallimard, 1951; *The Horseman on the Roof* (Jonathan Griffin), Knopf, 1954. *Jean le bleu*, Grasset, 1932; *Blue Boy* (Katherine A. Clarke), Viking, 1946. *Le Poids du ciel*, Gallimard, 1938. *Que ma joie demeure*, Gallimard, 1935; *Joy of Man's Desiring* (Katherine A. Clarke), Viking, 1940. *Regain*, Grasset, 1930; *Harvest* (Henri Fluchère and Geoffrey Myers), Viking, 1939. *Un de Baumugnes*, Gallimard, 1929; *Lovers Are Never Losers* (Jacques LeClerq), Viking, 1931. *Les Vraies Richesses*, Grasset, 1936. *Le Moulin de Pologne*, Gallimard, 1952; *The Malediction* (Peter de Mendelssohn), Criterion, 1955. *Le Bonheur Fou*, Gallimard, 1957; *The Straw Man* (Phyllis Johnson), Knopf, 1959.

Giraudoux, Jean. *Bella* Grasset, 1926; *Bella* (J. F. Scalan), Knopf, 1927. *Choix des Elues*, Grasset, 1939. *Siegfried et le Limousin*, Grasset, 1922; *My Friend from Limousin* (Louis C. Wilcox), Harper, 1923. *Simon le pathétique*, Grasset, 1918. *Suzanne et le Pacifique*, Emile-Paul, 1921; *Suzanne and the Pacific* (Ben Ray Redman), G. P. Putnam, 1923.

Gorz, André. *Le Traître*, Seuil, 1958; *The Traitor* (Richard Howard), Simon and Schuster, 1959.

Gracq, Julien. *Au Château d'Argol*, Corti, 1939; reprinted 1945; *The Castle of Argol* (Louise Varese), New Directions, 1951. *Un Beau Ténébreux*, Corti, 1945; *A Dark Stranger* (W. J. Strachan), New Directions, 1949. *Le Rivage des Syrtes*, Corti, 1952. *Un Balcon en forêt*, Corti, 1958; *Balcony in the Forest*, London: Hutchinson, and New York: Braziller, 1959.

Green, Julien. *Adrienne Mesurat*, Plon, 1927; *The Closed Garden* (Henry L. Stuart), Harper, 1928. *Christine*—suivi de *Léviathan*, Editions des Cahiers libres, 1928; *Christine and Other Stories* (Courtney Bruerton), London: Heinemann, 1931, contains *Christine, Leviathan, The Keys of Death, The Pilgrim on the Earth. Léviathan*, Plon, 1929; *The Dark Journey* (Vyvyan Holland), Harper, 1929. *Minuit*, Plon, 1936; *Midnight* (Vyvyan Holland), Harper, 1936. *Moïra*, Plon, 1950; *Moira* (Denise Folliot), London: Heinemann; Macmillan, 1951. *Mont Cinère*, Plon, 1926; *Avarice House* (Marshall Best), Harper, 1927. *Si j'étais vous*, Plon, 1947; *If I Were You* (J. H. P. McEwen), Harper, 1949. *Varouna*, Plon, 1940; *Then Shall the Dust Return* (James Whitall), Harper, 1941. *Le Visionnaire*, Plon, 1934; *The Dreamer* (Vyvyan Holland), Harper, 1934.

Guilloux, Louis. *Sang noir*, Gallimard, 1935; *Bitter Victory* (Samuel Putnam), McBride, 1936.

Hardy, René. *Le Fer de Dieu*, Laffont, 1953; *The Sword of God* (Humphrey Hare), London: Hamish Hamilton, 1954.

Hougron, Jean. *Soleil au ventre*, Domat, 1952; *Blaze of the Sun* (Mervyn Savill), Farrar, Straus & Young, 1954; London: Hurst & Blackett, 1954. *Tu récolteras la tempête*, Domat, 1950; *Reap the Whirlwind* (Mervyn Savill), Farrar, Straus & Young, 1953. *Mort en Fraude*, Domat, 1953; *The Fugitive* (Mervyn Savill), London: Hurst and Blackett, 1954.

Ikor, Roger. *Les Eaux mêlées*, Albin Michel, 1955; *The Sons of Avrom* (Leonard M. Friedman), Putnam, 1958.

Jacquemard, Simone. *Le Veilleur de nuit*, Seuil, 1962; *The Night Watchman* (L. D. Emmet), Holt, Rinehart and Winston, 1964.

Jouhandeau, Marcel. *Chaminadour*, Gallimard, 1934. *Elise*, Gallimard, 1933; *Marcel and Elise* (Martin Turnell), Pantheon, 1953 (contains selections from several volumes by Jouhandeau). *Monsieur Godeau intime*, Gallimard, 1926. *Monsieur Godeau marié*, Gallimard, 1933.

Kessel, Joseph. *L'Equipage. Les coeurs purs*, Gallimard, 1927; *The Pure in Heart* (n.t.), Dodd, Mead and Co., 1938, and London: Gollancz, 1938. *Le Lion*, Gallimard, 1958; *The Lion* (Peter Green), Knopf, 1959. *Tous n'étaient pas des anges*, Plon, 1963; *They Weren't All Angels* (Humphrey Hare), McKay, 1965.

Lacretelle, Jacques de. *La Bonifas*, Gallimard, 1925; *Marie Bonifas* (Winifred S. Whale), G. P. Putnam, 1927. *Le Retour de Silbermann*, Gallimard, 1929. *Silbermann*, Gallimard, 1922; *Silbermann* (Brian Lunn), London: Benn, 1923.

Larbaud, Valéry. *Amants, heureux amants*, Gallimard, 1923. *Fermina Marquez*, Plon, 1911.

Le Clézio, J. M. G. *Le Procès-Verbal*, Gallimard, 1963; *The Interrogation* (Daphne Woodward), Atheneum, 1964. *La Fièvre*, Gallimard, 1965; *Fever* (Daphne Woodward), Atheneum, 1966. *Le Déluge*, Gallimard, 1966.

Leduc, Violette. *La Bâtarde*, Gallimard, 1964; *La Bâtarde* (Derek Coltman), Farrar, Straus and Giroux, 1965. *La Femme au petit renard*, Gallimard, 1965; *The Woman with the Little Fox* (Derek Coltman), Farrar, Straus and Giroux, 1966.

Malaquais, Jean. *Le Gaffeur*, Corrêa, 1953; *The Joker* (Herma Briffault), Doubleday, 1954. *Les Javanais*, Denoël, 1939; *Men from Nowhere* (n.t.),

L. F. Fischer, 1943. *Planète sans visa*, Pré aux Clercs, 1937; *World without Visa* (Peter Grant), Doubleday, 1948.

Mallet-Joris, Françoise. *Le Rempart des Béguines*, Julliard, 1951; *The Illusionist* (Herma Briffault), Farrar, Straus and Young, 1952. *La Chambre rouge*, Julliard, 1955. *Cordelia*, Julliard, 1956; *Cordelia and Other Stories* (Peter Green), Farrar, Straus and Giroux, 1965. *L'Empire Céleste*, Julliard, 1959; *Café Céleste* (Herma Briffault), Farrar, Straus and Cudahy, 1959.

Malraux, André. *La Condition humaine*, Gallimard, 1933; *Man's Fate* (Haakon M. Chevalier), H. Smith & R. Haas, 1934; also The Modern Library, 1934; *Storm in Shanghai* (Alastair MacDonald), London: Methuen, 1935. *Les Conquérants*, Grasset, 1928; *The Conquerors* (Winifred Stephens Whale), Harcourt, Brace, 1929. *L'Espoir*, Gallimard, 1938; *Man's Hope* (Stuart Gilbert and Alastair MacDonald), Random House, 1938; also The Modern Library, 1941; as *Days of Hope*, London: G. Routledge & Sons, 1938. *Les Noyers de l'Altenburg* (*Combat avec l'ange* I), Gallimard, 1945; *The Walnut Trees of Altenburg* (A. W. Fielding), London: J. Lehmann, 1952. *Le Temps du mépris*, Gallimard, 1935; *Days of Wrath* (Haakon M. Chevalier), Random House, 1936; as *Days of Contempt*, London: Gollancz, 1936. *La Voie royale*, Grasset, 1930; *The Royal Way* (Stuart Gilbert), H. Smith & R. Haas, 1935.

Marchal, Lucie. *La Mèche*, Fortuny, 1948; *The Mesh* (Virgilia Peterson), Appleton-Century-Crofts, 1949.

Martin du Gard, Roger. *Jean Barois*, Gallimard, 1913; *Jean Barois* (Stuart Gilbert), Viking, 1949. *Les Thibault*, Gallimard, 1922–40, contains (1) *Le Cahier gris*, (2) *Le Pénitencier*, (3) *La Belle Saison*, (4) *La Consultation*, (5) *La Sorellina*, (6) *La Mort du père*, (7) *L'Eté 1914*, (8) *Epilogue; The Thibaults* includes Parts 1, 2, 3 (Madeleine Boyd), Boni & Liveright, 1926; *The Thibaults* includes Parts 1, 2, 3, 4, 5, 6 (Stuart Gilbert), Viking, 1939; *Summer 1914* includes Parts 7, 8 (Stuart Gilbert), Viking, 1941; *The World of the Thibaults: I, The Thibaults; II, Summer 1914* (Stuart Gilbert), Viking, 1941.

Marceau, Félicien. *L'Homme du roi*, Gallimard, 1952. *Bergère Légère*, Gallimard, 1953. *Les Élans du cœur*, Gallimard, 1955.

Mauriac, Claude. *Le Dîner en Ville*, Albin Michel, 1959; *Dinner in Town* (Merloyd Lawrence), London: Calder and Boyars, 1966; *The Dinner Party* (Merloyd Lawrence), Braziller, 1960. *La Marquise sortit à cinq heures*, Albin Michel, 1963; *The Marquise Went out at Five* (Richard Howard), Braziller, 1965.

Mauriac, François. *L'Agneau*, Flammarion, 1954; *The Lamb* (Gerard Hopkins), London: Eyre and Spottiswoode; Farrar, Straus and Cudahy, 1955. *Les Anges noirs*, Grasset, 1935; *The Mask of Innocence* (Gerard Hopkins),

Farrar, Straus & Young, 1953. *Le Baiser au lépreux*, Grasset, 1922; *A Kiss to the Leper* (James Whitall), London: Heinemann, 1923, subsequently, *A Kiss for the Leper* (Gerard Hopkins), London: Eyre & Spottiswoode, 1950, and also in *The Family*. *Le Désert de l'amour*, Grasset, 1925; *The Desert of Love* (Samuel Putnam), Covici-Friede, 1929; also (Gerard Hopkins), Pellegrini and Cudahy, 1951. *Destins*, Grasset, 1928; *Destinies* (Eric Sutton), Covici-Friede, 1929; also *Lines of Life* (Gerard Hopkins), Farrar, Straus and Cudahy, 1957. *Dieu et Mammon*, Capitole, 1930; *God and Mammon* (n.t.), London: Sheed & Ward, 1936. *La Fin de la nuit*, Grasset, 1935; *The End of the Night*, see *Thérèse Desqueyroux*. *Genitrix*, Grasset, 1923; *Genitrix* (in *The Family: A Kiss to the Leper and Genitrix*) (Lewis Galantière), Covici-Friede, 1930; also *A Kiss for the Leper and Genitrix* (Gerard Hopkins), London: Eyre & Spottiswoode, 1950. *Le Jeune Homme*, Hachette, 1926. *Le Mal*, Grasset, 1924; *The Enemy* (in *The Weakling* and *The Enemy*) (Gerard Hopkins), Pellegrini & Cudahy, 1952. *Le Noeud de vipères*, Grasset, 1932; *Vipers' Tangle* (Warre B. Wells), London: Gollancz, 1933; *The Knot of Vipers* (Gerard Hopkins), London: Eyre & Spottiswoode, 1952. *La Pharisienne*, Grasset, 1941; *A Woman of the Pharisees* (Gerard Hopkins), Holt, 1946; London: Eyre & Spottiswoode, 1946. *Le Sagouin*, Plon, 1951; *The Little Misery* (Gerard Hopkins), London: Eyre & Spottiswoode, 1952; also *The Weakling* in *The Weakling* and *The Enemy*. *Thérèse Desqueyroux*, Grasset, 1922; *Thérèse, A Portrait in Four Parts* (Gerard Hopkins) includes: *Thérèse Desqueyroux, Thérèse and the Doctor, Thérèse at the Hotel, The End of the Night*, Holt, 1947. *La Chair et le sang*, Emile-Paul, 1920; *Flesh and Blood* (Gerard Hopkins), Farrar, Straus and Cudahy, 1955. *Le Mystère Frontenac*, Grasset, 1933; *The Frontenacs* (Gerard Hopkins), Farrar, Straus and Cudahy, 1961.

Maurois, André. *Bernard Quesnay*, Gallimard, 1926; *Bernard Quesnay* (Brian W. Downs), Appleton, 1927; London: Jonathan Cape, 1927. *Le Cercle de famille*, Grasset, 1932; *The Family Circle* (Hamish Miles), Appleton, 1932. *Climats*, Grasset, 1928; *Atmosphere of Love* (Joseph Collins), Appleton, 1929. *L'Instinct du bonheur*, Grasset, 1934. *Les Silences du Colonel Bramble*, Grasset, 1918; *The Silence of Colonel Bramble* (Thurfrida Wake), Appleton, 1920; London: John Lane, 1920. *Les Roses de Septembre*, Flammarion, 1956.

Memmi, Albert. *La Statue de sel*, Corrêa, 1953. *Agar*, Corrêa, 1955; *Strangers* (Brian Rhys), Orion Press, 1960.

Merle, Robert. *Weekend à Zuydcote*, Gallimard, 1949; *Weekend at Dunkirk* (K. Rebillon-Lambley), Knopf, 1950; as *Week-end at Zuydcoote*, London: J. Lehmann, 1950. *L'Ile*, Gallimard, 1962; *The Island* (Humphrey Hare), St. Martin's Press, 1964.

Mohrt, Michel. *Mon Royaume pour un cheval*, Albin Michel, 1949. *Les Nomades*, Albin Michel, 1951. *Le Serviteur fidèle*, Albin Michel, 1955. *La*

Prison Maritime, Gallimard, 1961; *Mariner's Prison* (Xan Fielding), Viking, 1963. *La Campagne d'Italie,* Gallimard, 1965.

Moinot, Pierre. *La Chasse Royale,* Gallimard, 1954; *The Royal Hunt* (Ralph Manheim), Knopf, 1955.

Molaine, Pierre. *Les Orgues de l'enfer,* Corrêa, 1950; *Strange Laughter* (Eithne Wilkins), Roy, 1953; London: A. Redman, 1953.

Montherlant, Henry de. *Les Bestiaires,* Grasset, 1926. *Les Célibataires,* Grasset, 1934; *Perish in Their Pride* (Thomas McGreery), Knopf, 1936; as *Lament for the Death of an Upper Class,* London: J. Miles, 1935. *L'Histoire d'amour de la rose de sable,* Plon, 1954. *Les Jeunes Filles,* Grasset, 1936–39: (1) *Les Jeunes Filles,* 1936, (2) *Pitié pour les femmes,* 1936, (3) *Le Démon du bien,* 1937, (4) *Les Lépreuses,* 1939; *Pity for Women* contains 1, *Young Girls* (Thomas McGreevy) and 2, *Pity for Women* (John Rodker), Knopf, 1938; *Costals and the Hippogriff* contains 3, *The Demon of Good,* and 4, *The Lepers* (John Rodker), Knopf, 1940; Parts 3 and 4 as *The Lepers,* London: Routledge, 1940. *Le Songe,* Grasset, 1922; *The Dream* (Terence Kilmartin), London: Weidenfeld and Nicolson, 1962. *Le Chaos et la nuit,* Gallimard, 1963; *Chaos and Night* (Terence Kilmartin), London: Weidenfeld and Nicolson, 1964.

Morand, Paul. *Bouddha vivant,* Gallimard, 1927; *The Living Buddha* (Madeleine Boyd), Holt, 1928. *Fermé la nuit,* Gallimard, 1922; *Closed All Night* (G.P.C., C.B.P., and H.M.), T. Seltzer, 1925. *Ouvert la nuit,* Gallimard, 1923; *Open All Night* (H.B.V.), T. Seltzer, 1923. *Magie Noire,* Grasset, 1928; *Black Magic* (Hamish Miles), Viking, 1929.

Mouloudji, Marcel. *En Souvenir de Barbarie,* Gallimard, 1945. *Les Larmes,* Gallimard, 1957. *La Guerre buissonnière,* Gallimard, 1959.

Nels, Jacques. *Poussière de temps,* Bateau ivre, 1946; *A Man of Means* (Elaine Halperin), Chicago: Ziff-Davis, 1948.

Nimier, Roger. *Le Hussard bleu,* Gallimard, 1950; *The Blue Hussar* (Jacques LeClerq), Messner, 1953; *The Blue Hussar* (John Russell and Anthony Rhodes), London: McGibbon & Kee, 1953.

Nizan, Paul. *La Conspiration,* Gallimard, 1937; *Trojan Horse* (Charles Ashleigh), London: Lawrence and Wishart, 1937.

Oldenbourg, Zoë. *Argile,* Gallimard, 1946; *The World is Not Enough* (Willard A. Trask), Pantheon, 1948. *La Pierre Angulaire,* Gallimard, 1953; *The Cornerstone* (Edward Hyams), Pantheon, 1955. *Les Brûlés,* Gallimard, 1960; *Destiny of Fire* (Peter Green), London: Gollancz, 1961. *Le Bûcher de Montségur,* Gallimard, 1960; *Massacre at Montségur* (Peter Green), London:

Weidenfeld and Nicolson, 1961. *Les Cités Charnelles*, Gallimard, 1961; *Cities of the Flesh* (Anne Carter), Pantheon, 1963.

Pauwels, Louis. *Saint-Quelqu'un*, Seuil, 1946; *Not into Clean Hands* (Bernard Miall), London: Allen and Unwin, 1948.

Perec, Georges. *Les Choses*, Julliard, 1965.

Perret, Jacques. *Le Caporal épinglé*, Gallimard, 1951. *Le Vent dans les voiles*, Gallimard, 1948; *The Wind in the Sails* (F. G. Renier and Anne Cliff), London: Hart-Davis, 1954; Norton, 1955.

Perry, Jacques. *L'Amour de rien*, Julliard, 1952. *Monsieur d'Ustelles*, Julliard, 1954. *Le Mouton noir*, Julliard, 1953. *La Vie d'un païen*, Julliard, 1965.

Peyrefitte, Roger. *Les Ambassades*, Flammarion, 1951; *Diplomatic Diversions* (James FitzMaurice), London: Thames & Hudson, 1953. *Les Amitiés particulières*, Vigneau, 1945; *Special Friendships* (Felix Giovanelli), Vanguard, 1950. *La Fin des ambassades*, Flammarion, 1953. *Jeunes Proies*, Flammarion, 1956.

Pieyre de Mandiargues, André. *Le Lis de Mer*, Laffont, 1956. *La Motocyclette*, Gallimard, 1963; *The Motorcycle* (Richard Howard), Grove Press, 1965. *Porte Dévergondée*, Gallimard, 1965.

Pinget, Robert. *Le Fiston*, Minuit, 1959; *Monsieur Levert* (Richard Howard), Grove Press, 1961. *L'Inquisitoire*, Minuit, 1962. *Quelqu'un*, Minuit, 1965.

Proust, Marcel. *Jean Santeuil*, 3 vols., Gallimard, 1952. *Pastiches et Mélanges*, Gallimard, 1919. *Les Plaisirs et les jours*, C. Lévy, 1896; *Pleasures and Regrets* (Louise Varèse), Crown, 1948. *A la recherche du temps perdu*, 16 vols., Gallimard, 1913–27, (1) *Du Côté de chez Swann*, Grasset (subsequently Gallimard), 1913; *Swann's Way* (C. K. Scott-Moncrieff), London: Chatto & Windus, 1922; Holt, 1922; The Modern Library, 1928. (2) *A l'ombre des jeunes filles en fleur*, Gallimard, 1918; *Within a Budding Grove* (C. K. Scott-Moncrieff), London: Chatto & Windus, 1924; Seltzer, 1924; The Modern Library, 1930. (3) *Le Côté de Guermantes*, Gallimard, 1921; *The Guermantes Way* (C. K. Scott-Moncrieff), London: Chatto & Windus, 1925; Seltzer, 1925; The Modern Library, 1933. (4) *Le Côté de Guermantes*, II; *Sodome et Gomorrhe*, Gallimard, 1922; *Cities of the Plain* (C. K. Scott-Moncrieff), Boni, 1927 (subsequently Knopf); The Modern Library, 1938. (5) *La Prisonnière*, Gallimard, 1923; *The Captive* (C. K. Scott-Moncrieff), Boni, 1929 (subsequently Knopf); The Modern Library, 1934. (6) *Albertine disparue*, Gallimard, 1925; *The Sweet Cheat Gone* (C. K. Scott-Moncrieff), Boni, 1930 (subsequently Knopf); The Modern Library, 1934. (7) *Le Temps retrouvé*, Gallimard, 1927; *Time Regained* (Stephen Hudson), London: Chatto & Windus, 1931; *The Past Recaptured* (Frederick A. Blossom), Boni, 1932; The

Modern Library, 1951; *Remembrance of Things Past* (C. K. Scott-Moncrieff), Random House, 1934, 2 vols. (Vol. I: Parts 1–3; Vol. II: Parts 4–7).

Queffelec, Henri. *Un Recteur de l'Isle de Sein*, Stock, 1945; *Island Priest* (James Whitall), Dutton, 1952; *God Needs Men* is the film derived from this work. *Un Royaume sous la mer*, Presses de la Cité; *The Kingdom Under the Sea* (n.t.), London: Arthur Barker, 1959.

Queneau, Raymond. *Le Chiendent*, Gallimard, 1933. *Le Dimanche de la vie*, Gallimard, 1951. *Loin de Rueil*, Gallimard, 1944; *The Skin of Dreams* (H. J. Kaplan), Norfolk: New Directions, 1948. *Pierrot, Mon Ami*, Gallimard, 1945. *Un Rude Hiver*, Gallimard, 1939; *A Hard Winter* (Betty Askwith), London: Lehmann, 1948. *Zazie dans le métro*, Gallimard, 1959; *Zazie* (Barbara Wright), Harper, 1960.

Radiguet, Raymond. *Le Bal du Comte d'Orgel*, Grasset, 1924; *The Count's Ball* (Malcolm Cowley), Norton, 1929; *Count d'Orgel Opens the Ball* (Violet Schiff), London: Harvill Press, 1952; as *Count d'Orgel*, Grove Press, 1953. *Le Diable au corps*, Grasset, 1923; *The Devil in the Flesh* (Kay Boyle), H. Smith, 1932; New American Library, 1949.

Ramuz, Charles-Ferdinand. *La Beauté sur la terre*, Genève: Mermod, 1927; Grasset, 1928; *Beauty on Earth*, London & New York: G. P. Putnam, 1929. *Derborence*, Grasset, 1936; *When the Mountain Fell* (Sarah Fisher), Pantheon, 1947. *La Grande Peur dans la montagne*, Grasset, 1926. *Présence de la mort*, Lausanne: Mermod, 1922; *The Triumph of Death* (Allan Ross Macdougall), Pantheon, 1946; London: Routledge, 1946. *Le Règne de l'esprit malin*, Lausanne: Editions des cahiers vaudois (s.d.); Geneva: Georg, 1917; *The Reign of the Evil One* (James Whitall), Harcourt, Brace, 1922.

Réage, Pauline (attribution doubtful). *Histoire d'O*, Pauvert, 1954; *Story of O* (Sabine D'Estrée), Grove, 1966.

Roblès, Emmanuel. *Cela s'appelle l'aurore*, Seuil, 1953; *Dawn on Our Darkness* (Thérèse Pol), Messner, 1954. *La Remontée du fleuve*, Seuil, 1964. *Le Vésuve*, Seuil, 1961.

Rochefort, Christiane. *Le Repos du guerrier*, Grasset, 1958; *Warrior's Rest* (Lowell Bair), McKay, 1959. *Les Petits Enfants du siècle*, Grasset, 1961; *Children of Heaven* (Linda Asher), McKay, 1962.

Rolin, Dominique. *Le Souffle*, Seuil, 1952; *The Pulse of Life* (David Moore), London: Alvin Redman, 1954.

Romains, Jules. *Les Copains*, Figuière, 1913; *The Boys in the Back Room* (Jacques LeClerq), McBride, 1937. *Les Hommes de bonne volonté*, 27 vol.,

Flammarion, 1932–52 (Warre B. Wells, vol. I–III, Gerard Hopkins, vol. IV–XIV), Knopf, 1933–46. I. *Men of Good Will* contains (1) *The Sixth of October* (*Le 6 octobre*), (2) *Quinette's Crime* (*Le Crime de Quinette*), II. *Passion's Pilgrims* contains (3) *Childhood's Loves* (*Les Amours enfantines*), (4) *Eros in Paris* (*Eros de Paris*), III. *The Proud and the Meek* contains (5) *The Proud* (*Les Superbes*), (6) *The Meek* (*Les Humbles*), IV. *The World from Below* contains (7) *The Lonely* (*Recherche d'une église*), (8) *Provincial Interlude* (*Province*), V. *The Earth Trembles* contains (9) *Floor Warning* (*Montée des périls*), (10) *The Powers That Be* (*Les Pouvoirs*), VI. *The Depths and the Heights* contains (11) *To the Gutter* (*Recours à l'abîme*), (12) *To the Stars* (*Les Créatures*), VII. *Death of a World* contains (13) *Mission to Rome* (*Mission à Rome*), (14) *The Black Flag* (*Le Drapeau noir*), VIII. *Verdun* contains (15) *The Prelude* (*Prélude à Verdun*), (16) *The Battle* (*Verdun*), IX. *Aftermath* contains (17) *Vorge against Quinette* (*Vorge contre Quinette*), (18) *The Sweets of Life* (*La Douceur de la vie*), X. *The New Day* contains (19) *Promise of Dawn* (*Cette Grande Lueur à l'est*), (20) *The World Is Your Adventure* (*Le Monde est ton aventure*), XI. *Work and Play* contains (21) *Mountain Days* (*Journée dans la montagne*), (22) *Work and Play* (*Les Travaux et les joies*), XII. *The Wind Is Rising* contains (23) *The Gathering of the Gangs* (*Naissance de la bande*), (24) *Offered in Evidence* (*Comparutions*), XIII. *Escape in Passion* contains (25) *The Magic Carpet* (*Le Tapis magique*), (26) *Françoise* (*Françoise*), XIV. *The Seventh of October* (*Le 7 octobre*).

Mort de Quelqu'un, Gallimard, 1911; *The Death of a Nobody* (Desmond MacCarthy and Sidney Waterlow), London: Latimer, 1914; Huebsch, 1914; Knopf, 1944. *Psyché*, Gallimard, 1922–29; (1) *Lucienne*, Gallimard, 1922; *Lucienne* (Waldo Frank), Boni & Liveright, 1925, (2) *Le Dieu des corps*, Gallimard, 1925; *The Body's Rapture* (John Rodker), Liveright, 1937; Pocket Books, 1953, (3) *Quand le navire*, Gallimard, 1929.

Rossi, Jean-Baptiste. *Les Mal-Partis*, Laffont, 1950; *Awakening* (Prudence Griffin), Harper, 1952; Signet Books, 1954; as *The False Start*, London: Secker & Warburg, 1952.

Roy, Jules. *Le Navigateur*, Gallimard, 1954; *The Navigator* (Mervyn Savill), Knopf, 1955. *Le Femme infidèle*, Gallimard, 1955; *The Unfaithful Wife* (J. Robert Low), Knopf, 1956.

Sachs, Maurice. *Le Sabbat*, Corrêa, 1946; *Day of Wrath* (Robin King), London: Arthur Baker, 1953. *La Chasse à courre*, Gallimard, 1949; *The Hunt* (Richard Howard), Stern and Day, 1965.

Sagan, Françoise. *Aimez-vous Brahms?*, Julliard, 1959; (Peter Wiles), Dutton, 1960. *Bonjour Tristesse*, Julliard, 1955; (Irene Ash), London: Murray; Dutton, 1955. *La Chamade*, Julliard, 1966; *La Chamade* (Anne Green), Dutton, 1966. *Dans un Mois, dans un an*, Julliard, 1957; *Those without Shadows* (Frances

Frenaye), Dutton, 1957. *Ces Merveilleux Nuages,* Julliard, 1956; *The Wonderful Clouds* (Anne Green), Dutton, 1962. *Un Certain Sourire,* Julliard, 1956; *A Certain Smile* (Irene Ash), London: Murray; Dutton, 1956.

Saint-Exupéry, Antoine de. *Citadelle,* Gallimard, 1948; *The Wisdom of the Sands* (Stuart Gilbert), Harcourt, Brace, 1950. *Courrier-Sud,* Gallimard, 1929; *Southern Mail* (Stuart Gilbert), H. Smith & R. Haas, 1933. *Le Petit Prince,* Gallimard, 1945; Reynal & Hitchcock, 1943; *The Little Prince* (Katherine Woods), Reynal & Hitchcock, 1943. *Pilote de guerre,* Maison française, 1942; Gallimard, 1942; *Flight to Arras* (Lewis Galantière), Reynal & Hitchcock, 1942. *Terre des hommes,* Gallimard, 1939; *Wind, Sand and Stars* (Lewis Galantière), Reynal & Hitchcock, 1939. *Vol de nuit,* Gallimard, 1931; *Night Flight* (Stuart Gilbert), New York and London: The Century Co., 1932; also in *Airman's Odyssey* (contains *Wind, Sand and Stars, Night Flight, Flight to Arras*), Reynal & Hitchcock, 1943.

Sarraute, Nathalie. *Portrait d'un Inconnu,* Marin, 1948; *Portrait of a Man Unknown* (Maria Jolas), Braziller, 1958. *Martereau,* Gallimard, 1953; *Martereau* (Maria Jolas), Braziller, 1959. *Le Planetarium,* Gallimard, 1959; *The Planetarium* (Maria Jolas), London: Calder, 1962; Braziller, 1960. *Les Fruits d'or,* Gallimard, 1963; *The Golden Fruits* (Maria Jolas), Braziller, 1964. *Tropismes,* New Ed., Minuit, 1958; *Tropisms* and *The Age of Suspicion* (Maria Jolas), Braziller, 1963.

Sartre, Jean-Paul. *Les Chemins de la liberté,* 3 vols., Gallimard, 1945–49: (1) *L'Age de raison,* Gallimard, 1945; *The Age of Reason* (Eric Sutton), Knopf, 1947; London: Hamilton, 1947, (2) *Le Sursis,* Gallimard, 1945; *The Reprieve* (Eric Sutton), Knopf, 1947; London: Hamilton, 1947, (3) *La Mort dans l'âme,* Gallimard, 1949; *Iron in the Soul* (Gerard Hopkins), London: Hamilton, 1950; as *Troubled Sleep,* Knopf, 1951. *L'Etre et le néant,* Gallimard, 1943; only two long essays extracted from this book have been translated and published as *Existential Psychoanalysis* (Hazel Barnes), Philosophical Library, 1953. *Le Mur,* Gallimard, 1939; *Intimacy and Other Stories* (Lloyd Alexander), New Directions, 1948. *La Nausée,* Gallimard, 1938; *Nausea* (Lloyd Alexander), New Directions, 1949; *The Diary of Antoine Roquentin* (Lloyd Alexander), London: J. Lehmann, 1949. 'Qu'est-ce que la littérature?' in *Situations II,* Gallimard, 1948; *What Is Literature?* (Bernard Frechtman), Philosophical Library, 1949; London: Methuen, 1950. *Réflexions sur la question juive,* Morihien, 1946; 'Portrait of the Antisemite' (Mary Geggenheim), *The Partisan Review,* 1946; *Anti-Semite and Jew* (George J. Becker), Schocken Books, 1948; *Portrait of the Anti-Semite* (Erik de Mauny), London: Secker & Warburg, 1948.

Schwarz-Bart, André. *Le Dernier des Justes,* Seuil, 1959; *The Last of the Just* (Stephen Becker), London: Secker & Warburg; Atheneum, 1960.

Semprun, Jorge. *Le Grand Voyage*, Gallimard, 1963; *The Long Voyage* (Richard Seaver), London: Weidenfeld and Nicolson; Grove, 1964.

Simenon, Georges. Recent novels of a literary character are: *Les Anneaux de Bicêtre*, Presses de la Cité, 1963; *The Bells of Bicêtre* (Jean Steward), Harcourt, Brace, 1964. *Le Petit Saint*, Presses de la Cité, 1965.

Simon, Claude. *Le Vent*, Minuit, 1957; *The Wind* (Richard Howard), Braziller, 1959. *L'Herbe*, Minuit, 1959; *The Grass* (Richard Howard), Braziller, 1960. *La Route des Flandres*, Minuit, 1960; *The Flanders Road* (Richard Howard), London: Cape, 1962; Braziller, 1961. *Le Palace*, Minuit, 1962; *The Palace* (Richard Howard), Braziller, 1964.

Simon, Pierre-Henri. *Portrait d'un officier*, Seuil, 1959; *Portrait of an Officer* (Humphrey Hare), London: Secker & Warburg, 1961; and as *An End to Glory*, Harper, 1961. *Histoire d'un Bonheur*, Seuil, 1963.

Sollers, Philippe. *Une Curieuse Solitude*, Seuil, 1958; *A Strange Solitude* (Richard Howard), London: Eyre and Spottiswoode, 1961.

Tourville, Anne de. *Jabadao*, Stock, 1952; *Jabadao* (Mervyn Savill), London: Britannicus Liber, 1952; *Wedding Dance* (Mervyn Savill), Farrar, Straus & Young, 1953.

Triolet, Elsa. *Le Premier Accroc coûte deux cents francs*, Egloff, 1945; also Denoël, *A Fine of Two Hundred Francs* (n.t.), Reynal & Hitchcock, 1947 (includes also *The Lovers of Avignon, The Private Life of Alexis Slavsky, Notebooks Buried under a Peach Tree*).

Troyat, Henri. *L'Araigne*, Plon, 1938. *Faux Jour*, Plon, 1935. *Grandeur nature*, Plon, 1936; *One Minus Two* (James Whitall), Washburn, 1938. *Judith Madrier*, Plon, 1940; *Judith Madrier* (James Whitall), Washburn, 1941. *La Neige en deuil*, Flammarion, 1952; *The Mountain* (Constantine Fitzgibbon), Simon & Schuster, 1953. *Tant que la terre durera*, 3 vols., Table ronde, 1947-50: (1) *Tant que la terre durera*, 1947; *My Father's House* (David Hapgood), Duell, Sloan & Pearce, 1951, (2) *Le Sac et la cendre*, 1948, (3) *Etrangers sur la terre*, 1950.

Vailland, Roger. *Beau Masque*, Gallimard, 1951. *Bon Pied, Bon Oeil*, Corrêa, 1950. *Drôle de jeu*, Corrêa, 1965. *La Fête*, Gallimard, 1950; *Fête* (Peter Wiles), Knopf, 1961. *La Loi*, Gallimard, 1957; *The Law* (Peter Wiles), London: Cape, 1958; Knopf, 1958. *La Truite*, Gallimard, 1966; *A Young Trout* (Peter Wiles), London: Collins, 1965. *Drôle de jeu* had been translated in England by Gerard Hopkins and published in Boston, at Houghton Mifflin, as *Playing for Keeps*, 1948. *Les Mauvais Coups*, Sagittaire, 1948; *Turn of the Wheel* (Peter Wiles), Knopf, 1962.

Vercors (Jean Bruller). *Les Armes de la nuit*, Editions de minuit, 1946. *Les Animaux dénaturés*, Albin Michel, 1952; *You Shall Know Them* (Rita Barisse), Boston: Little, Brown, 1953. *L'Imprimerie de Verdun*, La Bibliothèque française, 1947; *The Verdun Press*, see *Le Silence de la mer*. *La Marche à l'étoile*, Editions de minuit, Cahiers du Silence, 1943; also French Pantheon Books, vol. 8, 1946. *Le Silence de la mer*, London & Paris: Editions de Minuit, Cahiers du Silence, 1943; *The Silence of the Sea* (Cyril Connolly), Macmillan, 1944. *Three Short Novels* (includes: *Guiding Star* (*La Marche à l'étoile*) (Eric Sutton), *Night and Fog* (*La Nuit et le brouillard*) (Haakon M. Chevalier), *The Verdun Press* (*L'Imprimerie de Verdun*) (Haakon M. Chevalier), Boston: Little, Brown, 1947. *La Liberté de Décembre, Monsieur Prousthe*, 1959; *Paths of Love* (Rita Barisse), Putnam, 1961. *Sylva*, Grasset, 1961; (Rita Barisse), Putnam, 1962.

Vian, Boris. *L'Écume des jours*, Gallimard, 1947. *L'Herbe rouge*, Gallimard, 1950. *L'Arrache-cœur*, Gallimard, 1953. New editions, J. J. Pauvert, 1963.

Vilmorin, Louise de. *Julietta*, Gallimard, 1951; *Julietta* (Alison Brothers), Messner, 1952. *Madame de*, Gallimard, 1951; *Madame de* (Duff Cooper), Messner, 1954. *Le Retour d'Erica*, Gallimard, 1948; *Erica's Return* (Sarah Fisher Scott), Random House, 1948. *Les Belles Amours*, Gallimard, 1954.

Wittig, Monique. *L'Opoponax*, Minuit, 1964; *The Opoponax* (Helen Weaver), London: Peter Owen; Simon and Schuster, 1966.

Yourcenar, Marguerite. *Mémoires d'Hadrien*, Plon, 1951; *Hadrian's Memoirs* (Grace Frick), Farrar, Straus & Young, 1954.

Zéraffa, Michel. *Le Temps des rencontres*, Albin Michel, 1948; *The Living and the Lost* (J. M. Cohen), London: The Bodley Head, 1952; Roy, 1953.

Bibliography of Essential
General Works on the Novel

Albérès, R. M., *Portrait de notre héros: Essai sur le roman actuel*. Le Portulan, Paris, 1945.

——, *La Révolte des écrivains d'aujourd'hui*. Corrêa, Paris, 1949.

——, *Histoire du roman moderne*. Albin Michel, Paris, 1962.

Aldington, Richard, 'Knowledge and the Novelist,' *The Times Literary Supplement*, July 2, 1938.

Ames, Van Meter, *Aesthetics of the Novel*. University of Chicago Press, Chicago, 1928.

——, 'Enjoying the Novel,' in *The Enjoyment of the Arts*, Max Schoen (ed.), The Philosophical Library, New York, 1944.

Arland, Marcel, 'Sur le roman,' *Nouvelle Revue Française*, No. 305, February 1939, 332–7.

Auerbach, Erich, *Mimesis: Dargestellte Wirklichkeit in der abendländischen Literatur*. Francke, Bern, 1946.

Barthes, Roland, *Le Degré zéro de l'ecriture*. Editions du Seuil, Paris, 1953. (Chapter on *L'écriture du roman*.)

Beach, Joseph Warren, *The Twentieth Century Novel: Studies in Technique*. Appleton-Century-Crofts, New York, 1932.

Bentley, Phyllis, 'The Armistice Period in British Fiction,' *The New York Times Book Review*, August 31, 1941.

Blanchot, Maurice, *Faux-Pas*. Gallimard, Paris, 1943. (Contains eighteen brief chapters on novelists.)

——, *La Part du feu*. Gallimard, Paris, 1949. (Essays on Kafka, Malraux, and Sartre.)

Bonnet, Henri, *Roman et poésie*. Nizet, Paris, 1951.

Bowen, Elizabeth, *English Novelists*. Collins, London, 1942.

Boylesve, René, *Opinions sur le roman*. Plon, Paris, 1929.

Brée, Germaine, and Guiton, Margaret, *An Age of Fiction*. Rutgers University Press, New Brunswick, New Jersey, 1957; Chatto and Windus, London, 1958.

Brooks, Cleanth, and Warren, Robert Penn, *Understanding Fiction*. Appleton-Century-Crofts, New York, 1943.

Burgum, Edwin Berry, *The Novel and the World's Dilemma*. Oxford University Press, New York, 1947. (Contains chapters on Proust and Malraux, as well as on Kafka, Mann, Joyce, and others.)

Caillois, Roger, *Puissances du roman*. Sagittaire, Marseille, 1943.

Camus, Albert, 'L'intelligence et l'échafaud,' in *Problèmes du Roman*, Jean Prévost (ed.) Confluences, Lyon et Paris, 1943, pp. 218–23.

Canby, Henry S., 'A Certain Condescension toward Fiction,' in *Definitions*. Harcourt, Brace and Company, New York, 1922.

Cather, Willa, 'The Novel *démeublé*,' in *Not Under Forty*. Alfred A. Knopf, New York, 1936.

Charbonneau, Robert, *Connaissance du personnage*. L'Arbre, Montreal, 1944.

Chauveau, Paul, 'A propos du roman,' *Les Nouvelles Littéraires*, April 14, 1928.

Chevalley, Abel, *Le Roman anglais de notre temps*. The Clarendon Press, Oxford, 1921.

Comfort, Alexander, *The Novel and Our Time*. Phoenix House, London, 1948.

Conrad, Joseph, *A Personal Record*. Harper and Brothers, New York, 1912.

——, *Prefaces to His Works*. J. M. Dent & Sons, London, 1937. (With an introductory essay by Edward Garnett.)

Cormeau, Nelly, *Physiologie du roman*. La Renaissance du Livre, Brussels, 1947.

Daiches, David, *The Novel and the Modern World*. University of Chicago Press, Chicago, 1939; new edition, 1960.

——, 'Problems for Modern Novelists,' *Accent*, Spring 1943, 144–51.

Daniel-Rops, 'Les Problèmes actuels du roman français,' *Bibliothèque Universelle et Revue de Genève*, August 1928, 932–45.

Dataller, Roger, *The Plain Man and the Novel*. Nelson, London, 1940.

Davis, Robert Gorham, 'Fiction as Thinking,' *Epoch*, I, 3, Spring 1948, 87–96.

De Voto, Bernard, *The World of Fiction*. Houghton Mifflin Company, Boston, 1950.

Dimic, Ivan, *La Crise psychologique dans le roman du XXe siècle*. Thesis, University of Strasbourg, 1961.

Duhamel, Georges, *Essai sur le roman*. Marcelle Lesage, Paris, 1925.

——, *Remarques sur les mémoires imaginaires*. Mercure de France, Paris, 1934.

Edgar, Pelham, *The Art of the Novel from 1700 to the Present Time*. Macmillan Company, New York, 1933.

Fernandez, Ramon, *Messages*. Gallimard, Paris, 1926.

——, 'Poétique du roman,' *Nouvelle Revue Française*, April 1929, 544–50.

Ferrero, Guglielmo and Leo, 'Remarques sur le roman,' *Les Nouvelles Littéraires*, March 23, 1929.

Fitch, Brian T., *Le Sentiment de l'aliénation dans le roman français entre 1930 et 1943*. Thesis, University of Strasbourg, 1962.

Follett, Wilson, *The Modern Novel: A Study of the Purpose and the Meaning of Fiction.* Alfred A. Knopf, New York, 1918.

Ford, Ford Madox, *The English Novel.* Constable, London, 1930.

Forster, E. M., *Aspects of the Novel.* Harcourt Brace and Company, New York, 1927.

Frank, Waldo, 'The Novel as Poem,' *The New Republic,* August 20, 1945.

Frierson, William C., *The English Novel in Transition, 1885–1940.* University of Oklahoma Press, Norman, Oklahoma, 1942.

Frohock, Wilbur M., *The Novel of Violence in America.* Southern Methodist Press, Dallas, Texas, 1950.

Gadenne, Paul, 'Efficacité du roman,' in *Problèmes du Roman,* Jean Prévost (ed.), Confluences, Lyon and Paris, 1943, pp. 248–57.

Galsworthy, John, *Castles in Spain and Other Scripts.* Heinemann, London, 1927.

————, *The Creation of Character in Fiction.* The Romanes Lecture, Clarendon Press, Oxford, 1931.

Gerould, Gordon Hall, *How To Read Fiction.* Princeton University Press, Princeton, New Jersey, 1937.

Gide, André, *Interviews imaginaires.* Pantheon Books, New York, 1943. (Interviews VIII–IX touch upon problems of the novel. The American translation was published in 1944 by Alfred A. Knopf.)

Girard, René, *Mensonge romantique et vérité romanesque.* Grasset, Paris, 1961.

Glasgow, Ellen, *A Certain Measure.* Harcourt Brace & Co., New York, 1943.

Gmelin, Hermann, *Der französische Zyklenroman der Gegenwart.* Quelle und Meyer, Heidelberg, 1950.

Goldmann, Lucien, *Pour une sociologie du roman.* Gallimard, Paris, 1964.

Hackett, Francis, 'The Novel and Human Personality,' *The New York Times Book Review,* August 15, 1948.

Haedens, Kleber, *Paradoxe sur le roman.* Sagittaire, Marseille, 1941.

Hamilton, Clayton, *Materials and Methods of Fiction.* The Chautauqua Press, Chautauqua, New York, 1911.

Henderson, Philip, *The Novel Today: Studies in Contemporary Attitudes.* John Lane, London, 1936.

Hoffmann, Frederick J., *Freudianism and the Literary Mind.* Louisiana University Press, Baton Rouge, Louisiana, 1945.

Hough, Graham, *The Dream and the Task. Literature and Morals in the Culture of Today.* W. W. Norton, New York, 1963.

Hytier, Jean, *Les Arts de littérature.* Charlot, Algiers, 1945. (Contains five very suggestive chapters on the art of fiction.)

Jaloux, Edmond, *Au Pays du roman.* Corrêa, Paris, 1931.

————, 'Préface à un roman mythique,' *Le Temps,* April 15, 1938.

————, 'Roman français et roman étranger,' *Le Temps,* March 1, 1939.

Jones, Howard Mumford, 'Fiction and the Art of Fiction,' *The New York Times Book Review,* July 26, 1946.

Karl, Frederick, *A Reader's Guide to the Contemporary English Novel.* Thames & Hudson, London, and Farrar, Straus & Cudahy, New York, 1962.

Lalou, René, *Le Roman français depuis 1900*. Presses Universitaires, Collection Que sais-je?, Paris, 1943.

Lawrence, D. H., 'The Novel,' in his *Reflections on the Death of a Porcupine*. Martin Secker, London, 1934.

———, 'Surgery for the Novel, or a Bomb,' 'Morality and the Novel,' 'Why the Novel Matters,' in *Phoenix: The Posthumous Papers of D.H.L.* Heinemann, London, 1936, pp. 517–20, 522–32, 533–38.

Leavis, D. Q., *Fiction and the Reading Public*. Chatto and Windus, London, 1932.

Leavis, F. R., *The Great Tradition*. Chatto and Windus, London, 1949.

Lesort, Paul A., 'Notes sur le roman,' *La Nef*, V, 40, March 1948, 7–18.

Levin, Harry, *The Gates of Horn*. Oxford University Press, New York, 1963.

Liddell, Robert, *A Treatise on the Novel*. Jonathan Cape, London, 1947.

London Magazine (The), 'The New Novelists,' Autumn number, 1958, V, ii, 13–31.

Lubbock, Percy, *The Craft of Fiction*. Jonathan Cape, London, 1929; and Charles Scribner's Sons, New York, 1929.

Magny, Claude-Edmonde, *L'Age du roman américain*. Editions du Seuil, Paris, 1948.

———, *Histoire du roman français depuis 1918*, I. Editions du Seuil, Paris, 1950.

Martin-Chauffier, Louis, 'Proust and the double "I,"' *The Partisan Review*, XVI, 10, October 1949, 1011–26. (Published in *Problèmes du Roman*, Jean Prévost (ed.), Confluences, Lyon and Paris, 1943).

Massis, Henri, *Réflexions sur l'art du roman*. Plon, Paris, 1927.

Mauriac, François, see Bibliographical Note to Chapter VI.

Maurois, André, *Le Roman et le romancier*. Société des Conférences, Monaco, 1929.

Merleau-Ponty, Maurice, 'Le Roman et la métaphysique,' in *Sens et nonsens*, Nagel, Paris, 1948.

Micha, René, 'La Marquise sortit à cinq heures,' *Cahiers du Sud*, No. 299, 1950, 120–32.

Mizener, Arthur, *The Sense of Life in the Modern Novel*. Houghton Mifflin, Boston, 1964, and Heinemann, London, 1965.

Moeller, Charles, *Littérature du XXᵉ Siècle et Christianisme*. Casterman, Paris et Tournai, 1953, Vol. 1.

Monroe, Elizabeth, *The Novel and Society: A Critical Study of the Modern Novel*. University of North Carolina Press, Chapel Hill, North Carolina, 1941.

Montesinos, José F., 'Imperfect Myths: Being an Observation on Detective Stories by a Continental Reader,' *Chimera*, V, 4, Summer 1947, 2–11.

Morgan, Charles, 'L'Avenir du roman,' *La Nouvelle Relève*, IV, 5, November 1945, 367–83.

Mottram, R. H., and Beresford, J. D., 'Tradition in the Novel,' 'Experiment in the Novel,' *Tradition and Experiment*. Oxford University Press, London, 1929.

Mounin, Georges, 'Mythologies de l'adolescence dans le roman contemporain, in *Problèmes du Roman*, Jean Prévost (ed.), Confluences, Lyon and Paris, 1943, pp. 36–52.

Muir, Edwin, *The Structure of the Novel*. Harcourt, Brace and Company, New York, 1929.

Muller, Herbert J., *Modern Fiction: A Study of Values*. Funk and Wagnalls Company, New York, 1937.

Murdoch, Iris, 'Against Dryness,' *Encounter*, XVI, i, January 1961, 16–21.

Murry, John Middleton, 'The Breakup of the Novel,' in his *Discoveries*. Collins, London, 1924.

Nadeau, Maurice, *Le Roman français depuis la guerre*. Gallimard, Paris, 1963.

The Novel of Tomorrow and the Scope of Fiction, by twelve American novelists. Bobbs-Merrill Company, Indianapolis, 1922.

The Novelist as Thinker, B. Rajan (ed.) Dennis Dobson, London, 1947.

O'Brien, Justin, *The Novel of Adolescence in France*. Columbia University Press, New York, 1937.

O'Connor, Frank (O'Donouan, Michael), *The Mirror in the Roadway*. A. Knopf, New York, 1956.

Onimus, Jean, 'L'Expression du temps dans le roman contemporain,' *Revue de Littérature Comparée*, XXVIII, 3, July–Sept. 1954, 299–317.

Ortega y Gasset, José, *The Dehumanization of Art and Notes on the Novel*. Princeton University Press, Princeton, New Jersey, 1948.

Overton, Grant, *The Philosophy of Fiction*. Appleton-Century-Crofts, New York, 1928.

Paul, David, 'Time and the Novelist,' *Partisan Review*, XXI, 6, Nov.–Dec. 1954, 636–49.

Pena, Carlos Hector de la, *La Novela moderna: Su Sentido y su Mensaje*. Editorial Jus, Mexico, 1944.

Penton, Brian, 'Note on Form in the Novel,' in *Scrutinies*, Edgell Rickword (ed.) Wishart, London, 1931, II, pp. 235–61.

Peyrade, Jena, *Recherche de la joie à travers le roman français contemporain*. Spes, Paris, 1946. (Mostly on Catholic novelists by a Catholic.)

Peyre, Henri, *Literature and Sincerity*. Yale University Press, New Haven, 1963.

Picon, Gaëtan, 'Définition du roman,' *La Gazette des lettres*, August 9, 1947.

——, 'D'une Philosophie du roman,' *Fontaine*, No. 57, December 1946–January 1947, 795–802.

Pouillon, Jean, *Temps et roman*. Gallimard, Paris, 1946.

Poulet, Georges, *La Distance intérieure*. Plon, Paris, 1952.

——, *Etudes sur le temps humain*. Plon, Paris, 1950.

Prévost, Jean, 'Le Métier de romancier,' *La Revue des Vivants*, February 1935, pp. 248–50.

——. Several articles in *Problèmes du roman*, Jean Prévost (ed.) Confluences, Lyon and Paris, 1943.

Pritchett, Victor J., *The Living Novel*. Chatto and Windus, London, 1946.

Rambaud, Henri, 'Sur le Génie du roman,' in *Problèmes du roman*, Jean Prévost (ed.) Confluences, Lyon and Paris, 1943, pp. 233–47.

Ransom, John Crowe, 'The Understanding of Fiction,' *The Kenyon Review*, XII, 2, Spring 1950, 189–218.

Rivière, Jacques, 'De Dostoevski et de l'insondable,' 'Marcel Proust et la tradition classique,' 'Le Roman d'aventures,' articles collected in *Nouvelles Etudes*. Gallimard, Paris, 1947.

Sartre, Jean-Paul, Preface to *Portrait d'un inconnu* by Nathalie Sarraute. Martin, Paris, 1948, pp. 7–16. (On the negative novels that Sartre defines as anti-novels.)

Seldes, Gilbert, 'Form and the Novel,' *The Bookman*, October 1929, pp. 128–31.

Sonnenfeld, Albert, 'Twentieth century Gothic: Reflections on the Catholic Novel,' *The Southern Review*, I, 2, Spring 1965, 288–405.

Stansbury, Milton H., *French Novelists of Today*. University of Pennsylvania Press, Philadelphia, 1935.

Swinnerton, Frank, 'Variations on Form in the Novel,' in *Essays and Studies by the English Association*. The Clarendon Press, Oxford, XXIII, 1938, pp. 79–92.

Thibaudet, Albert, *Réflexions sur le roman*. Gallimard, Paris, 1938. (Much of the author's earlier volume, *Le Liseur de romans*, Crès, Paris, 1925, is reprinted here.)

Tillyard, Eustace M., *The Epic Strain in the English Novel*. Chatto and Windus, London; and Essential Books, Fair Lawn, New Jersey, 1958.

Turnell, Martin, *The Art of French Fiction*. New Directions, New York, 1959 (new edition 1963).

Ullman, Stephen, *The Image in the Modern French Novel*. Cambridge University Press, Cambridge, England, 1960.

——, *Style in the French Novel*. Cambridge University Press, Cambridge, England, 1957.

Undset, Sigrid, 'Some Notes on Undercurrents of American Literature,' *The New York Times Book Review*, March 21, 1943.

Valéry, Paul, 'L'Art de Charles Morgan,' *Carrefours*, July 27, 1945.

——, 'Hommage' (to Marcel Proust) in *Variété* I. Gallimard, Paris, 1924, pp. 149–59.

——. Letter on the novel in *Problèmes du roman*, Jean Prévost (ed.) Confluences, Lyon and Paris, 1943, pp. 193–4.

Walpole, Hugh, and others, *Tendencies of the Modern Novel*. Allen and Unwin, London, 1934. (Contains a sketchy chapter, by Hamish Miles, on French fiction.)

Wharton, Edith, *The Writing of Fiction*. Charles Scribner's Sons, New York, 1925.

What's Novel in the Novel, *Yale French Studies*, No. 8, 1951. (Articles by thirteen authors.)

Woolf, Virginia, *Mr. Bennett and Mrs. Brown*. Hogarth Press, London, 1928.

Woolf, Virginia, 'The Russian Point of View,' 'Modern Fiction,' 'How It Strikes a
    Contemporary' in *The Common Reader*, First Series. Harcourt Brace,
    New York, 1929.
———, 'Phases of Fiction,' *The Bookman*, New York, April, May, and June
    1929, pp. 123–32, 269–79, 404–12. (See Solomon Fishman, 'Virginia
    Woolf and the Novel,' *The Sewanee Review*, XLI, Summer 1943,
    321–40.)

Index of Proper Names

473